Questioning God

INDIANA SERIES IN THE PHILOSOPHY OF RELIGION
MEROLD WESTPHAL, GENERAL EDITOR

Questioning God

Edited by
John D. Caputo, Mark Dooley, and Michael J. Scanlon

INDIANA UNIVERSITY PRESS
BLOOMINGTON AND INDIANAPOLIS

This book is a publication of

Indiana University Press
601 North Morton Street
Bloomington, IN 47404-3797 USA

http://iupress.indiana.edu

Telephone orders   800-842-6796
Fax orders   812-855-7931
Orders by e-mail   iuporder@indiana.edu

MANUFACTURED IN THE UNITED STATES OF AMERICA

Library of Congress Cataloging-in-Publication Data

Questioning God / edited by John D. Caputo, Mark Dooley, and Michael J. Scanlon.
  p.   cm.   — (Indiana series in the philosophy of religion)
Includes index.
  ISBN 0-253-33981-2 (cloth : alk. paper) — ISBN 0-253-21474-2 (pbk. : alk. paper)
1. Forgiveness—Religious aspects—Christianity—Congresses. 2. Derrida, Jacques—
Contributions in religious aspects of forgiveness—Congresses.
  I. Caputo, John D. II. Dooley, Mark. III. Scanlon, Michael J. IV. Series.
  BT795 .Q47 2001
  210—dc21   2001000985

1 2 3 4 5 06 05 04 03 02 01

To Dr. Helen Lafferty

The spirit of Saint Augustine,

The spirit of Villanova

Contents

Contents

ACKNOWLEDGMENTS

The editors wish to acknowledge the support of Villanova University in making possible the conference "Religion and Postmodernism 2: Questioning God" on October 14–16, 1999, upon which this volume is based. We thank in particular Rev. Edmond Dobbin, O.S.A., President of the University, for his continuing support and encouragement; Dr. John Johannes, Vice-President for Academic Affairs; Dr. Helen Lafferty, University Vice-President; and Rev. Kail Ellis, O.S.A., Dean of the College of Arts and Sciences, without whose generous financial assistance we would not have been able to organize this meeting.

We also thank the French Cultural Services for the grant administered by Mark Dooley in support of this conference.

Finally, we thank Terry Sousa, who met with her usual aplomb the daunting challenge of scheduling the meeting rooms and providing receptions and meals for some 500 people, and Anna Misticoni, the secretary to the David R. Cook Chair of Philosophy and the Josephine C. Connelly Chair of Theology, who time and again saved the organizers from themselves and managed the unmanageable complexities a meeting like this inevitably entails.

Questioning God

Introduction

God Forgive

John D. Caputo, Mark Dooley, and Michael J. Scanlon

In an entry in the log that he was keeping for *La Contre-Allée* at the time of the first "Religion and Postmodernism" conference in 1997, Derrida made a comment that we very much treasure. Here I am, he said, at Villanova University, a Catholic university conducted by the Augustinian friars, at a conference with the title "Religion and Postmodernism"—"two things that are strange to me, you know." Then he added, "my atheism gets on in the churches, all the churches, do you understand that?"[1] We think we do, or at least we have a theory. Derrida always worries about accepting our invitations, pointing out to us that he is not a trained theologian or Scriptural scholar and that he finds the distinguished philosophers and theologians we have assembled to speak with him "intimidating." Besides, as he has written, he "quite rightly passes for an atheist."[2] Add to all that the fact that, as he told us, when he was growing up in a Jewish family in Algeria "*les Catholiques*" meant everybody *else*, everybody who was *not* Jewish. To meet these concerns, we always say the same thing. First, "postmodernism" is just a word we use to draw a crowd. Second, we do not expect him to do theology, just his own work, and to leave it to us to

1

reinscribe his texts within the context of the great questions of theology and philosophical theology.

That is a delicate operation, to be sure, one that must resist co-opting Derrida's work for religion, distorting his insights, or above all confining the energy of deconstructive analysis within the limits of a determinate faith. But it is also one that cries out to be done. For what else can one do with a philosopher who writes about the gift and forgiveness, hospitality and friendship, justice and the messianic, with someone who has radicalized these notions in such a way that anyone with an ear for these matters, with half an ear, can hear the biblical resonance, even if that is not something that Derrida himself is conscious of or consciously monitors? What Derrida has variously called a "hyperbolic ethics," an ethics beyond or without ethics, the ethicity of ethics, or a "religion without religion" is, we think, a unique resource for reflection for anyone coming from a religious tradition. Moreover, and from the other side, bringing the energy of a deconstructive analysis to bear upon religion is an exercise for which we think religion itself, were there just one thing called "religion," also cries out. For how else can religion be faithful to itself, to its past and to its future, how else can it keep watch on its own worst tendencies and keep open to its best tendencies, apart from the vigilance of a deconstructive way of thinking? What better way to remind it repeatedly of the contingency and revisability of its inscriptions and of the open-endedness of the future?

Questioning God is based upon the second "Religion and Postmodernism" conference at Villanova, held in October 1999 (a third, on "Circumfession" and Augustine's *Confessions*, will have been held in September 2001). The main idea behind this conference, as in the past, was to bring Derrida into dialogue with an international constellation of theologians and theologically oriented philosophers, some of whom are sympathetic with his work and some of whom are not, at a moment when the old assurances forthcoming from "metaphysical theology" and the "philosophy of religion" have lost their grip. We are always asking, to adapt a question put by Jean-Luc Nancy, "what comes after the God of metaphysics?" In our view, what has been called the "philosophy of religion" has proven itself an ineffective way to reflect philosophically upon religion, while the work of exploring the implications of deconstruction for religion—which cannot avoid opening up the implications of religion for deconstruction—is, as we hope these conferences will show, a rich and rewarding one.

The present conference really had two—highly interactive—topics: God and forgiveness. Derrida gave the opening lecture on forgiveness, because that is what he is working on these days. Forgiveness was also the subject of the roundtable discussion with Derrida and the other speakers, moderated by Richard Kearney. There were also two other papers on forgiveness, one Jewish and one Christian—Robert Gibbs and John Milbank—each taking more theologically oriented points of view on forgiveness that differ from Derrida's. Co-editor Mark Dooley also contributed a piece disputing Milbank and defending Derrida on forgiveness. The remaining papers took up the announced theme of "questioning God." Similar to the way the first conference brought Derrida together with Jean-Luc Marion, the second conference also provided the occasion to bring Derrida and some philosophers influenced by Derrida together with the foremost representatives of a recent movement in the Anglican church entitled "radical orthodoxy." This conference thus offered the first opportunity to see these two different voices interact.

By way of introducing this volume, let us first try to get a fix on Derrida's view of forgiveness and then turn to the other contributions.

Forgiveness and Derrida's "Hyperbolic Ethics"

Derrida's presentation on the opening night of the conference, "To Forgive: The Unforgivable and the Imprescriptible," is the introductory lecture to a series of seminars on forgiveness that he has been giving in Paris for several years under the title "Forgiveness and Perjury" ("*Pardon et Parjure*"). Accordingly, in addition to sketching the aporia of "forgiveness in itself, if there is such a thing," the lecture is punctuated throughout by promises of more detailed analyses of difficulties that can only be mentioned here and that will have to await the eventual publication of these seminars for fuller discussion.

The present essay is framed within two words, *pardon* and *merci*, with which it begins and ends. "Pardon, yes, pardon. I have just said 'pardon,' in English." He begins with (*par*) the word *pardon*, which remind us of his analysis of the first line in the poem by Ponge "*Par le mot par commence donc ce texte / Dont la première ligne dit la vérité*," "With the word *with* this text begins / Of which the first line speaks the truth."[3] He begins with *pardon*: but with the word itself or the act? Is he using this word or mentioning it? In fact, he is doing both. For what is any lecture, speech, or discourse if not a continual exercise in asking forgiveness, in making one's apologies? Do we not always begin, implicitly and as a structural matter, with "Excuse me, may I please have a moment of your time, forgive me for presuming to have something to say," and do we not always end with "*Merci*, I thank you for your attention, and I beg your pardon for everything I failed to do, for failing to deliver on my promise, and I ask your mercy (*merci*)"? (pp. 49–50, this volume) So, then, how different are these two words, *pardon* and *merci*? For Derrida language itself is structured around a promise, an archi-promise to which our every word is a response. Every time we open our mouth we are implicated in the promise to deliver the truth, even as we are caught up in an unavoidable and structural ("destined") "perjury," a failure to keep our word of honor, for the thing itself always slips away, and for this we ask forgiveness. For Derrida, what Jean-Luc Marion says of theological language holds true for language itself: It is always implicated in a certain "hypocrisy" about what it pretends to say and it must always beg the reader's forgiveness.[4] So Derrida's essay *on* forgiveness and perjury is likewise a work *of* forgiveness and perjury.

Forgiveness, like the gift (*par/don, for/give*), begins by (*par*) the impossible, is driven by the same logic, or rather aporetic. It has the same poison/gift-like structure: as soon as it is present, this present can start to turn to poison. We can use forgiveness as a strategy, hold it over the other whom we have forgiven, secretly congratulate ourselves on our forgiving nature, and so forth. Like the gift, it depends upon the aporetics of "the" impossible, which is why the seminar on forgiveness is more a seminar on thinking the possible and the impossible "otherwise" than on classical metaphysics and modal logic. For the more "possible" forgiveness is, the more reasonable, sensible, and equitable it is, the more it slides into the rule of an economy, a "calculation," a way of squaring accounts and of producing symmetry, equilibrium, and reciprocity (pp. 45–46, this volume). Like the gift, forgiveness must resist becoming a system of exchange. In classical philosophy and theology, forgiveness is inscribed precisely within an economic order according to which it can be "given" only under certain conditions. If the offender admits that he is wrong and asks to be forgiven, expresses sorrow, means to make amends as far as possible, and promises to avoid repeating his offense in the future, then he is forgiven. The deal is struck, the exchange is made, and the reconciliation follows. The accounts on both sides are in order. The offender meets the conditions, pays off the debt, and thus is *owed* forgiveness. Anything else would be unfair.

Derrida does not say this is a bad deal; he does not denounce it or say that reconciliation is no different or no better than vengeance or endless retribution. He simply holds, as he says to Jean Greisch in the roundtable discussion that follows, that while it may be a "a noble and worthy calculation" (p. 57, this volume), the symmetrical balance of reconciliation remains a worldly inscription or correlate of "forgiveness," which is asymmetrical. Reconciliation and redemption are the way forgiveness enters the world; they belong to an economy that ought not to be confused with forgiveness, rather the way the law must not be confused with justice. For forgiveness in itself, if there is such a thing, is a gift, not a deal, good or bad, which means that to "give" or grant pardon to the other, is to do so unconditionally, apart from any economic considerations, even if the other does not ask for forgiveness, does not repent or plan to make amends or promise to sin no more. There is forgiveness as such just when there is no hint of a deal, no sign from the other side that they intend to keep the peace, no sign of equilibrium. There is forgiveness—and this is the aporia at the core of Derrida's position—even and especially if the other has done something unforgivable, which would represent an extreme disturbance of economy, equilibrium, and reciprocity. There is forgiveness just when forgiveness is "impossible," when it makes no sense to grant or expect forgiveness, just when forgiveness is not only not owed to the offender but when it is unimaginable. There is forgiveness not when what the offender has done is forgivable, proportionate, measurable, "venial" (p. 30, this volume), but just when forgiveness is faced with the unforgivable. The unforgivable is the only possible correlate of forgiveness and the only way for forgiveness to be a gift, which means to be itself. Forgiveness begins by the im-possible, where this "im-" is not a simple negation but an intensification, driving forgiveness to the most extreme possibility, impelling forgiveness to the possibility of the impossible. Indeed, Derrida suggests at the end of the lecture that if there is any limit to the analogy between the gift and forgiveness, it may lie in this, that this impossible forgiveness is not simply an application of the aporetic logic of the gift, but that it actually precedes it, that forgiveness is prior to the gift, more "urgent," more necessary, and also its "first and final truth" (p. 48, this volume).

The distinction between unconditional forgiveness and the conditioned state in which we find it "in the world" is slippery, and it ought not to be construed as a "simple opposition," for even though the two are heterogeneous, we are always beings in the world and so they are always "indissociable" (p. 45, this volume). The unconditional must always pass through conditions; we are constantly negotiating the distance between them, negotiating "the best response in an impossible situation" (p. 58, this volume). Derrida's position on forgiveness mirrors his position on the distinction between justice and the law. "Justice, in itself, if there is such a thing" must find a footing in the "law" if it wants to "exist," to have "force," so that justice flourishes in the world when there are as many just laws as possible. The same thing would be true of the distinction between unconditional hospitality and the mundane conditions under which it actually exists, in immigration policies, for example, or in the tightly closed circle of personal "friendships." Thus, here, in this essay, Derrida adds that "there is in the movement, in the motion of unconditional forgiveness, an inner exigency of becoming—effective, manifest, determined, and, in determining itself, bending to conditionality" (p. 45, this volume).

The idea behind this discourse on an unconditional "X in itself, if there is such a thing," to which Kevin Hart draws attention with his question in the roundtable discussion (p. 52, this volume), is to pry open the existing economies in which these structures are always inscribed, and in which they acquire effective existence, in order to keep them open to the future, to improve and revise them, to keep them open-ended and amendable so they do not contract into their "present" limitations. This task of negotiating the distance between the conditional and the unconditional is also the framework for Derrida's response to John Milbank in the same discussion. Milbank wonders if this "X in itself" is not a transcendental of such Kantian purity that it leaves us unable to differentiate our responsibilities and to discriminate the pressing claims of those immediately around us, to respond to them "in good conscience," as in Derrida's famous example of the cats in *The Gift of Death.* Derrida responds by saying that while, as a concretely situated and conditioned being, he is, to be sure, more responsive to his own cat, namely, to the sphere of his "own," he also thinks that the needs of everyone else are constantly and structurally tugging at him so that his obligation to these other others is like a wound that will never close over in a "good conscience" about himself. When we say a prayer before a meal we have put before our family or our close friends, we ask God to keep us mindful of all those other others who are hungry, those other others whose eyes press silently upon us at this table. We cannot enjoy this meal in *simple* good conscience. Nothing is simple, including good soup. We must love good soup and weep over the hungry, both at once; it is not a question of choosing between them. His conscience should never be "one," never *simply* good or simply bad. As he says to Regina Schwartz, who asks whether we can forgive ourselves, there is always someone inside us who is constantly forgiving us for our shortcomings and also another one "who is absolutely merciless," and the two are "constantly fighting" (p. 61, this volume). That is the structural "perjury" or "betrayal" of the other others to which he refers.

In a certain sense, it is more interesting to turn what Derrida is saying around so that he might be read as arguing not simply that the pure gift, or pure forgiveness, or pure hospitality does not exist but also that a pure economy does not exist, or if it did it would be a nightmare. We begin wherever we are in the world, in a text or context, in the midst of one economy or the other, or several at once. After all, all there "is" is one economy or another, and so the idea is always to keep these economies open-ended. A world where everything is run by laws and absolute reciprocity, where the lawyers run everything, where we simply take care of our own first, where there would be no gifts, would be monstrous. "Give economy a chance," give it some "give," pry open the various economies—social, political, religious, juridical, sexual, and so forth—and make an opening within them, a little crack or fissure here and there, where the flowers of the gift, of hospitality, and of forgiveness may spring up and blossom "without why."

A good deal of the present lecture is given to a discussion of the work of Vladimir Jankélévitch, who wrote two different essays on forgiveness upon which Derrida comments. Derrida, along with many other readers, takes these essays to be inconsistent with each other (p. 26, this volume), but he takes this inconsistency to be symptomatic of the tension or aporia within the classical concept of forgiveness. In the first book, *Le Pardon* (1967), which Jankélévitch says is very "philosophical" (implying that it is unrealistic and idealistic), Jankélévitch says that the scene of forgiveness is an ongoing struggle in which the infinite power of forgiveness, which is stronger than evil, does endless battle with the power of evil, which is also stronger than forgiveness. But in the second book, *L'imprescriptible* (1971), which contains a foreword entitled "Should We Forgive Them?," which is highly polemical, the ongoing dialectic between forgiveness and evil disappears, having been ground to a halt by what Jankélévitch insists is an unforgivable evil, the Shoah, for which granting forgiveness is not only not possible but would in fact be immoral. This foreword addresses a debate in France in the 1960s about whether to adopt the provisions of the United Nations resolution on the imprescriptibility of "crimes against humanity," which lifted any statute of limitations on the legal prosecution of such crimes.[5] "Imprescriptibility" is not the same thing as "unforgivability," Derrida points out, but is its legal or mundane correlate, no more than amnesty is forgiveness. Forgiveness or its refusal belongs to the sphere of "justice," of ethics, or of what Derrida calls here, using a word that he also finds Jankélévitch using, a "hyperbolic" ethics.

Jankélévitch emphatically refuses to forgive the Nazis or the Germans (he does not distinguish the two, Derrida points out). "Forgiveness died in the death camps," Jankélévitch writes. The history of forgiveness ended there, even though in *Le Pardon* Jankélévitch had said that forgiveness was infinite, endless and ongoing. In the name of the victims, Jankélévitch argues, we must not forgive, because: (1) the Germans have not acknowledged their guilt and asked for pardon, and (2) what they did is so monstrous as to surpass any human measure or proportion. To forgive a wrong, it must be on a human scale, and therefore punishable and expiable; there must be something one could do to restore symmetry and equilibrium. But what reparations could the Germans undertake? What measures can one take when faced with the immeasurable? Can the Germans bring the dead back to life, restore the peace of mind of the millions who survived the terror but whose lives were forever shattered? What they have done is "irreparable," representing a "radical evil" (Kant), and so it must remain forever unforgivable. The burning torch of this undying un-forgiveness will live always as a sign that the Jews remain loyal to the dead, as an inextinguishable memorial to their cruel murder. At least for Jankélévitch. For when Jankélévitch received a letter from a young German who had nothing to do with the death of the Jews but who expresses great guilt and sorrow for what the Nazis did, who asks for forgiveness for a crime that he did not commit, Jankélévitch's first condition had been met. He waited a long time to hear this "word" from a German, he says. But still, now that he has heard it, he begs to be excused. He is too old for forgiveness; this possibility belongs to future genera-tions of which he is not a part. The history of forgiveness will go on after all, but without Jankélévitch, and Derrida wonders whether what will be called recon-ciliation in the future will not always be for Jankélévitch forgetting the dead and "successful" mourning (pp. 41–42, this volume).

For Derrida, the dilemma in which Jankélévitch finds himself is ex-tremely "classical" and it exposes the "auto-deconstructibility" of the classical concept of forgiveness. On the one hand, Jankélévitch has rightly "calculated" that nothing can restore symmetry and equilibrium after such an immense and monstrous evil has been committed, that there is no proportionate punish-ment to balance the accounts, that things are indeed irreparable and as such unforgivable. Given that sound calculation, forgiveness is rightly withheld. On the other hand, Derrida writes:

John D. Caputo, Mark Dooley, and Michael J. Scanlon

> There is in forgiveness, in the very meaning of forgiveness, a force, a desire, an impetus, a movement, an appeal (call it what you will) that demands that forgiveness be granted, if it can be, even to someone who does not ask for it, who does not repent or confess or improve or redeem himself, beyond, consequently, an entire identificatory, spiritual, whether sublime or not, economy, beyond all expiation even. (p. 28, this volume)

The classical concept is inwardly disturbed by what Derrida calls here, using Jankélévitch's own language, a "hyperbolic" demand to surpass itself, so that forgiveness is forgiveness only in the face of the unforgivable, and thus only when, in classical terms, it is impossible, while forgiving the forgivable, something venial, is something less than forgiveness. The classical concept of forgiveness is aporetic, auto-deconstructing, "auto-interrupting," because it contains what it cannot contain, namely, a hyperbolic impetus or appeal or "call it what you will." It is astir with a longing, a force to forgive even and precisely when the conditions it itself sets forth are not met, even and precisely when it meets something that on its own terms and by its own calculations is unforgivable. Forgiving the unforgivable is not a demand that Derrida makes from without and imposes violently, or with some kind of excessive Kantian moralistic purism, on the classical concept, but rather a force that stirs within this concept itself and disturbs it from within, the result of which is that we can never rest with what in the world passes itself off as "forgiveness"—or "justice" or the "gift" or "hospitality."

"Forgiveness" then is pulled in two directions at once, and that is what keeps it both alive or effective and also unstable and auto-deconstructing. For, on the hand, it is moved by a force of *"becoming effective,"* making itself real, concretizing itself in the existing institutions (political, juridical, religious, etc.) in which it becomes practically effective, and, on the other hand, it is moved by a force of *"hyperbolic becoming,"* which is the becoming of the "to come," an impulse or impetus or desire, call it what you will, that keeps these structures open-ended, revisable, and turned toward an unforeseeable future.

The Essays

When Derrida focuses on the unconditional purity of forgiveness and not the conditioned economy of establishing peace and reconciliation between two parties, he takes leave of the predominant Christian and Jewish traditions on forgiveness, which have always calibrated the conditions of forgiveness, which Derrida referred to in the roundtable discussion as a "noble calculation" but a calculation nonetheless, not forgiveness as such. This comes out clearly in Robert Gibbs's probing study of the Jewish notion of Teshuvah, "repentance," but literally "returning," turning around and coming back to God and the neighbor whom one has offended. Unlike Derrida, Robert Gibbs argues, in the Jewish tradition the focus is somewhat more on "returning" than on forgiving. To return is to make an approach, an apology, while to forgive is

8

to accept someone back, to accept an apology. This distinction moves in tandem with another, the distinction between ethics, which concerns our relations with others, and theology, which concerns our relations with God. What, then, Gibbs asks, is the difference between seeking forgiveness from God and seeking it from the neighbor or companion, in particular from someone intimate, such as a parent, spouse, or child? What are the terms and the conditions of reconciliation (the very issues Derrida wants to separate out from forgiveness)?

Gibbs is discussing Levinas's commentary on the Talmud in dialogue with texts from the Mishnah and the Gemara. The Mishnah teaches that while it is true that the Day of Atonement atones an offense against God for us, the Day will not atone and we will not be forgiven until we make peace with our neighbor, which is for Gibbs the occasion of the invention of "social ethics." The relationship to God is indirect, but to the neighbor it is direct. Levinas comments that God, unlike my neighbor, can be counted on not to be fickle and to keep his promise of forgiveness if I sincerely ask to return, whereas satisfying the other human being, who is more unpredictable and to whom I am asymmetrically related, is a trickier business. Levinas follows the tradition that is disputed by Rabbi Joseph, who says that an offense against God is between God and the sinner and the relation to the neighbor is not a precondition of making things right with God. Levinas underlines my asymmetrical dependence upon the forgiveness of the neighbor whom I have offended, to whose will I am exposed. Levinas even goes along with Rabbi Isaac, who says that a sin against a neighbor, which may be a bodily act or completely verbal (such as a broken word), demands that appeasement take a monetary form. Someone must pay. Levinas explains that this translation of an ethical offense, which is not an economic issue, into an exchange of money, is an attempt to protect the seeking of forgiveness from degenerating into empty words and hypocrisy. But suppose the offended party will not relent no matter what I do? Then the rabbis recommend that I humiliate myself before the community. This public approach, as when I secure three lines of three people each to ask forgiveness on my behalf, which is recommended as a way to seek God's forgiveness, may also serve to prevail upon the offended neighbor, who must in turn also guard against becoming arrogant. Indeed, forgiveness might even be exacted from the dead, if we line up publicly before his grave. So, if we cannot simply seek forgiveness from God, who can always be counted on, we also need not be at the mercy of the arbitrariness of the offended neighbor, since we can constrain the neighbor to forgive by our public repentance. *Pace* Heidegger, "Only a god" *cannot* save us, Gibbs pointedly concludes, for until we save each other, not even God can save us.

In "Forgiveness and Incarnation," Anglican theologian John Milbank asks if forgiveness at a purely interhuman level is possible without divine mediation. In a masterful contribution that represents a kind of contemporary reprise of *Cur deus homo*, Milbank discusses what he calls the "five major aporias of forgiveness." Milbank concludes that only through the mediation of the Christian Incarnation can "positive" forgiveness be granted. For a theory of "negative" forgiveness, which is primarily secular in character, although not exclusively so ("a theology focused more upon divine fiat than upon the incarnation" is also considered negative), faces the seemingly insuperable problem of how it is possible to forgive and be forgiven if those whom we have wronged have either been erased from memory or cannot be found. Milbank contends that it is insufficient to respond to this aporia by stating that only God, as distinct from the God-Man, can forgive in the absence of the victims. For how, he ponders, can we be forgiven by God if these human victims against whom the wrong was committed have not forgiven us? Second, how can God truly forgive us if he, unlike the victims of suffering, is beyond all suffering? God, it seems, has nothing to forgive because he is beyond all victimage, and therefore beyond all offense which victimage inevitably causes. But, argues Milbank, the God-Man, through his suffering, humiliation, and death, is a "unique sovereign victim" who can forgive on behalf of all those who have been similarly brutalized. Through him humanity can forgive humanity, for, unlike purely human forgiveness, which is always preceded by hate and resentment, the forgiveness which the God-Man makes possible is free of such rancor. Hence, it is through the Trinity and the intercession of the Holy Spirit, according to Milbank, that positive, qua divine, forgiveness can be attained. In the second part of his essay, Milbank juxtaposes Aquinas's Christology to that of Duns Scotus, in order to show that while the former developed a strong and convincing argument in favor of divine/positive forgiveness, the latter, by undoing the connection between forgiveness and the Incarnation, promoted a "reign of aspiration" to purely negative forgiveness. In subjecting ontology to theology, Aquinas was able to show that unless the logic of theology transcends that of metaphysics, forgiveness is destined to remain but an "instance within divine goodness."

In "The Catastrophe of Memory," co-editor Mark Dooley takes up the notion of forgiveness in Jacques Derrida and John Milbank and presents a defense of Derrida's position. Dooley argues that Milbank's proposed answer to the question of whether pure forgiveness is possible, the God-Man as "sovereign victim," fails to meet the challenges posed by Derrida's controversial claim that absolute forgiveness is impossible. Dooley maintains that Milbank's belief in full reconciliation through the intercession of the God-Man is analogous to the trinitarian logic employed by Hegel, a circular economy of exchange which Derrida has from the beginning of his career sought to deconstruct. Derrida has done so by pointing out that we are always already cut from our origins by virtue of a "catastrophe of memory"—or an inability to fully gather up the ashes, cinders, and traces of which memory is comprised. By complicating any such trinitarian economy, Derrida shows, according to Dooley, that what deconstruction offers is not, as radical orthodoxy argues, a nebulous void, but a way of staying alert to the calls and cries of the faceless and nameless victims whose remains lie encrypted in the vast recesses of memory. If the certainty of resurrection is what motivates Milbank, the groundless faith that one day we shall be reconciled to such victims through a work of mourning is what impassions Derrida. Dooley concludes his discussion by defending Derrida against the charge, leveled by Milbank in the course of the Villanova roundtable, that the desire for impossible forgiveness leads to "absolute self-sacrifice" and "masochism."

The essays that follow shift from the topic of forgiveness to that of God.

In "The God Who May Be," Irish philosopher, novelist, and cultural analyst Richard Kearney proffers a third or median option between the two main interpretations of the tetragrammaton (Exodus 3:14), the ontological and the eschatological, which he calls the onto-eschatological. He suggests that we might do better to interpret the God of Exodus neither as being nor as non-being but as the possibility of either, that is, as May-Be. *'Ehyeh 'aser 'ehyeh* could thus be rendered as I-AM-WHO-MAY-BE. Kearney reviews the ontological tradition with its major moments in Augustine and Aquinas and then turns to recent biblical scholarship on the meaning of the Name. In different ways this scholarship focuses on the future tense, whereby the divine Name becomes a promise to God's people. To Moses, God reveals himself as *becoming different* from what he used to be in relation to his people—the God of their *Fathers* now discloses himself as the God of their *sons and daughters*. Kearney emphasizes that the Name, the eschatological promise, is granted within an I-Thou relationship of God with Moses, thereby indicating two sides to the promise, human as well as divine responsibility. While the promise is granted unconditionally, as pure gift and grace, the people are free to accept or refuse this gift. As an "I-Self in process," God takes on the risk of becoming with us, as dependent on us as we are on him. This new mutuality between God and humanity has revolutionary implications indeed. Kearney offers reflections on a contemporary strand of mystical postmodernism, described as a *teratology of the sublime* in that it focuses on the 'monstrous' character of God. He concludes with citations from Nicholas of Cusa, who taught that God alone "is what he is able to be." *Posse* replaces *esse* in this *poetics of the possible*. Atheistic and theistic certainty is replaced with *perhaps*! If we remain faithful to the promise, I-who-am-what-I-may-be may at last be a kingdom of justice and love.

The Australian theologian, philosopher, and poet Kevin Hart, in an essay entitled "On Interruption," undertakes an intriguing analysis of Derrida's "religion without religion," focusing especially on the latter's notion of "faith." Taking his cue from Derrida's "Faith and Knowledge: The Two Sources of Religion at the Limits of Reason Alone," Hart asks what the consequences for Christianity might be of a form of faith which is predicated upon a messianic hope for a justice to come. In order to arrive at a possible answer to this perplexing question, Hart reflects on the meaning of one of Derrida's most elusive phrases—"absolute interruption," for it is this phrase which best encapsulates what, for Derrida, is the experience of faith or belief, as distinct from knowledge or consciousness. An "absolute interruption" in the Derridean sense, argues Hart, marks the point where the "possible," or the ordinary horizon of expectation, is interrupted by an unforeseeable or unpredictable event, by what would have been considered "impossible" before such an event occurred. To hope for, or to have faith in, "the impossible," therefore, requires a hope against hope in what shatters, or absolutely interrupts, the present order. Hart concludes on the basis of this that Derrida's "religion" is not geared toward a kingdom (*basileia*) of this world but a "kingdom of the impossible," or a kingdom which is always to come. This same experience of faith, of faith in the impossible kingdom, is what, for Hart, characterizes Jesus's experience of God. This is a kingdom in which the parables of Jesus continually serve to undermine the sacred codes of the historical determinations. To experience God in the Christian context, thus, is to affirm God's trace in the singularity of Jesus's life and death, without trying to obviate all the problems and dilemmas which historical Jesus research brings to bear. This, argues Hart, is an "experience of absolute interruption," for it shatters the order of the same (the possible) in the name of what is considered, by present standards, impossible—the *basileia* of Jesus, a kingdom in which God is revealed through "a community of mutual otherness."

Regina M. Schwartz's essay advances the cause of conversation as a middle ground between Derrida and Jean-Luc Marion. Making use of two important theses of Marion, his distinction between idol and icon and his notion of praise as the third and iconic way beyond affirmation and negation, Schwartz argues that the sphere of the idol is not confined to the plastic or visual figure, which is the sphere of the biblical idol, nor to the "conceptual" idol that Marion identified in *God without Being*. She also includes within its range the considerable power of the narrative, which she takes to occupy a place analogous to causal metaphysical discourse. A great narrative gives us a commanding sense of knowing what is going on. One is reminded of the "Introduction" to *Being and Time*, when Heidegger is warning against treating Being as a being, in particular as a first cause; he says that we should not "tell a story" about Being (he is citing the *Sophist* 242c).[6] Both causes and stories try to catch God up in manmade terms. In order to avoid seeing the biblical narratives as constituting a people whom God jealously protects against their enemies, which then become an instrument, a weapon, to justify the worst evils, Schwartz proposes hearing the great biblical stories as performatives, as hymns of praise whose poetic qualities, rhythm, and meter thus come into play. Then the story of Cain, analyzed in her *The Curse of Cain*, is received not as a story of God siding with Abel, but as a story of the blood of Abel crying from the ground, a cry for justice.

Instead of causality or narrativity, Schwartz proposes the model of conversation. This analysis, in the second part of her essay, takes its point of departure from the religious power of poetry, or verse, by way of a commentary on

Herbert's *The Temple*, which she takes to be something of a seventeenth-century book of psalms. For Schwartz, the subject is constituted in and by the conversation and does not enjoy a prior existence that produces the conversation as an effect. The "I" does not use conversation as a tool but is brought into relation with the other by the conversation. The conversation is encounter, not an exchange of propositions, which Schwartz argues holds a middle position between the too little of "difference" (Derrida) and the too much of the "saturated phenomenon" (Marion). The model of conversation as a back-and-forth movement, a reciprocal speaking and hearing, "versing" to and fro is a biblical one, including above all the conversation that transpires between God and his people. Poetry is a performance, an enactment not a description, and hence like a liturgy, which illuminates the action of a conversation by enacting a dialogue between interlocutor and listener. Thus, if Marion regards the Eucharist as a saturated phenomenon, while Derrida might be expected to mark the distance between signifier and signified in it, Schwartz would treat it as the blood of Abel crying out from the ground through the blood of Christ, a cry for hearing.

One of the most confusing debates about "the condition of postmodernity" is the question of selfhood, a question that has become more urgent than ever, as Jean Greisch insists. In keeping with the conference theme Greisch attempts to link two questions: "Who are we?" and "What about God?" Given Villanova's Augustinian atmosphere and the recent death of Jean-François Lyotard, whose posthumous fragments have been published under the title, *La Confession d'Augustin*, Greisch returns to Augustine with his linked questions by way of a detour through Heidegger. Heidegger claimed the ontological primacy of the question, "Who?" in attempting to raise the question of the mode of being of the subject as over against the "What?" question of traditional ontology, which is still followed by Descartes and all of modern philosophy. Greisch finds it astonishing that Heidegger never raised the "Who?" question in relation to divine Selfhood. But Greisch insists that the style of questioning which best suits Lyotard's "postmodern condition" emerges at the intersection of the questions "Where is God?" and "Who is God?" While struggling with "the question" he had become to himself, Augustine discovered the divine Selfhood as synonymous with peace and plenitude in verse 9 of Psalm 4 in the Latin word, *idipsum* (the Self-same). This discovery of the Self-same is intimately linked with Augustine's discovery of his new self. The "Where" of the divine "Who" is in Augustine's innermost self, a self *in Te supra me*, as he confesses. Greisch explores the biblical presuppositions of Augustine's Self-same and moves forward to Eckhart's interpretation. For those who refuse to confuse postmodernity and post-Christianity, Augustine's route from the divine Self to the human self remains an option for the postmodern subject.

Concurring with Jean Greisch on the urgency of the question of selfhood, co-editor Michael J. Scanlon reviews the traditional dialogue between philosophy and theology on Christian anthropology from the Platonism of the Fathers through the Aristotelianism of the Scholastics to the theological reception of the modern "turn to the subject," raising the question of the continuation of this dialogue with postmodern philosophical anthropology, wherein the self is "humiliated" by Nietzsche and "erased" by Foucault. Arguing that theology requires an anthropology, he finds the postmodern "humiliated" self both congenial with the Christian tradition on the decentered self and particularly germane to the contemporary rhetorical task of theology, specifically to public theology. Given the postmodern challenge to rationality in all of the traditional disciplines, Scanlon turns to theologian J. Wentzel van Huyssteen's recent response to this challenge with his elaboration of "commonsense rationality." With the modern goal of *epistēmē* yielding to the more humble goal of *doxa* in postmodern thought the door is open to the contemporary rehabilitation of rhetoric. Recalling Augustine's contribution to the role of rhetoric in the ancient and medieval Western tradition, Scanlon moves to a consideration of contemporary rhetorical philosophy and theology toward a clarification of the rhetorical potential of public theology, described as the effort to discover and communicate the significance of the Christian tradition for issues under public discussion today. The theologically rhetorical self is a good illustration of the "humiliated" and thereby possibly effective self in addressing current situations.

In "Questioning God," Graham Ward contrasts the kind of question that Augustine is raising, which participates in an economy of love of and fealty to God and arises from a history in which God bears witness to this dialogue, with Derrida's questions about negative theology, which are put in such a way that we cannot be sure to whom they are addressed or how they are to be answered. Having reached today, by way of Derrida, the aporia of undecidability and the impossible, of the death of the God of onto-theo-logic, we now are on the cusp of another thinking of God foreshadowed in Augustine, who stood at the transition from paganism ("pluralism") to Christianity, even as we stand at the transition from Christianity to "pluralism" (paganism). When Augustine asks whether God is, what God is, and of what sort God is, he does so in a public act before a community of faith, hope, and love and in such a way that he himself is brought into question before God. Augustine thinks of an analogical likeness between God and the world, not of an "absolute interruption" by the wholly other into a continuum of immanence. Augustine thinks of God in terms of mystery and incomprehensibility and he thinks of the world as a gradually unfolding process, not something frozen in presence. Barth and Derrida, on the contrary, think of God's advent almost as an "alien invasion," as the coming of a "wholly other" who somehow or other must manage a terrestrial landing. Thus, for Ward, the name of God is not a "transcendental signifier" because it is the name of a questioning that never ends and because this questioning transpires within the Spirit in which and by which it questions. Augustine's God is not "logocentric," which means the absolutizing of the instantaneous and immediate (Certeau's "white ecstasy"). Hence the critique of logocentrism, which seeks something "wholly other," is not a critique of Augustine and indeed, by being in complicity with the modernist assumption that presence means the instant and univocal, this critique is seeking the remedy of a heterogeneity that is equally unbelievable. If Augustine and Derrida both want to suspend judgment in the face of ungraspable excess, Augustine does so in hope and in loving relation to the Good, whereas Derrida's questioning moves from aporia to aporia, locked in the impasse of Camus' Sisyphus, hence never really moving and never really reaching ethics, since we are always infinitely guilty. Derrida's is a questioning that opens up aporias for the sake of generating endless undecidability, a bad infinity, unhappy consciousness, onanism, *coitus interruptus.* Derrida is driven by the pleasure of the question and of not having what one desires, producing a "hermeneutical me-ontology" as opposed to Augustine's hermeneutical ontology, not an ethics of questioning, but an erotics or aesthetics, which does not entrust itself to what it questions, like the Starship Enterprise seeking further textual adventures. Still, Ward concludes, we question within a horizon that has been shaped in no small part by Derrida, and we cannot, even if we wished to, simply return to Augustine, which is something we learn from Derrida and Gadamer. Ward teases us with the possibility of a questioning "then," beyond onanistic logic, beyond deconstruction and the death of God, a "cybernetic questioning," about whose details we must await Ward's future publications.

Co-editor John D. Caputo rises to the defense of Derrida in a piece which questions Ward's "Questioning God." Caputo disputes Ward's treatment of Derrida and he goes on to voice a more general criticism of radical orthodoxy and the line it has adopted toward deconstruction. After analyzing the different view of Derrida that Ward has adopted in this piece as compared to his earlier more sympathetic treatment of Derrida in *Barth, Derrida and the Language of Theology*, Caputo contests Ward's understanding of undecidability. Undecidability is the condition of possibility of decision; its opposite is not "decision," but "decidability," a term borrowed from Gödel referring to the formalizability of a decision procedure. If a decision were "decidable," Caputo claims, we would not need good people, just good software. The difference between Augustine and Derrida for Caputo is *not* that Augustine is filled with faith and hope and love in the God before whom he confesses and whose actions are testified to in history while Derrida is adrift in undecidability. The difference is *not* that Augustine has "entrusted" or "delivered" himself over to the Good while Derrida is just seeking new adventures on the Starship Enterprise. That for Caputo is a polemical reading in which Ward has abandoned what he achieved in *Barth, Derrida and the Language of Theology*. The genuine difference is that for Augustine the object of his faith, hope, and love has a determinate historical name, that he has "entrusted" or "delivered" himself over to the proper names that have been transmitted to him by the Christian tradition, while for Derrida faith and hope and love have an ineradicable "determinability" such that they can always be determined otherwise, taking other forms in other historical contexts. In Caputo's view, Derrida makes explicit the determinability and undecidability that inhabits faith and hope, whereas Augustine comes to rest in an historically determinate Christian decision, a decision Augustine made in the midst of an undecidability that does not go away just because Augustine's faith is firm. Caputo writes, "The difference is *not* that Augustine decides and Derrida does not, that Derrida lapses into undecidability but Augustine does not, that Augustine has faith and hope and love while Derrida does not. Augustine's faith, no less than Derrida's, must be sustained across an abyss of undecidability. . . . *Unless* of course one has dogmatically decided that Augustine's *Christian* faith, hope, and love is the one definitive way of having faith, hope, and love and those who disagree with Augustinian Christianity are wrong, . . . are 'aesthetes' who cannot be serious." Caputo is worried that this kind of critique is endemic to the very idea of something like "radical orthodoxy."

In "The Scandals of the Sign: The Virgin Mary as Supplement in the Religions of the Book," Cleo McNelly Kearns puts the thought of Derrida to work in a different direction, offering an evocative interpretation of the Virgin Mary from a Derridean perspective. For Kearns, if Mary occupies a central place in one of the religions of the Book, in one of the great monotheistic faiths, she also represents a scandal to the faithful. For she is both the means by which the Word of God becomes incarnate and the moment that the Word undoes itself through supplementarity and dissemination. In responding affirmatively at the Annunciation, Mary the virgin declares that she is willing to become a vehicle for the divine logos, and, in so doing, she is drawn into the phallogocentric logic of what Derrida refers to as the concrete messianisms. But this affirmative response by Mary, argues Kearns, can also be interpreted as a deconstructive gesture, a gesture which "countersigns" that of Father Abraham himself. Like Abraham, Mary opens herself unequivocally to the divine summons, but she also brings an end to the sacrificial economy which characterizes the Genesis narrative of the *akedah*. For while she is the condition of "messianic sacrifice," she becomes "neither its celebrant nor its apostle." In Mary, Kearns identifies an openness to the in-coming of the other, a messianic affirmation of justice beyond the law. By surrendering herself to an openended future, Mary transcends the logocentric paradigm of established religion and assumes her place at the foot of the cross. At that point, continues Kearns, Mary's motherhood is disseminated across the ages. Kearns concludes with a reflection on what Chapter Twelve of the book of Revelation calls "The Woman Clothed with the Sun," a woman who, after giving birth to a man child of God, flees out into the wilderness. This wilderness Kearns associates with what both Derrida and Plato term *"khora"*—a cold and barren place which resists all revelation and interrogation. It is here, in *khora*, in a time before the time of the religions of the Book, that Mary is to be heard whispering that ancient deconstructive prayer *"Viens! oui, oui."*

Fittingly, *Questioning God* closes with a concluding and insightful review of the history and status of theological discourse about God. In "Being, Subjectivity, Otherness: The Idols of God," Francis Schüssler Fiorenza argues that an historical overview of theology's search for adequate language about God points out its need to reflect critically on the inadequacy of its God-talk. The categories of being (patristic and medieval theology), subjectivity (modern theology), and otherness (some modern and much postmodern theology) are the common sites for talking about God. These sites create idols of God to the extent that they pretend to be adequate. For some contemporary thinkers "Otherness" or "alterity" is the only appropriate category for God-talk in our postmodern age. Fiorenza does not concur. All three sites are problematic and ambiguous: each category must be recast, and yet each category has significance as a site for language about God. Fiorenza's contribution proffers a balanced argument in support of this conviction with critical appraisals of all three sites. Fiorenza rejects all sharp contrasts, especially the modern one between the God of Abraham and the God of philosophy, as well as the attuned synthesis between the two traditions in classical theology. He seeks to go beyond both dichotomies and syntheses to develop a path between the current contrast between otherness and sameness. Fiorenza argues that we should go beyond a naturalistic metaphysics by appealing to "fragile interpretive experiences," which should be elucidated not in terms of transcendental subjectivity but in relation to an ethical and religious intersubjectivity, and, finally, we should provide a thicker description of metaphysical language and the relation between sameness and otherness and show the ethical consequences of this thicker description. Fiorenza concludes that for the Christian tradition thus elucidated, language about God in and through a responsible community with its liturgical practice and concern for justice and for others is not supplementary but constitutive of knowledge and language about God.

NOTES

1. Jacques Derrida and Catherine Malabou, *Voyager avec Jacques Derrida-La Contre-Allée* (Paris: La Quainzaine Littéraire, 1999).

2. Jacques Derrida, "Circumfession: Fifty-nine Periods and Periphrases," in Geoffrey Bennington and Jacques Derrida, *Jacques Derrida* (Chicago: University of Chicago Press, 1993), p. 155.

3. See Jacques Derrida, "Psyche: Inventions of the Other," trans. Catherine Porter, in *Reading De Man Reading*, ed. Lindsay Waters and Wlad Godzich (Minneapolis: University of Minnesota Press, 1989), pp. 30–42; and for a fuller treatment of Ponge see *Signéponge/Signspong*, trans. Richard Rand (New York: Columbia University Press, 1984).

4. Jean-Luc Marion, *God without Being: Hors-texte*, trans. Thomas Carlson (Chicago: University of Chicago Press, 1991), p. 2.

5. According to the "Convention on Imprescriptibility of Crimes of War and Against Humanity," adopted by the General Assembly of the United Nations, Resolution 2391 (XXII) of 1968, and in the Council of Europe's treaty: Non-applicability of

John D. Caputo, Mark Dooley, and Michael J. Scanlon

Statutory Limitations to Crimes against Humanity and War Crimes, E. T. S. No.82, adopted on 25 January 1974, crimes against humanity are unaffected by statutes of limitation. This was reaffirmed in Article 29 of the Statute of the International Criminal Court.

6. Martin Heidegger, *Being and Time*, translated by John Macquarrie and Edward Robinson (New York: Harper & Row, 1962), 26.

PART I. FORGIVING

To Forgive

The Unforgivable and the Imprescriptible

Jacques Derrida

Pardon, yes, pardon.

I have just said "pardon," in English.

You don't understand anything by this for the moment, no doubt.

"Pardon."

It is a word, "pardon"; this word is a *noun*: one says *"un pardon,"* *"le pardon."* In the French language it is a noun. One finds its homonymic equivalent, more or less in the same state, with more or less the same meaning and with uses that are at least analogous in other languages; in English, for example ("pardon," in certain contexts that will be become clearer later on), although the word is, if not Latin, at least, in its tortuous filiation, of Latin origin (*perdon* in Spanish, *perdâo* in Portuguese, *perdono* in Italian). In the Latin origin of this word, and in too complex a way for us to tackle it head-on today, one finds a reference to the *"don,"* [the "gift"], to *"donation,"* [to "gift-giving"]. And more than once we would have to carry over the problems and aporias of the "gift" (such as I have tried to formalize them, for example, in *Given Time* and in particular in the last chapter of this book, entitled "The Excuse and Pardon"),[1] to transfer them, so to speak, to the problems and non-

Jacques Derrida

problems that are the aporias of forgiveness, aporias that are analogous and, what is more, linked. But one must neither yield to these analogies between the gift and forgiveness nor, of course, neglect their necessity; rather, one must attempt to articulate the two, to follow them to the point where, suddenly, they cease to be pertinent. Between giving and forgiving there is at least this affinity or this alliance that, beside their unconditionality of principle—one and the other, giving and forgiving, giving for giving [*don par don*]—have an essential relation to time, to the movement of temporalization; even though what seems to bind forgiveness to a past, which in a certain way does not pass, makes forgiveness an experience irreducible to that of the gift, to a gift one grants more commonly in the present, in the presentation or presence of the present.

I have just said "experience" of forgiveness or the gift, but the word "experience" may already seem abusive or precipitous here, where forgiveness and gift have perhaps this in common, that they never *present themselves as such* to what is commonly called an experience, a presentation to consciousness or to existence, precisely because of the aporias that we must take into account; and for example—to limit myself to this for the time being—the aporia that renders me incapable of giving enough, or of being hospitable enough, of being present enough to the present that I give, and to the welcome that I offer, such that I think, I am even certain of this, I always have to be forgiven, to ask forgiveness for not giving, for never giving enough, for never offering or welcoming enough. One is always guilty, one must always be forgiven the gift. And the aporia becomes more extreme when one becomes conscious of the fact that if one must ask forgiveness for not giving, for never giving enough, one may also feel guilty and thus have to ask forgiveness on the contrary, for giving, forgiveness for what one gives, which can become a poison, a weapon, an affirmation of sovereignty, or even omnipotence or an appeal for recognition. One always takes by giving: I have, in the past, insisted at length on this logic of giving-taking. One must a priori, thus, ask forgiveness for the gift itself, one has to be forgiven the gift, the sovereignty or the desire for sovereignty of the gift. And, pushing it farther, irresistibly, to the second degree, one would even have to be forgiven forgiveness, which may itself also include [*comporter*] the irreducible equivocation of an affirmation of sovereignty, indeed of mastery.

These are the abysses that await us and that will always lie in wait for us— not as accidents to avoid but as the ground [*fond*] itself, the ground without ground or groundless ground [*fond sans fond*] of the thing itself called gift or forgiveness. Thus, no gift without forgiveness and no forgiveness without gift; but the two are, above all, not the same thing. The verbal link of *don* to *pardon*, which is marked in Latin languages but not in Greek, for example, as far as I know (and we will have to ask ourselves about the apparent presence or absence of forgiveness in the strict sense in ancient Greek culture; an enormous and delicate question), this verbal link of *don* and *pardon* is also present in English and German: in English, *to forgive, forgiveness, asking for forgiveness*, and one will oppose *to give* and *to get* (this extraordinary word in the English language to which one would have to devote years of seminar) in *to forgive* versus *to forget*, forgiving is not forgetting (another enormous problem); in German, although *Verzeihen* is more common—*Verzeihung, jenen um Verzeihung bitten*: to ask someone for forgiveness—and this is the word Hegel uses in the *Phenomenology of Spirit* (we should return to this), one often uses *Entschuldigung* (more in the sense of an excuse) and *entschuldbar* in the equivocal sense of the forgivable-excusable, literally deculpabilizable, relieved of, exonerated from a debt remitted. There is nonetheless a word in German, a lexical family that maintains this link between the gift and forgiveness; *vergeben* means "to forgive," "*ich bitte um Vergebung*" [I ask for forgiveness], but its usage is usually reserved for solemn occasions, especially spiritual or religious occasions, occasions less common than those that elicit *Verzeihen* or *Entschuldigen*. This link between the uses of the word "pardon," those uses said to be common and everyday and light (for example when I say "pardon," "sorry" at the moment I must pass in front of someone as I get out of an elevator) and the serious uses, reflective, intense uses, this link between all types of uses in very different situations, this link should be one of our problems, both a semantic problem of the concept of forgiveness and a pragmatic problem of the acts of language or pre- or ultra-linguistic practice. *Vergebung* is used more frequently—but this frequency and this probability are precisely a question of practice, of context and social gesture—more foreseeably; thus, a religious sense (Biblical-Koranic here) of the remission of sins, although the use of the lexical family (*Vergeben, Vergebung, Vergabe*) is both flexible and perverse: *Vergeben* can mean the misdeal [*maldonne*], the corruption of the gift, *sich etwas vergeben*: to compromise oneself; and *Vergabe* is an invitation to tender [*marché attribué*], an auctioning . . .)

"Pardon": "pardon" is a noun. It can sometimes be preceded (in French) by a definite or indefinite article (*le pardon, un pardon*) and inscribed, for example as subject, in a constative sentence: forgiveness [*le pardon*] is this or that, forgiveness [*le pardon*] has been asked by someone or by an institution, a pardon [*un pardon*] has been granted or refused, and so forth. . . . Forgiveness asked by the Episcopate, by the police, by doctors, forgiveness that the university or the Vatican has not yet asked for, and so forth. This is the noun as reference of the constative—or theoretical—type. One could devote a lecture to the question, the subject, the theme of forgiveness, and this is basically what we are preparing to do (forgiveness thus becomes, to this extent, the name of a theme or of a theoretical problem, to be treated in a horizon of knowledge), unless the actors of the lecture ask or grant forgiveness in theoretically treating forgiveness. And when I opened this lecture by saying "pardon," you did not know, you still do not know, what I was doing, if I was begging your pardon or if, instead of using it, I was mentioning the noun "pardon" as the title of the lecture. For in the single word "pardon," with or without an exclamation point, one can, although nothing forces one to do so if a context does not require it, already hear an entire sentence implicit in it, a performative sentence: Pardon!

I am begging your pardon, I am begging you [*vous*] to pardon me, I am begging you [*te*] to pardon me, pardon me, I beg you [*pardonnez-moi, je vous prie*], pardon me, I am begging you [*pardonne-moi, je t'en prie*].

(I am already marking, I have just marked it as if in passing, beginning with a long digression in parentheses, this distinction between the *tu* and the *vous* in order to situate or announce a question that will long remain suspended but on which no doubt everything will also hang; if the "you" is not a "*vous*" of respect or distance, as this "*Vous*" that Lévinas says is preferable to Buber's "*Tu*," which signifies too much proximity or familiarity, or even fusion, and risks canceling out the infinite transcendence of the other; if thus the "you" of "I beg your pardon," "pardon me" is a collective and plural "you," the question then becomes one of a collective pardon—collective either because it involves a group of subjects, others, citizens, individuals, and so forth, or because it already involves, and this is even more complicated, but this complication is at the heart of "pardon," a multiplicity of agencies [*instances*] or moments, instances [*instances*] or instants, of "I"s inside the "I." Who forgives or who asks whom for forgiveness, at what moment? Who has the right or the power to do this, "who [to] whom?" And what does the "who" signify here? This will always be the almost ultimate form of the question, most often of the question insoluble by definition. However formidable it may be, this question is perhaps not the ultimate question. More than once we will be faced with the effects of a preliminary question, prior to this one, which is the question "who" or "what"? Does one forgive *someone* for a wrong committed, for example a perjury (but, as I would argue, a fault, an offense, a harm, a wrong committed is in a certain sense always a perjury), or does one forgive someone something, someone who, in whatever way, can never totally be confused with the wrongdoing and the moment of the past wrongdoing, nor with the past in general. This question—"who" or "what"—will not cease, in its many forms, to return and to haunt, to obsess the language of forgiveness and this not only by multiplying aporetic difficulties but also by forcing us finally to suspect or suspend the meaning of this opposition between "who" and "what," a little as if the experience of forgiveness (of a forgiveness asked for, hoped for, whether granted or not), as if, perhaps, the impossibility of a true, appropriate, appropriable experience of "forgiveness" signified the dismissal of this opposition between "who" and "what," its dismissal and thus its history, its passed historicity.

But between the "pardon" of the "pardon me" ["*pardonne-moi*"] and the "pardon" of the "pardon me" ["*pardonnez-moi*"] or the "pardon us" ["*pardonnez-nous*"] or the "pardon us" ["*pardonne-nous*"] (four essentially different possibilities, four different hands [*donnes*] of forgiveness between the singular and the plural that must be multiplied by all the alternatives of "who" and "what"—this makes a lot), the form that is the most massive, the most easily identifiable today of this formidable question, and we will begin with it, would be the one of a singular plural: can one, does one, have the right, is it in accordance with the meaning of "forgiveness" to ask more than one, to ask a group, a collectivity, a community for forgiveness? Is it possible to ask or to grant forgiveness to someone other than the singular other, for a harm or a singular crime? This is one of the first aporias in which we will constantly be entangled.

In a certain way, it seems to us that forgiveness can only be asked or granted "one to one," face to face, so to speak, between the one who has committed the irreparable or irreversible wrong and he or she who has suffered it and who is alone in being able to hear the request for forgiveness, to grant or refuse it. This solitude of two, in the scene of forgiveness, would seem to deprive any forgiveness of sense or authenticity that was asked for collectively, in the name of a community, a Church, an institution, a profession, a group of anonymous victims, sometimes dead, or their representatives, descendants, or survivors. In the same way, this singular, even quasi-secret solitude of forgiveness would turn forgiveness into an experience outside or heterogeneous [*étrangère*] to the rule of law, of punishment or penalty, of the public institution, of judiciary calculations, and so forth. As Vladimir Jankélévitch pointedly reminds us in *Le pardon*,[2] forgiveness of a sin defies penal logic. Where forgiveness exceeds penal logic, it lies outside, it is foreign to [*étranger*] any juridical space, even the juridical space in which the concept of a crime against humanity after the war, and, in 1964, in France, the law of the imprescriptibility of crimes against humanity appeared. The imprescriptible—namely, what is beyond any "statute of limitations"—is not the un-forgivable, and I am indicating here very quickly, too quickly, a critical and problematic space toward which we would have to return again and again. All of the public declarations of repentance that are multiplying in France today (*Eglise de France*, the police and the medical profession—still not the Vatican as such, nor the university in spite of its accomplishments [records] in the area in question), declarations that were preceded, at a certain rate and in various forms in other countries, through similar gestures—the Japanese prime minister or V. Havel presenting excuses to certain victims of the past, the episcopacy in Poland and Germany proceeding to an examination of conscience at the fiftieth anniversary of the liberation of Auschwitz; the attempt at reconciliation in South Africa, and so forth. All of these public manifestations of repentance (whether state sponsored or not), and most often of "forgiveness asked," very new manifestations in the history of politics, are determined by the background of the historical-juridical resources [*s'enlèvent sur ce fonds historico-juridique*] that carried the institution, the invention, the foundation of the juridical concept of Nuremberg in 1945, a concept still unknown then, of "crime against humanity." Be this as it may, the concept of forgiveness—or the unforgivable—which is often put forward in all of these discourses, and in their commentary, remains heterogeneous to the judiciary or penal dimension that determines both the time of prescription or the imprescriptibility of the crimes. That is, unless the non-juridical dimension of forgiveness, and of the unforgivable—there where it suspends and interrupts the usual order of law—

has not in fact come to inscribe itself, inscribe its interruption in the law itself. This is one of the difficulties that awaits us.

The little book of Jankélévitch that follows *Le pardon* and is entitled *L'imprescriptible* bears in epigraph several lines of Eluard, whose interest is paradoxical, and to my eyes usefully provocative, insofar as the lines oppose salvation, but salvation *on earth*, to forgiveness. Eluard says:

> There is no salvation on earth
> for as long as executioners can be forgiven.
>
> *Il n'y a pas de salut sur la terre*
> *tant qu'on peut pardonner aux bourreaux.*

Insofar as it almost always happens, and in a non-fortuitous way, that one associates—we will often return to this—expiation, salvation, redemption, and reconciliation with forgiveness, these remarks have at least the merit of breaking with common sense, which is also that of the greatest religious and spiritual traditions of forgiveness—the Judaic or Christian traditions, for example, that never remove forgiveness from a horizon of reconciliation, hope for redemption and salvation, through confession, remorse or regret, sacrifice, and expiation. In *L'imprescriptible*, from the very foreword of the text entitled "Should We Pardon Them?," a foreword that dates from 1971, Jankélévitch yields, without saying it in these terms, to a kind of repentance, since he admits that this text seems to contradict what he had written four years earlier in the book *Le pardon* of 1967. In addition, the short polemical essay "Should We Pardon Them?" was written in the context of the French debates of 1964 about the imprescriptibility of Hitler's crimes and the crimes against humanity. As Jankélévitch makes clear: "In *Le pardon*, a purely philosophical work that I have published elsewhere, the answer to the question Must we pardon? seems to contradict the one given here. Between the absolute of the law of love and the absolute of wicked (*méchante*) freedom there is a tear that cannot be entirely unsewn [*décousu*]. I have not attempted to reconcile the irrationality of evil with the omnipotence of love. Forgiveness is as strong as evil, but evil is as strong as forgiveness."[3]

Naturally, what we have here are statements and a logic that we have barely begun to debate, with which we are just beginning to struggle. Nonetheless, the texts of *L'imprescriptible*, participating as they do in the debate I have just evoked and to which we will return concerning imprescriptibility, firmly conclude with the impossibility and inopportuneness, indeed with the immorality, of forgiveness. And in order to do this, in this polemical and impassioned debate, they form a continuity of meanings that we must rigorously dissociate, and which, moreover, Jankélévitch himself dissociates in what he calls his "purely philosophical study," namely, for example, forgiveness, prescription, and forgetting. "Should We Pardon Them?" begins with this question: "Is it time to forgive, or at least to forget?"[4] Jankélévitch knows perfectly well that forgiveness is not forgetting, but in the spirit of a generous polemical demonstration, and in horrified fear before the risk of a forgiveness that might end up engendering a forgetting, Jankélévitch says "no" to forgiveness, alleging that one must not forget. He speaks to us, in short, of a duty of non-forgiveness, in the name of the victims. Forgiveness is impossible. Forgiveness should not be. One should not forgive. We will have to ask ourselves, again and again, what this "impossible" might mean, and if the possibility of forgiveness, if there is such a thing, is not to be measured against the ordeal [*épreuve*] of the impossible. Impossible, Jankélévitch tells us: This is what forgiveness is for what happened in the death camps. "Forgiveness," says Jankélévitch, "died in the death camps."

Among all of Jankélévitch's arguments to which we would have to return constantly, there are two I would like to bring to your attention. They are also two axioms that are far from self-evident.

A. *The first* is that forgiveness cannot be granted, or at least one cannot imagine the possibility of granting it, of forgiving thus, unless forgiveness is *asked* for, explicitly or implicitly asked for, and this difference is not nothing. Which would then mean that one will never forgive someone who does not admit his wrong, who does not repent and does not ask, explicitly or not, for forgiveness. This link between forgiveness granted and forgiveness asked for does not seem to me to be a given, even if here again it seems required by an entire religious and spiritual tradition of forgiveness. I wonder if a rupture of this reciprocity or this symmetry, if the very dissociation between forgiveness asked for and forgiveness granted, were not de rigueur for all forgiveness worthy of this name.

B. *The second axiom* is that when the crime is too serious, when it crosses the line of radical evil, or of the human, when it becomes monstrous, it can no longer be a question of forgiveness; forgiveness must remain, so to speak, between men, on a human scale—which seems to me as problematic, although very powerful and very classical.

Two quotations in support of these two axioms.

1. *The first* presupposes a *history of forgiveness*; it begins at the end of this history and it dates the end of the history of forgiveness (we might later say, with Hegel, of history as forgiveness) by the project of the extermination of the Jews by the Nazis; Jankélévitch emphasizes what in his eyes is the absolute singularity of this project, a project without precedent or analogy, an absolutely exceptional singularity which would allow one to think, retrospectively, a history of forgiveness. This history would have deployed itself and since exposed itself, precisely, since or starting from its final limit. The "final solution" would be in sum, so to speak, the final solution of a history and of a historical possibility of forgiveness—all the more so, and the two arguments are intertwined in the same reasoning, that the Germans, the German people, if such a thing exists, have never asked for forgiveness: How could we forgive someone who does not ask to be forgiven? Jankélévitch inquires more than once. And here I would repeat my question, a question that should never stop

echoing in our ears: Is forgiveness only possible, with its meaning as forgiveness, on condition that it be asked for?

Here then, before discussing them, are some of the strongest lines in Jankélévitch's argument:

"*Forgiveness! But have they ever asked us for forgiveness?* [the "they" and the "us" would obviously have to be determined and legitimated]. *It is only the distress and the dereliction of the guilty that would give forgiveness a meaning and a reason for being.*" [Thus, it is clear for Jankélévitch—as it is clear for more than one tradition, those traditions from which an idea of forgiveness comes to us in effect, but an idea of forgiveness the very legacy of which conveys a force of implosion whose deflagrations we will constantly be registering, a legacy that contradicts itself and gets carried away, fired up, I would say more coldly "deconstructs itself"—it is thus clear that for Jankélévitch forgiveness can be granted only if the guilty party mortifies himself, confesses himself, repents, accuses himself by asking for forgiveness, if consequently he expiates and thus identifies, in view of redemption and reconciliation, with the one of whom he asks forgiveness. It is this traditional axiom, which has great force, certainly, and great constancy, which I will be constantly tempted to contest, in the very name of the same legacy, of the semantics of one and the same legacy, namely that there is in forgiveness, in the very meaning of forgiveness a force, a desire, an impetus, a movement, an appeal (call it what you will) that demands that forgiveness be granted, if it can be, even to someone who does not ask for it, who does not repent or confess or improve or redeem himself, beyond, consequently, an entire identificatory, spiritual, whether sublime or not, economy, beyond all expiation even. But I will leave this suggestion in a virtual state, we would have to come back to it incessantly, in a way that is incessant; I return now to my quotation of this very violent text, as if carried away by an anger that is felt to be legitimate, righteous anger.]

> Forgiveness! But have they ever asked us for forgiveness? It is only the distress and the dereliction of the guilty that would give forgiveness a meaning and a reason for being. When the guilty are fat, well nourished, prosperous, enriched by the "economic miracle," forgiveness is a sinister joke. No, forgiveness is not for swine and their sows. Forgiveness died in the death camps. Our horror before that which understanding cannot, properly speaking, conceive of would stifle pity at its birth . . . if the accused "could inspire pity in us."[5]

What follow are remarks of such polemical violence and such anger against the Germans that I do not even want to have to read them or cite them. That this violence is unjust and unworthy of what Jankélévitch has elsewhere written on forgiveness it is only just to recognize that Jankélévitch himself knew. He knew he was letting himself get carried away, in a guilty way, by anger and indignation, even if this anger gave itself airs of righteous anger. That he should have been conscious of it comes through for example in an interview he gave several years later in 1977, in which Jankélévitch writes the following. I quote this *on the one hand* in order to note an expression that might well serve as the title of what I am trying to do here (namely a "hyperbolical ethics," or an ethics beyond ethics) and *on the other hand* in order to underline the more or less guilty tension that, along with Jankélévitch, we must admit to and try to be forgiven, a tension or a contradiction between the hyperbolical ethics that tends to push the exigency to the limit and beyond the limit of the possible *and* this everyday economy of forgiveness that dominates the religious, juridical, even political and psychological semantics of forgiveness, a forgiveness held within the human or anthropo-theological limits of repentance, confession, expiation, reconciliation, or redemption. Jankélévitch says this; he admits this:

> I have written two books on forgiveness: one of them, simple, very aggressive, very polemical [*pamphlétaire*] whose title is: *Pardonner?* [this is the one from which I have just quoted] and the other, *Le pardon*, which is a philosophy book in which I study forgiveness in itself, from the point of view of Christian and Jewish ethics. I draw out an *ethics* that could be qualified as *hyperbolical* [my emphasis], for which forgiveness is the highest commandment; and, on the other hand, evil always appears beyond. Forgiveness is stronger than evil and evil is stronger than forgiveness. I cannot get out of this. It is a species of oscillation that in philosophy one would describe as dialectical and which seems infinite to me. I believe in the immensity of forgiveness, in its supernaturality, I think I have repeated this enough, perhaps dangerously, and on the other hand, I believe in wickedness (*mechanité*).[6]

It is obvious that the passage I read before on the finite history of forgiveness, on the death of forgiveness in the death camps, on forgiveness not being for animals or for those who do not ask for forgiveness, that this passage obeys the so-called "polemical [*pamphlétaire*]" logic, which the logic of a hyperbolical ethics resists, and resists infinitely, a hyperbolical ethics that would command precisely, on the contrary, that forgiveness be granted where it is neither asked for nor deserved, and even for the worst radical evil, forgiveness only acquiring its meaning and its possibility of forgiveness where it is called on to do the im-possible and to forgive the un-forgivable. But the polemical [*pamphlétaire*] logic is not only a logic of circumstance; we must take it very seriously and pay it careful attention because it picks up on the strongest, the most strongly traditional, logic of the religious and spiritualist semantics of forgiveness, which grants it when there is repentance, confession, a request for forgiveness, a capacity to expiate, to redeem oneself, and so forth. One of the great difficulties that awaits us, in effect, stems from the fact that the hyperbolical ethics, which will also guide me, *both* lies in the wake of this tradition *and* is incompatible with it, as if this tradition itself carried in its heart an inconsistency, a virtual power of implosion or auto-deconstruction, a power of the impossible—that will require of us once again the force to re-think the meaning of the possibility of the im-possible or the im-possibility of the possible. Where, in effect, we find the un-forgivable as inexpiable, where, as Jan-kélévitch in effect concludes, forgiveness becomes impossible, and the history of forgiveness comes to an end, we will ask ourselves whether, paradoxically, the possibility of forgiveness as such, if there is such a thing, does not find its origin: We will ask ourselves if forgiveness does not begin in the place where it appears to end, where it appears im-possible, precisely at the end of the history of forgiveness, of history as the history of forgiveness. More than once we would have to put this formally empty and dry but implacably exigent aporia to the test, the aporia according to which forgiveness, if there is such a thing, must and can forgive only the un-forgivable, the inexpiable, and thus do the impossible. To forgive the forgivable (*pardonable*), the venial, the excusable, what one can always forgive, is not to forgive. Yet the nerve of Jankélévitch's argument in *L'imprescriptible*, and in the section of *L'imprescriptible* entitled "Should We Pardon Them?," is that the singularity of the Shoah reaches the dimensions of the *inexpiable*; and that for the inexpiable there is no possible forgiveness, or even a forgiveness that would have a sense, that would make sense (because the common axiom of tradition, finally, and that of Jankélé-vitch, the axiom we will perhaps have to call into question, is that forgiveness must still have a sense, and this sense must be determined on the basis of [*sur fond de*] salvation, reconciliation, redemption, expiation, I would even say sacrifice).

Jankélévitch had in fact previously declared that in the case of the Shoah:

> One cannot punish the criminal with a punishment proportionate to his crime . . . for next to the infinite all finite magnitudes tend to be equal; in such a way that the penalty becomes almost indifferent; what happened is literally *inexpiable*. One no longer even knows whom to put the blame on or whom to accuse."[7]

Jankélévitch seems to assume, like so many others, like Hannah Arendt, for example,[8] that forgiveness is a human thing. I insist that this anthropologi-cal feature that determines everything (for it will always be a matter of knowing whether forgiveness is a human thing or not) is always a correlate of the possibility of punishing—not of taking revenge, of course, which is something else, to which forgiveness is alien, she says, but of punishing and that, I quote:

> The alternative to forgiveness, but by no means its opposite, is punishment, and both have in common that they attempt to put an end to something that without interference could go on endlessly. It is therefore quite significant, a structural element in the realm of human affairs [my emphasis] that men are unable to forgive what they cannot punish and that they are unable to punish what has turned out to be unforgivable.

Thus Jankélévitch, in *L'imprescriptible*, and not in *Le pardon*, establishes this correlation, this proportionality, this symmetry, this common measure between the possibilities of punishing and forgiving, when he declares that forgiveness no longer has a sense where the crime has become, as has the

Shoah, "inexpiable," disproportionate, out of proportion with any human measure. He writes, in effect:[9]

> Properly speaking, the grandiose massacre [the Shoah, the "final solution"] is not a crime on a human scale any more than are astronomical magnitudes and light years. Also the reactions that it inspires are above all despair and a feeling of powerlessness before the *irreparable*.

[the irreparable: interrupting the quote, I underline this word for *three reasons*:

1. *First reason*. "Irreparable" will be Chirac's word to describe, in a text to which we will return, the crime against the Jews under Vichy ("France, that day," he declared, "accomplished the irreparable") ["*La France, ce jour-là accomplissait l'irréparable*"].

2. *Second reason* to underline "irreparable." We will have to ask ourselves if the irreparable means the unforgivable; I think "No," no more than the "imprescriptible," a juridical notion, belongs to the order of forgiveness and means the un-forgivable. Thus everything must be done to discern as subtly and as rigorously as possible between the unforgivable on the one hand and the imprescriptible on the other, but also all the related and different notions which are *the irreparable, the ineffaceable, the irremediable, the irreversible, the unforgettable, the irrevocable, the inexpiable*. All of these notions, in spite of the decisive differences that separate them, have in common a negativity, a "[do] not," the "[do] not" of an im-possible which sometimes, or at the same time, signifies "im-possible because one cannot," "impossible because one should not." But in all cases, one should not and/or cannot go back over a past. The past is past, the event took place, the wrong took place, and this past, the memory of this past, remains irreducible, uncompromising. This is one way in which forgiveness is different from the gift, which in principle does not concern the past. One will never have treated forgiveness if one does not take account of this being-past, a being-past that never lets itself be reduced, modified, modalized in a present past or a presentable or re-presentable past. It is a being past that does not pass, so to speak. It is this im-passableness, this im-passivity of the past as well, and of the past event that takes on different forms, which we would have to analyze relentlessly and which are those of the irreversible, the unforgettable, the ineffaceable, the irreparable, the irremediable, the irrevocable, the inexpiable, and so forth. Without this stubborn privileging of the past in the constitution of temporalization, there is no original problematic of forgiveness. Unless the desire and the promise of forgiveness, indeed of reconciliation and redemption, do not secretly signify this revolt or this revolution against a temporalization, or even a historicization that only makes sense if one takes into account this essence of the past, this being of the being-past, this *Gewesenheit*, this essence of the having been as the very essence of being. But also this eventness of being, the "it has been" ["*ça a été*"], the "it happened" ["*c'est arrivé*"]. It is in this horizon that we would have to reread all the thinking, which, like that of Hegel or, otherwise, Lévinas (and in Lévinas

differently at different moments in his trajectory), makes the experience of for-giveness, of the being-forgiven, of the forgiving-each-other, of the becoming-reconciled, so to speak, an essential and onto-logical (not only ethical or religious) structure of *temporal* constitution, the very movement of subjective and intersubjective experience, the relation to self as a relation to the other as temporal experience. Forgiveness, forgivenness [*la pardonnéité*], is time, the being of time insofar as it involves [*comporte*] the indisputable and the un-modifiable past. But this pastness of an eventness [*passéité d'une événemen-tialité*], the being past of something that happened is not enough to ground the concept of "forgiveness" (whether asked for or granted). What else is needed? Suppose we were to refer to this being-past of what happened by the seemingly simple term of "fact." Something has happened, a *fact* or a *deed* [*Il y a eu là un fait*] (past participle, which says that something took place, something that remains indisputable; something done, a deed). For there to be a scene of forgiveness, such a fact or deed (*fait*), such an event as done, must be not only an event, something that happens, a neuter/neutral and impersonal fact, this fact will have had to have been a *misdeed* or *wrongdoing* [*méfait*] and a *wrong done* [*méfait fait*] by someone to someone, a harm, a fault, implicating an author who is responsible and a victim. In other words, it is not enough for there to be a past event, a fact or even an irreversible misfortune for one to have to ask for forgiveness or to forgive. If, a century ago, an earthquake devastated a people or engulfed a community, if this past is a past harm, a terribly unfortu-nate and indisputable fact, no one will think, however, of forgiving or asking for forgiveness for this past event, for this "fact"—unless, that is, one still suspects some malevolent design or some malicious intent.

One would also have to discern, for you know, here as elsewhere, one must never give up distinguishing, dissociating as well, I will say relentlessly and without mercy—and the analysis of "forgiveness," of "pardon" is inter-minable—one must also discern between not only vengeance and punish-ment, but also between punishing or punishment and the right to punish, then between the right to punish in general and the juridical right to punish, penal legality. H. Arendt could still say that forgiveness is a correlative of *punishment* without concluding thereby that there is, necessarily, a juridical dimension to it; the example par excellence of an incarnation, I am indeed saying an in-carnation, of absolute and sovereign forgiveness as the right to forgive, as the right to punish, is the king's right to grant clemency [right of reprieve]. Of course, between forgiveness and clemency (just as between gift and "thank you [*merci*]," "to have at one's mercy [*merci*]"), there is this affinity that comes to us from an abyssal history, a religious, spiritual, political, theological-political history that should be at the center of our reflection. The only inscrip-tion of forgiveness in the law, in juridical legislation, is no doubt the right to grant clemency, the kingly right of theological-political origin that survives in modern democracies, in secular republics such as France or in semi-secular democracies such as the United States, where the governors and the president (who in the United States swears an oath of office on the Bible) have, if I am not mistaken, a sovereign right to "pardon" (moreover, one also says "pardon" in English in this case).

The king's right to grant clemency, this all-powerful sovereignty (most often of divine right) that places the right to forgive above the law, is no doubt the most political or juridical feature of the right to forgive as the right to punish, but it is also what interrupts, in the juridical-political itself, the order of the juridical-political. It is the exception to the juridical-political *within* the juridical-political, but a sovereign exception and a sovereign interruption that found the very thing from which they exclude or exempt themselves. As often, the foundation is excluded or exempted from the very structure that it founds. It is this logic of the exception, of forgiveness as absolute exception, as the logic of the infinite exception, that we would have to ponder over and over again. One should not be able to say "pardon," ask for or grant forgiveness, except in an infinitely exceptional way. If, furthermore, we listen to Kant (as we would often have to do, especially on the subject of "radical evil"), if we listen to him on the subject of the right to grant clemency, precisely in his *Doctrine of Right* (the first part of the *Metaphysics of Morals*) when he discusses Public Right, and in this the right to punish and to grant clemency (Introduction to §50 and following), what he tells us still has considerable scope if one transfers it onto forgiveness. The gist of what he says is this: that the right to grant clemency *(ius aggratiandi, Begnadigungsrecht)*, the right to lessen or remit the penalty of a criminal, is, of all sovereign rights, the most delicate, the slipperiest, the most equivocal *(das schlüpfrigste)*. It gives the most splendor to greatness, to the highness of the sovereign, to sovereignty (and we will have to ask ourselves whether forgiveness should or should not be "sovereign"), but the sovereign thereby runs the risk of being unjust, of acting unjustly *(unrecht zu tun)* in the highest degree. Nothing can be more unjust than clemency. And Kant adds a fundamental caveat here, he marks an inner limit to the sovereign's right to grant clemency: the latter does not, *should not under any circumstances*, have the right to grant clemency for a crime committed where he is not the one intended; he should not have the right to grant clemency for crimes committed by subjects against subjects—thus for crimes between those who for him are also third parties. Because this impunity *(impunitas criminis)* would be the greatest injustice toward the subjects. The right to grant clemency—and thus to pardon—should only be exercised where the crime is against the sovereign himself, a crime of *lèse majesté (crimen laesae maiestatis)*. And even in this case, the sovereign should not exercise his right to grant clemency except on condition that this clemency not constitute any danger for his subjects. Thus limited, severely limited, this right is the only one that deserves the name of majesty, the right of majesty *(Majestätsrecht)*.

At the very least, what one gathers from this fundamental remark, by extending it to forgiveness, is that forgiveness in general should only be permitted on the part of the victim. The question of forgiveness as such should only arise in the head-to-head or the face-to-face between the victim and the guilty party, never by a third for a third. Is this possible? Is such a head-to-head, such a face-to-face possible? We would have to return to this more than once. Forgiveness perhaps implies, from the outset, as if by hypothesis, the appearance on the scene of a third party whom it nonetheless must, should, exclude. In any case, according to common sense itself, no one seems to have the right to forgive an offense, a crime, a fault committed against someone else. One should never forgive in the name of a victim, especially if the latter is radically absent from the scene of forgiveness, for example, if this victim is dead. One cannot ask forgiveness of living beings, of survivors for the crimes whose victims are dead. As are sometimes its authors. This would be one of the angles from which to approach all the scenes and all the declarations of repentance and requests for forgiveness that have been multiplying for some time on the public scene (in France, the Catholic Church, the police, doctors, and perhaps one day, who knows, the university or the Vatican) and that we will have to analyze closely.

3. *Third reason* to underline "irreparable": As I will not cease to repeat, it is only against the unforgivable, and thus on the scale *without scale* of a certain inhumanity of the inexpiable, against the monstrosity of radical evil that forgiveness, if there is such a thing, measures itself.

I return now to my quotation of Jankélévitch:

> Also, the reactions it inspires are above all despair and a feeling of powerlessness before the irreparable. One can do nothing [A very strong sentence: everything becomes impossible, including forgiveness]. One cannot give life back to the immense mountain of miserable ashes. One cannot punish the criminal with a punishment proportionate to his crime: for next to the infinite all finite magnitudes tend to be equal [What Jankélévitch seems to exclude, with the full sense and common sense of a tradition, is the infinity of human forgiveness and thus the very hyperbolicity of the ethics by which he seemed to be and said he was inspired in his book on *Le pardon*], for next to the infinite all finite magnitudes tend to be equal, in such a way that the penalty becomes almost indifferent; what happened is literally *inexpiable*. One no longer even knows whom to attack or whom to accuse. (p. 558, modified)

Jankélévitch himself underlines the word "inexpiable"; and what he means to show is that where there is the inexpiable, there is the unforgivable, and where the unforgivable arises, forgiveness becomes impossible. It is the end of forgiveness and of the history of forgiveness: Forgiveness died in the death camps. We would have to ask ourselves, as far as we are concerned, if, on the contrary, forgiveness (both *in* and *against* the concept of forgiveness, in and beyond, or against the idea of forgiveness that we inherit—and whose legacy we must question, perhaps contest the legacy while inheriting from it—

and this is a reflection on inheritance that we are beginning here), if forgiveness must not free itself from its correlate of expiation and if its possibility is not called forth precisely and only where it seems to be impossible before the unforgivable, and possible only when grappling with the im-possible.

Since I have been quoting this page of *L'imprescriptible: "Pardonner?,"* about a forgiveness that *must* be asked for and about a forgiveness that would have died in the death camps, I think we would also be interested in what follows, and that concerns the *waiting* [*attente*] to be asked for forgiveness. Jankélévitch will tell us that he was *waiting* for the word "pardon," this word with which we began ("Pardon!") and which can have the value of a performative sentence (Pardon!, I ask your pardon, pardon me [*pardonnez-moi*], pardon me [*pardonne-moi*]), this word that asks for forgiveness. Jankélévitch will tell us that he was waiting, as were others, to be asked for forgiveness, implying thereby that forgiveness must be asked for, that it asks to be asked for. And in a certain way, by saying that he was waiting, as others were, and in vain, for a word of pardon, a request for forgiveness, Jankélévitch admits in short that he was asking for forgiveness to be asked for (this would be a problem for us, of course, but I would like to emphasize here a feature of this scene: It is asked, it is expected that the word pardon be uttered or implied, *signified*, in any case, as pardon beseeched). What is essential is not that the word be said but that it be *signified*, that a pardon-beseeched be signified, such as a plea for mercy [*grâce demandée*], a plea for "thank you" [*"merci" demandé*], and with this pardon-beseeched, before it, expiation, remorse, regret, confession, a way of accusing oneself, of pointing an accusatory and self-referential, auto-deictic finger at oneself, something that, as one says, rather quickly, the animal would be incapable of, the mea culpa of the one who can beat his breast and, by recognizing his crime, dissociate himself from the guilty subject, from the subject having been guilty. We should return to this structure of temporality and of temporal specularity. For the moment, I will quote this request for a forgiveness requested in order to associate *two references* to it.

Jankélévitch writes thus:[10]

> To ask for forgiveness! We have long been waiting for a word, a single word, a word of understanding and sympathy . . . we have hoped for it, this *fraternal* word!

I italicize the word "fraternal"; this word "fraternal" to describe a "fraternal word" must be given a very strong and very precise meaning; it does not only mean sympathy or effusion, compassion; it bespeaks the sharing of humanity, the fraternity of men, of sons recognizing their belonging to the human race, as will become clearer still; and it is hard to erase the profoundly Christian tradition of this humanist, familialist, and fraternalist universalism, in keeping with Jesus's message, among others, for example in Matthew 23: "Yes, you have one rabbi and you are all brothers, *unus est enim magister vester, omnes autem vos fratres estis, pantes de umeis adelphoi este.*"

Jacques Derrida

> We have hoped for it, this fraternal word! Certainly, we were not expecting
> our forgiveness to be implored. . . . But we would have received words of
> understanding with gratitude, with tears in our eyes. Alas, in the way of
> repentance, the Austrians have made us a present of the shameful acquittal
> of the executioners.

And a little further on, as often elsewhere, Jankélévitch violently attacks
Heidegger.[11] I would be tempted—this is the first of the two references that I
mentioned—to relate this remark to what many interpreters of Celan's poem
(*Todtnauberg*)—that he wrote in memory and in testimony to his visit to Heidegger—have read as the trace of a disappointed expectation [*attente*], of Celan's
anticipation [*attente*] of a *word* from Heidegger that would have signified a *pardon* beseeched. I myself will not venture to confirm or invalidate, I will not, out
of respect for the letter and the ellipsis of Celan's poem, rush into an interpretation so transparent and univocal; I abstain from this not only out of hermeneutic prudence or out of respect for the letter of the poem, but also because I would
like to suggest that forgiveness (granted or asked for), the address of forgiveness,
must forever remain, if there is such a thing, undecidably equivocal, by which I
do not mean ambiguous, shady, twilit, but heterogeneous to any determination
in the order of knowledge, of determinate theoretical judgment, of the self-
presentation of an appropriable sense [*de la présentation de soi d'un sens appropriable?*] (it is an aporetic logic that, at least from this point of view, forgiveness
would have [in common] with the gift, but I will leave this analogy in progress or
undeveloped here). What *Todtnauberg* says, Celan's poem that bears this title,
what it says and on the basis of which the interpreters who rush to transform
it into a clear narration find their authority (a narration of the type: "Celan-
came,-H.-did-not-ask-the-Jews-for-forgiveness-in-the-name-of-the-Germans,-
Celan-who-was-waiting-for-a-word-of-forgiveness,-a-"pardon!,"-a-request-for-
forgiveness-left-disappointed-and-he-made-a-poem-of-it-he-recorded-it-in-one-
of-his-poems), no, what the poem says, is at least this:[12]

> *Arnika, Augentrost, der*
> *Trunk aus dem Brunnen mit dem*
> *Sternwürfel drauf*
> *in der*
> *Hütte*
> *die in das Buch*
> *—wessen Namen nahms auf*
> *vor dem meinen?—,*
> *die in dies Buch*
> *geschriebene Zeile von*
> *einer Hoffnung, heute,*
> *auf eines Denkenden*
> *kommendes*
> *Wort*
> *im Herzen, [. . .]*

Arnica, eyebright, the / draft from the well with the starred die above it, / in the / hut, / the line / —whose name did the book / register before mine?—, / the line inscribed / in that book about / a hope, today, / of a thinking man's / coming / word / in the heart, [. . .]

Arnica, Casse-Lunettes (euphrasia, euphraise), la / gorgée à la fontaine surmontée du / dé étoilé, / dans la / hutte / la ligne dans le livre / le nom de qui a-t-il / accueilli avant le mien?— / la ligne écrite dans ce / livre d'un / espoir, aujourd'hui, en la / parole / à venir / au cur / d'un penseur; [. . .]

However one interprets the meaning and testimonial reference of such a poem, it links its signature as poem (and of a poem that signs itself by naming a signature in a book, a name left in a book [. . .] to, I quote, one must quote, the hope for words [parole], for a word (Wort) that comes in the heart, that comes from the heart, of a thinking being; and because it is a question of a past, of the signature and the trace of names left in the book of another, as that which is named, it is the hope for a word to come—or not—thus of a gift and a gift of thought, of a gift to come or not from a place or from a thinking being (kommendes, eines Denkenden—and you know how Heidegger is known for having often associated Denken and Danken: to thank, to acknowledge, to express one's gratitude, the thank you of acknowledgment, and think further of the relation between thanks and mercy [grâce], "to grace [faire grâce]" or "to beg for mercy, an act of grace [demander grâce]"), for all of these reasons, the motifs of the gift and acknowledgment belong as much to its thematics as they do to the act or essence of the poem, to the gift of the poem; and this poem says all of these things, the gift, and the gift of the poem and the gift of the poem which it itself is. As much because it gives as because it receives, from the past that it recalls and from the hope it calls forth [appelle], through its recall [rappel] and its calling forth [appel], it belongs to the element of the gift—and thus to the element of forgiveness, of a forgiveness asked for or a forgiveness granted, both at the same time no doubt, the moment it says the poetic experience both as appeal for acknowledgment (in the sense of consciousness, of the acknowledgment that recognizes and admits or the acknowledgment that gives thanks, acknowledgment as gratitude), the poetic experience as gift and forgiveness hoped for, asked for, granted, for the other, in the name of the other; as if there were no poetic experience, no experience of language as such without the experience of the gift and forgiveness—whether or not they are asked for, granted, given—the question mark around the name that comes before my own in the book (wessen Namen nahms auf vor dem meinen?— whose name was received before mine, with this untranslatable alliteration, Namen nahms auf, that evokes hospitality [aufnehmen]), the reception offered to the other, this question mark around the identity of the other, around the name of the other who will have preceded me and with whom I am, whether I want it or know it, bound, bound up in the strange community, the strange genealogy of this book: This question mark indeed marks this anguish or this

Jacques Derrida

anxiety as to the name of the other, as to this other to whom I am given over with my eyes blindfolded, passively, although I sign, the other having signed before me and marking, sur-marking in advance, my signature, appropriating my signature in advance, as if I always signed in the name of the other who also signs thus, in my place, the other whom I countersign or who countersigns me, who countersigns my own signature, the gift and forgiveness having taken place, or not, having taken place and having been nullified, carried away, without my ever even having to make a decision. This abyssal countersignature forms one body with the poem, with the experience of language itself, always as the language of the other, something that Celan knew and acknowledged so singularly, but which is also a universal experience of language (I must say that I myself signed this book in the hut, at the request of Heidegger's son, with as much anxiety, an anxiety that extended as much to all those in whose following, without knowing it, I signed, as to what I myself scribbled in haste, both things likely to be equally at fault, perhaps even judged unforgivable). Naturally, in order to begin doing justice to *Todtnauberg*, one would have to read as attentively what precedes and what follows each of the words, and the break after each word, for example "*Der Mensch*," the man, to designate the driver, *deutlich* to designate, so close to *deutsch* (a classical and quasi-proverbial association), to designate, thus, the univocal distinction between the words that were then uttered, once the words *Namen* and *Wort*, proper noun and words, had already found their echo in the poem, and especially the word "*viel*," many, innumerable, infinitely numerous, which is the last word of the poem and apparently, or figuratively, describes that which, like tracks or the humid thing (*Feuchtes*), is buried in the bog. . . . *Todtnauberg* remains thus to be read, to be received—as gift or forgiveness themselves, a gift and a forgiveness which are the poem before being, possibly, its themes or the theme of the poet's disappointed expectation.

2. The other, *the second* reference that I mentioned, involves an exchange of letters that took place in 1980 and 1981 between a young German and Jankélévitch following the publication of *L'imprescriptible*.[13] The young German who writes to Jankélévitch places in epigraph to his moving and troubling letter the words of Jankélévitch ("They killed six million Jews. But they sleep well. They eat well and the Mark is doing well."), and the long letter begins painfully as follows:

> I myself have not killed any Jews. Having been born German is not my fault, or my doing. No one asked my permission [thus is posed from the outset the immense question, which will remain with us, the question of guilt or forgiveness according to the legacy, the genealogy, the collectivity of a *we* and of which *we*]. I am completely innocent of Nazi crimes; but this does not console me at all. My conscience is not clear, and I feel a mixture of shame, pity, resignation, sadness, incredulity, revolt. I do not always sleep well. I often remain awake at night, and I think, and I imagine. I have nightmares that I cannot get rid of. I think of Anne Frank, and of

Auschwitz and of *Todesfuge* and of *Nuit et Brouillard*: *"Der Tod ist ein Meister aus Deutschland."*

Todesfuge is the title, as you know, of another of Celan's poems clearly referring to the death camps and in which the line *"Der Tod ist ein Meister aus Deutschland"* comes back four or five times; guilt without fault and repentance or forgiveness asked for a priori, infinitely, in the name of the other. Mixture of a "pardon beseeched," without the word "pardon" but this amounts to the same, of a pardon beseeched and a protest against what condemns one to admit and to ask forgiveness in the name of the other, for a fault that one has not oneself committed; as for the nightmare, it alerts us to the guilt, and the scene of forgiveness, and the mourning that is inseparable from it; when he says that he does not have a "clear conscience," Wiard Raveling no doubt knows that he is addressing the author of a book called *La mauvaise conscience*, which includes an entire chapter on "The Irreversible" and some very fine sub-sections on regret, the irremediable, remorse, and repentance. *La mauvaise conscience* is a book whose first edition dates from 1933 and of which the book *Le pardon*, in 1967, given all that you know, is a kind of sequel.

This young German also invited Vladimir Jankélévitch to visit him, thus offering him hospitality (hospitality, gift and pardon, tears: the gift is always insufficient, thus pardon, or else ghost [*revenant*] and mourning): "If ever, dear M. Jankélévitch, you pass through here, knock on our door and come in. You will be welcome. And be assured [this is the painful irony of the entire letter]. My parents will not be there. No one will speak to you of Hegel, or of Nietzsche, or of Jaspers, or of Heidegger or of any other of the great Teutonic thinkers. I will ask you about Descartes and Sartre. I like the music of Schubert and Schumann. But I will play a record of Chopin, or if you prefer Fauré and Debussy. [. . .] Let it be said in passing: I admire and respect Rubinstein; I like Menuhin."

Following this long letter, which, once again, I cannot read to you here, and which is both a pathos-filled complaint, a protest, a confession, a plea, and a summation, Wiard Raveling received two responses, both of which are also published in the *Magazine littéraire*. The first from Fr. Régis Bastide, on July 1st, 1980, from which I will cite several lines:

> Dear Sir, I cannot tell you for lack of time, the degree to which I was moved by your letter to Vladimir Jankélévitch. [. . .] I am an old friend of Vladimir Jankélévitch. But his attitude shocks me profoundly. This non-forgiveness is dreadful. It is up to us, to us Christians (even non-believers!) to be different. The fanatical Jew is just as bad as the Nazi. But I cannot say this to Vladimir Jankélévitch. [. . .] You are no doubt a French teacher to write so well and so powerfully. I agree absolutely with all the words of your letter that my friend will surely judge too sentimental, tinged as it is with the awful *Gemütlichkeit* that must seem to him the greatest of vices. But you are right. Do not judge all French Jews by the terrible words of my friend. [. . .] What is the origin of your last name, and your first name? Hungarian? Viking?

The other response came from Vladimir Jankélévitch himself. The word "forgiveness" is not uttered. But it clearly says that what was awaited (You remember these words: " . . . to ask for forgiveness! We have long been waiting for a word, a single word, a word of understanding and sympathy . . . We have hoped for it, this fraternal word!") has finally arrived:

> Dear Sir, I am moved by your letter. I have waited for this letter for thirty-five years. I mean a letter in which the abomination is fully assumed and by someone who has had no part in it [*n'y est pour rien*]. This is the first time I have received a letter from a German, a letter that was not a letter of a more or less disguised self-justification. Apparently, German philosophers, "my colleagues" (if I dare to use this term) have nothing to say to me, nothing to explain. Their good conscience is unperturbable. [Injustice or ignorance of Vladimir Jankélévitch: as if a letter addressed to him personally were the only reparation possible.] You alone, you the first and no doubt the last, have found the necessary words outside the political commonplaces and the pious clichés. It is rare for generosity, spontaneity, and a keen sensitivity to find their language in the words we use. And such is your case. There is no mistaking it. Thank you [pardon beseeched: a gift that calls for thanks]. No, I will not come see you in Germany. I will not go that far. I am too old to inaugurate this new era. Because for me it is a new era all the same. For which I have waited too long. But you are young, you do not have the same reasons as I. You do not have this uncrossable barrier to cross. It is my turn to say to you: When you come to Paris, do as everyone does, knock on my door. . . . We will sit down at the piano.

I underline this allusion, on both sides, on the part of both correspondents, to music, to a musical correspondence, to music played or listened to together, a sharing of music. I underline it not only because Vladimir Jankélévitch was, as you know, a musician, an interpreter of music and a music lover, but also because between a certain beyond the *word* required, perhaps by forgiveness (a theme to which I should return later—the theme of verbal language, of discourse as the disastrous condition of forgiveness, which makes possible forgiveness but which also destroys it), between a certain beyond the word required, perhaps by forgiveness, and music, and even wordless song, there is perhaps an essential affinity, a correspondence which is not only that of reconciliation.

And in fact, Wiard Raveling recounts that he visited Vladimir Jankélévitch only once, that everything took place very cordially but that Jankélévitch always "systematically avoided" returning to these questions. Even in the correspondence that followed. But you will have remarked in Vladimir Jankélévitch's letter that I have just quoted and which speaks of a "new era" for which "I am too old" ("You do not have this uncrossable barrier to cross": "the uncrossable to cross"), Jankélévitch, in a way which is exemplary for us, causes two discourses to cross each other [*croise entre eux deux discours*], two logics, two axiomatics, which are contradictory, incompatible, irreconcilable, one of which is, precisely, that of conciliation or reconciliation, the other that of the irreconcilable. On one side, he welcomes the idea of a process, of a history that continues, of the passage from one generation to the other, and thus of the work of memory, as the work of mourning that makes what was not possible for him, forgiveness, possible in the future. Forgiveness will be good for you, for the next generation, the work will have been done, the work of mourning and memory, history, the work of the negative that will make reconciliation possible, and expiation, and healing, and so forth. But at the same time, he makes it known, more than he says it, that if this barrier—which will perhaps be crossed by new generations—remains uncrossable for him, this is because it must and can only remain uncrossable.

In other words, history, as the history of forgiveness, has stopped and it has stopped forever, it will have to have remained stopped by radical evil. It has stopped forever. And one feels this double conviction, both sincere and contradictory, self-contradictory. He does not doubt, he even hopes, and sincerely, that history will continue, that forgiveness and reconciliation will be possible for the new generation. But at the same time, he does not want this, he does not want this for himself, thus he does not want what he wants and what he accepts wanting, what he wants to want, what he would like to want, he believes in it but he does not believe in it, he believes that this reconciliation, this forgiveness will be illusory and false; they will not be authentic forgivenesses, but symptoms, the symptoms of a work of mourning, of a therapy of forgetting, of healing away, of the passage of time; in short, a sort of narcissism, reparation and self-reparation, a healing that re-narcissizes (and we would have to study in the Hegelian problematic of forgiveness this logic of the identification with the other that is assumed by the scene of forgiveness, on both sides, of the forgiver or the forgiven, an identification that forgiveness assumes but which also compromises and neutralizes, cancels out in advance, the truth of forgiveness as forgiveness from the other to the other as such). The uncrossable will remain uncrossable at the very same moment it will have been crossed over. Forgiveness will remain im-possible and with it history, the continuation of history, even if it becomes possible one day. What is it one senses at the heart of Jankélévitch's letter—and that I call to your attention because it should remain a great paradigmatic lesson for us? One senses the unaltered conviction, unalterable, that even when forgiveness of the inexpiable will have taken place, in the future, in the generations to come, it will not have taken place, it will have remained illusory, inauthentic, illegitimate, scandalous, equivocal, mixed with forgetting (even when its subjects are and believe themselves to be sincere and generous). History will continue and with it reconciliation, but with the equivocation of a forgiveness mixed up with the work of mourning, with forgetting, an assimilation of the wrong, as if, in short, if I can summarize here this unfinished development in a formula, tomorrow's forgiveness, the promised forgiveness will have had not only to become the work of mourning (a therapy, a healing away, even an ecology of memory, a manner of better-being with the other and with oneself in order to continue to work and to live and to enjoy) but, more seriously, the work of mourning forgiveness itself, forgiveness mourning forgiveness. History continues on the background of [*sur fond de*] an interruption of history, in the abyss, rather, of an infinite wound, which, in its very scarring, will have to remain an open and unsuturable wound. In any case it is in the zone of hyperbole, of aporia and paradox that we should often have to stand or move in this reflection on forgiveness.

Before leaving, at least provisionally, these texts of Jankélévitch, I would like to return to another of the paradoxes of the "inexpiable," of the logic of the "inexpiable" that he puts to work under this word in *L'imprescriptible*. The word "inexpiable" is used at least twice in a disturbing face-to-face (p. 24, p. 29, and again, p. 62; Eng. tr. p. 554, p. 558). You will remember that Jankélévitch said, I quoted it earlier, that "what happened [namely the Shoah, which defies all judgment, all logic, all logic of punishment, and so forth] is literally inexpiable." Before this, he has already described the will to exterminate the Jews as a singular, exceptional, incomparable movement of hatred against an existence, the existence of the Jew insofar as this existence is felt to be an "inexpiable" sin of existence. In this context, it is more particularly a matter of the human, anthropocentric dimension that structures the problem—and which will interest us precisely when it becomes a problem, a problematic, contestable and contested by the very idea of forgiveness.

A little earlier in his text (p. 22 ff.; Eng. tr. p. 554 ff.), in fact, precisely at the beginning of the chapter that bears the title "The Imprescriptible," (at the very moment of the vote in France on the imprescriptibility of crimes against humanity) Jankélévitch reminds us that these crimes are aimed at the essence of the human, "or, if one prefers, the 'humanness' ['*l'hominité*'] of man in general."

> The German [he says, hypostasizing in turn, in a way that is problematic, something like the essence of Germanity], the German did not want, strictly speaking, to destroy beliefs judged to be erroneous or doctrines considered to be pernicious: it was the very being of man, *Esse*, that the racist genocide attempted to annihilate in the suffering flesh of these millions of martyrs. Racist crimes are an assault against man as man: not against this or that man (*quatenus . . .*), not against man insofar as he is this or that, for example, communist, Freemason, or ideological adversary. No! the racist was truly aiming at the ipseity of being, that is, the human in all men. Anti-Semitism is a grave offense against man in general. The Jews were persecuted because it was they, and not at all because of their opinions or their faith: it is existence itself that was refused them; one was not reproaching them for professing this or that, one was reproaching them for being. (p. 555, modified)

Here, through some gap in the argument that does not explain why an aggression against the humanity of man is aimed at the Jew alone (and even

Israel, for he extends the same reasoning to the existence of the State of Israel, in a way that is even less convincing), Jankélévitch goes so far as to reverse, in some sense, the logic of the inexpiable. What becomes inexpiable, and this is Jankélévitch's word for the Nazis, is the very existence of the Jew. For the German, the Germans, the Nazis (and Jankélévitch passes easily from one to the other or others),

> it is not obvious that a Jew must exist: a Jew must always justify himself, excuse himself for living and breathing; his arrogance in fighting for subsistence and survival is in itself an incomprehensible scandal and there is something outrageous about it; the idea that "*sub-humans*" [my emphasis] may defend themselves fills the *superhumans* [my emphasis] with indignant stupefaction. A Jew does not have the right to be, existing is his sin. (p. 23; p. 555, modified)

I take up and underline the expression, polemical here, "sin of existing," removing it a little from its context: "A Jew does not have the right to be, existing is his sin." Implicit is: for the German. I am taking up the expression, I am exporting it out of its context and I am indicating in it a horizon of possible generality in order to point out one of the paths of the problematic of forgiveness—which will, furthermore, be illustrated quite strongly and classically by thinkers as powerful and as diverse as Kant, Hegel, Nietzsche, Heidegger, Lévinas, and others, no doubt: It is a matter of forgiveness—asked for, granted or not—a priori, and always asked for, whose request is originary and without end, because of a guilt or a debt, an original liability or imputability, infinite and indeterminate, in some sense, such that existence, or consciousness, or the "I," before any determined fault is at fault and in the process, consequently, of asking at least implicitly for forgiveness for the simple fact, finally, of being-there. This being-there, this existence, would be both responsible and guilty in a way that is constitutive ("sin of existing") and could only constitute itself, persevere in its being, sur-vive by asking for forgiveness (knowing or without knowing of whom or why) and by assuming forgiveness to be, if not granted, at least promised, hoped for, enough to be able to continue to persevere in one's being. And along with forgiveness, reconciliation and redemption, atonement for this "sin of existing"—which would not be reserved for the Jew here, unless the Jew, what one understands by this word, is once again interpreted as exemplary of the humanity of man, with all the problems that this claim to exemplarity would engender and on the subject of which I have often questioned myself. In all of these cases, forgiveness can be just as constantly hoped for, assumed to come, as desperately deferred, for if the sin is the sin of existing, if guilt is originary and attached from birth, stained by birth, so to speak, forgiveness, redemption, expiation will remain forever impossible. We would all be in that inexpiable state of which Jankélévitch speaks regarding the Jew for the German: if the fault consists in being-there, only death, only annihilation can put an end to it and feign salvation, mimic atonement or redemption, silence the plaint or the accusation. Naturally, the problem is enormous and we should return to it more than once, for we would have to ask ourselves what relation there may be among all these determinations of the "sin of existing," of an originary scene of "forgiving," first among them, between, let's say, a Hegelian type, a Heideggerian type or a Lévinassian type in the description and interpretation of this structure, and what relation there might be between this general structure, universal and supposedly originary, aneventful, pre-eventful, and on the other hand determined faults, crimes, events of malice or viciousness, effective perjury for which I must accuse myself and for which I could ask for forgiveness.]

I am closing my digression here on the expression "inexpiable" I noted earlier. On the next page, in the spirit of the same logic, one thus finds this word "inexpiable" again, this time not to describe the crime of Hitler's Germany but the being-Jew as being-human for the Nazis. For the latter, Jan-kélévitch says, and I quote (p. 24; p. 556), "the crime of being a Jew is inexpia-ble. Nothing can erase that curse: neither political affiliation, nor wealth, nor conversion."

Conveyed by the same word, "inexpiable," (and it is to an entire history of this word and to the expiatory that we are summoned here: what does "to expiate" mean?), we have two antagonistic and complementary movements: as if it were because the Nazis treated the being of their victim, the Jew, as an *inexpiable* crime (it is not *forgivable* to be Jewish), that they behaved in a way that was itself *inexpiable*, beyond all possible forgiveness. If one takes account of these two occurrences of the word "inexpiable" in Jankélévitch's text, and of their logic, one will say that the crime of the Nazis seems inexpiable because they themselves considered their victims to be guilty of the (inexpiable) sin of existing or of claiming to exist as men. And this always takes place around the limit of man, of the human figure. This is why I emphasized the words *sub-human* and *superhuman* a moment ago. It is because they have taken them-selves to be superhuman and have treated the Jews as sub-human, it is because from both sides the Nazis believed they could pass over the limit of man that they committed these *inexpiable* crimes against humanity, that is, imprescript-ible crimes—according to the juridical translation and the human right, ac-cording to the right of man which is here at the horizon of our problem.

I insist on this point for two reasons, two programmatic or problematic reasons, two ways of announcing today what should subsequently give us steady pause. Thus two questions.

1. *First question*. Is forgiveness a thing of man, something that belongs to man, a power of man—or else is it reserved for God, and thus already the opening of experience or existence onto a supernaturality just as to a super-humanity: divine, transcendent, or immanent, sacred, whether saintly or not? All the debates around forgiveness are also regularly debates around this

"limit" and the passage of this limit. Such a limit passes between what one calls the human and the divine and also between what one calls the animal, the human, and the divine. In a moment, we will perhaps say a word about "animal" forgiveness.

2. *Second question.* Because this limit is not just a limit among others, everything that depends on it will also affect it, as it will affect this difference—or distinction—that we have already recalled more than once today, between pure or unconditional forgiveness and these related and heterogeneous forms of remission, heterogeneous among themselves and heterogeneous to forgiveness and that are called excuse, regret, prescription, amnesty, and so forth, so many forms of conditional forgiveness (hence impure), and sometimes juridical-political forms. We thus dissociated *on the one hand* unconditional forgiveness, absolute forgiveness—I am not saying absolution in the Christian sense—absolutely unconditional forgiveness that allows us to think [*donne à penser*] the essence of forgiveness, if there is such a thing—and which ultimately should even be able to do without repentance and the request for forgiveness, *and on the other hand* conditional forgiveness, for example, that forgiveness which is inscribed within a set of conditions of all kinds, psychological, political, juridical above all (since forgiveness is bound up with the judiciary as penal order). Yet the distinction between unconditionality and conditionality is shifty [*retorse*] enough not to let itself be determined as a simple opposition. The unconditional and the conditional are, certainly, absolutely heterogeneous, and this forever, on either side of a limit, but they are also indissociable. There is in the movement, in the motion of unconditional forgiveness, an inner exigency of becoming-effective, manifest, determined, and, in determining itself, bending to conditionality. In such a way that, for example, and I am saying it too quickly for the moment, phenomenality or juridical or political conditionality is both outside and inside the motion of forgiveness—which will not make things easy. Even if the "imprescriptible" does not mean the "unforgivable," the contamination of the two orders will not be an accident that is itself reducible; and this will be valid of all the distinctions we will have to make.

We started by considering cases in which the noun "pardon" belonged to a performative utterance (Pardon!, I ask your pardon [*je te demande pardon/je vous demande pardon*], We ask your pardon [*nous te demandons, nous vous demandons pardon*]). You will note that in French it can only be used alone (*Pardon!*) in an act of performative language in the sense of "pardon beseeched," never in the case of forgiveness granted or refused. Is it true that for forgiveness to be granted or even only envisaged, it must be asked for and asked for on the basis of [*sur fond*] confession and regret? In my eyes, this is not a given and might even have to be excluded as the first fault of anyone who grants forgiveness; if I grant forgiveness on condition that the other confess, that the other begin to redeem himself, to transfigure his fault, to dissociate himself from it in order to ask me for forgiveness, then my forgiveness begins to let itself be contaminated by an economy, a calculation that corrupts it.

As soon as the word "pardon!"—the performative of forgiveness as speech act—is uttered, is there not the beginning of a reappropriation, a mourning process, a process of redemption, of a transfiguring calculation which, through language, the sharing of language (see Hegel on the subject) rushes toward the economy of a reconciliation that causes the wrong itself to be simply forgotten or annihilated, and thus this unforgivable as well, this unforgivable that is the only possible correlate of a forgiveness worthy of the name, of an absolutely singular forgiveness as unique event, unique but necessarily iterable, as always? The result of this law of iterable unicity, promised to repetition, divided by the promise that haunts all forgiveness, the result of this law of iterable unicity is that at the same time there is no sense in asking for forgiveness collectively of a community, a family, an ethnic or religious group—and at the same time multiplicity and the third and the witness are involved from the outset [d'entrée de jeu de la partie]. This may be one of the reasons, certainly not the only one, why forgiveness is often asked of God. Of God not because he alone would be capable of forgiveness, of a power-to-forgive otherwise inaccessible to man, but because, in the absence of the singularity of a victim who is sometimes no longer there to receive the request or to grant forgiveness, or in the absence of the criminal or the sinner, God is the only name, the name of the name of an absolute and namable singularity as such. Of the absolute substitute. Of the absolute witness, the absolute *superstes*, the absolute surviving witness. But inversely, if the address of forgiveness (I say the *address of forgiveness* to designate both the act of asking for forgiveness, of addressing a request for forgiveness, and the place from which forgiveness, once the request is received by the addressee of the request, is either granted or not granted), if the address of forgiveness is always singular, singular as to the fault, the sin, the crime, the harm, and singular as to the perpetrator or his victim, nonetheless it calls forth not only repetition but through or as this repetition, a disidentification, a disseminating multiplication, all of whose modes we would have to analyze.

Three suspension points before concluding.

1. Why did I begin with the single word "pardon," with the noun "pardon" about which it was impossible to know, to decide at the beginning, out of context, whether I was quoting, whether I was mentioning a noun, a theme, a problem or whether I was asking your pardon, performatively, not by mentioning but by using the noun (mention/use distinction in speech act theory)? I began in this way not only because I have an infinite number of reasons for asking your forgiveness (and in particular for keeping you too long: this is always the first fault of anyone who asks forgiveness: to think he has the right to interest the other and to keep his attention—"Listen to me, I am begging your pardon; wait, don't leave, I am begging your pardon; pay attention, pay atten-

tion to me, I am begging your pardon"—this can become an odious strategy or an odious and ridiculous calculation of false mortification that can go as far as tears; and we are very familiar with situations in which the person who does this is a pain in the neck and you pretend to forgive him or her in order to change the subject and to interrupt the conversation: "OK, give me a break, I am not even accusing you, enough already; OK, I forgive you but I don't want to see you again . . . , my mind is elsewhere, let's talk about something else, I don't even take you seriously enough to be accusing you").

No, I began in this way to quote a performative (neither to *mention*, nor to *use*, but to mention a use) in order to draw your attention to the question of the word, the performative word as speech, as verb (pardon, I ask your [*te-vous*] pardon). Like everyone, like all those who wait and think, they must wait for forgiveness to be asked for; it is a *word* of forgiveness, a verb, a verbal-noun that Jankélévitch was waiting for ("I have been waiting for this letter for thirty-five years . . . , Have we ever been asked for forgiveness?") and even, according to his interpreters, it was a *word* that Celan was waiting for, (*von/ einer Hoffnung, heute, / auf eines Denkenden / kommendes / Wort / im Herzen*). Must forgiveness pass through words or must it pass [beyond] words? Must it pass through word-verbs or must it pass [beyond] them, these word-verbs? Can one only forgive or ask forgiveness when speaking or sharing the language of the other, that is to say, by already identifying sufficiently with the other for this, and, by identifying with the other, making forgiveness both possible and impossible? Must one refuse the experience of forgiveness to whoever does not speak? Or, on the contrary, must one make silence the very element of forgiveness, if there is such a thing? This question is not only that of music, which I alluded to earlier; it is also, even if it is not only this, the question of the animal and of that which is said to "belong to man." Does forgiveness belong to man or does it belong to God? This question seems to exclude the animal, that which one calls by this confused general term "animal" or the animality of the beast or of man. Yet we know that it would be very imprudent to deny all animality access to forms of sociality in which guilt, and therefore procedures of reparation, even of mercy—begged or granted—are implicated in a very differentiated way. There is no doubt an animal thank you or mercy. You know that certain animals are just as capable of manifesting what can be interpreted as an act of war, an aggressive accusation, as they are capable of manifesting guilt, shame, discomfort, regret, anxiety in the face of punishment, and so forth. I am sure you have seen shameful animals, animals giving all the signs of "feeling guilty," thus of remorse and regret, and animals fearing judgment or punishment, animals hiding or exposing themselves to reproach or chastisement. One also knows that in the often-overloaded symbolism of combat or war, of fights between animals, well, that movements and even rites of reconciliation, of the interruption of hostility, of peace, even of mercy, of mercy begged and granted, are possible. The moment an animal is, I would say, at the mercy of another, it can admit to being defeated and make signs that put it at the mercy of the other who then sovereignly grants it its life unharmed as a sign of peace. Certain animals make war and peace. Not all, not always, but neither do men. So, without confusing everything and without erasing all sorts of ruptures that arise with the articulation of a verbal language, one cannot deny this possibility, even this necessity of extra-verbal forgiveness, even un-human [*an-humain*] forgiveness.

2. We constantly struggle in the snares of an aporia whose abstract and dry form, whose logical formality is as implacable as it is indisputable: There is only forgiveness, if there is such a thing, of the un-forgivable. Thus forgiveness, if it is possible, if there is such a thing, is not possible, it does not exist as possible, it only exists by exempting itself from the law of the possible, by impossibilizing itself, so to speak, and in the infinite endurance of the im-possible as impossible; and this is what it would have in common with the gift; but besides the fact that this enjoins us to try to think the possible and the impossible otherwise, the very history of what one calls the possible and "power" in our culture and in culture as philosophy or as knowledge, we must ask ourselves, breaking the symmetry or the analogy between gift and forgiveness, if the urgency of an im-possible forgiveness is not first what the enduring and non-conscious experience of the im-possible gives to be forgiven, as if forgiveness, far from being a modification or a secondary complication or a complication that arises out of the gift, were in truth its first and final truth. Forgiveness as the impossible truth of the impossible gift. Before the gift, forgiveness. Before this im-possible, and as the impossible of this latter im-possible, the other. The other im-possible. You understand that this lecture could also have been a lecture on the possible and on the "im-" that comes in front of it, of an im-possible which is neither negative, nor non-negative, nor dialectical.

3. Finally, perjury. Today I must justify the articulation (proposed as the title of this seminar) of pardon and perjury. Pardon/Perjury: As you can imagine, if I associate these two nouns, it is not because "[parleying] with the syllable *par* thus begin these words [*par la syllabe par commencent donc ces mots*]," as a certain Ponge would have said, Ponge's *Fable* which I am parodying here (*Par le mot par commence donc ce texte / Dont la première ligne dit la vérité* [With the word *with* thus begins this text / Whose first line tells the truth]), *Fable* which would not be without relation, nonetheless, to the scene of forgiveness, since it revolves around a judgment, on the one hand, and on the other, of the breaking of a mirror, of the interruption of a specular identification: "(*Par le mot par commence donc ce texte / Dont la première ligne dit la vérité / Mais ce tain sous l'une et l'autre / peut-il être toléré? / Cher lecteur déjà tu juges. Là de nos difficultés* . . . /*APRES sept ans de malheurs / Elle brisa son miroir* [With the word *with* thus begins this text / Whose first line tells the truth / But this tain under one and the other / can it be tolerated? / Dear reader, already you judge. There as to our difficulties . . . /AFTER seven years of bad luck / She broke her mirror.])"[14]

The reader, apostrophized as judge ("you judge": performative and constative), is being asked to forgive—and this is perhaps the truth of which the text speaks as the truth of any scene of writing and reading: to ask the reader's pardon by confessing. One always writes in order to confess, one always writes in order to ask forgiveness; I wrote something like this somewhere, forgive me for quoting myself. No doubt one always teaches, also, in order to ask forgiveness; this is perhaps why I think I will no longer change, henceforth, the title of this seminar, for as long as it may be destined to last. If I have associated pardon and perjury, it is thus not to begin with words that begin with *par*. . . . But for a reason that here again I will state dryly, I will lay out abstractly, before returning to it later. I will draw a broad outline of it in two strokes.

1. Any fault, any crime, anything there might be to forgive or for which one might have to ask forgiveness is or assumes some perjury; any fault, any wrong, is first a perjury, namely the breach of some promise (implicit or explicit), the breach of some engagement, of some responsibility before a law one has sworn to respect, that one is supposed to have sworn to respect. Forgiveness always concerns a perjury—and we will (would) then have to ask ourselves what in fact perjury is, what an abjuration is, what it is to break a vow, an oath, a conjuration, and so forth. And thus first what it means to swear, to take an oath, to give one's word, and so forth.

2. The second feature, even more aporetic, more impossible, if this is possible. Perjury is not an accident; it is not an event that happens or does not happen to a promise or to a prior oath. Perjury is inscribed in advance, as its destiny, its fatality, its inexpiable destination, in the structure of the promise and the oath, in the word of honor, in justice, in the desire for justice. As if the oath were already a perjury (something of which the Greeks, as we will see, had more than a premonition). And this, I have already spoken of this in the wake [*sillage*] of Lévinas but by dangerously complicating the trajectory of this Lévinassian path [*sillage*], from the moment that in the face-to-face there are more than two, from the moment that the question of justice and law arises. From the moment there is *law* and *three*. And there are at least three from the first dawn of the face-to-face, from the first look [*regard*], from the crossing of the first look that sees itself looking. Then it is justice itself that makes me perjure myself and throws me into a scene of forgiveness.

I must ask forgiveness—*pour être juste* [*for* being just/*to be* just]. Listen carefully to the equivocation of this "*pour*." I must ask forgiveness in order to be just, *to be* just, with a view to being just; but I must also ask forgiveness for being just, for the fact of being just, because I am just, because in order to be just, I am unjust and I betray. I must ask forgiveness for (the fact of) being just. Because it is unjust to be just. I always betray someone to be just; I always betray one for the other, I perjure myself like I breathe. And this is endless, for not only am I always asking forgiveness for a perjury but I always risk perjuring myself by forgiving, of betraying someone else by forgiving, for one is always doomed to forgive (thus abusively) in the name of another.

Forgive me for having taken so long, and without mercy [*merci*], so much of your time, thank you [*merci*]. When one says "thank you," does one say "thank you," I am thanking you for what you give me and what I acknowledge with gratitude? Or else "mercy," I ask for your mercy, I ask you not to be "*merciless*," I ask your forgiveness for what you give me, I give you thanks [*grâce*] for mercy [*grâce*], for the forgiveness that I am still asking you to give me, and so forth. In short, you will never know what it is I am saying to you when I say to you, to conclude, as in the beginning, pardon, thank you/mercy [*merci*]. In the beginning, there will have been the word "pardon," "thank you/mercy [*merci*]."

TRANSLATED BY ELIZABETH ROTTENBERG

NOTES

1. *Given Time, I: Counterfeit Money*, trans. Peggy Kamuf (Chicago: University of Chicago Press, 1991).

2. Vladimir Jankélévitch, *Le Pardon* (Paris: Aubier-Montaigne, 1967), p. 165. See also the little book that was published shortly after Jankélévitch's death under the title *L'imprescriptible: Pardonner? Dans l'honneur et la dignité* (Paris: Seuil, 1986), which brings together essays and talks from 1948, 1956, and 1971. [*Le Pardon* is also available in Vladimir Jankélévitch, *Philosophie Morale*, ed. Françoise Schwab (Paris: Flammarion, 1998), pp. 991–1149. The articles "Should We Pardon Them?" and "Do Not Listen to What They Say, Look At What They Do" are translated by Ann Hobart in the journal *Critical Inquiry* 22 (Spring 1996): 549–572, which also contains brief "Introductory Remarks" by Arnold Davidson (545–548). There is also a translation of "Irony: A French Approach" in *The Sewanee Review Quarterly* 47 (1939). See also Emmanuel Levinas, *Outside the Subject*, trans. Michael B. Smith (Stanford: Stanford University Press, 1993), especially "Vladimir Jankélévitch," pp. 84–89. All of these articles use the spelling of his name with a "J" rather than a "Y".—Eds.]

3. "Should We Pardon Them?," p. 553 (translation modified).

4. Ibid.

5. Ibid., p. 567 (translation modified). (This is on pp. 50–51 of the original edition of *Le Pardon*, same pagination in the *Points* edition.)

6. This is cited by Alain Gouhier in an article entitled "*Le temps de l'impardonnable et le temps du pardon selon Jankélévitch* [The Time of the Unforgivable and the Time of Forgiveness According to Jankélévitch]," published in the proceedings of a remarkable colloquium devoted to forgiveness in *Le Point Théologique, Forgiveness*, Proceedings of the Colloquium organized by the Centre Histoire des Idées, Université de Picardie, ed. Michel Perrin (Paris: Beauchesnes, 1987).

7. "Should We Pardon Them?," p. 558 (translation modified).

8. In a passage in *The Human Condition* (Chicago: University of Chicago Press, 1958), p. 241.

9. "Should We Pardon Them?," p. 558.

10. "Should We Pardon Them?," p. 567 (translation modified); *Le pardon*, p. 51.

11. For example: "Robert Minder forcefully asserts that Heidegger is responsible not only for everything he said under Nazism but also for everything he abstained from saying in 1945." "Should We Pardon Them?," p. 568 (translation modified); *Le Pardon*,

p. 53. See Robert Minder, "Hebel et Heidegger: Lumière et obscurantisme," in *Utopies et institutions au dix-huitième siècle*, ed. P. Francastel (Paris: 1963).

12. "Todtnauberg," in *Poems of Paul Celan*, trans. Michael Hamburger (New York: Persea Books, 1989), pp. 292–293.

13. This exchange is too long for me to cite here, but it was published in an issue of the *Magazine Littéraire* devoted to Vladimir Jankélévitch in June 1995 (no. 333), and it can be consulted there.

14. See Jacques Derrida, "Psyche: Inventions of the Other," trans. Catherine Porter, in *Reading De Man Reading*, ed. Lindsay Waters and Wlad Godzich (Minneapolis: University of Minnesota Press, 1989), pp. 30–42. [—Eds.]

On Forgiveness

A Roundtable Discussion
with Jacques Derrida

Moderated by Richard Kearney

Richard Kearney: I am going to ask each speaker to pose a question to Jacques Derrida on the theme of forgiveness and, in so doing, to try to keep the discussion as informal and conversational as possible.

Kevin Hart: Jacques, I wonder if I might get things going by reminding you of a phrase which you used two or three times last night. You use the locution, "forgiveness, if there is such a thing." I think I know why you use that prudent phrasing. You explained the other night that there is a relation between forgiveness and the figure of the impossible: Forgiveness, if there is such a thing, would exceed the economy of the philosophical. However, I would like to know if you could imagine the circumstance that you have stepped outside the economy of philosophy, that you stand on that non-place you have evoked so often, would there ever be forgiveness? From that vantage point is there such a thing as forgiveness? If there is such a thing, what would it be? What circumstances, what constraints, could one imagine that would give us forgiveness?

Jacques Derrida: It so happens that I often and regularly use this phrase, *s'il y en a,* "if there is such a thing," not only for forgiveness but for a number of related concepts, or quasi-concepts—for the gift, hospitality, and so on. What I mean by this is that when an impossible something happens or becomes possible *as* impossible, then the criteria provided by what you call the economy of philosophy should become unavailable. When I say "if there is such a thing," I do not mean that I doubt the possible occurrence of such a thing. I mean that, if forgiveness happens, then this experience should not become the object of a sentence of the kind "S is *p*," "this is, this presents itself as forgiveness," because forgiveness should not present itself. If it happens, it should not be in the form of something present. I have said the same thing for the gift. So as soon as I am sure that I forgive, for example—I cannot be sure that the other forgives—if I say that I know that I forgive, if I say, lightly, "I forgive you," this sentence in the present, with a verb in the present tense, is absolutely the destruction of forgiveness. That is because it implies that I am able to forgive, that I have the power to forgive, the sovereign power to forgive, which introduces me into the scene of the economy of exchange. You have to recognize that I forgive you, and this is recognizable, which is, of course, the beginning of the destruction of what forgiveness should be.

This means that forgiveness should exceed the very category of presence and, of course, of objectivity, of anything that could become the object of a theoretical statement; there is no theoretical statement about forgiveness. Each time I make a theoretical statement about the event of forgiveness I am sure that I miss it. Even more than that, the consciousness or the self-consciousness of the forgiver, as well as of the one who is forgiven, has the same effects. That is, if I am conscious that I forgive, then I not only recognize myself but I thank myself, or I am waiting for the other to thank me, which is already the reinscription of forgiveness into an economy of exchange and hence the annihilation of forgiveness. So if forgiveness happens, *if* it happens, it should exceed the order of presence, the order of being, the order of consciousness, and happen in the night. The night is its element.

Now then, I come back to the most difficult question, these themes which I try to explore again and again. What, then, regulates my use of the word forgiveness? What should forgiveness mean, if it is not something of that sort? Well, here I must say I do not know. I have no knowledge of this. I can know what is inscribed in the concept of forgiveness that I inherit, so I work on this heritage. I found the word and the concept, and a certain number of conflicts surrounding the concept in our tradition, in a number of traditions. This can be the object of knowledge, and from within this possible knowledge, I discover this extraordinary excess that I mentioned a moment ago. And about this excess itself I have no knowledge, and I cannot speak of it in a theoretical fashion. But I can nevertheless think—I can think what I cannot know—I can think of a desire to forgive beyond economy, or to be forgiven beyond economy. I have a thought of this gracious and unconditional forgiveness. I have a thought which is given to me by, or rather through, this heritage. Even if nothing can be adequate to this thought, I have the thought or the desire of this motion. It is out of this desire or thought, which exceeds knowledge, that I speak, that I organize this discourse; but it's a very unsafe discourse, as you realize. That is why I use quotation marks, as if to say, "that is what they used to call forgiveness," "that is what I myself as a subject inscribed in this tradition call forgiveness." But who knows? Perhaps, since nothing can be adequate to it, this word is just useless. Perhaps we will have to get rid of it. Perhaps that is what is going on today on a worldwide scene. On the one hand, forgiveness dominates the whole scene, and on the other hand, it has become hollow, void, attenuated. Perhaps that is what we are experiencing right now. But perhaps Richard will not forgive me for going on.

Kearney: Kevin, would you like to comment on that?

Hart: No, let us go on.

Derrida: Let me add just one thing. As you can imagine, I have reflected on my insistence of the *s'il y en a* in a number of contexts. In a recent text on Jean-Luc Nancy[1]—who, by the way, is trying to write something on deconstruction and Christianity to be entitled *La déconstruction du christianisme*—and in rereading his work, I found that he does not say, "if there is something." He repeatedly says, *"il n'y a pas le langage," "il n'y a pas la technique," "il n'y a pas le toucher,"* and so forth. We should not speak of *"le" langage* or *"la" technique* or *"le" toucher* in the singular, as if there were a singular word or concept. Nevertheless, he uses these words; having said this, he goes on using these words. I was comparing the two strategies. They have something in common, but they are not the same. The signature is different. There is some idiomatic gesture here.

Robert Gibbs: I will start with a citation and then go on to a question. I hope this won't be very long.

Derrida: To save time, just ask unanswerable questions.

Gibbs: In *Thus Spoke Zarathustra*, when Zarathustra comes down from the mountain, the first person he meets is the saint. And as he leaves the saint, he says to himself "Is it possible? The old saint in his forest has not heard that God is dead?" You build off of Jankélévitch the notion that forgiveness is dead, impossible, and that somehow we are now in a new era that we might call, not postmodern, but post-forgiveness. So a new possibility of forgiveness arises in this moment of post-forgiveness. Now Nietzsche has his reasons for saying that God is dead, and Jankélévitch obviously links his claim to the Shoah. I think some of us, working with theological traditions, find themselves in a situation where we might be like that holy saint. We are not so sure that forgiveness from before the Shoah is impossible after the Shoah. The question I want to put, what I want to ask you to explain a bit more, is this. You speak of the inheritance from these traditions, and you use a language of being in the wake of them, of following after them, and you also indicate a kind of continuity with them. Obviously it is both a rupture and a continuity. I think I understand how that works. But that particular event of inexpiable violence seems to occupy a specific place in the way you want to examine forgiveness. Now I will make the question just a little bit longer, but not too much longer. In Jewish philosophical and theological reflection, there are a lot of people who made such a claim, Fackenheim, Arthur Cohen, and others. But there are others who say "Well, you know, actually this is something which the Jews have been struggling with since the destruction of the Second Temple. The normal economy was destroyed when the Temple was destroyed and it turns out that the economy has been impossible ever since, and yet there has been the recovery of forgiveness. So this particular rupture for Jewish thought does not represent such a big rupture. It is another terrible rupture, but we are familiar with ruptures." The topic that I want to hear your thoughts about is to what extent are we in a post-forgiveness situation, a situation of forgiveness after the death of forgiveness? To what extent is that really different from before? And insofar as it may not be so different, then the recultivation of those theological traditions might in fact have more resources precisely for addressing some of these cataclysmic evils.

Derrida: Thank you. I think we agree more than you seem to think. You attribute to me Jankélévitch's thought, which I criticize or question. Jankélévitch says that forgiveness has come to an end, has died in the death camps. I oppose this. It is exactly the opposite. It is because forgiveness seems to become impossible that forgiveness finds a starting point, a new starting point. So I would not say that we are entering a post-forgiveness era at all. I said almost exactly the opposite. Of course I agree with you that, whatever originality there may be in the Shoah, this is repeating a long history. I come back to this question of the Shoah, and not only the Shoah, but all the inexpiable monstrosities of this century. If I do not think we are entering an era of post-forgiveness, nevertheless I think that something new is happening today in the world and that this has to do precisely with what happened in the second part of the century. In the process of globalization we see the theatricality of forgiveness, with heads of state asking for forgiveness, and so forth. By reference, I add to this the juridical concept of "crimes against humanity," which was coined for diplomatic reasons, produced by the Nuremberg court, and a new "Declaration of the Rights of Man," which is different from the previous one. So there is a new space in which the universalization of the notion of the inexpiable provokes new urges for forgiveness, for asking forgiveness, even if it is in a confused language, in a language full of equivocations. There is this universal potential agreement about crimes against humanity, the rights of man, and so on. We have had a lot of progress. Nevertheless, the international community, international law, with the institution of a universal penal court, and so on, are indications that humanity is entering a phase in which the inexpiable should be denounced and judged as such, the inexpiable as such.

That is why I take so much interest in the French law about imprescriptibility. Of course, I insisted on the fact that this law has nothing to do with forgiveness. If something is imprescriptible, that does not mean it is unforgivable. Nevertheless, in this law there is a sign toward the eternal right to judge crimes which are held inexpiable, beyond history, beyond time, beyond any given period of time. That means that the horizon of the forgiving of the unforgivable is now determining the human community, at least potentially. That is what interests me. From that point of view I would say that we are in something new. I would not call it post-forgiveness, and if I call this a new epoch, I would historicize it again. I think it is not a history, not a part of a history, but something more than historical that is happening now. What in the act or the experience or in the thought, not the concept but the thought, of forgiveness is meta-historical, not unhistorical but historical in a different way? Forgiveness should imply a break with the ordinary course of time, an interruption, and we are now experiencing this interruption in our history and in our concept of history. You cannot open a newspaper without being informed about the new scene of forgiveness, asked for and granted, or not. I think what is happening today is perhaps this new era of forgiveness. I am sure that in order to think what is coming, we need the old history and tradition, not the tradition but traditions and all conflicts within the traditions. Yesterday I referred to the heterogeneity of these traditions. We need constantly to look back and to reread these texts, even as you said in your paper in a very striking way. Each time we reread a text—the Bible, your texts, mine—it looks like a repentance. We are asking for forgiveness by reading. Somewhere I wrote that as soon as I write, I am asking for forgiveness, without of course knowing what will happen. But forgiveness is inscribed in the very first speech act. I cannot perform what I would like to perform. That is why things happen.

Kearney: Before we move on to Jean Greisch, I wish to invite Jean and each of the subsequent speakers also to feel free to pick up on any of the points made by previous speakers.

Jean Greisch: Thank you, Richard. My question is immediately linked to what you said about interruption and forgiveness as breaking the ordinary course of time and history. I would relate this to what you hinted at yesterday evening, namely, Benjamin's paradox of forgiveness without reconciliation (*Vergebung ohne Versöhnung*).[2] This is a very challenging topic. Something that troubles me nevertheless is to what extent we can dissociate forgiveness and reconciliation? Why must the notion of reconciliation be rejected or excluded? To give a sharper formulation to my question: Does this rejection apply to every possible notion of reconciliation or only to Hegel's image of the wounds of the spirit which heals our wounds without leaving scars, an image he uses precisely in the context of discussing *Vergebung*?

Derrida: Thank you. Of course, it is not a matter of rejecting or excluding reconciliation. I tried to refine the purity, the possible purity, the rigor of the concept of forgiveness. So if forgiveness has a finality, if it is given in view of reconciliation, that is, of being at peace with the other or, as they say in the Truth and Reconciliation Commission, of "healing away" the traumatic experience, if forgiveness has such a finality, then it is not pure, gracious, and unconditional forgiveness. Let us come back to the situation of the world today. Speaking of this equivocal use of the word forgiveness, we see that all these political scenes of forgiveness, of asking for forgiveness and repentance, are often strategic calculations made in view of healing away. I have nothing against that. I have something against the use of the word forgiveness to describe these cases. "Healing away" is a major term in South Africa. In France, each time the head of state, the prime minister, wants to grant amnesty and to erase the crimes of the past, it is in the name of "national reconciliation," to reconstitute the healthy body of the nation, of the national community. I have nothing against that. But if the word forgiveness is used in view of such an ecology or therapy I would say no, that is not to forgive. It is perhaps a very useful, a very noble strategy, but it is not forgiveness. So forgiveness, if there is such a thing, should be devoid of any attempt to heal or reconcile, or even to save or redeem. If I forgive, or ask to be forgiven, in order to be redeemed, that is a noble and worthy calculation, an economy. I ask for forgiveness, so I pay, and then you pay me back by forgiving me, and we are reconciled. There is a reconciliation of the victim and the perpetrator. We are, both of us, saved and redeemed. So I am trying—and I know how violent this is—to disassociate true forgiveness from all these finalities—of reconciliation, salvation, redemption, and so on.

If by reconciliation—now I go back to the sharpest point of your question—I refer to something which has no identification, no recovery, no therapy, as simply a certain relation to the other as such, then I say yes, that is what I have in mind by forgiveness. But that is not what one usually has in mind when one speaks of reconciliation, not only in Hegel but in others who speak of reconciliation, for whom reconciliation implies community, education, complicity, and so on. But in that case, this would not be pure forgiveness.

I would like to add just one more point, since you refer to a text of Benjamin, a very enigmatic one-page text, in which he speaks of the Jewish God as forgiving without reconciliation, as falling like a tempest or a hurricane that strikes the land.[3] That is the asymmetry of forgiveness, an eschatological asymmetry. Now forgiveness should keep this asymmetry. If this asymmetry is kept in the reconciliation, then I have nothing against reconciliation. This asymmetry is part of the scene of forgiveness. The most violent violence is when you not only victimize someone but you victimize someone to the point that the victim cannot even forgive, cannot even speak, cannot even witness, and then is not in a position to be asked to forgive. That is an absolute asymmetry. So we must constantly take into account this interruption, this asymmetry. The word forgiveness, once it is rigorously dissociated from all these motives associated with it by religion—redemption, salvation, justification, which are very biblical—once we have purified the concept of forgiveness, so to speak, then, even if it is inaccessible, we start at least to know what we are speaking about; we have at least a measure to control political rhetoric. We know that this reference to forgiveness is often empty rhetoric, hypocritical rhetoric. If you do not have this point of reference for a rigorous use of the concept, however difficult it might be, then you cannot as a practical matter have a critical response to the political abuses of the concept, of which, as we know, there are more and more today. This is also a political precaution.

Kearney: I would just like to reiterate, given the fact that Derrida, as we know, nearly always turns an answer into another question, each speaker can respond to Derrida's answer, which is also another question, as well as posing their own question.

Cleo McNelly Kearns: I think this will be in line with what Richard just said, because I think my question is perhaps just a reiteration of what I am hearing on both sides of the discussion at the moment. It has two parts. My question in a simple form is a re-posing of Robert Gibbs's question. I can see that forgiveness exceeds economy, but I am curious as to whether it exceeds heritage. Let me come back to that for a moment because I want to just add a loop in there. Jacques Derrida has spoken, very well, I think, and I am pondering it very deeply, of the corruption of the process of forgiveness, whatever it may be, by therapeutic discourse. I think this is really a very fertile and fruitful thing to pursue, although I think we would have to distinguish between many different kinds of therapeutic discourse. I want to use, or I want to invite you to use, if you wish, as a case in point some of the complexities of that. I have in mind another novum, as it were, in terms of the war crimes and crimes against humanity issue, which is the elevation, if that is the word, of a rape into a war crime, which is, as you know, a highly debated thing in feminist legal circles, a very complex business. I mention only one of its complexities, which is that it is a crime where even to announce that one has been the victim increases the victimization. That is to say, we have now a situation in Bosnia where men are refusing to accept back their wives who have confessed that they have been raped. So you have a kind of double indemnity there, if you like, which is extremely complicated by the issue of therapeutic discourse because in matters of sexual violation, therapeutic discourse has just proliferated, making a great claim to be able to heal.

Derrida: Thank you. You realize that when I opposed the conditional to the unconditional I immediately added that they were absolutely irreducible to one another but indissociable. That is, if we want to embody an unconditional forgiveness in history and society, we have to go through conditions. We have to negotiate between the unconditional and conditional. They cannot be dissociated, although we know they are absolutely heterogeneous and incommensurable. It is because these incommensurable poles are indissociable that we have to take responsibility, a difficult responsibility, to negotiate the best response in an impossible situation.

Then the second part of this question has to do with the possibility of exceeding the heritage. What is the heritage? The way I address this question implies that as soon as we speak, we are inheriting; we speak out of a heritage. But the heritage itself is heterogeneous and multiple; it gives us contradictory injunctions. For example, the heritage of the concept of forgiveness is not a given. On the one hand it prescribes unconditional forgiveness and on the other hand it prescribes conditional forgiveness, conditioned by repentance, or by asking for forgiveness, and so on. The heritage is not something I receive. It is something I have to interpret and reinterpret through an active responsibility. So nothing exceeds the heritage, but the heritage exceeds itself. Within the heritage you have such conflicts, such irreducibly conflicting motives that the excess is within the heritage. What we inherit is an idea of the excess. Everything that we have discussed here today has to do with the excess within the heritage. Everything we inherit, especially in religion, in faith, whatever we want to call it, is a heritage of excess, and the excess is part of any heritage, not only a religious heritage. When my father leaves me something, it leaves me free. My freedom is the condition of my inheritance. So he gives me something which is infinite, which exceeds myself, and I have to assume this excess. So the excess is part of the heritage.

To go quickly—because Richard is looking at me—I want to go back to the last part of your question, about the abuse of the language of forgiveness and therapy and especially your reference to the woman. I can take another example, from another part of the world. I refer to a wonderful and moving book by Antjie Krog.[4] She is a woman poet from South Africa, whom I met and who attended the sessions of the Truth and Reconciliation Commission. She is an Afrikaner and she was absolutely traumatized, overwhelmed, by what she saw and heard. In this book, she reports—and this refers to the victims who cannot bear witness—that women in South Africa were often raped and could not come forth and bear witness before the commission because they would have to tell the stories of their being raped or they would have to show the scars and expose their nakedness. So they could not come before the commission and testify. There was also the case of a remarkable woman who became a minister after the end of Apartheid and who had an important political position, but who could not publicly testify to the violence. Many of them told the "Gender Commission"—this is described in a chapter entitled "Does Truth Have a Gender?"[5]—the story of the way they were arrested. The first gesture of the black policemen was to tell them, "You are not an activist; you are not acting politically; you are a whore, a prostitute." They were denied the dignity of their political involvement and then, after their terrible experiences, they could not come before the commission. These are victims who could not simply publicly testify. There was the story of another woman who came before the commission and met one of the policemen who killed her husband, and she was asked whether she could forgive him. She spoke in her own language—there are eleven languages in South Africa—and so we are not sure what she said because this was translated into English. She said, "First, no government can forgive, no commission can forgive, only I could forgive and I am not ready to forgive." This sentence translated into English remains very obscure because it may mean "I am not ready to forgive because of the violence," or "I am not ready to forgive because I am not ready today"; this would require a time of healing away, a work of mourning. Or it may mean "I am not ready to forgive because I am a victim but the main victim is my husband, who is dead, who would be the only one entitled to forgive." So we cannot even understand what she meant by this "I am not ready to forgive." In any case, she was pointing out that no institution as such, no commission appointed by the government, no government is entitled to forgive. Forgiveness is something else. She probably did not use the word "forgive" but this was translated into Anglo-Christian English. There was a case of another woman who was in the same situation who said, "Well, the only thing I wanted was to know what happened. Now I know what happened. I want no revenge. I forgive."

Regina Schwartz: You've inspired a lot of questions, so I have to choose among them. Early in your talk last evening, you were talking about the problem of who can forgive whom. You said that one individual can forgive another individual, or one community can forgive another community. At the time I thought, there are two other options. One is forgiving yourself, and I am curious to know what you would say about that problem. In order to forgive yourself, do you need a prior forgiveness? Is that what we mean by divine forgiveness? Is it a self-acceptance after you have done something horrible? The fourth and final possibility is a little risky to bring up, but where else can I say it than at a conference called "Questioning God"? Can you forgive God? Is that a question that we can ask? For instance, when I was quoting Psalm 22, "My God, why have you forsaken me?," the answer for Christ is that he is not forsaken. What about those who ask the question and do not get that answer, or who do not feel they got that answer? Can they legitimately ask that question of God? The question, I suppose, is the old one of divine justice, but now in the context of contemporary thought.

Derrida: Thank you. "Forgiving oneself"—if I had to answer, I would say, on the one hand, I never forgive myself, and on the other hand, I always forgive myself. In both cases, it would imply that I am not alone with myself, either when I forgive myself, because I summon someone who helps me, or when I do not forgive myself, because there is another one of me who will not forgive me. Freud tells the story of Heinrich Heine, who was converted, and the conversation concerned the Christian God. When he was lying on his death-bed, and there was a priest there, and someone asked him "Do you think God will forgive you?" His answer was, "Well, he will forgive me because that is his profession!" The very genesis of the idea of a God in that case would be to produce someone who is available for forgiveness each time we need it. So then I may have someone who does that job for me. I constantly have to forgive myself just to survive, just to go on. As you know, the young Levinas wrote in one of his essays before the war—I don't remember the title—that forgiveness and reconciliation were part of the constitution of the temporalization of the ego.[6] It is not simply a moral, ethical, or religious experience, but simply in order to go on and to produce the synthesis that you need to be yourself, and to identify yourself through time, you have to forgive yourself constantly. Forgiveness then is part of the temporal constitution of the ego, self-forgiveness. So from that point of view, yes and no, I forgive myself, I never forgive myself; it depends. We are a scene of multiple egos, persons. There is in me someone who is always ready to forgive and another who is absolutely merciless, and we are constantly fighting. Sometimes I can sleep, sometimes I cannot.

Now I turn to the phrase "forgiving God." We know that we, especially the Jews, often make God appear before a court. After the Shoah, there were scenarios in which some Jewish communities called upon God to appear and to respond, to account for his misdeeds. But even without these theatrical and sometimes unbelievable scenarios, we are constantly trying to judge God. Even if we forgive him, even if we think finally that we cannot judge God, nevertheless the movement to evaluate God ethically, trying to understand the will and the strategies and designs of God, is a way of judging him. Finally, the believers are those who think that they do not have the right to judge, that a priori they forgive God for whatever God does. I am not sure that all the believers do that constantly. The people who have faith in God—since faith is not certainty and since faith is a risk—are also the people who are constantly tempted not to forgive God, tempted to accuse or to denounce God. That is part of the risk of faith. I am sure that we are constantly struggling with the temptation to judge God, constantly.

Graham Ward: You just mentioned Levinas and I want to ask you a question about Levinas. I am aware that there has been long conversation between you and Levinas, a dialogue between your work. What I am interested in is your first essay on Levinas, "Violence and Metaphysics," where you seem to me to question the residue of transcendentalism that is going on in Levinas. So I was really surprised last night that you structured your argument around a series of transcendentals, such as absolute forgiveness, absolute otherness, radical evil, interruption. I thought those things would be deconstructed, but they are not and so I would like to ask you, what is happening there? But more importantly, and following from that, if you structure your argument about forgiveness in that way, then is there not the danger that you make aporia itself a transcendental, so that we are just paralyzed in front of an absolute abyss and therefore unable to do anything, let alone forgive?

Derrida: Thank you. First of all, in this early text on Levinas, I did not charge him with transcendentalism. On the contrary, I tried to question him, at least provisionally, from an ontological and transcendental point of view. My objections were made to him from a transcendental point of view. So in that respect I have nothing against transcendentalism. On the contrary, I was trying to say that a transcendental philosophy such as Husserl's could resist, could more than resist, Levinas's objections. So my strategy in that article was rather transcendentalist, at least in that essay. But in other places, my relationship with transcendental philosophy is more complex, as you suppose. I have nothing against transcendentality. In *Of Grammatology* I spoke of an ultra-transcendentality. I tried a discourse which had to be even more than transcendental.[7] I question the history of the concept of the transcendental, but not in order to go back to the opposite of the transcendental, to empiricism or positivism. I make the option of the more transcendentalist, so to speak, than the traditional transcendental, and I often use the word "quasi-transcendental," to define the key concept that I use in certain contexts. The quasi-transcendentals function like the classical transcendentals, but they are not transcendentals in that sense. We need them for many reasons. Now to come back to the question of forgiveness, we need a pure concept of forgiveness, even if there is no forgiveness. We need at least a reference to an absolute forgiveness, an unconditional something, in order, first of all, to know what we mean as much as possible, and to think what we think, even if we cannot know it. So I am exactly the opposite of an anti-transcendentalist. The strategy is more complex here.

As to the aporia, on the one hand, I often say, perhaps not enough last night, that the aporia is not a paralyzing structure, something that simply blocks the way with a simple negative effect. The aporia is the experience of responsibility. It is only by going through a set of contradictory injunctions, impossible choices, that we make a choice. If I know what I have to do, if I know in advance what has to be done, then there is no responsibility. For the responsible decision to be envisaged or taken, we have to go through pain and aporia, a situation in which I do not know what to do. I have to do this and this, and they do not go together. I have to face two incompatible injunctions, and that is what I have to do every day in every situation, ethical, political, or not. So the aporia is not paralyzing, not the way I understand it. I often say the aporia is not something I can refer to as a phenomenon. In the small book entitled *Aporias* I say that what is aporetic in the aporia is that the aporia never presents itself as such.[8] The aporia consists in the fact you cannot do a phenomenology of the aporia; the aporia does not appear as an aporia, as such. So I am not referring to some object, to a set of quiet poles of opposition. An aporia is an experience, enduring an experience, in which nothing—such as forgiveness—presents itself as such. That is because absolute forgiveness never presents itself as such and is irreducible to conditional forgiveness. That is the reason the aporia does not present itself as such, either. Of course, when I say that the aporia is what we have to go through in order to take responsibility and to act or to decide, that does not mean that it is easy to do. On the contrary, I will never know that I have made a good decision. If someone tells us, "I have made a decision, I have taken this responsibility," for me, to my ears, this sounds absolutely ridiculous and obscene. One never knows who is taking the responsibility, or if it is the right one, and so on. So not only "I forgive," but also "I am responsible," or "I've made a decision"—that is to me not only unjustified but unbearable.

Francis Schüssler-Fiorenza: I would like to ask you about something that you indirectly alluded to but did not discuss in detail in your talk last night. My question concerns the significance of two elements that are indeed distinct from forgiveness but are nevertheless related to the topic of forgiveness:

namely, collective guilt and collective repentance. Collective guilt is a common Christian theme in its theological tradition on original sin. However, as you mentioned in your talk, a German could say: "My grandparents were involved in the Holocaust, but I wasn't," or an American could say, "My ancestors were involved in slavery, but I wasn't."

Nevertheless, I would like to note that in America today we still live off the benefits of that slavery. I may not have been a colonialist and I may not have trafficked in slaves, but I live off the benefits of colonialism and the results of slavery. The very shirt that I wear may be cheaper than it would be because of underpaid labor in a colonialized country. Therefore, the question of collective guilt emerges in relation to the enjoyment of benefits that result from injuries to others, even if done in the past or by others. Even though one may have not been directly involved, one nonetheless still enjoys the benefits of the injustice. Therefore, I would like to point to the notion of a collective repentance. The acknowledgment of the obligation of repentance is an acknowledgment of an obligation that follows from collective guilt. I would argue that in the United States, the question of affirmative action toward minorities (for example, affirmative action in admitting of minorities to universities) should be a part of the collective repentance for evil that was done in the past and whose effects still exist. To those individuals today who might complain that affirmative action treats them unjustly for they were not directly guilty, one could point out that affirmative action is required because collective guilt should entail collective repentance. What I am interested in and what I am asking you is, how do you understand and interrelate such a notion of collective guilt and repentance with your understanding of forgiveness?

Derrida: I totally agree with you. Let me come back for a second to something I just said in order to say something even more shocking. The fact that I cannot, I should not be able to, say, "I forgive," or "I am responsible," or "I make a decision," does not exonerate me from my responsibility, but it implies that the one who forgives in me or decides in me or takes responsibility in me is the other. If my gesture, forgiving, deciding, being responsible, is simply the explication of what I am or of what is possible for me, for my power, then I do nothing. For me to do something, which is forgiving or deciding, I must do something that is higher, larger and other than me, that is, the other makes the decision in me, which does not mean that I am passive, that I am simply obeying the other. But the one who forgives, the one who decides, the one who takes responsibility is the other in me. That comes back to the relative complexity of the scenario within ourselves.

Now I come back to your question. I totally agree with you. Yesterday I said that although we often presuppose that the scene of forgiveness is face to face and that it implies singularity, I also added immediately that a third one was implied. There is no scene of forgiveness without language, even if it is a silent language. We are in the possibility of a community and of heritage. Now, while I agree with you, I would disassociate the scene of forgiveness from the scene of repentance. I think it is a good thing that the community repents, and I totally agree with you when you say that Americans today and others have benefited from slavery. That is obvious every day. So Americans today have to recognize their current guilt and to repent. That is what Clinton did when he was traveling in South Africa and met Nelson Mandela. He did not repent but he recognized that there was some guilt, that slavery is the Americans' responsibility, but without drawing any consequences, because in that case repentance requires precisely starting a process of repairing, repaying. On the international scene, as soon as you acknowledge a crime, then you have to repay. There are procedures of compensation, which is what happened with the Jews in Germany. So if Clinton or the American government wanted to be consistent with their recognition of slavery, they should provide deep transformations, endless transformations, in the current state of society. This would not have anything to do with forgiveness. They would not be forgiven; they would not have asked for forgiveness. They have to simply acknowledge what happened and be consistent with this recognition. Of course, everyone, not only the Americans, should participate in this transformation of society. When I was lecturing in Australia on forgiveness, I was asked by a journalist at a press conference, should our government apologize for the treatment of the Aborigines? My first response was, I am a visitor here and it is your responsibility. I will not give advice. Nevertheless, if you insist, I would say, yes, the government should apologize because that would be a promise to improve the situation, to change a terrible situation. The next day, in the newspaper, the headline read, "French Philosopher Urges Government to Apologize."

Hart: And the Prime Minister refused.

John Milbank: I think I would like to pick up on what Graham Ward said. Your reply, Jacques, was of course absolutely right, that you are a transcendentalist philosopher, even of a new sort, an extreme sort. So really what I want to ask is, why is that not called into question? Why are you a Kantian? The question really has two parts, relating both to ethics and to theoretical philosophy. So, first of all, in relation to ethics, it seems that there's a repeated structure that you share with Levinas and Patočka, whereby you say, if such and such an ethical concept can be purged of certain religious elements, having to do with reward and salvation, it would become purer and thereby more religious.

Derrida: More religious?

Milbank: Yes. Now what I would like to ask is this. Is this in danger actually of being too moralistic, in the sense that it is not looking at how the purer the ethical becomes, the more anti-ethical it becomes. What I mean by that is that if I insist on pure absolute self-sacrifice I am indeed suggesting a kind of obliteration of myself, and one might ask, well, is this ethical? It does seem to me that secularity of itself almost encourages that, because if death is the ultimate horizon in the future rather than eternity as the ultimate horizon, then one tends to say that the noblest thing is for the individual to sacrifice himself or herself to the future or to the state or whatever. So that what we have seen is that ever since the nineteenth century, the more secular things have become, the more people talk about sacrifice. You get this in Comte and Durkheim, and what I worry about in somebody like Patočka is whether that sort of thing isn't still going on. It is the same with talk about a very pure gift or very pure forgiveness. If you demand that they be really pure, then they are impossible, but should we actually want them to be really pure? Up to a point I strongly agree with you about asymmetry, that you have got to be prepared if necessary to sacrifice yourself, and that you shouldn't be forgiving the other just so that you can be forgiven. But nonetheless, is pure forgiveness the name of the good or, as Robert Schemann, a German philosopher, argues, would the name of the gift, the name of the good, rather be, in the end, something like us all sitting down for the eschatological feast? In other words, if there isn't enough to go around then I should give my share away to the other, but obviously I hope that I will be able to eat alongside of the other, too. That is the religious image, the religious beyond the ethical, a sort of hyper-ethical. You could argue that it is actually more ethical, and that in a very strange kind of way, secularity encourages a kind of masochism.

Derrida: Masochism?

Milbank: Yes. Whereas the traditional religious view does not. So it does seem to me that there is a common thread of Kantianism, seeing the ethical as purity of will and so forth, and an unpreparedness to examine something like the eudaimonistic. That is the first part of the question.

The second part is this. You have this notion, indeed, of some sort of transcendental horizon, of something that is absolutely impossible that is nonetheless the condition of possibility for the possible. But it then tends to happen that when that impossible is expressed, it is betrayed. Absence founds presence, but as soon as the thing is, it is present, and then it is concealing absence, and so on. You are arguing that that is rigorous transcendental philosophy, indeed almost a kind of phenomenology, that that is what appears to us. But what I want to ask, then, is, well, there's a sort of objectivism about that, and could that be concealing a decision you are making or a subjective judgment that you are making? I wondered actually in "Circumfession," in the text underneath the Bennington book, whether you were raising that question yourself, whether you started to say, well, maybe what I have concluded is actually autobiographical. That does seem to be a serious question. If we're talking about something like the boundary between the known and the unknown, is it correct to think like Kant, that one can somehow state what the limits of possible knowledge are, even if one states them as aporias? One still claims in that way that one can fix the boundary between the known and the unknown, and of course, in the wake of Kant, Jacobi called that into question. It does seem that perhaps Jacobi is actually somehow beyond the postmodern, if one wants to think of you as a postmodernist. I am not worried about the term. The question is really, Are not so-called transcendentalist issues, setting out a transcendental framework, really not always themselves a matter of interpretation? Have you not owned up to something like an act of interpretation? It is here that the issues with theology I think become crucial because I agree with you, against Kevin Hart, that ultimate aporias are not a lot of use to theology. An aporia might, as you say, be a gift, and it might be a poison. But if it is a matter of interpretation, does it somehow still remain possible for theology to say, well, in my interpretation, in my experience, presence and absence are not related like that, but somehow presence in its very presence is mediating an absence? So, in other words, one has the idea that the unknown, the horizon beyond, is always somehow mediated, is always coming through the known in such a way that there is not really any fixable boundary, but the unknown makes itself present because one has interpreted the unknown more as a plenitude than as an abyss. The question is, is that not an equally possible interpretation once one has abandoned the assumption that one can even do transcendental philosophy, even of the kind that you carry out?

Derrida: I would need twenty-four hours at least to answer all these questions. So let me try something. I take the risk of saying this abruptly. First, on the one hand, pure forgiveness should be in a certain way beyond any interpretation, because interpretation, the process of interpreting, is already taken in an economic way—reconciliation, healing away, negotiating. So in certain way, forgiveness should go beyond interpretation understood in that sense. In another sense, because of the reasons I gave, there is only interpretation in the night about forgiveness. I would say both at the same time. I leave this as an aporia. Now I will try to answer some of your questions.

The first one has to do with the transcendental tradition. Here again I am in a heritage. I am struggling, as we all are, with the heritage of philosophy. I learned a lot from Plato, Kant, Husserl, and I try to be true to their lessons and the request for transcendentality is one of them. Nevertheless, this does not prevent me from objecting to Kant on many points, especially on the point of duty and the moral law. I said somewhere[9] that if I act ethically, not only in conformity with duty (*Pflichtmässig*), but out of duty (*aus Pflicht*), then I am just paying a debt. In that case, I am not behaving ethically. I should do what I have to do beyond the duty. So I am ultra-Kantian. I am Kantian, but I am more than Kantian. I am constantly taking up this struggle within tradition. The same would be true with the question of the boundary between the known and the unknown. When I referred to this classical distinction between knowing and thinking a moment ago, I did not imply that I knew where to draw the boundary. It is unclear to me. So again I am here in this difficult position. I must confess that I am struggling with things which remain problematic and unclear to me and I have no response. Having worked, like all of us, within the heritage, I am in the process of understanding a little more, of transforming the heritage, and going I do not know where. I really do not know where.

Now the danger of becoming moralistic is obviously a danger. I agree with you. Personally, I am someone who is constantly described as an immoralist and an atheist and also as a priest. I have to respond to these two sets of imperatives and I am taken in this way. That is why the question of sacrifice, which is at the center of what we are discussing, is not addressed much. Again, in what I write, which I cannot reconstitute here, I am constantly against the logic of sacrifice, especially in the question of forgiveness. I am trying to deconstruct the logic of sacrifice, which is at the center of Kant, Levinas, Lacan, Heidegger. In that case, deconstruction consists in identifying the sacrificial logic even if it is hidden in these great thinkers. So I try not to be simply sacrificialistic but at the same time I cannot deny that sacrifice is unavoidable. I try to think what a sacrifice is and I am against it and for it. You said that today, in what you call secularity, the secular dimension of our time, one speaks more and more of sacrifice. The concept of secularity to me is very, very obscure. I do not think that there is anything secular in our time. First of all, the concept of secularity is a religious concept. So when you are describing something as secular you already understanding and interpreting it as religious. So I think our time is less secular than ever. If I am interested in forgiveness and the gift it is because I think what is at stake today in our time is something that is neither secular nor religious in the traditional sense. It is something else.

Milbank: But if I said something "immanentist," thinking of someone such as Durkheim?

Derrida: But if I ask you what you mean by immanence and you tell me the Incarnation is the mediation of God and man, is that transcendence or immanence?

Milbank: It is both, but is predicated on transcendence, whereas I do not think that worshiping society is transcendence.

Derrida: Judaism would say that the Incarnation is a way of immanentizing transcendence. So I do not know. Each time I face this couplet of concepts I just resign myself. We have learned, especially from Kant and from Husserl, that there is transcendence in immanence, and so on. I do not want to choose between the two. Now at some point you used the word "betrayal." I do not remember the sentence but I remember the question. You wanted to avoid betrayal or urge me to avoid betrayal and unfortunately I think we are, that I am, constantly betraying. I tried in a short essay on Levinas to show that from the very beginning of ethics, in the very relation to the face, *visage*, in a dual relation, since the third one was required and the third one is already comparison, the betrayal, the perjury, is already there. The perjury does not fall upon the promise or the sworn faith; the perjury is at the heart of the sworn faith. That is why the seminar I am currently giving is not simply on "Forgiveness." It is called "Forgiveness and Perjury." I think that perjury is unfortunately at the very beginning of the most moralistic ethics, the most ethical ethics. That might sound difficult, but in a certain way it is trivial: As soon as I am true to you, I am betraying you, or the other one, one as/or the other, and I know that from the beginning. So Levinas was suffering from this. He asked

Richard Kearney

why there is another of the other, and why I am compelled to compare, to refer to justice in the sense of the law, the legal institution, to comparison, to reason, and so on. Because as soon as I relate to an irreducible singular one, I am betraying another one, or I introduce a third one who disturbs or corrupts the singular relation to the other. So I betray or I am perjuring. The fact that there is betrayal at the beginning does not mean that I am free to betray.

Milbank: I would like to say something very quickly about betrayal. I was really more talking about transcendental betrayal . . .

Derrida: I am too sensitive to transcendental betrayal.

Milbank: I wanted to ask whether one could also conceive the ultimate ontological scenario in another way. I cannot spell this out now but, roughly speaking, I think something like the *analogia entis* conceives this scenario in another way. But I think that is not irrelevant to what you are talking about. Because I think if one has this model of transcendental betrayal, then one somehow thinks that difference is taken to be the ultimate, that, if you have got a sort of transcendental difference, and difference is the ultimate, then there is a sense in which everything is on a level and there is a certain kind of indifference and then transcendental betrayal. So you will end up saying, well, I have an equal duty to this person and this person. As you put it very wittily in one of your books, you say, why should I look after this cat and not other cats?[10] That seems to be a consequence of this transcendentalism about betrayal. You will end up thinking "nothing has more weight than anything else."

Derrida: It is not "nothing," but "no one."

Milbank: That there is no sort of sort of real, imbued order to the universe. I want to ask, is that necessarily the case? Do we not usually experience the sense that—even if we can agree that there are lots of situations where we can never be absolutely sure of this—somebody has some sort of prior claim? Also, if you look at this on a social level, are not such aporias to do with a sort of absolute breakdown of community? If there are a lot of stray cats, then it's a problem. In Italy it would be a problem, but in cat-loving England it is not a problem, because everybody there looks after their cat. So obviously you can look after your cat with a good conscience, because you know that other people are looking after their cats.

Derrida: You might change the example!

Milbank: Yes, I might change the example. I think it is important to do so. The idea that charity is an absolutely general obligation to everybody—again, I am not so sure about that. In the Middle Ages they tended to interpret charity in terms of notions of kinship, quasi-kinship, and friendship, so that there was a higher duty to look after those closer to you. Aquinas says that you should love your wife and your family more than other people. It is only later on that people have real problems with that. In the Middle Ages they were not thinking of charity as some sort of indifference to Eros, friendship, and affection, to affinity, if you like. What you are saying seems to me not to take seriously affinity and the erotic. So, again, it seems almost that *because* you are being too moralistic, you will also end up saying that one cannot do anything moral.

Derrida: You might call this indifference, but if you think that the only moral duty you owe is the duty to the people—or the animals—with whom you have affinity, kinship, friendship, neighborhood, brotherhood, then you can imagine the consequences of that. I, of course, have preferences. I am one of the common people who prefer their cat to their neighbor's cat and my family to others. But I do not have a good conscience about that. I know that if I transform this into a general rule it would be the ruin of ethics. If I put as a principle that I will feed first of all my cat, my family, my nation, that would be the end of any ethical politics. So when I give a preference to my cat, which I do, that will not prevent me from having some remorse for the cat dying or starving next door, or, to change the example, for all the people on earth who are starving and dying today. So you cannot prevent me from having a bad conscience, and that is the main motivation of my ethics and my politics. If I speak of "national preference," as we do in France, and we say that we will give work to French-born citizens and not to the immigrant . . .

Milbank: No, I do not mean that at all.

Derrida: . . . but that is kinship and affinity and a common language. Then you can see where that leads. It is not because I am indifferent, but because I am not indifferent, that I try not to make a difference, not to make a difference ethically and politically, between my family and his family and your family. I confess that it is not easy. I know that practically I grant a privilege to kinship, to my language, to France, to my family, and so on. But I do not have a good conscience about that.

Kearney: We have time now for questions from the floor.

Audience: Throughout the conversation, the phrase has been going through my head "Father forgive them, they know not what they do." I ought to say that I am mentioning this as a quotation and not offering it as a prayer for this group. Both would do, of course. That seems to me to raise a question, well, very many questions, that cannot be answered in five minutes. But there's a question there about forgiving those who do not know what they do and of forgiveness being pleaded for by a third party (or perhaps a second-and-a-half party, if we are going to be trinitarian), which adds another dimension. That also relates to another question that occurs to me, which is, are Christianity's contributions to the heritage the concept of the unforgivable, rather than some exalted sense of forgiveness, that it is Christianity that brings in the idea of unforgivable sin, the unforgivable sin of nailing god on a cross, which then relates to the other unforgivable sin or the punishment that a heritage metes on the Jews as having resigned any right to forgiveness, if you take the Gospel passages at face value. That is a complex question.

Derrida: Two points. First, "Forgive them, they do not know what they do"—that is of course a very famous and difficult statement that I try to interpret in my seminar, and it takes a long, long time. But on two occasions, once when I gave a lecture at the Institut Catholique de Paris, and once last spring when I was having a debate with Ricoeur on the question of forgiveness before legal theorists, the same question occurred, and of course it is an unavoidable one. No one had mentioned this in the debate until someone like you brought it up. I tell you what I tried to answer. I tried two possible answers, which differ in tone. One, of course, is the trivial one: Since they do not know what they do, they are not responsible for what they do. They did wrong but with no intention of doing wrong, so they were not wicked themselves and so we can forgive them. They are not responsible, not knowing what they do. That is a trivial answer. The other, more sophisticated answer that I take the risk of formulating is that between what one does when one harms someone, when one sins or does something criminal, between what one does and knowledge there is a gap and you cannot reduce the gap between doing and knowing, in a certain way. Forgiveness has nothing to do with knowledge. That is why St. Augustine, when he confesses, asks God, why should I confess before You when You know everything in advance? That means that the confession does not consist in letting the other know. The other knows. In order to confess, you have to imply that the other knows already, that in confessing you do something else than to inform the other. So confession, forgiveness, have nothing to do with knowledge. Sinning, doing something wrong, or causing harm have nothing to do with knowledge. So forgive them because what they did has nothing to do with their consciousness or knowledge. That is a more risky interpretation.

You say, in a very interesting way, that perhaps Christianity has taught us the unforgivable rather than forgiving. Now, we can connect this statement with what is happening today, crimes against humanity. What is unforgivable today before the law, in France and elsewhere, is a crime against humanity, that is what is inexpiable and unforgivable. That means that what becomes unforgivable is a crime directed against what is most sacred in humanity, in the humanness of the human, the most sacred. The concept of a crime against humanity implies something sacred. It is an absolute principle; no one would oppose that. Today the cornerstone of international law is the sacred, what is sacred in humanity. You should not kill. You should not be responsible for a crime against this sacredness, the sacredness of man as your neighbor, your brother, the Christian man, made by God or by God made man. That is, God-made man. Man is divine, sacred, and the crime of what is inexpiable is crucifixion, a crime against the most sacred dimension of humanity. In that sense, the concept of crime against humanity is a Christian concept and I think there would be no such thing in the law today without the Christian heritage, the Abrahamic heritage, the biblical heritage. That is why I do not think there is anything secular in international law today. The idea of crime against humanity is a religious law. I am in favor of that. I think it is a radical mutation, a progress, but this does not prevent me from thinking that it has some religious origin.

Kearney: I would like to thank Jacques Derrida on behalf of all of us, in particular for the extraordinary gift, yet again, of his generosity, time, energy, intellectual dexterity, and wisdom, and not just with regard to philosophical and theological concepts and arguments, but with regard to very ordinary, everyday, concrete moral and political issues, ranging from Yugoslavia to South Africa to crimes against humanity to the Holocaust. It is a unique combination of the philosophical and the ethical and we have been very privileged to witness this yet a second time here in Villanova. There is talk, and it is only a rumor, of a third conference on religion and postmodernism, probably a mad dream in the minds of Michael Scanlon and Jack Caputo. But if it comes to pass, you might all remember an old legend about the Augustinians and visitors to their monasteries, which is that if a visitor comes back for a third time and knocks at their door and enters, he or she shall become a novice. So, if Jacques Derrida returns and takes on for a third time this debate in this Augustinian institution, the question remains undecidable for the moment as to whether he becomes a novice or this Augustinian institution becomes deconstructed, or both. But you are all invited back to the next one to find out. So on behalf of all of you, I would like to thank Jacques Derrida for his extraordinary generosity.

Derrida: Thank you, Richard, and thank all of you for your hospitality. I very much enjoyed this new experience. Forgive me for improvising in my awkward English. For me an improvised discussion is always a nightmare, especially in a foreign language for which I have no affinity or kinship. In order to thank you, I wanted to add an anecdote to what Richard said. Before giving a seminar on forgiveness and perjury, I gave a three-year seminar on hospitality, in which I often refer not just to Christianity or to Judaism, but also to pre-Islamic culture. The hospitality which was required among nomadic communities was such that when someone lost his way in the desert, the nomadic communities should receive him, should offer him hospitality, for three days. For three days they had the obligation to feed him and look after him, but after three days they could kill him.

Kearney: Thank you, Jacques.

NOTES

1. Jacques Derrida, *Le toucher, Jean-Luc Nancy* (Paris: Galilée, 2000).

2. Walter Benjamin, *Gesammelte Schriften,* vol. IV (Frankfurt: Suhrkamp, 1991), Fr. 71, pp. 97–98.

3. "Wie der reinigende Orkan vor dem Gewitter dahinzieht, so braust Gottes Zorn in Sturm der Vergebung durch die Geschichte, um alles dahinzufegen, was in den Blitzen des göttlichen Wetters auf immer verzehrt werden müßte." Benjamin, *Gesammelte Schriften,* IV, p. 98.

4. Antjie Krog, *Country of My Skull: Guilt, Sorrow, and the Limits of Forgiveness in the New South Africa* (New York: Three Rivers Press, 1999).

5. Chapter 16 is entitled "Truth Is a Woman."

6. Emmanuel Levinas, *Time and the Other*, trans. Richard A. Cohen (Pittsburgh: Duquesne University Press, 1987).

7. Jacques Derrida, *Of Grammatology*, corrected edition, trans. Gayatri Chakravorty Spivak (Baltimore: Johns Hopkins University Press, 1997), pp. 60–61.

8. Jacques Derrida, *Aporias*, trans. Thomas Dutoit (Stanford: Stanford University Press, 1993).

9. See Derrida, *Aporias*, pp. 16–17; Derrida, *On the Name*, ed. Thomas Dutoit (Stanford: Stanford University Press, 1995), p. 8.

10. Jacques Derrida, *The Gift of Death*, trans. David Wills (Chicago: University of Chicago Press, 1995), p. 71.

Returning/Forgiving

Ethics and Theology

Robert Gibbs

"Return, Israel, to THE LORD, your God." My first word, "Return," is a citation of a biblical command, and it is a citation of the first word in the first word-pair of my title: returning/forgiving. I cite the command, the exhortation in Hosea (14:2) addressed to the community, to re-cite and so to alert us to the other side paired with forgiveness. Hosea's text is the earliest Hebrew text about returning. The Hebrew word for repentance, *Teshuvah*, means returning and is from the root that means to turn. It is clearly a relational term: We return to God and to other people. In the Jewish tradition, the problems, even the aporias, focus more on the task and the impossible possibility to return. Forgiveness, although less the focus, is also a relational term. Indeed, both terms are not primarily self-relations, but relations with others, with others as agents who are able to act. Of our social relations, these two relations (returning/ forgiving) are the most other-centered, depending most on another person. To return is to re-approach, to come near again, placing me back in relations with someone I harmed. To forgive, on the other hand, is to accept someone back, to overlook the harm or better still to remedy what went wrong. To accept apologies. These two performances are different, however, and not only is my responsibility as returner different from my responsibility as forgiver, but also what I must risk in returning to another is distinct from my risk in waiting for another to ask for my forgiveness. The two performances make different demands of me, different risks in relation to the other depending on which side of the relation with another I am located. These relations enact a complexity of asymmetry.

The other relation I will explore, ethics and theology, is construed on a different plane. The double contingency of forgiveness and return structures the performances in the social realm; the possible relations of ethics and theology occur in the realm of discourse about responsibilities. My point of departure would be that ethics concerns our relations with each other, our responsibilities for other people, and so in the specific context of this paper, our responsibilities to return to and to seek reconciliation with those we have harmed—and the other responsibility to welcome the other back and accept the offering of appeasement. Theology, on the other hand, concerns not simply the nature of God, but more important, our relations with God, particularly when we have damaged that relationship through sin. Here, too, there is a responsibility to return to the one I have harmed, but here the task in forgiveness is to accept God's forgiveness—a task whose complexity we could learn from Kierkegaard. To what extent is our return to God like our return to another person? To what extent is the expectation of forgiveness parallel? Must we understand our responsibility to forgive others to be like God's, or is it somehow different? Those direct questions point to the deeper issue: How must the discourse about our responsibilities for each other be linked or unlinked from a discourse about our responsibilities to God?

For myself, I would not choose to identify myself as a theologian, but that is not due to any commitment to exclude God or even theological matters from philosophy, but rather due to a commitment to translate and so run risks of misapprehension in the effort to re-invigorate and redevelop each discourse. I wish to strain these discourses and their disciplines in order to think what philosophy needs most today: a thinking and, even more so, a performance of repentance. Let me conclude my preamble with one almost-slogan: The task of theology for our moment is to translate the teaching of Teshuvah, of return, into a philosophical teaching. Teshuvah is not a private act of contrition but is a social performance and is the key to understanding a task of reconciliation fundamentally different from Hegel's. Its vulnerability and one-sidedness is vital to the ethics of reconciliation, where the goodwill of the survivors must not be coerced, demanded, or even presumed. Both within philosophy's own domain and in our world, the work of reconciliation requires insight into both returning and forgiving—an insight that when introduced from theology can also give us hope to take responsibility for our pasts.

What I can try to develop in this chapter is really only the beginning of a perspective on returning and forgiveness. When I presented this paper, I depended on a handout with texts and an overhead projector, relying on the listeners to be readers. In this written form, I will attempt to let my readers also listen to the presentation and so preserve some of the orality of the performance. Your task, however, will be to follow the complex layering of texts here. I proceed by way of commentary. My focus is a text from the Talmud, which itself is a commentary (the Gemara) on another text, the Mishnah. All translations are mine.* I will be commenting on longer passages from the Talmud and the Mishnah, but I break those passages into chunks, each of which is lettered, so that text 4 is broken into 4a, 4b, 4c, and so forth. The talmudic texts will be marked by a bold t (**T**) with a citation to the standard Vilna pagination of the Babylonian Talmud. The text itself is from the last chapter of the tractate *Yoma*, (*The Day*, the usual rabbinic term for The Day of Atonement). The mishnaic texts will be marked by a bold m (**M**) and will be cited to chapter and mishnah (e.g. **M** 4:5) of the tractate *Yoma*. When either Mishnah or Talmud cite a biblical text, I will then quote that text (with a reference to the book, chapter and verse), marking the biblical text with underlining to accent the words or phrases that were cited. The Mishnah was edited at the beginning of the third century of the Common Era, the Gemara—its commentary—in the late fifth century. These are fundamental texts for Jewish traditions, but we will be reading them not on the basis of their authority. They are the backbone of what is called the Oral Torah, and they are not organized as commentary on the Jewish Holy Scriptures or Bible (called the Written Torah). The Mishnah set out to be *not* a commentary on the Written Torah, although you will see it doing the work of commentary in a few moments. The Gemara of the Talmud understood itself as commentary on the Mishnah. Emmanuel Levinas, along with a few other Jewish thinkers in this century, has re-opened these texts to philosophical engagement, in part by delivering oral commentary on them. His readings of the mishnaic and talmudic texts will also appear, in each case marked by his name in bold (**Levinas**), and a reference to the page numbers in both French and the available English translation (**Levinas** 47/35), and those texts will also be parceled out in chunks. My goal is not to provide a definitive interpretation either of the Talmud or of Levinas's commentary, but rather to explore the questions in order to allow these texts to speak to us, to be resources for our thinking about repentance. Thus I explore Levinas's commentary on the Talmud by moving first from the Mishnah to Levinas, and then from the Gemara to Levinas. You will then be reading texts from four different strata of Jewish texts: biblical, mishnaic, talmudic, and a contemporary commentary (Levinas). Those texts are the pretext of my words.

Of course, what I am doing is in one way a return to a tradition of thought,

---

*I have consulted both Soncino and Neusner for translations of the Rabbinic texts and the New JPS and other translations for the Bible. For Levinas I have cited *Nine Talmudic Readings*, trans. Annette Aronowicz (Bloomington: Indiana University Press, 1990), but I have provided my own English version. The original Levinas text is from his *Quatre Lectures Talmudiques* (Paris: Les Editions de Minuit, 1968).

to a way to think. But that is one of the most important points I cannot describe for you in my short essay (although I can perform it here)—that the work of commentary is a task of return (repentance), and that return itself is interpreted to be a textually explicit return to previous texts in order to re-open them and to take responsibility for both missed readings and for mis-readings of the past and even of the present generation. The Torah is not an inheritance but requires a re-reading in which new questions produce new resources in the text. This recasting of repentance and forgiveness as linguistic practices has been happening in the Jewish tradition since the time of Hosea, in the eighth century BCE, and finds so much of its fullest articulation in rabbinic texts from the fifth century of the Common Era. This need to re-read and return is not first found in Derrida's deconstructions, nor, more important, is it an invented in the hermeneutics of Heidegger re-reading the philosophical tradition. It is the broken heart of Scriptural religion.

§1. The Invention of Social Ethics: The Mishnah

While from a philosophical viewpoint we might need to make a serious argument to recognize that ethics is originally social ethics, that the relations to other people (and not solely to my own ends and to my own will) are the focus of ethics, from a theological viewpoint, the possibility of ethics is quite a different kind of problem. While there may be moral responsibilities that are simply independent and thus subordinate to our responsibilities to God, the possibility for a range of ethical responsibilities that stand alongside the specifically private relationship to God is a complex question. All the more so when the topic is forgiveness: Doesn't the need to forgive others stand in an intimate relationship to being forgiven by God? And does the need to repent, to return, to other people follow the same structure as before God?

I begin with a much-cited text from the Mishnah. The text concerns the Day of Atonement (Yom Kippur), which in biblical times was a day for special sacrifices in the Temple, a day that provided for the cleansing of the priests and the people before God for the various sins committed. At the time of Mishnah, the Temple is destroyed, but it still explores the Day in relation to the Temple, and in another sense in relation to the Temple destroyed.

1a) **M** 8:9. Transgressions between a human and God—the Day of Atonement atones. Transgressions between a human and his companion—the Day of Atonement does not atone until he has satisfied his companion.

The basic division is between the sins a person does against God and those against his companion. The latter, for our purposes, represents the rabbinic invention of social ethics. For both kinds of sin, THE DAY OF ATONEMENT ATONES—and this means that even without the sacrifices, even without priests to officiate and a Temple to make offerings, the very day in the calendar, just about one month ago, itself is capable of atoning. Even in our time, the day is observed with fasting and prayer, and Jews understand that atonement is given for sins against God. The relations with God are mended in this atonement—but the relations with another person are separate, or at least different. Even If I return to God and confess my sin, God cannot forgive, the day cannot do its work, unless first I have appeased my companion. This sin against my neighbor is both *a sin*, and so against God, requiring divine forgiveness, and *against my neighbor*, requiring my neighbor's forgiveness. What sequence is required? Divine forgiveness (atonement) is impossible until the companion HAS BEEN SATISFIED. Human forgiveness has been identified and indeed elevated here. The task of returning has been doubled: first to seek my neighbor's reconciliation, and then to seek God's.

This text continues with a Scriptural interpretation to justify this claim. Throughout this chapter of the Mishnah there had been no Scriptural interpretation to justify a various group of claims—and I believe that the move to find a Scriptural warrant here is a confession that what is happening is a bolder and more dubious move, and therefore in need of some support.

> 1b) Rabbi Elazar ben Azariah interpreted: "From all your sins before THE LORD, you will be clean" [Leviticus 16:30]: transgressions between a human and God—the Day of Atonement atones; transgressions between a human and his companion—the Day of Atonement does not atone until he has satisfied his companion."

R. Elazar cites a basic text from the Bible, a text that prescribes the observances for the holiday at the time of the Temple. He first cites it and then proceeds to break apart the confusing sentence in order to support the interpretation of social sins.

> 2) Leviticus 16:29. And this shall be a law for you forever: In the seventh month, on the tenth day of the month, you shall afflict your souls and do no work at all, neither the citizen nor the resident alien in your midst. 30. Because on that day atonement will be made for you to cleanse you <u>from all your sins; before THE LORD you will be clean.</u>

The first verse from Leviticus (29) establishes the key elements of the day: a fixed moment in the calendar, the practices of rest and affliction, and the inclusion of all who live among the people.

In this inclusion of the resident alien (pilgrims) we may see some light on the reconciliation between people. But R. Elazar is looking at verse (30). I have <u>underlined</u> the words he actually cites. The verb "cleanse" is used twice, and the grammar causes some confusion. The plain sense is to insert a break between *sins* and *before*. The second clause, then, is the resulting cleanliness before God that the atonement and the cleansing of the Day brings. The problem in the verse is that if in the first part the Day does cleanse the people, then the second part is redundant: Of course they are clean before God—before whom else could they be clean? R. Elazar, however, pushes against this break, and interprets FROM ALL OUR SINS BEFORE GOD YOU WILL BE CLEANSED. R. Elazar, therefore, argues that the first time the root "to clean" appears, it concludes a phrase by stating that the purpose of the Day is to clean. The second half, then, explains not that the cleansing is before God, but that the relevant sins are those committed before God. Hence, R. Elazar restricts the "sins" to only those "before God," and so claims that the interhuman ones are not cleansed by the Day. The first half refers to the appeasement of the companion, the second to atonement before God.

Why does the Mishnah need R. Elazar's interpretation? What is novel here is that the Day alone cannot atone for the sins between people. The Mishnah is substantializing a category of interhuman relations (we call it *ethics*), and separates it from the category of sins against God. If we are right, however, to say that the ethical infractions also partake of sin against God, we still have the production of a category that would be characterized as social sins, and the remedy includes working things out with someone who has been harmed. The other person is clearly in control: He must be satisfied. The point is not that before the Mishnah was edited, Judaism did not know that when another person has been hurt, I must first satisfy her. Rather, the formalizing of this concept helps to focus our attention on the social repair. The recourse to the biblical interpretation both authorizes the new category and allows us to see its novelty. As we proceed, we will also see that God's role in our repentance shifts from a direct relation to an indirect one through the production of this new category.

Levinas offered a commentary on this text in a talmudic reading in 1963. Levinas's reading develops an interpretation of the Mishnah we have just read and then goes on to read the talmudic commentary on this Mishnah (the Gemara). I will first look briefly at Levinas on the Mishnah, and then we will expand our discussion by reading first the Gemara and then Levinas's commentary on it.

> 3a) **Levinas** 36/16. My sins in relation to God are forgiven without my depending on his good will! God is in one sense *the Other* par excellence, the other as other, the absolutely other—and nonetheless my disposition with this God depends only on me. The instrument of forgiveness is in my hands.

Levinas claims that the distinction between the sins against God and those against the other person shows me in control of the dispensation of God's forgiveness (DEPENDS ONLY ON ME). God is so other that forgiveness is not a question of satisfying the other but only of repenting—or of repenting and the Day. There is a security in relation to God: His provision and promise of forgiveness allows me to return with perfect certainty. Although God is the ABSOLUTELY OTHER, God is not fickle and has bound his freedom in the promise of forgiveness. God's direct intervention breaks through my anxiety, encouraging me to make the return.

> 3b) **Levinas** 36–37/16. In contrast, the neighbor, my brother, a human, infinitely less other than the absolutely other is, in a certain sense, more other than God: To obtain his forgiveness on the Day of Atonement, I must as a precondition appease him. And if he refuses? As soon as there are two, everything is in danger. The other may refuse to forgive and leave me forever unforgiven.

The contrast, however, accentuates just how much harder it is to be forgiven by another person. I am in her hands. I must respond to her freedom to forgive or not. The other person becomes more free, MORE OTHER THAN GOD! Levinas notes this paradox and that the structure of asymmetry with another person is in some ways more rigorous than the relationship with God—because of the profound unpredictability of the other's response. While Levinas does emphasize how vulnerable we are in relation to others, especially to those others we have harmed, he also integrates the unexpectable fact that others do forgive, do allow us to return. While the forgiveness is harder to expect with other people, Levinas in a later comment notes that the act of return is hardest in relation to God, indicating an account of deep moral corruption akin to Kant's account of radical evil in the *Religion within the Limits of Reason Alone*. Our point here, however, is that forgiveness can be expected from God, if we can return, but it is much less certain with another person—leaving unexamined the question about how forgiving we are supposed to be with someone who has harmed us.

§2. Returning the Spirit of the Text

The sages debated and interpreted the material in the Mishnah for 300 years before compiling the Gemara, a commentary of sorts upon it. One task in these commentaries is to mark the discontinuity between biblical texts and the Mishnah and to raise the question of how to justify that gap. We now turn to the commentaries upon our Mishnah:

> a) **T 87a.** "Transgressions between a human and God, etc.": R. Joseph bar Havu raised an objection to R. Abbahu: "'Transgressions between a human and his companion—the Day of Atonement does not atone?' But it is written: 'If a man sin against a man, God will mediate' [I Samuel 2:25]."

The discussion begins with an objection raised by one sage to another against the Mishnah. In question is the legitimacy of the new category we are calling social sin. R. Joseph firmly argues that the Day itself must be able to atone, even for sins against another person. The issue of sin is between God and an individual, and so repentance and forgiveness can atone for the sin. He does not regard satisfaction of the other as a precondition. He, like R. Elazar, has a verse to make his case. His verse comes from the midst of a tragic story. Eli is speaking to his sons, who in their role as priests have been abusing the people and desecrating the worship of God.

> 5) I Samuel 2:25. "If a man sin against a man, God will mediate; but if against THE LORD, who will mediate for him?" But they did not listen to the voice of their father because THE LORD was pleased that they should die.

Shortly after this speech, God appoints Samuel to succeed Eli, and not long after, Eli's sons are struck dead. Hence the conclusion of this verse points both toward revenge for God's honor and toward clearing the way for the accession of Samuel. But what of Eli's address to the sons? Clearly he is warning them that they should not offend God. He seems to recognize the twofold categorization: sins against other people and sins against God. What is striking is that there seems to be no intercessor, and hence no forgiveness for sins against God! In contrast, God himself seems to intercede to make peace in broken relations between people. R. Joseph brings this verse, therefore, to argue that God intervenes and so makes atonement when human relations are harmed—in clear opposition to the Mishnah that insisted that the people themselves must make good the damage. His point seems to be that the restoration of relations between the people is made possible by Yom Kippur and its relation with God as a third that transcends the relation with another person. Rabbi Abbahu, however, answers:

> 4b) **T** 87a. "What does *Elohim* mean? The judge."

He re-reads the verse. In the first half, the name of God—the tetragrammaton—is not used, so he proposes that we read the more general word "Elohim" as a human judge. Since in the second part of the verse God is named by the proper name, when only the general term "Elohim" is written in the first, it does not likely refer to God. R. Abbahu, therefore, claims that when a person harms another person, THE JUDGE intercedes, restoring justice. Transgressions require adjudication and mediation, and so the simplest meaning of the Mishnah, that the other person can tell me when I have satisfied him, is qualified by this response. Yes, a third party may be needed to make peace between us—but it will be a human third, not God. Such a third party serves the interests of the Mishnah: to distinguish the social realm where reconciliation must be worked out. While the entry of this judge represents a rationalizing of the need to satisfy, the judge still is not a representative of the Day of Atonement. Unlike God, who acts as the Divine Judge of us for life and death, a human judge is on the same plane as me and the person I have harmed.

R. Joseph, however, is less satisfied. He objects:

> 4c) **T** 87a. "Then how do you interpret the conclusion: 'And if a man sin against THE LORD, who will mediate for him?'"

The problem seems to be that the second piece of the verse clearly points to sins against God. Surely if it is the judge who mediates between people, then God can mediate for the sins against God—that is, God can forgive or justify the sinner. But Eli's point seems to be that God fixes things only between people and that there will be no higher court, no higher authority capable of repairing the betrayed relations with God—like misusing sacrifices intended for God. R. Abbahu's reading allowed for someone equal to the interested parties to intervene; R. Joseph argues that the text requires someone absolutely higher than the parties (God). The judge is indeed God, but not God as the one who has been sinned against, not as the one who has to forgive. The Name (translated as THE LORD) marks the intimacy of the sin and of the relation, and of the impossibility of repair! The biblical priest Eli seems, on this reading, to be without a Day of Atonement in any form.

R. Abbahu responds (and indeed has the last word) [the biblical verse is underlined].

> 4d) "This is what it says: 'If a man sins against a man, and appeases him—God will forgive him; and if a man sins against THE LORD—who can appease? Only repentance and good deeds.'"

The same word which we have translated "mediate" is from the root for prayer, intercede, and in that sense, "appease." R. Abbahu is forced to accept that the problem is appeasement in the two-party relationship, particularly with God, and so abandons the thought of the judge and the third. But he argues that a sinner can both appease his companion and appease God. In neither case is a third party needed. Rather, his new reading is that first the sinner appeases his companion, and then GOD WILL FORGIVE HIM; and that for sins against God REPENTANCE AND GOOD DEEDS serve as appeasement. His interpretation of Eli's warning is that the sons must repent and do well, else God will not forgive them. Hence, despite the despair of the biblical text, R. Abbahu now reads in the possibility and the power of repentance. He makes human repentance (with good deeds) equal to the task of God's forgiveness, indeed a parallel or even a replacement for it. Clearly the rhetorical question from the biblical text (WHO CAN APPEASE?) is troubling. R. Abbahu suggests that Eli can only mean that no one else can intervene or appease God for them; the sons themselves must repent. However forgiveness is to occur, there can be no detour from the initial effort of return, whether toward God or toward the other person I have harmed. R. Abbahu, thus, interprets the verse as opening a way for the sons—but perhaps R. Joseph is correct, for the verse concludes that neither the sons nor God wanted the sons to repent.

We turn to Levinas's commentary with this very moment: when R. Abbahu responds to R. Joseph's question: how do you read the rest of the verse (4c)?

> 6a) **Levinas** 42/19. But the gemara decidedly rejects this position. Here is the version it proposes: [Levinas's translation] "If a man commits a sin

against a man, and *appeases him*—God will forgive him; but if the sin is against God—who can intercede for him? *Only repentance and good deeds.* The solution consists of inserting the italicized words into the biblical verse, to bend it to the spirit of the Mishnah. One could not be less attached to the letter and more enamored of the spirit.

Levinas examined the narrative of the text, following it step by step. He was sure that R. Joseph's position stands rejected. Here he offers his own read-ing of the response, where he calls attention to the interpolated words with italics. Levinas's commentary explains and justifies the ways the sages argue. Out of loyalty to the Mishnah, R. Abbahu is willing to re-vise the biblical verse. The question of SPIRIT and LETTER is a rhetorical gesture of response to the Christian polemic against Jewish reading, a polemic that has become a cliché and a commonplace in the intellectual world. Levinas is gesticulating: See, the rabbis love the spirit at the expense of the letter. Their own interpola-tion, inserting words into the verse, performs a fidelity to THE SPIRIT OF THE MISHNAH—to its interests. But we can note that that textual move is itself a performance of repentance: they cultivate the possibility of repentance in the words of Eli, transforming the text from one which threatened the sinner with despair into one that offers hope of appeasing God. Offering hope where there was none, they alter the way the biblical text works, re-reading it in line with a richer view of repentance. Moreover, in the process it also offers a commen-tary on the Mishnah, emphasizing that I can appease someone I have harmed. Thus, the commentary serves the spirit in the sense of elevating repentance and the realm of the social.

> 6b) **Levinas** 42–43/19. It is thus very serious to have offended a human. Forgiveness depends on him, one finds oneself in his hands. There is no forgiveness that has not been requested by the guilty. The guilty must recognize his sin; the offended one must want to welcome the supplica-tions of the offender. Moreover, no one can forgive, if he has not had forgiveness requested by the offender, if the guilty has not sought to ap-pease the offended.

Levinas now explains the import of this exchange between R. Joseph and R. Abbahu. He limits the text to the relation with another person, ignoring the most convoluted part (and the focus of their problem), the relation with God. To offend is to put myself IN the other's HANDS. In a few short phrases, Levinas explains exactly the asymmetries and the responsibilities and dependencies on each other in this situation. I cannot forgive myself, but I also cannot forgive the other unless the other seeks forgiveness, yet I must welcome the one who seeks me. Even if I do admit my guilt and seek forgiveness, the other person may refuse me. I cannot produce forgiveness—from either side—without the responsive performance by the other. There are at least two roles, but they are utterly unexchangeable, and so responsibility is response to another's action.

Both the offended and the offending in turn must wait upon the other to act. My responsibility, even to forgive, is relational and asymmetric—and my responsibility to repent is one that exposes me to another's will. This is why the mishnaic requirement of satisfying the other person is so threatening. The forgiver is not simply in control, but the offending party must simply place himself in the other person's control and cannot seek God's forgiveness until the offended one accepts the apology. The asymmetries are comparable to those between God and the individual, but also they are different—as we have seen in the Mishnah.

§3. An Economy of Repair: Paying for Words

The Talmud's commentary then continues, focusing on the question of what counts as sin against one's neighbor and how one must appease him. The previous text seems to make the repenter almost powerless. Are there limits? The Talmud goes on to explore the possibility of limits in the context of verbal sins. Some might think only bodily actions can be sins, but the sages focus precisely on the sins which are verbal. To offend a companion it is not necessary to do a bodily action—indeed, the verbal harm seems to become primary.

> 4e) T 87a. R. Isaac said: Whoever vexes his companion, even if only with words, he must pacify him, as it is written: "My son, if you become surety for your neighbor, if you have shaken hands for a stranger—, you are snared by the words of your mouth. . . . Do this, now, my son, and deliver yourself, seeing you are come into the hand of your neighbor; go humble yourself and urge your neighbor." (Proverbs 6:1–3)

R. Isaac demands that I return to my companion even for "mere words"— that the rift that is caused by insult or harsh words equally requires a return and an attempt to PACIFY my companion. He then makes his point by citing a text from Proverbs, another text of fatherly advice.

> 7) Proverbs 6:1. My son, if you become surety for your neighbor, if you have shaken hands for a stranger—, 2. you are snared by the words of your mouth, caught *by the* words of your mouth. 3. Do this, now, my son, and deliver yourself, seeing you are come into the hand of your neighbor; go humble yourself and urge your neighbor.

The context in Proverbs is less significant, being a compilation of fatherly advice. (I will have more to say about fathers later.) If you pledge SURETY (and, the text suggests, surety as a third party for another's loan), then you are obliged. You will have to HUMBLE YOURSELF. The father is reprimanding his son and teaching him the financial side of appeasing.

> 4f) T 87a. If he has a claim of money upon you, open the palm of your hand to him, and if not, send many friends to him.

R. Isaac interprets the verse by expanding the possibility of release. The one to be appeased does not forgive the debt easily; instead, the one who is surety is still caught. You, the guarantor, cannot be forgiven the debt owed to the loaner if the debtor defaults. You must make good the debt. Appeasement must be monetary. Even when the obligation is not monetary, still you must seek appeasement verbally. The promise of surety is now expanded to be the promise that is not financial, the promise we might think of as a promise about another's worth (a letter of reference, for instance). R. Isaac's innovation, however, is to imagine appeasement coming by sending MANY FRIENDS. The repair to the broken promise is made through the sincerity of other people—not just a single third person, but other friends, a plurality of trustworthiness that can repair the breach of trust in words.

Levinas offers an extensive commentary on this saying of R. Isaac, and I will excerpt a little to help us understand the issues here—according to Levinas and in some complex anticipation of Derrida.

> 8a) **Levinas 45–46/20.** Indeed, the Talmud wants to shows the seriousness of a verbal insult. If you have said one word too many to your neighbor, you are as guilty as if you had caused a material injury. No forgiveness is possible without having obtained the appeasement of the offended! And in order to prove this, a passage from the Book of Proverbs is quoted in which the question is not insults but money. John lends money to Paul and you have guaranteed the repayment of the loan. You are certainly henceforth prisoner of the word you pledged. But in what respect does this principle of commercial law have anything to do with hurtful words?

Levinas explains the principle of "verbal" harms but is puzzled by the problem of the text from Proverbs. It begins by dealing with someone who gives his word, or shakes hands, to secure a loan for someone else. Obviously, this is not an insult, or even a willful deceit. The issue is not about insult but about giving one's word, about the need to stand surety in COMMERCIAL LAW. The harm seems not insult but financial loss. Levinas continues:

> 8b) **Levinas 46/20–21.** Could it teach us about the identity of injury and "monetary loss"?
>
> Or could it teach us the essence of speech? How could speech cause harm if it were only *flatus vocis*, empty speech, "mere word"? This recourse to a quotation which seems totally unrelated to the topic, and to which only a seemingly forced reading brings us back from afar, teaches us that speech, in its original essence, is a commitment in relation to a third party on behalf of our neighbor; the act par excellence, the institution of society. The original function of speech consists not in designating an object in order to communicate with another person in a game with no consequences but in assuming toward someone a responsibility on behalf

of someone else. To speak is to engage the interests of men. Responsibility would be the essence of language.

Levinas makes two comparisons: 1) from INJURY to "MONETARY LOSS"— that a sin against another person is intrinsically economic (more on this later), and 2) that speech is always about social relations, that THE ESSENCE OF SPEECH is giving my word about one person to a third person. The struggle to make repentance and forgiveness relationships with only two roles keeps slipping into three-part relations. Levinas recognizes that speech to another is not merely communicating information, but what we sometimes don't see in our readings of Levinas is that he also recognizes speech as involving three people. Indeed, the heart of the matter here is that I give my word not about what I will do but about what others are committing to do for other others. Trust in someone is engendered by my promise for that one to another person who trusts that someone because she first trusts me. The need to repent for verbal sins arises because language binds us in its promise of trusts, of surety for others. It is not just words, not just talk, but someone must pay. And so Levinas explores the paying, and indeed, the first claim (that a sin against another is intrinsically economic).

8c) **Levinas** 46–47/21. We can now understand the "misreadings" of the Talmudic interpretation. "Insist energetically and mount an assault upon your neighbor" means, to be sure, in the first place, insisting to the debtor to whom you have given your guarantee that he fulfil his obligation. But what does insistence mean if not the willingness to pay from one's own pocket? That the extent of the commitment is measured in cash, that the sacrifice of money is, in a way, the one which costs the most, is a Talmudic constant. Far from expressing some sordid materialism, it denounces the hypocrisy that harbors the ethereal spiritualism of possessors. The "insisting to the debtor" and the "mounting an assault upon one's neighbor" of which the Book of Proverbs speaks are necessary to redress the wrong done to the creditor if this redress is not to be gratuitous or spiritual. Verbal injury demands no less. Without the hard work of reconciling numerous wills, without material sacrifice, the asking for forgiveness, and even the moral humiliation it involves, make room for cowardice and laziness. Pious wishes are easy. The effort inherent in action begins when one strips oneself of one's goods and when one mobilizes wills.

Levinas now finds the place for economics in these relations—economics in relations where there is no closed economy and no zero sum. Precisely because the guarantor has no right and no reasonable expectation to expect the debtor to forgive the debt, his need to appease is a genuine responsibility, an infinitely obliging responsibility. Levinas lauds the Talmud for recognizing that sacrifice is not merely spiritual but must include MONEY. To appease the creditor is to pay him back, no less. And returning after verbal injury must then require a parallel effort, A MATERIAL SACRIFICE. What seems to us as the most inward of moral states, repentance, becomes something that can be counted out. No money, no cost, no real repentance—and hence no forgiveness. The alternative, from the perspective of the repenter, is a lax and vague, even cowardly, inner change. But when someone is hurt (their life savings on the line, their good name in the community besmirched, their own graciousness at risk), then even a guarantor must be willing to pay. One STRIPS ONESELF OF GOODS, as though possessions adhered to me, and now I will be naked, and one MOBILIZES WILLS—the friends whose trustworthiness can repair the damage done to the *"economy"* of trust.

§4. At the Limit of Repentance

I return now to the Talmud itself for three more teachings on the responsibility to pacify the person I have harmed. The first tries to find the limits when the offended person refuses to be satisfied—limits obviously needed because the balance has shifted from the repenter to the forgiver. Just what is the limit of what the repenter must do?

> 4g) **T** 87a. R. Hisda said: He needs to appease him with three lines of three people each, as it is said: "He lines up men and says: 'I have sinned and I have perverted what was right and it did not benefit me.'" (Job 33:27)

The reluctant forgiver is now compelled by a procedure. It is not a simple procedure, for the offender must collect groups of three people to come before the one he offended and ask for forgiveness. For rabbinic Judaism, a set of three witnesses makes a court, represents the public. Hence, I must go public with my injury and entreat you in public for forgiveness. (And I must do it three times!) Reconciliation seems to depend on this public event—if you refuse me in private, then I humiliate myself publicly, but I also draw on the publicity to entice you to forgive me. Indeed, you might then say, "What does it matter to me? You will be considered appeased if only you gather this committee to meet three times." It is in the public interest, the community's, that we be reconciled, and they will regard us as so if only I am willing to humiliate myself three times in public.

But what of R. Hisda's biblical verse (the only one that is not a fatherly injunction)? Job has frustrated his three comforters, and Elihu, who is a younger man, explodes in anger, charging Job not to claim to be free from sin. Elihu praises God, claiming that God will redeem Job from the pit, as he redeems the pious. He continues: [I underlined the words R. Hisda cited]

> 9) Job 33:26. "He will pray to God, and he will be favorable to Him. He will see His face in joy, for He renders to a man his righteousness. 27. He

lines up men and says: 'I have sinned and I have perverted what was right
and it did not benefit me.'"

This speech is somewhat obscure, but R. Hisda interprets the first word of
verse 27 to be setting up a line, even a quorum of ten people, as a context in
which to confess his sins against God. God will accept the sinner who prays to
God and who confesses in front of others. Whether Elihu sees this public
repentance as a means of restoring God's good name in the eyes of the others
who come to witness or sees the public humiliation as a positive achievement
for the one who returns to God is unclear. Following our own ruminations on
how the public approach to the offended one encourages the offended to
forgive, perhaps God can be more readily forgiving in this public performance.

But the much more interesting issue here is that the sins for which one
assembles this line of people are sins against God. Even for those "private"
sins, a public performance is required—Yom Kippur is, of course, a communal
holiday, with communal confession and fasting, and so forth. But Hisda is
making a much more striking claim here: The practices by which one returns
to God and is forgiven by God can be adopted for receiving forgiveness from
another person I have harmed. If lining up people helps secure God's forgiveness, then we can use it to establish the need for the other person to forgive me.
Remember, the central question is What is the difference between the sins
against another and the sins against God? Here the procedure for repenting
before another person is constructed as an imitation of the procedure before
God. The publicity serves to make the community the guarantor of access to
human forgiveness—just as it also secured the access to Divine forgiveness. We
then continue with R. Jose:

> 4h) T 87a. R. Jose b. Hanina said: Anyone who asks pardon of his compan-
> ion does not ask him more than three times, as it is said: "Forgive, I pray
> you now . . . and now we pray you." (Genesis 50:17)

R. Jose now focuses our attention on the three requests. Whereas R. Hisda
was most concerned about the public nature of forgiveness and, indeed, was
making use of the public setting to transfer the expectation that God forgives to
a situation in which the offended one refuses to forgive, R. Jose is more
concerned with limiting the number of times. His text makes no reference to
the line of three witnesses—either indicating that he waives that requirement
or, more likely, that within the context of needing a public, he will limit
himself to the question of how many times. Three is enough; more is inviting
the offender to grovel and the offended one to become arrogant. But again we
need to look at the text from which he draws his insight.

The passage comes from Genesis, when Jacob has died and the brothers
fear that Joseph will now take his deserved revenge upon him. They plot to
plea before him [I have underlined the words cited]:

10) Genesis 50:16. And they sent to Joseph, saying, "Your father commanded before his death, saying, 17. 'So shall you say to Joseph, "Forgive, I pray you please, the trespass of your brothers and their sin; for they did evil to you: and now we pray you, forgive the trespass of the servants of the God of your father."'" And Joseph wept as they spoke to him.

The first thing to notice is the repetitive phrases in their address: They use two different words of entreaty (pray, please) and for a total of three times. But that would be a mechanical reading, to say the least. The Jewish commentators notice that, of course, Jacob never told them to come and say this to Joseph. The brothers fabricate an address, and we do not know whether Joseph intended evil or not. But clearly the address works well: Joseph is in tears and then promises not to take revenge. The image of his father is enough to move him to forgive. Fabrication, indeed, fabrication of a citation (He said, tell him this. . . .—all those quotation marks!) seems at least to be effective. Our interest, moreover, goes farther because we see the image of the dead father encouraging the offended one to forgive. Reconciliation that lasts depends on the memory of the father, indeed, on the ascription of fatherly advice (by the ones who need forgiveness). I will have more to say about the fathers in a moment. But first, let us look briefly at Levinas's commentary on this text (and mention in passing that he does not even translate, much less comment upon, either the next passage [4i], nor upon the position of R. Hisda [4g]).

11) **Levinas 48–49/22.** In this passage there would be three entreaties or a ternary rhythm which would prove the thesis of Rav Jose bar Hanina. The commentators discuss its cogency. What does it matter? I would like to fasten on the choice of Biblical verse. What example of an offense was sought in the Bible for the occasion? The story of the brothers who sold their brother into slavery. The exploitation of man by man would therefore be the prototype of offense, imitated by all offenses (even verbal).

Levinas can count the use of "please" words, too. But he also looks at the context and notices something much more basic: The offense in question is the betrayal of a BROTHER. Offenses are in the first instance between those who are closest to us (which is why the word I have steadily translated *companion* is sometimes translated *neighbor*. My point was to accentuate the very intimacy of the one whom I have sinned against. A companion is someone we share with, not merely someone near us). Sin then disrupts the sharing with our intimates.

While the Talmudic passage will continue beyond our texts (4i), telling stories of botched attempts at appeasing another person, I wish to quote only one more line, the one that immediately follows the citation from Genesis:

4i) **T 87a.** And if he died? He brings ten people and stands them by his grave and says: "I have sinned against the Lord, the God of Israel, and against this one, whom I have wronged."

How do I reconcile with someone who is dead? Line up another public at the grave and confess. While the three times before an irreconcilable wronged companion produced the legal fiction of forgiveness, the corpse, too, can be made to forgive. Precisely to address our keen sense that I could die unreconciled, legitimately blocking the healing for someone who harmed me, the Gemara forces the dead to forgive. If I am willing to convene a public group and confess before them, the dead are unable to withhold forgiveness. The power of the offended one, the freedom to leave me unforgiven, is withdrawn in death.

§5. Fathers and Brothers

I wish to explore with you the fathers (Eli, in Proverbs, and Jacob) in order to come to a stopping point. My own first reading of these texts was drawn to see how only a father's reproach could get the sons to seek reconciliation. The editors of the Gemara took some pains to find paternal texts, texts that accentuated fathers' advice, but to what end? That paternal voice seemed to borrow the authority of the Divine (as in the Job citation). For the Job citation argued that public performance of the repentance in human affairs must follow repentance before God, thus the power to elicit God's forgiveness could be transformed into the power to elicit a human being's forgiveness. It seemed to me that not only could two people not reconcile themselves, but that they needed a third who had authority over both of them, a third who was either God or a surrogate, a father, even a dead father.

Now, however, I suspect here a more radical teaching about human reconciliation, one that displaces both fathers and God. First, I wonder if a maternal voice might be more likely to get the boys to apologize. Is it only fear of the patriarchy that keeps us in some solidarity? This opens key questions for a feminist critique of repentance in this passage—for the possibility of a public performance, as well as the possibility of a Temple performance, are exclusive of women. Is this account of return an account of men's returning only? The earliest roots of this image are entangled in the extremely problematic image of Israel as an adulteress returning to her husband, God. These concerns open up because the familial violence and almost impossible reconciliation are made the center of the Talmudic discussion (brothers, fathers and sons, and dead fathers). Is this different from the relation of wife and husband?

But second, one can easily notice that the most effective advice was the fictive voice of Jacob—invented out of fear by the brothers themselves. Eli's warning, in contrast, was a failure. Is the *idea* of authority more valuable in teaching us to seek reconciliation and to grant forgiveness than real authority? That is, I began to wonder if the father as authority was most effective when he was not present making the plea to his sons but was only available in citation, in the mouths of the boys. That shift is accentuated for the readers in the Joseph story because the sons themselves have to invent the fatherly advice, have to think like a father, like a father that Joseph might heed (with loud echoes of Jacob deceiving his father by sounding like his brother—an echo with the profound change in the equality of the speakers and listeners, the great discovery of brotherly justice in Genesis as a book). And lest we miss the point, the citation is itself an instruction on what the brothers are to say to Joseph—they are ad-libbing but pretending only to be the instruments of the father. Jacob seemed incapable of working reconciliation between the brothers throughout the story—but the idea of Jacob in the mouths of the sons is capable of producing reconciliation.

But this fictive, absent father in place of a present authoritarian father is itself a theological idea. It arises as a commentary on the development of repentance and forgiveness between human beings in their sin against each other, the sphere where God cannot forgive us first. Might God, too, be better able to inspire us to seek reconciliation, to make the painful return to those we have harmed and to teach us to welcome those who do return if God withdraws from the scene? I think that the Gemara's commentary on the Mishnah is a means of developing and emphasizing the theological insight that lurks in the idea I have called the invention of social ethics. For what the Mishnah produced—the insight that the Day of Atonement (and God's willingness to forgive us) does not atone until I have appeased my companion—requires a different account of the relation of theology and ethics.

If I tell the story as I have in the past, then I understand the focus of Yom Kippur as the relationship with God—it seems to be the holiest day of the year, the day most devoted to God. The social sins are a nuisance that must be relieved by appeasing my companions, but the task is to become cleansed before God on that day—so the text from Leviticus instructs us and institutes the Temple atonement procedure. At first the cleansing was achieved by the high priest, but when the Temple was destroyed again, prayer and repentance and good works were accounted as adequate—again for cleansing us before God. But lest people depend on a too-lazy relationship with their fellows, the social sins were pulled out and a special treatment was required.

But let us tell the story in a different way: Yom Kippur was instituted to repair the harms people had done to each other. It institutionalized a time for people to confess and to repent and to mend their ways—especially their ways with other people. Because we despair of our ability to change ourselves and we prefer to deny to ourselves the harms we have done others and we incline to bear a grudge against others who have harmed us, recourse was had to a direct intervention of God into this process. Repentance was secondary because God's forgiveness broke up the structures in our lives that cried out for repair. Depending on divine forgiveness allowed us to reconstruct our ways.

Except that it did not work that way. Depending on God's interruption relieved our responsibility too much. The tasks of repenting and forgiving depend too much on asymmetrical human relations; the other person has to be involved, and I have responsibility directly in relation to that other. The sages dispatched God from the central role: The other person is in control. This yielded a severe imbalance in the requirement of appeasement, which was then redressed through public constraint on the one who forgives. The constraint now lies in the public sphere and not solely in God's hands. God, the father, is citeable but lies outside the scene of what we must do before each other. If we cannot seek to reconcile ourselves, we might invoke God's call, but we must still do the work ourselves. The earlier attempt to make God forgive failed because it did not depend enough on our own efforts of repentance and forgiveness. Better than holy sacrifice and direct action is the action that responds to God's call, an action undertaken between a person and a wronged companion. Yom Kippur is now elevated through the Gemara's interpretation of the Mishnah, finding in the practices and the commandments a higher form of cleansing—a cleansing of each other. That new relation lives in the danger of the infinite authority of each in performing his or her own role, and it confines that danger only by recourse to the human community. God calls us to return to each other and gives us hope, but in our vital social relations we become the actors. God's role is not hereby exhausted, but it is all too clear that "only a God" cannot save us now. We must save each other, for until then, even God cannot save us.

Forgiveness and Incarnation

John Milbank

1. Forgiveness as Negative or Positive

If we are to be saved, in the Christian West, then we must partake of the waters of forgiveness which flow down the slopes of Mount Purgatory. However, right from the top, these waters divide: down the near slope pour the waters of Lethe, or of forgetting; down the farther side rush the waters of Eunoe, or of positive remembrance. According to Dante, this stream "*non-adopra / se quinci a quindi pria non ē / gustato* [it works not if first it be not tasted on this side and on that]."[1]

Forgiveness, therefore—the forgiveness that we in the West have been given to remember—is poised vertiginously between obliteration and a recollection that amounts to a restoration. It is either, or both, a negative gesture and a positive deed. The most ancient, pre-Christian cognates for something at least akin to "forgiveness" suggest mostly the former: Greek *aphesis* is a letting go, or dismissal; Latin *ignoscere* is an overlooking or not-knowing, and in the Old Testament the God of mercy is said to hide human faults behind his back. If there was any question, for the Romans, of a deed here, or of an active donation, then the gesture of forgiving was not itself seen as a gift, but what was offered (*dare*) was either impunity (*venia*) or, once again, oblivion as to the past.[2]

Only in a later era at once Christian and feudal do the vernacular tongues suggest that forgiveness is a positive offering. Both the Latinate and Germanic languages now deploy words designating a hyperbolic giving: *pardonner, perdonare, perdonar, vergeben*, forgive.[3] In both cases the main force of the prefix seems to be one of emphasis—here giving is extreme because one-sided and unprompted, a gift to the undeserving. At the same time, it is not clear that negativity is not also connoted. In English the prefix "for-" may be an intensifier (as in forread, forfrighted), but it may also be a negator (as in foredeem, forhale).[4] Perhaps forgiveness, since it gives up, or *for*swears a legitimate ground of complaint, suggests a kind of negative giving which benignly removes—the giving of a gift which fortunately destroys. This is exactly how, in *Works of Love*, Søren Kierkegaard understood forgiveness: namely, as the counterpart of creation, which miraculously brings being out of nothing; and of hope, which turns an absence into a presence.[5] By contrast, for Kierkegaard, forgiveness with equal miraculousness decreates, and causes what is not merely to be as if it were not, but literally not to be. It is precisely this absurdity of forgiveness which leads the Danish philosopher to insist that it is a reality only of divine grace and only to be known as real by human faith. Indeed, since, for Kierkegaard, the gift of creation appears to bring about existence, while the negating anti-gift of forgiving grace removes it, he seems to invoke here a meta-ontological register of "donology."

However, one may already pose the question as to whether, in this respect, and with regard to his exclusive understanding of forgiveness as negation, Kierkegaard is not the heir to specifically late-medieval, early modern, and Reformation developments. For whatever the linguistic evidence, there is no doubt that for the earlier Christian era, negativity was doubly qualified by something positive. By our human efforts alone, we could, indeed, for this period, like the pagan Virgil, arrive at the waters of Lethe, but to arrive at the waters of positive remembrance we required already prevenient grace, personified in Dante by the figure of Matilda who presides as a new Proserpine (that earlier female *figura* of a necessary half-and-half) over the earthly paradise.[6] Thus, for the high Middle Ages, the forgiveness and repentance which is specifically the grant of grace was mediated only through the sacrament of penance, which is the first instance of a new, positive dimension to forgiveness. In penitence, repentance is more than an attitude, it is also a public sign, a gesture, an offering which somehow "makes up" for a past error. But this positivity might indeed appear to be a mere prelude to the negating anti-gift of pardon as mediated by the priest, a prelude required by the legalism of medieval Christian thought. Such legalism may seem to be exemplified in Thomas Aquinas's stipulation that whereas *human* forgiveness may be offered in the absence of repentance, divine forgiveness cannot be so offered.[7] However, it turns out that legalism is not what is in evidence here, but something almost like the reverse: Whereas human forgiving may or may not induce repentance, says Aquinas, divine forgiveness necessarily does so. Therefore, for Aquinas, archetypal, exemplary divine forgiveness is not a mere blotting out, as it frequently becomes in later theologies, for which a putatively pure, utterly un-elicited divine forgiveness only forgets and ignores the past, whereas the forgiveness realized through repentance looks initially at damaged past events which it then seems to transform. Following this latter model, divine forgiveness for Aquinas is the provision to the one forgiven of the positive means not merely to make restitution for an injustice, but to make a restitution so complete that one is utterly reconciled with the one wronged (here God himself) and one's relationship with Him can flow in future so smoothly that it is exactly, as Kierkegaard later put it, as if it had never suffered any "jolt" whatsoever.[8] And since divine forgiveness was, for Aquinas and the Middle Ages in general, mediated by the Church through the sacrament of penance, it was to some extent the case that, at an interhuman level also, to forgive someone was actively to bring about reconciliation through the provision to the other of a positive means of recompense.[9]

However, at times this action might go beyond merely providing opportunity for recompense and become a matter of oneself offering recompense in an act of substitution. Thus, the second positive dimension to medieval pardon concerns the proximity of this notion to ideas of atonement. Supremely, of course, God was held to have offered us forgiveness, even for original sin, through his incarnation, suffering, and death as a man. Whether God could, nonetheless, have forgiven our sins without such recourse was a crucial matter of debate within medieval theology: Yet whatever was concluded on this issue, it was unavoidable that, as a matter of fact, divine forgiveness had taken the initial form of suffering in our stead. Here, one is tempted to say, forgiveness had become literally for-giving, giving the gift on behalf of the other; in this Christological instance it is the divine Son through his assumed human nature making the return offering of true worship to the Father—a return which humanity should make, but since the fall can make no longer. Such an assimilation of the prefix "for" to its prepositional use, may well be without etymological warrant; nevertheless, it appropriately conveys the Christian assimilation of forgiveness to substitutionary atonement. Here it is the case that guilt so incapacitates the habitus, that first of all an innocent other must show one the way of penitence, which only thenceforward becomes imitable, even by the guilty. And of course such a logic was not confined to the supreme Christological instance; rather, the intersubjective contagion of works of piety and intercession was central for medieval faith and practice.

One could say that the double addition of positivity to forgiveness belonged within a cultural matrix which did not firmly distinguish mercy from justice and thought of all giving, including forgiving, not as ideally pure, free, and disinterested, but rather as situated within an economy of exchange and obligation.[10] This was not, however, a capitalist exchange, even in disguised or latent form (as Marxists such as Pierre Bourdieu have claimed). As I have suggested elsewhere, the gift was not a commodity refusing to declare itself, because it returned non-identically, at no absolutely required time, and thereby always preserved a reciprocity that was asymmetrical and in consequence not abstractly equivalent to other reciprocities.[11] In a somewhat parallel fashion, the circulating economy of forgiveness could not be reduced to a workable calculus of self-interest, trading sin for sin, like debt for debt, in the ultimate interest of one's eternal self-preservation. No such simple reduction was possible, because the high medieval theology of forgiveness was a paradoxical attempt to economize the aneconomic. For this theology, sin was the refusal not simply of a measurable divine justice, but rather an immeasurable divine grace. As such a refusal of an infinite free gift, it was without human, calculable remedy and was only to be remedied by the incalculable mystery of God himself enduring, innocently, this lack of his own grace, and so giving us, once again, this grace in the mode of a suffering that heals.[12] Therefore, for this outlook, what we are offered once again through Christ's atonement is without measure and without price, and the only penance demanded of us in return for this forgiveness is the non-price of acceptance, even if such acceptance must be shown, manifest and realized in this or that appropriate action according to time and place. Likewise, the contagion of merit and intercession, though it was still, and crucially, a trade of sorts, was an impossible and miraculous trade in the infinite, a seeking to restore, by all and for all, the repayment of a debt due which is nothing but an infinite free accepting. Just for this reason, Aquinas insisted that human forgiveness could not wait on a human penance which it could not, like divine forgiveness, guarantee; instead, forgiveness, as negative cancellation only attained through positive enabling and substitutionary undergoing, had to be freely and infinitely offered without price to the neighbor, as the gospels had demanded. Thus forgiveness obeyed no ordinary, calculable economy, since it was without finite price. Nonetheless, the aim of forgiveness was not a lone, self-righteous certainty of the will to exonerate (without regard to circumstances or the repentance of the other), but rather charity, which the Middle Ages regarded less as a performance than as a *state* of fraternal, friendly, and harmonious co-existence. The aim, in other words, was reconciliation, where the bond of love is an exchange of infinite charity. However, since this exchange, though without limits, was also according to finite measure, concrete issues of fair distribution and the rectification of past unfairness and violent seizures were here not to be ignored. (Hence there was no sense of an infinite obligation to give which we always fail to realize.) Infinite giving, in order to be participated in, must be manifest for now in an aesthetic sense of who is to give, what, where and when, and what might be an appropriately shaped response or recompense, in the case of something judged to be lacking. Just because the goal sought was not the private subjective sustaining (with indifference to objects) of a pure and absolute negative commitment to ignore all faults one suffers from others, but rather concrete reconciliation based on mutual agreements as to the right distribution of objects (and an agreement whose justice must be validated by a third party), forgiveness in this era was not as yet interruptively counterposed to justice and issues of positive recompense. Instead, one could say, for the Christian understanding up to the high medieval era, forgiveness was the name of the order which carried justice into the infinite, a justice beyond justice which assumed that if all was to be fairly set right, then all must be reconciled in the truth, whose pattern is such that the reconciliation is infinite and beyond all possible finite undoing. It is just for this reason, that before going to meet Beatrice in the celestial paradise, Dante must become reconciled with her under the auspices of Matilda in the earthly paradise.[13] Indeed, this sequence makes clear that there will be no individual preceding to heaven *until* the fallen order of the earth is restored through a measured reconciliation.

From the high medieval era, therefore, we have been bequeathed a certain legacy of forgiveness as unlimited positive circulation, which contrasts with the antique understanding of forgiveness as mere negative gesture. Nevertheless, since this era, the increasing sundering of gift from contract, and of mercy (including divine mercy) from justice, encouraged first by new theological assumptions and new ecclesial practices, has apparently ensured an overwhelming cultural re-insertion of forgiveness as negativity. This notion of a simple re-insertion is, however, misleading: For in classical times there was mostly no real recommendation of forgiveness in a post-Christian sense. In this period, the "overlooking" of fault referred either to a pragmatic ignoring of it for self-interested reasons, or else to the taking into account of mitigating circumstances and involuntary motions.[14] And, in fact, acts of arbitrary "mercy" were viewed with suspicion as exonerating malefactors and raising benefactors above the normal sway of legality. Within, for example, the ancient Greek *strictly finite* regime of justice and gift-exchange, *aphesis* was indeed often regarded as an arbitrary intrusion, breaking maliciously into a balanced and regular interchange between equals.[15] For the sake of this interchange, the Greeks were prepared, mostly, to sacrifice the difficult exception and the unreconciled and aggrieved individual (though one must read Plato's *Laws* and Aristotle's *Ethics* as protesting against this). Preparedness to violate the law in the name of charity or mercy was much more associated with oriental despotic empires, from which Israel herself learned much.[16] Here, however, forgiveness was very much an act of sovereign whim, a gesture of pure negative cancellation, and an act quite prepared to violate justice. Insofar as many modern Christian versions of forgiveness, as exemplified by Kierkegaard, recommend a unilateral act of ontological cancellation, then they would seem to be long-term legatees of this oriental despotism, protracted to infinity in the late medieval reconception of God as a reserve of absolute, infinite untrammeled power and will. (One should note here that there was already a *theological* invention of pure unasked-for forgiveness, and that postmodern versions of this merely repeat in secular guise this later theology.)

It might be claimed here, notwithstanding, that this modern Christian position is a legitimate extrapolation from the Bible. For up until the time of the Babylonian exile, there is little evidence for a strong Hebraic notion of forgiveness, other than ideas of mitigation according to circumstance and for future mutual interest.[17] Strong notions of forgiveness seem rather to have arisen from that epochal Hebraic projection of empire into the transcendent as a power able to overrule and belittle all human despotism.[18] Hence in Deutero-Isaiah, Ezekiel, and Jeremiah, God is endowed with an unlimited will to forgive. However, the Hebrew projection is scarcely to be understood as itself an exaltation of the despotic, and in consequence the will to forgive of the Hebrew god is not a will to pure forgetfulness of fault. To the contrary, a new sense of the need for, and the possibility of, a far-reaching divine forgiveness for extreme sins is accompanied, in texts of a mainly priestly origin, by a renewed sense of the need for ritual purifications and acts of atonement. And so far from these two considerations running in counterpoise, it is rather the case that there is an increasing expectation of an eschatological day when God will offer—perhaps in the shape of some shadowy human figure—a new possibility of final expiation. Here, one might say, forgiveness has entered into a mixed constitution: The monarchic component of interruption of legal process by fiat has become blended with an aristocratic sense of appropriate equity in time and place and a democratic sense of restitution from within, according to immanently absorbed norms. And of course such a mixed constitution of forgiveness is supremely realized in the Incarnation, where the estranged and alien sovereign is restored to rule through the consensual self-legislation of humanity (in Christ and his body the Church) under norms of taught and received objective measure. After the Incarnation, contrary to Jewish expectation, there is held to begin not a reign of realized forgiveness, but a time when divine forgiveness can be mediated by human beings: a time for which justice is infinitized as forgiveness.

Thus, already I wish provisionally to suggest that the most compelling Western legacy of forgiveness is as a positive mixed constitution—exemplified ideally not in an oriental empire, but in something like the Logres of King Arthur (who, in the romance of *Tristram*, is shown to offer forgiveness and reconciliation to the adulterous lovers, in opposition to the unmerciful justice of King Mark of Cornwall).[19] By contrast, the negative and unilateral post–late-medieval and Reformation sense of forgiveness perverts this constitution into a despotism now to be exercised as anarchy. If there is something legitimate in forgiveness as negation, then this surely is but a negation of negation, an overlooking, an absorption into the positive through suffering of evil, which is of its nature privative in the first place. In consequence, forgiveness is not, as for Kierkegaard, a decreation, but rather the uninterrupted flow of the one initial creation through and despite, as he puts it, the "jolt" of fault. Here the donological remains ontological.

2. The Aporias of Forgiveness

So far I have traced the tension between forgiveness as negative gesture and forgiveness as positive gift. Already, though, we have glimpsed the lineaments of a second tension, between forgiveness as human and forgiveness as divine. Let us suppose, first of all, that we are asking whether or not forgiveness can be enacted between human beings today in terms of the resources for thinking about forgiveness in both negative and positive terms as so far described.

It seems to me that a purely interhuman forgiveness will then appear to be impossible in terms of five major aporias.

(a) Who is to forgive?

First of all, there is the question of who is to forgive. Here, one signpost at the divided way reads "the victim," while the other reads "sovereign authority." Of course, as now reiterated piously ad nauseam, only the victim can forgive, since only she has suffered the wrong and only she can be reconciled. But even this chosen fork of victimage proves a path that cannot really be taken. Quite simply, the victims will never appear to exonerate us. First of all, they are far too numerous: Since evil is contagious, it is impossible to know how far the consequences of even the simplest and most minor misdemeanors extend. That is its terror; that is why all wrong is so absolutely wrong. Therefore, the infinite jury of victims can never be summoned to the consistorial court of penitence. And second, as is often pointed out, the true victims do not survive at all, to be able to proffer pardon. Forgiveness is, always for us in time, only a reality that is proven to be possible for the weaker, the easier cases: Those dead and pulverized in their fury and despair will never rise in time to prove they can surmount these attitudes.

However, even if we could locate and summon the victims, which we cannot do exhaustively, and so not into adequate exoneration, do they really enjoy an exclusive or primary right to exonerate? Part of the problem here is already latent in what has just been said: Since there is never only *one* victim, the claim of this victim exclusively to forgive a fault is like an anarchic appropriation of sovereignty; all the other, often untraceable victims are thereby betrayed. Moreover, private forgiveness always implies an interruption of public justice which is associated with the perspective of a third party. If it is thought of in negative terms, then a fault is simply overlooked; the raped girl, victim of a man who was once her lover, forgives him and never brings him to court. If it is rather thought of in positive terms, then the upshot is still the same: The raped girl exacts from her ex-lover her own conditions for recompense and reconciliation, but if these are *just* conditions, do not they then require public, third-party assessment? (Although, according to the New Testament, all Christians are expected to settle things among themselves out of the secular court, a certain ecclesial trial is still involved.) Thereby, however, the forgiving victim might legitimately incur public outrage: Her loyalty to a friend may betray other women, past or future possible victims of the same man, or else still other women rendered more vulnerable to similar acts in parallel situations by the girl's refusal to expose, and make an example of, this particular criminal. What makes her, after all, the right one to do the forgiving, rather than all these other women? Moreover, such a relinquishing of justice gives her a power over the offender and obliterates his fault by turning it into the means of such power. Finally, since any rape renders all women less secure and all men less trusted and more liable themselves to false accusations of rape and therefore *also* less secure, this crime is an attack on the whole community. It follows, therefore, that only the sovereign representative of this community should be properly empowered to forgive. But if it were to do so, it would be offering the chance for making reparation and achieving rehabilitation to a dangerous rapist, while his actual, damaged victims persisted in hatred and bitterness toward him; then we should not feel that he had been forgiven. And where are we to locate the sovereign power to represent all those injured who may lie unknown beyond any traceable boundary of space and time? Therefore, neither the victim nor the sovereign power may forgive, and there is no human forgiveness.

(b) Forgiveness in Time

Second, there is the question of how, in any sense at all, a past fault can be removed. The problem is one of *time*. For there is no problem with a spatial mistake: The person blocking the entrance can simply be removed. But *that* he blocked the entrance for a time, and prevented such and such another person from getting through, so crucially delaying her, and so forth, can never be altered, or changed, ever. Writers such as Vladimir Jankélévitch have asked, in the wake of the Holocaust, whether an absolute imperative to forgive is not nihilistic, since it amounts to the will to abolish misdeeds from our memory, thereby ensuring a complicity with the perpetrators.[20] For Jankélévitch, more specifically, the order of time runs counter to forgiveness, because, first of all, if past events can be wiped out from our reckoning, we are ignoring the ineluctable discreteness of past moments, through which alone time occurs and finite being arises at all. Second, it runs counter to forgiveness, because certain events perpetrated in time, and supremely the Holocaust, manifest a radical evil, to which wickedness is unmotivated by even the illusion of good. Whereas, in the case of an inadequate will to the good resulting in a deficient deed, one may appeal to the fundamentally good will of the perpetrator and redeem his deed through a remembering of it in its aspects of a positive desire for the good, thereby shedding only what was lacking and perverted about it (and therefore never fully there in the first place), in the case of an absolutely perverse will, there is no seed of conscience to be cultivated, and its resulting deed is pure positive horror. Such horror cannot, like a privation, be legitimately forgotten and yet, if remembered, it cannot possibly be redeemed. This wound must forever fester.

Besides Jankélévitch's issues of the reversibility of time and of radical evil, one may mention a third problematic of time and forgiveness, which involves, once again, the vanishing of the victim. As we have already seen, the primary problem here is that the most victimized are always already dead, such that apologizing to them in one's own name or in the name of one's ancestors, seems smug and futile and even in a certain way patronizing to the villains of the past, who did not enjoy our interests or perspectives—which themselves, indeed, may be less absolute than we imagine. Hence, we may well deplore the millennial futility of apologizing to Galileo, the victims of the crusades, exterminated Native Americans, and so forth. Either apologizing for, or else offering forgiveness on behalf of, one's ancestors, seems a dubious procedure. But does not the same dubiety invade also one's relationship even to one's own past self? How can I apologize now, after the heat of the moment, for my anger then, within it? More crucially, how can I forgive now, when the effects of injury have somewhat abated, the wrong I suffered then, enduring its full and unmitigated impact? One may say, indeed, that this problem is only serious if one entertains a Humean skepticism as to the continuity of identity; however, even if one does not go that far, there remains a rupture between the person first injured and the same person later offering forgiveness, even were it to occur merely one minute later. For one *cannot* receive injury at the psychic level, which is alone relevant here, without experiencing a weakening, and resentment and anger about that weakening. And where the cause of the injury is received as personal, one receives a malicious intent, concerning which one cannot fail to feel fury. There can be no distinguishing the sin from the sinner here, because sin is a manifestation of personality and is always specifically characterized as proceeding from *this* specific individual or set of individuals. Refusing to hate the sinner despite his sin can only mean endeavoring to attend to what remains positively loveable in him despite his sin, not pretending to love what is not loveable and does not deserve love. (The reverse view is actually yet more post–late-medieval distortion of the gospel). Thus, inevitably and unavoidably, victims pass through a moment of hatred for those who have offended them. This is why victims are dangerous, this is why victims—which means all of us—are corrupted, weakened, and poisoned by that which they at first innocently suffer. But if victims must at first hate, then what worth their eventual offering of forgiveness? Is it that they later repent their first hatred, thereby betraying from their newfound relative comfort their earlier violated selves? And is not such a gesture futile, since it cannot wipe out the fact of this earlier hatred, nor even perhaps entirely expunge it from memory?

Having stated these three dimensions to the aporia of forgiveness and time, it must however immediately be asked whether they can be mitigated if one invokes the Augustinian account of the inseparability of time and memory. For does not what has so far been said assume that time is a series of punctual, discrete moments? Yet this is clearly not the case, since every past moment has always already become present, and then, in turn, future. Therefore, as Augustine perhaps first realized, the past only occurs initially through the supplement of the trace it leaves in the future—a trace which, in *De Musica*, Augustine clearly regards as ontological, although in the *Confessions* he explicates the psyche as the most intense, complex, and reflexive site of such traces.[21] The past, on this understanding, only *is* through memory, and while this does not abolish the ontological inviolability and irreversibility of pastness, it does mean that the event in its very originality is open to alteration and mutation. As Augustine correctly saw, one cannot imagine, and there could not be, any entirely discrete past event unaffected by what came later, just as, to use his example, a note in music is only situated and defined by its place in a sequence, such that the end of a musical composition still to be heard can change the nature of what we have already heard.[22] Certainly there are limits to alteration, even though they cannot be specified: The note remains this note, however far the new relations it enters into may re-disclose it. Nevertheless, these reflections reveal that the past is not strictly unalterable and that the remembered past, although provisional and revisable, is not a sort of hypothesis that can never be confirmed, but is rather itself the ontologically real past.

Now of course it is no accident that Augustine began to develop a temporal rather than spatial ontology of finitude in the course of writing a work of *confession*, in which he seeks to obtain forgiveness for his past life and reconciliation with God. Augustine realized, in effect, that the Christian promotion of forgiveness in time demanded drastic ontological revision, if certain aporias were to be overcome. Thus with respect to the first of our problematics, forgiveness, as stated by Jankélévitch: It is not that forgiveness nihilistically pretends to obliterate past evidence, but rather than this past existence is itself preserved, developed, and altered through re-narration. In this re-narration one comes to understand why oneself or others made errors, in terms of the delusions that arose through mistaking lesser goods for the greater. As to the third of our problematics of time and forgiveness (all aspects of the one aporia), the inevitable past hatred undergone by the victim, this also is not to be regarded as something punctual and static, as if the "first" past were still somehow really there. While Jankélévitch is right to insist on a certain stubborn resistance of "pastness," he is wrong to ignore the fact that the "passing away" of time does reveal a complicity of time with the nothingness of finitude in itself—a complicity which nonetheless furnishes the ground for the possibility of redemption. For since evil is only of the finite, not of the infinite, which as infinite and enduring is without rupture or impairment of power, it can indeed absolutely fall away, because finitude in its own right is nothing whatsoever and only receives being as participation in the infinite. Hence time, which was first the time of gift, becomes, after the intrusion of evil, the time of mercy. The victim comes to remember and revise his past hatred more objectively as a correct refusal of the negative and of the impairment of his own power; but at the same time through re-narration he is able to situate and qualify this hatred in relation to a renewed understanding of the deluded motives of his violater. Most crucially, his offering of forgiveness involves not simply a cancellation of his earlier hatred, but a kind of dispossession of his own hatred, as he comes to understand (in a fashion well described by Spinoza) how his negative reaction belonged to a whole sequence of (nonetheless not Spinozistically fated) events mostly outside his control.

Eventually, at the heart of his hatred, he re-discovers the love for his own and others' real good, which essentially motivated it, and sees indeed that this love is the entire, real, actual content of hatred, since what was really hated was the negative impairment of love and the good. What was hated was nothing, and in consequence, hatred actually falls away from the positively remembered reconstituted past which is the real past. One has passed through Lethe to the waters of Eunoe, where all flows through the earthly paradise without one jolt, as if horror has never been, as, indeed, in a sense it has not. It is as Borges put it in his story "The Rose of Paracelsus"—the fall means, precisely, not to realize that one is still in the earthly paradise; redemption, conversely, is the restoration of paradise to our perception.[23]

From the above we can see that there is a clear connection between the Augustinian theory of time as memory which permits forgiveness, on the one hand, and his account of evil as privation on the other. For evil can only pass away, be forgiven and forgotten, if not only the past can be revised, but also what is deficient in the past can be revised out of existence. This means that what really and fully occurs and has the capacity to recur in memory is the good and positive: Hence, in a much more drastic and radical sense than Nietzsche, Augustine really did think that "only the active returns" (and not the reactive). But of course what arises here is a question with respect to Jankélévitch's second problematic: Can one sustain this Christian ontology of forgiveness in the wake of the Holocaust of Jewry? In my view, one must say yes, not out of a kind of sustaining of nerve, but because precisely the Holocaust requires all the more such a visionary response. By contrast, talk of radical evil, an absolutely corrupted will, a motiveless crime that can never be atoned, and so forth, falsely *glamorizes* this (perhaps) most terrible of events, by rendering it outside all comprehension whatsoever, and absolutizes it, granting it a demonic state equivalent to divinity, and finally perpetuates its terror, since what is unredeemed remains in force. The argument which runs "*This* evil was so terrible that we belittle its horror if we describe it as negative" effectively means that this evil was really so impressive that we had better accord it a status in being equivalent to the good.[24] Thus, whereas the soldiers simply and rightly, if belatedly, sent in the tanks and arrested the perpetrators, the philosophers choose rather to resurrect this horror as ontological victory. Bowing down to the remains of the camps as though before an idol, they solemnly proclaim a surd and ineliminable evil so serious that art from henceforward must confine itself to fashioning little figurines of atrocity.

One prefers, surely, the crude common sense of the soldiers. The greatest atrocity requires all the more an access of hope, the greatest evil calls out all the more for an impossible forgiveness and reconciliation, else, quite simply, such evil *remains in force*; as uncomprehended, unresumed, we must still live in the echoes of its illusions (as the return of neo-Darwinism [despite the current crisis of Darwinism as science[25]], eugenicism, and an art of pure sublime rupture would all seem to indicate). In contrast to myths of "radical evil," one should rather recognize that the most terrible thing about the Holocaust was that *even this* event was brought about through a chain of seemingly "good reasons"—economic, cultural, scientific, even peace-seeking—whose delusory appeal is unfortunately *not* alien to our common humanity. Mere lack of good, we can now all the more see, is a sufficiently terrible thing in itself. Moreover, this status of mere lack allows us still to ascribe the holocaust to the contingency of perversity, and therefore to realize that its malice need never be repeated either in deed or in unhealed memory.

It has been seen therefore that the aporia of forgiveness and time may be overcome through the double Augustinian vision—first of ecstatic time which is already memory and second of evil as privation. However, it must now be made explicit that this is necessarily a theological vision. Time as remembered in its ontological positivity is only real because it participates in the divine, infinite eternal memory. Otherwise it would be destined to pass away, like the original merely past past, into pure oblivion, thereby rendering the good and actual ontologically as nugatory as the privative and deficient. For where, indeed, there is no creation ex nihilo, but only the pure irruption of being through time out of a nothingness with which it is contradictorily identical (as for Heidegger), then it may well be arguable that what negates or deprives is in every way as positive as the seemingly good and actual, since all being must for this vision only arise as the secret concealment of a simultaneous deprivation: the ontic being regarded as the mask of an ontological ultimacy which manifests itself only as irreducible removal.[26] Likewise, since here ontological recollection by resolute Dasein dissipates the appearance of discrete ontic moments into the contentless pure flux of immanent ontological passage (without any analogical mediation of the ontological through the ontic), such recollection, if we are to continue to think at all, must return us to the necessary illusion of discrete present instances, as proffering indeed the only serious basis for human ethical life. Thus, unlike the Augustinian ecstatis of time, the Heideggerean version cannot be ethically lived, and delivers us, after all, to the calculus of momentary instances. Therefore, it does indeed leave us with past facts unalterable in their record of horror and ontologically positive in their very negativity. Likewise, it underwrites a dualism between infinite forgiveness and finite justice. A supposedly pure and negative forgiveness equated with the ontological can only be actualized via its manifestation in the calculus of just exchange between finite ontic instances whereby it is cancelled as pure forgiveness. This disallows the possibility that the finite exchange of reconciliation, achieved through a positive ontological remembering and transformation of past time, might itself mediate an infinite forgiveness. For such a perspective, this infinite forgiveness is seen as a divine plenitude of exchange and not as a transcendental abyss of one-way passage from nothing to nothing.

It follows, therefore, that if we seek forgiveness in purely human terms according to the canons of pure immanence, that the aporias of forgiveness and time will indeed stand, offering us no possibility of forgiveness whatsoever.

(c) Forgiveness and Forgetting

A third aporia of human forgiveness concerns the question of forgiving and forgetting. If, as we have just seen, for a purely immanentist perspective, past events must remain marooned in their pastness (for all that this is an ontic illusion), then it would seem that the only possibility of forgiveness resides in a negative forgetting. The truth of such forgetting would, however, be on a level with the truth of all forgetting of purely ontic experience, which is bound up with an inevitable "anxiety" as to ultimate meaning and purpose. Hence we would here only forgive and forget to the same non-ethical measure that we were able to surmount finitude itself.

However, even allowing this problem as to whether one is here speaking of ethical forgiveness at all, there is a further difficulty. Where, as for the immanentist perspective, past hatred is immutable and subject to no alchemy of transformation, then so long as one hates one does not forgive, and so long as there remains a fault present for one, one does not forgive. By contrast, in a case where this fault no longer impinges, then this must be because it has been entirely forgotten. Once forgotten, the fault can be forgiven. But of course, once the fault has been forgotten it no longer needs to be forgiven, and therefore as soon as forgiveness becomes possible, it is already redundant.

An immanentist account of time confines one, therefore, to a view of forgiveness as negation. But this turns out, for the reason just given, to be a gesture impossible to perform.

(d) The Trade in Forgiveness

The fourth aporia of forgiveness concerns the question of purity of motive. We have seen that where forgiveness is thought of as having positive dimensions of penance and substitution, it is inherently a matter of exchange and reconciliation. Here the question of purity of motive does not really arise, because what the forgiver seeks to achieve is not a state of personal disinterested benevolence, but rather an instance of ontological harmony between himself and another, such that his own self-realization and happiness is ineluctably bound up with the other's, and vice versa. For this Christianized eudaimonism, my interest in my own happiness cannot compromise the disinterest of my will to forgive, since my happiness is from the outset less a possession than a relational ecstatis: my fulfilling myself by orientating myself beyond myself to the other, my realizing myself by expressing myself and letting myself go and receiving back from the other a new interpretation of myself.[27] Here to forgive is to restore that order of free unlimited exchange of charity which was interrupted by sin. For this reason, to forgive is, as the gospels insist, immediately to receive forgiveness: Thus Kierkegaard says that my forgiving and being forgiven belong together as the sky reflected in the sea and the sky itself.[28] It might seem, of course, that if one forgives in order, or partly in order, to be forgiven, there is a trade in forgiveness such that, after all, Christian forgiveness does not escape the calculative prudence of Greek *aphesia* and Latin *ignoscere*. However, this would be again to overlook the aneconomic economy of pardon. For this economy, to offer charity, whether as original gift or restorative forgiveness, is only possible if one is *already* receiving the infinite divine charity, since charity is not an empty disposition (as it later became), but the ontological bond between God and creatures, whereby creatures only are as the receiving of the divine gift and the unqualified return of this gift in the very act of receiving. Because this bond is also the ground of a correct harmonious relation between creatures, such a return is impossible if the gift is not also passed on from creature to creature in accord with the divine spirit of generosity. Hence giving, since it is not enacted in order to achieve purity of motive but to establish a reciprocity, is already a receiving according to a reception transcendentally *prior* to any purely possessive calculation of what one might, perhaps, receive by giving. And, likewise, to forgive is to re-establish a reciprocity only possible as the attainment of a mysterious harmony through its participation in the divine infinite harmony. As the human forgiver is himself a sinner, he must re-receive this harmony in order to be able to forgive. His forgiving of the other, therefore, shows that he is divinely forgiven, or rather his forgiving of the other is the very instance of himself being divinely forgiven.

There is, therefore, no question of a secret trade in forgiveness, nor of an inevitably contaminating motive of hope for forgiveness for oneself within the terms of a construal of forgiveness as both divine and positive. These issues arise only for an immanent and negative perspective. Here, as we have seen, to forgive must mean a gesture of negating the past, and must be regarded as genuine, not in terms of a positive upshot of reconciliation—since this cannot here come about with the perpetrator *as* perpetrator—but rather in terms of the forgiveness being done entirely for its own sake of refusing resentment and ignoring wrong. But the trouble then, of course, is that forgiveness never can be offered for its own sake. Rather, every pardoner is indeed Chaucer's pardoner, who tells narratives showing that greed leads to death but himself hopes that pardon can break this chain of fatality.[29] Thus he deploys pardon calculatively as a warding-off of, or absolute escape from, death. To this end he receives payment for his telling of narratives about greed leading to death and for his offering of papal pardons that will suspend this logic. But finally his own offering of pardons to temper the upshot of greed is itself motivated by the basest of all greed: An easy, wandering life of cheap prestige, petty power, and worldly goods at the cost of little effort. This trade in pardon does indeed condone and increase human injustice, according to the worst fears of the ancient democratic and egalitarian Greeks. The pardoner is the anarchic agent of the remote Roman tyrant.

Chaucer depicts, perhaps, the growing corruption of the medieval economy of forgiveness, whereby it was turning into a cheap forgiveness of mere negative gesture, which nonetheless had to be bought dearly. It may seem as if the Reformation removed this price and ended the trade, but at a profound level that is not so. For every habitual and humble pardoner, in the very awareness of his free pardoning, congratulates himself and awards himself a high status if his goal be purity of motive rather than actual concrete reconciliation, *which no possessed virtue can guarantee*, and which arrives always, miraculously, by grace. Such a sense of high status carries with it also a consciousness of anarchic power and of the binding of those remitted in an infinite indebtedness. Furthermore, it guarantees an easy, picaresque lifestyle, again like that of Chaucer's pardoner, since the habitual and easy forgiver travels light through time by instantly ridding himself of the terrible burdens of injuries done to him and the terrible difficulties involved in seeking reconciliation (within infinite justice) with others. Since to forgive, negatively and easily, does not necessarily improve the character of the one forgiven, and may have the opposite effect, it seems that the real motivation of pure disinterested forgiveness is rather the avoiding of suffering, by pretending one has not been injured after all. Therefore the secular, negative pardoner is an adept of cheap forgiveness, as far from the genuine struggles of Christian existence as Bonhoeffer's adept of cheap grace. By contrast, although Aquinas, indeed, as we saw, insists that human beings must offer forgiveness even in the absence of penitence, he only regards this offer as an initial and incomplete stage in the bringing about of reconciliation: The initiating gesture creates a negative space for an eventual positive upshot.

(e) Forgiveness and Finality

The fifth aporia of forgiveness concerns forgiveness and finality. Where, again, forgiveness is regarded as negative, then the total forgetting of a fault implies that forgiveness has the last word over and against both fault and just indignation. As Vladimir Jankélévitch points out, however, that "last word" might be regarded as both dangerous and deluding. For if, indeed, one should not harbor resentment, then equally one should not forget injustice, not only in order to honor the memories of its victims, but also in order to remind oneself of possible future danger. By merely forgiving, by contrast, one forgets this danger or the possibility that a past malefactor may act viciously once again, perhaps precisely by abusing one's very forgiveness. As Jankélévitch puts it, "Where grace abounds, sin may abound all the more," as well as vice versa.[30] Therefore, it seems that to forgive one must utterly forget, as if this alone guarantees an ultimate and irreversible reconciliation, and yet in forgetting one is blinding oneself to an actual or possible absence of reconciliation.

In this way every secular performance of forgiveness poses as an illusory eschaton. And because its finality is a chimera, it offers not more security within human relationships, but rather an undesirable hesitation between increased security and increased insecurity. This arises in the following fashion. The implication of secular forgiving is that its obliterative finality has established an unshakable security hitherto absent. For, hitherto, within a given specific human relationship, where all has gone smoothly without fault or grievance, there remains a sense of something untested. Will love survive the breaking of faith by one party? It seems that only forgiveness demonstrates that it can, and therefore discloses, irreplaceably, the depth of the relationship. However, if the offense is merely forgotten, then nothing after all has been gained. But if, to the contrary, it is remembered, then there is no forgiveness, precisely because the retained fact that a bond *could* be ruptured seems to place an insurpassable barrier before the gate of Eden and to suggest that the bond was weaker than supposed. Therefore, since human forgiveness is not really final, it no more strengthens a relationship than a fault weakens it.

The above reflections upon this last aporia illuminate by contrast the significance of positive and divine forgiveness. Where the offender has positively offered penance, then indeed forgiveness may tilt the balance toward stability, since repentance can indicate an improvement of character beyond the latent tendency which led to the commission of a fault. Because the fault has exposed this tendency and permits its extirpation, it becomes indeed a kind of *felix culpa*, and forgiveness can be regarded as a gain on an erstwhile semi-illusory innocence of interaction. At the same time, the revelation of the possibility of fault still does, indeed, insinuate a germ of insecurity. And here forgiveness can only offer finality—without which security, indeed, *there could be no reconciliation*—through a participation in real, divine, eschatological finality. Thus, there is an inescapable logic to the original Biblical notion of positive forgiveness as only arriving with the eschaton, or else as its anticipation.

3. Forgiveness as Human or Divine

The foregoing consideration of the five aporias of forgiveness has confirmed that positive notions of forgiveness tend to regard it as first of all divine, since the prime paradigm for positive forgiveness is the Incarnation and atonement. By contrast, negative notions are associated first of all with a theology focused more upon the divine fiat than upon the Incarnation, and second with a secular outlook unable to countenance the recuperation of time by eternity.

As we have seen, the aporias of time, forgetting, motive, and finality apply only to these negative accounts, especially in their secular form. However, the first aporia of the appropriate pardonee crosses the threshold between negative and positive, human and divine.

For this aporia seems to suggest that no human forgiveness, negative or positive, is possible, since the victims cannot be found, and neither victim nor sovereign may adequately forgive. Perhaps, then, this suggests that only God can forgive, since he alone is an adequate sovereign authority who can represent us all. Such a conclusion is partially correct, but it of course runs up against the problem of how we can be forgiven by God if human victims do not in fact forgive us. Such a forgiveness would surely be no more than nominal. Furthermore, a human sovereign power in some measure suffers what those it represents suffer, but not so God, who is perfect in act, beyond all suffering. Thus God is so disconnected from all victimage, so impervious to offense, that it seems that he has nothing to forgive. Indeed, one mystical theologian of the late medieval period, Julian of Norwich, roundly declared that God does not forgive, since he cannot be offended, but only continues to give, despite our rejection of his gift. For Julian, sin as negative remains so entirely outside the divine comprehension (as negative it is not really something to be known) that from the divine point of view it is simply as if humanity has suffered an incomprehensible and even involuntary disaster, since no will enjoying beatitude could genuinely choose evil.[31]

It would appear then that neither human beings nor God can offer forgiveness. God may go on giving despite sin, but how is his gift, which is always of peace, mediated to us, if no human reconciliation can be affected?

4. Forgiveness as Divine and Human

(a) The Sovereign Victim

If, however, forgiveness is neither human nor divine, then it would seem appropriate to ask whether this is why, for us in the West, forgiveness began as the work of, and was made possible by, precisely a God-Man. It may not, indeed, be the case that the notion of Incarnation resolves in a fully satisfactory manner the aporia of the pardonee, or of who is to forgive. But perhaps, by pointing to the mystery of the God-Man, it points to the only imaginable site of such resolution.

For here we have the unique instance of the sovereign victim. As Thomas Aquinas put it: "the most efficacious argument for His Divinity has been this: without the support of the secular power he has changed the whole world for the better."[32] As unique sovereign victim, perhaps, the God-Man was alone able to inaugurate forgiveness; for here was not a single human nature, victimized like all humans by other humans, but also a human victim suffering the maximum possible victimage, by virtue of its personification by the divine *logos*, all-wise and all-innocent and therefore able to let the human nature plumb the full depths and implications of suffering. In this way a single suffering became also a sovereign suffering, capable of representing all suffering and to forgive on behalf of all victims. (One can note here that it is also a uniquely personal sovereignty, whereas human sovereignty—which only exists in *modern* political theory—is necessarily an impersonal cipher to which all our freedoms are initially sacrificed.) And also able to forgive, unlike other human beings, at the very original instance of hurt without a single jolt of rancor, since in the divinely enhypostasized human nature, suffering is paradoxically undergone in a wholly accepting, actively receptive fashion, such that this undergoing is itself offered as a gift. Indeed, the suffering Christ is without qualification forgiveness from the outset, and not merely after repenting of his initial anger as a victim (which we cannot avoid) precisely because his human nature and will is imbued with the shape, character, idiom, or *tropos* of the pure divine gift, which, as we have seen, never needs to forgive since it is never offended. (As Maximus the Confessor establishes, Christ's human will, being imbued by the divine *tropos*, is a separate will by nature, but not by *gnomē* or intention—see *Opusculum* 3.) Such a gift only becomes forgiveness when in Christ it is *not* God forgiving us (since he has no need to) but humanity forgiving humanity. Therefore divine redemption is not God's forgiving us, but rather his giving us the gift of the capacity for forgiveness. And this can only be given in the first instance by the Trinity to the God-Man, because, first of all, only his victimage will be sovereign, and second, only he will be able absolutely and entirely and without trace to break with that rancor which normally must precede forgiveness and continue to contaminate it. Normally, forgiveness is occasioned by resentment and so remains somewhat grudging: With the God-Man alone there arises a pure forgiveness, since this really *surpasses* forgiveness and is rather the unbroken continued giving of the divine gift as also the offering of a suffering actively undergone.

Yet nevertheless, despite this suggestion of how forgiveness might be possible, a disquiet must remain, a disquiet felt by those who asked Christ, By what right do you forgive sins? One can answer, by right of conjoined divinity and humanity, by right of sovereign victimhood. And yet, if Christ, by reason of his enhypostasization by the infinite and innocent *logos* is, as it were, "virtually" all victims, able to speak in their name, still he may not usurp their freedom, and if we are forgiven by Christ, but not, say, by Beatrice, we may still feel that we hover between the waters of Lethe and the waters of Eunoe. But it is for this reason that the gift of intrahuman forgiveness offered by the whole Trinity to the God-Man is passed on by the God-Man to us as the Holy Spirit, the bond of exchange and mutual giving within the Trinity. As participators through the sacraments and membership of the body of Christ in the divine humanity, we now also begin to be capable of a forgiveness on sufficient authority and without taint of rancor. However, it remains our task to forgive and to go on receiving the forgiveness of other human beings, since what God offers us is *not* his negative forgiveness but the positive possibility of intrahuman reconciliation. God is already reconciled to us, but only when Queen Matilda shows us once again the earthly paradise will we be reconciled to God.

(b) The Three Impossibilities

If the above gives the lineaments of a theology of incarnational forgiveness, one may still nonetheless ask about its ontological foundation. Just how is the sovereign also a victim? Is this mysterious impossibility entirely impenetrable? Can we hope further to lift the veil of the aporia?

One may note here, first of all, that perhaps it should be untroubling to us that forgiveness appear, to our understanding, impossible. For theology considers what are, to us, three absolute impossibilities. First of all, there is the impossibility that anything else should exist outside of God, who is replete Being. For this to be possible, God must have gone outside of himself, and yet there is no exterior to God, no sum which might add to his amount. But then on top of this impossibility of creation, theology overlays the second impossibility of sin, namely that creatures enjoying to their appropriate degree the absolute, and enjoying this only by grace of the absolute, might discover an illusory "of themselves" wherewith to reject the absolute in the name of something lesser. Although, indeed, sin in itself is only loss and the desire of something less, the first sin that imagined sin does indeed appear to be a surd, ungrounded, "radical evil." Finally, on top of this impossibility, theology overlays the third impossibility of redemption for a fault which, since it cuts finite being off from (infinite) reality, would appear to be without redress, even by that reality. It should surely result in absolute extinction, and one may note here that theology up to the high Middle Ages generally maintained that Creation only remained in being after the fall through the proleptic working of the Incarnation.

In consequence of this theological vision, the Western Christian legacy has worked in terms of not one, but three ontologies of the impossible, all seamlessly laid on top of each other without break, and yet without necessary connection, like a palimpsest. We now only glimpse the impossibility of creation through the impossibility of the fall, and both through the impossibility of redemption, even though creation does not entail fall, nor fall, redemption. For us, now, the impossible reality of a retrieval of absolute loss preserves and discloses again the impossibility of this loss, which in turn preserves and discloses the impossibility that anything could first have been received from absolute plenitude.

It is difficult, however, for theology to remain with the thought of the impossibility of redemption, which is precisely the impossibility of forgiveness. The temptation is to claim too strong an insight into the ground of its possibility, thereby rendering it a kind of ineluctable necessity or a mere rebound effect of interrupted contractual exchange. Thus Anselm, for all the brilliant subtlety and correctness of much of his Christology, which certainly describes an aneconomic sacrifice of God to us and not a measurable debt paid by us to God,[33] nevertheless perhaps too much suggests that he can grasp how an infinite loss may be rectified. In some sense, certainly, as he suggests, this must be through the re-offering of the finite to the infinite by the infinite in person, but to imply that this logic is more than aesthetically compelling (if he does so, and he may not) is to advance too far. First of all, the suggestion that God cannot of necessity suffer loss and dishonor to his glory tends to overlook the point that any such loss is strictly "impossible" for God. God cannot become a victim, and therefore is in no way drawn by absolute necessity into forgiveness. In the second place, since sin is the absolute refusal of the absolute, or a totally "impossible" negation of what cannot be negated, it is not clear that even the absolute can now retrieve the finite from within itself.

Indeed, for reasons not totally unlike these two considerations, these aspects of Anselm's position were frequently rejected in later High Scholastic theology. Thus, divine redemption and forgiveness came to be grounded not in an automatic reaction to the loss of glory but rather in the free divine willing of the good, even though such willing was taken absolutely to characterize the divine nature and not to be a matter of caprice.[34] At the same time, the possibility of divine redemption and forgiveness came to be grounded not in an Anselmian equation of infinite with finite, but rather in the mysterious depths of divine creative capacity, deemed somehow able to restore that which has refused its own created status. These positions were common both to Thomas Aquinas and to Duns Scotus, even though their respective explications of those positions dramatically diverged. (It is terribly tempting in this instance to compare Anselm with Hegel and Aquinas and Scotus with the later Schelling.) In the remainder of this chapter, I want to show how Aquinas's Christology thought through as far as possible the problematic of a divine-human commencement of forgiveness conceived as positive, while Scotus's Christology undid the vital link between forgiveness and Incarnation, thereby inaugurating the reign of aspiration to purely negative forgiveness which, as we have seen, cannot be achieved and effects no reconciliation. I will also show that whereas Aquinas's subordination of ontology to theology permits him to ground forgiveness in ultimate reality, Scotus's first beginning of onto-theology involves also an onto-Christology which renders forgiveness a secondary, restricted, and arbitrary instance within the divine goodness. Hence, it turns out that a unilateral and negative conception of good belongs from the outset within the logic of onto-theology (whereas it is frequently presented as its opposite). Inversely, an account of forgiveness as a positive exchange and reconciliation belongs to the logic of a theology that is in excess of metaphysics.

(c) Aquinas, Incarnation, and Forgiveness

For Aquinas, it is possible that God, according to his *potentia absoluta*, might have forgiven us without the incarnation of the *Logos*.[35] A divine decree of negative obliteration allied to an act of positive recreation would in theory have been sufficient. By this assertion, Thomas assures us that God had no need to be appeased in order to become reconciled to us and that instead, in himself, he always and eternally was reconciled to us. One can express this in the terms already favored which declare that God does not need to forgive since he goes on giving. For Aquinas, therefore, the Incarnation does not bring about this reconciliation for God, but rather mediates this reconciliation to us, making it effective for us and in us, so ensuring that we, too, are reconciled. He argues that the actual means of incarnation and atonement adopted for our salvation, while not absolutely necessitated, were nonetheless "convenient," fitting, suitable for this purpose.[36] They possess the necessity, in Aquinas's own illustration, not of going in a certain direction to reach a certain goal, but of traveling most conveniently, or appropriately—for example, on horseback.[37] This sense of *convenientia* hovers, therefore, between the necessitated and the arbitrary and as such (as Gilbert Narcisse has argued at length) it is clearly an *aesthetic* notion closely allied to terms such as *proportio, harmonia, ordinatio*, and *analogia*.[38] A certain pleasing *logos* is exhibited here beyond merely capricious arrangement, and yet God is not obliged to this order, as he is obliged to conclude that *a = a* and is not *not-a*. Nevertheless, for Aquinas, the counter-factual invocation of *potentia absoluta* is an essentially abstract, logical moment, designed to indicate where God is not impersonally, ineluctably constrained. It is not, as for later Scholastics, following more a model derived from later canon law, a kind of reserve power which may, at a whim, intervene to interrupt the conventional norms of *potentia ordinata*.[39] Rather, for Aquinas, *all* that God actually does belongs to his *potentia ordinata*, which is not an order of caprice, but rather itself reflects the eternal divine sense of justice and appropriateness. Therefore Aquinas's God is "compelled" not only by the absolute exigencies of logical possibility, but also by something one may dub "actual necessity," or the agreeable that appears in the harmonious proportions of an infinite actual order. This is then reflected in the divine economy.

Aquinas lists several different ways in which the order of incarnation was "convenient" and declares that he only cites a few, since their number is infinite.[40] But especially relevant to present considerations are, first of all, the notion that it is aesthetically fitting that since we fell from Adam's pride and rebellion of the sensual, we should be restored through divine humility and re-education of the understanding by the senses. Christ follows and shows us the path through suffering and despair to a despising of our mortality and the regaining of eternal life.[41] This shows that while, for Aquinas, God *could* have restored us just through his continued gift, he nonetheless so respects human freedom and the legacy of human history that he seeks also positively to forgive us by tracing himself, as only an innocent man can, the perfect ways of penitence which we are to follow.

A second instance of *convenientia* is also instructive. It is appropriate that God should draw near to humanity in this most radical and unexpected fashion, because God as infinite and replete cannot possibly be rivaled, and therefore can give himself entirely—even his own divine nature to human nature.[42] Here Aquinas is exploiting to the full (as he does elsewhere, when insisting on the place of secondary causality) the mystery of the first theological impossibility, that of creation. Just because there is no outside to God, God can most freely and ecstatically exceed himself; just because God cannot share *any-thing*, he can share *everything*. It is partially because of his intense sense of this paradox that Aquinas espouses ontologically strong notions of deification. Adam was created to enjoy the beatific vision and to share without reserve, but to the (for us, unknown) measure of human personhood, in the divine nature.[43] And, significantly, Aquinas cites this predestination of Adam as a further ground for the *convenientia* of the Incarnation; humanity has a *natural* kinship with the supernatural; humanity bears the image of God, rather as the Son bears the image of the Father; finally, humanity as a rational animal synthesizes the whole work of Creation in a way the angels do not—it is "appropriate" that this finite totality be conjoined with infinite plenitude.[44]

All this is also relevant to the thematic of forgiveness. Aquinas's account of divine non-rivalry means that God, being all, is uniquely only able to give of himself. Since all that is is of God, things only suspire by a return to God, which is realized through man the microcosm, the crown of creation. Hence while, for Aquinas, creation is in one sense an entirely one-way gift, in another it is an absolute exchange, since the gift is only received in its return to God, just as deified humanity comes more and more to participate in the Son's return to the Father within the Trinity. And since, for Aquinas, the Creation is not really outside of God, it is, through humanity, able to make an adequate return of love and honor to God. *Without the Incarnation,* for Aquinas (we shall shortly see the contrast with Scotus here), God is able in the Creation to realize a *telos* commensurate with his own infinite nature. One might ask how can this be, since anything other than God is less than God? But the point here is that this very *other* to God is so problematic that Aquinas realizes that it can only be possible as a *self-exceeding*—that is to say as the lesser and other to God which only exists (through humanity) as always canceling this lesserness and otherness. Here the final upshot—deification—is extraordinarily in excess of the original goal—Creation—since it would be pointless for God to aim for deification, which is already himself. This strange structure—outcome in excess of goal—only applies to the relation between God and Creation, and is an upshot of its "impossibility."

Given this structure of exchange between infinite and finite, whereby it belongs intrinsically to human nature "to exact"—albeit through the divine grace by which alone it is human—deification, God does not, for Aquinas, gain an adequate return for his infinite love only through the Incarnation. The ground of incarnation is not, then, for him, the completion of the infinite-finite gift exchange. Rather, the occasion for incarnation is God's free will to redeem according to his goodness, and hence the occasion for incarnation is the offer of *forgiveness*—although in the sense already described of an offering of the possibility of reconciliation with God and other human beings. The difficulty though, of imagining how God can offer us this reconciliation, is, as we have seen, the sheer apparent impossibility of retrieving a deficient act which is itself an impossible will to destruction. Here, as we have also already seen, Aquinas seems to claim less insight than Anselm: He does not exactly "grasp" the conjoining of finite to infinite as necessitated, but nonetheless he can envisage something of its "appropriateness" in the beauty of the narratives which relate this conjoining. It is not so much that God *had* to become incarnate in order to retrieve us, and that we can comprehend the "possibility" of this, as rather that it seems "fitting" that a God whose absolute giving has been thwarted (inconceivably) should somehow miraculously redouble this giving. Hence the intimate link established by Aquinas between deification and hominization: Where deification is refused by us, God still wills nonetheless to bring it about through the making of a human nature actually to subsist in a divine hypostasis. And here, once again, Aquinas insists that *of necessity* this did not have to be the person of the *Logos*; rather, this was merely aesthetically "right" because of the affinity between the Son as image and humanity as image.[45]

But the problem here, it would seem, is how, if God in Creation gave absolutely, such that deification adequately completes the infinite-finite gift exchange, he can possibly give anything more. The answer may be that in Creation God gave himself unreservedly to creatures, including the grace of beatification, and never gives *to creatures* anything more than this. However, in the Incarnation he causes a human creature not just to receive as finite the infinite in due measure, but actually to be, in its entire, unrepeatable, specifically characterized and incommunicable *suppositum* or self-subsistence, God himself, as "appropriate" to that persona which is the *Logos*. This is not so much a new gift of God to humanity, as a making of a human nature also to be the means of absolute uninterrupted giving, by which means, as I have suggested, it is alone able to inaugurate forgiveness on earth.

Nevertheless, if the Incarnation is not a further gift, it still brings about something in excess even of absolute divine gift, namely the conjoining of humanity to divinity. This is indeed a sharing in excess of gift, in excess of creation, even though there was nothing originally withheld. Thus, while the occasion and goal of incarnation for Aquinas was *not* (as later for Scotus, as we shall describe) ontological completion of the Creation, but rather the offering of forgiveness (in the sense of the possibility of positive reconciliation), nonetheless there appears to arise as an outcome of this purpose something ontologically in excess of it, something therefore ontologically in excess even of forgiveness and reconciliation. For the Incarnation was no temporary instrument to be left behind: Now, for always in time, and so from eternity, human nature through Christ is directly impersonated by the *Logos* in such a way that we may worship Christ's human appearance without idolatry. If Christ's humanity eternally subsists in the *Logos*, meaning that the *Logos* is both *sup-*

positum of divinity and *also suppositum* of this humanity, then in some sense the world was created by and through the baby in Bethlehem. In some sense also, the human offense which required the Incarnation was always, also, an offense against the incarnate one. We are to rejoice in and adore the resurrected humanity *not* because it has redeemed us (as if we were paying a due price) but simply because it is glorious and causes us to exult.

Thus Aquinas explicitly calls attention to the *felix culpa* pronounced at the lighting of the Easter candle, and is apprised also of the fact that, via redemption, Mary also has received a status beyond that of Adam, since her assent to the Incarnation was essential to human recreation (whereas Adam did not assent to his creation) and the enhypostasis of the human nature.[46] Aquinas (unlike Scotus) was in tune with the thrust of the famous lines of the folkloric carol: "O' n'ere had the apple taken been. . . N'ere had our Lady a' been Heaven's Queen." (It is significant that Scotus had to resort to an alternative mode of exalting Mary—namely the doctrine of her immaculate conception—which focuses not on her own will but on divine predetermination.)

However, does it *really* seen "fitting" (and it did not, later, to Scotus) that through fault a higher status should eventually be realized? Does not this downgrading of innocence to secondary status conversely elevate the merely *reactive* virtue of forgiveness over the purity of original giving? And does this notion not seem to underwrite the dubious view, as described, that forgiveness is more final than fault? Lastly, as Scotus argued, if the conjoining of humanity in person to the divinity is a higher good (as it is) even than the saving of humanity, then must not this have been God's primary intent in the Incarnation?[47]

None of these problems should be lightly dismissed, and indeed the *felix culpa* is too easily celebrated in sermons of tipsy casualness. However, let us attempt to deal with them in order. First of all, there is no sense, in Aquinas, that pre-fallen innocence was lacking in any perfection, any more than was the case for the original created order without incarnation. And one must remember that real innocence is unknown to us: It is a state where malice is unimaginable for the good and so not, after all, equivalent to a seemingly secure untested good relationship prior to any serious fault, such as we might encounter in our fallen state. We distrust the untested character of such a relationship, precisely because we know that its participants are already creatures susceptible to temptation, since unlike our unfallen first parents, they already know what temptation is.

In the second place, real, positive, Christological forgiveness is, as has been shown, not reactive, since it is only the sustained giving of the original gift, despite its refusal. For this reason, forgiveness in response to fault is not a reaction superior to an original action, since it still is only this action, neither more nor less.

In the third place, it may indeed be the case that in human experience, to know reconciliation after rupture is yet more joyous than an original state of tranquility. Yet we should hesitate over this too-facile analogy. Once again, we have never known real innocence and therefore cannot compare the joys of reconciliation with the joys of innocence. If, nonetheless, it be insisted here that we have known innocence to some degree and yet do experience a more intense joy in the arrival of reconciliation after the rupture of this innocence, then one should still note that this is partly because one has a sense of something final—of a relationship tested and shown to be absolutely binding; were we to imagine in reconciliation that there might be further ruptures, our joy would no longer be unconfined. In a sense, therefore, there is something in the outcome of forgiveness which exceeds its occasion and goal, which is the instrumental healing of a relationship. However, as we have seen, such finality in human forgiveness is only more than illusion where it participates (after the Incarnation and before the *parousia*) in eschatological finality itself. Therefore, only the advance arrival of the eschaton in the middle of history guarantees the finality of forgiveness, and, in consequence, forgiveness as such. But precisely what is it which renders Christ's forgiveness final, and ensures that, whereas the deified Adam could fall, those deified through participation in Christ's humanity enhypostasized by the *logos* can never fall again (a point which Christian theology found at first difficult to establish, as Origen's writings indicate)? Presumably one must say just this new absolute degree of conjoining between infinite and finite, whereby the reality of victimage, which may seek to forgive, does so absolutely and before rancor, since it is infused with the idiom of uninterrupted sovereign gift. (In this fashion, following Maximus, there is in Christ no hesitant, wavering human *gnomē*, independent of the divine *gnomē* which expresses the divine *tropos*.)

In the fourth place, one must still deal with the Scotist point that God must will, primarily, the higher goal first. However, this objection, first of all, too easily assumes that there can be something for creatures higher than deification. The Incarnation stands higher than deification for Aquinas's understanding, not because it realizes a higher *finite* goal for the creation but because here God's own infinite *telos* in himself has become also the realization (though incomprehensibly with no real addition to God, and no "real relation" to him, as Thomas puts it)[48] of this particular human nature *in atomo*. This is the case for Aquinas in the *Tertia Pars*, because he recognizes only one *esse* in Christ, which is the divine *esse* itself.[49] For this reason, God gains nothing in glory through the Incarnation, since he gains only himself, which is no gain.

In the second place, the Scotist objection fails to realize that, as we have seen, the paradoxical structure of outcome exceeding occasion and cause is not peculiar only to the Thomist account of Incarnation as motivated by the will to forgive, but is already the structure of all divine activity, since its explicates the impossibility of creation. God's goal is the existence of creatures outside himself, yet since there is nothing outside God, all creatures suspire through humanity (and I am conscious of supplementing Aquinas with Maximus here) only in returning to God and attaining an outcome in excess of their first occasioning. The structure of divine redemption simply repeats this structure of divine creation, and therefore the ontological excess of the hypostatic union over its instrumental occasion in turn explicates the impossibility of this redemption. God can only restore what has gone wrong by rendering it also at one point (but to which all other points are connected—and there are many thorny problems here) united with him, identical in subsistent character to him, even though this "adds" nothing to his own character.

However, there is also a further, crucial consideration. Just a little earlier it was suggested that the structure "outcome exceeding occasion" is *also* the structure of all forgiveness, insofar as it requires finality, even though this finality can only be genuinely provided Christologically. Hence indeed it seems that while the Incarnation is ontologically in excess of our being forgiven, this circumstance alone is precisely what ensures that we *are* forgiven. To receive forgiveness is to receive that which is in excess of forgiveness; to receive forgiveness is not only to continue to receive the gift through and despite Kierkegaard's "jolt," it is also to receive the intensified gift of identity with the giver, an identity of shared *character*, idiom, ethos, or *tropos* which still respects independence of will—although the wills unite in a shared intention. (In this way, we need to add Maximus's Christological insight to Augustine's insights on time in order fully to grasp forgiveness.) Where people differ, struggle, and quarrel, then finally the only solution is to become one flesh, to forge one shared identity, one harmony, one tone, one flavor, which does not mean that asymmetrical contributions to this are denied (though in the case of the divine-human union, there is, of course, really no intrinsic human contribution to the shared *persona*). It may be unpopular to say this, but reconciliation is the absoluteness of shared taste, the freedom of the dance in joint measure which is the gift, of lovers, to an audience—their transmitted bond which binds a community to them, just as the bond of the Holy Spirit forges the hypostatic union.

Forgiveness, therefore, perfects gift-exchange as *fusion*. If gift-exchange retains free gift as non-identical repetition and asymmetrical reciprocity, then forgiveness exceeds this to the measure that in perfected exchange every surprise is anticipated by the other, since the surprise she offers is also the surprise he arrives at at that very instance as requiring a perfectly *improvised*, and yet absolutely consensual, dance. But since, as we have seen, forgiveness is only inaugurated by the sovereign victim, this perfection of exchange as fusion is first granted to us in the idiomatic characterizing of victim as sovereign, sovereign as victim. It is their relation, their dance, that first and alone reconciles.

However, all this seems to point to a further inescapable mystery. To receive forgiveness, we have discovered, can only mean to receive the God-Man, and to receive him as an outcome which infinitely exceeds the forgiveness he proffers, although this exceeding *is* forgiveness, since forgiveness is unshakable finality. This implies that while there is indeed no Hegelian necessity for fault if we are to reach the highest human goal, and no reason too blithely to celebrate fault, that all the same a narrative course of alienation and restoration *does* appear to occasion an ontological revision (it is this cautiously "Hegelian" Thomism which the subtle exegesis of Michel Corbin appears to point toward).[50] This is not, indeed, as for Hegel, an ontological revision for God, but it is still an ontological revision for the Creation in relation to God, since for forgiveness to become possible, it is necessary that *now the logos comes to be* not merely the *suppositum* of the divine nature but also of human nature as manifest in this individual, Jesus Christ. Certainly this hypostatic union is for Aquinas created and in no real relation to God—in such a way that it is not, for God, a new thing that he is now the subsistent base of a creature, but rather there is this new mode of being only for the creature and for us. All the same, not just the Creation in itself but its relation to God is thereby revised. *Now* it begins to be true, although it must also be retrospectively true (just as Adam, according to Aquinas, even though he did not know he was to fall, still proleptically anticipated Christ in his enjoyment of the beatific vision),[51] that the Creation is sustained not only through participation in, but—in a mediated sense—through union with, God. Equally, *now* it begins to be true, though it must have been true always, that *analogia* or *convenientia* is not just approximation of man to God but even the appropriate blending together in one idiom or *tropos* of the one with the other.

So if forgiveness is a reality, then it seems that it is somehow not subordinate to ontology, or rather that being is now shown in time as forgiveness and finality and as revisable via narrative. Here, therefore, finite ontology does not yield to, but nonetheless coincides with, eschatology.

One must deliberately refrain, however, from any actual ascription of "event" to God: This would be incompatible with his aseity. Nevertheless, the implication of Chaledonian doctrine appears to be that God is not only infinite *esse*, outside time, but also the subject of this particular series of events in time resumed as a resurrected human nature through all eternity. Moreover, Aquinas's peculiar metaphysics deliberately negotiate this circumstance in a way, perhaps, that has never been fully noted. For Aquinas, the notion of God as *esse* exceeds metaphysics and belongs to *sacra doctrina*, since metaphysics (as Aristotle failed to realize), in thinking only general, transcendental categories, *cannot*, after all, think the transgeneric character of being (as recognized by Aristotle), since *esse* is as much present in the individual and accidental as in the general and the substantive.[52] Hence, the knowledge enjoyed by the divine *esse*, unlike the knowledge of the metaphysician, stretches down to every last particular.[53] And so from the divine perspective of *esse*, there *is indeed* a comprehension of event in excess of the mere falling of events under general ontological categories, since the yet more "general" perspective of *esse* fractures the sway of generality itself. From the point of view of *esse*, an instance can break out of a preceding framework, just as the perfection of the divine eminent knowledge of a fallen thrush is identical in the divine essence to his knowledge of the category "birds."

It is this understanding of the divine transgeneric *esse* which then forms the ground for Aquinas's insistence that there is only the one, divine, *esse* in the divine humanity. There cannot, for Aquinas, be another finite, human *esse* (although there is, of course, a human *essentia*), because this would either be an accident added to the divine *suppositum*—which cannot receive accidents any more than it can be accidentally conjoined to the humanity (since God cannot be the accident of a creature)—or else another substance so added, which would be equally impossible since the divine substance is infinite and replete.

For many commentators, and perhaps most medieval Scholastic theologians, this refusal of either substantive or accidental additions to the *Logos* has seemed to exhaust all possibilities of union with humanity.[54] However, this is to fail to grasp the subtleties of Thomas's metaphysical innovations. Since *esse* is non-generically common to substance and accident, it is indifferent to either, and yet God is supremely *esse*. Therefore, he lies beyond the substance/accident contrast in his *essentia*, and since the persons of the Trinity are identical with this *essentia*, this self-subsistence also exceeds the contrast of essential versus additional. Inversely, the divine *esse* is identical with, and manifest as, the three "incommunicablities" of personhood. It *is* their peculiar, through subsistently interrelated, "ways" of being.

Hence, when Aquinas speaks of the one *esse* of the divine humanity, he means, somewhat like Maximus the Confessor (though he is less explicit), that all that there *is* in Christ is the one way of being that characterizes the eternal *Logos*.[55] Because *esse* is as much event and instance as general structure, and because as a "way" of being it is somewhat like an eternal "narrative" constitution that forms character (in the *perichoresis* of the Trinity), it is able to be entirely communicated to a finite instance. A "way" of being slips out of the infinite into a perfect reflection in the finite. Both finite and infinite, it seems, can exhibit one and the same specific character of love in the perfect fusion that is forgiveness. Thus, while, for Aquinas, Jesus's humanity has a fully human mind, will, and even individuality, it still does not possess a human personhood or *suppositum*, because this involves absolute self-subsistence, incommunicability, and uniqueness, and all of Jesus's individual human nature subsists in and is held together in consistency of character by (again this is more explicit in Maximus) the eternal hypostasis of the Son.[56] This hypostasis, as a "way" of being, is beyond substance and accident, and just for this reason is able to receive an "addition" to itself which is not really an addition (to its essence) and yet is not accidental either. Aquinas gives many instances at the finite level of "proper accident," or of additions to essence which still belong properly to a thing's being or "character." In the Christological instance also he cites finite analogues, specifically the relation of a body to a hand.[57] Here he explains that one can have a body without a hand, and yet a hand is not an entirely accidental instrument of the body as, for example, is an ax. A hand is rather an "organic" instrument of the human body, and here it is important to bear in mind that Aquinas, in his commentary on the *De Anima*, supports and augments the remarkable Aristotelian view that only men of extreme sensitivity of touch are intelligent.[58] Thus while, of course, Aquinas considers that handless men are men, he can scarcely think that hands are purely "accidental" to a rational animal. An organic instrument is neither substantial nor accidental, but is still an integral part of the *esse* and specific personal *suppositum* of the individual. And with charming brilliance Aquinas notes that a sixth finger on a hand may be an accidental deformity, yet since it is *useful* to his owner, it has become an integral part of him.[59] And he compares the hypostatic union precisely to the growth of a sixth finger.

For Aquinas, therefore, since God is both *esse* and tri-personal, he is open to the arrival of an event which causes something else to belong to him, not accidentally and not essentially, but rather as exhibiting precisely the same way of being—the same dance, in the same measure. But for Aquinas's metaphysics, this existential character *is* the real, is the true concrete reality which upholds everything. Hence to be conjoined this way is not to be weakly or metaphorically conjoined, or *merely* conjoined by like *habitus* (a position he specifically rejects),[60] but to be joined in substantive actuality.

Nevertheless, for Aquinas, this event, this arrival, involves nothing new for God; it is not a real relation for him. Thus the human nature of Christ belongs integrally to the *Logos* and its being is only the being of the *Logos*, and yet, to its human attribute, the *Logos* is not really related. This seems highly strange, yet it is really an outcome of the same old impossibility of something being outside God when there is no outside of God. God, for Aquinas, is not really related to the Creation, and yet the Creation is real, and really participates in him. Likewise, God is not really related to the divine humanity, and yet the latter also is real and is really so fused with God that now God is, also, human (since the *Logos* is the subject, also, of human attributes). However, just as Aquinas says that God perfectly knows the Creation through knowledge of how his essence may be participated, so it would seem that one must also say (as Aquinas, however, explicitly does not), that God knows perfectly the hypostatic union through knowledge of how a finite event may be absolutely conjoined to his *esse*. And also that just as for Aquinas God foreknows that he will create and so utters the *Logos* in this foreknowledge, so also one should add to Aquinas (to be consistent with his thought) that God utter the *Logos* in foreknowledge of sin and his appropriate, fitting response to it through the hypostatic union.

But in that case, always and from eternity, God as giver is also the God who proffers divine-human forgiveness. Always and from eternity *esse* is also event. Always and from eternity, God is also man. Always and from eternity, ontologic is also eschatalogic and what is must also be told.

This need to tell even of God, since he is also in himself a telling, arises from the mysterious and incomprehensible paradox that God is as originally forgiving (or rather the giver of forgiving) as he is giving.

Thus, our reflections on Aquinas have shown that if forgiveness can only be commenced by the divine sovereign victim, this also reveals forgiveness to be an outcome exceeding its own occasion and the perfection of gift-exchange with fusion. Finally, we have seen that the recognition of God as the provider of forgiveness so correctly characterized, entails that the infinite always was, if certainly not (as for Hegel) really related to the finite, nonetheless eminently fused with it at a certain incomprehensible point of identity.

(d) Scotus, Incarnation, and Forgiveness

As a melancholy postscript to these reflections, it can now be explained how Duns Scotus removed, for a time, the possibility of an authentic under-standing of forgiveness along the lines I have indicated.

For Duns Scotus, as is well known, the ultimate motivation for incarna-tion was not the forgiveness of humanity. We have already seen the weakness of much of the reasoning to this conclusion. However, his position is only fully comprehensible when one realizes that he did not grant to Adam in the earthly paradise an orientation by nature to the beatific vision.[61] Since, for Scotus, being is transcendentally indifferent to infinite and finite, as also to active and potential, albeit that the former terms are allowed to be more exemplary as to intensity or degree or *gradus*, the finite Creation fully *is*, in its own right as Creation, and holds ground ontologically, simply as what God has determined it shall be.[62] Lost from this perspective is a full sense of the impossibility of creation: For where this is grasped, as by Aquinas, then it is also seen that finitude as constituted only by the infinite must, in order to suspire, be self-canceling. Hence, the finite creature fully conscious of its finitude must aspire to return to God and to comprehend his finitude in the vision of his maker. In consequence, for Aquinas, human beings simply as human were ordained to the beatific vision and to deification.

For Scotus, by contrast, such ordination is merely a divinely willed supple-ment. But in consequence, creatures as creatures do not appear to Scotus as capable of making a return of love to the Creator commensurate with the gift of creation. For this reason God, who for Scotus is bound of his own necessity to will the highest good, is inevitably inclined to will (albeit freely) the Incar-nation, in order that here a creature via his conjunction with the infinite *Logos* may offer back to God an infinite return of love.[63] The problem with this conception is that it appears to downgrade humanity and not to allow that humans of their very nature (if this be followed) offer the highest return possible by creatures. And as we have already seen, Christ in a sense offers nothing higher within and from a creature considered only *as* creature. Thus, for Aquinas, there is no question of the Incarnation increasing God's reception of finite glory, as there appears to be for Duns Scotus.

But the most curious thing about Scotus's scheme is that while, in a sense, it offers incarnation instead of deification, where Aquinas sees deification as the ground of possibility of incarnation (shocking as this may seem), the inhibition regarding deification, founded on univocity of being, actually restricts also any strong account of the hypostatic union. Thus, in Scotus's view, while indeed Christ's humanity somehow makes an infinite return of love to God through the *Logos*, as purely human it enjoys only finite merit; whereas for Aquinas, who developed a strong Alexandrian view of the *communicatio idiomatum*, this merit was infinite.[64] Likewise, for Scotus, again in contrast to Aquinas, Christ's human nature is not engraced, is not indefectible, and does not enjoy the beatific vision through fusion with the divine nature in the one divine hypostasis, but instead is elevated in these three ways purely by divine decree which need not have been enacted.[65] In like fashion, for Scotus, the indefeasibility of the final persistence of the blessed in enjoying the beatific vision does not derive from the vision itself as secured by our participation in the hypostatic union, but rather is, once again, a merely intrinsic grant of the divine will.[66]

Thus, while the ground of incarnation is for Scotus onto-Christological rather than redemptive, it is difficult to see how in fact this union, which is supposed to perfect the Creation, is any reality of itself, as opposed to a kind of imposed structure. Hence Scotus, knowing no medium between substance and accident, regarded Christ's humanity as an accidental addition to the *Logos*, though of course the *Logos* was still for him in no real relation to it.[67] Supposedly, Scotus thought that an accident in dependence on a substance need not realize any potential in that substance (which would be inappropriate for God); but one cannot come to possess any accident which comes in some, albeit temporary, way to characterize oneself without it realizing some potential in one—otherwise an accident is just an eternal possession. If that indeed is what Scotus is really talking about (or even if one allowed that there can be an accident not realizing a potential), then it still is the case that God cannot receive anything into his *esse* or *persona* that is not essential and not assimilated to his own essence. Scotus only thinks in these terms because his elevation of finite being to ontological equality with infinite being in terms of sharing in a transgeneric attribute—if not in terms of mode and degree—ensures that a real sense of its participatory character is lost, and it must be thought as standing spatially alongside the infinite. Thus, in the Christological instance, Christ's humanity, if it is to remain real for Scotus, must enjoy an *esse* of its own. And indeed, its individuality seems in effect to amount for him to human personhood, since he understands human personhood only negatively, as a not-being dependent on something higher.[68] Thus, all the essential ingredients of human personality—individuality, animality, rationality—are there in Christ for Scotus; it is simply that all this is included in a purer self-subsistence. While Aquinas indeed thinks in somewhat similar terms, he also allows personality as a positive, specifically characterized incommunicability, which as something human *really is not there* in Christ, whereas a positive divine personality *is* present.

It appears, then, that while one might be attracted by the Scotist view of the Incarnation as pure active *gift*, and not reactive forgiveness, that the divine-human union accompanying this account is in fact extremely tenuous. This has implications for how Scotus conceives the secondary purpose of the Incarnation, contingent upon sin, which is indeed the forgiveness of human sins. Here once again a weak sense of participation (reduced to a matter of degrees of perfection that stops short of the infinite, thought of as a positively different *modus*, whereas for Aquinas it is a negative term related primarily to our *modus significandi*)[69] means that Scotus thinks that even original sin is only finite and only requires finite merit, which a mere human being could render in compensation.[70] Thus God could, by his *potentia absoluta*, have appointed a merely human savior, and indeed, since Christ's human merits are finite, it would seem that even through the Incarnation we are only humanly redeemed. And as a result of all this, forgiveness as conceived by Aquinas has been in every way lost to view.

First of all, Christ's offering of finite merit and satisfaction fulfills the demands of divine justice, not of divine mercy. The latter operates much more by fiat, and since the *pattern* of satisfaction realized by Christ is no longer its means of operation, it is difficult to see how this fiat any longer expresses itself in what is "convenient." God simply decrees the adequacy of what Christ does and conjoins with it his forgiveness. For Scotus, the divine justice and mercy are now "formally distinct," just as happiness (as self-realization) and justice are formally distinct (the devil being held to have fallen through a neglect only of the latter).[71] In either case, Scotus assumes that where, from our point of view, concepts can be conceptually distinguished, this is because they directly indicate distinct essences external to our perception (where Aquinas locates essence much more in the mind and describes much more of a gulf between mental understanding and ontological states of affairs).[72] Such essences are simple and inviolate, so that if we project them to the infinite, this may increase their intensity but not alter their inner core of identity. Thus, divine justice and mercy and happiness are essentially the same in nature as ours and remain "formally distinct" in God. Even though they are "really identical" in him, this is only insofar as they reside "virtually" in his single essence which is infinite. God's understanding of this infinite essence is his "first instance," but in his consequent "instants" he produces from his understanding the essences of things as *finite* and as formally distinguished from himself and each other.[73] Hence, through the formal distinction, Scotus over-elevates the absoluteness of finite simplicities and simultaneously compromises the absoluteness of the divine simplicity. Indeed, he says explicitly that since simplicity is univocally shared between God and creatures, infinity and not simplicity must primarily characterize God.[74] Thus, he interprets Anselm's *Monologion* to mean that we know God in terms of infinite degrees of perfections that we grasp in their simple essence quite apart from God, arguing that to refer a perfection analogously to God adds nothing to our knowledge of this perfection.[75] This totally obliterates the "phenemonological" dimension implicit in Aquinas (and in Anselm), which assumes that to grasp a perfection *is* to see the infinite shining through the finite and calling the finite above itself.[76]

For Scotus, therefore, we can grasp "mercy" and "justice" nontheologically as distinct in their essences—else why would there be two concepts, he reasons, disallowing the notion that perhaps they are *really* distinct only for our deficient ontological experience. In this way he already thinks of mercy in "secular" terms, and so as outside of justice. As such it becomes a matter of mere negative decree or withholding—this notion of mercy he then projects upon God.

Thus we can see that, in the first instance, Scotus loses Aquinas's sense of forgiveness as positive and inherently divine. In the second instance, he also loses Aquinas's sense of it being only possible through the Incarnation as the work of the God-Man, or the sovereign victim. This is because he is scarcely able to think of the hypostatic union at all, and has to patch it up with divine decrees, in any case deemed adequate for our forgiveness without the mediating work of penance and substitution. Scotus never, like Aquinas, allows that merit automatically elicits grace, since it is (for Aquinas) itself the result and manifestation of grace.[77] Once more Scotus's ontic conception of God makes him think of divine initiative and human response as external to each other, in such a way that our merit becomes too much ours, or at any rate something that does not of itself return to God, but rather something which God may or may not graciously receive. One consequence of this loss of a sense of participation is therefore a loss also of a sense of exchange between infinite and finite. God becomes more of a one-way giver and, significantly, this unilateralism of the gift seems here to be a *consequence* of a reduction of God to one ontic pole within a common univocalized being. Thus, whereas a finite being that *was not* of itself had of itself to return, and indeed God as loyal to his own *esse* and its transcendental norms of beauty and justice "had to" guarantee this return, now a finite being need not of itself return, and God is not of himself bound to receive it. Already, therefore, the Scotist God has become more like a bestowing tyrant and the "mixed constitution" of gift-exchange and positive forgiveness has begun to be lost.

In the third instance, Scotus loses also Aquinas's sense of forgiveness as "outcome exceeding occasion." As we have seen, he rejects this essentially because his doctrine of univocity obscures a sense of the impossibility of creation and the way in which, as a consequence, the whole divine economy involves an outcome exceeding occasion. But with this loss, Scotus can no longer think a finality intrinsic to forgiveness, but must resort to a God who simply "decides" that the blessed need not fall again, though he withheld this benefit from Adam.

In the fourth instance, Scotus loses forgiveness as fusion, because he disallows deification as a ground for incarnation and in consequence cannot think the divine-human union through character or *tropos*.

In the fifth and final instance, Scotus loses divine *esse* as conjoined to event, and the divine gift as also eternally divine forgiveness. His onto-theology necessitates also an onto-Christology because it disallows deification and requires something to compensate the divine requirement of glory from the creation. But an onto-Christology, when conjoined to the view that a merely finite human fault could have been corrected by minor, finite means, ensures that none of the narrative, typological, and aesthetic seriousness of Christ's suffering and passion is carried up into his preordained eternal destiny in an organic rather than a merely accidental fashion. Thus, while the Scotist God is eternally also man, this man also remains accidentally outside God, and in consequence it does not seem that this God is eternally also forgiveness. By contrast, in the Thomist scheme, where Christological outcome is ontologically in excess of Christological purpose, and this excess over forgiveness nonetheless *is* forgiveness, God is seen as from eternity in his own foreordination also human, and therefore, through this fusion, as eternally forgiving.

NOTES

1. Dante Alighieri, *Purgatorio*, Canto 28. And see Jacques Madaule, "Dante: Une Liturgie Poetique du Pardon," in *Le Pardon*, ed. Michel Perrin (Paris: Beauchesne, 1987). I am grateful to Alison Milbank for discussions about the *Purgatorio*.

2. In Michel Perrin, ed., *Le Pardon* (Paris: Beauchesne, 1987), see Danièle Aubriot, "Quelques Refléxions sur le Pardon en Grèce Ancienne," 25–27, and Alain Michel, "Le Pardon dans 'Antiquite de Platon à St. Augustine,'" 49–60. See also Chong-Hyoun Sung, *Vergebung der Sünden* (Tübingen: J.C.B. Mohr, 1993), especially pp. 75–77.

3. See Michel, "Le Pardon dans 'Antiquite de Platon à St. Augustine,'" and André Crepin, "Pardon Chrétien et vengeance germanique dans 'Angleterre du Haut Moyen Age,'" also in Perrin, *Le Pardon*.

4. See the *Oxford English Dictionary* entries for these words.

5. Søren Kierkegaard, *Works of Love*, trans. H. V. and E. H. Hong (Princeton, N.J.: Princeton University Press, 1995), 294–295.

6. *Purgatorio*, Cantos 28 and 33.

7. S.T. III Q. 86 a 2.

8. Kierkegaard, *Works of Love*, Supplement, p. 314.

9. S.T. III, Q. 86. a 4 resp.; a 6. See also John Bossy, *Christianity in the West 1400–1700* (Oxford: Oxford University Press, 1985).

10. S.T. III Q. 86 a 2; a 4 resp.; a 6. See Bossy, *Christianity in the West*, and Catherine Pickstock, *After Writing: On the Liturgical Consummation of Philosophy* (Oxford: Blackwell, 1998).

11. John Milbank, "Can a Gift Be Given?: Prolegomena to a Future Trinitarian Metaphysics," *Modern Theology* 2, no. 1 (January 1995): 119–161.

12. See David Hart's brilliant article "A Gift Exceeding Every Debt," in *Pro Ecclesia* VII, no. 3, pp. 333–349.

13. *Purgatorio*, Canto 33.

14. See Aubriot, "Quelques Refléxions sur le Pardon en Grèce Ancienne" and Michel, "Le Pardon dans 'Antiquite de Platon à St. Augustine.'"

15. See Aubriot, "Quelques Refléxions sur le Pardon en Grèce Ancienne."

16. See Sung, *Vergebung des Sünden,* pp. 66; K. Koch, "Suhne und Sünden-bergebung um die Wende von der exilischem zur nachexilischen Zeit," *Evangelische Theologischeszeitschrift* 26 (1966): 217–239; John Milbank, "History of the One God," *The Heythrop Journal* XXXVIII (October 1997): 371–400.

17. See Sung, *Vergebung des Sünden,* and Koch, "Suhne und Sündenbergebung um die Wende von der exilischem zur nachexilischen Zeit."

18. See John Milbank, "History of the One God"; and "I Will Gasp and Pant: Deutero-Isaiah and the Birth of the Suffering Subject," *Semeia* (1992): 59–73.

19. See Jacques Ribard, "Du Don au Pardon: a L'écoute des oeuvres littéraires des XIIᵉ et XIIIᵉ Siècles," in Perrin, *Le Pardon,* 117–130, esp. 129. See also Christiane Marchello-Nizid, "Adultère et Pardon dans le Roman Courtois," in the same volume, 131–139.

20. Vladimir Jankelevitch, *Pardonner?* (Paris: Le Pavillion, 1971) and *Le Pardon* (Paris: Aubier, 1967); and Alain Gouhier, "Le temps de L'impardonnable selon Jan-kélevitch," in Perrin, *Le Pardon,* 269–282.

21. See John Milbank, "Sacred Triads: Augustine and the Indo-European Soul," *Modern Theology* 13, no. 4 (October 1997): 451–474; and Catherine Pickstock, "Music: Soul, City and Cosmos after Augustine," in *Radical Orthodoxy,* ed. J. Milbank, C. Pickstock, and G. Ward (London and New York: Routledge, 1999).

22. Augustine, *Confessions,* XI, 26.

23. Jorge Luis Borges, "The Rose of Paracelsus," in *Collected Fictions,* trans. Andrew Hurley (New York: Penguin, 1998), 504–508.

24. See Joan Copjec, ed., *Radical Evil* (London: Verso, 1996); Jean-Luc Nancy, *The Experience of Freedom,* trans. Bridget McDonald (Stanford: Stanford University Press, 1993); Slavoj Žižek, *For They Know Not What They Do: Enjoyment as a Political Factor* (London: Verso, 1991).

25. See David J. Depew and Bruce H. Weber's magnificent *Darwinism Evolving* (Cambridge, Mass.: MIT Press, 1997), passim.

26. See John Milbank, "Problematizing the Secular: The Post-Postmodern Problematic," in *Shadow of Spirit,* ed. P. Berry and A. Wernick (London and New York: Routledge, 1993), 30–44; and "La fin des Lumières: Postmoderne and postseculière," *Concilium,* no. 2 (1992): 57–68.

27. See Robert Spaemann, *Glück und Wohlwollen: Versuch über Ethik* (Stuttgart: Le Lette-cotta, 1990).

28. Kierkegaard, *Works of Love,* 380.

29. Geoffrey Chaucer, *The Pardoner's Prologue and Tale,* ed. A. C. Spearing (Cambridge and New York: Cambridge University Press, 1994).

30. Cited in Gouhier, "Le temps de L'impardonnable selon Jankélevitch."

31. Julian of Norwich, *Revelations of Divine Love,* trans. Elizabeth Spearing (Harmondsworth: Penguin, 1998), passim.

32. S.C.G. IV. 55 (15).

33. See David Hart, "A Gift Exceeding Every Debt."

34. See Frederick Bauerschmidt, *Julian of Norwich and the Mystical Body of Christ* (Notre Dame, Ind.: Notre Dame University Press, 1999), introduction and passim.

35. S.T. III. Q. 1 a 2.

36. S.T. III. Q. 1 aa 1–4.

37. S.T. III. Q. 1 a 2.

38. Gilbert Narcisse, O.P., *Les Raisons de Dieu: Arguments de Convenance et Esthetique Thélogique Selon St. Thomas d'Aquin de Hans Urs von Balthasar* (Fribourg: Editions Universitaires Fribourg Suisse, 1997), esp. 165–180.

39. See Bauerschmidt, *Julian of Norwich and the Mystical Body of Christ.*

40. S.T. III. Q. 1 a 2. resp.: "and there are many other advantages which accrue, above man's apprehension."

41. S.T. III. Q. a. 1 a 3 ad 1; S.C.G. IV. 42 (4).

42. S.C.G. IV. 55 (3); S.T. III Q. 1 a 1.

43. S.T. I. Q. 95. a 1; . 99 a 1 a d 3. See Richard Cross, *Duns Scotus* (Oxford: Oxford University Press, 1999), 113–126, for a clear exposition of the difference from Scotus at this point.

44. S.C.G. 55 (2): The Incarnation is "not contrary to the order of things . . . because, although the divine nature exceeds the human nature to infinity, man in the order of his nature has God himself for end, and has been born to be united to God by his intellect." Also 55 (4)–(17). In addition, see S.T. III Q. 1 a 2 resp: the Incarnation is "convenient . . . with regard to the full participation of the Divinity, which is the true bliss of man and end of human life; and this is bestowed upon us by Christ's life."

45. S.T. III Q. 3 a 5.

46. S.T. III. Q. 1 a 3. ad 5.

47. On this entire issue, see Michel Corbin, *L'Inoui de Dieu: six Etudes Christologiques* (Paris: Desclée de Brouwer, 1979).

48. S.T. III A. 16 a b ad 2; Q. 17 a 2 resp; Q 2 a 7 ad 3. And see Richard Cross, *Duns Scotus*, and his article (unfavorable to Aquinas) "Aquinas on Nature, Hypostasis and the Metaphysics of the Incarnation," *The Thomist* 60, no. 2 (April 1996): 171–202.

49. For example, S.T. III. Q. 17 a 2. resp.

50. Corbin, *L'Inoui de Dieu.*

51. See note 48 above, and S.T. II. II. Q 2 a 7; Q 5 a 1; III Q. 1a 3. And see also John Milbank and Catherine Pickstock, *Truth in Aquinas* (London and New York: Routledge, 2000), Chapter 2.

52. See Milbank and Pickstock, *Truth in Aquinas*, Chapter 2.

53. Ibid.

54. See Richard Cross, *Duns Scotus*, and Rowan Williams's article on later medieval Christology, "Jesus Christus III: Mittelalter," *TRE* 16 (1987): pp. 748–753.

55. See Andrew Louth, *Maximus the Confessor* (London and New York: Routledge, 1996), 54–59.

56. S.T. III 2. a 1 ad 1 and ad 2; a 3 resp. and ad 2; a 5 ad 2; a 12 ad 2; 16 a 1 resp.

57. SCG IV 41 (7) (11); S.T. III a 3 ad 2. For a much fuller discussion of the significance of the hand analogy, see John Milbank and Catherine Pickstock, *Truth in Aquinas*, Chapter 3.

58. Aristotle, *On the Soul*, trans. W. S. Hett (Cambridge, Mass.: Harvard University Press, Loeb Editions 1995), Books II and III; Thomas Aquinas, *A Commentary on Aristotle's De Anima*, trans. Robert Pasnau (New Haven: Yale University Press, 1999), § 54–82. Again, for a much fuller development of this thematic, see Milbank and Pickstock, *Truth in Aquinas.*

59. SCG IV 41 (12).

60. S.T. III Q. 2 a 3 resp.

61. See Richard Cross, *Duns Scotus*; and Olivier Boulnois's article "Duns Scotus:

John Milbank

Jean," in *Dictionnaire Critique de Théologie*, ed. J.-Y. Lacoste (Paris: Presses universitaires de France, 1998).

62. Duns Scotus, *Ordinatio* I d 3 q i; d 8 q iii.

63. See Cross, *Duns Scotus*; Williams, "Jesus Christus III: Mittelalter"; and Boulnois, "Duns Scotus: Jean."

64. S.T. III Q. 2 a 1 ad 2; a 3 resp.; Q. 17 a 2 resp. See also Williams, "Jesus Christus III: Mittelalter."

65. Again see Cross, *Duns Scotus*; Williams, "Jesus Christus III: Mittelalter"; and Boulnois, "Duns Scotus: Jean."

66. Cross, *Duns Scotus*; and Boulnois, "Duns Scotus: Jean."

67. See Cross, *Duns Scotus*.

68. See Cross, *Duns Scotus*; and Williams, "Jesus Christus III: Mittelalter."

69. For Scotus's view that we cannot love negations, see Duns Scotus, *Ordinatio* I d 3 Part I, Q 2.

70. See Cross, *Duns Scotus*; and Boulnois, "Duns Scotus: Jean."

71. See Boulnois, "Duns Scotus: Jean"; and Cross, *Duns Scotus*, passim. For the formal distinction of attributes in general in Duns Scotus, see *Ordinatio* I. dist. 8 Part I Q. 4.

72. See Milbank and Pickstock, *Truth in Aquinas*, chapter 2.

73. Duns Scotus, *Ordinatio* I d 8, Part 1 q. 4; *Quodlibet* 14. 14, 5 S.

74. Duns Scotus, *Ordinatio* I d 8, pars I q. 3.

75. Duns Scotus, *Ordinatio* I d 3 q. 3.

76. See Milbank and Pickstock, *Truth in Aquinas*, Chapter 2. See also Catherine Pickstock's unpublished essay on Anselm's *Prologion*.

77. See Boulnois, "Duns Scotus: Jean"; and Cross, *Duns Scotus*.

five

The Catastrophe of Memory

Derrida, Milbank, and the (Im)possibility of Forgiveness

Mark Dooley

The movement known as radical orthodoxy, the most notable exponents of which include John Milbank, Graham Ward, and Catherine Pickstock, has, since its inception, crusaded against what it sees as the plagues and nuisances of secularism and postmodernism. Its fundamental aspiration, we are told, is to "reclaim the world by situating its concerns and activities within a theological framework," one which is much more than a "leisure-time activity of private commitment."[1] The theology of radical orthodoxy, so its mission statement reveals, is predicated upon the firmly held principle that "the self-conscious superficiality of today's secularism" has led to a regrettable state of nihilistic despair. The objective, thus, is to still the "impersonal chaos" which lies at the heart of the postmodern predicament by reconfiguring "theological truth." They do so by reaffirming their commitment "to credal Christianity and the exemplarity of its patristic matrix," thus "recovering and extending a fully Christianized ontology and practical philosophy consonant with authentic Christian doctrine."[2] What this amounts to is an attempt to have everything "participate" in God, for if such participation does not obtain, then eternal stability gives way to "a purely immanent security," to a void or a nothingness which makes all questions of ultimate meaning meaningless. If Derrida and his defenders opt for the void (a void which they try to conceal through appeals to the saving power of *différance*), the high priests of radical orthodoxy insist that behind the phenomena lies an "eternal source," one which gives to "bodies, their art, language, sexual and political union" a more profound and permanent density. The choice then is clear: either participation in the eternal source or nihilism, either permanence and stability or an anonymous vortex devoid of rhyme or reason. Postmodernism can only offer, in good Nietzschean style, an anonymous rumbling, while radical orthodoxy makes sense of our world by affirming its participation in a divine order, one which is given expression through language, culture, sexuality, religious practice, and politics.

It may seem somewhat strange, therefore, that the principal harbinger of the good news of radical orthodoxy, John Milbank, contributed an essay to a book edited by his fellow traveler, Graham Ward, entitled *The Postmodern God.*[3] However, Milbank, Ward, Pickstock, and Philip Blond consider themselves to be "postmodern" in the sense that they see the dawn of modernity as having heralded the demise of true and genuine theological discourse. With the collapse of modernity this "modern predicament of theology" has been overcome, for now "it no longer has to measure up to accepted secular standards of scientific truth or normative rationality."[4] As such, it can reclaim its premodern roots as an alternative means of making sense of reality, one which assiduously avoids the confusion and lack of cohesion which postmodernism of the Parisian variety generates. So when Milbank uses the term "postmodern theology," he is not referring to the work of Mark C. Taylor, John D. Caputo, Edith Wyschogrod, Kevin Hart, or Charles Winquist—each of whom has been influenced by Derrida in one way or another, but rather he is adverting both to himself and to the radical orthodoxy set writ large. The former, on Milbank's reading, ought to be categorized as postmodern nihilists who "embrace contingency and arbitrariness as the real natural good."[5] Having given up on the eternal source, having called into question the divine origin, and having disregarded all talk of ontological foundations, such thinkers appear to have surrendered themselves to a formless flux in which nothingness prevails. As such, they should not be considered theologians *stricto sensu*, but preachers of the abyss, prophets of the dark night into which we are all aimlessly and hopelessly wandering.

Milbank's response to the efforts of postmodernists such as Caputo and Taylor and others is thus to advance a "postmodern" theology of his own, one which is founded on the most sacred tenets of radical orthodoxy. Such a theology, he argues, "can only proceed by explicating Christian practice." For Milbank, Christianity ought not to be thought of as simply one discourse competing with others. Rather, we should think of it as more "internally" postmodern than competing religions because of its celebration of difference. "Christianity," he continues, "pursued from the outset a universalism which

tried to subsume rather than merely abolish difference: Christians could remain in their many cities, languages, and cultures, yet still belong to one
eternal city ruled by Christ, in whom all 'humanity' was fulfilled."[6] Christianity is nevertheless "peculiar" in that while it admits of difference, it is
simultaneously committed to a harmonization of those differences "in the
body of Christ." So while Christianity manifests for Milbank the perfect form
of community, one in which, by virtue of the resurrection, everyone is admitted, so-called "nihilistic postmodernism" represents the breakdown of dialectics, resolving in indifference, fragmentation, and the sundering of community
and self-identity. He argues:

> Christian theology, by contrast to nihilistic postmodernism, yet with equal
> validity, imagines temporal process as, in its very temporality, reflecting
> eternity; as the possibility of a historical progress into God, and as some-
> thing recuperable within memory whose ultimate point is the allowing of
> forgiveness and reconciliation.[7]

It is this sentiment, and all that underpins it, which goes to the heart of the
debate held at the second Religion and Postmodernism conference held at
Villanova in September 1999. While much of the debate between radical
orthodoxy and deconstruction at the conference appeared, ostensibly at least,
to focus primarily on the notion of "forgiveness"—both Jacques Derrida and
John Milbank gave difficult and intricate papers on that subject—much more
was indeed at stake. First, this was the occasion of the first live encounter
between two movements which are currently battling it out for the minds and
souls of many theological faculties throughout the United States and beyond;
second, it allowed postmodernism—in the form of Derrida—to respond to the
criticisms which radical orthodoxy has been inexorably launching at it for
much of the past decade, the essence of which I have outlined above; third, it
put under the spotlight the contention, advanced by Milbank, that because
time reflects eternity, forgiveness and reconciliation are indeed possible. What
I will endeavor to do in the remainder of this chapter is show how this "debate"
between Derrida and Milbank unfolded. In so doing, I will argue that the
critique advanced by Milbank of Derrida as both a nihilist and as someone for
whom absolute self-sacrifice is essential is indicative of a thorough lack of
understanding of what has driven deconstruction since its inception. In so
doing, I shall pay close attention to the question of forgiveness as dealt with in
both conference papers and in the course of the roundtable which followed.

Overcoming the Void in the Instant of the God-Man

As stated, radical orthodoxy tries to reclaim from secularism "aesthetics,
politics, sex, the body, personhood, visibility, [and] space," by resituating them
"in terms of the Trinity, Christology, the Church, and the Eucharist."[8] This
emphasis on a highly Christianized approach to theological and philosophical

matters becomes starkly evident once more in John Milbank's scholarly conference paper, "Forgiveness and Incarnation." The crux of this article centers on what the author designates as the "five major aporias" of a "purely interhuman forgiveness."[9] For Milbank, as his title suggests, real and genuine forgiveness can only be attained in and through the Christian Incarnation, for this announces a "time when divine forgiveness can be mediated by human beings: a time for which justice is infinitized as forgiveness."[10] But for those of a secular frame of mind, and perhaps also for those of another denominational persuasion, forgiveness appears impossible. Before attempting to delineate the differences between Milbank and Derrida on this rather complex issue, let me detail the nature of the five aporias which Milbank argues are an insuperable obstacle for those seeking forgiveness without the intercession of the Incarnation.

The first aporia to be faced by those who strive after such purely interhuman forgiveness revolves around the question Who is to forgive? Milbank contends that because only the victims of injustice can forgive, and because any harmful or injurious action will never be limited to one victim alone—in that an evil action tends to have innumerable unforeseen consequences and ramifications for many other innocent victims—the culprit can never be fully exonerated. For "it is impossible to know how far the consequences of even the simplest and most minor misdemeanors extend." "The infinite jury of victims," declares Milbank, "can never be summoned to the consistorial court of penitence."[11] Moreover, the "true victims" of injustice—those whose bodies lie "pulverised in their fury and despair," cannot, and indeed should not, be spoken for in their absence. For if a living victim forgives in the name of those who are either dead or forgotten, "all the other, often untraceable victims are thereby betrayed."[12]

This applies also to the sovereign power who has the right to pardon those whose crimes have left a trail of shattered bodies. Milbank argues that if such sovereigns, in forgiving the perpetrator—a rapist in this example—were to offer "the chance for making reparation and achieving rehabilitation to a dangerous rapist, while his [the rapist's] actual, damaged victims persisted in hatred and bitterness toward him, then we should not feel that he had been forgiven." The sovereign, in other words, cannot forgive the living in the name of the dead; neither he nor she can "represent all those injured who may lie unknown beyond any traceable boundary of space and time." No one, that is, can speak for those whom Paul Ricoeur calls the "anonymous forces of history." Hence, Milbank concludes, "neither the victim nor the sovereign power may forgive, and there is no human forgiveness."[13]

The second aporia, "forgiveness and time," focuses on the following problem: How can a wrongdoing be elided from memory through an act of forgiveness, such that the wrongdoing appears never to have happened, without thereby risking irresponsible amnesia and thus a repetition and a revisitation of that same wrongdoing on a future generation? In analyzing this conundrum,

Milbank appeals to the insights of Vladimir Jankélévitch, an author about whom Derrida also has a lot to say. Milbank points out that for Jankélévitch, "the order of time runs counter to forgiveness," and this because any attempt to erase a past event ignores "the ineluctable discreteness of past moments, through which alone time occurs and finite being arises."[14] While forgiveness demands that the wrongdoing be elided from memory, the future demands that it be retained as a warning from history. The horror of the Holocaust, for example, bears witness to a "radical evil" which ought never to be forgotten or expunged.

Milbank does, however, identify a possible way of obviating this aporia in the form of Augustine's argument to the effect that time and memory are inseparable. This argument which is central to Ricoeur's treatment of narrative selfhood in his monumental *Time and Narrative*[15] is founded on the assumption that the past, as Milbank puts it, "only *is* through memory, and while this does not abolish the ontological inviolability and irreversibility of pastness, it does mean that the event in its very originality is open to alteration and mutation."[16] Consequently, pace Jankélévitch, forgiveness on this Augustinian reading does not seek to undo the past but rather strives to "re-narrate the past." In so doing, "one comes to understand why oneself or others made errors, in terms of the delusions that arose through mistaking lesser goods for the greater."

Moreover, because the finite is of itself a "nothingness," and because evil "is only of the finite, not of the infinite," it follows that evil, once again contra Jankélévitch, may be abrogated. Hence the victim who "positively remembers" the past, or who re-narrates the past, will come to understand that the object of his hatred—the evil or horror perpetrated by his aggressor—was in fact *nothing*. To think otherwise allows evil to acquire a firm foothold, for "what is unredeemed remains in force." So when Jankélévitch declares that the Holocaust is unforgivable, Milbank rejoins that "the greatest atrocity requires all the more an access of hope, the greatest evil calls out all the more for an impossible forgiveness and reconciliation."[17] Before turning to his third aporia of forgiveness, Milbank makes clear that this "Augustinian vision" is "necessarily a theological vision," one which insists that unless time "participates in the divine, infinite eternal memory . . . it would be destined to pass away . . . into pure oblivion, thereby rendering the good and actual ontologically as nugatory as the privative and deficient."[18] Where no such vision abides, forgiveness truly did, as Jankélévitch believed, perish in the death camps.

The third aporia is dealt with under the title "Forgiveness and Forgetting." Following on from the conclusion drawn in the discussion of the previous aporia regarding the necessity of a theological approach to questions of time and forgiveness, Milbank argues that for those who do not hold to the theological vision advanced—those of a "purely immanentist perspective"—the past cannot be transformed or re-narrated in accordance with the Augustinian schema of time and memory. The problem for one with an immanentist frame of mind is that because hatred, and the fault which provoked it, cannot be transformed in the manner described above, no forgiveness seems possible. The only way the fault can be forgiven is if it has been, as Milbank suggests, entirely forgotten. The problem here consists in the fact that if the fault has been forgotten it no longer requires forgiveness. So "as soon as forgiveness becomes possible, it is already redundant."[19] This is the paradox of "negative," or purely human, forgiveness.

The penultimate aporia considered by Milbank, "The Trade in Forgiveness," is especially significant, because it is here that he tries to counter many of the arguments put forward by Derrida in *Donner le mort* (*The Gift of Death*) and elsewhere,[20] to the effect that Christian charity is regulated by a sophisticated form of celestial economics. Although Milbank does not mention Derrida by name in this context, it is obvious from the analysis that it is the latter he has in mind. For Milbank, forgiveness should not be thought of as an act of what Levinas calls "total altruism."[21] Rather, we ought to consider it in terms of a "Christianized eudaimonism," in which forgiveness marks the site of a self-reorientation by way of a dialectical engagement with another. Milbank describes this process in the following terms:

> For this Christianized eudaimonism, my interest in my own happiness cannot compromise the disinterest of my will to forgive, since my happiness is from the outset less a possession than a relational ecstatis: my fulfilling myself by orientating myself beyond myself to the other, my realizing myself by expressing myself and letting myself go and receiving back from the other a new interpretation of myself. Here to forgive is to restore that order of free unlimited exchange of charity which was interrupted by sin.[22]

Such is the paradoxical "aneconomic economy of pardon"—an economy which is founded on the belief that unless one is already receiving "infinite divine charity" one cannot offer charity or forgiveness to another. For divine charity is "the ontological bond between God and creatures," the means by which the latter can forgive and be forgiven. Due to the fact that one is always already divinely forgiven, one has no need to engage in the secret trade of counterfeit forgiveness. One can forgive freely without compromising one's purity of motive. Indeed, it is because we are already the recipients of divine charity, of a divine gift, that we can establish what Milbank refers to as "a correct harmonious relation between creatures."[23] This is so because in receiving the gift we can freely, without thought of how we might profit from such an exercise in generosity, pass it on to fellow creatures. In so doing, our motives remain pure as a consequence of the fact that we give not to receive, for we have already received. But those who do not recognize divine charity, those who believe that the gift of forgiveness comes from them alone, run the risk of binding those whom one forgives "in an infinite indebtedness." Furthermore, such a person will not seek to embrace the pain and suffering which positive or divine forgiveness demands; not only does such counterfeit forgiveness release the forgiver from the "injuries done to him and the terrible difficulties involved in seeking reconciliation (within infinite justice) with others," but it also leaves open the possibility that the one to be forgiven will not be rehabilitated. Purely human forgiveness is, according to Milbank, too easy—it is cheap forgiveness, forgiveness at a below-cost price.

Finally, the fifth aporia—"Forgiveness and Finality"—deals with the vexed issue, touched on above, of how to forgive while at the same time retaining a sense of the injury caused so as to prevent such a thing ever recurring again. For Milbank, the negative or purely human forgiver, in simply forgetting the past wrong, naively thinks that mere forgiveness alone will immunize him against some future threat posed by the one he has forgiven. Reconciliation between the wronged and the wrongdoer, that is, is not a natural consequence of mere forgiveness qua forgetting. Such is the insecurity in human relationships caused by forgiveness which is not grounded in a divine source. If, however, divine forgiveness is sought, we can be sure that the wrongdoer has actively "offered penance" and that his repentance has resolved in "an improvement of character beyond the latent tendency which led to the commission of a fault." It is only through participation in what Milbank calls "real, divine, eschatological finality"[24] that forgiveness can engender the security in human affairs which any act of genuine reconciliation promises.

For Milbank, thus, positive forgiveness requires the intercession of the Incarnation. For, as he goes on to argue in the remainder of his chapter, the God-Man, as "unique sovereign victim" for the reason that he suffered "the maximum possible victimage," can forgive *in the name of* those countless victims whose forgiveness we desire but can never receive. Through him humanity can forgive humanity. As such, it is not God himself who forgives us, but rather he gives us the capacity to forgive one another. Unlike negative forgiveness, no hate or bitterness precedes the forgiveness afforded in and through the incarnate Christ. Consequently, "with the God-Man alone there arises a pure forgiveness, since this really surpasses forgiveness and is rather the unbroken continued giving of the divine gift as also the offering of a suffering actively undergone."[25] Through the Holy Spirit, thus, we may access the gift of divine charity which the Trinity embodies and purveys.

The most obvious concern which Milbank's analysis arouses, as I intimated earlier, has to do with whether or not those who do not believe in the Incarnation can be saved. It never seems to occur to Milbank, either here or throughout his other writings, that it is not simply a stark choice between credal Christianity, on the one hand, and secularism, nihilism, and postmodernism (all of which are synonymous for him) on the other. The logical upshot of this extreme Christocentric position is that forgiveness and reconciliation appear to be impossible not only for those of a secular or nihilistic frame of mind but also for those of a non-Christian religious disposition. This may not be what Milbank intends to suggest, but I can locate nothing in his argument which leads me to any other conclusion. Indeed, his analysis of forgiveness sits comfortably with that advanced by Hegel in his early essay of 1799, "The Spirit of Christianity,"[26] in which the negative forgiveness of the Jews is compared unfavorably to that of the positive forgiveness of the mediator and redeemer, Jesus Christ.

In fact, it could plausibly be argued that Milbank's version of radical orthodoxy shares many of the same fundamental gestures and axioms which characterize Hegel's philosophy of religion, even though the latter is not normally considered one of the theological precursors of radical orthodoxy. For is it not the case that when Milbank says such things as "Christian theology . . . imagines temporal process as, in its very temporality, reflecting eternity; as the possibility of a historical progress into God, and as something recuperable within memory"[27] he is echoing Hegel's belief that it is only by virtue of the Incarnation, only by virtue of the fact that time does indeed reflect eternity, that we can dialectically surmount the division, alienation, and sin which block the passage to full reconciliation and atonement in the form of a full-fledged Christian community? But for those who do not believe that God has entered history in the form of the God-Man, for those who continue to look to the future for the coming of the kingdom, positive forgiveness appears unavailable. Just like Abraham in Hegel's depiction of the Jewish condition, those who reject the Trinity are condemned to wander the barren deserts without hope of returning to the place whence they came.

Giving Economy a Chance

If observed from this perspective, it becomes somewhat easier to analyze Milbank's stance in relation to Derrida. To recall, Milbank contends that postmodernism generally, and Derrida in particular, opts for a nihilistic brand of secularism which espouses the view that out of nothing we came and into nothing we shall go. Hence, the pure positive forgiveness of which Milbank speaks is rejected in favor of a purely human form of forgiveness which resolves in negativity, insecurity, despair, and alienation. But to accuse Derrida of propounding such a view is quite simply a mistake. For Derrida has never spoken in these negative terms; he has never, that is, declared himself on the side of those who champion either neo-Nietzschean nihilism or postmodern relativism. Tirelessly, he insists that deconstruction is neither nihilism nor negativity, but affirmation and hope. It is true, of course, that Derrida would consider problematic (for all the reasons I shall give below) the type of Trinitarian position to which Milbank holds, but it in no way follows that because of this he is a knight of infinite despair. For Derrida is one of those individuals who serves to complicate and confound Milbank's stark and rigid dichotomy between Christianity and secularism/nihilism. He is one of those for whom the lines of demarcation are not so clearly drawn.

In his previous writings, Milbank has described Derrida's work as "unregenerate Hegelianism."[28] I consider this to be a rather accurate description of what Derrida is up to, even if I don't agree with the spirit in which it is employed in that context. For, as I have argued elsewhere,[29] Derrida's entire enterprise has been an attempt to make trouble for the logic of self-presence and closure which characterizes Hegel's dialectics, the same type of self-presence and closure which I am arguing is a significant feature of Milbank's oeuvre. But for all his criticism of teleology and the dialectics of closure, Derrida is still a Hegelian insofar as he considers Hegel to have been correct in assuming that identity is predicated upon difference and also by virtue of the fact that he too considers history, unlike those who quest for transcendental or metaphysical purity, to be central to our self-understanding . More important, however, it is Hegel's emphasis on the pivotal role of "recollection" or "memory" and the way in which it is employed by Derrida which most interests me here. For it is in and through their respective theories on the function, role, and power of *memory* that the differences between radical orthodoxy and deconstruction become clearly identifiable.

On my reading, as argued above, Milbank considers memory to be that faculty which permits us access to eternity as it is reflected in temporality. This suggests that it is by virtue of our recollection of the God-Man that we can breach the rupture between finitude and the infinite. In other words, through the forgiveness of sins the God-Man provides the occasion for a reconciliation of the temporal and eternal components of the self. Even though, as we have seen, Milbank considers it impossible for us to offer forgiveness in the name of the dead, for the reason that countless victims have been lost to memory, he nevertheless believes that we can, through a Trinitarian ontology, tap into a divine source, recover or re-member it, as it were, from the vagaries of time and chance. While we might forget the victim, we cannot forget the occasion of the God-Man—the *sovereign victim*. Either we accept that we can indeed surmount the alienation which temporality necessitates through the forgiveness of sins or we surrender ourselves, like Abraham on Moriah, to an impersonal void.

We can move toward a greater understanding of the issues here by attending to a chapter in Milbank's recent book, *The Word Made Strange*,[30] in which he severely criticizes Derrida's distinction between speech and writing as well as his distinction between writing and "the Book." For Milbank,

> Derrida's written difference, defined by its possibility of surviving the death of every speaker, is necessarily a deferred difference, a difference that never arrives, that is therefore nothing, no-difference. For a regime of the primacy of writing is perforce a disembodied, ahistorical regime, in which sign does not finally decay along with its speaker; in which, therefore, sign is falsely hypostasized in abstraction from figured event, and construed as a "pure value" which never can be, and is in consequence "nothing."[31]

In analyzing Derrida's use of the distinction between speech and writing in such literal terms, Milbank misses the more general point which is being made here: In employing this distinction, Derrida is endeavoring to drive home the point that throughout its history, philosophy, qua metaphysics–onto-theology, has tended to privilege the notion of self-presence and purity above a notion of selfhood which admits of loss and contamination. The metaphor of speech is used to convey the idea that in hearing itself speak, the self is fully present to itself, while the metaphor of writing is used to convey the idea that any attempt to circumscribe speech within a frame or between borders (in a "Book") so as to keep it safe is bound to fail. For once I open my mouth, I draw on a language which is not my own, but which is an admixture of many different languages and tongues. My language, Derrida insists, is not *my* language, but the language of the other, of the other who inhabits me. Quite simply, languages and traditions have a history, a long and convoluted history which is by no means transparent. All traditions and languages are multi-layered and multi-textured; they contain within themselves voices which have long since been repressed by the weight of the dominant tongue or the dominant tradition. Hence, there is no *one* tradition or language, no *one* lineage or history, but traditions within traditions, languages within languages.

The consequence of all this, for Derrida, is that even while speaking, the self is always already disjointed, always already somewhat lost (*destin-errant*). For it is never the case that we can twist free of our sociolinguistic-cum-historical moorings; we can never, that is, fully, trace our origins through a systematic unraveling of contexts which have been occulted either by the dominant tradition or simply through the wear and tear of time. No grand narrative, myth, or supreme plot can account for the fact that, whether we like it or not, our past is composed of multifarious contexts, all of which have bled into one another to such an extent that even the most skilled historian, archaeologist, anthropologist, or geologist cannot hope to comprehensively disentangle them. All we have to work with are signs and traces, archives and museums, bones and ashes, testimonies and narratives. As such, memory—personal or communal—delivers a past which is always already, to appropriate one of Derrida's most misunderstood slogans, "under erasure," or a past which has always already begun to decay. Traces, signs, and testimonies do not afford us full access to a world lost from view, to the mind or intentions of others whose only remnant is ash, or to those whose marks or traces never made it into the archive.

The importance of this for Derrida lies in the fact that any community which declares itself pure all the way down has lost sight of the fact that its identity is ineluctably contaminated from within, that it contains within itself traces of strangers and foreigners. So any community which attempts to reinforce its identity by insisting that it can trace its origins, or that it can, by way of its sacred books, take aim at the heart of the real or the true, is impervious to the fact that books have a history and a context, that they too had authors who were situated in a particular sociolinguistic framework. Hence, books demand interpretation; they demand to be read and re-read not as documents which contain within themselves the full and pure intention of their authors but as traces of a context bound up with innumerable other contexts. Consequently, because communities are generally founded on myths, stories, and books, they too cry out for interpretation, they too summon us to look beyond or beneath their borders and frames for the marks and traces of the other both within (the suppressed other) and without (the excluded other). As such, the identity of a community is always already incised and permeated by difference. It is a community or an identity which is plagued by gaps in its memory and haunted by the ghosts of those who were either colonized, expelled, or killed in its name. So while communities might give the impression of being completely organic, they are in fact as disjointed and as fractured as any other entity which attempts to erect borders in an effort to block the exile. All communities are inhabited by other communities and identities.

What drives Derrida's deconstruction, thus, is a passion to keep us sensitive to the unavoidability of context, to the fact that all contexts are inhabited by others and that because of such contamination the notion of the absolute origin is undermined. His aim is to encourage us to move beyond the dominant readings of our past, to look between the lines of our sacred books in an effort to identify the traces of those whose voices were censored, those who were denied entry. Deconstruction, in other words, wants to sensitize us to the faceless and nameless who have been buried beneath the weight of officially sanctioned history. It asks us to keep watch for signs of a past which has never been present to us in the form of a grand narrative.

It is incorrect of Milbank to suggest, therefore, that Derrida's "written difference" is a "nothing," for such a view entirely misconstrues the fact that, for Derrida, "writing" equates to the marks and inscriptions of those who have been victimized in the quest for purity and full self-presence, even when such marks have been, either intentionally or unintentionally, turned to ash or cinders. If, as I have claimed, the driving passion of deconstruction is to alert us to the muffled calls and cries of the faceless, which, in turn, alert us to the poverty of memory, then I think it is fair to say that Derrida's "written difference" amounts to an affirmation of the otherness which has been written out of, or elided from, consciousness, or of the muted and censored difference which lies deep within the depths of the self.

Every country, state, and context, argues Derrida, has its own "economy of memory"—its own way of being economical with memory. Such an economy is predicated upon "several layers of forgetting," which issues in a "capitalization of silence." Deconstruction is an attempt to initiate "a movement towards the liberation of memory," toward the liberation of "specters" or "ghosts." It is an attempt to give them a future, to let them come again (*revenir*). For deconstruction is all about giving hope to those whose time is out of mind. The book (historical, religious, political, philosophical), thus, has no end, for there is always the possibility of dissecting it further, of uncovering hidden intentions, of reinterpreting it in the light of new findings and newly disclosed marks. So, for Derrida, "the axiom of deconstruction—the basis on which it has always set itself in motion," is justice—justice for those who have fallen between the lines of the page or for those who have been exiled beyond the borders of the book. Such is what links deconstruction "to the priceless dignity of otherness."[32] This "work of mourning," the work of trying desperately to keep the promise of hope alive, is what a deconstructive meditation on writing sets out to do:

> To meditate on writing, which is to say also on effacement—and the production of writing is also the production of a system of effacement, the trace is at once what inscribes and what effaces—is to meditate constantly on what renders unreadable or what is rendered unreadable. . . . But there is also the unreadability that stems from the violence of foreclosure, exclusion, all of history being a conflictual field of forces in which it is a matter of making unreadable, excluding, of positing by excluding, of imposing a dominant force by excluding, that is to say, not only by marginalizing, by setting aside the victims, but also by doing so in such a way that no trace remains of the victims, so that no one can testify to the fact that they are victims or so that they cannot even testify to it themselves. The meditation on writing is a meditation on this *absolute weakness*, the weakness of what you are calling the victim.[33]

To meditate upon writing, therefore, is not to surrender oneself to a "nothing" or to an impersonal void. It is to open oneself to one's heritage, to come to terms with the fact that "memory is not just the opposite of forgetting," but it is "tied to the future and not only to the past."[34] It is to contemplate the possibility that, as Derrida likes to say, we have forgotten that we have forgotten, that there has been a "destruction of memory," that the name of the victim has been effaced.[35]

Now I think the implications of all this for Milbank's brand of radical orthodoxy, and for his related belief in the possibility of pure forgiveness, are quite significant, so significant, in fact, that I believe this is the reason why he continues to read Derrida's "speech-writing" distinction so literally. For if Derrida's analysis of memory holds, the belief that we can somehow, in a manner analogous to Hegel, return to the divine source through the mediation of the God-Man is complicated somewhat. This is so not because at bottom there is nothing but simply because scripture, like any other text, has a context and a history. In saying this, Derrida is not out to destroy Christianity, or any other religion for that matter, but to make it a little more honest about its origins, to make it face up to the possibility that it might just have forgotten that it has forgotten. For example, if placed in context, it is probable that much of what we read in scripture cannot be taken literally. For the historical Jesus scholars, as well as many contemporary theologians, have taught us to be highly circumspect with regard to the *facts* of the "Book"; in reading between the lines on the page, they have exposed us to the many whose accounts were pilloried and excluded because they challenged the official version of events.

They have taught us that most of the events of the New Testament do not correspond to actuality, that they were manufactured after the fact in an effort to "protect the faith." They have, moreover, highlighted the fact that the so-called "religions of the Book" have presided over a catastrophe of memory by "imposing a dominant force . . . so that no one can testify to the fact that they are victims."[36] What these Jesus scholars tend to emphasize above all else is the Jewishness of Jesus, the fact that he never set out to cause trouble for Judaism but only to revivify it. His social teachings were geared to bring about a new kingdom for the Jewish people and to soften the hearts of his fellow rabbis. It must not be forgotten that Jesus liked to be called "Rabbi." This Jesus—Jesus the Jewish rabbi—is the one which the deconstructive techniques of the scholars have exposed, few traces of whom can be found in the "Book."

This, of course, is not to say that deconstruction, as John D. Caputo repeatedly reminds us, is a cold atheism. Due to the fact that it calls our attention to the difficulties involved in recollecting and memorizing the origin, it can hardly then definitively declare that there is no God. Like the rest of us, all Derrida can do is take what Enda McDonagh has so powerfully called the "risk of God."[37] Like Abraham, he hears a voice summoning him from the darkness, from the pit of his psyche, a voice which cannot be traced. To respond to such a voice, to risk responding to its demands, requires courage and faith. For one will never know who or what is calling, or where one might be led if one chooses to respond to the call. The trials of responsibility go hand in hand with fear and trembling.

Unlike Milbank, who thinks that *pure* forgiveness is possible through the redeeming power of the God-Man, through the occasion of the resurrection when fissure and rupture in the form of sin are healed, and when the self becomes one with itself through the intercession of the Holy Spirit, Derrida, for all the reasons proffered above, can only hope against hope that, like Abraham, he too will one day make it home. For he dreams of a day when the work of mourning will come to an end. Such is Derrida's impossible dream: the hope that one day justice for all the ghosts who summon us to mourn them will be realized. It is an *impossible* dream because the work of mourning is interminable and the meditation on writing is a passion which cannot be assuaged—that is, of course, unless you have forgotten that you have indeed forgotten. To try to recover oneself from the ruins of memory—even the memory of the God-Man, given what deconstructive analysis has taught us about Jesus the Jew—or to return to one's roots and origins, is to pray and beg for the impossible. It is an attempt, as Derrida said to me in the course of a recent interview, to "make possible what I am sure is impossible."[38]

But let me reiterate: What inspires deconstruction is the hope against hope—the passionate *faith*—that one day the impossible might become possible, that the Messiah may show up, that one day the promise of my heritage may be fulfilled. This is why Derrida begins the first chapter of *Given Time*—a text which has everything to do with resurrection, reconciliation, and forgiveness—with the words: "Let us begin by the impossible."[39] For, pace Milbank and radical orthodoxy, Derrida's work does not resolve in hopelessness and despair, but, as I said at the outset, in affirmation and longing. He does not say "Let us be content with mere possibility, with the here and now," but "Let the desire for *the* impossible impassion us." The responsibility of deconstruction is to try to go one better than mere possibility. Its aim is to teleologically suspend all laws of equivalence in the name of what exceeds the order of the same.

But this does not mean, as Milbank and others suggest, that deconstruction does not have preferences, that it is a pure affirmation of otherness which strives to annul all sameness, presence, or self-possession. As I have tried to make clear, deconstruction always works from within a heritage; it insists that one cannot entirely escape from one's tradition, home, culture, or language. One belongs from the very outset to an *oikonomia*—to a home or an economy which is subject to laws and regulations. So the first "principle"—a word Derrida would be loathe to use, but one which I shall employ for the sake of convenience—of deconstruction is that we cannot evade the law of the home—that we have a self, an identity, a history, a family—but that this inheritance cannot be traced back to its origins. We are, to a certain extent, to invoke Julia Kristeva's charming expression, "strangers to ourselves."

The work of mourning is an impossible attempt to recover this loss as best we can. It is an impossible attempt to welcome the strangers back home—impossible because they are, alas, dead, but also because some are not even inscribed in memory. But this should not deter or inhibit us from probing further, or from desiring beyond desire that, at some point, a trace or mark may come into view and, as a consequence, the strange will become less alien. While I cannot, in other words, escape the law of the home, I can endeavor nevertheless to make it a little less uninviting and a lot more welcoming to those who challenge my rigid sense of identity, self, and context in the name of an opening of the borders, in the name of hospitality.

This is why in his conference paper at Villanova, "To Forgive: the Unforgivable and the Imprescriptible," Derrida argues, pace Jankélévitch, that "there is only forgiveness, if there is such a thing, of the un-forgivable. Thus, forgiveness, if there is such a thing, is not possible, it does not exist as possible, it only exists by exempting itself from the law of the possible, by impossibilizing itself, so to speak, and in the infinite endurance of the im-possible as impossible; and this is what it would have in common with the gift."[40] The big difference between Milbank and Derrida here is that for the former the aporias of forgiveness outlined above can be surmounted through the Incarnation. Even those whose marks and traces have been erased are brought to life again, are resurrected through the sovereign victim. For Milbank, the work of mourning is indeed interminable unless divine forgiveness can be availed of, unless the law of the home, the *oikonomia*, is fully functioning. There is no uncertainty or undecidability in Milbank, no fear and trembling, no faith. The manifold layers of history do not present an obstacle to full self-recovery, for the wounds and scars of temporality are salved, healed, and purified by the blood of Golgotha.

What worries Derrida about all of this is the fact that it is predicated upon the belief that the impossible can become possible, that the catastrophe of memory can be overcome. For if the impossible becomes possible, the passage to the other—the other deep within myself whose time has yet to come—is blocked off. In saying that we can avail of pure or divine forgiveness, Milbank is overlooking the fact that what we call "the divine" is no less contextual, no less historical, and therefore no less deconstructable than anything else. While Derrida dreams and hopes that there might be a savior, he cannot say for sure that there is one. To do so would be to destroy faith, to confuse it with knowledge. It would be to give a concrete messianism the edge over its rivals, thus insulating itself against any unforeseen ghosts, any unnoticed traces, and any smoldering cinders. It would be to block up the home, to secure the self against foreign invasion. In such circumstances the fully conditional law of the home would prevail:

> That the without-ground of this impossible can nevertheless take place is . . . the ruin or the absolute ashes, the threat that must be thought, and, why not, exorcised yet again. To exorcise not in order to chase away the ghosts, but this time to grant them the right, if it means making them come back alive, as *revenants* who would no longer be *revenants*, but as other arrivants to whom a hospitable memory or promise must offer welcome— without certainty, ever, that they present themselves as such. Not in order to grant them the right in this sense but out of a concern for justice. Present existence or essence has never been the condition, object, or the *thing* (*chose*) of justice.[41]

Derrida tries always to situate himself between what is possible and the impossible, between the conditional and the unconditional. He endeavors, that is, to ensure that the law of the *oikonomia* does not become too conditional and rigid by exposing it to the unconditional demand. To begin by the impossible, thus, is a way of sensitizing to the fact that our current traditions and institutions can never acquire absolute status, that they can always be reformed in the light of unforeseen appeals for justice. To have a passion for the impossible or the unconditional means that you desire what you know to be impossible—due to the claim which language and tradition make upon you—so as to prevent the conditional from becoming *too* conditional. So when Derrida says that *pure* forgiveness is impossible and that this is what it has in common with the gift, he is simply saying that because forgiveness by its very nature must be afforded unconditionally, and because I cannot actually grant forgiveness without *wanting* or *desiring* to do so, thus reconciling myself to and domesticating the other (by drawing her into an economy), forgiveness is always already annulled. Like the gift in Derrida's analysis, once "I" *want* to forgive or once "I" *desire* forgiveness, I draw the other into a circle of exchange in which there is a remission of *debt* through the *giving* of pardon (*don*, gift), hence nullifying the gift. In saying that something is unforgivable, therefore, Jankélévitch is insisting that only under the most extreme conditions will forgiveness be afforded. But for Derrida, what Jankélévitch is here referring to as forgiveness in no way resembles forgiveness. For the more conditions, the less forgiveness.

To say that I have been reconciled with an other is to say that our differences have been surmounted, that we have balanced our payments and put the economy in order. But when I am engaged in the work of mourning, I can never say that I have been reconciled with those who summon me from the embers of history, for the trace bespeaks loss and disjointedness. Milbank agrees, and that is why he insists that we must have divine forgiveness. But Derrida insists, on the other hand, that because we cannot rise above context, divine forgiveness is an impossible dream. For it would be the height of injustice to say that mourning the dead reconciles me to them *in full*. But the dream that someday I may be reconciled to them is what keeps us mourning all the harder. It is what prompts us to keep digging further and further beneath the surface, even if we are simply sifting through ashes and dust. Indeed, to say that because there is a "supreme victim" pure forgiveness and absolute reconciliation is possible would be to say that now that we have been forgiven, and now that we have the capacity to forgive, we need no longer mourn. Mourning, however, is a process in which *singular* traces and marks enjoin us testify on behalf of *proper names*. It is a process whereby we try as best we can, given the constraints of temporality and history, to bear witness to individuals and to the memory of broken lives. Even though we know it to be impossible, we try indefatigably to bring them home. If Milbank's resolution to the five aporias amounts to a forgetting of proper names and of singularities, Derrida's notion of impossible forgiveness keeps hope for singular victims alive.

So for Derrida, it is always a case of beginning by the impossible, of desiring what you cannot have so as to keep the self desiring beyond desire, or to keep the self from closing in upon itself. It is never a case of surrendering oneself to the other, of becoming one with the other, as Levinas instructs, to the point of substitution—for that is the impossible—but of coming to terms with the fact while I cannot escape my heritage (*oikonomia*), I can, however, try to keep the borders sufficiently porous and permeable. It is a case of trying for what Milbank thinks is possible while knowing all the while that self-recovery on such a grand scale is beyond the capacity of a poor existing individual who has no means of tapping into an eternal source. It is a matter of understanding that mourning is not forgiveness, for the reason that it is undertaken by a subject or a self who wants and *desires* pardon for the victimhood which a meditation on writing reveals. For once forgiveness is sought, as Derrida asks, "Is there not the beginning of a reappropriation, a mourning process, a process of redemption, of a transfiguring calculation which, through language, the sharing of language . . . rushes toward the economy of a reconciliation that causes the wrong itself to be simply forgotten or annihilated?"[42]

It is a matter, therefore, of moving between the dream of absolutely unconditional forgiveness, "which ultimately should even be able to do without repentance and the request for forgiveness," and conditional forgiveness, "which is inscribed within a set of conditions of all kinds." For, as Derrida reminds us again and again, "the unconditional and the conditional are, certainly, absolutely heterogeneous, and this forever, on either side of a limit, but they are also indissociable."[43] In other words, the desire for pure forgiveness serves to prevent conditional forgiveness from becoming simply a judicial pardon, a situation in which forgiveness is given only on the condition that the accused appeals for clemency, or *gives* of his time, or shows signs that he has repented. Such a sphere is governed by what Paul Ricoeur calls "the logic of equivalence"—the logic of give and take, or the logic of retribution—as distinct from the "logic of superabundance"—the absurd logic of forgiveness in which clemency is offered without condition.

Self-Sacrifice versus Hospitable Narcissisms

We are now in a better position to understand why, I think, Milbank's questions to Derrida in the course of the Villanova roundtable were somewhat off the mark. When Milbank asks if Derrida is in danger of becoming too moralistic because he insists on "pure absolute self-sacrifice" or because he demands that we strive after "a very pure gift or very pure forgiveness," he shows that he has profoundly misunderstood Derrida's work on the gift and on forgiveness, a misunderstanding which has serious implications for the way in which radical orthodoxy interprets Derrida across the board. For, as I have argued, the whole point of Derrida's discourse is to suggest that "pure absolute self-sacrifice" is impossible, that no matter how hard I try I can never abandon my heritage, my language, or my tradition. I can, to repeat, never escape the law or the economy of the home. But I can, by keeping the impossible dream alive, prevent this law from becoming an obstacle to those who do not come under its jurisdiction. Pure gifts and pure forgiveness are, for Derrida, impossible. This is why he urges that "without a movement of narcissistic reappropriation, the relation to the other would be absolutely destroyed, it would be destroyed in advance." "The relation to the other," he continues, "even if it remains asymmetrical, open, without possible reappropriation—must trace a movement of reappropriation in the image of oneself for love to be possible."[44] Without a sense of self how could I love the other? In other words, how could I be a host if I did not have a home?

On my reading, thus, it is because Derrida insists on the fact that *absolute* self-sacrifice is impossible that he cannot be accused, as he is by Milbank, of wanting to give to the other to the point where he neglects his own. As such, it is wrong of Milbank to accuse Derrida of "masochism," a masochism which is the inevitable result of secularity. If, for Milbank, the religious disposition is one in which I will give away what I have to the other if there is not enough to go around but one in which I also hope that "I will be able to eat alongside the other, too," then Derrida is, pace Milbank, "religious beyond the ethical." He embraces the sort of "hyper-ethical" position that Milbank accuses him of neglecting in favor of moralistic indifference. Derrida's reply to these charges in the roundtable sums up nicely what I have been trying claim on his behalf in the course of this paper:

> You might call this indifference, but if you think that the only moral duty you owe is the duty to the people—or the animals—with whom you have affinity, kinship, friendship, neighborhood, brotherhood, then, you can imagine the consequences of that. I, of course, have preferences. . . . But I do not have a good conscience about that. I know that if I transform this into a general rule it would be the ruin of ethics. . . . So when I give a preference to my cat, which I do, that will not prevent me from having some remorse for the cat dying or starving next door, or . . . for all the people on earth who are starving and dying today. So you cannot prevent me from having a bad conscience, and that is the main motivation of my ethics and politics.[45]

If John D. Caputo were to ask me, therefore, to tell him "in a nutshell" what Derrida is endeavoring to say throughout his paper on forgiveness in this volume, I think I might paraphrase what Derrida himself says so incisively of the gift elsewhere:[46] *Know* still what forgiving wants to say, know how to forgive, know what you want and want to say when you forgive, know why you intend to forgive, know how forgiveness annuls itself when it is drawn into an economy, commit yourself even if commitment is the destruction of (pure) forgiveness by (conditional) forgiveness, give economy its chance. For, finally, the overrunning of the circle (*oikonomia*) by forgiveness, if there is any, does not lead to a simple, ineffable exteriority that would be transcendent and without relation. It is this unconditional forgiveness, this exteriority, that sets the circle going, that puts the economy in motion. It is this unconditional forgiveness that engages in the circle and makes it turn. We ought not to think of the distinction between unconditional and conditional forgiveness in terms of a simple opposition. They are indissociable. Like unconditional hospitality, justice beyond the law, and the democracy to come, pure forgiveness is the stuff that dreams are made of. Without such dreams all economy would simply freeze over, and the promise to those for whom no tears are spilled would be broken beyond repair.

NOTES

1. John Milbank, Catherine Pickstock, and Graham Ward, eds., *Radical Orthodoxy: A New Theology* (London: Routledge, 1999), p. 1.
2. Ibid., p. 2.
3. See John Milbank, "Postmodern Critical Augustinianism: A Short Summa in Forty-two Responses to Unasked Questions," in *The Postmodern God: A Theological Reader*, ed. Graham Ward (Oxford: Blackwell Publishers, 1997), pp. 265–278.
4. Ibid., p. 265.

5. Ibid., p. 267.

6. Ibid., p. 268.

7. Ibid., p. 266.

8. *Radical Orthodoxy*, p. 1.

9. John Milbank, "Forgiveness and Incarnation," this volume, pp. 97–98.

10. Ibid., pp. 97–98.

11. Ibid., pp. 98–99.

12. Ibid., pp. 98–99.

13. Ibid., p. 99.

14. Ibid.

15. See Paul Ricoeur, *Time and Narrative*, vol. I (Chicago: University of Chicago Press, 1984).

16. Milbank, "Forgiveness and Incarnation," this volume, p. 101.

17. Ibid., pp. 102–103.

18. Ibid., pp. 102–104.

19. Ibid., p. 104.

20. See primarily Chapter 4 of *The Gift of Death* (Chicago: University of Chicago Press, 1995), entitled "Toute autre est tout autre," pp. 82–115. For a remarkable reflection on this text, see John D. Caputo, *The Prayers and Tears of Jacques Derrida* (Bloomington: Indiana University Press, 1997), pp. 188–211.

21. Emmanuel Levinas, "Existence and Ethics," in *Kierkegaard: A Critical Reader*, ed. Jonathan Ree and Jane Chamberlain (Oxford: Blackwell, 1998), p. 34.

22. Milbank, "Forgiveness and Incarnation," pp. 104–105.

23. Ibid., p. 105.

24. Ibid., p. 107.

25. Ibid., p. 109.

26. G. W. F. Hegel, "The Spirit of Christianity and Its Fate," in *On Christianity: Early Theological Writings by Friedrich Hegel* (Gloucester, Mass.: Peter Smith, 1970), pp. 192–301.

27. Milbank, "Postmodern Critical Augustinianism," p. 266.

28. John Milbank, *The Word Made Strange: Theology, Language, Culture* (Blackwell: Oxford University Press, 1997), p. 61.

29. See Mark Dooley, *The Politics of Exodus: Soren Kierkegaard's Ethics of Responsibility* (New York: Fordham University Press, 2001); "Kierkegaard on the Margins of Philosophy," *Philosophy and Social Criticism* 21, no. 2 (March 1995): 95–107; "Murder on Moriah: A Paradoxical Representation," *Philosophy Today* 39 (Spring 1995): 67–83; "Playing on the Pyramid: Resituating the 'Self' in Kierkegaard and Derrida," *Imprimatur* 1, nos. 2/3 (Spring 1996): 151–162; "Risking Responsibility: A Politics of the Emigré," in *Kierkegaard: The Self and Society*, ed. George Pattison and Steven Shakespeare (New York: Macmillan, 1998), pp. 65–89; "The Politics of Exodus: 'Hospitality' in Derrida, Kierkegaard, and Levinas," in *The International Kierkegaard Commentary: Works of Love*, ed. Robert L. Perkins (Macon: Mercer University Press, 1999), pp. 125–142.

30. Milbank, "Pleonasm, Speech and Writing," in *The Word Made Strange*, pp. 55–83.

31. Ibid., p. 70.

32. "The Deconstruction of Actuality: An Interview with Jacques Derrida," *Radical Philosophy* 68 (Autumn 1994): 36. As with so many of his interviews, this one with

Brigitte Sohm, Cristina de Peretti, Stephane Douailler, Patrice Vermeren, and Emile Malet is a lucid and insightful guide to the many complex issues which characterize Derrida's prodigious output over forty years.

33. "Passages—from Traumatism to Promise," in *Points . . . Interviews 1974–1994*, ed. Elisabeth Weber (Stanford: Stanford University Press, 1995), p. 389.

34. Ibid., p. 383.

35. Ibid., p. 389.

36. Ibid.

37. Enda McDonagh, "Friendship, Marriage, and the Risk of God," *INTAMS Review* 5/1 (1999).

38. "The Becoming Possible of the Impossible: An Interview with Jacques Derrida," in *From Aquinas to Derrida: John D. Caputo in Focus*, ed. Mark Dooley (forthcoming).

39. Jacques Derrida, *Given Time I: Counterfeit Money* (Chicago: University of Chicago Press, 1992).

40. Jacques Derrida, "To Forgive: The Unforgivable and the Imprescriptible," this volume, p. 48. See also John D. Caputo, "The Time of Giving, the Time of Forgiving" (forthcoming); his excellent discussion of forgiveness in both Hannah Arendt and Derrida in both *Against Ethics: Contributions to a Poetics of Obligation with Constant Reference to Deconstruction* (Bloomington: Indiana University Press, 1993), pp. 106–112; and "Reason, History, and a Little Madness: Towards an Ethics of the Kingdom," in *Questioning Ethics: Contemporary Debates in Philosophy*, ed. Richard Kearney and Mark Dooley (London: Routledge, 1999), pp. 84–104. See also Paul Ricoeur, "Reflections on a New Ethos for Europe," in *Paul Ricoeur: The Hermeneutics of Action*, ed. Richard Kearney (London: SAGE, 1996), pp. 3–14; and "Memory and Forgetting" in *Questioning Ethics*, pp. 5–11, as well as our interview with Ricoeur, "Imagination, Testimony, and Trust: A Dialogue with Paul Ricoeur," also published in *Questioning Ethics*, pp. 12–17. While there are differences between Ricoeur and Derrida on the notion of "forgiveness," these differences ought not to obscure the striking convergences which are also very apparent, especially as Ricoeur also situates forgiveness within "the logic of the gift."

41. Jacques Derrida, *Specters of Marx: The State of the Debt, the Work of Mourning, and the New International* (New York: Routledge, 1994), p. 175.

42. Derrida, "To Forgive," pp. 45–46.

43. Ibid., p. 45.

44. Derrida, "There is No One Narcissism," in *Points . . .* , p. 199.

45. "On Forgiveness: A Roundtable with Jacques Derrida," this volume.

46. Derrida, *Given Time*, pp. 30–31. The figure of the circle has long been a feature of Derrida's work. From the very beginning, he has been preoccupied with the way in which the relationship with the other is predicated on a circle of exchange in which the self gives of itself to the other only so as to reappropriate in full the gain from the investment. This, of course, is the dialectical logic of giving and receiving which lies at the heart of Hegel's systematics, a logic which I am suggesting Milbank shares. In Hegel, the loss of oneself, the gift of oneself to the other, is always negated through a recuperation of the loss. The self, thus, is resurrected or reconciled to itself *via* the other. Consequently, Hegel's theory of self-becoming runs on a *circle* of exchange, in which what I give is returned to me in equal measure. As Hegel repeatedly argues, the end is the beginning and the beginning is the end. Such a notion of full self-recovery is

what set the wheels of deconstruction turning. This is why I have always felt that it is in the reader's best interest to approach Derrida as someone who is trying to thwart the logic of circularity inherent in Hegel before turning to the way in which deconstruction goes to work on the logic of presence in both Husserl and Heidegger. For the motifs of anamnesis, of resurrection (*relever, aufheben*), and of reclaiming the origin through a circular recovery of expenditure are typically Hegelian gestures. In contradistinction to this rather "restricted economy," (*oikonomia*—homecoming), Derrida proposes a general economy which does not seek a full return on its investments. He grants to Hegel that it is only by virtue of the economy between self and other that self-awareness and possession is possible. But he then tries to ensure that the economy does not close in upon itself by insisting that full self-reappropriation is impossible because the self is, from the outset, cut from the origin. Derrida inhabits the circle, thus, in an effort to show how its beginning and its end are incommensurable. Due to the fact that we have always already forgotten that we have forgotten, and due also to the fact that we cannot cleanse ourselves of our acculturation, the self is irreparably wounded. This explains further why the motif of "circumcision" is so central to the Derridean text: for Derrida, the circle of exchange, the circle of absolute recovery, is always already severed and cut.

For a more detailed explication of these rather complex matters, and for a fuller account of the way in which Derrida deals with the Hegelian notion of absolute returns through a negation of death, see my "Murder on Moriah" and "Playing on the Pyramid."

PART II. GOD

The God Who May Be

Richard Kearney

Introduction

In Exodus 3:14, Moses meets his maker. Leading his flock to the desert mountain of Horeb, he is summoned by a voice from the midst of a flaming bush. From this strange fire which burns without being consumed, the voice calls and Moses answers "Here I am." The voice bids him stand back and take off his sandals. And revealing himself as the Lord of his ancestors—of Abraham, Isaac, and Jacob—God says he has heard the cry of his people and has come to deliver them from bondage.

But it is not enough for Moses. Standing there under the midday sun, he surely wonders if this is not some mirage, some hoax. Perhaps the voice is an inner demon prompting him to a fit of madness. After all, wasn't it just such a dark angel who appeared to Jacob late one night and shattered his hip before disclosing the name of Israel? And wasn't it another strange voice which summoned Abraham to Mount Moriah to murder his own son? That was a cruel command. A trick, of course. Only a test of faith. But still, he must tread carefully. Moses isn't quite sure he wants to do business with such a mercurial God: one who sends visitors to maim you in the middle of the night and commandeers blood sacrifice (even if he isn't really serious). Every angel is terrible in a way, isn't it?

Moses longed for a God of justice and liberty. A God who would remain constant and faithful to his people. But who was he to question God—if this really was God and not some counterfeit conjured by his dizzy mind? He would have to proceed cautiously. So instead of asking straight out Who are you?, Moses puts it another way, the other way around: "Who am I?" "Who am I," he inquires, that I should go unto Pharaoh and lead the children of Israel out of Egypt? To which God replies with a second, though still indirect, revelation of himself: "I will be with Thee." The ancestral God is now declaring himself a faithful God—one who will stand by Moses as he embarks on his mission to a promised land.

Still Moses is unsure, but he is beginning to like the sound of things. There is maybe more to this deity than meets the eye, he muses. Something more than the tribal divinity of his forebears, a hint of something new. Not just a God of ancestry, it seems, but a God of advent: a promise for the future.

Emboldened by this surmise, Moses asks God, one last time, to reveal himself, to say who he truly is, to disclose his real name. Feet still bare on the hot sand, Moses takes a small step forward. He wipes perspiration from his forehead, and addresses the burning bush: "When I come unto the children of Israel and shall say unto them, The God of your fathers hath sent me unto you; and they shall say to me, What is his name? what shall I say to them?" (Exodus 3:13). To which God responds, bolder and brasher this time—his third and final reply: ʿehyeh ʿaser ʿehyeh. The King James version reads: "And God said unto Moses, I AM THAT I AM: and he said, Thus shalt thou say unto the children of Israel, I AM hath sent me unto you." And lest there be any lingering doubt, God adds the binding promise: "This is my name forever and this is my memorial unto all generations" (Exodus 3:15).

So there we have it. Holy Moses, a tired shepherd with a price on his head, dusty and parched after days of wandering about with his father-in-law's sheep in the desert, is confronted with a fire that doesn't burn out and a voice that answers his questions with a riddle! If Moses is to lead his people out of bondage in Egypt, he needs to know the credentials of the one who speaks to him. He must be able to convince his own people, after all, that this God is a better bet than the magic deity of Pharaoh and the Egyptians. So how does God respond to Moses? How does he reassure His bewildered shepherd, racked with doubt and insecurity? He reassures by repeating Himself, by not really replying at all, turning his answer into a tautology, an enigmatic turn of phrase which not only puzzles Moses but all those after him who profess the Name: ʿehyeh ʿaser ʿehyeh—I am who am!

This formula, translated into Greek as ego eimi ho on and into Latin as ego sum qui sum, was to fascinate commentators for centuries. Talmudists and exegetes, mullahs and prophets, Church Fathers and angelic doctors, theologians and philosophers, have pored over this riddling Name and offered countless conjectures. And the riddle remains. In Exodus 3:14, God declares his own incognito and presents himself in terms of a divine self-definition which cannot be defined. Unlike other passages in the Torah where God reveals himself in the position of the divine "I" ("I Yahweh"), this passage is rare in that it adds the copulative "is." Indeed it adds it twice, first in terms of 'ehyeh—I am—and then by adding 'aser 'ehyeh: I am who am. The tetragrammaton thus appears to partake in the semantic field of the verb traditionally rendered as "to be." How best to translate this verb is a complex matter dividing scholars throughout the ages and resisting final consensus. In more contemporary idiom, it compels us to wonder if God is here reducing himself to a metaphysics of presence or rendering himself immune to it for good and all.

In what follows, I will discuss two main traditions of interpretation under the headings ontological and eschatological before offering a third or median option which I will call onto-eschatological. My ultimate suggestion is that we might do better to reinterpret the God of Exodus 3 as neither being nor as non-being but as the possibility of either, that is, as May-Be. 'Ehyeh 'aser 'ehyeh could thus be rendered as "I-Am-Who-May-Be." That is, in a word, my wager.

1. The Ontological Reading

From the outset, the Greeks rendered Exodus 3 in terms of the verb "to be," or *einai*. Inheriting the Hellenic formula *ego eimi ho on*—I am the one who is—Augustine and the Latins claimed there was no fundamental difference between this *ego sum qui sum* and the *esse* of metaphysics. The Exodic formula was considered by early and medieval Christian theologians to be the highest way of saying *vere esse, ipsum esse*, that is, Being-itself, timeless, immutable, incorporeal, understood as the subsisting act of all existing. While the human soul is split apart into memory (it was), attention (it is) and expectation (it will be), God suffers no such *distentio animi*. The God revealed in Exodus is what He is in Himself, one and the same: his own *essentia*—*Idipsum esse* existing beyond all time, all history, all movement.[1]

Already in the Confessions (XIII, 31, 46), Augustine turns the verbal "is" of God into a substantive formula. And this move becomes more explicit when Augustine comments directly on Exodus 3:14 (which he renders as "*Qui est, misit me ad vos*")—"Because he is Is," that is to say, God is Being itself, *Ipsum esse*, in its most absolute and full sense. "*Esset tibi nomen ipsum esse*," he says to God (*Enarrationes in Psalmos* 101: 10).[2] Consolidating this quasi-Parmenidean reading, Augustine makes an important distinction between what God is "for us" (his *nomen misericordiae*) and what He is "in himself" (his *nomen substantiae*) in the Exodus 3 revelation. While the former, more historico-anthropomorphic perspective is conveyed by the formula "I am the God of Abraham, Isaac, and Jacob," the latter—safeguarding the absolute, inaccessible and transcendent character of God—is expressed by the "*ego sum qui sum*." It is this latter sense that Augustine has in mind in the *De Trinitate* when he identifies the God of Exodus with the Greek-Platonic notion of substance (*ousia*) understood as an atemporal, ahistoric immutable essence: "He is no doubt *substantia*, or if one prefers, he is the *essentia* which the Greeks called *ousia*. . . . *Essentia* comes from *esse*. And who 'is' more than He who said to his servant Moses: '*ego sum qui sum*.' . . . That is why there is only one substance or immutable essence which is God and to which being itself (*ipsum esse*) properly belongs" (*De Trinitate*, V, 2, 3). Augustine concludes from this that anything that changes or is capable of "becoming something which he was not already" cannot be said to possess being itself. We can say of God therefore that "He is" precisely because he is that which does not change and cannot change.[3]

Aquinas developed the Augustinian view that the *qui est* of Exodus is the principal name of God and the highest formulation of being. The revelation of Exodus, he affirmed, designates "true being, that is being that is eternal, immutable, simple self-sufficient, and the cause and principle of every creature."[4] For Aquinas, as for Augustine, the *esse* of God is nothing other than his *essentia* and as such exists eternally in the present without past or future: that is, without movement, change, desire or possibility—*Deus est actus purus non habens aliquid de potentialitate*. With Aquinas and the Scholastics, the God of Exodus is thus unequivocally enthroned as the most fully fledged "act of Being." In both his *Commentary on the Sentences* and *De Substantiis Separatis*, the Exodus verse is invoked by Thomas to corroborate speculative thought about the most ultimate mode of Being. For Being says more of God than either the Good or the One. The proper name of God revealed in Exodus 3:14 is none other than the absolute identity of divine being and essence. *Esse* is the *essentia* of God. This obtains for Aquinas no matter how much the divine essence surpasses the limits of rational speculation, approaching God only in an analogical way in the proofs for his existence. Aquinas concedes, after all, that while we can prove that God exists, we cannot know what he is. But these reservations notwithstanding, Aquinas has no hesitation in citing Exodus 3:14 as confirmation of his proofs in the *Summa* (Ad 3). This is how he justifies his conviction that the Exodic formula provides us with the ultimate name for God:

The reason for this name is that in its reference it exceeds every form, because it signifies being itself (*ipsum esse*). Moreover, the less determined the names the better they pertain to God, by virtue of their common and absolute character. Every other name in fact connotes a restrictive modality. Now "He who is" does not define any particular modality of being, but it envelops all indeterminate modes. Nevertheless, the sacred tetragrammaton preserves better still the incommunicability and singularity of God (*Summa Theologiae*, q 13, a 11).

Without the encounter of Greek metaphysics with biblical religious thought, philosophers "would have never reached the idea that Being is the proper name of God and that this name designates God's very essence."[5] Or, as

Etienne Gilson remarked in *The Spirit of Medieval Philosophy*, "Exodus lays down the principle from which Christian philosophy will be suspended. . . . There is but one God and this God is Being, that is the corner-stone of all Christian philosophy."[6] With this Scholastic verdict, the traditional notion of faith seeking understanding reaches its logical culmination. The conflation of Yahweh with the supreme Being of the philosophers is sealed. And this conjunction of God and Being was to survive for at least 1500 years—from Bonaventure and Aquinas to Gilson and the neo-Scholastics. Thus did the God of Exodus secure ontological tenure in the God of metaphysics. And this tenure has come to be known, after Heidegger, as "onto-theology": a practice of reifying God by reducing Him to a being (*Seiende*)—albeit the highest, first, and most indeterminate of all beings.[7]

Onto-theology, we might say, sought to have its cake and eat it too: to equate God with a modality of being while safeguarding His ultimately ineffable and transcendent nature. Unlike the negative theology of Dionysius and the Christian neo-Platonists, however, most Scholastics identified God with Being by means of proofs and analogies, seeking some sort of balance between Being's universality and indeterminacy on the one hand, and God's density as a quasi-subject or person (which holds God from descent into infinite dispersion) on the other.[8] It is, arguably, but a short step from such onto-theological equilibrium to Hegel's notion of a "concrete universal"; or Schelling's famous equation of the divine "I am" with the self-identification of the transcendental Ego. Indeed, Schelling will go so far as to claim that the "I Am" is "one and the same thing with our immediate self-consciousness."[9] This unification of divine and human consciousness finds modern echoes not only in German Idealism and Romanticism (Schelling, Fichte, Hegel, Coleridge), but also in a contemporary strand of New Age mysticism.[10]

In short, if one pole of the ontological reading of the I Am leads to onto-theology (the conceptual capture of God as a category of substance), another pole comprises what we might call mystical ontologism (the conflation of divine and human consciousness).[11] We shall revisit these positions in the third part of this chapter, entitled "Critical Considerations."

2. The Eschatological Reading

But there is a powerful countertradition which resists ontological approaches to God. This second tradition of interpretation—which I call eschatological—is generally more attuned to the original biblical context of meaning. Here the emphasis is on the ethical and dynamic character of God. The very framing of the Exodic self-revelation in terms of a response to Moses's question—Who shall I say sent me?—opens the phrase toward the "mark of becoming."[12] This reading points to the fact that Exodus 3:14 falls within the framework of a solicitation, that is, assumes the task of summoning us toward an eschatological horizon. Such an understanding of the Exodic Name contrasts sharply with the more essentialist conceptions of divine Being in medieval and post-medieval metaphysics.

It is important to recall here that Moses responds to the call of the burning bush—"Moses! Moses!"—with the reply "Here I am." The self-revelation of God that precedes and follows Moses's reply is less predicative than appellative. Above all else, it is a call and a promise: "This is the name I shall bear forever, by which future generations will call me" (Exodus 3:15). We should be chary, therefore, of hypostatizing the I-Am-Who-Am and try to relocate the metaphysics of the Name where it properly belongs, namely, "within the ethical orbit of the mandate."[13] By amplifying the meaning of the I-Am in this way we allow for a plurality of interpretations of the verb "to be" used by God in his address to Moses. This means reading the formula in terms of function rather than substance, in terms of narrative rather than syllogism, in terms of relation rather than abstraction. God's I-Am appears to need Moses's response "Here I am" in order to enter history and blaze the path toward the Kingdom.

One consequence of the infiltration of the Mosaic God into the history of Greek and Latin metaphysics was to inject the latter with an ethical charge. Smoke from the burning bush blurred the clear blue sky of Graeco-Roman assurance; nobody slept quite so well at night anymore or breathed quite so easily during the day. There was a whiff of anxiety and expectation in the air now. Dogmatic definitions of God began to fritter and come undone. And even those neo-Platonists who recognized the unknowable nature of God found it difficult to handle the urgency of this eschatological summons. God, it seemed, was undergoing an identity crisis. (Though not a gender one yet; He was still called He for a long while yet). And while it was all very well to agree with the likes of the Pseudo-Denys that the accompaniment of every affirmation with a negation points, apophatically, to a God beyond the proper names of Being, one was still left facing the quandary: If God is devoid of all historical being, is He not then also deprived of the power to act and call and love—a God so distant as to be defunct? So whether it was a question of the metaphysical God of essence or hyper-essence, it was hard to square either with a burning bush. God resolved to retrieve the past and inaugurate a new begining.[14]

But let us return to Moses in front of his bush. In Exodus 3:14, Moses raises the question of God's identity in the context of the cultic-magical power systems prevalent at the time in most religions of the ancient Near East. Near Eastern gods bore a variety of names for general consumption but were considered to have a secret inaccessible name, unavailable to humans, bearing enormous power. One exegetical commentator, André LaCocque, suggests that Moses's question to God may in part be an attempt to acquire this unknown name of divine power, particularly when we remember his competition with the Egyptian magicians. Moses's request, on this reading, is for just such a "Name of Power"; and God's response to his request may be read accordingly as a refusal of this request. The very circularity and indeterminacy of the nameless name—I-Am-who-Am—confounds the attempt to glean magical power from it. What God resists is not being addressed by Moses as such—He is invoked on countless occasions in the personal form of "Thou" throughout the Psalms (e.g., Psalm 99:6). No, what he resists is being reduced to the status of an idol. In short, God is repudiating any name that would seek to appropriate Him here and now as some thaumaturgical presence. Instead, God keeps Himself open for a future, allowing for a more radical translation of his nameless name as "I am as I shall show myself."[15] In this respect, the linguistic root "*hyh*" in '*ehyeh 'aser 'ehyeh* is to be understood, LaCocque argues, less as a mere copula than as a token of agency: more like "to be with, to become, to show oneself . . . to befall, to happen" (*cadere, evenire*).[16]

Other paraphrasitic translations of Exodus 3:14 include Buber's "As the one who will always be there, so shall I be present in every time" or Rosenzweig's "I will be there as I will be there."[17] These commentators share the view that what the suffering Hebrews needed from Moses was not some metaphysical proof about the existence of God as *ipsum esse* but an assurance that He would remain close to them. The promise of the speaking God which begins with the word '*ehyeh*, "I shall be," means a pledge to his people that he will not abandon them. It is not, Buber observes, the self-exposure of some occult magical power but a clarification of the kind of God he is, an indication of the "meaning and character of a name (YHVH)."[18] The God revealed in Exodus is more, however, than a demystification of pagan tendencies to invoke divine Names as mythical powers.

It also marks a step beyond the capricious deity inherited by the Hebrews themselves from certain narratives of their ancestors recorded in Genesis—in particular the sacrificial episode with Abraham and Isaac on Mount Moriah in Genesis 22. Exodus 3:14 may be read accordingly not only as a biblical critique of other mystery-rite religions but as a self-critique of such traces in the biblical religion itself![19]

According to this view, the Greek rendition of Exodus as *ego eimi ho on*/I am the one who is misses too much of the original dynamism of the Hebrew expression and already concedes too much to Hellenistic ontology.[20] God's I Am is to be understood less as an ontological substance in opposition to nonbeing than as a self-generating event, like the Burning Bush from which it announces itself. An agent is designated whose "work is actualised in Israel's exodus from Egypt"—namely, the self-revealing agency of the "Thou in dialogue with the divine I."[21]

In such light, Moses's question in Exodus 3:13 may be reinterpreted as a radical challenge to the One who has revealed himself as the God of his ancestors to proclaim a new program of action by "becoming different from what he used to be and has been until now."[22] The fact that Moses returns to Egypt and delivers a message of emancipation to his people signals the inauguration of a "new mode of divine relation to them."[23] The One who was experienced by them as the God of their Fathers now discloses himself as the God of their sons and daughters.

So the "I Am", we may surmise, is both an "I" that is identical with itself in its past and a "Thou" that goes forth into the future. It reveals God as he is, at the same time as it commits God, and his emissary Moses, to an action of salvation. This is why the Exodic Name is both theophanic and performative.[24] It serves as the pre-name and sur-name of that which cannot be objectively nominated. And it is this excess or surplus that saves God from being reduced to a mere signified—transcendental or otherwise. In short, the revelation of the nameless Name in Exodus is intimately connected with Moses's commission to announce to his fellow Hebrews their liberation and redemption. "You shall know that I am Yhwh your God, who frees you from the burden of the Egyptians." Henceforth, Yhwh is to be experienced as a saving-enabling God, a God whose performance will bear out his pledges. As Psalm 138 makes clear, "You have made your promised word well above your name."[25]

It is worth repeating here that this eschatological promise is granted within an I-Thou relationship (of God with Moses), thereby indicating two sides to the promise, human as well as divine responsibility. The double relation in turn carries a dual injunction not to become too distant or too familiar with God. Moses, remember, is summoned to approach but also to remove his sandals and keep his distance. A safe distance, a sacred reserve. This twofold summons—Come! but not too near!—is itself parallel to the shift from past to future. The revelation of Exodus 3 marks a displacement from an ancestral deity (of magic, territory, and inheritance) to a salvific God who vows to free the faithful from bondage in Egypt and prise open the more universal horizon of a "Promised Land." Here God commits Himself to a kingdom of justice if his faithful commit themselves to it too; the promise of Sinai calls forth a corresponding decision on behalf of the people. To phrase this otherwise: The "I" puts it to the "Thou" that the promise can only be realized if those who receive it do not betray its potential for the future. Not that this is a matter of conditional exchange, turning the Exodus revelation into a economy of give-and-take. No, the promise is granted unconditionally, as pure gift and grace. But God is simply reminding his people that they are free to accept or refuse this gift. A gift cannot be imposed; it can only be offered. A gift neither is nor is not (as Derrida reminds us); it gives.

This liberty to receive or reject the promise of the Name is epitomized by the character of discretion contained in the paronomasis—that is, the circular, tautological, indeterminate quality of the expression (similar to the proverbial shaggy dog story that undoes itself: a literary device not unknown to several postmodern narrators, from Beckett and Borges to Calvino and Eco). Indeed, even when Moses reports the revelation of the Name to his people, he does not do so in the objectifying form of the third person but once more in repetition of the I-Thou commission "'Ehyeh has sent me." In this manner also, the unnameable Name refuses not only the temptation of ritual incantation but also the danger of ideological appropriation. Yhwh does not possess and cannot be possessed. Paronomasis serves, accordingly, as a guarantee of radical dispossession.[26]

God does not reveal himself, therefore, as an essence *in se* but as an I-Self for us. And the most appropriate mode of human response to this Exodic revelation is precisely that: commitment to a response.[27] Such commitment shows Yhwh as "God-the-agent," whose co-respondents, from Moses to the exilic prophets and Jesus, see themselves as implicated in the revelation as receivers of a gift—a Word given by someone who calls them to cooperate with Him in his actions. That is why Moses is called to be as "God for Aaron" and "for the Pharaoh" (Exodus 4:16 and 7:1). Moses and the prophets are implicated in the revelation, showing us how Yhwh acts concretely through his human emissaries. With the revelation of his Name, "God tells of himself something like 'With you, Moses—and with Israel throughout history—I stand or fall!'" Exodus 3 is the proclamation that God has invested the whole of Himself in his emissary's history.[28]

We may say, consequently, that the identity-formula of I-am-who-am signals an inextricable communion between God and humans, a commitment to a shared history of "becoming," beginning with the emancipation from bondage in Egypt. God may henceforth be recognized as someone who "becomes with" us, someone as dependent on us as we are on Him. God's relation with mortals is, in other words, less one of conceptuality than of covenant, from which it follows that most philosophical reflections on God are in need of revision. Certainly, the orthodox onto-theological categories of omnipotence, omniscience and self-causality, originally forged *sub specie aeternitatis*, could do with a radical rethink *sub specie historiae*. Before the burning bush one doesn't merely speculate; one runs, or, if one stays, one praises, dances, acts.[29]

The eschatological wager here reaches its most dramatic stakes. Once the "unaccomplished form of the verb"—*'ehyeh*—is taken in its full implications, one realizes that the claim that God is what he is actually prefigures what he will be when he becomes his Kingdom and his Kingdom comes on this earth. "At the eschaton, God will be God" (cf. Isaiah 11:9; Psalm 110:1; I Corinthians 15:24–28). Meanwhile, God is in the process of establishing his lordship on earth, and the *'ehyeh 'aser 'ehyeh* may be rendered accordingly as "I will be what I will be; I will become what I will become." And so, in addition to the unaccomplished form of the verb we find an "uncannily taut drama" signaled by the relative pronoun *aser* (what/who), "for its content essentially depends on the quality of history that Moses and his people will pour into it."[30]

Thus does the Exodic Name come to supplement Elohim as the name for the living God. For if Elohim—a name derived from a common noun—is the transcendent God who sat in heaven (Psalm 2), created earth, and demanded sacrifice (e.g., of Isaac), Yhwh is more a name of invocation which makes the living God more accessible to human relation and history (i.e., more personal and more eschatological). With the revelation of Exodus, "God ceases to be the Unnameable, the inaccessible, the one *a se et per se*. He ceases to be impassible—if he ever was."[31] Yhwh is now revealed as affected and vulnerable, henceforth showing himself as one who wrestles with himself (Hosea), who laments (Jeremiah), who regrets (Samuel), who seduces and forgives (Psalms). Here we witness a God who persuades rather than coerces; invites rather than imposes; asks rather than impels. This God of Mosaic manifestation cannot be God without relating to his other—humanity.[32] Nowhere is this wager on human testimony so clearly expressed as in the following Midrash on Isaiah 43:12: "If you are not My witnesses, I am, as it were, not God."[33]

In the final analysis, what makes Exodus 3:14 a call to human attestation through a history of effectivity (*Wirkungsgeschichte*) is not just the unaccomplished nature of the verb and pronoun but the first person present tense—I Am. The formulation is performative rather than predicative, appellative rather than attributive, conative rather than constative. It takes the form of an address that solicits action from the addressee rather than some kind of superdetermination from on high which leaves us too cold, or too hot, to act; that is, with no real option of response. This is surely why commentators as different as Fromm, Ricoeur, and LaCocque see in the presence of the first person the call to a Thou—the very condition of divinity as an eschatological colloquy where I and Thou engage in a relationship of mutual answerability and co-creation.[34]

The existential implications of this inauguration of a personal God are revolutionary. For what we are witnessing here is a radical alteration of the metaphysical use of the copula. What is crucial for Greek thought is to be, since divine being is ultimately timeless and permanent, ontological rather than moral (just think of Aristotle's God). For the Hebrews, by contrast, what is most important is to become, to be able. Thus while the Hellenists will translate Exodus 3:14 as "I am the Being who is eternal," a non-Hellenic Jew such as Maimonides encourages us to conceive of Yhwh as an agent with an active purpose, a God who does rather than a being which is (*Guide to the Perplexed* 1.54–58).[35]

The consequences for a Christian reading are no less radical. The early Church saw the incarnate Christ as the Exodic Name made flesh. As Revelation 1:8 proclaims: "I am the one who is, who was, and who is to come." In this manner, the recognition of the Name as eschatological vocation is charged with a goal which for Christianity finds its realization in the coming, or second coming, of Christ. In several passages in John we find the formula "*ego eimi*/I am" (John 1:15; I John 1:1). And it is also in John that we find Christ identifying himself explicitly with the Name: "I have made your Name known to those whom you gave me from the world. . . . Now they know . . . in truth that I came from you" (John 17:6).

I-Am-Who-Am is, in short, God's way of appearing-disappearing in a burning bush that never burns away. The Exodic revelation is an ingenious wordplay which heralds an eschatological transcendence—a transcendence with the wherewithal to resist the lures of logocentric immanence.

3. Critical Considerations

Transcendence can, however, become too transcendent. If removed entirely from historical being, God can become so unknowable, invisible, and unimaginable as to escape all identification whatsoever. Such a numinous deity often takes the form of a theology.

This tendency to construe the God of Exodus as a God without being, a summons devoid of all ontology, is especially evident in a contemporary thinker such as Jean-Luc Marion.[36] The more theologically inclined Marion cites Denys and the apophatic tradition in his argument that the whole metaphysics of naming God must give way to a new understanding of God as pure gift. To subordinate the God of love to speculative distinctions of being and non-being is to resort to principles of reason which God radically transcends. Indeed for Marion, Nietzsche's and Heidegger's conceptual atheism is curiously one of the best weapons against the "conceptual idolatry" of onto-theology. Why? Because it permits a new logic to emerge: that of superabundance and gratuity. The statement "God is One" thus gives way to the utterance "God loves."

But there are, I believe, problems with Marion's mystical theology when it comes to the name of God. In *God without Being*, Marion directly relates Exodus 3:14 to what he considers to be privileged mystical revelations in the Christian scriptures (John 8:24 and 58; or Luke 24:39, where Christ says "I am me, *ego eimi autos*"). In so doing, Marion invokes the authority of a eucharistic hermeneutic. The "hermeneutic of the text by the community," he writes, is conditioned by that community itself being "interpreted by the Word." But this can only be ultimately guaranteed "thanks to the liturgical service of the theologian par excellence, the bishop."[37] In the heel of the Marionesque hunt, "only the bishop merits, in the full sense, the title of theologian."[38] To remain true to such a mystical-authoritarian hermeneutic we must accept that the "saturation" of signs (words, names, texts, speech) by the "unspeakable Word" means that "we find all already given, gained, available."[39] And this is so because the referent of the religious sign is not something to be "taught" and, by extension, debated. No, it is "encountered by mystical union."[40] Consequently, only he who knows the "Word nonverbally," in mystical communion and the Eucharist, has the wisdom to subsequently interpret it.[41] (So where does that leave non-communicant non-Catholics?)

But how does Marion come to such an authoritarian-fideistic position? In his essay "Au Nom," Marion clarifies the underlying implications of his thinking. Here he points to a God beyond both the affirmation and negation of names, where words assume a purely pragmatic function: "Beyond every name and every denegation of the name . . . the word says just as little as it negates—it acts by referring to the One who de-nominates (*dé-nomme*)."[42] As such, Marion argues that the "hyper" invoked by the Pseudo-Denys and others to indicate the "ineffability" of God (*The Divine Names*, VII, I, 865c) is not of the order of essence or knowledge but transgresses both in favor of a praise of that which precedes every essence. The "hyper" of negative theology would thus point to a Levinasian God "otherwise than being," safely beyond the reaches of onto-theology understood as a metaphysics of presence. Marion distils negative theology (as enunciated by Denys and Gregory of Nyssa) into an uncompromising "theology of absence." The "saturated phenomenon" of mystical eucharistic encounter with the divine is informed by such a hyper-excess that it can be neither seen, known, nor understood. Its very superabundance surpasses all predication, nomination, and narration. Or, to put it in Marion's own words: This mystical experience takes the form of a certain "stupor" or "terror" which its very "incomprehensibility imposes on us."[43]

We hit here upon a serious hermeneutic muddle. If the saturating phenomenon is really as bedazzling as Marion suggests, how can we tell the difference between God and madness? How are we to distinguish between enabling and disabling revelations? Who is it that speaks when God speaks from the burning bush? And if it is true indeed, as Paul concedes, that the Messiah comes like a thief in the night, in the very same passage (I Thessalonians 5), Paul, pace Marion, calls for sober and enlightened vigilance: "But you, beloved, are not in darkness, for that day to surprise you like a thief; for you are children of light and children of the day; we are not of the night or of darkness. . . . So let us keep awake and be sober." Or as John D. Caputo adroitly inquires, when we are confronted with the saturated phenomenon of God, how can we discriminate between excess and defect—"How do we know that we have been visited by a supereminent excess and not just invaded by *khora*?"[44] How indeed!

***

But in addition to the conceptual atheists and negative theologians, there exists a third strand of mystical postmodernism which challenges attempts to reduce divine alterity to the knowable. This third approach I term—borrowing from medieval parlance—a teratology of the sublime in that it focuses on the "monstrous" character of God.[45]

In the realm of the sublime, the upwardly transcendent finds its mirror image in the downwardly monstrous—or what Kant called "radical evil." Both extremes transgress the limits of representation, and for several postmodern authors such as Lyotard and Zizek, the two are virtually indistinguishable.[46] In this schema, the monstrosity of horror is just as "ineffable" as the vertical transcendence of God (invoked by Levinas and the negative theologians). There is, in short, an apophasis of the monstrous as there is an apophasis of the divine. To render these two apophatic extremes interchangeable is to revert to the *tohu bohu* of the *il y a*, which, as I understand it, resists an ethical notion of the divine as unequivocally good. Pushing this argument ad absurdum—to the point of absolute horror—Peter Haidu puts the dilemma thus in "The Dialectics of Unspeakability":

> The impossibility that attends the representations of the Event (the Shoah) as well as its designation as a unique event with a special status of "exceptionality," looks very much like the initial stage of the institutionalization of the divine. As such, it will be a divinity unlike that which we inherit as Jews, as Christians, or as atheists. The unspeakability of the Event, the horror which comes upon the historian as his gaze fixes on the documents of his research, enters into a tradition of the ineffability which attends appearances of the divine. The topos of ineffability is associated both with the experience of horror and with that of the sublime. What I wish to designate, however, precedes that distinction: the irruptions into human life of the divine as that which is awesome, that which strikes us with terror, inexplicable because of the unpredictability of its violence as well as the force of that violence. Divinity here might be the name given that violence Walter Benjamin considered constitutive.

This, claims Haidu, is a notion of divinity which pre-exists the moralization of divinity under the sign of monotheism. It is a concept of divinity, he concludes, "that is pre-Judaic, intractable in moral terms, in which divinity bypasses human understanding, not necessarily as desirable perfection, but equally as an object of profound repugnance. It is a concept of divinity which culture and civilisation as we know them, hold at bay, rendering it also 'unspeakable.' "[47]

More ominously, Himmler endorsed such an apophasis of the monstrous when he spoke of the Holocaust as a sublime and sacred glory that could never be written, spoken, or represented (*ein niemals geschriebenes und niemals zu schreibendes Ruhmesblatt unserer Geschichte*). The order to exterminate the Jews, he proclaimed, partakes of an "unspeakable sacred order" (*Heiligkeit des Befehls*).[48] By this reading, the exemption of the Holocaust from the experience of human historicity, and its absolution from all limits of human comprehension and context, made it a "sacred" event, an absolute secret whose very strangeness and uncanniness (*Unheimlichkeit*) constitute its gloriously apophatic monstrosity.[49] One shudders before such logic.

Postmodern thinkers such as Zizek and Lyotard could not, of course, be farther removed, politically, from National Socialism. Granted. My point is rather that their readings of the sublime leave them virtually speechless before the horror of evil. By way of unpacking some unsettling consequences of such speechlessness, let me say a word about each in turn.

Lyotard's reading of Kant's notion of the sublime shows it aiming "not to supply reality but to invent allusions to (that) which cannot be presented."[50] It is because the "terror" of the Holocaust has become "absolute," by virtue of its incomparable singularity, that it cannot be said or represented. Qua unspeakable trauma, it requires not a "talking cure" but silence, a silence which

Lyotard relates explicitly to a postmodern version of the Kantian aesthetics of the sublime. Lyotard's post-Holocaust poetics thus radicalizes Adorno's dictum that after Auschwitz, poetry is impossible. His impossible poetics signals an uncompromising rejection of all modes of narrative representation and discourse; it announces a post-poetics of silence.[51]

Zizek, for his part, drives this postmodern aesthetic of the sublime further still.[52] Observing that for Kant both the monstrous (*das Ungeheure*) and the supra-sensible realm of the good/law belong to the domain of the noumenal, Zizek surmises that they are therefore the same. As soon as we come too close to the Law, "its sublime majesty turns into obscene abhorrent monstrosity."[53] What appears as good from our subjective humanist perspective is, in fact, in itself evil. "What our finite mind perceives as the sublime majesty of the moral Law is in itself the monstrosity of a crazy sadistic God."[54] Which is perhaps one reason why Lacan, Zizek's mentor, was so obsessed with the relation between Kant and de Sade.

In Kant, these postmoderns argue, the sublime Law comes to occupy the place of the noumenal God of Exodus. We know that the Law is but not what it is. Law somehow withdraws from its various temporal incarnations, leaving us guilty and often terrified.[55] Citing Kant's equation of "diabolical evil" with the monstrous sublime in the Third Critique, Zizek claims that "the impossible content of the moral Law as pure form is 'diabolical evil.' "[56] In other words, in the highest instance of noumenal experience—contact with the Law—the human subject finds itself obliterated in a sort of Kafkaesque confusion of sublime proportions. For what it encounters here is nothing other than the "unconscious" of the Good: that is, the monstrous. "The subject disintegrates, obliterates itself, the moment it comes too close to the impossible Thing whose symbolic stand-in is in the empty Law."[57] Exposure to the noumenal God leads to madness. "If we gained direct access to the noumenal sphere," Zizek contends, "we would be confronted with the 'terrible majesty' of God in his *Ungeheure*, horrifying real."[58] Here we discover that "de Sade is the truth of Kant," for Kant is compelled to formulate the "hypothesis of a perverse, diabolical God" and make the "the ethical Good and Evil indistinguishable." The logic of Kant's monstrous sublime follows that of Milton's Satan: "Evil, be thou my good."[59] Or that of Conrad's Kurtz faced with the heart of darkness. Or that of Melville's Pip in *Moby Dick*, who, cast to the bottom of the ocean, spied the demon God: "Carried down alive to wondrous depths, where strange shapes of the unwarped primal world glided to and fro before his passive eyes . . . Pip saw the multitudinous, God-omnipresent, coral insects, that out of the firmament of waters heaved the colossal orbs. He saw God's foot upon the treadle of the loom, and spoke it; and therefore his shipmates called him mad."

Kant himself stopped short of the "abyss of the Monstrous," realizing that to suspend the limit separating good and evil would be to embrace a form of amoral nihilism. But Zizek has no such compunctions. Mixing a postmodern cocktail of Lacan and Hegel, he follows the logic of the monstrous sublime through to its dark, unbearable end. What Kant called radical or diabolical evil is just another word, in Zizek's psychoanalytic reading, for the "death drive"—a drive which embraces the negative horror of the "real," an anarchy which exists before and beyond the Law. Lacan already made a move beyond the ethics of good and evil, as did Hegel before him when his dialectics of the negative reverted to the "pagan fascination with a dark God who demands sacrifices."[60] But Zizek's conclusion is more unblinking in its audacity: "Hegel's (and Lacan's . . .) point is that it is possible to move 'beyond good and evil', beyond the horizon of the Law and constitutive guilt, into drive (which is the Freudian term for the Hegelian 'infinite play of the Idea with itself'). [The] implicit thesis is that diabolical Evil is another name for the Good itself; for the concept 'in itself', the two are indistinguishable; the difference is purely formal, and concerns only the point of view of the perceiving subject."[61]

But I have some anxieties about this. For as soon as the human subject dissolves into the void of the Monstrous "real," it seems to me we no longer have a stay against regression to the radical indifferentiation of pure drive—the chilling indifference of the There is (*il y a*). Do we not thus regress to the traumatism of tohu bohu—the condition of the Real before the ethical God spoke the symbolic Word and the world divided into good and evil?

Now I am all for shaking up doctrinaire conservatives and shocking the self-righteous. Good philosophy, like good avant-garde art, has a duty to *épater la bourgeoisie*. But Zizek and his postmodern teratologists sometimes go too far. By contrast, a rebel iconoclast such as Moses shows how we can break open a new order of existence without dissolving into a void. He confronts the Burning Bush without succumbing to the monstrous. His encounter with the absolutely Other reveals a deity who calls us to an ethico-political task— the eschatological quest for liberty and justice.

Conclusion

The danger of God without being is that of an alterity so "other" that it becomes impossible to distinguish it from monstrosity—mystical or sublime. To avoid this, I suggest, it might be wiser to reinterpret the God of Exodus 3:14 as neither being (onto-theology) nor non-being (negative theology, hysterical postmodernism), but as something between the two: an eschatological promise that may be? Such a third way might help us eschew the excesses of both mystical authoritarianism on the one hand (Marion and certain negative theologians) and apocalyptic anarchism on the other (Zizek and the prophets of the sublime).

To this end, I propose in conclusion to briefly revisit the hermeneutic trajectory of Exodus 3, sketching out the possibility of an eschatological retrieval (*Wiederholung*) of the ontological I Am. My wager here is that at the chiasmus where Yahweh meets *einai* a revolutionary exchange operates—with God putting being into question just as being gives flesh to God. And at this very border crossing, divine flesh always carries with it a certain *noli me tangere*—a name that remains unnameable, a narrative that refuses to end (in the historical present), a presencing that transfigures itself to the point of self-withdrawal even as it flares in the Burning Bush.

From this onto-eschatological perspective, I will try, by way of a few final remarks, to reread some high points in the historical interpretations of the Exodic Name. Such re-reading is necessarily tentative and selective. When Philo translated the Exodus passage into Greek—as *ego eimi ho on*—he insisted that God here reveals not his content (whatness-essence) but only that he exists (the verb *einai*). And Christian authors translating the Gospel into Greek would seek to render this passage in the light of the variations of self-revelation in the Gospel of John—for example, "The one who is, and who was, and who is coming" (1:14), or again, "Before Abraham was, I am" (8:58). This translation of the Hebrew into Greek (*einai*) and later into Latin (*esse*) was to radicalize the existing plurality and equivocity of the Hellenic and Latin terms for being (recognized since Aristotle). It provoked an extraordinary variety of interpretations throughout the history of Western thought. Indeed, it is Paul Ricoeur's view that this very plurality of interpretations actually safeguards against the danger of "conceptual idolatry" (so rightly feared by Marion and other postmoderns) and reinforces the enigmatic resonance of the original phrase as heard by Moses and his Hebrew followers.[62] In short, why not assume that Exodus 3:14 was "ready from the very beginning to add a new region of significance to the rich polysemy of the verb being, explored in other terms by the Greeks and their Muslim, Jewish and Christian heirs?"[63]

The prefatory command of God to Moses to remove the sandals from his feet may now be seen in its original innovative implications, as is also the fact that it is far from his own people, captured in Egypt, that Moses receives his revelation from God. For it is only in the solitary estrangement from his native home that the Other shows itself (as self-consuming fire) and speaks itself (as tautological pun). In this manner, the "dangerous liaisons" between being and God are, as Stanislas Breton suggests, a way of showing God in his transcendence without abandoning all traces of existence: For if there was no burning bush to see or no voice, however riddling, to hear, there would be nothing to witness, and so nothing to remember or promise! There would only be regress to the chaos of pre-creation: the dark before the Word. *Tohu bohu.*

Revisiting Meister Eckhart's much-neglected intervention in the Exodus 3 debate, we might note how this subtle Dominican managed to twist inherited ontological categories in the direction of an eschatological intent. Under his gaze, the "I" of the I Am tautology is seen to accentuate the sense of God's difference: the epithet *discretivum*, with which Eckhart qualifies the "I," connoting a measure of "distance."[64] By extension, Eckhart's use of the term *substantia* may be understood in the curious sense of a "being that stands on its own, by its own energy"—the quasi-being encountered at the heart of nothingness, which "carries all things according to the Word." This pure separateness of the divine "I" declines all additions of "this or that" and outstrips the familiar Aristotelian categories of substance utilized by conventional Scholasticism.

Eckhart's commentary on the verb *sum* also radically reinterprets the traditional being of God. "Being-as-copula" becomes being in "solitude and separation."[65] Qua *sum*, God here absolves himself from all predication, announcing both the ontological difference between Being and beings and the theological difference between divine and human. Here is a *sum* whose very burning-bush indeterminacy, in Breton's words, "expresses the purificatory fire of a certain iconoclasm."[66]

And what, finally, of the "who"? Here again, Eckhart may be seen as stressing the dynamism of the self-revealing God: "The repetition which says twice 'I am who I am' is the purity of affirmation which excludes all negation. . . . It indicates a certain reflexive conversion in itself and on itself, a sanctuary or repose which holds in itself; what is more, it indicates a specific effervescence (or bubbling over) or birth of self: this being, in fact, conceals a fervour which expands within itself and onto itself in a sort of bubbling; light within light, it penetrates everything."[67] By means of such hyperbole, Eckhart's rendering of the Exodic verse actually destabilizes and redefines traditional metaphysics. Behind their ostensible orthodoxy, the ontological proposition *esse est Deus* and the theological proposition *Deus est esse* mutually deconstruct each other. But this bilateral deconstruction does not ignore the fundamental co-implication of being and God in flesh. On the contrary, it shows that God's self-nomination cannot dispense with the detour through being, lest it become so unknowable as to pass us by unseen, unheard. There's more to God than being. Granted. But to pass beyond being you have to pass through it.

Thus, the ontological commentaries on the *ego sum qui sum* found in Eckhart may be seen—from an eschatological viewpoint—to carry a presentiment of God as pure gift and passage. Pure gift in the sense, noted by Derrida, of self-giving beyond the economic condition of return. "Being," as the Meister put it, "is so superior in rank and purity and so much God's own that no one can give it but he—as he gives himself."[68] But God is also pure passage in the sense that while he always stays faithful to his promise, He never stays put. Eckhart's own best defense against the charges of onto-theology or mystical ontologism is the reminder that he deemed the dialogue between God and being to be provisional rather than final. God passes through being just as we beings pass through God—but the primary verb is just that: passage, understood as transition and migration. Reinterpreted from an eschatological perspective, God is "the imperative of transit." "This is a God who disturbs, uproots, reiterates the call of Yahweh to Abraham to 'leave his house'; a God who shakes every edifice, even the venerable *esse subsistens.*"[69] Which is surely why Eckhart takes his leave of being only after he has rendered homage to its imprescribable necessity. His famous formula—"I pray God to rid me of God"—may be read consequently as an echo of the imperative to transit. The move beyond ontology has as its corollary the move beyond essentialist theology, surpassing the essence of God toward God's ultimate promise. In this wise, the metaphysics of exodus (being-word-abyss) becomes an exodus of metaphysics: a self-emptying movement of metaphysics beyond itself, the revelation of God as pure passage.[70]

In transiting through and beyond metaphysics, God reveals himself, in keeping with his promissory character in Exodus, as a God that neither is nor is not but may be. And here we might add the intellectual dexterity of Cusanus to the deconstructive daring of Eckhart. God, as Nicholas of Cusa put it, is best considered neither as *esse*, nor as *nihil*, but as *possest*. Transgressing the traditional Scholastic capture of God as *esse*, Cusanus redefines God as *possest* (absolute possibility which includes all that is actual). "Existence (*esse*) presupposes possibility (*posse*)," writes Cusanus, "since it is not the case that anything exists unless there is possibility from which it exists." "God alone," he concludes, "is what he is able to be."[71] This calls, I believe, for a new hermeneutic of the God as May-Be. What I term an onto-eschatological hermeneutics, or, more simply, a poetics of the possible.[72]

We are here surely not a million miles away from Derrida's recent pronouncements on the messianic function of "perhaps." ("There will occur, perhaps, the event of that which arrives, and this will be the hour of joy, an hour of birth but also of resurrection. . . . The promise promises in that fundamental mode of perhaps . . . The possibilisation of the impossible possible must remain at one and the same time as undecidable—and therefore as decisive—as the future itself.").[73] But that is work for another day.

Let me conclude the above explorations with the following final surmises: In the circular words I-Am-Who-May-Be, God demythicizes and exceeds being. His *esse* reveals itself as *posse*. The Exodus 3 exchange between God and Moses, I am thus suggesting, might be usefully revisited not as the manifestation of some secret name or essence but as a pledge to remain constant to a promise. God is really saying, isn't he—I am who may be if you continue to keep my word and struggle for the coming of justice? The God who reveals himself in the Burning Bush both is and is not, neither is nor is not. It is a God who puns and tautologizes, flares up and withdraws, promising always to return, to become again, to come to be what he is not yet for us. This God is the coming God who may-be, the one who resists quietism as much as zealotry, who renounces both the onto-theology of essence and the voluntarist impatience to appropriate holy lands. This Exodic God obviates the extremes of atheistic and theistic dogmatism in the name of a still small voice that whispers and cries in the wilderness, perhaps. Yes, perhaps if we remain faithful to the promise, one day, some day, we know not when, I-who-am-what-I-may-be may at last be. Be what? we ask. Be how? Be what is promised as it is promised. And what is that? A kingdom of justice and love. Democracy to come. There and then, to the human "Here I am," God may in turn respond, "Here I am." But not yet.

NOTES

1. Emile Zum Brunn, "L'exégèse augustinienne de 'Ego sum qui sum' et la 'Métaphysique de l'Exode," in *Dieu et L'être: Exégèses d'Exode 3, 14* (Paris: Etudes Augustiniennes, 1978), pp. 246–72.

2. Quoted by Dominique Dubarle in his chapter "La Nomination ontologique de Dieu," in *L'Ontologie de Thomas D'Aquin* (Paris: Éditions du Cerf, 1996), p. 45. Dubarle suggests that this equation of the God of Exodus with the "Is" of Parmenides and Greek ontology prefigures "la locution nominale de saint Thomas disant Dieu *ipsum esse per se subsistens.*"

3. Dubarle considers this Augustinian equation of Greek as *"substantia/essentia"* with the biblical God of Exodus 15 to be a decisive determination for subsequent Christian theology influencing not only Aquinas but the whole Scholastic tradition. Commenting about the above text from the *De Trinitate*, he writes:

> Le texte fondamental de l'Exode y sert de base à l'édifice entier. Le *sum* de L'Ecriture y est identifié à *l'essentia* pure et simple qui, à son tour, est identifiée à l'immutabilité. Au-dessous de cet Est absolu, s'ordonnent hiérarchiquement les autres *essentiae* selon qu'elles sont 'plus ou moins', mais elles lui doivent toutes ce qu'elles ont d'être. Enfin *l'essentia* latine déclare ouvertement la filiation qui la relie à *l'ousia* grecque. Tout se passe comme si le Dieu chrétien assumait ici l'héritage de *l'auto kat'auto* de Platon. . . . Le Dieu-Etre augustinien est une positivité de plénitude absolue de l'être. (Dubarle, "La Nomination ontologique de Dieu," pp. 48–50)

Extending this reading beyond Augustine, Dubarle points out that the same God of Exodus—le "Qui est"—is also for Aquinas and Scholasticism "la nomination la plus propre de Dieu lui même" (*Summa Theologiae*, Ia., qu.13, art. 11). For a more elaborate development of this thesis see Dominique Dubarle, "La Nomination ontologique de Dieu," pp. 51 ff., and Dubarle, *Dieu avec L'être: de Parménide à Saint Thomas, essai d'ontologie théologale* (Paris: Éditions Beauchesne, 1986), especially pp. 245–253. In the latter text, Dubarle argues that Augustine must not be reduced, as he so often is in the Christian speculative tradition, to a purely onto-theological God:

> On peut aussi penser à une signification bien plus existentielle de Moïse et de son peuple, sans qu'il s'agisse d'un enseignement de Dieu sur lui-même et sur sa propre nature: "Je serai avec toi, je serai ce que je serai, ferai ce que j'entends faire, et on verra bien ce que je ferai". De même *'Qui est'* dénomme celui qui agit avec Moïse, son envoyé. . . . Dieu ne se fait pas professeur de théologie, ni d'ontologie. (p. 247)

For another post-metaphysical reading of Augustine's formative interpretation of Exodus 15, see Goulven Madec, *Le Dieu D'Augustin* (Paris: Éditions du Cerf, 1998), pp. 104, 117–118, 127f., 147f. (For Madec, Augustine's God of Exodus 15 is a biblical-ethical God of the living more than a God of ontology per se.)

4. See Paul Ricoeur, "From Interpretation to Translation," in *Thinking Biblically: Exegetical and Hermeneutical Studies*, trans. D. Pellauer (Chicago: University of Chicago Press, 1998), p. 350. Ricoeur's text offers here an illuminating summary of the

main metaphysical readings of Exodus 3:14 from Augustine and the Pseudo-Denys to Bonaventure and Thomas, pp. 341–355.

5. Ibid., p. 353.

6. Etienne Gilson, *The Spirit of Medieval Philosophy* (Paris: Vrin, 1941), p. 51. See also Gilson's neo-Thomist reading of Exodus 3:14 in the section entitled "HE WHO IS" in *The Elements of Christian Philosophy* (Mentor-Omega, The New American Library, 1960) pp. 135–145.

7. Although the term "onto-theology" originally came from Heidegger's critique of metaphysics, it has been increasingly invoked by contemporary Christian thinkers (Jean-Luc Marion, Joseph O'Leary, Kevin Hart, John Caputo, David Tracy) eager to dissociate themselves from the substantialist metaphysics of Scholastic philosophy. The danger they denounce is that of conceptual idolatry. For a daring post-Heideggerean reading of the onto-theological interpretations of Exodus 3:14, see, for example, Joseph S. O'Leary, *Questioning Back: The Overcoming of Metaphysics in Christian Tradition* (Minneapolis: Winston Press, 1985), pp. 178–191; and *La vérité chrétienne à l'âge du pluralisme religieux* (Paris: Éditions du Cerf, 1994), pp. 219–227 (Eng. trans. *Religious Pluralism and Christian Truth* [Edinburgh: Edinburgh University Press, 1996], pp. 159–165). O'Leary claims, in his reading of Augustine for instance, that "despite the ultimate irreducibility of the divine 'Thou' to metaphysics, Augustine's God remains nine-tenths a metaphysical construction" (*Questioning Back*, p. 186). O'Leary does not deny, however, the radical deconstructive import of the remaining one-tenth: "To draw out the more primordial biblical sense of God from the prevailing metaphysical discourse about God, great attention to the tone and narrative movement of the text is required. . . . [For] even if biblical elements irreducible to metaphysics are marginalised in the text, they can constitute a quintessential instance of the treacherous margin, calling in question the entire metaphysical order which seeks in vain to integrate them" (pp. 186, 182). In the later book, *La Vérité Chrétienne* O'Leary develops his radical thesis thus:

> 'Dieu' n'est jamais un terme neutre; il signifie un choix; un jugement polémique. . . . Il "déconstruit" non pas en tant que pur absolu mettant en évidence la faiblesse et la complexité de nos langages, mais en tant qu'il se nomme. Ce n'est pas par son silence, mais quand il parle, que ce Dieu nous déroute. . . . Le nom qui signifiait la réponse ultime à toutes nos questions . . . est devenu le chiffre d'une question insondable. (pp. 220–221)

8. Quoted by S. Breton in "Je Suis (celui) qui Suis (Ontologie et Métaphysique)," in *Libres Commentaires* (Paris: Éditions du Cerf, 1990), p. 64.

9. Cited and commented on by Gabriel Marcel in *Coleridge et Schelling* (Paris: Aubier-Montaigne, 1951). This Schellingian equation of the Exodic God with the Transcendental "I Am" is what the romantic critic Samuel Coleridge would call "primary imagination"—that is, "the repetition in the finite mind of the eternal act of creation in the infinite 'I Am'" (*Biographia Literaria*, xiii). It might also be noted here that Heidegger's ontology of Dasein is itself greatly influenced by the German mystical-romantic-idealist theory of the "I am" and "imagination" (*Einbildungskraft*). See J. D. Caputo's illuminating analysis of the Heidegger-Eckhart connection in *The Mystical Element in Heidegger's Thought* (New York: Fordham University Press, 1982); and the recent critical genealogies of Heidegger's mystical notion of Being in Theodore Kisiel, *The Genesis of Being and Time* (Berkeley: University of California Press, 1993) and

John Van Buren, *The Young Heidegger* (Bloomington: Indiana University Press, 1994). See also T. Kisiel and J. Van Buren, eds., *Reading Heidegger from the Start* (Albany: SUNY Press, 1994). For a somewhat contrasting account of Heidegger's theory of the "I am," see P. Ricoeur, "Heidegger et la Question du Sujet," in *Le Conflit des Interpréta-tions* (Paris: Éditions du Seuil, 1969), pp. 222 ff. Just to take one example of how deep an echo exists between the "I Am Who I Am" and Heidegger's definition of authentic Dasein, see his definition of Dasein in *Being and Time* as the Being who has for its end its own Being or his cryptic rendition of Being in "The Letter on Humanism . . . Being Is Its Own Being (*Doch das Sein—was ist das Sein? Es ist Es selbst*)." Here Heidegger betrays a debt not only to Judeo-Christian theology but also, and perhaps more funda-mentally, to the notion of the "I Am" as the transcendental ego/imagination of German idealism and romanticism—a notion of which Derrida writes: "L'essence interne de l'absolu est une éternelle *In-Eins-Bildung* qui se répand à profusion; son émanation (*Ausfluss*) traverse le monde des phénomènes à travers la raison et l'imagination. On ne peut donc séparer philosophie et poèsie, affirmation sans cesse répétée par Schelling" (J. Derrida, "Théologie de la Traduction," in *Qu'est-ce que Dieu?* [Brussels: Publica-tions des Facultés universitaires Saint-Louis, 1985], pp. 170–171 ff).

10. This New Age mysticism is often an eclectic mix of Eastern Zen Buddhism, Jung, comparative mythologism à la Joseph Campbell, ecological paganisms, and even a certain strand of neo-Christian mysticism drawn (often liberally) from such figures as Thomas Merton, Theilhard de Chardin, and Thomas Moore. The following reading of Exodus 3 by Thomas Merton is a case in point: "When Moses saw the bush in flames, burning in the desert but not consumed, You did not answer his question with a definition. You said, 'I Am'. How shall we begin to know You who are if we do not begin ourselves to be something of what You are? . . . We come to live in Him alone" (*No Man Is an Island* [Kent: Burns and Oates, 1997], pp. 212, 226).

11. We might also mention here the radical, if frequently misunderstood, influ-ence of Meister Eckhart's interpretation of Exodus 3 on the Christian mystical readings of the divine name. Writing in the fourteenth century, Eckhart deployed the onto-theological terms inherited from Bonaventure and Thomas to render Exodus 3, but he pushed the metaphysical language to its limits and, some would argue, beyond. Let us take the following commentary on the tetragrammaton from Eckhart's *Lateinische Werke*, 11, 20; *In Exodum*, 3, 14:

> First the three words: "I", "am", "who", belong, in their most strict and proper sense, to God. The pronoun "I" is of the first person. This pronoun, as a separator (*discretivum*) signifies pure substance; pure, I say, without anything accidental or alien, substance without quality, without this form or that, without any addition of this or that. Now all this pertains to God and to Him only, who is beyond all accidents, kinds and genres. . . . Similarly, the "who" is an infinite (or indefinite) name. Such infinite and immense being can belong only to God. And likewise the verb "am" (*sum*) is of the order of pure substance. It is a word: "and the word is God": a substantive verb: "carrying all things by virtue of its word," as it is written in the first letter to the Hebrews. (Quoted in Breton, "Je Suis (celui) qui Suis (Ontologie et Métaphysique)," pp. 59–60.)

In another text, *Von der Abgeschiedenheit* (*About Disinterest*), Meister Eckhart offers a more mystical variation on Exodus 3:14. He glosses the self-revelation as follows: "We might say: The unchanging One hath sent me!," and explains how it represents a privileged self-manifestation of God as "unmoved disinterest." To illustrate this, he claims that Christ partook of this disinterest even as he cried out "My soul is sorrowful unto death," as did Mary, his mother, as she stood beneath the Cross. "Whatever about the lamentations of our Lady, inwardly she was still unmoved and disinterested." Moreover, Eckhart is prepared to extend this analogy to human beings. While their outer agents and actions are subject to change and movement, the internal soul can partake of eternity. The outward man, or sensual person operating with the five senses, is only one part of us; the inner self lives in unmoved disinterestedness and disengagement. "A man may be ever so active outwardly and still leave the inner man unmoved and passive." The inner person is the divine "word of Eternity" giving birth to itself in us. Using the illustration of the swinging door, he explains: "A door swings to and fro through an angle. I compare the breadth of the door to the outward man and the hinge to the inner person. When the door swings to and fro, the breadth of the door moves back and forth, but the hinge is still unmoved and unchanged" ("About Disinterest," in *Meister Eckhart: A Modern Translation*, ed. and trans. R. B. Blakney [New York: Harper and Row, 1941], pp. 86–87). On this theme, see Oliver Davies' very insightful commentary in *Meister Eckhart: Mystical Theologian* (London: SPCK, 1991), pp. 162–176. The most curious thing about this passage is, arguably, that while God seems identical with Himself as "he-who-is," this does not, as we might expect, rule out the possibility of human beings becoming identical with God by attaining to this same inner point of silent, still disinterest. On the contrary, it secures it. "God became man," suggests Eckhart, "so that I might be born to be God—yes, identically God" (ibid., p. 194). Or, more explicit still, "Between the Son and the soul there is no distinction" (p. 213). "The eye by which I see God and the eye by which God sees me are one and the same" (p. 206). "God's isness (*Istigkeit*) is my isness" (p. 180). We encounter here a startling paradox. For while most orthodox theologies read the Exodus passage as the mark of absolute separateness between a transcendent God (the divine *a-se-esse*) and transient humans eager to grasp his name, Eckhart appears to claim a radical identity between the two. The human person who abandons its own outer will and enters fully into the desert of its own emptiness becomes one with the Godhead of God. "When both God and you have forsaken self, what remains between you is an indivisible union. It is in this unity that the Father begets his Son in the secret spring of your nature" (p. 127). Just as "life is only to live," so God is only to be (p. 127). God's being is without why. "In him there is neither idea nor form" (p. 180). Such divine Being "ranks higher than life or knowledge. . . . Being is a name above all names" (p. 171). It is beyond all opposites (good and evil, etc.) and even beyond all our notions of "God and Godhead" (pp. 172–173). God is pure Being, isness, *esse*, substance, I am.

12. Paul Ricoeur, "From Interpretation to Translation," in *Thinking Biblically*, p. 334. See also Ricoeur's suggestive reading of Exodus 3:14 in terms of a hermeneutic of narrative mission and prescription, "D'un Testament à l'autre: Essai d'hérméneutique biblique," in *La Mémoire et le Temps: Mélanges offerts à Pierre Bonnard* (Geneva: Labor et Fides, 1991), pp. 299–309. See in particular pp. 300–301, where Ricoeur insists that the ontological predication of the divine "I Am Who Am" be framed within a narrative and prescriptive context, made clear in Exodus 20:

> C'est moi Jahve, ton Dieu, qui t'ai fait sortir du pays d'Egypt, de la maison de servitude; tu n'auras pas d'autre Dieu que moi (Ex. 20). La proposition relative de forme narrative—"c'est moi qui . . . t'ai fait sortir"—et le grand commandement qui

suit immédiatement, constituent ensemble ce qu'on peut appeler la nomination prédicative de Dieu, laquelle explique, déploie le nom purement appellative contenu dans la clause d'autoprésentation: "Je (suis) Jahvé". Sous sa forme narrative, ce nom prédicatif résume toute l'histoire de l'Exode; sous sa forme préscriptive, il résume toute la révélation sinaïque de la Torah. (p. 300)

Ricoeur adds: "La proclamation de l'unicité de Dieu ne se laisse pas décomposer en deux enoncés: premièrement 'Dieu existe', deuxièmement, 'il est un (seul)'. Les prédicats éthico-narratifs, qui expliquent la shéma ('écoute!') équivalent à une acte de confiance dans l'efficacité historique et dans l'efficacité éthique du nom, rendent superflue toute assertion prétendument distincte d'existence" (p. 301). The ethico-narrative character of the Exodus revelation is rooted, for Ricoeur, in the fact that the actual moment—when God says "I am who am" and Moses replies "Here I am"—is intrinsically related to past and future, to memory and promise, to ancestry and eschatology. That is why what Gilson calls the "metaphysics of Exodus" needs to be checked and challenged by both the narrative character of the call and the indeterminate-repetitive-excessive character of Yahweh's triple use of the verb *eyeh*—a verb translated by Rosenzweig and Buber in terms of "becoming" (*werden*) rather than "being" (*sein*). As Ricoeur writes: "le cadre même du récit de vocation empêche de suréstimer et d'hypostasier le triple 'Je suis', culminant dans le nom 'Jahvé' " (p. 302). Likewise, this triple use of *eyeh* engenders a surplus of meaning, opening up a history of multiple interpretation and constantly renewed fidelity to action (*wirken*): "Cet excès . . . n'engendre-t-il pas une situation herméneutique d'un genre unique, à savoir l'ouverture, la signification d'Exode 3: 14 ne peut plus être séparée de l'histoire de ses effets, de sa *Wirkungsgeschichte*" (p. 302).

13. On this point see Paul Ricoeur, "From Interpretation to Translation," p. 337 ff.; and Joseph O'Leary, "God Deconstructs," in *Religious Pluralism and Christian Truth* (Edinburgh: Edinburgh University Press, 1997), pp. 159–204.

14. At times, it must be admitted, the neo-Platonic Christian tradition of negative theology did equate the God beyond being with the Good per se. And even Aquinas, who favored an analogical rather than apophatic approach to the naming of God, recognized that Being is not as good as Yahweh! The Scholastic tradition inaugurated by Albert the Great and Thomas sought to grant speculative theology the status of a science, but, true to a certain neo-Platonic influence, it never denied the transcendence of divine being as such. We can never know, as Aquinas admitted, what God is. As the neo-Platonist tradition in Christian theology frequently repeated, we can only speak of God as or as if (*sicut/quasi/quatenus*) he was this or that kind of being—which, taken literally or non-figurally, he is not. See Bernard Dupuy, "Heidegger et Le Dieu inconnu," and Stanislas Breton, "La querelle des dénominations," in *Heidegger et la Question de Dieu*, ed. R. Kearney and J. S. O'Leary (Paris: Grasset, 1981). Dupuy argues, for example, that "the attempts to harmonise the revelation of Sinai with Greek ontology have long obscured the sense of the disclosure of the divine name. It entails the rejection of all anthropomorphism, the relativisation of all the figures used to apprehend Him who is beyond being and non-being and thus 'without analogy' " (p. 119). For a contrasting reading, see Fran O'Rourke, *Pseudo-Dionysius and the Metaphysics of Thomas Aquinas* (Leiden: Brill, 1992).

15. Gese translates Exodus 3:14 as "ich erweise mich, als der ich mich erweisen werde, ich bin, als der ich mich erweisen werde [I shall show myself in that I shall show

myself, I am as I shall show myself]," Gese, "Der Name Gottes," quoted in André LaCocque, "The Revelation of Revelations," in *Thinking Biblically*, p. 312.

16. LaCocque, "The Revelation of Revelations," p. 312. For other post-metaphysical readings of Exodus 3:15 see also J. S. O'Leary, *Religious Pluralism and Christian Truth* (Edinburgh: Edinburgh University Press, 1996), especially the section "The Name of God" in Part 6, "God Deconstructs," pp. 159–165; and Derrida's intriguing comments on the possibility of a hyper-ethical God/Gift/alterity beyond the "proper names" of ontology, "Sauf le Nom," in *On the Name* (Stanford, Calif.: Stanford University Press, 1995), pp. 33–85; *The Gift of Death* (Chicago: University of Chicago Press, 1995), p. 71; "Comment ne pas parler," in *Psyché: Inventions de L'autre* (Paris: Galilée, 1987); and *Circonfession/Derridabase*, by J. Derrida and Geoffrey Bennington (Paris: le Seuil, 1991), especially p. 103 ff. and p. 91, where Derrida calls himself "l'eschatologiste le plus avancé." Elsewhere, Derrida insists that the alterity that precedes and exceeds us cannot be "seen" as a primal object or "read" as a proper name, here and now, but calls for another kind of seeing—a "seeing beyond," a "vision-beyond-vision," a "sur-vision"; see J. Derrida, "Living On: Border Lines," in *Deconstruction and Criticism* (London: Routledge, 1979), pp. 90–91 ff. This line of thinking is perfectly consistent with Derrida's claim that "God deconstructs": "La guerre qu'il déclare, elle a d'abord fait rage au-dedans de son nom: divisé, bifide, ambivalent, polysémique: Dieu déconstruit" (*Psyché*, p. 207).

17. Quoted in Ricoeur, "From Interpretation to Translation," pp. 360–361.

18. M. Buber, *Moses: The Revelation and the Covenant* (New York: Harper and Row, 1958), p. 49. Buber develops this point as follows:

> As replay to his question about the name, Moses is told: Ehyeh asher ehyeh. This is usually understood to mean: "I am that I am" in the sense that YHVH describes himself as the being One or even the Everlasting One, the one unalterably persisting in his being. But that would be abstraction of a kind which does not usually come about in periods of increasing religious vitality; while in addition the verb in the Biblical language does not carry this particular shade of meaning of pure existence. It means: happening, coming into being, being there, being present, being thus and thus; but not being in an abstract sense. "I am that I am" could only be understood as an avoiding of the question, as a statement that unfolds without any information. Should we however, really assume that in the view of the narrator the God who came to inform his people of their liberation wishes, at that hour of all hours, merely to secure his distance, and not to grant and warrant proximity as well? This concept is certainly discouraged by the twofold ehyeh, "I shall be present," which precedes and follows the statement with unmistakable intention, and in which God promises to be present with those chosen by him, to remain present with them, to assist them. This promise is given unconditional validity in the first part of the statement: "I shall be present. . . .I am and remain present." Behind it stands the implied reply to those influenced by the magical practices of Egypt, those infected by technical magic: it is superfluous for you to wish to invoke me; in accordance with my character I again and again stand by those whom I befriend. . . . In the revelation at the Burning Bush religion is demagicized. . . . YHVH is "He who will be present." . . . He who is present here; not merely some time and some where but in every now and in every here. Now the name expresses his character and assures the faithful of the richly protective presence of their Lord.

Buber alerts us here to the presence-absence enigma of the Exodic God, an enigma which provokes us to rethink God not as a *deus absconditus* but as a *deus adventurus*. A similar shift of emphasis onto the futural potentiality of God is found in Moltmann and the theology of liberation, as well as in Whitehead and process theology. See in particular Whitehead's notion of God's "consequent nature," comprising a reservoir of possibilities to be creatively realized as world, in *Process and Reality* (New York: Free Press, 1978). See also John B. Cobb, "A Whiteheadian Doctrine of God," in *Process Philosophy and Christian Thought*, ed. D. Brown, R. James, and G. Reeves (Indianapolis: Bobbs-Merrill, 1971), pp. 215–243; William Dean, "Deconstruction and Process Theology," *Journal of Religion* 64 (1984): 1–19; and David. R. Griffin, "Postmodern Theology and A/Theology," in *Varieties of Postmodern Theology*, ed. D. Griffin, W. Beardslee, and J. Holland (Albany: SUNY Press, 1989), pp. 29–61.

19. Because the indicative imperfect of the root *hyh* (as used in Exodus 3:12—*'ehyeh*) suggests the futural sense of "I shall be with thee," it points to a "transitional" meaning of the verb. It prefigures future alteration in present circumstances. That is, *hyh* has the force of a "temporal indicator" opening up the ancestral past toward an eschaton yet to be realized. It is this kind of exegesis which tempers any hasty attempts to convert the Exodic Name into an ontological abstraction or ecclesiastical icon, particularly under the influence of speculative thinking from the West (e.g., the translation of *'ehyeh* as *ho on*, or "the one who is" in LXX). See here the analysis of the grammar of the Exodic formula by G. S. Ogden, cited by A. LaCocque in *Thinking Biblically*, pp. 313–314.

20. LaCocque, *Thinking Biblically*, p. 314.

21. Ibid.

22. Ibid., p. 315.

23. Ibid.

24. LaCocque writes:

> It elicits recognition and worship as the recipients are not just made privy to a divine secret but are the objects of an action of salvation. "It is I who am Yhwh" goes far beyond a rhetorical statement—it reveals the ultimate meaning of the redeeming event. Thus we see why the Name is no atemporal, ahistorical, abstract axiom about the divine aseity. God says "ehyeh" and the unaccomplished tense helps us see the action as a process. It is not a question of divine essence, but it is a promissory statement that God, as it were, "stands or falls" with his people, and in the first place with Moses about to return to Egypt where a price is set upon his head. (*Thinking Biblically*, p. 316)

See also Eric Fromm, *You Shall Be as Gods: A Radical Interpretation of the Old Testament* (New York: Fawcett, 1966); and M. Buber, *Moses: The Revelation and the Covenant* (New York: Harper, 1958), pp. 48–54.

25. *Yhwh* thus comes, as LaCocque notes, to "promise a history of merciful guidance whose onset, namely the Exodus, constitutes both its beginning and its end, its apex and the figure of things to come at the eschaton, because the Event in question is paradigmatic *kat'exochen*" (*Thinking Biblically*, p. 317).

26. Here we are confronted with what Zimmerli describes as a "mystery without a definition," a mystery whose "potency" (*Wirkung*) goes beyond conceptual speculation and imagistic fixation in favor of a divine "calling for decision on the part of Moses and his people—the recipients of the self-revelation." Walter Zimmerli, *I Am Yahweh* (At-

lanta: John Knox, 1982), p. 153, cited in *Thinking Biblically*, p. 322. The fact that the revelation of Exodus is given in terms of a "word" rather than an "image" is perfectly consistent with the Hebraic interdiction of divine figuration and iconography. God does not here propose some divine icon in contradistinction to an anthropocentric idol (as Christian thinkers such as Marion or Von Balthasar might like to believe). "The revelation of the Name is granted by an imageless God who desires to be accessible and known": LaCocque, *Thinking Biblically*, p. 319. See also Gerhard von Rad, *Old Testament Theology* (New York: Harper and Row, 1962); and Gese, "Der Name Gottes," p. 86. Mediated relationships with God through visual representation (third person) are here replaced by the more immediate relationship of the one to one (second person). But as the Decalogue makes plain, God can only be fully honored and respected by refusing both objectification (through the mediation of images and idols) and identification (through the inordinately immediate).

27. LaCocque is adamant on this point, arguing that "recognition of the lordship of God is no metaphysical knowledge" and that the tetragrammaton is "no invitation to speculation upon the aseity of God." It does not refer to a divine *causa sui* but takes place within very concrete events. (LaCocque, *Thinking Biblically*, p. 323).

28. Even his judgment over (and his condemnation of) his people may be seen from the perspective of God's personal commitment. See LaCocque, *Thinking Biblically*, pp. 322–323.

29. Ibid., p. 324: "Praise is the proper human response to revelation, rather than speculation on how it is that God made himself dependent on the human to be Yhwh, as the human is dependent on the divine to be the *imago Dei*." On this biblical enigma of human-divine interdependency and interlocution, see E. Levinas, *Totality and Infinity* (1961; Pittsburgh: University of Duquesne Press, 1969). See also J. Derrida's tantalizing commentary on Levinas's notion of the "face of God" in his "Violence and Metaphysics," in *Writing and Difference* (New York: Routledge, 1981), pp. 108–109:

> The foundation of metaphysics—in Levinas' sense—is to be encountered in the return to things themselves, where we find the common root of humanism and theology: the resemblance between man and God, man's visage and the Face of God. "The Other resembles God." Via the passageway of this resemblance, man's speech can be lifted up toward God, an almost unheard-of analogy which is the very movement of Levinas's discourse on discourse. Analogy as dialogue with God: "Discourse is discourse with God. . . . Metaphysics is the essence of this language with God." Discourse with God, and not in God as participation. Discourse with God, and not discourse on God and his attributes as theology. And the dissymmetry of my relation to the other, this "curvature of inter-subjective space signifies the divine intention of all truth." It "is, perhaps, the very presence of God." Presence as separation, presence-absence—again the break with Parmenides, Spinoza, Hegel, which only "the idea of creation ex nihilo" can consummate. . . . A resemblance which can be understood neither in terms of communion or knowledge, nor in terms of participation and incarnation. A resemblance which is neither a sign nor an effect of God. Neither the sign nor the effect exceeds the same. We are "in the Trace of God." A proposition which risks incompatability with every allusion to the "very presence of God." A proposition readily converted into atheism; and if God was an effect of the trace? If the idea of divine presence (life, existence, parousia, etc.), if the name of God was but the movement of erasure of the trace in

presence? Here it is a question of knowing whether the trace permits us to think presence in its system, or whether the reverse order is the true one. . . . The face of God disappears forever in showing itself. Thus are reassembled in the unity of their metaphysical signification, at the very heart of the experience denuded by Levinas, the diverse evocations of the Face of Yahweh. . . . The face of Yahweh is the total person and the total presence of the "Eternal speaking face to face with Moses," but saying to him also: "Thou canst not see my face: for there shall be no man see me and live. . . . Thou shalt stand upon a rock; and it shall come to pass, while my glory passeth by, that I will put thee in a cleft of the rock, and will cover thee with my hand while I pass by: And I will take away mine hand, and thou shalt see my back parts: but my face shall not be seen" (Exodus 33:20–23). The face of God which commands while hiding itself is at once more and less a face than all faces. Whence, perhaps, despite all Levinas's precautions, the equivocal complicity of theology and metaphysics in *Totality and Infinity*. Would Levinas subscribe to this infinitely ambiguous sentence from the *Book of Questions* by Edmond Jabes: "All faces are His; this is why He has no face"? The tensive relationship between Levinas's eschatology of divine transcendence and his phenomenological human-ism of the face is underlined here in dramatic fashion. The reference of the Eternal speaking face to face with Moses bears a telling allusion to Exodus 33:11 and to the burning bush episode.

30. LaCocque, *Thinking Biblically*, p. 324.

31. Ibid., p. 325.

32. "Justice triumphs in the prayer, faith, hope, and love, of those whose who seek justice. God is God only through the proclamation of his people. Yhwh malakh! (God reigns! cf. Psalm 93:1, 96:10, 97:1, 99:1, etc.). In this acclamation is redeemed the human abandonment of God reported in the myth of Genesis 2–3. God's risky wager, which he lost from the outset of creation, is now salvaged in Israel's liturgy celebrated in the temple." (Ibid.)

33. *Sifre Deuteronomy* 346, cited in LaCocque, *Thinking Biblically*, p. 325.

34. "I posits another person, the one who, being as he is, completely external to me, becomes my echo to whom I say you and who says you to me" (Emile Benveniste, *Problems in General Linguistics* [Miami: University of Miami Press, 1971], p. 224). Cited in LaCocque, *Thinking Biblically*, p. 326. See also LaCocque, ibid.: "Within Israel's consciousness, the Exodus inaugurates not only its history as a people . . . but also the world's redemption. The exodus from Egypt is toward the Promised Land, the microcosm and 'bridge-head' from where the whole of creation has started its trans-figuration into the Kingdom of God. The Exodus is thus the event par excellence, the 'V-Day' of history, the day when the world is changed into itself by eternity."

35. It is this temporal, historical, dynamic God-in-process who is evoked again and again in the Jewish Agadic tradition. The Midrash *Agadah*, for instance, renders Ex-odus 3:14 as "I who used to be the One is I who shall be the One"; while *Mekhita Bahodesh* 5 offers this variation: "I was in Egypt, I was at the sea, I was at Sinai, I was in the past, I will be in the future" (Footnote, quoted in LaCocque, *Thinking Biblically*, p. 327). In a similar vein, *Targum Yerushalmi* I reads: "I who was, who am and who shall be, sends me to you." Or again: "The one who says to the world—be! and it is; and who will say to it—be! and it is . . . it is He who sent me to you." Here again the emphasis is not so much on the magic or essence denoted by the Name itself but the invocation of

the Name—an invocation that is at the same time a vocation: "This will you tell the child of Israel: 'ehyeh sent me to you'" (cited in LaCocque, *Thinking Biblically*, p. 328). In his 1992 Cambridge lecture, "The Great Tautology," Steiner adds an interesting semantic inflection to the hermeneutic tradition of Exodus 3:14. Confirming this Exodic text to be one of the most foundational and seminal passages of Western and Middle Eastern religion, Steiner remarks how the untensed Hebrew wordplay disturbs the various attempted translations into the Indo-European language systems and injects ambiguity into the very heart of theological reflection, from the post-Exodic books of the Bible down to the Fourth Gospel and beyond. The recurrent question becomes: Who speaks in the burning bush? Is it being or non-being? Is it radical absence or real presence? Steiner identifies this voice as one of "spiritual and existential duplicity." Only by wagering on transcendence, he says, on an ultimate mystery beyond ourselves, can we begin to hear the voice of the burning bush. This Exodic passage calls for a conversion from the "symmetries of immanence" to a new theology of transcendence (see R. P. Carroll, "On Steiner the Theologian," in *Reading George Steiner*, ed. Nathan Scott and Ronald Sharp [Baltimore: John Hopkins University Press, 1994], p. 271).

36. Jean-Luc Marion, *God without Being*, trans. T. Carlson (Chicago: University of Chicago Press, 1991), p. 123. Marion is greatly indebted here to Levinas's discussion of transcendence in *Totality and Infinity* (The Hague: Nijhoff, 1961); in *Otherwise Than Being* (The Hague: Nijhoff, 1981); and in *De Dieu qui vient à l'idée* (Paris: Vrin, 1982).

37. Marion, *God without Being*, p. 152.

38. Ibid. p. 153

39. Ibid. pp. 156–158.

40. Ibid. p. 155.

41. Ibid.

42. J.-L. Marion, "In the Name: How to Avoid Speaking of Negative Theology," in *God, the Gift, and Postmodernism*, ed. J. Caputo and M. Scanlon (Bloomington: Indiana University Press, 1999). The title and theme of this paper critically echo Derrida's "Comment ne pas parler," in *Psyché*. For the most pioneering and illuminating treatment of Derrida and Levinas on the God question and negative theology, see J. D. Caputo, *The Prayer and Tears of Jacques Derrida: Religion without Religion* (Bloomington: Indiana University Press, 1997).

43. Marion, "In the Name."

44. J. D. Caputo, "On the Gift," discussion on the phenomenology of the gift with J. Derrida, J.-L. Marion, and R. Kearney and response by J. Caputo, Villanova University, in *God, the Gift, and Postmodernism*, pp. 54–78.

45. Even Derridean deconstruction can, on occasion, lend itself to this postmodern taste for sublime apocalypse. In *On the Name*, Derrida confronts us with the radically unindentifiable character of God's alterity, beyond all horizons of human or historical anticipation: "The other, that is, God and no matter who . . . as soon as every other is wholly other. For the most difficult, indeed the impossible, dwells there: there where the other loses his name or is able to change it in order to become no matter what other" (J. Derrida, *On the Name*, ed. and trans. T. Dutoit [Stanford, Calif.: Stanford University Press, 1995], p. 74). Here God becomes so unrecognizable in his irreducible otherness as to become indistinguishable, virtually, from anything at all. There is no way of telling. So in the last analysis, there may be no way of discerning between monsters and Messiahs. In the name of pure openness toward the other, this approach

argues that "the newcomer may be good or evil, but if you exclude the possibility that the newcomer is coming to destroy your house, if you want to control this and exclude this terrible possibility in advance, there is no hospitality. . . . The other, like the Messiah, must arrive wherever he or she wants" (J. Derrida, "Hospitality, Justice and Responsibility," in *Questioning Ethics*, ed. R. Kearney and M. Dooley [New York: Routledge, 1999], pp. 70–71). Some commentators, notably Simon Critchley, push this deconstructive logic to the ropes. "Does the impossible experience of the *es spukt*, the spectrality of the messianic," he asks, "look upwards to a divinity, divine justice, or even the starry heaven that frames the moral law?" Or does it not rather "look into the radically atheistic transcendence of the *il y a*, the absence, dis-aster and pure energy of the night that is beyond law?" (Simon Critchley, "On Derrida's Specters of Marx," in *Philosophy and Social Criticism* 21, no. 3 [1995]: 19). In short, how are we to link Derrida's atheological undecidability with decision and action, if God is not somehow present in his absence, as he is in the burning bush from which He speaks in Exodus, identifying Himself as a God of memory, covenant, and promise? What can deconstruction ultimately say about the Exodic God who can be seen (as a burning bush), heard (as one who promises to liberate his people) and believed (as God of past and future)? If the God of Exodus were to remain as anonymous as the *il y a* of primordial confusion and disaster (the *tohu bohu* of Genesis), surely Moses would not have been mobilized to go and emancipate his people from slavery and lead them toward a promised land of justice. He wouldn't even have been able to find his sandals again, would he? To overemphasize the undecidable, unspeakable, and ultimately "impossible" character of the Exodic deity may lead, I suspect, less to praxis than to paralysis, less toward new tasks of communal liberation than to a certain bedazzlement before the mystical sublimity of the event itself (as non-event *ici et maintenant sans présence*), a return to the night in which all gods are black. *Khora.* Although Derrida stops short of equating the alterity of God with that of the Monster, some of his postmodern contemporaries have no such hesitations. In all, Derrida's treatment of the eschatological a-God (*a-dieu*) is highly suggestive, if characteristically elusive. Writing of the "open circumcised word" in Paul Célan's poetry, Derrida offers the following comment on the complex and often disturbing relation between alterity, monstrosity, and what he calls the "messianic or eschatological prophet," Elijah:

> Ouverte d'abord comme une porte, ouverte à l'étranger, à l'autre, au prochain, à l'hote ou à quiconque. A quiconque sans doute dans la figure de l'avenir absolu (celui qui viendra, plus precisément qui viendrait car cet avenir, celui à venir, sa venue ne doit pas être assurée ni calculable), donc dans la figure de la créature monstrueuse. L'avenir absolu ne peut s'annoncer que sous l'espèce de la monstruosité, au-délà de toutes les formes ou les normes anticipables, au-délà des genres. Et je passe ici sur ce que l'apparition du Rabbi Loew nous rappelle du Golem, l'inventeur du monstre. . . . Parole ouverte à quiconque dans la figure aussi, peut-être, de quelque prophète Elie, de son fantôme ou de son double. Il est méconnaissable, à travers cette monstration de monstre, mais il faut savoir le reconnaître. Elie est celui à qui l'hospitalité est due, promise, préscrite. Il peut venir, on doit le savoir, à tout moment. . . . Ici-même le monstre, ou Elie, l'hôte ou l'autre se tient devant la porte. (*Shibboleth* [Paris: Galilée, 1986], pp. 102–103)

See also Derrida's development of the links between the monstrous, the sublime, and the incalculable/incommensurable/incomparable character of alterity in *The Truth in*

Painting (Chicago: University of Chicago Press, 1987), pp. 142–143, 349–351. These links are teased out in Section 4 of this work entitled "The Colossal," where Derrida revisits Kant's analytic of the sublime in *The Critique of Judgment*. He explores Kant's definition of the "monstrous" (*ungeheuer*) as anything whose size "defeats the end that forms its concept." The related notion of the "colossal" (*kolossalisch*) is understood as "the mere presentation of a concept which is almost too great for presentation, i.e., borders on the relatively monstrous." The sublime and the monstrous both operate according to a double sentiment of attraction/recoil which acknowledges the sublime character of the colossal/monstrous as both an "excess," "surplus," and "superabundance" on the one hand, and a implosive, negative "abyss" on the other. In order to try to apprehend what is uncontainable and unpresentable by our imagination, we are compelled to recoil, take a distance, from the sublime/monstrous/colossal. And here, curiously, at the very limit of perception, comprehension, and imagination, Derrida seems to recognize a certain demand for narrative: "Does not the distance required for the experience of the sublime open up perception to the space of narrative?" (p. 142). Perhaps Moses's experience of the burning bush is, in these respects, not unrelated to the sublime (as understood by Derrida). A suspicion confirmed by Derrida's invocation, later in the same book, of Moses removing his sandals in Exodus 3 in order to mark an appropriate distance from the holy event unfolding before him—a common Hebraic gesture of respect and awe before the sacred as witnessed in the Mishnah prohibiting the wearing of shoes on the Sabbath (pp. 350–351). Derrida returns to the "I Am" revelation of Exodus 3 on a number of suggestive, if characteristically allusive, occasions, for example, his discussion of "Jahweh spricht nur immer 'Ja'" in "Nombre de Oui," in *Psyché* (Paris: Galilée, 1987), pp. 639 ff.; his reference to YAHWE as "I am he who is . . ." in relation to James Joyce's use of "HE WAR" in *Finnegan's Wake*, in "Two Words for Joyce," in *Post-structuralist Joyce*, ed. D. Attridge and D. Ferrer (New York: Cambridge University Press, 1984), pp. 145–146, 151; and in *The Postcard* (Chicago: University of Chicago Press, 1987), pp. 141–142; the commentary on "the Eternal speaking face to face with Moses" in his essay on Levinas, "Violence and Metaphysics," in *Writing and Difference* (New York: Routledge, 1981), pp. 108–109; the analysis of the "unpronounceable name" of the Jewish God in "Shibboleth for Paul Celan," in *Wordtraces: Readings of Paul Celan*, ed. A. Fiorefos (Baltimore: John Hopkins University Press, 1994), pp. 54–55; and, finally, the description of God-memory in terms of "*desseins-d'aveugles*" and the eschatological temporal tension within the tetragrammaton in *Memoirs of the Blind* (Chicago: University of Chicago Press, 1993), p. 54: "It is theological through and through, to the point, sometimes included, sometimes excluded, where the self-eclipsing trait cannot even say itself in the present, since it is not gathered, since it does not gather itself, into any present, 'I am who I am' (a formula whose original grammatical form, as we know, implies the future). The outline or tracing separates and separates itself; it retraces only border lines, intervals, a spacing grid with no possible appropriation."

46. Berel Lang, "The Representation of Limits," in *Probing the Limits of Representation*, ed. Saul Friedlander (Cambridge, Mass.: Harvard University Press, 1992).

47. Peter Haidu, "The Dialectics of Unspeakability," in *Probing the Limits of Representation*, p. 284.

48. Cited in ibid., p. 288.

49. Ibid. p. 292

50. J.-F. Lyotard, *The Postmodern Condition* (Minneapolis: University of Minnesota Press, 1984), pp. 79 ff.

51. For a more sympathetic reading of Lyotard's post-Holocaust aesthetic of the sublime, see Geoffrey Hartman, "The Book of Destruction," in *Probing the Limits of Representation*, pp. 320 ff.

52. Slavoj Zizek, *The Plague of Fantasies* (London: Verso, 1997), pp. 218–229.

53. Zizek, "The Unconscious Law," in *The Plague of Fantasies*, p. 219.

54. Ibid.

55. See Gilles Deleuze, another radical postmodern theorist, on this subject: "By establishing THE LAW as an ultimate ground . . . the object of the law is by definition unknowable and elusive. Clearly THE LAW, as defined by its pure form, without substance or object of any determination whatsoever, is such that no one knows nor can know what it is. It operates without making itself known. It defines a realm of transgression where one is already guilty and where one oversteps the bounds without knowing what they are." (Gilles Deleuze, *Coldness and Cruelty* [New York: Zone Books, 1991], pp. 82–83. See Zizek's psychoanalytic commentary on this in ibid., pp. 225–227).

56. Zizek, *The Plague of Fantasies*, p. 227.

57. Ibid.

58. Ibid., p. 229.

59. Ibid. pp. 229–230. See, from a very different philosophical viewpoint, William Desmond's reading of Kant's notion of "genius," "terror," and "transgression" in the Third Critique. In spite of the difference of perspective, Desmond's conclusion is remarkably similar to that of the postmoderns on certain points; for example, his conclusion: "If we say something other gives the rule to the self, then either there is an inward otherness of selfhood which is beyond complete autonomy, or the self is a manifestation of something more primordial, and what is primordial is not itself lawlike and ordered and regular: the primordial is beyond the law. . . . When self proclaims its complete autonomy, it is only masking from itself its issue from something that is not reasonable, or intelligible, or morally benign. . . . More often it is wildness, frenzy, the primitive, the ugly, the excremental, the senseless. Genius and madness become indistinguishable. And we seem hard put to discriminate between divine madness and mad madness" ("Kant and the Terror of Genius," in *Kant's Aesthetics*, ed. Walter de Gruyter [Berlin and New York, 1998], p. 614). Unlike Zizek and fellow devotees of the equivocal sublime, Desmond is clearly uneasy before such lack of discrimination.

60. Zizek, *The Plague of Fantasies*, p. 228. Such dialectical conflations of God and monstrosity are not, however, the prerogative of postmodern philosophers. One finds similar evocations of sublime transgression of good and evil in the neo-gnostic writings of several New Age authors. And this represents what we might call a fourth, more populist, approach to the monstrous God. Joseph Campbell, one of the leading theorists of New Age mysticism and myth, epitomizes this conflation of the unknowable deity with the monstrous when he writes: "By monster I mean some horrendous presence or apparition that explodes all your standards for harmony, order and ethical conduct. . . . That's God in the role of destroyer. Such experiences go past ethical judgements. Ethics is wiped out. . . . God is horrific" (*The Power of Myth* [New York: Doubleday, 1988], p. 222). The book in which this statement appears, *The Power of Myth*, was not some occult curiosity but the number one bestseller in North America for three years and the basis of an extraordinarily popular TV series that was broadcast

internationally in the late 1980s and the 1990s. Such a return to the mythic indistinction of monstrosity is also evidenced, albeit innocuously, in the growing fascination of Hollywood and the Internet with "aliens"—a high-tech breed of extraterrestrial monsters who confound the boundaries of good and evil, exploit our obsession with the hysterical sublime, and blur distinctions between gods and demons. But the rapport between aliens and monsters is another day's work. (See my papers on "Others and Aliens: Between Good and Evil," University of Virginia, March 1998, and "God and Desire," Villanova University, September 1987, published in *God, the Gift, and Postmodernism.*)

61. Zizek, *The Plague of Fantasies*, pp. 228–229. See here Levinas's description of the "there is" as radically godless in his early essay, "There Is: Existence without Existents," first published in 1946 as a section of *De l'existence à l'existant* (Paris: Vrin) and reprinted in *The Levinas Reader*, ed. S. Hand (London: Blackwell, 1989). Levinas talks of the "there is" or *il y a* as a "mute, absolutely indeterminate menace," a nocturnal space without exit or response and utterly impervious to God. "Rather than to a God the notion of the there is leads us to the absence of God, the absence of any being . . . before the light comes" (pp. 32–33).

62. Ricoeur, "From Interpretation to Translation," p. 341:

This resonance would already have at least a double sense: the enigma of a positive revelation giving rise to thought (about existence, efficacity, faithfulness, accompanying through history), and of a negative revelation dissociating the Name from those utilitarian and magical values concerning power that were ordinarily associated with it. And perhaps the even greater enigma of a revelation, in the usual sense of a theophany, or a nonrevelation, in the sense of a withdrawal into the incognito.

63. Ibid.

64. S. Breton, *Libres Commentaires*, p. 59.

65. Ibid., p. 60.

66. Ibid., p. 64. See Derrida's subtle and suggestive reading of Eckhart's negative theology in "Comment ne pas parler," *Dénégations* (1986), in *Psyché* (Paris: Galilée, 1987), trans. K. Frieden in *Languages of the Unsayable: The Play of Negativity in Literature and Literary Theory*, ed. Sanford Budick and Wolfgang Iser (New York: Columbia University Press, 1989), pp. 3–70.

67. Eckhart, *In Exodum*, 3:14, *Lateinische Werke*, II, 21. Cited by Breton, *Libres Commentaires*, pp. 61–62. See Stanislas Breton's suggestive gloss on this, ibid., p. 62:

L'acte d'être, sous la flamme du buisson ardent, devient flamme à son tour, élan de vie, feu originel, déployé en un groupe d'opérations, de mouvements et de relations qu'entretient une énergie bouillonnante qui se répand au-dedans comme au-dehors. Le mot ferveur est ici décisif. Il projette sur l'abstrait dynamisme de la *causa sui* l'irradiation d'une source de lumière et de chaleur qui entraine, en son tourbillon, le monde et la divinité elle-même. L'univers est un buisson d'étincelles. Ephémères ou durables, ces 'fleurs du feu' naissent d'un espace festif qui n'est autre que la surabondance de l'acte pur.

On this metaphor of the God of Exodus 3:14 as an overspilling, bubbling, superabundant source, see also A. Gesche, "Apprendre de Dieu ce qu'il est" in *Qu'est-ce que*

Dieu? (Brussels: Publications des Facultés universitaires Saint-Louis, 1985), p. 743:

> La tradition chrétienne parle de Dieu comme *pègè*, Source intarissable. C'est sans doute parce que Dieu est source débordante qu'il peut ainsi 'se vider' (Ph. 2,7) et donner sans rien perdre, se perdre sans rien perdre. Qu'il peut même donner 'ce qu'il n'est pas', si l'on peut se permettre d'exprimer ainsi ce qu'est la création, position et surgissement d'une véritable altérité. La surabondance divine explique cette priorité de Dieu, d'un Dieu toujours en avance, jamais en retard sur l'être. 'Je suis qui je suis' (Ex 3,14). Superbe tautologie, qui signifie que Dieu n'est pas déterminé par une antériorité qui le limiterait, comme il en est des Idées éternelles incréées de Platon. Surtout, il n'est pas précédé par nos définitions. Dieu est 'dès-avant' (*prior*), il est Sur-Sum. Non pas, comme l'être précédé ("*cogito/ergo sum*"), mais le précédant, puisqu'il y a infiniment plus dans le mot Dieu que dans le mot être'. Seigneur, ainsi que nous l'avons vu plus haut,—termes plus adéquats que celui de personne,—que Dieu peut ainsi perdre l'initiative d'une priorité et le risque d'un premier pas, qui chez tout autre serait faux pas?

One might usefully compare and contrast this Eckhartian reading of Exodus 3:14 with Franz Rosenweig's radical reading from a more Jewish perspective. See "The Eternal," in F. Rosenweig and M. Buber, *Scripture and Translation* (Bloomington: Indiana University Press, 1994).

68. Meister Eckhart, "The Sermons, 16," in *Meister Eckhart*, p. 171.

69. S. Breton, *Libres Commentaires*, p. 66. He adds: "Having divinised being one must go beyond it by passing through it."

70. Ibid., p. 67

71. Nicholas of Cusa, "Dialogus de Possest," in *A Concise Introduction to the Philosophy of Nicholas of Cusa*, ed. J. Hopkins (Minneapolis: University of Minnesota Press, 1980), pp. 120, 69. See also my commentary on Nicholas of Cusa's discussion of God as *possest* in *The Wake of Imagination* (New York: Routledge, 1988), pp. 75–78.

72. See my development of this notion of God as possest/possibility/may-be—in analogy with Heidegger's notion of Being as *Vermögen*/power/can-be—in *Poétique du Possible* (Paris: Éditions de Beauchesne, 1984), in particular Part 4, where I adumbrate a new eschatological hermeneutic of God as *posse* in critical comparison and contrast with Heidegger's ontological hermeneutic of being as *Vermögend-Mögende* in his "Letter on Humanism" and elsewhere (in *Phenomenology and Humanism*, ed. R. Zaner and D. Ihde [New York: Capricorn Books, 1973], pp. 147–181).

73. Jacques Derrida, "Loving in Friendship: Perhaps—the Noun and the Adverb," in *The Politics of Friendship*, trans. G. Collins (New York: Verso, 1997), pp. 28–29. See also Derrida's development of this notion of the "perhaps" of impossible-possibilization in "Comme si c'était possible, 'within such limits' . . . ," *Revue Internationale de Philosophie* 3, no. 205 (1998); and John Caputo's illuminating "Apology for the Impossible," in *God, the Gift, and Postmodernism*.

"Absolute Interruption"

On Faith

Kevin Hart

I would like to begin by listening to Jacques Derrida telling us about "the experience of faith."[1] To be sure, one does not expect such a tale from someone who assures us that he can "quite rightly pass for an atheist," but his readers have long since come to expect the unexpected from him.[2] With that in mind, let us hear him speaking toward the end of "Faith and Knowledge: The Two Sources of 'Religion' at the Limits of Reason Alone," a remarkable text he composed several years after his confession of atheism, if indeed that is what it was.[3] Immediately before I break in, he has been telling us about testimony and a "social bond" that unravels itself. And then he says, "If belief [*la croyance*] is the ether of the address and relation to the utterly other, it is to be found in the experience itself of non-relationship or of absolute *interruption* (indicies: "Blanchot," "Levinas" . . .)."[4]

I stop him there: He has given us enough to think about in a title and a sentence. Derrida's title is of course a weaving together of others, two of which have been silently changed, and so we recall canonical texts in the philosophy of religion by Hegel, Bergson, and Kant. The title of Kant's *Die Religion innerhalb der Grenzen der blossen Vernunft* (1793) has been altered: once in the middle of the subtitle where *innerhalb* ("within") is reset as *aux* ("at the"), thereby foregrounding the question of what happens at a limit; and once at the very border of the subtitle, where Kant and Bergson meet, by placing "religion" in quotation marks and therefore signaling that the word is being used in a special sense. Both these changes are important, and I will return to them. What particularly strikes me, though, is the expression "absolute *interruption*." Perhaps it should not trouble me, since Derrida explicitly reminds us that it can be traced to Maurice Blanchot and Emmanuel Levinas. Then again, very different attitudes to faith could be developed starting from Blanchot or Levinas. So maybe there is a reason to be apprehensive.

"Absolute *interruption*": the expression recalls several others familiar to theologians, beginning with Spinoza's definition of God as "absolutely infinite."[5] I think of Hegel's doctrine of "Absolute Spirit," and at the same time of something he disliked intensely, namely Schleiermacher's founding of religion on the consciousness of being "absolutely dependent."[6] This network could easily be extended eastward to include "*absolute* nothingness," a notion proposed to amplify the doctrine of Christ's kenosis.[7] Or, returning to France, we could find ourselves brooding over Jean-Yves Lacoste's meditations in *Expérience et Absolu*.[8] Unlike "absolute," the word "interruption" plays a less conspicuous role in theology; nevertheless, the concept has been a powerful one, especially since the Reformation, and I will touch on this a little later. Now, though, I would like to pose two questions. Could it be that Derrida is quietly working himself into this complicated philosophical and theological network? Could it be that he is suggesting "absolute *interruption*" as a rival to "absolutely infinite," "Absolute Spirit" or "absolute dependence"?

These questions cannot be answered quickly, for two reasons. First, it would take some time to establish the ways in which the word "absolute" works in Derrida's writings. Kant notes that the adjective "absolute" must be used with caution, for it can indicate both "that which is in itself possible" and "that something is valid in all respects, without limitation."[9] Derrida also uses the adjective in different senses: to suggest a discharge of debt, that which cannot be calculated, or the strange logic of stricture. All are relevant to my discussion, and a close examination would doubtless reveal others. Second, we would need to determine the scope, strength, and status of the word "interruption" in "Faith and Knowledge" and other texts by Derrida. To begin to do this effectively, we would have to read Blanchot and Levinas in a patient and thorough manner, taking care to differentiate them whenever a word such as "faith" or "God" is used. Although Derrida cites these great thinkers in the one context of "absolute *interruption*," in truth both are more gripped by interruption than by talk of the absolute. More challenging, because less likely, is the task of reading "interruption" from the perspectives of theology. And since the word as cited occurs in an essay devoted to faith and knowledge, a contribution to a symposium on "religion today," itself a title chosen by Derrida, one can hardly be accused of diverting a discourse heading elsewhere. And yet one should not presume to know where, if anywhere in particular, that discourse is aimed. For Derrida's contribution to "religion today" declares that it is not about religion but about "religion," whatever that may be.

***

Early in "Faith and Knowledge" Derrida distinguishes faith from religion. He has drawn similar lines before, separating faith and theology, prophetic messianism and religious institution, and he is well aware of other ways in which a cut could be made.[10] Whether a vinculum should separate faith and religion is of course a traditional topic in theology, and in Derrida's essay this tradition appears principally in Kant's critique of it. At first his reference to Kant may lead to confusion, because what Kant calls religion is associated with what Derrida wishes to construe as faith, *croyance* rather than *foi*. There is only "*one* (true) *religion*," Kant says, which is "hidden within and has to do with moral dispositions," while there can be external "*faiths* of several kinds."[11] These historical faiths are vehicles for religion, and it is desirable to pass from the historical faith in which one finds oneself to the universal religion. In doing so, one gains a "*saving* faith," which consists in a faith in atonement and a faith that in conforming to our duty we will become pleasing to God.[12] Ecclesiastical faith begins with atonement, while religious faith prizes moral action; and the two are to be harmonized in a liberal Christology: The true object of saving faith is not the historical Jesus but rather Christ, the God-Man, "the archetype, lying in our reason."[13]

Derrida seeks to revive this enlightenment understanding of faith by radicalizing it: Belief in atonement is dropped and religious faith is reworked in an expanded context. Faith is not to be accommodated in Christology; indeed, since faith, *croyance*, eschews predication, it is not to be accommodated anywhere. Yet what Derrida retains from Kant is something older than a liberalization of faith. I am thinking of Jesus's preaching of the kingdom, which started to attract close attention only with the Enlightenment. For Kant, the kingdom was to be understood in purely ethical terms, and this thought has remained in play in theology for the past two centuries, even when the kingdom has come to be interpreted by way of eschatology, even apocalypse.[14] The *basileia* for Derrida is not an eschatological reign of God; it has no parousia as horizon; it is unequal to itself and is always "to come" (*à venir*) rather than abiding in a future present (*l'avenir*). Nor is this *basileia* to be achieved by the slow and certain progress of human society, informed by reading the Bible, as one often finds in nineteenth- and early twentieth-century Protestant liberalism. One can find this view in Albrecht Ritschl, although that venerable father of the liberal tradition also affirmed that the transformative quality of God's reign comes from its standing at variance with the mundane human order.[15] Some of his admirers, evangelists of the social gospel, interpreted him otherwise and sought to spread the kingdom here and now and thus revive our life on earth.[16]

I have never liked to translate *basileia* as "kingdom," as happens in the King James Version of the Bible, for the word brings with it too many associations of British regnal politics. To be sure, the *basileia* is compared to a secular reign (Matthew 18:23), yet this parable needs to be kept within the perspective set by Luke 17:20–21. The *basileia* cannot be experienced in the same way as the political administration of a land, if it can be experienced at all. I imagine that for other reasons Derrida might be uneasy about the word *basileia*, even if I leave it in Greek. And yet I wish to retain the word; perhaps something in his writing obliges me to do so. Derrida's *basileia*, if I can continue to call it that, falls outside what the word usually means; it is not motivated by redemptive faith, and it carries more of a stress than one finds in liberalism of the sheer verticality of the kingdom. The reign of justice does not submit to calculation. Also, though, the *basileia* intervenes in this world; it seeks to influence material decisions and to question the limit dividing law from justice. Such is the burden of Derrida's recent work on friendship and forgiveness, not to mention justice itself. To put it rather sharply, in terms I shall have to explain and refine in a moment, he attends to the possibility of an impossible kingdom or, if you like, a kingdom of the impossible.

I will return to this *basileia* a little later. Before then, I would like to look back past Kant to a moment of the tradition which he seeks to redirect. I have in mind the admirably lucid analysis of the relations between faith and religion that St. Thomas furnishes in both his early commentary on Boethius's *De Trinitate* and the *Summa Theologiæ*. Religion is a moral virtue, he notes early and late, a species of justice: In the practice of religion, we act justly toward God. On the other hand, faith is a theological virtue; it is given to us by God and leads us directly to him. Because the act of faith occurs within religion, faith and religion are materially the same; yet because faith and religion have different objects, they are formally distinct.[17] So we can discriminate between faith and religion without changing the nature of religion. Even were he to have known of them, St. Thomas would have had no need to place quotation marks around the word "religion."

When Derrida adjusts the relations between religion and faith, however, he has no doubt that "religion" should be placed in inverted commas. Excluding the subtitle, the first time these little marks appear is on the second page of the text. He has been speaking of "the evil of abstraction," and he passes from thinking of "religion today" to talking of "religion." This is not because he suddenly attends to the word or the concept "religion." Rather, it seems that he has just become aware that the word is unclean or unclear. It is tempting to call on the little taxonomy of quotation marks devised by I. A. Richards and debate whether on any given page Derrida means ^{w}religion^{w} or ^{q}religion^{q} or ^{r}religion^{r} or any of the rest, including !religion!.[18] Doubtless religion may be complicated by its dual sources in holiness and faith or seen to be escaping in all directions like spilt mercury because of its many meanings. And so quotation marks are imposed. It is as though Derrida has realized that the word "religion" must be held with pincers, or as though the word has just realized that Derrida has taken it up and so raises its eyebrows in astonishment. Does religion scare Derrida, or should it be scared of him? Perhaps a little of both. The practice of placing "religion" in quotation marks is far from consistent in "Faith and Knowledge," though, which of course will raise other eyebrows, and in any case there may be other reasons why the word deserves those inverted commas in the first place.

Hegel dominates the title "Faith and Knowledge," leaving Bergson and Kant to meet in the subtitle, "The Two Sources of 'Religion' at the Limits of Reason Alone." Now if we recall Bergson's book—*The Two Sources of Morality and Religion*—we can see that Derrida omits the word "morality" when fabricating his title. Or maybe "morality" is not so much occluded in the title as absorbed by "Religion." Perhaps those quotation marks indicate morality. Were that so, morality would suspend religion for us to view it all the better; it would hold it aloft on either side like two angels slightly too large to dance on the head of a pin. Something in this thought makes me recall how Levinas uses the word "religion," and I recall one sentence in particular: "For the relation between the being here below and the transcendent being that results in no community of concept or totality—a relation without relation—we reserve the term religion."[19] For there to be true religion, according to Levinas, humanity must be separated from God. It is atheism, the state of being without God, that "conditions a veritable relationship with a true God *kath auto*."[20] Defining religion in this way performs two theological tasks at the same time: It creates a space for and welcomes revelation while rejecting what Levinas takes to be mysticism. In *Totality and Infinity* and beyond, Levinas will earth revelation in ethics, confiding that "the kingdom of heaven is ethical," and he will oppose ethics to Christian mysticism, which he associates—all too hastily, I think—with immediacy and fusion.[21]

"Religion," for Derrida, would therefore be formed at the limit of ethics and revelation, and the man himself would be "religious" while quite rightly passing for an atheist. His position should not be confused with what Karl Jaspers calls "philosophical faith": the conviction, underived from revelation, although sometimes in harmony with it, that human beings are open to transcendence.[22] Derrida speaks of faith, *croyance*, granted at the limit of a "religion" that offers no experience of knowledge. I think of Kant, of course, but also of Levinas, for whom equally there could be no cognition of God: A "you" is always inserted between the "I" and "absolute He," breaking any correlation between me and the divinity.[23] Remaining agnostic about this "absolute He," Derrida stands at a distance from the word "God," using it as an example for a hardened presence or, at best, "a reality that would constitute the object of an indisputably determining experience."[24] No mistake about it: Derrida's "religion" will be exercised wholly in relations with the "utterly other," the movement toward whom is holiness itself, and as we have seen that these relations will occur in "the ether of the address," in the testimonary faith that is presumed in any encounter with the other. This is a faith without religion or, for that matter, without any determinate knowledge: a credence that universally underwrites and unsettles all discourses, including those of faith and knowledge.[25]

* * *

Once Derrida's notion of credence is grasped, the possibility arises that a positive religion such as Christianity is open to a deconstruction in its name. I should say at the outset that this is a rather different enterprise from that broached by Jean-Luc Nancy.[26] Derrida is not concerned to rethink a notion such as sense (*sens*) that has been obscured by Christianity but to affirm faith as testimonary credence. Deconstruction, here, involves a reduction: not in Husserl's sense of the word but in Levinas's, namely a leading back from the Said to the Saying and, if it can be countenanced, a perpetual unsaying of the Said.[27] Faith would not be open to deconstruction; rather, it would be both its impetus and medium, even were it not done in the name of faith.

Now there are internal limits to this disarrangement or rearrangement of religion, even though they are divided and equivocal. In the first place, it is fundamental to the gospel that human beings are always and already in relation with others and with God: Our identity is not frozen in self-identity, whether imagined as a ground or a horizon. More generally, Christianity is a singular name for a plural phenomenon: adherence to the credal formulations of Chalcedon or Nicea does not always imply agreement between different groups, even about quite basic matters such as the Eucharist. And furthermore, it is deep in the nature of Christianity that no lines be drawn between insiders and outsiders. As soon as someone tries to separate Christians from non-Christians, one finds people outside who seem more Christian than many of those inside. One does not have to rely on Karl Rahner's notion of "anonymous Christians" or "implicit Christianity" for support.[28] It is what the gospel tells us to expect: Many people outside the fold are closer to the *basileia* than some of those within.

As Derrida himself says when answering a question at Villanova in 1994, a deconstruction of religion would be aimed at "a set of beliefs, dogmas, or institutions." Yet, as he readily concedes, in religions there are "tensions, heterogeneity, disruptive volcanoes . . . which cannot be reduced to an institution, to a corpus, to a system."[29] To this reservation I would merely add that the *fides qua* and the *fides quae* are in a fluid and dynamic relationship that does not allow an easy separation of faith and dogma, and that in any case religion involves a greater mix of elements than is entertained here. Experiences, rituals, and sacred narratives: these deeply inform dogma and faith, and one can hardly imagine an institution that does not answer to an anterior ritual. While a de-sedimenting of the Church at its deepest institutional levels, the magisterium and the papacy, would undoubtedly have effects on ritual, there is no reason to suppose that the mass would be any the less Christian because of the changes that would follow. In fact one could argue that Paul, the earliest documenter of the resurrection, invites us to consider the gospel as a blow that comes from outside all human knowledge, including religious knowledge.

I am thinking of I Corinthians 1:19, "I will destroy the wisdom of the wise," itself a quotation of Isaiah 29:14. Overlaying that thought is a memory of Martin Luther citing Paul in the *Heidelberg Disputation* (1518). In his twentieth thesis, Luther follows the standard translation of the verse and renders the Greek verb "*apollumi*" by the Latin *perdere*: "*apolv thn sofian tvn sofvn*" becomes *perdit sapientiam sapientum*. In thesis twenty-one, however, he speaks of how the cross demolishes human works and the natural man: *quia per crucem destruuntur opera et crucifigitur Adam*. Faith must make its way past the speculations of the *theologia gloriæ* to its ground—or, better, non-ground—in the *theologia crucis*. As we know, Heidegger drew this very thread from Luther's *Disputation* in his early seminars when he started to speak of *Destruktion*.[30] Now Luther's *destructio* participates in contexts other than those of Heidegger's *Destruktion*, and the same is true of *déconstruction*. That said, one should not presume that deconstruction is alien to Christianity. On the contrary, Christianity has frequently been tied to different styles of deconstruction, and these have been pursued in tension with other concerns. In Meister Eckhart, for instance, one can find contrary movements of neo-Platonism and deconstruction. To this suggestion, I would like to add a related thought. It is this: The vocabulary of the West is so thoroughly saturated in Christian themes and motifs that no discourse can proclaim itself not to be Christian in some of its effects without risk of embarrassment. As I have suggested, not only is the *basileia* folded into Derrida's refiguring of religion but also it helps to animate what is ethically valuable in his writing. Derrida himself openly recognizes that the very idea of deconstructing Christianity in the name of faith can be traced to Søren Kierkegaard.[31] And with appropriate qualifications, one could say the same of Karl Barth, for whom religion is unbelief.[32]

St. Thomas would not have felt a need to place "religion" in quotation marks, even had they been available to him. Nevertheless, he would have known what Derrida means by "faith," and in his commentary on Boethius he fully defends that usage:

> And because in human society one person must make use of another just as he does himself in matters in which he is not self-sufficient, he must take his stand on what another knows and is unknown to himself, just as he does on what he himself knows. As a consequence, faith is necessary in human society, one person believing what another says. As Cicero remarks, this is the basis of justice. That is why there is no lie without moral fault, for every lie does some harm to this so essential faith.[33]

Yet St. Thomas also distinguishes human faith from faith as a theological virtue. A slash divides what enables us to communicate with one another and "our hope for blessedness."[34]

This line does not fall sufficiently obliquely for my liking, since Derrida is speaking at the limits of "religion." In the first place, his emphasis that credence escapes all predicative attribution means that credence crosses the apophatic tradition. Even Derrida's confession of atheism involves a little faith and a little negative theology; and when he places those quotation marks around "religion" we should be aware that they indicate that a negative theology of religion has already started. Perhaps we could expand Richards's taxonomy of quotation marks by adding the convention $^{\eta\theta}$religion$^{\eta\theta}$ where "$\eta\theta$" stands for "a negative theology." And in the second place, Derrida's concept of faith comes within cooee of some liberal Christians, regardless of his personal confession. Unlike Derrida, I quite rightly pass for a believer. I agree with Gerhard Ebeling that faith is a medium, although for reasons that will become apparent I would not say with him that it is also a ground.[35] It is an opening and a risk. And so, without contesting the broad lines of Derrida's argument about the apophaticism of human faith, I wish to retain a faith that can criticize religion but that comes from God rather than circulates solely among human beings.

∗ ∗ ∗

"The shortest definition of religion: interruption." So writes Johann Baptist Metz in a selection of aphorisms.[36] This may indeed be one of the shortest definitions of religion, although as Jürgen Moltmann observes, it is not adequate, for in any state of affairs a single interruption can always be deflected or absorbed, thereby allowing things to continue as usual. "'Interruption,'" he writes, "is not an eschatological category. The eschatological category is conversion."[37] Would it help Metz, I wonder, if someone proposed one of the second shortest definitions of religion: "absolute interruption"? For the moment, I leave aside whose suggestion this is and simply note that the expression first occurs in Blanchot's meditation, "Interruption (As on a Riemann Surface)."[38]

Blanchot distinguishes three modalities of relation: one in which the other is dialectically suborned by the same, another in which the same is ecstatically fused with the other, and one he calls "the third relation," in which no unity is established. In this third relation, the transcendent other does not appear in my horizon or project a horizon, for he or she cannot be reduced to a phenomenon. Being is therefore interrupted by the other, which means in part that the other cannot be approached by way of possibility. I cannot have reciprocal relations with the other because we do not relate as one subject to another; our relationship is marked by an irreducible strangeness which we experience in speaking with one another or even in being silent together. If we ask what sort of disturbance is at issue here, Blanchot tells us there are two kinds of rupture. Some interruptions are allowed or encouraged in order to facilitate understanding: for example, a conversation with its alternation of speech and silence. Others are "more enigmatic and more grave" because they fracture all attempts to form a unity, and it is the latter which obtains in relations with the other.[39]

So the image of the man without horizon appears on the far side of phenomenology, and Blanchot remains interested in that borderland. And yet he is distracted. His allusion to a Riemannian surface hesitates between an analogy of proportionality and a metaphor and, when judged as a metaphor, it fails rather badly. Blanchot's chief concern in "Interruption" is to commend a new sense of writing which disturbs unity, and the thought of an n-sheeted surface on which a complex variable elaborates itself by passing from one sheet to another strikes him as an apt image for that brave new world. Yet unless this surface has an infinite number of sheets, unity is not compromised, and not even the bridges between sheets can rightly be seen as interruptions.[40] Far more intriguing, however, are Blanchot's remarks that touch the limit of a phenomenological exercise, those ruptures that arise from affliction or fatigue when one waits for nothing and to no end. These experiences may not be as barren as they seem to those who suffer them, Blanchot thinks. They may open onto the impossible. Of particular interest is the speculation that follows these borderline cases. "Let us suppose an interruption that would in some sense be absolute and absolutely neutral."[41] This Outside, as he calls it, would be "exterior and anterior to all speech"; it would be brought into expression by a speech that contests all law, even its own, and would take the form of fragments such as those of René Char rather than aphorisms such as those of Johann Baptist Metz.[42] For Blanchot, the poet writes without horizon, while the theologian must write within one, even when he or she is not composing aphorisms.

An absolute interruption, then, could not be reappropriated by its contexts. At once, though, a counter-example presents itself, and since it comes from a text signed by Derrida, I should quote it immediately. On close inspection, it is not "Derrida" I cite but a speaker in a dialogue he has composed which turns, now closely and now distantly, on the poetry of Angelus Silesius and the negative theologies at work there. "The possibility of the impossible, of the 'more possible' that as such is also possible ('more impossible than the impossible'), marks an *absolute interruption* in the regime of the possible that nonetheless remains, if this can be said, in place."[43] Now "the impossible" here is not tied to the endlessness of dying, which Blanchot calls the "impossibility of possibility."[44] It is what is unforeseen and unpredictable as seen, after the fact, from the perspective of the possible. So Derrida contends that what is unforeseen comes, disturbs the order of things, and unconditionally changes this order in one or more ways but without disordering the whole. It is not a matter of changing an essence but rather of another register being introduced into the order of the possible. It is a kingdom that is more of a haunting than an inhabiting.

When talking of the absolute, Derrida, like Heidegger, invites us to hear the Latin *ab-solvere*, meaning "unfastened from something or someone."[45]

We may recall Derrida reading the third *Critique* and concerning himself there with the "absolute interruption" that for Kant yields free beauty and that for Derrida leads us to find a "without" as a trace in the thing of beauty.[46] Or we may recall him in a Kierkegaardian moment speaking of "the mad moment of decision, at the point of its absolute interruption."[47] No decision can be calculated, and so we may quietly add what he does not say, then, that a decision will carry in its wake a supplement of indecision. Or, again, we may recall him brooding over how in Levinas there occurs a possible trace "of absolute interruptions, of the ab-solute as interruption."[48] Examples can be multiplied, but the point is evident: An interruption may be absolute but it can never be pure. A border is always in the background, never quite able to be disengaged from what is framed. An interruption is absolute not when there is a pure cut, were such a thing possible, but when the other person is recognized as not a modification of the same—that is, when the ties that bind other to self are loosened—and ethical relations with this other person are thereby opened up.[49]

* * *

"As with a blare of trumpets from another world it interrupts one's reflections concerning himself and his life, concerning his duties to family, calling, and country. It interrupts even the cultivation of his religious thoughts and feelings!"[50] So says the young Karl Barth of conscience in tones reminiscent of the Blumhardts, although within a short time he will not hesitate to speak of God rather than conscience. His God will rise up in the midst of life "like an immense boundary-wall shutting out some poor neighbor's view; or like a fortress occupied by the enemy; or like a boxer's closed fist."[51] For all the passionate violence imagined in the second edition of his *Romans*, Barth is not speaking of an absolute interruption. His duo of possibility and impossibility dances to a more staccato rhythm than Derrida's, as does his later dynamic of "Therefore" and "Nevertheless."[52] Barth is stirred by the thought of the "thief in the night"; Derrida remains closer to the rumor of "the *other* night."

In his final maturity as a theologian, Barth speaks more expansively of absolute interruption than of interruption. To be sure, a legalism is never quite shaken off, yet deep down, especially in the account of "Jesus Christ, the Lord as Servant," the *Church Dogmatics* murmurs that absolute interruption precedes interruption.[53] I take Barth's early introduction of the Trinity in the *Dogmatics* to be a sign of that. Searching, though, for a more manageable body of work to discuss, I settle on Barth's most illuminating commentator, Eberhard Jüngel, who is himself a theologian of considerable strength. It is Jüngel whom I had in mind a while back as the one who suggests that the second shortest definition of "religion" might be "absolute interruption." Truth be told, he prefers to speak of "elemental interruption," which he takes to be the truth that breaks into life:

> The elemental interruption of the continuity of life would be negative only if the continuity of life remained permanently interrupted. However, this is in no way the case. On the contrary, interruption by the truth leads to an *enhancement* of the continuity of life which is interrupted, conferring a new quality on this life.[54]

This enhancement is consequent on an "experience with experience (*Erfarhung mit der Erfahrung*)": an encounter with non-being that leads to a reevaluation of all one's relations with others. Jüngel stresses the ambiguity of this event: It can lead to anxiety, as Heidegger has forcefully shown, or it can result in thankfulness that one is preserved from non-being. In the latter case, the experience will have been "the *revelation of God*"; it will have been made possible not by virtue of a natural receptivity for revelation but by dint of the Cross.[55] That Christ has suffered death, and that the Word of God is fundamentally an address to men and women concerning this death and its triumphant overcoming, is what enables one to affirm experience unreservedly.

It is plain that Jüngel is attempting to sublate Bultmann and Barth or, taking a longer perspective, to show that Schleiermacher is correct to value the feeling of absolute dependence but mistaken to ground it in nature rather than revelation.[56] Either way, the position is not without its difficulties. One large set of problems can be indicated by placing Jüngel and Rahner in conjunction. The experience with experience occurs with no reference to the subject's historical and cultural situation. Without an awareness of the gospel, one would not know that an enhancing experience is the revelation of the Christian God; and since Jüngel construes the call for universal salvation in terms of what follows from the Christ event, he cannot adopt Rahner's broader understanding of grace. That, for him, would be the subsumption of revelation by natural theology.[57] Jüngel makes much of experience, and of course "experience of God" is one of Rahner's central themes: I experience God unthematically in my self-transcendence. What becomes clear in setting Rahner beside Jüngel, however, is just how little experience, in the sense of *Erfahrung*, Rahner allows there to be of God. The rapport between transcendental and categorical schemas offers the divinity little room to surprise the subject, while the steady emphasis on self-transcendence minimizes attention to the transcendence of self. In Rahner's late work, of course, it is not easy to distinguish self-transcendence from transcendence of self, in the mystical sense of the expression. Early and late, the centrality of the subject means that "being toward the Other" overrides "being with others."

That Jüngel understands interruption to be absolute is evident: The revelation of God opens a relationship in faith that resets all experience—past, present, and future—and the very idea of experience. And yet Jüngel also tends to regard interruption as pure. While he goes a fair way to overcome the rift between Barth and Bultmann, he retains a doctrine of the Word as event and renders it more deeply subjective than one finds in anything by the Whale of

Basel.[58] Faith for Barth is an acknowledgement of God's revealing Word, while for Jüngel the revelation of God and the act of faith are given together in an experience with experience. On this understanding, faith is mediated only by the revelation of God from which it can be formally, but not materially, distinguished. Historical mediation is limited to what allows us to recognize this event as the revelation of the Christian God. It is this affirmation that faith grounds the content of faith that draws the ire of Wolfhart Pannenberg, for it forgets that the revelation of God historically precedes a subjective act of faith. In other words, one must know God in his actions before one can trust him, his pre-eminent act being the resurrection of Jesus.[59] Faced with this objection, Jüngel will respond that Pannenberg is asking us to accept a "grotesque para-dox": The fact that allows us to ground faith must itself be believed outside any and all grounds of faith.[60] The only way that faith can be grounded is in the object of faith, God himself.[61]

I would phrase matters differently than either Jüngel or Pannenberg. Faith in the Christian God is an endless negotiation of an aporia between relative historical knowledge and absolute trust in God. In this sense Barth was right to criticize Harnack in their famous encounter: There is no faith without an interruption of historical determinations. And in this sense Kierkegaard was also right to call the decision of faith a moment of madness; although what he did not know, certainly not as well as we know today, is the tremendous pressure placed on the content of faith, especially as it surrounds the historical witness of Jesus as the Christ. Unlike Bultmann, I do not think one can disregard or diffuse that pressure and rely on kerygmatic assurances; and un-like Pannenberg, I do not think that one can find a realm of fact outside faith that authenticates faith. We need to keep passing from the Said of Christianity to its Saying, indeed to its Unsaying. This is not a matter of denying or down-playing belief in the resurrection of Jesus; it is a question of trying to see, with the resurrection as our vantage point, what Jesus taught in the parables of the kingdom. These are the founding stories of Christianity, and they are stories that provocatively unsay the Said. It is here that we come as close as we can to Jesus's experience of God, what he called the *basileia*.

The word "experience" returns us to Derrida's evocation of the experi-ence of faith, and it reminds us that he can speak in this way only if he refigures "experience."[62] For faith cannot be presented to consciousness and turned into knowledge. It is an opening of experience, one that must be reaffirmed in its irresolvable tension so long as it is lived; and if it is not lived—risked, chal-lenged—it is not faith at all but merely a sacred code.

* * *

Following Heidegger, although cautiously and at a distance, Derrida draws a line between revelation and revealability, *Offenbarung* and *Offen-barkeit*.[63] The distinction recalls a long history of debate between theological positivism and liberalism, culminating in Barth's sharp "No!" to Emile Brunner's question whether there might be a natural place in human beings where revelation inserts itself. Here is Derrida thinking about revelation:

> "In fact," "in truth," it would be only the event of revelation that would open—like a breaking-in, making it possible after the event—the field of the possible in which it appeared to spring forth, and for that matter actually did so. The event of revelation would reveal not only this or that—God, for example—but revealability itself. By the same token, this would forbid us saying "God, for example."[64]

The quotation marks around "in fact" and "in truth" remind us that the author believes he can "quite rightly pass for an atheist." Of more interest than Derrida's lack of faith is how he pictures those with faith. I can imagine someone reading the passage I have just quoted out of context—finding it scribbled on a piece of paper in the Christian dogmatics section of a theology library, say—and thinking it was written by the young Barth or by a dialectical theologian whose name does not quite come to mind. For revelation, here, is a case of breaking and entering. On this understanding, revelation would contest its condition of possibility, revealability, by showing it to be a consequence of revelation.

Absolute interruption is so close to pure interruption here that the former seems to have been contaminated by the latter. Given that for Derrida revelation turns on the singular, it should come as no surprise that he offers iterability as a possible way of thinking other than in terms of revelation and revealability.[65] This is perfectly reasonable: Revelation and revealability would be tied in an aporia, and I can imagine re-reading not only Brunner with this in mind but also, and perhaps more rewardingly, Rahner as well. And yet, even knowing this, perhaps the very person who found this passage scribbled on a piece of paper might still think that it was originally written by a dialectical theologian. The model of revelation as radical communication from outside the world remains firmly in place. To dislodge it one would need a supplementary theology of the Trinity as community. Such a theology would have little room for talk of pure cuts, but absolute interruption would be central to it. The problem of revelation and revealability would be secondary, in this theology, to the doctrine of God. And faith would be situated within this doctrine.

When one says that faith in God can come only from God, one is talking about a relationship inaugurated by God that can develop in many different ways and that can be nourished by reference to tradition and biblical criticism. The Christian experience of God is that he has left his trace in the life and death of Jesus, and consequently it both is and is not an experience. One could say, rather loosely, that Christianity involves an experience of absolute interruption: In responding to God another register is introduced into life, one that invites us to acknowledge the otherness of the other and, on that basis, to relate ourselves differently to one another and to God. Yet nothing in this register can be presented to consciousness. Faith may always be in quest of understanding, but it does not always pass by way of experience. To read John of the Cross is to recognize that non-experience contains the decisive trait of experience.[66] Luther would have agreed: Hebrews 11:1 ("Now faith is the substance of things hoped for, the evidence of things not seen") remained a horizon for his theology, even though his understanding of it deepened over the years.[67] I should add that Luther also tells us that faith gives us a good conscience, but my reasoning—and dare I say, my experience?—makes me doubt that things can ever be that nicely settled. After modern biblical criticism, faith cannot be centered in *fiducia*; It must answer to determinate knowledge as well as absolute trust. Because this trust is never able to be calculated, one can never know if one is trusting enough; yet to make faith wholly a matter of trust is to erase the margin of criticism and self-criticism that protects one from fideism, false piety, integralism, and all the rest. The gift of faith is the gift of an aporia. Induction into the divine mystery never erases or suspends anxiety.

If one cannot experience the trace of God in the life and death of Jesus, one can perhaps find that very trace in experience. Of course, this trace can only be looked for in faith and is never presentable. At the same time, it is always possible for an experience to be the unexpected point of entry of divine love into the world. Faith does not simply cross experience; it promises new events, and it can never be exhausted by any number of events that may take place in a future present. It turns each and every event toward the break in the horizon from which the unforeseen and perhaps undesired encounter with the Other comes. W. H. Auden tells us that in the modern age "interruption is what we expect," although it is equally true that there are interruptions that can never be expected or solicited.[68] God is not a horizon, at least not in Blanchot's sense, although the advent of God sets fresh horizons and longer offings. The verticality of the *basileia* prevents any identification of the Church and the kingdom, and that disjunction exposes the Church to Jesus's preaching and the preaching about Jesus. Were that not so, even the most passionate *theologia crucis* would slip back into an abstract *theologia gloriæ*.

These references to Luther and the cross bring me back to that other theologian of the cross, Jüngel, and to my conclusion. Over the years Jüngel has come to appreciate that interruption is absolute before it is anything else, and this recognition is at heart eschatological. He says, rightly I think, that eschatology is the "definitive being-together of the Creator with his creation and of the creatures with one another."[69] Turning the observation around, one could understand creation as absolute interruption: God establishes relations of mutual dependence and development in everything that is created and in that way institutes a trace of himself. Like many another contemporary theologian, Jüngel stresses the primacy of relations within God, a view which goes back to the Cappadocians.[70] In his phrasing, the Trinity is "a *community of mutual otherness*," and without risk of confuting Jüngel I would only add that this community exists in an eternal *perichoresis* rather than arising from a divine essence. Jüngel goes on to say that this idea of the Trinity "could be an incentive to develop models of earthly being-together," and here I depart from him.[71] For this way of putting things presupposes a gap between the idea of the Trinity and models of how we should live.

A pure interruption will always posit such a gap: It requires divine communication to precede divine community, and its terms of discussion will eventually turn on the relative priority of communication and communicability. Absolute interruption, however, presumes no such thing. God's revelation is always a self-communication; and since his selfhood is a community of mutual otherness, the revelation of God is the founding of being-in-relation with others and, first of all, with himself. Our humanity is principally revealed in worship. Absolute interruption does not reveal our being to be a substance, a *res cogitans* or anything of the sort, but a being-in-relation. Utterly inexhaustible, this divine self-communication can never coincide with the communities it founds: The economic Trinity never consumes the immanent Trinity. When turned toward itself rather than God, any relationship will allow a process of closure to begin and it will establish itself as a communion rather than a community. The Church remains a community and a sign of the *basileia* only when it remains freely exposed to the God whose very act of being is otherness.

Derrida's Response to Kevin Hart

I will not be able to say anything valuable now because it is impossible for me to improvise in English. At the same time, I do not want to keep silent, as if I were trying to avoid speaking. So I want to simply thank you and all of our colleagues who gave such powerful papers. I am overwhelmed by everything I have been listening to, especially by the reinscription of my modest essays into this powerful tradition, with which I am not familiar, as you know. I feel at the same time, of course, relegitimated and delegitimated and that I should just sit down and read all of the theologians to whom you refer. All I can do in a few minutes, in English, is just to react in a very spontaneous fashion to what you said.

First, you asked me a while back in Paris why I put quotation marks around "religion."[72] I had forgotten that I had put quotation marks around religion and why I did so. So, I try today to understand and to justify this, after the fact. And, of course, you asked a moment ago, what is the difference between putting quotation mark around religion and not. I see no good reason. I could have also put other words in quotation marks. So why did I put quotation marks only around religion? A quick answer to this would be that in this context, in "Faith and Knowledge," I wanted first to report the use that others make of the word "religion," what is happening to the word "religion." As you know the main object of this essay is to report what is happening today with the Latin word "religion" in what I call "globalatinization" (*mondialati-*

nazation).[73] That is exactly what I did last night with the word "pardon." I started using, without using, just mentioning, the word "pardon." I said that you do not know if I use it or if I mention it. I was trying to understand what is going on today on the globalized scene with the word "forgiveness" and what is going on with the word "religion." I tried in this essay to show that in fact it is a part of a process of *mondialatinazation*, that is, the Latin Roman word "religion" is now used to describe everything, even if it has nothing to do with Judaism, Christianity, or Islam. So what is happening with the word "religion"? Then, as you know, I tried in this essay to follow two threads, the two etymologies by which some people try to account for the word "religion." So that is why I put the word in quotation marks. What do they mean? What do we mean? I was doing just an analysis of the semantics of globalized humanity today, and of course it is a political problem too, and a legal problem, a cultural problem, and so on. I tried to do the same thing with "pardon" last night. Now I could have done this in different contexts with every word.

When you quoted a passage from *Sauf le nom* about *Offenbarung* and *Offenbarkeit*, you yourself paid attention to the fact that this was a voice in a fictional dialogue, in which I make now one voice speak and now another voice, not in order to withdraw myself, but simply in order to let a number of voices speak through me—"me" in quotation marks. That is just to relate this gesture, which is constantly my own concern, to your point about interruption. It is in order to do justice to the other voice in me that I use this fictional mode and these quotation marks. This is an experience of interruption, that someone could say this and I have to listen to it from another place, and so on. So you could perhaps reinterpret everything I said about absolute interruption through this staging of the quotation mark and of the fictional dialogue—not only dialogue but polylogue—in which I cannot find my place, a sure and safe place.

I also want to follow up on what you said about presence and absence. On the one hand, I understand the gesture which has been often represented by many people according to which God manifests himself as absent, through interruption. You protest against this and you say that is not the way you experience God. God for you is too close. Then I say, well, when one speaks of the infinite distance of God, that is a figure to describe alterity. When Levinas speaks of infinite distance, he means that God is absolutely other. It is not a distance, of course. So there is no contradiction between what you said about the God close to myself, or even more interior to myself than myself, and God's infinite distance. It is the same. So if I had to write a dialogue I would put this into quotation marks and have the two voices agree and disagree one with the other. Then, when you have two or more than two voices agreeing and disagreeing at the same time, you start asking, where am I? What's going on? Not simply in an academic debate or dialogue, but in the world, where you have these conflicting voices.

The last point concerns what you said about the aporia as a gift. As soon as

I interpret the aporia in which I suffer as a gift, if I really experience the aporia—the aporia is not simply just a theme or a formalized logic but simply the tragedy of my life—as a gift, if I am sure that aporia has been given to me by God, then that is the end; that is a reconciliation. To experience the aporia I will never know if it is being given to me as a gift or if it has been given to me as death or as a blow or as a punishment or torture. If you are sure that aporia was given as a gift, I envy you.

* * *

Hart: Thank you so much. I will respond very briefly to your last point. In Christianity we talk of the "gifts of the Spirit" and, more generally, of faith and grace as God's free gifts. Now there is a good deal one could say about rethinking these gifts in terms of what you have written about the gift, but I won't do that now. My paper turned on the existential situation of accepting faith as a gift. When one accepts the free gift of faith, nothing is thereby made simple. Not at all: One's experience as a Christian is always structured as what you call an aporia. We have to try to balance an absolute trust in God with the relative historical knowledge we have about the life, suffering, and death of Jesus. We have to hold an incalculable revelation of divine love in tandem with the calculations involved in revealability. We have to keep the contrary tugs of faith and reason in some sort of relation, and we never emerge securely from that situation: It pushes us on, ever on, though without any positive assurance because we are pulled ever more deeply into a mystery. Christian experience does not neatly resolve itself into knowledge: A good deal of it remains desire, intuition, wonder, puzzlement.

There is a tremendous joy in the Christian life, which I would not wish to diminish. At the same time I would not wish to downplay the anguish involved: We live in a space of acknowledgment, not knowledge. The old conjunction of "faith and reason" never resolves itself in favor of knowledge. Augustine speaks of seeking understanding, not knowing. One lives, or tries to live, in the trace of God, which in its deepest sense is the trace of the Trinity. God withdraws in the very act of his self-communication, and he leaves us with each other. When we love each other, as Jesus taught us, we are letting the *basileia* break into the world. In loving each other, the Trinity has passed through us as a trace.

A Christian is exposed to risk at each and every moment, not just because I can always ruin my life but because I am always exposed to God. No one can contain God within a horizon of expectation. We remain vulnerable to his surprise. He can interrupt our lives, even though He is closer to us than our own breathing. A moment ago I said that He was not infinitely distant from us but infinitely close to us: we can never step back far enough and bring him into focus. If we could step back that far, we would make him into an idol. But we cannot take such a backward step with God.

NOTES

1. Jacques Derrida, "Faith and Knowledge: The Two Sources of 'Religion' at the Limits of Reason Alone," trans. Samuel Weber, in *Religion*, ed. Jacques Derrida and Gianni Vattimo (Cambridge: Polity Press, 1998). The text was first published in French in 1996.

2. Derrida, "Circumfession," in *Jacques Derrida*, by Geoffrey Bennington and Jacques Derrida (Chicago: University of Chicago Press, 1993), 155. The text was first published in French in 1991.

3. On this question, see my essay "The God Effect" in *Post-Secular Philosophy: Between Philosophy and Theology*, ed. Phillip Blond (London: Routledge, 1998).

4. Derrida, "Faith and Knowledge," 64.

5. Benedict de Spinoza, *Ethics: Preceded by "On the Improvement of the Understanding,"* ed. and intro. by James Gutmann (New York: Hafner Pub. Co., 1949), I, def. vi.

6. Friedrich Schleiermacher, *The Christian Faith*, ed. H. R. Macintosh and J. S. Stewart, intro. by Richard R. Niebuhr, 2 vols. (New York: Harper and Row, 1963), I, §4.

7. See, for example, Masao Abe, "Kenotic God and Dynamic Sunyata," in John B. Cobb, Jr., and Christopher Ives, eds., *The Emptying God* (Maryknoll, N.Y.: Orbis, 1990), 4–17. The expression cited occurs on p. 16.

8. Jean-Yves Lacoste, *Expérience et Absolu* (Paris: Presses universitaires de France, 1994).

9. Immanuel Kant, *Critique of Pure Reason*, trans. Norman Kemp Smith (London: Macmillan, 1933), A324–26.

10. Derrida observes that "from the perspective of faith, deconstruction can at least be a very useful technique when Aristotelianism or Thomism are to be criticized or, even from an institutional perspective, when what needs to be criticized is a whole theological institution which supposedly has covered over, dissimulated an authentic Christian message." James Creech, Peggy Kamuf, and Jane Todd, "Deconstruction in America: An Interview with Jacques Derrida," *Critical Exchange* 17 (1985): 12. Also see *Spectres of Marx: The State of the Debt, the Work of Mourning, and the New International*, trans. Peggy Kamuf, intro. by Bernd Magnus and Stephen Cullenberg (New York: Routledge, 1994), 59. For other ways of distinguishing religion, see "Faith and Knowledge," 36.

11. Immanuel Kant, *Religion within the Limits of Reason Alone*, trans., intro., and notes by Theodore M. Greene and Hoyt H. Hudson, corrected and revised ed. (New York: Harper and Row, 1960), 98–99.

12. Ibid., 106.

13. Ibid., 110.

14. Ibid., 92. For Kant, the kingdom of God is what Calvinists call the "invisible church"; it is to be distinguished from the kingdom of ends.

15. Consider, for instance, the apparent tension between these two remarks: "The idea of the Kingdom of God, as the moral fellowship of men proper to their nature, had its way to influence prepared by the fact that it was preceded by the moral fellowship of the *Family*, national fellowship in the *State*, and, lastly, the combination of several nations in the *World-empire*. The Christian conception of the Kingdom of God in part stands in the closest analogy with all these graduated forms, and in part it is genetically

203

derived from them"; and "Now, in the Christian view of the world, the Kingdom of God is the supramundane final end of the world, an end which at the same time is fixed by the conception of God as love, as the content of the Divine personal end," Albrecht Ritschl, *The Christian Doctrine of Justification and Reconciliation*, 3 vols., III, trans. H. R. Macintosh and A. B. Macaulay (Edinburgh: T. and T. Clark, 1900), 309, 511.

16. See Walter Rauschenbusch, *A Theology for the Social Gospel* (New York: Macmillan, 1917).

17. Thomas Aquinas, *Faith, Reason and Theology: Questions I–IV of his Commentary on the "De Trinitate" of Boethius*, trans. and intro. by Armand Maurer, Mediaeval Sources in Translation (Toronto: Pontifical Institute of Mediaeval Studies, 1987), q. III art. 2. Also see *Summa Theologiæ*, 2a2æ, q. 81 art. 5.

18. For Richards, the "w" around each word indicates "that the word—merely as the word in general—is being talked about; the 'q' indicates that our problem is, What does this word say here? . . . The marks are equivalent to Query; and the 'r' indicates 'that some special sense of the word or phrase is being *referred* to'; the '!' indicates 'surprise or derision, a Good Heavens!'" For these and the other special quotation marks, see I. A. Richards, *How to Read a Page: A Course in Effective Reading with an Introduction to a Hundred Great Words* (London: Routledge and Kegan Paul, 1943), 68–69.

19. Emmanuel Levinas, *Totality and Infinity: An Essay on Exteriority*, trans. Alphonso Lingis (The Hague: Martinus Nijhoff, 1979), 80.

20. Levinas, *Totality and Infinity*, 77.

21. Levinas, *Otherwise Than Being, or Beyond Essence*, trans. Alphonso Lingis (The Hague: Martinus Nijhoff, 1981), 183. Also on this question see the introduction to the revised edition of my *The Trespass of the Sign* (New York: Fordham University Press, 2000).

22. See Karl Jaspers, *Philosophical Faith and Revelation*, trans. E. B. Ashton (London: Collins, 1967).

23. Levinas, "Phenomenon and Enigma," in *Collected Philosophical Papers*, trans. Alphonso Lingis (The Hague: Martinus Nijhoff, 1987), 73.

24. See, for example, Derrida, "Violence and Metaphysics," in *Writing and Difference*, trans., intro., and notes by Alan Bass (London: Routledge and Kegan Paul, 1978), 143; and *Aporias*, trans. Thomas Dutoit (Stanford, Calif.: Stanford University Press, 1993), 22.

25. Derrida, "Faith and Knowledge," 18.

26. Jean-Luc Nancy, *The Sense of the World*, trans. and foreword by Jeffrey S. Librett (Minneapolis: University of Minnesota Press, 1997), 55. Whereas Derrida is concerned with the deconstruction of religion, Nancy is explicitly addressing the deconstruction of Christianity. See p. 183 n. 50. Nancy is currently writing a study on this theme.

27. Levinas, *Otherwise Than Being*, 45, 181.

28. See Karl Rahner, "Anonymous Christians," in *Theological Investigations*, vol. 6, trans. Karl-H. and Boniface Kruger (London: Darton, Longman and Todd, 1969), pp. 390–398; and "Atheism and Implicit Christianity," in *Theological Investigations*, vol. 9, trans. Graham Harrison (London: Darton, Longman and Todd, 1972).

29. John D. Caputo, ed., *Deconstruction in a Nutshell: A Conversation with Jacques Derrida* (New York: Fordham University Press, 1997), 21.

30. Martin Luther, *Heidelberg Disputation* (1518), in *Luther's Works*, 55 vols., gen.

ed. Helmut T. Lehmann (Philadelphia: Muhlenberg Press, 1958–86), vol. 31: *Career of the Reformer* (vol. I), ed. Harold J. Grimm. John van Buren offers an illuminating account of Heidegger's investment in Luther's appropriation of I Corinthians 1:19 in his *The Young Heidegger: Rumor of the Hidden King* (Bloomington: Indiana University Press, 1994), 160–165.

31. See Derrida, *Deconstruction in a Nutshell*, 21–22.

32. See Karl Barth, *Church Dogmatics*, I.ii, ed. G. W. Bromiley and T. F. Torrance, trans. G. T. Thomson and Harold Knight (Edinburgh: T. and T. Clark, 1956), 299f.

33. Aquinas, *Faith, Reason and Theology*, q. III, art. 1.

34. Aquinas, *Summa Theologica* 2a2æ q. 4 art. 1.

35. Gerhard Ebeling, *The Nature of Faith*, trans. Ronald Gregor Smith (Philadelphia: Fortress Press, 1961), 157.

36. Johann Baptist Metz, *Faith in History and Society: Toward a Practical Fundamental Theology*, trans. David Smith (London: Burns and Oates, 1980), 171.

37. Jürgen Moltmann, *The Coming of God: Christian Eschatology*, trans. Margaret Kohl (Minneapolis: Fortress Press, 1996), 22.

38. Maurice Blanchot's "L'Interruption" appeared in *Nouvelle Revue Française* 142 (October 1964): 674–685, and the more general section of the essay which concerns me was reprinted in *L'Entretien infini* (Paris: Gallimard, 1969), 106–112. The word "interruption" is used several times in Levinas's "Enigme et phénomène." Perhaps the most important forerunner of *Otherwise Than Being*; it was first published in *Esprit* 33 (June 1965): 1128–1142. As is often the case with Blanchot and Levinas, it is extremely difficult to establish the direction of influence and, in any case, beside the point. In *Otherwise Than Being*, Levinas uses "interruption" often, though never, to my knowledge, does he speak of absolute interruption. See pp. 20, 44, 150, 152, 160, 168, 169f., 170.

39. Blanchot, *The Infinite Conversation*, trans. and foreword by Susan Hanson (Minneapolis: University of Minnesota Press, 1993), 76.

40. Blanchot's use of Riemannian surfaces is rather vague. His main claim concerns "a change in the form or the structure of language (when speaking is first of all writing)—a change metaphorically comparable to what which made Euclid's geometry into that of Riemann" (*The Infinite Conversation*, 77). However, he goes on to suggest a kind of writing that would occur on a Riemannian surface. Although Blanchot derives the idea of writing on a Riemannian surface from Paul Valéry, he takes the notion of Riemannian space from Levinas: "'curvature of space' expresses the relation between human beings" (*Totality and Infinity*, 291). The relation between Riemmanian space and surfaces for Blanchot remains obscure. It is doubtful, for example, that he is aware that a Riemannian surface is one type of two-dimensional Riemannian manifold.

41. Blanchot, *The Infinite Conversation*, 78.

42. See René Char, "Feuillets d'Hypnos," in *Fureur et mystère*, préf. Yves Berger (Paris: Gallimard, 1967). Blanchot speaks of the fragment in Char in "The Fragment Word" in *The Infinite Conversation*.

43. Derrida, *On the Name*, ed. Thomas Dutoit, trans. David Wood, John P. Leavey, Jr., and Ian McLeod (Stanford, Calif.: Stanford University Press, 1995), 43, my emphasis. See Levinas, "A rupture which would be caused by a movement coming from outside, but a rupture which, paradoxically, would not alienate this rational self-sufficiency," in *Beyond the Verse: Talmudic Readings and Lectures*, trans. Gary D. Mole

(Bloomington: Indiana University Press, 1994), 145–146. Without belaboring the obvious, I simply note that Derrida's recent penchant for dialogues—learned from Heidegger and Blanchot—shows his desire to stage interruptions as well as discuss them.

44. See Blanchot, *The Space of Literature*, trans. Ann Smock (Lincoln: University of Nebraska Press, 1982), 240.

45. Heidegger, *Hegel's Concept of Experience* (San Francisco: Harper and Row, 1970), 38.

46. Derrida, *The Truth in Painting*, trans. Geoff Bennington and Ian McLeod (Chicago: University of Chicago Press, 1987), 87, 98.

47. Derrida, "By Force of Mourning," trans. Pascale-Anne Brault and Michael Naas, *Critical Inquiry* 22, no. 2 (1996): 177.

48. Derrida, "At This Very Moment in This Work Here I Am," in *Re-reading Levinas*, ed. Robert Bernasconi and Simon Critchley (Bloomington: Indiana University Press, 1991), 28.

49. See Derrida and Pierre-Jean Labarrière, *Altérités: avec des études de Francis Guibal et Stanislas Breton* (Paris: Editions Osiris, 1986), 82. Also see Derrida's remarks on the logic of stricture in *The Truth in Painting*, esp. 340; his question to Hans-Georg Gadamer on *Verstehen* in *Dialogue and Deconstruction: The Gadamer-Derrida Encounter*, ed. Diane P. Michelfelder and Richard E. Palmer (Albany: SUNY, 1989), 53; and his comments on the social bond as an experience of unbinding in *Adieu: To Emmanuel Levinas*, trans. Pascale-Anne Brault and Michael Naas (Stanford: Stanford University Press, 1999), 92.

50. Karl Barth, "The Righteousness of God," in *The Word of God and the Word of Man*, trans. and new foreword by Douglas Horton (New York: Harper and Row, 1957), 10.

51. Barth, *Epistle to the Romans*, trans. Edwyn C. Hoskins (Oxford: Oxford University Press, 1933), 259. For the influence of the Blumhardts on Barth, see H. Martin Rumscheidt, *Revelation and Theology: An Analysis of the Barth-Harnack Correspondence of 1923*, Monograph Supplements to the *Scottish Journal of Theology* (Cambridge: Cambridge University Press, 1972), 10. It is worth recalling Ernst Fuchs speaking of obstacles to our understanding of Jesus. The first one he mentions is "that the context of earthly events has been interrupted by the resurrection of Jesus, and by this alone. However, this is not the opinion of the New Testament. For there both the Holy Spirit and faith break in upon the earthly reality or the context of earthly events, with the result that many things change, including things in our daily life." "Preface to the English Edition," *Studies of the Historical Jesus* (London: SCM Press, 1964), 7.

52. Barth, *Church Dogmatics*, II.ii, ed. G. W. Bromiley and T. F. Torrance, trans. G. W. Bromiley et al. (Edinburgh: T. and T. Clark, 1957), 315.

53. See Barth, *Church Dogmatics*, IV.i, ed. G. W. Bromiley and T. F. Torrance, trans. G. W. Bromiley (Edinburgh: T. and T. Clark, 1956), §62.

54. Eberhard Jüngel, "Value-Free Truth: The Christian Experience of Truth in the Struggle against the 'Tyranny of Values,'" in *Theological Essays*, II, ed. J. B. Webster, trans. Arnold Neufeldt-Fast and J. B. Webster (Edinburgh: T. and T. Clark, 1995), 205.

55. Eberhard Jüngel, *God as the Mystery of the World: On the Foundation of the Theology of the Crucified One in the Dispute between Theism and Atheism*, trans. Darrell L. Guder (Grand Rapids, Mich.: William E. Eerdmans, 1983), 33, ix. Else-

where, Jüngel speaks of faith disclosing "an *absolutely new* sphere of meaning," *The Freedom of a Christian: Luther's Significance for Contemporary Theology*, trans. Roy A. Harrisville (Minneapolis: Augsburg Publishing House, 1988), 43.

56. The importance of the conjunction of "Bultmann" and "Barth" goes without saying for theologians of Jüngel's age. Nevertheless, Jüngel has explicitly oriented his thought in terms of this polarity. For an early instance, see his remarks in the preface to the first edition (1962) of his *Paulus und Jesus: Eine Untersuchung zur Präzisierung der Frage nach dem Ursprung der Christologie* (Tübingen: J. C. B. Mohr [Paul Siebeck]), 1986), v.

57. See Jüngel's "Extra Christum Nulla Salus—A Principle of Natural Theology?: Protestant Reflections on the 'Anonymity' of the Christian," in *Theological Essays*, I, trans. and ed. J. B. Webster (Edinburgh: T. and T. Clark, 1989).

58. For example, see Eberhard Jüngel, *The Doctrine of the Trinity: God's Being Is in Becoming*, trans. Horton Harris (Edinburgh: Scottish Academic Press, 1976), 13–14.

59. Wolfhart Pannenberg's most persuasive criticism of Jüngel's account of faith (although he is not named here) is in his *Systematic Theology*, 3, trans. Geoffrey W. Bromiley (Grand Rapids, Mich.: William B. Eerdmans, 1998), 153. Pannenberg criticizes the hermeneutic on which Jüngel's account of "experience with experience" is based in his *Theology and the Philosophy of Science*, trans. Francis McDonagh (London: Darton, Longman and Todd, 1976), 169–177.

60. Eberhard Jüngel, "Womit steht und fällt heute der christliche Glaube? Elementare Verantwortung gegenwärtigen Glaubens," in *Spricht Gott in der Geschichte?* (Frieburg: Herder, 1972), 169. Also see his *The Doctrine of the Trinity*, xix.

61. See Eberhard Jüngel, "Das Dilemma der natürlichen Theologie und die Wahrheit ihres Problems: Überlegungen für ein Gespräch mit Wolfhart Pannenberg," in *Entsprechungen: Gott, Warheit, Mensch* (München: Chr. Kaiser Verlag, 1980), 171–175.

62. For a more full account of this, see my essay "The Experience of God," in *The Religious*, ed. John D. Caputo (Oxford: Basil Blackwell, 2001).

63. See Derrida, "How to Avoid Speaking: Denials," in *Derrida and Negative Theology*, ed. Harold Coward and Toby Foshay (Albany, N.Y.: SUNY, 1992), 124.

64. Derrida, *Politics of Friendship*, trans. George Collins (London: Verso, 1997), 18.

65. Ibid., 25 n. 26.

66. See my essay "The Experience of Non-Experience," in *Mystics: Presence and Aporia*, ed. Christopher Sheppard and Michael Kessler (Chicago: University of Chicago Press, 2001).

67. See *Luther's Works*, vol. 27: *Lectures on Galatians*, ed. Jaroslav Pelikan, assoc. ed. Walter A. Hansen (St Louis, Mo.: Concordia Press, 1965), 377.

68. W. H. Auden, "Metalogue to the Magic Flute," in *Collected Shorter Poems* (New York: Random House, 1966), 276.

69. Eberhard Jüngel, "Toward the Heart of the Matter," *The Christian Century* 108, no. 7 (1991): 232.

70. Three prominent instances are Moltmann, *The Trinity and the Kingdom: The Doctrine of God*, trans. Margaret Kohl (San Francisco: Harper and Row, 1981); Leonardo Boff, *Trinity and Society*, trans. Paul Burns (London: Burns and Oates, 1988); and Catherine Mowry LaCugna, *God for Us: The Trinity and Christian Life* (New York: HarperCollins, 1991).

71. Jüngel, "Toward the Heart of the Matter," 233. I take this phrasing to mark a development in his thought on the Trinity. See *God as the Mystery of the World*, 369–370.

72. Derrida is referring to Jacques Derrida, "Faith and Knowledge: The Two Sources of 'Religion' within the Limits of Reason Alone," in Jacques Derrida and Gianni Vattimo, eds. *Religion* (Stanford: Stanford University Press, 1998).

73. Derrida, "Faith and Knowledge," pp. 29–30.

Questioning Narratives of God

The Immeasurable in Measures

Regina Mara Schwartz

One evening the son of a minister, seated at his family dinner table, turned to his father and asked "Daddy, is god really everywhere?" His father patiently replied "Yes, son, he is." His son pressed the issue further: "Well, does that mean he is here, in this dining room?" His bemused father replied, "Yes." "Well, if he is here," his son pressed further, "does that mean he's at the dinner table with us?" "I suppose so," his father indulged. And then his son picked up the lid to the sugar bowl, clamped it on the bowl, and proclaimed triumphantly, "Got you, God!"

Two preoccupations govern this essay. The first reflects my suspicion of narrative, a suspicion that grows even as my respect for the power of narrative deepens. That suspicion questions the adequacy of narratives about God—not only because such narratives tend to be projections of human life, human desire, and human conflict but because of the impossibility, indeed, the idolatry, of any such description. To speak of representation as idolatry is not new: it is several thousand years old. But to speak of the idol not as a visual representation, a statue, a painting, but a verbal one, a narrative, seems to be still somewhat controversial.[1] My second concern is to attend to the question of conversation itself, not to the addressor and addressee—in fact, I very much want to set aside their much-discussed identity—but rather to heed the *process* of conversation, its turnings, its rhythms, its silences, especially its silences, to discern if it can escape narrative idolatry.[2] The parable of the sugar bowl is helpful for approaching both the problem of idolatry and the question of conversation, exposing the dangers of trying to delimit meaning, to possess the ineffable (the child made off stealthily with the sugar bowl to his bedroom), but also exposing the hazard of conversation itself. For in conversation, it is the moment when the respondent looks at you knowingly and nods with confidence, muttering "Got it" or even worse, "Gotchyou" that only one thing is sure: neither *it* nor *you* have been gotten.

For some time now, I have been in conversation with Jacques Derrida, and more recently Jean-Luc Marion has joined us. (The fact that neither of them knew they were in this conversation is, in this case, irrelevant). Exiled from Florence, Macchiavelli consoles himself: "When evening comes, I return to my home, and I go into my study, and on the threshold, I take off my everyday clothes, which are covered with mud and mire, and I put on regal and curial robes; and dressed in a more appropriate manner I enter into the ancient courts of ancient men and am welcomed by them kindly, and there I taste the food that alone is mine, and for which I was born; and there I am not ashamed to speak to them . . . and they, in their humanity, answer me; and for four hours . . . I dismiss every affliction, I no longer fear poverty nor do I tremble at the thought of death."[3] From different angles, both Derrida and Marion have critiqued onto-theology: Derrida for its metaphysics of presence, Marion for its metaphysical concept of God as a causal Being. But as Marion notes, Heidegger himself saw the problems of a conception of God as equivalent to *causa sui*. He wrote: "Man can neither pray nor sacrifice to this God. . . . The god-less thinking which must abandon the God of philosophy, God as *causa sui*, is thus perhaps closer to the divine God."[4] I would add that it may be that the "god-less thinking which must abandon the God of narrative" is perhaps closer to the divine God. Like the God of metaphysics, narrative tries to offer up a God of determinate meaning. And like the God of metaphysics, narrative tries to offer up a God of causes. To ask, as I do, how can the divine God break through narrative is similar to asking how the divine God can survive metaphysics. Both are human stories, preoccupied with Being and beings, cause and effect, motive and meaning. If we were to search for the more divine god, we would need, as Marion puts it, "to think God without pretending to inscribe him or to describe him."[5] We would turn to a different understanding of language—not one that pretends to convey meaning, but one that, quite simply, praises.

In this context, it will be helpful to distinguish between two views of language: first, *descriptions* that claim to inscribe, describe, explain, or capture (gotchya God, gotchyou); that purport to answer questions (who, what, where, when, and why); that leave hearer with either a false sense of epistemological satisfaction or frustration that all their questions have not been answered—in short, language as utility, working as a tool to convey meaning, trying to impart a sense of something either understood or mis-understood. This instrumental, idolatrous use of language differs little, it seems to me, from turning to a golden calf to ensure prosperity. As an instrument, language is destined to "miss its mark," to "misfire" (the violence of these metaphors is not mine; they are in common circulation). Derrida showed in his powerful critique of Austin's speech-act theory that whatever the illocutionary intent, the perlocutionary effect is not the same; the conditions of an utterance are infelicitous for such success.[6] If I use language instrumentally, then, I have taken up an unruly tool, one that does not do what I mean for it to do. If I use it to convey meaning, what I intended to convey is not received. Sins multiply. Using language as a tool to convey meaning is one idolatry, and that violence breeds further violence: the misfire, mis-understanding is an injury, and added to this unintended injury are intentional misuses of language; soon, using language as a tool becomes more like using language as a weapon. Whatever the biblical story in Genesis 9 describing the curse of Canaan intended to convey, it certainly misfired (the narrative is even known, erroneously, as the "curse of Ham" in order to better "explain" that curse). The bullets have ricocheted throughout history. Genesis 9:25–26 reads "Accursed be Canaan. The lowest of slaves will he be to his brothers. Blessed be the Lord, the God of Shem. May Canaan be the slave of Shem." What are we doing when we ask, "What meaning is this narrative trying to convey?" "Why is Canaan cursed? What is the explanation?" Or with a different ideological lens, "Why should Canaan be victim to this terrible curse?" All of these questions presume that the narrative is a tool conveying a meaning, but this presumption of instrumentality is, in turn, the condition for its legacy of violent uses. The curse falls where it will, far beyond the ancient Canaanites. The narrative was used as a weapon to justify slavery in the antebellum south: Josiah Priest was among the ministers who used a version of the story to preach that a whole race of humankind was cursed by Noah to be subjugated to another race and that this was this will of God. "Accursed be Ham [in his version, as in Hamites, Africans]. He shall be his brothers' meanest slave; blessed be Yhwh God of Shem, let Ham be his slave. May God extend Japheth, may he live in the tents of Shem and may Ham be his slave."[7] This kind of reading has recently been revived by white supremacists. One writes in a manifesto he alarmingly titled "A Scriptural Justification of Racism":

> The curse was in his descendants in the form of spiritual and moral deformity, and Canaan's descendants were a cursed people. [He is presuming Canaan's descendants were black.] These were the sinful people living in the Promised Land when the Israelites entered it. In Deuteronomy 7, God's people were told to destroy them and not intermarry with them, but Israel disobeyed and consequently these people were always in trouble in the land, acting as pricks and thorns.

The violence of such overt instrumentality is apparent. Elsewhere, I have called it not the curse of Canaan but of Cain—to recall the violence between the first brothers.[8] This kind of idolatry, the use of language to convey meaning, is not limited to biblical readers. For some audiences, Shakespeare's *Othello* is only about a Moor who murdered his Venetian wife in Cyprus just after the war with the Turks because he was insanely jealous. But fortunately, others are moved and for them the play seems to take on the function of ritual or, to be more accurate, seems to reclaim the function of ritual in which early drama was born—some shared cry of pain.

Is there a way to approach narrative, including biblical stories, without instrumentality? Is there a way to overcome the curse of Canaan, the curse of Cain? Certainly, there *is* a very different view of language that is not instrumental, that does not purport to capture, describe, or explain (however unsuccessfully); there is even a language explicitly concerned with divinity that does not pretend, through its representations, to capture it: no "gotchya God". This language does not try to convey meaning, but it does perform otherwise: praising, lamenting. To hear such language, we would not attend to functions of referentiality or predication but to rhythm, the rhythm that marks poetry, drama, ritual, and even conversation. Because the term unfolds into so many nuances, I allude to "conversation" in its enhanced sense: con*verse*, going to and fro, versing to and fro, but also it suggests dwelling among, living (as Macchiavelli did with his ancients), and then, *con*verse, the opposite, the negation of verse, and *conversio*, a transformation, and *conversio realis*, the *conversio realis*. It is in all of these senses that conversation can overcome the curse of Cain.

For instance, what happens when we hear the creation narrative in Genesis 1 as a conversation instead of as an idolatrous description of divine activity? Is it possible to read an account of the beginning without satisfying or frustrating our craving for an explanation of the beginning? Can the creation narrative be read not as an instrument or vehicle but perhaps as an expression of gratitude, a hymn of praise? Or can it only presume to *describe* performance— albeit the magnificent first performance of creation—rather than perform? After all, the divine performative is framed by a narrative that does explain: "When in the beginning, God created the heavens and the earth, now the earth was a formless void, there was darkness over the deep and the spirit of God hovered over the water. And God said (*vayomer Elohim*) 'Let there be light' [*vayahi or*]." Here, the divine performative is embedded in description; not only introduced but also followed by more description, "And there was light (*vayahi or*)." Is it possible that this description of creation is idolatrous because of its attempts to describe? Or does it demur from putting either creation or God in the sugar bowl and achieve something more, something beyond description, something more like poetry, like praise? The prose is marked by a strong rhythm; each day is punctuated by the repetitive praise, *qui tov* ("and it was good"), and it even breaks into verse to describe the creation of man:

God created man in the image of himself,
in the image of God he created him,
male and female he created them. (Genesis 1:27)

That dramatic, liturgical quality (among other reasons) has even prompted biblical scholars to call this biblical source the "priestly writer."

But instead of attending to the features of the creation narrative/poem itself, should we not be asking about the attitude of the reader? For in the end, there are no reliable verbal clues that could answer the question of whether the narrative *describes* or *acts*, for whether we read Genesis as an idolatrous narrative of description or a liturgical poetry of praise is a question of perception. The point is not that sometimes language describes performance and sometimes it performs, for the same passage can have different effects on different hearers at different times in differing contexts. Like the statue in Marion's description of idols and icons at the opening of *God without Being*, narrative and poetry are not two classes of beings or two genres but two manners of apprehending.

Let us shift, then, to that perspective: whether the story is *received* as idolatrous (describing and containing) or whether it is received as performing (praising what cannot possibly be contained). While I will use the terms *narrative* for description and *poetry* for enactment, my distinction here is not generic. The genre termed poetry describes for some, transforms others. The genre called narrative can do either. For some readers, Genesis 1 describes the creation of the world; for others, it creates the world. Hoping to do their part to keep chaos at bay another year, on Rosh Hashanah, many experience Genesis 1 as creating. And I know that in his blindness and defeat, John Milton read it that way, for he implored his Muse to repeat the creative act in him: "What is dark in me illumine, what is low, raise and support."[9] If one way of apprehending biblical narratives sees God described and inscribed as a Being who constitutes a people, protects them, secures their borders, and guarantees the destruction of their enemies, these very narratives *can* be and *are* experienced differently, as a poetry that praises and laments.

Here, I must confess that I am guilty of idolatry, for I have used the narratives of the Bible (albeit with the best of intentions) to inspire toleration, even respect, for the other, to deplore violence against our brothers, especially the outrageous notion that God could sanction genocide. And, idolater that I am, my intention has often misfired. When I turned my attention to Cain and Abel, pained that we continue to murder our brothers, I wondered if the story offered an explanation for man's inhumanity to man. Looking to be satisfied by some explanation or description, I found explanations and descriptions: the pain of a rejected gift, the humiliation of injured merit, failed efforts to please, competition for favor, sibling rivalry, jealous rage, murderous envy, the pain of punishment, the pain of exile—any or all of these familiar mental landscapes were described in the story that I read as saying so little about divinity but too much about humanity. And I was preoccupied with a problem: If the narrative wanted to depict human competition and violence that way, why did it also seem to implicate God in that scenario? Why did it not describe God valuing the sower and the shepherd equally so that then there would be cooperation rather than violent competition between the first brothers?

> Abel kept flocks and Cain worked the soil. In the course of time Cain brought some of the fruits of the soil as an offering to the Lord. But Abel brought fat portions from some of the firstborn of his flock. The Lord looked with favor upon Abel and his offering, but on Cain and his offering he did not look with favor. So Cain was very angry and his face was downcast. (Genesis 4:2–5)

My suspicion that God is implicitly described as playing favorites was confirmed by later narratives of sibling rivalry, ones that describe one brother prospering at the expense of the other with the suggestion that this was the will of God.

In the story of Jacob and Esau, after Jacob steals his elder brother's blessing, the unsuspecting Esau approaches his father to ask for his blessing—only to learn that because his younger brother has already been blessed, there is no blessing left for him.

> When Esau heard his father's words, he burst out with a loud and bitter cry and said to his father, "Bless me—me too, my father!" But he said, "Your brother came deceitfully and took your blessing." ". . . Haven't you reserved any blessing for me?" Isaac answered Esau, "I have made him lord over you and have made all his relatives his servants and I have sustained him with grain and new wine. So what can I possibly do for you, my son?" (Genesis 27:34–37)

And then Esau asks a profound question, one that reverberates from the ancient Israelites and Edomites through the subsequent history of religious strife between peoples: "Have you only one blessing, my father? Bless me—me too, my father." And he weeps: "He burst out with a loud and bitter cry."

All of these narratives of neglected, rejected, or exiled brothers have been used instrumentally, and the use to which they were put most often involved justifying some hatred, hurting, even killing the other in the name of God. Examples are rife: not only slavery in the United States but the expulsion, persecution, and genocide of Jews; of indigenous peoples in the New World; and, more recently, ethnic cleansing in Bosnia. In *The Curse of Cain*, I understood these stories of scarce blessings and pain as proleptic of historical tragedy.[10] But if I had turned to the story of Jacob and Esau attending not to description but to performance, not to its narrative but to its poetry, what would I have heard? Not descriptions of the divine sanctioning of injury and the terrible purposes to which that has been put, but the weeping of Esau. And what would we hear from the story of Cain and Abel? The blood of Abel crying from the ground. Cries from the injured, cries for justice.

And what if, instead of charting the fate of brothers who succeed Cain and Abel, we follow the fate of grain? In another story—the story of manna—it is not offered *to* God, but *by* God. Exodus 16 does not describe God as being short on blessings but as infinitely charitable, infinitely giving, with blessings for all. This narrative describes a God who rains bread from the heavens, enough for everyone. Greed, the notion that some would take more than they need and hoard it, is addressed in a didactic narrative that schools the ancient Israelites in an equitable distribution of their resource.

> "That" said Moses to them, "is the bread God gives you to eat. This is God's command: Everyone must gather enough of it for his needs." . . . When they measured in an omer of what they had gathered, the man who had gathered more had not too much, the man who had gathered less had not too little. Each found he had gathered what he needed. (Exodus 16:15–18)

But the Israelites fail to accept this divinely ordained distribution of resources—of each according to his needs. When they hoard their food, it rots:

> Moses said to them, "No one must keep any of it for tomorrow." But some would not listen and kept part of it for the following day, and it bred maggots and smelt foul; and Moses was angry with them. (Exodus 16:19–20)

What message does this narrative seem to convey? That despite all evidence of dearth, despite their starving in the wilderness, the Israelites are asked to trust in a God who will provide for them, and they are asked to base their actions on that belief in divine generosity so that they will not hoard their resources. This kind of faith and this vision of bounty recur in the New Testament, where Jesus is described as miraculously multiplying the loaves and fishes so he can feed everyone.

Surely these narratives are not liable to the charge of a tragic historical realism, for they neither spawn intolerance and violence nor do they inspire a remarkable generosity. The heavens do not rain bread when the needy cry for it. Children are hungry. When people are dying of starvation, loaves and fishes do not multiply for them. Furthermore, the instrumental afterlife of these narratives is not reassuring. Well-meaning efforts to hold up such narratives for ethical purposes—to inspire giving—can collapse under the weight of the opposite purpose, greed. In an op-ed in an Italian newspaper about the Albanian refugees fleeing to Italy, a spokesperson for the right wrote: "We can offer them a plate of pasta but not open the cafeterias. Even Jesus who multiplied bread and fishes did not open trattorias. He transformed water into wine, but, it seems to me, only once, and even then, for a wedding. Albania, like Bosnia, is not our problem, but the problem of Europe." But because the manna and the loaves and fishes miracles fail on the level of verisimilitude, does that mean that they succeed in other terms? Has something of transcendence shone through? An endless divine giving? The glory of the Lord? Neither a realistic nor a utopian *description* can capture divinity, because no description, not even beautiful ones, capture the divine.

There is another way to understand grain: not part of the curse of Cain nor the blessing of manna, not a description of a withholding deity or a bountiful one—not descriptions at all—but in the context of effects, transformations. The murder of Abel, the tears of Esau, and curse of Canaan can *do*. Indeed, these narratives are performed every time there is a mass. And the murder of our brother, the breaking of his body, is performed and transformed as a sacrifice. "Then he took some bread, and when he had given thanks, broke it and gave it to them, saying, 'This is my body which is given for you; do this in remembrance of me.'" Unlike the murder of Abel, the violence of the sacrifice does not destroy another but it is transformed into a gift by that other. Abel's blood crying from the ground of an unjust murder has been transformed from robbing to giving life. "He did the same with the cup after supper, and said, 'This cup is the new covenant in my blood which is poured out for you.'" The bread rained from heaven in the wilderness no longer describes a superabundant generosity that feeds the starving, it is transformed into a bread that nourishes beyond material feeding: Take, eat, this is my body which is broken for you. But the Eucharist is not just a way of reading a narrative, it is also a religious ritual, so how can it describe the performance of narrative, how contrast with the idolatry of narrative?

Versing/Conversing

I turn now to poetry to make the case that language does not only act in religious ritual, but also in verse; the immeasurable is in measures, in meter, rhythm, in the spaces in between words, the spaces that make poetry, that make verse, and that make conversation. Surely it was the Reformation's insistence on democratizing the ritual transformation, taking away the power of *conversio realis* from the priesthood, that led to such an overtly sacramental poetry among Protestants. If the wine was not transformed into the blood through the Priest's words of institution, it was still transformed in that most democratic of forms—as Derrida once referred to it—literature.[11] A poem by the Anglican pastor George Herbert is illustrative of this movement from liturgy to poetry, one I would maintain could be extended to the performative transformative quality of all language. That is, the ritual function of language is not lost; rather, it is broadened into the sphere of the everyday, a sphere commonly known as secular, but only under the most narrow understanding of "the sacred."

The poem "Love III" (sacred or secular, or inextricably both?) is the third poem on love in George Herbert's anthology of lyrics, *The Temple*, but the final poem in the main section, "The Church." It is the crown of a work that was then and is now widely regarded as the greatest compendium of religious lyrics written in the seventeenth century, England's great age of religious poetry. While these lyrics are now regarded as a triumph of *literary* imagination, they were also perceived in their own time as not only a source of religious inspiration but even a model for practical devotion. So well did the lyrics do something that they inspired doing. In *The Poetry of Meditation*, Louis Martz says of *The Temple* that it is "hardly too much" to call it "a book of seventeenth-century psalmody."[12] Barbara Lewalski writes that "Herbert seems to have conceived his book of lyrics as a book of Christian psalms, and his speaker as a new David, a Christian Psalmist."[13] The translation of the psalms by Sir Philip Sidney, with their metrical variety and simplicity of phrasing, has been seen as the closest precedent to Herbert's poetry. But in his poetry, Herbert does not render biblical verse in English; he speaks scripture in his own voice. It is as if scripture entered him, like Ezekiel, who had eaten the scripture and it tasted like honey: That is precisely the image he invokes to open his poem on the Bible, *Holy Scriptures I*: "Oh Book! Infinite Sweetness! Let my heart Suck ev'ry letter." He also understands the Bible as in dialogue with itself; in his other poem on the scriptures, he writes that one biblical allusion points to the next, in an intratextuality that forms a constellation of references.

The Holy Scriptures II

Oh that I knew how all thy lights combine,
And the configurations of their glorie!
Seeing not only how each verse doth shine,
But all the constellations of the storie.
This verse marks that, and both do make a motion
Unto a third, that ten leaves off doth lie.

Verses go to and fro, verses con-verse.

"Love III" is a conversation that issues in *conversio realis*. Marked by such deceptive simplicity, ease, even grace at presenting a deep theological and emotional drama, it is Herbert's quintessential poem.

Love III

Love bade me welcome. Yet my soul drew back
    Guilty of dust and sin
But quick-eyed Love, observing me grow slack
    From my first entrance in,
Drew nearer to me, sweetly questioning,
    If I lacked any thing.
A guest, I answered, worthy to be here:
    Love said, You shall be he.
I the unkind, ungrateful? Ah my dear,
    I cannot look on thee.
Love took my hand, and smiling did reply,
    Who made the eyes but I?
Truth Lord, but I have marred them: let my shame
    Go where it doth deserve.
And know you not, says Love, who bore the blame?
    My dear, then I will serve.
You must sit down, says Love, and taste my meat:
    So I did sit and eat.

The feast of love to which God has invited man suggests both the earthy communion—with the implied pun on host—and the heavenly apocalyptic marriage banquet it anticipates.[14] *The Book of Common Prayer* makes that very association, invoking the parables of the marriage feast and the wedding garment in the communion service. The prayer book exhorts those who are "negligent to come to the holy Communion," alluding, as Herbert does, to the parable of the great supper. "Ye know how grievous and unkind a thing it is, when a man hath prepared a rich feast, decked his table with all kind of provision, so that there lacketh nothing but the guests to sit downe, and yet they which be called (without any cause) most unthankfully refuse to come. . . . If any man say, I am a grievous sinner, and therefore am afraide to come: wherefore then doe you not repent and amend? When God calleth you, be you not ashamed to say yee will not come?"[15]

In contrast to the parable where the unwilling and hence unworthy guests are condemned, in the Song of Songs, love is not angered by her rejection: "I opened to my beloved, but my beloved had withdrawn himself, and was gone." There, love does not condemn her beloved but is determined to win him back. Herbert relies on these biblical scenes and more that depict God inviting man to a feast to create his verse: the 23rd Psalm, where God is a gracious Host; Matthew 26:29, "I tell you I shall not drink again of this fruit of the vine until that day when I drink it new with you in my Father's kingdom"; Luke 12:37, where the master comes and serves his servants; Revelation 3:20, the promised messianic banquet: "Behold I stand at the door and knock; if any one hears my voice and opens the door, I will come in to him and eat with him, and he with me"; Matthew 22:1–10 and Luke 14:7–24 (the parables of the great supper). And in Herbert's poem there are also protestations of unworthiness. They are not punished; they are heard. And each protest provokes a response.

In "Love III," Love does not simply invite a guest who says I am not coming (Matthew) and then is pronounced unworthy and someone else is invited; nor are the guests claiming to be unworthy and so the host gives up on them (Luke). Love does not give up with the invitation. Love will not be refused. She invites him not only to her meal but into a conversation—sweetly questioning if he lacked anything. In the course of this conversation, the guest claims that he is not worthy and is told that another has imputed worthiness to him. But this is more than a discussion about worthiness; in the course of the conversation, the guest *becomes* worthy—first by acknowledging his lack of worth, next by listening when he is told that this unworthiness has been acknowledged and accounted for; and all of these change him, qualify him, for the communion when he finally demonstrates his worthiness by eating. That is, his subjectivity is not constituted before the conversation (as the speaker who is unworthy) or after the conversation (as the speaker who is worthy); rather, it is constituted actively, in the course of the conversation. I am making the claim that subjectivity is constituted in dialogue. We cannot ask who is speaking and who is spoken to as though they are prior to the conversation because it is only in being addressed and responding that they become the addresser and addressee. Who issues this invitation? God? Christ? the Son? Love? But what is love? Love is welcoming, observing, questioning, offering, explaining, inviting, insisting. And who is invited? One who is reluctant, self-deprecating, self-piteous, self-absorbed, then abject, and finally, one who abandons his will and accepts the invitation.

In conversation, the concern is less to designate, to nominate—for after all, every entry into the conversation requires a shift in such designations—less to describe or inscribe the speakers than to attend to the conversation. Attentiveness suggests hearing and then saying, saying and then hearing, back and forth, con-versing, versing across. What is received is not precisely what is said, and the response is not precisely what is anticipated. And the space between the said and the heard, the response and the anticipated response, is very much part of the conversation too. That space, that in-between, that listening and anticipating silence is key for conversation to transpire; the anticipation of hearing, the anticipation of responding is what turns two monologues into a dialogue. These occur in a special kind of silence: the silence we hear between sounds, between measures. It is a silence that signals not only something to hear but also a hearer. It is a silence that marks time, both the rhythm of sound and the rhythm of conversation. This silence is not the absence of a response, it *is* a response. Derrida writes in *Faith and Knowledge* that response is at the very heart of religion. There, he questions speaking of religion in the singular: "Religion, in the singular? Response: Religion is *the Response*. Is it not there, perhaps, that we must seek the beginning of a response? Assuming, that is, that one knows what responding means, and also responsibility. Assuming, that is, that one knows it—and believes in it. No response, indeed, without a principle of responsibility: one must respond to the other, before the other, and for oneself."[16]

In his theophany to Moses in Exodus 3, God is famously unwilling to name his name, and Pseudo-Dionysus makes much of this—the divine is both all names and no name. But before there is even any discussion of naming, before Moses asks Who shall I say sent me?, God tells Moses that he is the one who *hears* and knows of the Israelites' affliction. Indeed, this is why he appears to Moses, to say *he has heard and seen and means to save*: "I have seen the affliction of my people who are in Egypt, and have heard their cry because of their taskmasters; I know their sufferings, and I have come down to deliver them out of the hand of the Egyptians, and to bring them up out of that land to a good and broad land" (Exodus 3:7–8). In this passage, hearing, seeing, and saving are versions of the same act: response. Exodus 6:5 reiterates this claim that God has heard: "Moreover I have heard the groaning of the people of Israel whom the Egyptians hold in bondage and I have remembered my covenant." That is, I have remembered my promise to hear. The Lord hearing the people contrasts markedly with the people's deafness to the divine message that Moses delivers: "Moses spoke to the people of Israel; they did not listen to

Moses." Nonetheless, as the prophets say, the word of the Lord does not come back empty. The words that God has given man are heard and a response proceeds. This dialogue—dialogue as such—deserves our attention; Hans Urs von Balthassar has remarked that

> looking back over two thousand years of Christian theology, it is astonishing how little attention it [dialogue] has received. . . . After all, at the very center of the biblical events lies the Covenant between God and man, in which God gives man, whom he has created and endowed with freedom, an area of independent being, an area where he can freely hear and answer and ultimately cooperate responsibly with God. . . . There is also . . . taking up a position, possible refusal. . . .His astounding masterpiece is to elicit the Yes of his free partner from the latter's innermost freedom.[17]

According to Herbert, if we are unable to be heard, we are unable to speak. There is no cry when there is no anticipation of a response. Only if we are heard can we speak.

Deniall

When my devotions could not pierce
    Thy silent ears;
Then was my heart broken, as was my verse:
My breast was full of fears
    And disorder
Cheer and tune my heartless breast,
    Defer no time;
That so thy favours granting my request,
    They and my mind may chime,
    And mend my rime.

Here, Herbert suggests that we can only verse when we converse. In another lyric, "A True Hymn," he maintains that "the fineness which a hymn or psalm affords / Is, when the soul unto the lines accords." This congruence between the soul and a line of poetry can also be regarded as con-verse. Later in the lyric, Herbert explains that a poet who wants to offer everything in his poem— all mind, soul, strength, and time—has every right to be disappointed if he produces merely a rhyme—and to make the point, he offers just such a stanza.

He who craves all the minde,
And all the soul, and strength, and time,
If the words only ryme,
Justly complains, that somewhat is behinde
To make his verse, or write a hymne in kinde.

"Thou shalt love the Lord thy God, with all thy heart, with all thy soul and with all thy might," according to Deuteronomy 6:5. Luke 10:27 changes it to "all thy heart, soul, strength, and *mind*." Neither speak of time. But Herbert's poem speaks of mind, soul, strength and *time*, thereby substituting time—poetic meter—for the heart. But if the heart is missing in this stanza, it appears twice in the final one, where it ultimately stops, and stops time, including poetic time.

> Whereas if th' heart be moved,
> Although the verse be somewhat scant,
> God doth supply the want.
> As when th' heart says (sighing to be approved)
> O, *could I love!* And stops: God writeth *Loved.*

The poet offers a verse too short, too scant, but God supplies the rest of the line.[18] Poet speaks; God responds. They verse together, converse. And then the lamenting heart sighs and stops. The heart stops, the verse stops, time stops, life stops. But it turns out that this is not an end; only a stop, a silence that is a pause, for it issues in a response. God adds more: a response to the lament. His obvious answer to the cry, "O could I Love" would be "You *can* love," but the response is different: "Loved." This is God's word, from scripture: "We love him because he first loved us" (I John 4:19); "loved" answers the desire *to* love.

For Herbert, the "true hymn" is God's word, and only one word—no description, no explanation, just "loved." Note too the repetition of "somewhat"— "somewhat it fain would say" "somewhat is behind," "somewhat scant"; "somewhat" is not even "some thing"—no category of being, no attribution—but repeating *somewhat* contributes to the true hymn through its very lack of content. It matters not what is said, what matters is the saying. In this, Herbert anticipates Emmanuel Levinas's distinction between the Saying (*Dire*) and the Said (*le Dit*): the Said is the language of ontology, a theme, topic, thesis, argument; Saying is prior to any Said, a silence ahead of all words, and it presupposes the subject's responsibility for the other.[19] But Herbert's "somewhat" also echoes Pseudo-Dionysius on the impossibility of naming the Divine, for it is beyond all names. Not only did Pseudo-Dionysius enjoy a resurgence in seventeenth-century England, England had its own mystical tradition, including the anonymous *Cloud of Unknowing.* Implicit elsewhere, Herbert's "The Quidditee" makes his connection to apophatic theology explicit. In Scholastic philosophy, the quiddity was the nature of a thing, but in Herbert's lyric, that allusion is ironic for he can only approach the nature of a thing—specifically, verse—through negations.

> My God, a verse is not a crown
> No point of honour, or gay suit,
> No hawk, or banquet, or renown,
> Nor a good sword, nor yet a lute.
>
> It cannot vault, or dance or play,
> It never was in France or Spain.

Then, after all these negations that include courtly love poetry, heroic verse, Homeric song, Virgilian pastoral, he offers his affirmation of what verse is. And in his formulation, it has no predicate:

Regina Mara Schwartz

> But it is that which while I use
> I am with thee

This remarkable conclusion challenges the common understanding of instrument (that which I use), for nothing is used and nothing is conveyed by the user; rather, the user of verse is brought into a relation: "that which while I use *I am with thee*" (my italics). Verse is no thing; it is that which (impossible to nominate) brings me into the presence of God.

Given the rhythm of verse—the stops that mark its time—it is no accident that Pseudo-Dionysius's *Mystical Theology* begins with a poem. That poem evokes an alternative revelation to the one at Sinai—not descriptions of thunder and lightening, but the experience of silence and darkness; not descriptions of words graven on stone tablets soon dashed to pieces, but allusion to a mystic scripture whose words need not be cut or broken, for they "lie simple" in the brilliant darkness of a hidden silence. To approach them, we too must be silent and blind. The revelation only occurs when our senses and our understanding are left behind, so that our sightless minds can be filled with treasures beyond—beyond being, divinity, goodness, and all beauty. The eloquence of this silence challenges us to think silence without a determinate meaning: a silence that listens, a silence that hears. This silence betrays neither a discernible origin—Which is the first silence?—nor a seamless continuity, for it disrupts, erupts into speech, marking the measures of the immeasurable. The measures of this verse make no attempt to measure, to describe, inscribe, or otherwise try to contain what is beyond them, in silence and darkness.

This resistance to containing, this pointing *beyond*, yearning for more, signifying more—more than the language can say, more than the hymn can express—is as much a part of a sacramental poetry as desire is part of praise, impelling it beyond any designations or denominations. Herbert makes this clear in "Providence," where a sign cannot only point to one thing, but more, and that more is impelled by desire to praise; and in the providential scheme, all things are impelled to praise.

> Each thing that is, although in use and name
> It go for one, hath many wayes in store
> To honour thee; and so each hymne thy fame
> Extolleth many ways, yet this one more.

To live is to praise. The ancient Israelites understood death as the state when we can no longer praise: "For Sheol does not sing thy praise, Death does not celebrate thee" (Isaiah 38:18). "The dead, they do not praise Yahweh, nor any who sink to the silent land. But we, we will bless Yahweh from this time forth and for evermore" (Psalm 115:17). One of the oldest meanings of converse (indeed, so apt that it would be tempting to invent had it not already meant this) is "to live." And so not only is to live to praise, but also to converse is to live, and to praise is to converse. But what do we mean by "praise"? The question is not who delivers or who receives the praise, it is praise itself.[20]

Jean-Luc Marion understands praise as the return of the gift given to us. Praise is enabled by that gift.[21] Such praise, I would add, expresses not only gratitude but also desire. Henri de Lubec writes that the desire we have for God, like the longing for the beyond that informs mystical theology, is no accident; rather, it belongs to the humanity that is called, and that desire itself is our response to the call. The prayer/poem that opens Pseudo-Dionysius's poem in *Mystical Theology* reveals the desire that inheres in praise: "Trinity! Higher than any being, any divinity, any goodness! Lead us up!" But how can one express gratitude when his request is not yet granted? "Lead us up," says Pseudo-Dionysus amidst his praise, but we are not yet led up, so why is he already grateful? Grateful for what? For desire, for what is *given* is this desire. Hence, to feel desire is to be grateful, and when we express gratitude, we inevitably express our desire. "God is not governed by our desire," writes de Lubac, "the relation is precisely the other way around—it is the giver who awakens desire. . . . It remains true that once such a desire exists in the creature it becomes the sign, not merely of a possible gift from God, but of a certain gift. It is the evidence of a promise."[22] This desiring subject, whose very heart is inscribed with want, is himself, by virtue of his very desire, evidence that the promised gift has been made. As such, he is not only the receiver; rather, he becomes an offering made back to God, a gift that is first given. The logic of offering a gift that has already been given, offering it even with the strongest desire, informs the logic of Herbert's poem "The Altar," where each part of the poet's heart, cut by God, desires only to praise. The subject *is* the offering made at the altar, and so the poem is visibly shaped not only like an altar but to form the shape of the pronoun "I."

The Altar

A broken Altar, Lord, thy servant reares,
Made of a heart, and cemented with teares:
Whose parts are as thy hand did frame;
No workmans tool hath touch'd the same.
A heart alone
Is such a stone
As nothing but
Thy pow'r doth cut.
Wherefore each part
Of my hard heart
Meets in this frame
To praise thy Name:
That, if I chance to hold my peace,
These stones to praise thee may not cease.
O let thy blessed sacrifice be mine,
And sanctifie this Altar to be thine.

While the speaker's words are also figured as the stones of the altar, his praise, his tears, and his heart, Herbert arranges them in the shape of an altar, making his gift, like the sacrament in Augustinian parlance, include both the word and the visible word. Wanting to be the sacrifice but enabled only by another's sacrifice, the subject can only constitute an altar rather than a hardened heart when he is sanctified by another. Praise is a giving, a giving of thanks, a thanks-giving; literally, a eucharist.

But if mystical theology asks us to think of praise as a gift that has been made to us and as an offering that we return, praise is also, in a seeming paradox, a lament. In contrast to the prayer that hungers for what is not, praise celebrates what is, and when that is gone, praise gives way to lament. But underlying that mourning is gratitude for what is lost. In lament, something beyond the subject gives him the sense that something is lacking—and to even know *that* is a gift. Furthermore, in the very act of lamenting, he celebrates what he already does have: a listener, someone to hear. Long before a request is made or honored, there is a prior response to it, the very presupposition of responsiveness and, with that, gratitude. In this sense, praise is prior to prayer.[23] The heart of this paradox governs liturgical language, and we should not be surprised that the psalms repeatedly express the interdependence of praise and lament. While Sigmund Mowickel has separated psalms of lamentation from psalms of praise as heuristic structures, he acknowledges that liturgically the distinction does not hold. Even as the speaker laments, he shows his confi-dence that God will not fail him; and conversely, in the very act of celebrating God, the speaker expresses his painful longing for him.

> "Here, Yahweh, take pity on me;
>   Yahweh, help me!"
> You turn my mourning into dancing,
> you strip off my sackcloth and wrap me in gladness;
> and now my heart, silent no longer, will play you music;
> Yahweh, my God, I will praise you for ever.
> (Psalm 30:11–12)

Furthermore, the vow usually contained in the psalms of lamentation indi-cates that they were probably offered in a cultic setting when some distress had been overcome, as a song of thanksgiving.[24] The *todha*, or thanksgiving psalm, had two functions: to offer testimony to the saving work of God and then to thank God for that salvation. These psalms begin with praise: "I will extol thee, Yahweh, for thou hast lifted me up" (Psalm 30:1) and proceed to an account of affliction and an account of salvation. "On the very day I cried unto thee / Thou answeredst me at once" (Psalm 138:3). The verb *hvdh*, generally trans-lated as "to praise," properly means "to confess" or "to accept" so that praising includes a confession (of unworthiness) and acceptance (of the judgment for that unworthiness). Gerhard von Rad points to the "avowal" component of praise: "in accepting a justly imposed judgment, the man confesses his trans-gression, and he clothes what he says in the mantle of an avowal, giving God the glory."[25] This is praise from the depths, as it says hauntingly in the Bible,

"God gives these songs in the night" (Job 35:10). It is the praise of Jonah from the belly of the whale; it is the praise of Job; and it is the praise of Christ from the Cross: "My God my God, why have you forsaken me?," echoing Psalm 22—a psalm not only of lament but also of praise.

> My God, I cry by day, but thou does not answer;
> and by night, but find no rest. (Psalm 22:2)

Herbert's brief lyric "Bitter-sweet" compresses both understandings of praise that we find in the psalms, as lament and gratitude, lack and fullness, desire and love. That compression begins with the hyphenated title—one word that combines the bitterness of affliction with the sweetness of praise:

Bitter-sweet

> Ah my deare angrie Lord
> Since thou dost love, yet strike:
> Cast down, yet help afford;
> Sure I will do the like.
>
> I will complain, yet praise;
> I will bewail, approve;
> And all my sour-sweet days
> I will lament, and love.

We saw that for Herbert, the "true hymn" is constituted by a cry and an answer: "O could I love," God writeth "Loved." Not a cry that goes unheard, however short and to the point, it is part of a conversation. In "The Collar" another call is answered with a pointed response. The title puns on "cholar" as anger, "collar" as a yoke, and finally, on "caller" as one who calls. The speaker is frustrated, angry, lamenting his constraints, when suddenly, a voice breaks in:

> But as I rav'd and grew more fierce and wilde
> At every word
> Me thoughts I heard one calling, Child!
> And I reply'd, My Lord.

Shifting from cholar to caller, from man to God, this lyric offers an eloquent testimonial that the divine call enables the human response. Pseudo-Dionysius writes of the Unnameable with all Names, "They especially call it *loving* toward humanity, because in one of its persons it accepted a true share of what it is we are, and thereby *issued a call* to man's lowly state to rise up to it" (my emphasis).[26] The Incarnation itself is described as part of a dialogue, a call to man which is framed in a way that man can respond. "Since the unknowing of what is beyond being is something above and beyond speech, mind, or being itself, one should ascribe to it an understanding beyond being. . . . In our reverent awe, let us be drawn together toward the divine splendor. For . . . the things of God are revealed to each mind in proportion to its capacities; and the divine goodness is such that, out of concern for our salvation, *it deals out the immeasurable and infinite in limited measures*" (my emphasis).[27] When these limited measures are understood not only as an accommodation to finite knowledge and mortality but also as the *measures* of poetry, then the immeasurable is made proportionate to man not only in the Incarnation but also in another kind of incarnation—poetry—the Word made words. Indeed, *Mystical Theology* offers an apt description of the much later metaphors in Herbert's poetry: "The Transcendent [comes to us] clothed in the terms of being, with shape and form on things which have neither, and numerous symbols are employed to convey the varied attributes of what is an imageless and supranatural simplicity. . . . We now grasp these things in the best way we can, and as they come to us, wrapped in the sacred veils of that love toward humanity with which scripture and traditions cover the truths of the mind with things derived from the realm of the senses." But if God offers a revelation proportionate to man's capacities, how could man respond? What could be our answer? Thanksgiving, the hymn of praise awakened by the desire that invites us beyond ourselves. This is a conversation, not a thunderous clap from the beyond that flattens the listener into shock—a conversation, not a devastation. Nor is it a human call that echoes in a cavern, a lonely call left unanswered, only deferred endlessly until its echo fades away. The mystery of this conversation "according to our proportion" is the mystery of the Eucharist, of Christ assuming a body and our liturgical response. And this mystery is called Love, by Pseudo-Dionysius and by George Herbert, who turns the sacrifice into not just a gift or invitation accepted but, more specifically, into a conversation.

The rhythm of conversation is marked by silence. It is in this silence—unspoken and unwritten—that response is located. Such silence is anticipatory, full of expectation of an answer. It is the silence of attention, of hearing, that precedes and occasions a response. Sometimes, it can be the briefest of silences, barely noticeable for the overlapping of voices; sometimes, an agonizingly long, even interminable, silence. To speak, to write, to cry, is to engage in an act of faith—to believe someone will answer. "I cried out to the Lord," says the psalmist, "and he answered me." Our first breath is a cry that signals our entry into conversation, into response and responsibility.

But sometimes the expectation of an answer becomes exhausted, waiting gives up, belief gives way to hopelessness, and there is no reason to cry, for no one is listening—there will be no response. This is another kind of silence—not of expectation but of indifference. This silence is no caesura in a verse, nor a pause in the conversation, but the stunning silence that signals no answer. Where is the answer to the cry during earthquakes, massacres, death camps? It is met with a deafening silence. How can we know when the conversation is going on, when there is still hope for a response, and when it is over? And when it is over, how can we know if that last silence is a full silence or an empty one? Perhaps attention to conversations in the Bible might help, for the Bible offers both poignant accounts of the human cry and a virtual taxonomy of conversation. Many biblical examples seem to compel the hearer to response as the seraph touching Isaiah's unclean lips, or Yahweh reaching out his hand to touch the mouth of Jeremiah, saying "There! I am putting my words into your mouth" (Jeremiah 1:9). Jeremiah's plaintive response betrays this compulsion to speak: "The word of Yahweh has meant for me insult, derision, all day long. I used to say, 'I will not speak in his name any more.' Then there seemed to be a fire burning in my heart, imprisoned in my bones. The effort to restrain it wearied me" (Jeremiah 20:9). Jeremiah wants to fall silent but cannot.

In contrast, the suffering servant of Psalm 22 fears silence, interpreting it not as freedom but indifference.

> My God, my God, why have you deserted me?
> How far from saving me, the words I groan!
> I call all day, my God, but you never answer,
> all night long I call and cannot rest.

The speaker recalls that his calls once were answered; that history constitutes his very genealogy.

> In you our fathers put their trust,
> they trusted and you rescued them;
> they called to you for help and they were saved,
> they never trusted you in vain.

But then he abandons the temporary comfort of seeing himself in that lineage and returns to the present, sees himself, not in terms of a history of salvation, but through the eyes of his contemporaries, constituted by them as a victim.

> Yet here am I, now more worm than man,
> scorn of mankind, jest of the people,
> all who see me jeer at me,
> they toss their heads and sneer,
> "Rely on Yahweh, let Yahweh save him!
> If Yahweh is his friend, let Him rescue him!"

This is the language that Matthew invokes to describe the taunting of Jesus before his crucifixion. And in Psalm 22, as at the crucifixion narrative, this cry *is* answered. Those who taunt that God could save him speak the truth unwittingly: Rely on Yahweh, let Yahweh save him.

> For he has not despised
> or disdained the poor man in his poverty,
> has not hidden his face from him,
> but has answered him when he called. (Psalm 22:24)

Jonah offers another mockery of the notion that our cries go unheard: he cries out from the belly of a fish with laments that are also allusions to the psalms, and yet, even as he cries out, the fish is carrying him, delivering him to shore. In the end, the joke is on Jonah.

From the belly of the fish he prayed to Yahweh, his God; he said:
"Out of my distress I cried to Yahweh
and he answered me;
from the belly of Sheol I cried
And you have heard my voice.
You cast me into the abyss, into the heart of the sea,
and the flood surrounded me,
All your waves, your billows,
washed over me.
And I said, I am cast out
from your sight.
But I with a song of praise
will sacrifice to you.
The vow I have made, I will fulfill.
Salvation comes from Yahweh."
Yahweh spoke to the fish, which then vomited Jonah on to the shore.
(Jonah 2:2–11)

The cry of Jonah is part of a biblical pattern: in Exodus, when the ancient Israelites cry, God hears, responds to their pain, and delivers them from distress, even as they are murmuring in the wilderness; the ancestral history of the Israelites begins with the call to Abraham to leave his father's house, that is, everything he has known, and go to a new place. His loss is enveloped in the larger gift of the covenant, just as the cry of the forsaken Jesus is folded into a larger salvation. As the psalmist says, "Those who sow in tears shall reap in joy." Similar calls are made to Moses, to Samuel, to Isaiah and the other prophets, to Sarah, Hannah, and Mary. While the seemingly unheard cry is embraced by a larger hearing, when the response comes, the addressee is often deaf to it—so loudly is he lamenting the answer of silence.[28]

But for this soteriological pattern to work is to assent to that larger hearing or a final answer; in short, it is to believe. And when it fails? What then? Can only the cries of believers be heard? If so, how can secular verse, how can apostrophe, hope to offer a cry and an answer, a call and response? How can any response be performed that is other than the response to a God and from a God who delivers? Without the profession of faith, on what ground? To answer that question, we must return to the distinction between story and literature, between when a story *describes* a response and when poetry *performs* one. Poetry does not discover a world that it describes; it creates worlds by performing them. Its performative words are analogous to the divine fiat; let there be worlds. And man is in the *image of* God—*imago Dei*—not God, but his image, when he so creates. Let there be light, says the voice of God. Let there be a hearer, says the voice of the poet. While the performance of poetry shares the functions of liturgy, it differs from the kataphatic tradition of naming, from prayer to someone for something, or the apophatic tradition of un-naming, a call to a hearer beyond names. The performance of poetry calls out to one who is performed into hearing, that is, performed into performing. Because the performance that is poetry is different from either a prayer to someone for some thing or a call to a someone that cannot be named, like apostrophe, it simply calls out to *a hearing*. When the blood of Abel cries out from ground, this crying blood calls out for a response. Theological responses include that he is ultimately saved from his enemy, given an eternal life in Christ, but the poetic response (if, indeed, they can be separated, which is doubtful) to the cry is more modest, a cry for a hearing, and with it, a demand for justice. Attentive to the performative character of poetry, literary critics Barbara Johnson, Paul De Man, and Jonathan Culler have discerned that "the fundamental tropes of lyric are apostrophe (the address to something that is not an empirical listener—as in Shelley's 'O wild West Wind') and prosopopoeia (the giving of face and voice to and thus the animation of what would not otherwise be a living interlocutor)."[29] What is performed in poetry is an interlocutor and a listener—conversation. But then, as Marion asks, how can we be sure that the addressee is not an idol, the reflection of my intentionality, the image of my heart's desire, and therefore not an other, but a projection of the same? There is only one way around this: I was addressed by the other before I could address him. Theology calls this grace. Poetry calls it inspiration.

Having demonstrated the oppressiveness that can inhere in onto-theology's commitment to presence, Derrida has opened up for us difference and replaced the obsession with presence with the trace, an indicator of lack, of deferral—not here, not now. Marion, seeing the subject constituted by a call from without, a call that precedes it, has offered us a third reduction in the givenness of phenomena and, in the limit case, the phenomena that dazzle, that overwhelm with their saturation.[30] Acknowledging my debt to both powerful models of difference and givenness, I propose a third for signifying, for constituting the subject, and for responsibility: conversation. As von Balthassar says of our encounter with the revelation in the world, "If the two parties involved in the encounter are to do more than give a nod of recognition in passing, this first encounter must be followed by a conversation. . . . For God's revelation is not an object to be looked at: it is his action in and upon the world, and the world can only respond, and hence 'understand,' through action on *its* part."[31] Poetry can illuminate that "action." Its conversation, including its eloquent silences, offers neither too much to apprehend, like the saturated phenomenon of Jean-Luc Marion, nor too little to grasp, like the perpetual difference of Jacques Derrida. Rather, like the last of Goldilock's three bears, conversation may be "just right." Just right, because it says neither less nor more than we can say. Just right, because in it, we hear neither less nor more than we can hear. In the poetry of conversation, the immeasurable comes to us in measures.

Finally, for Derrida, the Eucharist would mark difference, the distance between signifier—the wafer—and signified—the body of Christ. For Marion, the Eucharist is the saturated phenomenon par excellence, marked not by lack but by its unique hermeneutical success.[32] For Schwartz, the blood of Abel cries out from the ground through the blood of Christ, not for retribution, not even for reconciliation, but for a hearing, so that pain can praise.

Whether or not that praise is heard is the anxiety that attends the very performance that calls forth the hearing: apostrophe. "Hail holy light, off-spring of heaven first-born, or of the eternal co-eternal beam, may I express thee unblamed?" opens John Milton's third invocation in *Paradise Lost.* This address suggests that the speaker is unsure if anyone is listening, unsure who he addresses and unsure if he dare to speak (unworthy as he is), and yet through all this anxiety, his desire to praise the light and what it illumines bursts forth from the blind poet: "So much the rather thou celestial light, shine inward. There plant eyes. All mist from thence purge and disperse, that I may see and tell of things invisible to mortal sight"[33]—that I may praise through my pain, verse to converse.

Derrida's Response to Regina M. Schwartz

Derrida: If I say thank you, is that praise? This leads to one small question about the definition of praise. Would you distinguish between praise in the way you used it and prayer, or an apostrophe—since you are constantly speaking of the call as an apostrophe? In a discussion with Marion, in a footnote,[34] I tried to distinguish between praise, which keeps some description—there is some narrative in praise—and prayer, which just addresses the other without praise. Of course, they are often linked with each another; in prayer, one addresses the other through a praise, but that does not mean that two elements are homogeneous. But that is my question: Is there not an apostrophe or a prayer or a call which is absolutely heterogeneous to the minimal description, evaluation, or narration that there is in a praise? Would you distinguish between a prayer and praise?

Schwartz: I am familiar with your distinction, which, as I recall, is in "Comment ne pas parler: Dénégations," translated as "How to Avoid Speaking." As I think about it, there are two points to be made. One is Marion's response, that one is "praised as," so that a praise is not really of someone who is thereby denominated. There is an index of inadequation, which means that whatever or whoever you are praising you are not calling into being. So I find praise safeguards against that arrogance. Prayer worries me: because the focus of my argument is the danger of instrumentality, I fear the instrumentality of prayer. What do we get when we engage in praise or lament? Silence, the anticipation of a response, the aporia of whether that response will come or not. Too many prayers sound instrumental to my ears, asking, as they do, for something.

Derrida: Well, everyone may have his or her interpretation of a prayer. But can you accept the dissociation of prayer and instrumentalization? Of course, there is a instrumentalization in a prayer, obviously. But there is something in a prayer that gives up any usefulness. I pray not to ask for something, not to request, but just simply to address the other in an apostrophe without even being sure that there is a responsiveness. To pray, you must, of course, as you rightly pointed out, presuppose a responsiveness, but you cannot be sure that there is someone responsive on the other side. So you may pray without asking for anything, just calling the other, and without describing the other, because in the praise there is already some constative structure, that is, the other is worthy of being praised. It is a description, a narration, and there is some element of the non-performative in the praise. There is some performative in the praise, but there is also a non-performative. It is not a pure performative; it implies some knowledge or implied knowledge, some supposed knowledge, a description of who God is or who you are, and so on. So I would distinguish between praise and prayer. This would have some consequences in the organization of the logic of your discussion. Perhaps in the Roundtable we will discuss this again.

This is not to speak against the insistent and indispensable reference to performativity, as you do, and as everyone does today. I am very grateful for this distinction between the constative and the performative. But at some point, especially when we reach the question of calling, of referring to the other in a call, in a prayer, and waiting for the event, for a possible event, not a sure event, I know that the event, that is, the possible response of the other, if it happens, will have nothing to do with any performative. The eventness of the event not only defeats the constative but it also defeats the performative. The eventness of the event has no power. Performativity implies some power. A poetic performative implies that I am able to perform. But there is a point in what happens where you lose the performative power. What happens is the arriving of the other. Now the happening of the other, if it is an authentic happening, an unpredictable happening, should just defeat performativity—and constativity even more. So there is a point here, where the way we, all of us, rely on performativity more and more in the university becomes suspect, because I think that we tend to forget that performativity implies power, implies some control, some mastery about what happens, what we make happen. I am able, when I perform, to make this happen, through my speech act and through my verse and through my verse in conversation.

Let us go back to conversation. If in conversation something happens with the other, from the other, it should at some point again exceed any performativity, and that is so even in poetry. I am aware, as you are, of the performative power of any poetry worthy of its name. But I am even more interested in the fact that there is in poetry something that exceeds performativity. The poet controls a lot of things, performs a lot of things, and produces events through poetic language. But at some point the poet is weak, passive, finite, that is, unable to take the measure, to use your language; the poet cannot measure his or her own performativity to the event, which is more than anything that can be measured. So here is the incommensurability between the event of what happened, the other as happening, let us say, and the performative, any performative power, in the conversation. Could you imagine a conversation, even a silence—the way you rightly describe a certain silence—which would not interrupt performative acts? There must be something more than the performative in conversation, and I would relate this to desire and prayer and not simply to praise.

Schwartz: Thank you for that response. I am grateful. To respond just briefly to it, if I can: I felt like you have—and please do correct me if I am mistaken—brought a third person into the discussion. That is, when I heard you talk about the passivity that has to set in when you relinquish the power of performativity, when the event happens to you and you are just receiving, I heard the strains of the thinking also of Jean-Luc Marion, with his very enhanced understanding of passivity. I hardly dare to use the word passivity. I rarely would. But in his "saturated phenomenon" that dazzles, which certainly exceeds performativity, he is saying something that would be very much in agreement with you. So we would have a very interesting moment in which I would be on one side of the conversation and the two of you would be on the other, together. I would be holding up my end by arguing for a humbler conversation, only because I really do worry about the implication of being dazzled or devastated by the event. Because how are you going to then stand up and speak the next sentence? When the conversation exceeds performativity, then your voice can be crushed.[35]

NOTES

1. On idolatry, I am indebted to Jean-Luc Marion's *God without Being*, trans. Thomas Carlson (Chicago: University of Chicago Press, 1991), originally *Dieu sans l'etre: Hors-texte* (Paris, 1982); and Marion, *L'Idole et la distance* (Paris: Grasset, 1977).

2. I first began developing the model of conversation in a paper on the Eucharist delivered at the University of Chicago Conference on Mystics. It is forthcoming in a volume edited by Chris Sheppard and Michael Kessler, University of Chicago Press. I want to thank them for their helpfulness as I addressed the question of conversation.

3. Niccolo Macchiavelli, "To Francesco Vettori in Rome, Dec. 10, 1513," in *The Portable Macchiavelli*, trans. Peter Bondanella and Mark Musa (New York: Penguin, 1979), p. 69.

4. Marion, *God without Being*, p. 35.

5. Ibid., p. 45.

6. Jacques Derrida, "Signature, Event, Context," *Glyph* 1 (1977): 172–197; the response by John Searle, "Reiterating the Differences: A Reply to Derrida," *Glyph* 1 (1977): 198–208, and Derrida, "Limited Inc.," *Glyph* 2 (1977): 162–254.

7. Josiah Priest, *Slavery, as It Relates to the Negro, or African Race, Examined in the Light of Circumstances, History, and the Holy Scriptures; with an Account of the Origin of the Black Man's Color, Causes of His State of Servitude and Traces of His Character as Well in Ancient and in Modern Times* (Albany: C. Van Benthuysen and Co., 1843), 15. This book was reprinted five times in eight years.

8. Regina Schwartz, *The Curse of Cain: The Violent Legacy of Monotheism* (Chicago: University of Chicago Press, 1998).

9. *Paradise Lost*, in *John Milton: Complete Poetry and Major Prose*, ed. Merritt Hughes (New York: Odyssey Press, 1957), Book I, ll. 22–23.

10. I do not argue that these biblical narratives of violence *cause* historical violence, but that the violence of humanity is reflected in these stories and that they are used to authorize violence that is motivated by the same causes the stories describe: competition, greed, possessiveness, and anxious identity formation. See especially pp. 1–28, *The Curse of Cain.*

11. Jacques Derrida, "This Strange Institution Called Literature: An Interview," in *Acts of Literature*, ed. Derek Attridge (New York: Routledge, 1992), p. 37.

12. Louis Martz, *The Poetry of Meditation: A Study in English Religious Literature of the Seventeenth Century* (New Haven: Yale University Press, 1962), p. 280.

13. Barbara Lewalski, *Protestant Poetics and the Seventeenth-Century Religious Lyric* (Princeton: Princeton University Press, 1979), p. 300.

14. Chana Bloch, *Spelling the Word* (Berkeley: University of California Press, 1985), p. 100.

15. *Book of Common Prayer*, 1604.

16. "Faith and Knowledge" trans. Samuel Weber, in *Religion*, ed. Jacques Derrida and Gianni Vattimo (Stanford, Calif.: Stanford University Press, 1998), p. 26. Orig. *La Religion: Seminaire de Capri* (Paris: Editions de Seuil et Editions Laterza).

17. Hans Urs Von Balthassar, *Theo-Drama: Theological Dramatic Theory*, trans. Graham Harrison (San Francisco: Ignatius Press, 1988), vol. 1, p. 34. Orig. *Theo-dramatik: Erster Band* (*Prolegomena* [Einsiedeln: Johannes Verlag, 1983]).

18. See the discussion of Chana Bloch, *Spelling the Word*, p. 59–61.

19. Emmanuel Levinas, *Otherwise Than Being, or Beyond Essence*, trans. Alphonso Lingis (The Hague: M. Nijhoff, 1981). Orig. *Autrement qu'etre*.

20. See Marion, *God without Being*, p. 49 ff., and the discussion of Marion's understanding of the impossibility of predication for praise in Thomas Carlson, *Indiscretion: Finitude and the Naming of God* (Chicago: University of Chicago Press, 1999), pp. 197–203.

21. Marion, ibid.

22. Henri de Lubec, *The Mystery of the Supernatural*, trans. Rosemary Sheed (New York: Crossroad Herder, 1998), p. 207. Orig. *Le Mystere du surnatural* (Paris, 1965).

23. Here I depart explicitly from Derrida's emphasis on "prayer" which holds forth the possibility for instrumentality, for a motivated request, that pure praise does not. While Derrida asserts that praise implies predication—we praise some *thing*—I maintain the opposite: *we pray for some thing*, whereas praise suggests neither predication nor instrumentality. I agree with Marion that within the language of praise, God is always praised "*as . . .*" and the *as* constitutes an "index of inadequation," so praise does not claim to describe, to inscribe. It admits the inaccessibility of what we praise. What Derrida says of prayer is precisely how I would define praise, "demands only that the other hear it, receive it, be present at it, be the other as such, a gift, a call, and cause of [praise]." See Jacques Derrida, "How to Avoid Speaking: Denials," trans. Ken Friedan, in *Derrida and Negative Theology*, eds. Howard Coward and Toby Foshay (Albany: SUNY Press, 1992). Our difference on the nature of praise springs from my debt to the biblical understandings of praise, which escapes the instrumentality of prayer. If Der-

rida's "prayer" for the impossible that never can come reflects his passion for justice, how can praise (of what is) or lament (of what is lost) avoid the charge of an inherent conservativism? Praise escapes the charge of the apolitical by virtue of what it embraces: praise is not of a being, but of justice—a justice once here and now gone, an imagined justice, a thought of justice. Caputo goes so far as to contrast Derridean religion with the apophatic tradition: "Derrida's religion is more prophetic than apophatic, more in touch with Jewish prophets than with Christian Neoplatonists, more messianic and more eschatological than mystical" (John Caputo, *The Prayers and Tears of Jacques Derridas: Religion without Religion* [Bloomington, Ind.: Indiana University Press, 1997], p. xxiv). But this binary of the ethico-political prophets versus the mystical apophatic tradition invites deconstructing. For just as Isaiah's lips are touched by the seraph's flame in a mystical experience, so the political effect of "singing the unnameable name" in apophatic theology is surely an unwillingness to master by means of naming. While Derrida has indeed spoken convincingly of justice linked to his "hoping sighing dreaming" for the impossible, there is another justice that is not born of lack, but of gratitude. See John Caputo's rich discussion in *The Prayers and Tears of Jacques Derrida*, esp. 1–26.

24. Sigmund Mowinckel, *The Psalms in Israel's Worship*, trans. D. R. Ap-Thomas, 2 vols. (Nashville: Abington Press, 1962), II, pp. 30–43.

25. Gerhard von Rad, *Old Testament Theology*, trans. D. M. G. Stalker (New York: Harper and Row, 1962), I, p. 359. Orig. *Theologie des Alten Testaments* (Munich: Verlag, 1957).

26. *Pseudo-Dionysius: The Complete Works*, trans. Colm Luibheid (New York: Paulist Press, 1987) p. 52.

27. *Pseudo-Dionysius*, p. 49.

28. In their work, von Rad, von Balthassar, Levinas, and Marion have focused on the call that is prior, that calls us into a covenant, into subjectivity, responsibility, and into love.

29. Jonathan Culler, "Deconstruction and the Lyric," in *Deconstruction Is/In America*, ed. Anselm Haverkamp (New York: New York University Press, 1995), 30.

30. Marion, "The Saturated Phenomenon," *Philosophy Today* 40, no. 1 (Spring 1996). Translated by Tom Carlson.

31. Von Balthassar, *Theo-Drama*, vol. I, p. 15.

32. Marion, *God without Being*, pp. 139–158.

33. *Paradise Lost*, III, ll. 51–55.

34. Jacques Derrida, "How to Avoid Speaking: Denials," trans. Ken Friedan, in *Derrida and Negative Theology*, eds. Howard Coward and Toby Foshay (Albany: SUNY Press, 1992), pp. 136–38, note 16.

35. For more on Regina Schwartz's response to the problem of "silence" in conversation, see the paper she gave at the Continental Philosophy of Religion Conference in Lancaster, UK, July, 2000, which is forthcoming in a volume edited by Philip Goodchild entitled *Continental Philosophy of Religion*.

nine

"Idipsum"

Divine Selfhood and the
Postmodern Subject

Jean Greisch

*Denkwege bergen in sich das Geheimnisvolle, daß wir sie vorwärts und
rückwärts gehen können, daß sogar der Weg zurück uns erst vorwärts führt.*

—Martin Heidegger, *Unterwegs zur Sprache*, p. 99

On the 11th of August this summer, I watched the last complete solar
eclipse of the present millennium in a small village in Normandy. Of course, I
was not the only witness of this event. All around, the cliffs were crowded with
people, young and old, lifting their black glasses up to the sky. At the most
fascinating moment, while a strange darkness shrouded the whole landscape
and Venus suddenly made a brilliant appearance in the sky, the crowd clapped
their hands, as if they were beholding a happening specially organized for
them by some invisible showmaster.

This unexpected reaction of my fellow spectators, a reaction I did not
share, stirred in me some disturbing questions. Was this merely the expression
of a childish marveling, or did it confirm Heidegger's thesis that we are all
children of the "age of representation," whether we know it or not? *Who* were
these people who clapped their hands at the meteorological showdown: modern or postmodern subjects?

Some weeks later, approaching the city of Paris, my eyes were caught by
huge advertising panels, announcing the creation of the Internet site of a

Jean Greisch

broadcasting company under the title "*Et Dieu dans tout ça?* (And what about God?)" with this recommendation: "Questioning—that's essential."

The central thread of the following reflections will consist of an attempt to link the question "Who are we?" with the question "And what about God?"

The Augustinian catchword in the title of this paper is not just a diplomatic nod to St. Augustine, the *genius loci* of Villanova University, nor to Jean-François Lyotard, who died on the 20th of April 1998 and whose posthumous fragments have just been published under the title *La Confession d'Augustin.*[1] My intention is to show that in the context of this second Religion and Postmodernity conference, dedicated to the topic "Questioning God," it might be helpful to go back to Augustine who, long before Heidegger, highlighted the relation between questioning (*quaerere*), worrying (*curare*), and selfhood: "*quaestio mihi factus sum* (I have become a question to myself.)" Moreover, Augustine could help us to not forget that the title "Questioning God" leaves open the question who questions whom.

1. "Who Are We?": A Heideggerian Question and Its Implications

Trag vor dir her
Das Eine Wer?
Wer ist der Mensch?

—Martin Heidegger, *Besinnung*, p. 5[2]

In Descartes' second *Metaphysical Meditation*, we find the following well-known proposition: "So we must conclude and hold firmly that this proposition: 'I am, I exist' is necessarily true each time that I utter it, or that I conceive it in my mind." "*Sum, existo*": This is the first announcement of an intellectual victory after the fierce battle of doubt in the first meditation. It leads immediately to the question of "*what* I am, I who am certain *that* I am?" This question implies an "inquiry into the list of predicates which can be attributed to this 'I' who is ascertained to exist in the nakedness of the 'I am.'"[3]

a) The Ontological Primacy of the Question "Who?"

Both statements—the apodictic certainty: "I am, I exist" as well as the open question: "*What* am I, I who am certain that I am?"—have obviously an ontological meaning. In Descartes and in Kant, the question of the subject is that of its ontological status. It cannot be reduced to a mere gnoseological question (What can I know about myself?), and even less to a psychological question (to put it in Montaigne's words, who is the "shadow" of Descartes: Am I able to draw a true picture of myself?). Nor is it an epistemological question (How can we qualify self-knowledge and which kind of science can we construct upon it?). Among other texts, the *Conversations with Burman* make it clear that in his second meditation Descartes intended to raise an ontological question regarding the cogito.

But how does he state this question? Obviously, he uses the framework of traditional ontology, which goes back to the medievals and even to Aristotle: every being, therefore also the cogito, can be submitted to the twofold question of its *anitas* (*an sit*: does *x* exist?) and its *quidditas* (*quid sit*: what is *x*?). The true question is whether the traditional distinction of existence and essence enables us to clarify the ontological status of the "I," that is, the meaning of "*sum*" in the proposition "*sum, existo.*"

During his Marburg teachings, Martin Heidegger tried to work out an answer to this question. In his opinion, the only way of clarifying the ontological status of the "I" is to let oneself be guided by the question "Who?" which is neither reducible to that of *anitas* (*do* I exist?) nor to that of *quidditas* (*What* am I, I who am certain *that* I exist?, etc.). Heidegger's discussion of the fundamental thesis of modern ontology in Chapter 3 of his *Fundamental Problems of Phenomenology*[4] shows that in his opinion we need to introduce a new ontological "category," better attuned to the question "Who?" In fact, it is more than a category, insofar as it replaces the category of *ousia*, which is dominant in traditional ontology. Heidegger calls it *Werheit*, a neologism which Jean-François Courtine translates quite literally as "*quissité,*" which could be rendered in English as "Who-ness" or "*quissity.*"[5]

This new category of *Werheit* plays a fundamental role in Heidegger's answer to the question whether modern philosophy, which elects subjectivity as its major topic, has been able to elucidate the ontological status of selfhood or not. I propose to summarize his answer to this question, an answer which can be found in the 1927 Marburg lecture in the following four points.

1. No philosophy whatever can exclude from its aim at universal understanding the questioning of the ontological status of the subject, for the simple reason that "where philosophy appears, *Dasein* stands already on the horizon."[6] This is why we must avoid opposing ancient and modern philosophy as a philosophy *without subject* against a philosophy *of subject*. This opposition is just as misleading as the opposition of "cultures with history" and "cultures without history" or writing and non-writing societies. In his book *Aristote et la question du monde*, Rémi Brague has shown the implications of this thesis for a phenomenological reading of Aristotle's conception of the world.[7] It is unnecessary to add that what holds for premodern thinking also holds for the so-called postmodern thinking: In any case, postmodern thinking cannot mean that the question of selfhood as such becomes meaningless.

2. The main characteristic of modern philosophy is its focus on the idea that the cogito is the fundamental principle of philosophical thinking as such. Subjectivity, which thus far had been a philosophical topic among many others, becomes from now on its primordial theme. The fact that in starting with the ego, modern philosophy has brought about a "total turning of philosophical questioning"[8] cannot be denied.

But does this amount to a revolution in ontological thinking?

Heidegger's answer is clearly negative: Descartes and all his followers up to Kant, Hegel, Fichte, and Husserl were unable to raise the question of the *mode of being* of the subject. In this respect, the philosophical revolution started by Descartes' discovery of the cogito is no revolution at all or, in other words, the real revolution is yet to come![9]

3. The reason for this failure, which explains why, as far as ontology goes, modern philosophy is not modern at all, can be clearly indicated: Descartes and his followers still speak the language of medieval ontology, especially in its Suarezian idiolect. This is why the question of the meaning of the *"sum"* is eluded instead of being treated.

4. How can this obstacle be surmounted? *Fundamental Problems of Phenomenology* highlights the importance of a suggestion which was already at work in *Being and Time*: Only if we allow ourselves to be guided by the question "Who?" do we have a chance to develop a quite different ontology. It begins with a question Heidegger formulates in connection with Kant's account of the person as an "end in itself": "How can we qualify the self *ontologically*, which reveals itself *ontically* as the 'I' in the moral feeling of respect?"[10]

In this paper I cannot engage in a thorough discussion of Heidegger's position or ask myself to what extent I subscribe to his arguments. Many well-qualified historians of philosophy have undertaken this task in relation to Descartes, Kant, Fichte, and Husserl. In the context of our discussions, it is more interesting to follow the track of the question "Who?" in Heidegger's later thinking, from the "metaphysics of *Dasein*," elaborated in the years after the publication of *Being and Time*, up to the post-metaphysical notion of *Ereignis*.

Regarding the former notion, it is important to keep in mind that the notion of "metaphysics of *Dasein*" is closely linked to Heidegger's thesis that Kant's fourth question: *"Was ist der Mensch?* (What is the human being?)" should be regarded as the first question of philosophy, that is to say, the decisive question of ontology as first philosophy. Does this mean that Heidegger himself falls back into traditional ontological questioning, applying the formal structure: "What is *x*?" to human beings? Not at all! A thorough analysis of Heidegger's "metaphysical" lectures during the years 1928–1934 shows that he is still struggling with the ontological enigma of selfhood as such, one of his major insights being that selfhood must not be reduced to self-determination. In other words, *Dasein* can only understand itself if it resists the temptation of thinking that it is the originary source of its selfhood.

b) From the "Question of the Subject" to "Putting the Subject in Question": Selfhood and *Ereignis*

This leads to our second question: What about the "Who?" in Heidegger's later post-metaphysical thought? Is it wiped out, neutralized, or does it receive a new meaning? A close look at Heidegger's texts in which the "turn" (*Kehre*) "takes place," or is "accomplished," shows that the question "Who?" does indeed receive a new meaning. This can be illustrated by several especially interesting pages of the manuscript entitled *Besinnung*, a text which Heidegger penned during the years 1938–1939, in continuity with *Beiträge zur Philosophie*, written in 1936–1938.

Besinnung, recently published as Volume 66 of the *Gesamtausgabe*, opens with seven poetic texts. The third poem, entitled "Der Sprung (The Leap)," consists of five strophes. Three of them relate directly to our problem:

Trag vor dir her	Bear before thee
das Eine Wer?	The one Who?
Wer ist der Mensch?	Who is Man?
Sag ohne Unterlaß	Say ceaselessly
das Eine Was	The one What?
Was ist das Seyn	What is Being?
Mißachte nie	Never disdain
das Eine Wie?	The one How?
Wie ist ihr Bund?	How is their Alliance?[11]

Several paragraphs in the same volume, especially those gathered in Section VII under the title "Being and Man" can be read as a philosophical exegesis of this rather strange "poem." Instead of giving a linear commentary on this section, I shall simply point out the most interesting aspects relating to our topic.

1. The Non-anthropological Meaning of *Being and Time*

Heidegger stresses first that in a *"hermeneutical and phenomenological"*[12] perspective, *Being and Time* is *"neither* any kind of anthropology" "*nor* any kind of metaphysics,"[13] which could eventually lead to "some kind of existential ethics."[14] But this does not mean at all that we are rid of the question of human selfhood. Rather, we need an entirely new mode of questioning: We need "to question about man *starting with the question of the truth of Being* and *only* in that way."[15] The assumption that "*Da-sein*" is a solipsistic and individualistic entity can not be neutralized by simply insisting on human plurality, community, and society. This is exactly what the Nazi ideology did in glorifying the collective personality of a mythic *Volkssubjekt*. Heidegger dismisses this dangerous illusion with the words "*Die armen Tröpfe!* (The wretched oafs!)"

2. *Wasfrage* and *Werfrage*

After the 1936 "turn" to a post-metaphysical thinking, the question "Who?" does not fade away; on the contrary, it crops up again as a kind of unavoidable "feedback" (*Rückschlag*) of questioning the Truth of Being as such.

Of course, it receives thus a new meaning. The leading question is no longer that of the "metaphysics of *Dasein*," asking with Kant: "What is man?," but the question: "*Who* are 'we'?"[16] For this reason, Heidegger now strongly stresses the distinction between the question "What?" and the question "Who?" The question "What?" can be put without difficulty in the plural. This is not the case with the question "Who?," which must be taken in its *singularity*: That which is at stake in the *Werfrage* is nothing other than the "*self*hood (*Selbst*theit) of man."[17]

3. *Wesensflucht:* The Avoidance of the Most Essential Question

Are we ready to ask this singular question? Not at all! We avoid it, fleeing from it. This *Wesensflucht* (escape from essence) exhibits several aspects. The first is the conviction that we already know the answer—the essence of man is given in the definition: a "rational animal"! This makes us blind to the historical variability of human self-understanding. The typical modern expression of this *Wesensflucht* consists in the conviction that self-understanding means nothing more than free self-determination. The *Wesensflucht* of which Heidegger is speaking does not necessarily manifest itself as avoiding "introspection" in the name of the so-called external and objective Reality. It can also express itself through individualism and its communitarian or collectivistic equivalents.

4. *Frage an den Menschen:* The "Destinal" Meaning of the Question

If it is understood in Heidegger's way, the question of selfhood implies what he calls a "*genitivus essentialis.*" It is not only an essential question "about man," but a question in which the human being itself is at stake, a question which strikes the self even before it can ask it. In other words: it is a *destinal* question. This is probably the reason why Heidegger formulates the *Wesensfrage* in a temporal mode: "But when and how is he *himself*?"[18]

5. *Vermenschlichung* and *Vermenschung:*
The True Meaning of Anthropomorphism

The distinction between *Wasfrage* and *Werfrage* is completed by a second, just as important, terminological distinction: Heidegger distinguishes between "anthropomorphizing" (*Vermenschlichung*) and "humanizing" (*Vermenschung*).[19] Anthropologism, or anthropomorphism, as it is usually understood, can be reduced to some contemporary version of Protagoras's axiom: "*Homo mensura*"—the human being is the measure of everything else. One of the most trivial readings of this axiom is the supposition that nothing is more interesting than humans, so that every question, whether metaphysical or theological, can be transformed into a question about man. This is the leading principle of Feuerbach's well known anthropological interpretation of Christian religion.

But this *Vermenschlichung*, consisting in looking at the totality of beings with human, all-too-human, eyes, presupposes already a decision regarding human self-understanding. This is what Heidegger has in mind when he speaks of *Vermenschung*. Man has already decided about his own essence: He understands himself as an animal *plus* something else. In the spiritualistic tradition this "plus" is interpreted as "soul," Bergson's famous, often-quoted and often-misunderstood *"supplément d'âme."* But paradoxically this supplement can also be understood as a "minus," a burden, as is the case in Rilke's "Eighth Duino Elegy." Whether the human being celebrates its superiority over the animal world or whether it envies the assurance which characterizes animal life, the principle of self-understanding remains the same: Humanity must be understood in reference to animality.

Heidegger refuses to take part in the "phantom battle" (*Scheingefecht*[20]) about the hierarchy between the terms "body, soul, spirit," opposing the spiritualistic and humanistic defenders of "spiritual values" to their materialistic adversaries. In his opinion, this debate is a perfect illustration of an ideological controversy which avoids the essential question: "Who are we?" Paradoxically, both camps share a common presupposition: They know already the answer to the question of what man is; their disagreement refers only to whether we should stress our superiority over animals, or, on the contrary, rediscover our animality.

In this context, Heidegger makes an ironic remark that reveals the depth of his anti-Christian and anti-Catholic resentment: In his opinion the enemies of religious spiritualism are even more "catholic" than the Catholics themselves ("more catholic than the Pope," so to speak), insofar as the formula "body-mind-soul" in purely Catholic style "serves all purposes yet remains shielded against all objections."[21]

Heidegger's main thesis is that the "abandonment by Being" (*Seinsverlassenheit*) whose cultural manifestation is nihilism is most triumphant in the panicky avoidance of the question of our selfhood. In order to put an end to this *Wesensflucht*, we need more than a voluntaristic decision—"Enough is enough!"—because voluntarism and decisionism are the very symptoms of this *Wesensflucht*. What we need, says Heidegger, are three things: a new "fundamental position" (*Grund-stellung*), grounded in a new "fundamental experience" (*Grund-erfahrung*), which presupposes first of all a "fundamental distress" (*Grund-not*).[22]

Although I do not share all the presuppositions of Heidegger's *Ereignisdenken*, and although I am not at all sure that the expressions "post-metaphysical" and "postmodern" must be taken as synonymous, I think that Heidegger's reflections may help us focus the fundamental questions at stake in the often-confusing debates about the condition of postmodernity. One of these questions is certainly that of selfhood.

Even if we have good reason to criticize the modern understanding of the subject (including Nietzsche's "anti-cogito," which belongs to the same *Grund-stellung*), we still have to deal with the question of selfhood. This question has become more urgent than ever. At the same time, the pluri-vocality of the question "Who?" gives rise to several ideas of selfhood, which we find in recent philosophical literature. The self can be understood as the Levinasian "Here I am" of responsibility, which puts the subject in the accu-sative, as the dative of Heidegger's *Da-sein*; as an *"advenant,"* in the line of Claude Romano's *"herméneutique événementiale"*;[23] as *"l'interloqué"* (the "overtaken") who is also an *"adonné"* (the given to, or the "addicted") in Jean-Luc Marion's sense;[24] or with Ricoeur as the "self as another," suggesting that alterity—a plurivocal notion—is constitutive of selfhood as such.[25]

2. The Epochal Meanings of the Question of God

Thus far, I have deliberately left out the problem of divine Selfhood, that is to say, the question of whether the idea of God should also be developed in the light of the question "Who?" Now we need to lift these brackets in order to deal with the question "What about God?"

I will start with an idea developed by Ernst Jüngel in his book *Gott als Geheimnis der Welt*. Instead of supposing that the question of God belongs to an unchanging *philosophia perennis*, historical consciousness shows us that there are many different ways of questioning God philosophically or theologi-cally. Therefore, one could say that each age has the question of God that it deserves, or rather that fits its historical situation. These different ways of questioning can be illustrated through the spectrum of interrogative forms: "Does God exist?" "What is God?" "Where is God?" "Who is God?" The classical proofs of divine existence belong to an age in which the crucial question was that of the existence of God. The question "What is God?" seems to play a central role in modern philosophical theologies from Descartes to Fichte, Schelling, and Hegel, not forgetting Spinoza, Leibniz, and Kant.

In Jüngel's understanding, the modern age, which developed a meta-physics of subjectivity, seems to favor the question "Where is God?,"[26] which receives its most dramatic expression in Nietzsche's *Fröhliche Wissenschaft*: "*Wohin ist Gott?*" ("Where has God gone?"). In the mouth of Nietzsche's madman, who proclaims the death of God, this seems to be a purely rhetorical question, calling attention to an event whose consequences we have not yet measured. But the question also troubles all Nietzsche's contemporaries, whether they are believers or not.

One of the most interesting ideas developed by Jüngel is the link he establishes between this question and the problematization of the essence of God.[27] Three apparently incompatible sentences highlight, in his view, the way in which metaphysics of subjectivity deals with the possibility of thinking God. Each of them can be read as a new formulation of the famous Augustin-ian dictum: "If you understand, it will not be God."[28]

1. The first is Fichte's statement in his defense against the accusation of being a concealed atheist: God "must not be thought at all, because such a

thing is impossible."[29] Fichte appears thus to be the first thinker working with the hypothesis that philosophical theology consists in "conceptual idolatry," a hypothesis defended nowadays by Jean-Luc Marion. The same idea was already stated by Fichte in the following words:

> *In Summa*: the very fact that something is understood conceptually implies that it is no longer God; and each so-called concept of God is necessarily that of an idol. He who says: you must not make a concept of God says in other words: you must not make an idol and this commandment has the same spiritual meaning as the ancient Mosaic commandment has on the sensual level: you must not make an image nor anything which pretends to be a resemblance (*Gleichnis*).[30]

This Fichtean interpretation of Augustine's "*si comprehenderis, non erit Deus*" seems to turn into its contrary in Feuerbach's statement: "Only if you think *God*, are you *thinking*, rigorously speaking."[31] This thesis could be translated back into Augustinian Latin in the following way: "*Si comprehendis, eris Deus* (If you understand, you will be God)." At first sight, this seems to be the expression of a hyperbolic theologization of human thinking. In fact, as we well know, Feuerbach's thesis is the principle of a radical reduction of all theological statements to anthropological statements. In thinking God, human reason celebrates its highest abilities. God, says Feuerbach, is nothing else than the other name of "reason which proclaims itself to be the Supreme Being and which affirms itself as such."[32]

3. Is it possible to imagine an Augustinian gloss on the rhetorical question "Could you *think* a God?" which Nietzsche's Zarathustra addresses to his listeners as an ultimate challenge, in the passage entitled "Auf den glückseligen Inseln." This question confronts human reason again with the Infinite, the abyss of divine immensity which Nietzsche symbolizes in the image of the open sea. But he also indicates the price that must be paid by those who want to be delivered of the nauseating vertigo which Anselm's *id quo majus cogitari nequit* introduced in the human mind: the *Übermensch* alone can get rid of religious and metaphysical transcendence. "*Si comprehenderis, creaveris deum* (If you understand, you will create God)": This could be the Augustinian "translation" of Zarathustra's question.

I agree with Jüngel that, regarding God-thinking, we still move within the triangle of these three statements.[33] My question is the following: What is the place of the question: "Who is God?" in this epochal vision of the history of thought? Is it premodern, modern, or postmodern? Instead of giving an immediate answer, we need to reflect more thoroughly upon the "hermeneutical situations" (individual as well as collective) in which all the questions mentioned thus far are rooted.

1. It is only under precise circumstances that human reason feels the need of producing a "proof" of the existence of God, or of defining a rational access to God, an *itinerarium mentis in Deum*. This is the case whenever human

reason has to deal with the problem of different religions or when it has to confront the challenge of science.

2. The "hermeneutical situation" in which the question "What is God?" is grounded, corresponds to an age of reason in which the very idea of God is at stake. This leads to focusing on the problem of the coherence of divine attributes, as well as to the problem of theodicy. Descartes' philosophical theology—described by Jean-Luc Marion as a "white" theology, contrasting with his "gray" ontology—is a good example of this way of questioning; it deals with the ideas of substance, *causa sui*, infinity and absolute perfection, which, in Marion's interpretation, correspond to three different, and even incompatible, theologies.[34]

Heidegger has elaborated his own answer to the question of the status of "onto-theo-logy," which constitutes metaphysical thinking as such: the God of onto-theology, that is to say the metaphysical name of God, is *causa sui* and nothing else. This onto-theological structure receives its most perfect expression in what Heidegger calls Hegel's "onto-theo-*ego*-logy."[35]

Neither Heidegger's question "How does the God come into philosophy as such?" (*Wie kommt der Gott in die Philosophie?*) nor his answer—the metaphysical name of God is *causa sui*—is self-evident. In his book *Nietzsche et l'ombre de Dieu*, Didier Franck has drawn attention to the hidden presupposition behind Heidegger's use of the definite article, which corresponds to the Greek *to theion*. Franck himself suggests that this formulation ought to be replaced by a more accurate question, which fits better Nietzsche's thinking: "How does God (that is to say the God of Judeo-Christian Revelation) come into philosophy?"[36]

3. How can we characterize the "hermeneutical situation" in which the question "Where is God?" emerges? No doubt this question has a specific relation to the problem of evil, on the existential as well as on the intellectual level. But if it is taken in the directional meaning of Nietzsche's *Wohin*, it also relates to the experience of the "flight of the gods," as Heidegger calls it, following Hölderlin.

4. What about the question "Who?" We have seen that in Heidegger's opinion this is the most important question regarding the essence of man. Astonishingly, he never asked whether the same question can also be related to God. Instead of following Heidegger, limiting the question to the selfhood of *Dasein*, I think that it not only can, but it also must, be related to divine Selfhood. I am fully aware that the consequence of this suggestion is that, in a certain sense, we would have to speak of God's *Da-sein*—which is obviously an anti-Heideggerian heresy.

At the end of these "epochal considerations," let me introduce a rather daring hypothesis: The style of questioning which best suits the situation we have in mind when we use Lyotard's thoroughly problematic notion of "postmodern condition" emerges at the intersection between the questions "Where is God?" and "Who is God?" This point of intersection needs a more thorough examination.

3. The "Selfsame": A Forgotten Name for God

Cuius participatio in idipsum. *Here, my Brothers, I entreat whoever lifts up the gaze of the mind, whoever puts aside the obscurity of the flesh, whoever cleanses the eye of his heart, let him lift up his mind to contemplate the Selfsame. What is the Selfsame? How express it if not as the Selfsame? Understand the Selfsame, my Brothers, if you can. For in using any other word I do not express the Selfsame.*

—St. Augustine, *Enarrationes in Psalmos* 121, 3[37]

Taking the *"causa sui"* as the metaphysical name of God implies the risk of masking other equally important, or even more important, names produced by the tradition of philosophical theology which cannot be reduced without further distinctions to the massive and monolithic notion of onto-theology. In the line of my hypothesis, which invites us to intersect the questions: "Where is God?" and "Who is God?," let us consider for a while the name through which Augustine designates the mystery of divine selfhood: *Idipsum.*

"*Tu autem idem ipse es*": How can this statement be understood?[38] In his recent book, *Le Dieu d'Augustin*, Goulven Madec reminds us that the fascination which the mystery of divine Selfhood aroused in Augustine played an important role in his conversion,[39] especially during the time of Cassiciacum and Ostia. The *Soliloquia*, as well as Book IX of the *Confessions*, allows us to trace his discovery back to his philosophical and Christian retreat during autumn and winter of the year 386. Meditating *"cum ipso me solo coram Te"*[40] alongside the topics of wisdom and happiness, and reading at the same time the Psalms, he was struck by a formula in verse 9 of Psalm 4, which reads thus in the version of the *Vetus latina*: *"in pace in idipsum obdormiam . . . quoniam tu domine, singulariter in spe constituisti me."* Still struggling with the temptations of vanity, Augustine suddenly discovered a Selfhood which is synonymous with peace and plenitude. Throughout his further work, it was to become his masterword for God's own life. Its importance is not only documented by its frequency (the *Corpus Augustinianum Glissense* counts 1,685 occurrences of *"idipsum,"* and 107 occurrences of *"id ipsum"*), but also by its role in Augustine's exegesis of the revelation of the Name of God in Exodus 3:14. Together with its Johannine resonances, this exesis invites us to join, instead of severing, the *nomen substantiae: "Sum qui sum"* and the *nomen misericordiae: "*the God of your fathers, the God of Abraham, Isaac and Jacob."[41]

The difficulties of translating the term *Idipsum* indicate already the problem of its interpretation. Should it be translated as "Being itself" (*"l'Etre même"*), following the suggestion of Solignac; as "Selfbeing" (*Selbstsein*) as

Dieter Hattrup does; as "The Identical," as proposed by Madec; or as the "Selfsame," as in the current English translations?[42] Although I like the latter expression very much, I will add my own less qualified voice to the concert of these eminent Augustinian specialists in venturing to propose a translation inspired by Ricoeur's hermeneutics of selfhood: "The Self Himself." If one focuses only on the coherence of divine attributes, one can certainly say, as does W. C. Gundersdoff von Jess, that in Augustine's thinking the terms *vere esse, incommutabilitas, aeternitas, manentia, idipsum et simplicitas* have the same truth-value. But does this way of considering the matter really do justice to the originality of Augustine's way of speaking? Only an ear which listens to Augustine's way of uttering (*dire*), instead of focusing exclusively on his utterances (*dit*), can perceive that *Idipsum* is what Hattrup calls Augustine's "favourite philosophical term" (*philosophisches Lieblingswort*)[43] and Solignac his "typical expression for the mystery of Divine Being."[44]

To illustrate this I quote the exclamation, directly "inspired" by the language of the Psalms, which announces the discovery of the *Idipsum* in Book IX of the *Confessions:* "O in peace! O in the selfsame! . . . You supremely are that selfsame, for You are not changed and in You is that rest in which all cares are forgotten, since there is no other besides You and we have not to seek other things which are not what You are: but You, Lord, alone have made me dwell in hope."[45] In Book XII, Augustine celebrates the Creator of heaven and earth in an even more lyrical and almost liturgical language, which it is better to quote first in Latin: "*idipsum et idipsum et idipsum, 'sanctus, sanctus, dominus deus' omnipotens.*"[46] "You who do not change as things and circumstances change, but are the Self-same, and the Self-same and the Self-same, Holy, Holy, Holy Lord God Almighty": Could one imagine the *causa sui* becoming the object of the same vibrant language?

I am well aware that there are good reasons to ask whether the term *idipsum* has a neo-Platonic rather than a Christian origin.[47] But I think it important to pay close attention to the circumstances in which this term imposed itself on Augustine's mind, or, in other words, to reflect upon the "linguistic event," the *Sprachereignis,* which it constitutes. If we look at the textual data of the fourth chapter of Book IX, we soon discover to what extent Augustine's discovery of the Selfsame is intimately linked with the birth of a new self.

At the risk of being accused of practicing an abusive "psychologism," I will point out several aspects of this textual dynamic that culminate in the statement that God is the Selfsame.

Right from the start the question resounds: "Who am I and what kind of man am I?" (*quis ego et qualis ego?*)[48] In the context of Book IX, the term *qualis* can even be punningly understood in the sense of the German word *Qual:* It is a tormented man, torn apart by contradictory desires, who presents himself to his reader. His desire is not to violently get rid of his teaching of Rhetoric: "And I thought it would be good in Your sight if I did not dramatically snatch my tongue's service from the speech-market, but quietly withdrew."[49] But a somatic symptom, ambiguous as are most symptoms, indicates that withdrawing from his teaching and renouncing the prestige attached to this function was more painful than he had thought it would be. Alluding to his difficulties in breathing and the aphasia which they induced, Augustine notes with astonishing psychological acuteness that his illness brought him what a Freudian would call some "subsidiary benefits": "Furthermore that very summer, under the too heavy labor of teaching, my lungs had begun to give way and I breathed with difficulty; the pain in my breast showed that they had been affected and they no longer let me talk with any strength for a too long time. At first, this disturbed me, because it made it practically a matter of necessity that I should lay down the burden of teaching, or at least give it up for a time if I was to be cured and grow well again."[50] Earlier in the text, he gives one of the "reasons" which led to his feeling of oppression: The literary works he wrote at that time show that "this breathing-space still smacked of the school of pride."[51]

In this particular situation Augustine begins to "read" the Psalms of David. They not only help him to recover his voice, but they literally allow him to "give his voice to God": "What cries did I utter to You (*quas tibi voces dabam*) in those Psalms and how was I inflamed towards You by them, and on fire to set them sounding through all the world, if I could, against the pride of man!"[52] These expressions suggest not only that Augustine speaks with a loud voice ("*il donne de la voix*," as one would say in French), but that he gives his voice to God, which makes him an *adonné*, in Marion's sense.

This description of reading the Psalms applies especially to the reading of Psalm 4, which Augustine recounts in great detail, insisting upon its "performative" and transforming effects. What he wants to tell is "what that Psalm did in me" (*quid de me fecerit ille psalmus*: literally, "what this Psalm made of me").[53] Of course he read this Psalm again and again. But if "reading" means that someone takes the initiative of appropriating the meaning contained in a text, we should rather say that it was Psalm 4 which "read" and "understood" Augustine better than he understood himself!

The first effect of what this Psalm "made" of him is that it "put him at large" (*dilatasti mihi*). This "enlargement" has nothing to do with what Romain Rolland would call an "oceanic feeling." It is rather a feeling of being set free, directly linked with this new "way of speaking with myself and to myself before Thee."[54] It is this new speech-situation, and not only his new idea of God, which liberates him from the Manichees. Still further in the text, we come across a description of Augustine's new situation which could well mark its irreducible difference from our postmodern practices of reading: "I cried out as I read this aloud and realized it within."[55] This is exactly the situation in which the "reading and burning" discovery of the Selfsame, induced by verse 9 of the same Psalm, takes place.

I close my scrutiny of the narrative sequence in the fourth chapter of Book IX with a note of humor. Augustine's story ends with a little miracle: the healing of a very severe toothache "which had grown so agonizing that I could not speak."[56]

Our analysis of the textual dynamics of Book IX also helps us understand how Augustine raises the problem of self-knowledge at the beginning of Book X. It seems that this problem can be raised properly only after the *Idipsum* has come to his mind.

One famous formula shows why the question "Where?" is so important for Augustine and how he tries to answer it: "In what place then did I find You to learn of You? For You were not in my memory, before I learned of You. When did I find You to learn of You, save in Yourself, above myself (*in Te supra me*)?"[57] The question of where God can be found and met cannot be separated from the question of what I am in the innermost of myself (*quid ipse intus sim*), a question Augustine thematizes right from the start of Book X.[58] In his commentary on this book, Johann Kreuzer insists that "the self which knows that it is known by God is not the presupposition, but the result of the stories which it remembers."[59] Memory, which thus far had functioned in the mode of a narrative voice, giving profile to what one could call the "narrative identity" of the confessor, becomes now the principle of self-knowledge and knowledge of God, which are absolutely inseparable. The literary composition of Book X, as well as its contents, show that we have to do with a "metaphysics of conversion" combining two movements: the movement of ascension, which is accomplished by a loving and desiring memory (*memoria amans*), and the descending movement of "care" (*cura*), leading back to the experience of finitude, especially through the three fundamental forms of temptation. It is significant that in his own attempt at a phenomenological interpretation of Book X, Heidegger focused much more on the second than on the first movement.

In Augustine's use, the term *Idipsum* designates the biblical name of God the Father, in contrast to the vanity of the material God of the Manichees, who is simply much bigger than an elephant. But it designates also the divine "*esse a se*," which brings peace and plenitude and thus puts an end to all vanity. Taken in this sense, the "word self-being (*idipsum*) is the fundamental word by which Augustine designates the very life of God. God has a Self which human beings desire, but do not possess."[60]

How can we inscribe Augustine's *Idipsum* in a reflection upon the onto-theological constitution of metaphysics? The Selfsame gives an answer to the question "Who is God?," which Heidegger avoids almost systematically. Besides a few rather vague allusions to divine aseity, he has never reflected upon this terminological invention. To help explain this omission, we can take seriously an expression in the *Letter on Humanism*: In Heidegger's understanding, "*Idipsum*" is the designation of Being itself, insofar as it is understood as *Ereignis*.[61]

This chapter cannot possibly reconstruct in greater detail the *Wirkungsgeschichte* of Augustine's formula. This would, for instance, imply an investigation of the *Ipsum esse subsistens* in Thomas Aquinas and its complex relationship to the Augustinian heritage. The question we have to deal with is much more radical: It is the question whether in our postmodern condition, this topic is still of some interest, or whether we must conclude that the history of its reception is definitely closed.

Before addressing such a frightful question, it helps to highlight the notion of the *Idipsum* by two complementary considerations. The first leads us back to the biblical background of the notion; the second relates to a particular moment in the history of its reception.

4. The Biblical Background of the Notion of Divine Selfhood

Who can say anokhi, *besides God?*

—A Hassidic anecdote

Would the *Idipsum* have come to Augustine's mind if his retreat in Cassiciacum had not been so strongly influenced by his enthusiastic reading of the Psalms—which was much more than a quotation in the postmodern sense of the word? Obviously not! Augustine himself tells us that the Psalms accompanied him everywhere, even to the toilet. Does the hermeneutical fact that his thinking is "entirely regulated by formulas taken from Scripture,"[62] to the point that the Scripture becomes the principle of a new self-understanding,[63] mean that we modern or postmodern thinkers, who have learned not to mingle any longer the voices of philosophy and of theology, which are as different as water and fire, must send the Selfsame back to its biblical background and reject it as a philosophical concept? But maybe the postmodern condition allows a new relationship to the non-philosophical sources of philosophy, different from that which characterized the modern age. This does not necessarily mean that philosophy must be "retheologized," which some philosophers are suspected of doing. Precisely because Augustine's thinking does not yet entail the scholarly distinctions between philosophy and theology, he can become an interesting interlocutor for us.

The way in which he speaks of the Selfsame shows the possibility of a "poetics of reading" the biblical texts, which has nothing in common with a "poetic" or purely emotional reading. Therefore it is interesting to look also at the biblical intersection between the questions "Who?" and "Where?" related to God. This is what Paul Ricoeur does in his book *Penser la Bible*,[64] which he wrote in common with André LaCocque, a specialist of the Hebrew Bible. The six reading exercises which compose this book contain many interesting elements that help us deepen our understanding of Divine Selfhood.

The main interest of an exegetical approach is that it allows us to enlarge the textual base beyond the classical passages of Psalm 9 and the famous verse Exodus 3:14. Recent exegetical research, including the works of Claus Westermann and Walter Zimmerli, has shown that the prophet Ezekiel created a new type of discourse, which Zimmerli calls "proof of identity." It is reflected in the typical formula: "You will know that I am YHWH," of which we find about seventy-two occurrences in Ezekiel alone. One of the most important of them appears at the end of the vision of the dry bones: "Then you shall live and you shall know that I, YHWH, have spoken and I have done it, says the Lord." (Ezekiel 37:14). Zimmerli emphasizes that this formulation "of the proof of identity never appeals to speculation or to human (intellectual) effort, but expresses always a human acknowledgment after a divine action."[65] It is never the first, but always the last, word of a story.

A literary analysis of the typical structure of prophetic oracles confirms the same fact. They start with the formula of the messenger, unfold through the announcement of judgment or salvation, and end by formulating the acknowledgment of God's action.

The opening formula already suggests a specific relation between the divine "I" and the "I" of the human envoy. "Insofar as the prophetic saying is the saying of Another, its utterance, similar to that of prayer, still bears the mark of a personal 'event'; something 'arrives' to somebody; it arrives that he is struck by the word of Another."[66] On the side of the prophet, the consequence of this event is that he is ever more strongly implicated in the message he delivers.

As to the prophetic announcement, it is based upon the intimate relation between the prophetic *Erweiswort* and the divine *Selbsterweis* (C. Westermann). The apodictic future of prophetic oracles must not be confounded with prediction or prevision. "The prophet is a messenger who is certain to have been sent by God to say what God will certainly do."[67] Ricoeur uses the expression "sentry of imminence" to characterize Ezekiel's existential attitude. It sees the prophet's particular relationship to history as traumatizing, contrary to the traditional reassuring history of mythic discourse. This view covers all the literary forms of biblical prophetism, even the visions which are also "exercises of vigilance entrusted to the sentry of imminence."[68] This is what highlights the contrast between eschatological and apocalyptical discourse: The sentry of imminence has to deal with intrahistorical events. This implies quite another attitude than that of the apocalyptic "decoding of enigmas."[69] The task of the sentry is not to tell the fulfillment of his prophecy; the prophet can only anticipate a date.

The formula of acknowledgment is of special interest, insofar as it establishes a strong relation between events which are interpreted as signs of a divine intervention and the knowledge of God himself. Taking the whole of humanity as witness, and even the whole universe, the formula has a dialectic relation with the formula of the envoy, which highlights the singularity of the envoy. On both sides we have a hiatus between signifying and showing, which leaves open the "possibility of multiple and even conflicting interpretations."[70]

The primordial object of acknowledgment is nothing else than Divine Selfhood itself: "I am YHWH." What must be acknowledged "is not a *What*, but a *Who*, the *Who* of the one who says of himself: 'I am.' "[71] The messenger neither gives his mandate to himself, nor does he become an agent of the knowledge of God, which would allow him to say: "I know better who God is than anybody else." "God, the subject of his own doings, remains the self-attesting subject in the heart of knowledge."[72] His self-presentation appeals to the risk of interpretation implied in the act of recognition: "The purity and nakedness of the 'I am YHWH' seals, in a certain manner, the irreducible indeterminacy of human judgment, which has to 'recognize' God through 'proofs which are signs' exhibited in history."[73]

This analysis contains many important issues for our problem. Even from a strictly exegetical point of view, we are invited to compare the prophetic formula for divine self-presentation with the revelation of the tetragramma in Exodus 3:14. LaCocque reminds us that despite the frequent occurrences of the tetragramma in the Hebrew Bible, it is as a "strange philological formation,"[74] whose religious roots raise difficult problems. The episode of the burning bush can only be understood if it is put in the context of the mission of Moses and, more generally, related to the Egyptian quest for a "secret name of power" characteristic of magical religion. Moses's question about God's identity is no idle question, as his confrontation with the Egyptian magicians shows. It "must not be understood as if it merely asked God to reveal his Name. It intends to ask the meaning of this name. What is the secret hidden within the Name of God?"[75]

If Moses's question intends to get at a "Name of Power," must we conclude, as a certain number of commentators do, that the *'ehyeh 'asher 'ehyeh* has no other meaning than God's refusal to play such an ambiguous game? LaCocque's interpretation is more subtle, although his warnings against any kind of "ontological abstraction regarding Being"[76] cannot be overheard. In his eyes, the Septuagint translation is already "an exaggerated concession to Hellenistic ontology."[77] More generally, philosophers are tempted to take the tetragramma as an "invitation to speculate about the essence of God,"[78] a tendency which culminates in the opinion that the *causa sui* is the quintessence of the metaphysical knowledge of God.

Does this mean that all questioning regarding Divine Selfhood must be rejected from a biblical standpoint? Absolutely not! LaCocque suggests that the revelation of God's own Name has a symbolic equivalent in the burning bush, which signifies an indefectible active and dynamic Presence. Only if we relate the tetragramma to divine activity does it show its real meaning: "I am really here." The exclusivity of the Divine Name appears also in the fact that it singularizes the human beings for whom it is destined: "He who faces God receives a proper name in relation with a God who himself is not anonymous."[79] Thus the revelation of the Name establishes an intimate relationship between Divine selfhood and the human self: "The greatest paradox is that He who alone has the right to say 'I' and who is the only *'ehyeh*, has a Name which includes the second person, a thou."[80] To illustrate this interpretation, LaCocque quotes a Hassidic anecdote of the Rabbi who refuses to open his door to a disciple who knocks at the door saying: "It's me!," to which the master replies: "Who can say *anokhi* besides God?" Alluding to the title of one of Derrida's books, we could call this the biblical version of "*la passion du Nom.*"

Perhaps we understand better now the interest of comparing the revelation of the Name in Exodus with the prophetic formula for divine self-presentation. We can now give a positive meaning to the revelation of the Name and nevertheless preserve God's incognito, which is inseparable from the horizon of Promise. The interdiction of any kind of figurative representation of God, that is to say, the prohibition of idolatry, is only half the truth. Even if there is no doubt that "the revelation of the Name is given by an non-iconic God," this God is no *agnôstos théos*. Although he remains a "hidden God," or, rather, exactly for this reason, he "wants to become accessible and known."[81] This interpretation also sheds new light on the decalogue, which LaCocque reads as a "legal commentary on the divine Name."[82]

When he spoke of a "*métaphysique de l'Exode,*" E. Gilson echoed a long tradition of ontological readings of Exodus 3:14. Meanwhile this meeting-place of philosophy and theology more and more resembles a battlefield. It is almost impossible to count the articles which deploy a battery of exegetical arguments which seem to disqualify forever any attempt at an ontological reading of the "revelation of revelations" on Mount Horeb. Could the "intellectual event"[83] of the Septuagint translation and the numerous philosophical and theological speculations which it induced be simply the fruit of a philological mistake?

Like Ricoeur, I believe it is impossible to ignore or wipe out readings which have shaped to some extent "the intellectual and spiritual identity of the Christian West."[84] We had better ask under which conditions the so-called ontological readings of Exodus 3:14 can become "if not legitimate, at least plausible" despite the "almost professional mistrust"[85] of specialists in biblical exegesis.

Therefore (distinguishing carefully the problems of translation and interpretation!) we need to consider the singularity of this text within the biblical corpus itself in order to become conscious of all its enigmas. Only thus can we discover the legitimate margin of interpretation between what Ricoeur calls a "*minimizing*" reading (as that of LaCocque) and an "*amplifying*" reading (that which he himself practices). We could also say that the first reading mainly pays attention to the setting of the jewel, whereas the second pays attention to the jewel of verse 14 itself. The second reading stresses that the formula exceeds its function as well as its context. This "exceptional hermeneutical situation"[86] allows several interpretations of the verb, beginning with that which the Septuagint translation has made possible. In Ricoeur's eyes, this translation has "an intellectual and spiritual fecundity whose effects are not yet exhausted."[87]

One of the most important effects of the transplantation of the Greek verb *einai* on the Hebrew verse is that the Hebrew begins to resonate with the plurivocality of the Greek. Rather than seeing this encounter as a lethal contamination, the Greek translation sheds new light on the threefold *'ehyeh* itself. Instead of dissolving the enigma of the revelation of the Name (which is the biblical equivalent of Augustine's Selfsame), the "ontological" translation helps highlight it. This is Ricoeur's most innovative suggestion: "Why not suppose that Exodus 3:14 invites us, right from the start, to add a totally new region of meaning to the rich polysemy of the verb 'being,' which the Greeks and their Islamic, Jewish and Christian heirs have explored elsewhere?"[88]

The true question has to do with this new region of meaning. In this respect an investigation of the "strange pair"[89] which Augustine and the Pseudo-Dionysius constitute throughout the Middle Ages is most instructive. Regarding Augustine, Ricoeur stresses that in his thinking the *"qui est* does not give access to any *quid est."*[90] It is the poverty of ontological language, and not its richness, which makes it adequate to God, that is to say to the both interior and superior transcendence, which Augustine calls *ipsum esse* or *idipsum esse*.

Medieval interpretations of Exodus 3:14 show clearly that the alternative of apophatic and ontological readings is overwhelmed by speculations about the meaning of the *qui* in the *qui est*. This magnetic attraction, linking the question *quid est?* to the question *qui est?* explains why at the very moment when the Scholastic *disputatio* broke free from the *lectio divina*, the christianization of hellenistic thinking remained stronger than the hellenization of Christianity. In Ricoeur's opinion, nothing allows us to conclude that the "convergence without fusion" between the biblical verse and ontological language, inherited from Greek philosophy, was an "intellectual aberration."[91]

5. "Istikeit": Philosophy of Selfhood and "Onto-theo-logical Solipsism"

> *Du solt alzemal entzinken diner dinisheit und solt zer fliesen in sine sinesheit und sol din din und sin sin ein min werden als genzlich, das du mit ime verstandet ewiklich sin ungewordene istikeit und sin ungenanten nitheit.*[92]

—Meister Eckhart, "Sermon 83," 19–21[93]

Nothing shows better that the so-called ontological translations of the divine Name are not an intellectual scandal than the echoes of the rabbinic question "Who can say *anokhi* besides God?" in a philosophical tradition which meditated intensively upon the Augustinian *Idipsum*, inscribing it at the same time in a new climate of thinking. Alain de Libera[94] has shown that one of the most interesting stages in the history of the reception of Augustine's Selfsame is to be found in the Cologne school founded by Albertus Magnus. Ulrich of Strassburg and Eckhart are the main representatives of the original synthesis of the Augustinian heritage and the Dionysian apophatism already mentioned above. De Libera's general characterization of their attempt attracts our attention to a most important point: "In the Cologne school Augustine's metaphysics of Exodus did not hide his metaphysics of conversion: The evolution of this school, from Ulrich to Eckhart, is marked by a permanent deepening shift of the theology of God as Being towards a theology of *Being*-God, of the desire of being towards the desire of being-Himself, of a philosophy of the *esse* towards a philosophy of the *ipsum esse*."[95]

De Libera designates this philosophy by the technical term: "onto-theological solipsism."[96] His analysis of the "well argued and systematic attempts at a conciliation between Augustinian and Dionysian Neo-platonism,"[97] which constitutes in his eyes the hallmark of the Cologne school, contains several topics which relate directly to our subject.

1. A first point regards the way in which this school presents the radical difference between Divine "Aseity" and the "Ab-aliety" of the creature. Instead of leading us back to the notion of *causa sui*, we are invited to reject it, as in a statement from the fourth chapter in the *Summa de Bono* of Ulrich of Strassburg: "He is not the cause of Himself, but he subsists in such a way that nothing ever affected him in the past and nothing will ever affect him in the future and the present will never fail him in one way or another." De Libera comments on this statement in the following way: "The Being-God subsists in Himself. There is nothing in him but his Being. In Him there is nothing but Himself. Because God is Himself, he is without cause. Being his Self, he is not his own cause."[98]

2. The German and the Latin works of Meister Eckhart constitute the summit of this "onto-theological solipsism," which has its primal source in the Augustinian Selfsame, an expression which Eckhart translates into German as *isticheit* or *istikeit*. It is the divine Selfhood he has in mind when he declares in one of his sermons that " 'Ego,' the word 'I,' is proper to none, but to God in his oneness."[99] Paradoxically, this exclusiveness does not imply that God is separated from all things. On the contrary: For this very reason he is more intimate to all things than they are to themselves.[100] The Augustinian topic of the *"intimior intimo meo"* becomes in Eckhart a task which is both spiritual and ontological: "God must really become I, and I must really become God, so fully one that this 'he' and this 'I' become and are one 'is' and eternally work one work in that isness."[101]

De Libera shows also that the five stages of Eckhart's exegesis of Exodus 3:14 can be read as five ways of approaching the mystery of divine Selfhood. Right from the start, the grammatical explanation of the divine Name develops a complex argument of convenience, in showing that the pronoun *Ego*, the indefinite *qui*, and the substantive *sum* suit God alone. As to the meaning of the *sum*, it designates nothing else than the pure and naked Being of the divine subject himself. "Pure Being," "naked Being," and "Being Himself" are synonymous expressions.

One of the most remarkable aspects of this "onto-theological solipsism" is the idea that in the divine *sum*, "Being" and "Life" melt entirely in a constant "boiling" (*bullitio*) and giving birth to the essence of Deity. This "primordial and impersonal life, which expands and liquefies itself in the outflowing of the Persons," is, as de Libera says, "the model of all life, and the preamble of every being."[102] Here we can pay attention to the "complex interplay" of an exegesis which on the one hand "posits the I (*Ego: sum*) as the Self of the Being which is not yet manifested," and, on the other, "hides it in its own manifestation (*sum qui sum*), in the Life of the self which is essentially not his own, but which is properly lived."[103]

The fourth exegesis shows that Eckhart's meditation upon divine Aseity is dominated by the question: "Who?," a question which Heidegger restricted to the sole *Dasein*. Eckhart's answer to this question is no less original: God is the "*Qui est.*" On this level, the *quid* and the *quis* presuppose each other. In consequence, ontology and spirituality become inseparable: "Who is God? God is *qui est*. What is God? God is this *What*. Ontology and spirituality link the *Who* and the *What*, thus realizing the inseparable unity of metaphysics and mystic of Exodus."[104]

The fifth and last stage of Eckhart's exegesis takes up Maimonides' analysis of divine self-sufficiency. Eckhart insists that God is his own being, and vice versa. This last approach to the mystery of the Selfsame fully justifies the notion of onto-theological solipsism: "Therefore Being means being God in God, it means being the very *Ipse* of Being."[105]

Conclusion

I am aware that in claiming that the enigma of selfhood can no longer be resolved by invoking self-determination, I am not a very radical postmodernist. Does this mean that in stepping back to Augustine's Selfsame and its biblical presuppositions and moving forward to Eckhart's interpretation of the same topic, I have eluded the most difficult question: what kind of relationship the postmodern subject can have, or can no longer have, with God? Was my *Schritt zurück* to Augustine a mere avoidance of our postmodern condition? For those who confuse postmodernity and post-Christianity—they are ever more numerous today—things are very clear: We must apply Hegel's analysis of the Greek religion of art to Christian religion. "*Der Geist ist Künstler*": we can only establish a purely esthetic relationship with a religion whose truth-claims are no longer believable.

Does this mean that Augustine's question—"What happened in your heart when you heard the word 'God'? What happened in my heart when I said God'?"[106]—has become purely rhetorical? Is it a question which can only be quoted (as we can quote any other text in our culture of generalized quotation which evokes irresistibly Hegel's description of the world of the alienated spirit[107]), but which no longer evokes any echo within ourselves?

1. An elegant way of eluding the question would use an argument from

authority (forgetting for a while that, apparently, there are no authorities in the postmodern age): Wittgenstein greeted the *Confessions* "as the most serious book ever written,"[108] Derrida met Augustine in writing his autobiographical text "Circonfession," Lyotard died before finishing his text *La Confession d'Augustin*. Is the attraction which the author of the *Confessions* has exercised on a certain number of contemporary thinkers just a curious coincidence?

From my phenomenological and hermeneutical perspective, I add to this list Heidegger's conclusion to his 1921 lecture on "Augustine and Neoplatonism." I quote a passage entitled significantly "The Being of the self": " 'Vita' (Life) is not a mere word, a formal concept, but a structural connexion which Augustine himself had in mind, although he lacked the required conceptual precision. This precision cannot either be gained today, because Descartes gave our reflection on the self as a fundamental phenomenon a downward direction, from which modern philosophy has not recovered."[109]

"Augustine's ideas," adds Heidegger, "were diluted by Descartes. The self-certainty and the way the self possesses himself in Augustine's sense are something totally different from the Cartesian evidence of the 'cogito.' "[110] Heidegger's claim that one of the best ways of getting rid of the presuppositions of the modern philosophy of subjectivity is to rediscover Augustine's intuitions should be taken as seriously as other interpretations of this break.

As for what we gain from this hermeneutical and phenomenological *Schritt zurück* to Augustine, Heidegger makes the following conclusive remarks:

> Self-certainty must be interpreted starting with factical being, and it is possible only through faith.
>
> From a methodological point of view, we must not take this evidence as being isolated, which would mean a downward perspective.
>
> The evidence of the *cogito* is there, but it must be grounded in the factical. At the end, all science depends also on the factical existence.[111]

2. Leaving aside these arguments from authority, let me recall my main thesis: In the postmodern condition, the question "Who?" (especially if it is related to Derrida's questions: Who forgives whom? Who forgives what?) loses neither its pertinence nor its urgency. Contrary to Heidegger, and together with Augustine, I think we are not obliged to restrict the "Who?" to the human self, understood as *Dasein*. In this sense, I agree with Didier Franck's suggestion that Heidegger's question "How does the god come into philosophy?" ought to be completed by the question "How does God come into philosophy?" This question becomes especially important if we unfold it in the horizon of the twofold question "Who/Where is God?"

3. Regarding Nietzsche's question "Would you be able to think a God?" my meditation upon the *Idipsum* and its echoes in the Rhine mystics leads me to complete his question in the following way: "Would you be able to think a *living* God?" In this respect, we can ask whether Eckhart's speculations upon

the inner *bullitio* of divine Life and the self-sufficiency of Divine essence could not meet the preoccupations of contemporary phenomenologists; for instance, the motif of self-sufficient life (*Selbstgenügsamkeit*) in Heidegger's early teachings or Michel Henry's characterization of life as "self-affection." In Henry, Eckhartian intuitions, which were already present in his early book *L'essence de la manifestation,* have been unfolded in his recent phenomenological interpretation of Christianity. The central Christological thesis of his book *C'est moi la Vérité* shows that Henry endeavors to think a Selfhood which is the source of Life itself.[112]

4. Even if it is impossible to simply repeat the strange coupling of Augustine and Pseudo-Dionysius which found its strongest expression in Eckhart, we have good reasons to ponder again the mystery of the Selfsame as such, without assimilating it at once to the *ipsum esse* or the *ipsum esse subsistens.* If my suggestion that *Idipsum* could be translated by the "Self Himself" is accurate, we can apply to the Divine Self Ricoeur's distinction between two concepts of human identity: It can be approached either under the sign of "sameness" (*mêmeté*) or under the sign of "selfhood" (*ipséité*).

Maybe this distinction helps us liberate the concept of God from "ontotheology" as it is usually understood. If, following Derrida, we refuse to limit forgiveness to the human sphere, we will have to ask what understanding of the Selfsame fits a radical notion of forgiveness—a question which makes no sense if God is merely defined as *causa sui.*

Of course, one could object to the current definition of God as being "the Other par excellence," the "other as other," or the "absolutely other." My answer to this objection consists in saying that Augustine's Selfsame does not imply the negation of God's Otherness; on the contrary, it emphasizes its meaning.

5. Unlike the United States of America, contemporary philosophy is no longer "God's own country." The landscape of contemporary thinking is ever more that of a *regio dissimilitudinis.* It is here where the postmodern subject confronts more than once the experience of his lack of identity. Does this mean that the question "Who am I?" becomes totally meaningless? In my opinion, the best answer is that given by Ricoeur, speaking of the "nights of personal identity" which are documented in many stories of conversion (among which we find Augustine's account of his own conversion): "In these moments of extreme bareness, the absence of an answer to the question *Who am I?* leads not to the vacuity, but to the nakedness of the question itself."[113]

6. Could the same statement not be applied, *mutatis mutandis,* to the twofold question "Where/Who is God?," through which I attempted to define our postmodern condition? Another formula of Ricoeur's, which he uses as a hermeneutical key in interpreting Exodus 3:14, suggests constructing a bridge between human, fundamentally problematic selfhood and the abysmal selfhood of God: "Thus an extreme gap opens between the unknown, unnameable God and humans who are committed to the abyss of the question: Who

am I? Any relationship between these two extremes can only be an interval which is precisely spanned by other modes of naming, which, in a certain manner, narrow the gap between God and human beings. But here, proximity can only be a distance which has been crossed, without forgetting the far distance, as in the strong German expression *Ent-fernung*, which suggests etymologically something like a de-distancing."[114]

Perhaps our present task is to better understand this movement of "de-distancing." If we are thus confronted "not with the vacuity, but with the nakedness of the question itself," we ought to ponder again the words of an old Meister: "It is a stumbling-block to many a learned cleric! It is a strange and desert-place, and is rather nameless than possessed of a name, and is more unknown than it is known. If you could naught yourself for an instant, indeed I say less than an instant, you would possess all that this is in itself. But as long as you mind yourself or for any other thing at all, you do know better no more of God than my mouth knows of colour or my eye of taste: so little do you know or discern what God is."[115]

NOTES

1. Jean-François Lyotard, *La Confession d'Augustin* (Paris: Ed. Galilée, 1998).

2. Martin Heidegger, *Gesamtausgabe*, vol. 66, *Besinnung* (Frankfurt: Klostermann, 1997). Works in Heidegger's *Gesamtausgabe* will hereafter be cited as "Ga" followed by the volume number.

3. Paul Ricoeur, *Soi-même comme un autre* (Paris: Ed. du Seuil, 1990), p. 17 n. 3.

4. Martin Heidegger, *Fundamental Problems of Phenomenology*, Ga 24, 172–251.

5. Ibid., 170.

6. Ibid., 173.

7. Rémi Brague, *Aristote et la question du monde. Essai sur le contexte anthropologique et cosmologique de l'ontologie* (Paris: Presses universitaires de France, 1988). The following short sentence summarizes Brague's central thesis: "Greek thinking tells us everything about the world, but the fact that *we are in it*" (p. 46).

8. Ga 24, 174.

9. Ibid., 175.

10. Ibid., 194.

11. Martin Heidegger, *Besinnung*, Ga 66 (Frankfurt: Klostermann, 1998), p. 5.

12. Ibid., 145.

13. Ibid., 146.

14. Ibid., 143.

15. Ibid., 146.

16. Ibid., 153.

17. Ibid., 148.

18. Ibid., 155.

19. Ibid., 153.

20. Ibid., 141.

21. Ibid., 142.

22. Ibid., 147.

23. Claude Romano, *L'événement et le monde* (Paris: Presses universitaires de France, 1998), pp. 79–192; and Romano, *L'événement et le temps* (Paris: Presses universitaires de France, 1999), pp. 129–143, 248–308.

24. Jean-Luc Marion, *Etant donné. Essai d'une phénoménologie de la donation* (Paris: Presses universitaires de France, 1997), pp. 343–438. For a more thorough confrontation with Marion's position, see my article *"Index sui et non dati. Les paradoxes de la phénoménologie de la donation,"* *Transversalités: Revue de l'Institut Catholique de Paris* no. 70 (avril–juin 1999): 27–54.

25. Ricoeur, *Soi-même comme un autre*, p. 367.

26. Eberhard Jüngel, *Gott als Geheimnis der Welt. Zur Begründung der Theologie des Gekreuzigten im Streit zwischen Theismus und Atheismus* (Tübingen: Mohr-Siebeck, 1978), p. 67.

27. Ibid., pp. 132–137.

28. "De Deo loquimur, quid mirum, si non comprehendis? Si enim comprehendis, non est Deus. Si pia confessio ignorantiae magis quam temeraria professio scientiae. Attingere aliquantum mente Deum magna beatitudo est; comprehendere autem, omnino impossibile." Saint Augustine, *Sermo* 117, 3, 5, MPL 38, 663, quoted by Jüngel, *Gott als Geheimnis der Welt*, p. 7.

29. J. G. Fichte, ed., *Fichtes Werke*, vol. 5, *Gerichtliche Verantwortungsschriften* (Berlin: Veit, 1845), p. 265s, quoted in Jüngel, *Gott als Geheimnis der Welt*, p. 180.

30. Ibid., p. 267, quoted by Jüngel, *Gott als Geheimnis der Welt*, p. 187.

31. Ludwig Feuerbach, *Das Wesen des Christentums*, ed. W. Schaffenhauer, vol. 1 (Stuttgart: Reclam, 1971; Frankfurt: Klostermann, 1980), p. 85.

32. Ibid., p. 85, quoted by Jüngel, *Gott als Geheimnis der Welt*, p. 193.

33. Jüngel, *Gott als Geheimnis der Welt*, p. 168.

34. Jean-Luc Marion, *Sur le prisme métaphysique de Descartes. Constitution et limites de l'onto-théo-logie dans la pensée cartésienne* (Paris: Presses universitaires de France, 1986), pp. 217–292.

35. Martin Heidegger, *Hegels Phänomenologie des Geistes* (Frankfurt am Main: Klosterman, 1980), Ga 32, 183.

36. Didier Franck, *Nietzsche et l'ombre de Dieu* (Paris: Presses universitaires de France, 1998), pp. 139–158. "If the name 'god' is preceded by the definite article or not, its identity changes and this in turn changes the problem of the theological character of metaphysics" (p. 147). This thesis is most important for a questioning regarding divine Selfhood. In Franck's opinion, it leads to inverting Heidegger's questioning, which no longer relates to an "anonymous god without any religious quality" but to the God of the Judeo-Christian Revelation. In that case, the true problem is that "of understanding how God himself has introduced himself into metaphysics, and why the Revelation, which is not a philosophical event, has nevertheless become an event for philosophy" (p. 148).

37. Augustine of Hippo, *Selected Writings*, trans. Mary T. Clark (New York: Paulist Press, 1984), p. 235.

38. *Sermo* 7, 7 (*Patrologia Latina* [Paris: Migne, 1835], 38, 66–67).

39. Goulven Madec, *Le Dieu d'Augustin* (Paris: Ed. du Cerf, 1998), p. 129.

40. Augustine, *Confessions* IX, 4, 7, trans. F. J. Sheed (Indianapolis: Hackett Publishing Company, 1993), p. 151.

41. Compare Emilie Zum Brunn, "L'exégèse augustinienne de 'Ego sum qui sum'

et la métaphysique de l'Exode," in *Dieu et l'Etre. Exégèses d'Exode 3, 14 et de Coran 20, 11–24* (Paris: Bibliothèque des Etudes augustiniennes, 1978), pp. 141–164.

42. Madec, *Le Dieu d'Augustin*, p. 129.

43. Dieter Hattrup, "Die Mystik von Cassiacicum und Ostia," in *Die Confessiones des Augustinus von Hippo: Einführung und Interpretation zu den 13 Büchern*, ed. Norbert Fischer and Cornelius Mayer (Freiburg: Herder, 1998), p. 408.

44. Aimé Solignac, "Notes Complémentaires: Idipsum," in *Bibliothèque Augustinienne: Oeuvres de saint Augustin*, ed. A. Solignac, Vol. 14: *Les Confessions: VIII-XIII* (Paris: Desclée de Brouwer, 1962), pp. 550–552; see F. Berrouard, "Idipsum," in *Bibliothèque Augustinienne: Oeuvres de saint Augustin*, vol. 71, pp. 845–684.

45. *Confessions* IX, 4, 11 (p. 157).

46. *Confessions* XII, 7 (p. 237).

47. Compare James Swetnam, "A Note on Idipsum in S. Augustine," *The Modern Schoolman*, vol. XXX (1953), pp. 328–331.

48. *Confessions* IX, 1.

49. Ibid., 2, 2 (p. 152).

50. Ibid., 4 (p. 152).

51. Ibid., 4, 7 (p. 151).

52. Ibid., 4, 8 (p. 155).

53. Ibid., 4, 8 (p. 151).

54. Ibid., 4, 8.

55. Ibid., 4, 10 (p. 157).

56. Ibid., 4, 12; *Bibliothèque Augustinienne: Oeuvres de saint Augustin*, vol. 14, p. 93.

57. *Confessions* X, 26, 37 (p. 192). For the meaning of this formulation, see Goulven Madec, " 'In te supra me.' Le sujet dans les *Confessions* de saint Augustin," *Revue de l'Institut Catholique de Paris*, no. 28 (1988): 45–63.

58. On this topic, see Norbert Fischer, "Unsicherheit und Zweideutigkeit der Selbsterkenntnis. Augustins Antwort auf die Frage 'quid ipse intus sim' im 10. Buch der *Confessiones*," in *Geschichte und Vorgeschichte der modernen Subjektivität*, ed. Roland Hagenbucher, Reto Luzius Fetz, and Peter Schulz, vol. I (Berlin: de Gruyter, 1998), pp. 340–367.

59. Johann Kreuzer, "Der Abgrund des Bewußtseins. Erinnerung und Selbsterkenntnis im 10. Buch," in Fischer and Mayer, eds., *Die Confessiones des Augustinus von Hippo*, p. 446.

60. Hattrup, "Die Mystik von Cassiacicum und Ostia," p. 408.

61. "Doch Das Sein—was ist das Sein? Es ist Es selbst. Dies zu erfahren muß das künftige Denken lernen." Martin Heidegger, *Brief über den "Humanismus,"* in *Wegmarken* (Frankfurt: Klostermann, 1967), p. 162.

62. Madec, *Le Dieu d'Augustin*, p. 89.

63. Compare Isabelle Bochet, "Interprétation scripturaire et compréhension de soi. Du *De doctrina christiana* aux *Confessions* de saint Augustin," in *Comprendre et interpréter. Le paradigme herméneutique de la raison*, ed. Jean Greisch (Paris: Ed. Beauchêne, 1993), pp. 21–50.

64. Paul Ricoeur and André LaCocque, *Penser la Bible* (Paris: Ed. du Seuil, 1999).

65. Ibid., p. 198.

66. Ibid., p. 226.

67. Ibid., p. 228.

68. Ibid., p. 229.
69. Ibid., p. 230.
70. Ibid., p. 234.
71. Ibid., p. 235.
72. Ibid.
73. Ibid., p. 236.
74. Ibid., p. 305.
75. Ibid., p. 309.
76. Ibid., p. 311.
77. Ibid., p. 313.
78. Ibid., p. 323.
79. Ibid., p. 315.
80. Ibid.
81. Ibid., p. 319.
82. Ibid., p. 321.
83. Ibid., p. 335.
84. Ibid., p. 336.
85. Ibid., p. 337.
86. Ibid., p. 343.
87. Ibid.
88. Ibid., p. 347.
89. Ibid., p. 352.
90. Ibid., p. 351.
91. Ibid., p. 360.
92. "You should wholly sink away from your youness and dissolve into his His-ness, and your 'you' and his 'His' should become so completely one 'Mine' that with him you understand his unbecome Isness and his nameless Nothingness." Eckhart, *Sermons & Treatises*, vol. II. Trans. and ed. by M. O'C. Walshe (Shaftesbury: Element Books, 1987), p. 333.
93. Meister Eckhart, *Die deutschen Werke*, ed. Josef Quindt (Stuttgart: Kohlham-mer, 1936). Hereafter DW.
94. Alain de Libera, "L'être et le bien: Exode 3, 14 dans la théologie rhénane," in Alain de Libera and Emilie Zum Brunn, *Celui qui est. Interprétations juives et chrétiennes d'Exode 3, 14* (Paris: Ed. du Cerf, 1986), pp. 127–162.
95. Ibid., p. 128.
96. Ibid., p. 127
97. Ibid., p. 138.
98. Ibid., p. 149.
99. Eckhart, "Sermon 28," in *Sermons & Treatises*, in *Die deutschen Werke*, ed. Josef Quint, vol. II (Stuttgart: W. Kohlhammer, 1958), 68, 4–69, 2; in Walshe transla-tion, vol. I, p. 145.
100. Eckhart, "Sermon 77," in *Sermons & Treatises*, in *Die deutschen Werke*, vol. III, 340, 1–3.
101. Eckhart, "Sermon 83," in *Sermons & Treatises*, in *Die deutschen Werke*, vol. III, 447, 10–11; in Walshe translation, vol. II, p. 334.
102. de Libera, "L'être et le bien: Exode 3, 14 dans la théologie rhénane," p. 155.
103. Ibid., p. 155.
104. Ibid., p. 157.

105. Ibid., p. 159.

106. *Homélies sur L'Evangile de Jean* I,8, in *Bibliothèque Augustinienne: Oeuvres de saint Augustin*, vol. 71, pp. 144–145.

107. On the dangers of postmodern estheticism from a religious point of view see also H. J. Adriaanse: *"Devotio postmoderna. Stades sur le chemin de la mémoire religieuse,"* in *Penser la religion. Recherches en philosophie de la religion*, ed. J. Greisch (Paris: Ed. Beauchêne, 1991), pp. 277–295.

108. Rush Rhees, ed., *Ludwig Wittgenstein: Porträts und Gespräche* (Frankfurt: Suhrkamp, 1987), pp. 132–134.

109. Ga 60, 298.

110. Martin Heidegger, *Phänomenologie des religiösen Lebens* (Frankfurt: Klostermann, 1995), Ga 60, 298.

111. Ibid., p. 299.

112. "No living transcendental ego is possible if not within a Selfhood which it presupposes without being able to create it—for the same reason that it does not create its own life—, a Selfhood which is co-generated in the self-affection of absolute Life, the phenomenological efficiency of which is precisely the Archi-Son. Being the Firstborn of Life and the first Living, the Archi-Son holds the essential Selfhood in which the self-affection of life becomes effective." Michel Henry, *C'est moi la Vérité. Une philosophie du christianisme* (Paris: Ed. du Seuil, 1996), p. 140.

113. Ricoeur, *Soi-même comme un autre*, p. 197.

114. Paul Ricoeur and André LaCocque, *Penser la Bible* (Paris: Ed. du Seuil, 1998), p. 165.

115. Eckhart, "Sermon 28," in Walshe translation, p. 325.

ten

The Humiliated Self as the Rhetorical Self

Michael J. Scanlon

Many would concur with Jean Greisch's judgment that the "condition of postmodernity" has made the question of selfhood more urgent than ever. This question is especially urgent for theologians and philosophers with theological concerns. From the time of St. Augustine, Western theology has been characteristically a long and troubled discourse on the third article of the creed, the gift of the Spirit as the source of a Christian anthropology. While the New Testament's portrayal of Jesus of Nazareth, confessed as the Christ, has provided the paradigm for this Christian anthropology, its development has been influenced by the traditional dialogue between theology and philosophy over the centuries. Platonic interest in the spirituality of the soul and Aristotelian concern with the intrinsic relationship between soul and body inform patristic and Scholastic anthropologies respectively. Modern Christian anthropology in turn has been significantly shaped by the "turn to the subject" and, more recently, by the sociopolitical turn in philosophy. This philosophical-theological tradition in theological anthropology raises the question as to what extent the biblical self might resonate with the postmodern critique of the modern self—the rational, autonomous self so humiliated by Nietzsche (the godfather of postmodern discourse) and, more recently, erased by Foucault. The dialogue between Athens and Jerusalem continues.

It seems clear by now that the philosophy of modern subjectivity generally overlooked the necessary mediation of language in the self's auto-constitution in its noetic performances. Paul Ricoeur avers that "Nietzsche brings to light the rhetorical strategies that have been buried, forgotten, and even hypo-critically repressed and denied, in the name of the immediacy of reflection."[1] For theologians, Ricoeur suggests an anthropology of the summoned or mandated self, the biblical self of the prophetic tradition.[2]

Congenial with this biblical self is the postmodern humiliated self. Etymologically, the humiliated self is the down-to-earth self for whom timely *doxa* (belief) is far more effective than timeless *epistēmē* (science or, better, knowledge). The rhetorical self is a good illustration of this down-to-earth self. And theology, as a practical discipline, is a good illustration of rhetoric, language which seeks to persuade people to *praxis* here and now.

Among the contemporary tasks of theology is the development of a public theology, which, even though it is a form of faith seeking understanding for the public theologian, does not restrict its addressees to the faithful. Not depending on a shared faith for its reception, public theology explores forms of rationality different from the modern, theory-centered style of philosophizing that "poses problems and seeks solutions, stated in timeless, universal terms."[3] Self-consciously rhetorical, theology (and particularly public theology) delights in "the revival of practical philosophy in our own day."[4]

The Postmodern Challenge

Public theology can be described as "the effort to discover and communicate the socially significant meanings of Christian symbols and tradition."[5] The effort to communicate these meanings raises the question of the form of rationality to be employed. It has become clear that philosophy, theology, the natural sciences, and the social sciences all find themselves challenged by postmodernism with regard to the issue of rationality. Universal epistemological guarantees have disappeared with the contemporary critique of modern foundationalism. There is no Archimedean, non-historical, non-cultural place to stand for indubitable grounding for the various disciplines.

In response to this critique, different forms of "non-foundationalism" have emerged in philosophy and theology. Some current narrative and post-liberal theologies are non-foundationalist forms of postmodern theology. These narrative theologies are based on a correlation between the temporal character of human life and experience and the stories that make time human.[6] In a rather well-known article, Gary Comstock tried to link the extremes of revisionist and post-liberal American theology by identifying two groups of narrative theologians, the "pure narrativists" and the "impure narrativists."[7] The "pure narrativists" hold that Christian theology is fundamentally descriptive and regulative and that, therefore, it should do its work within the confessing communities formed and determined by the biblical narratives. The "impure narrativists" agree on the centrality of the biblical narratives in communicating the Christian story, but they insist that these narratives make cognitive claims that must be justified by the methods of revisionist theology.

Lindbeck's post-liberal theology is a good example of pure narrativism. Christian doctrines are regulative rules for a confessing community and as such make no factual or ontological claims. The theological tradition receives its justification pragmatically, by showing how it nurtures an authentic way of life. Non-foundationalist narrative theology exhausts its purpose in serving the reflective needs of the household of faith. This type of isolationist theologizing can be described as a language game, embedded in a religious form of life, immune from external criticism. We often hear it described as "Wittgensteinian fideism" despite the fact that it is not Wittgensteinian![8]

An interesting response to the postmodern challenge is that of theologian J. Wentzel van Huyssteen, currently at Princeton University. His work should receive a positive reception from Catholic theologians, since the Catholic tradition has always defended human reason as part of God's gift of creation. He has written extensively on theology and science, but his most recent book, *The Shaping of Rationality: Toward Interdisciplinarity in Theology and Science*,[9] is unique in its special focus on the problem of rationality in theology and the sciences in response to the intellectual challenges raised by postmodern thought. His choice of relating theology to science is not just a matter of personal interest. He seeks emphatically to reject the modern prejudice that celebrates the superior rationality of the natural sciences to the extent that they are taken as the paradigmatic instance of human rationality and objectivity. Religion and theology as reflections on religious experience were relegated by modernity to the subjective sphere of non-rational, interior, private experience. Van Huyssteen seeks not only to retrieve the public nature of theology but to insist on its interdisciplinary nature over against modernity's "clear and distinct" division of academic disciplines into tightly closed departments of specialization.

Van Huyssteen recognizes the appeal of non- or anti-foundationalism for theologians, since, against modernist and universalist notions of rationality, non-foundationalism celebrates the fact that every historical context, and every cultural or social group, has its own distinct rationality. But now we have "many rationalities" thriving in isolation from each other. Against this insulated isolationism, Van Huyssteen holds that the biggest challenge of our new and pervasive postmodern culture for both science and religion is its attack on rationality itself, that which gives us our identity as human beings. In response to this challenge, he explores the many faces of human rationality as they relate to a pre-theoretical reasonableness, a "common-sense rationality" that informs and is present in all our everyday goal-directed actions. He contends that shared rational resources may actually be identified for the sciences, for theology, and for other forms of inquiry. He may remind some of the similar project of Bernard Lonergan long before the postmodern challenge. Van Huyssteen is obviously a postmodern theologian, but for him postmodern is not anti-modern. It is an effort to retrieve the enduring accomplishments of modernity by appropriating a constructive form of postmodern critique, which he calls "postfoundationalism."

Van Huyssteen locates the nature of human rationality in our pursuit of particular goals and values, of which intelligibility may be the most important. Theology shares this quest for intelligibility with all other reasoning strategies. Chastened by the postmodern critique of modern foundationalist rationalism, we do not look for indubitable certitude. We seek to make responsible judgments about those beliefs which are part of our interpreted religious experience. Van Huyssteen reminds us that the high degree of personal involvement and commitment in religious faith present a special challenge to any theory of rationality in theology—together with the radical contextuality of religious experience. He argues for a theory of rationality in theological reflection that encompasses both experiential and theoretical adequacy. Like postmodern science, postmodern theology recognizes the fact that it is an intellectual activity of a specific community with specific practices in a specific local context. While we must engage with our local contexts and traditions, we must stand in a critical relation to tradition by stepping beyond its epistemic boundaries in cross-contextual conversation. All intellectual inquiry rests upon that broad "common-sense rationality" which informs all our everyday goal-directed actions. It is within this broad context that theology should seek to achieve its cognitive goals.

For Van Huyssteen, our human quest for optimal understanding is fundamentally shaped by our value judgments, that is, by the way we see ourselves, one another, and the world we share. These value judgments often function as prejudgments which show our embeddedness in linguistic communities and involvement in social practices. The understanding that flows from our participation in concrete life-worlds is primarily practical, rendering rationality itself a refigured form of praxis. Thus, theology will not display an abstract, theoretical rationality but one that is operative in our words and deeds. Indeed, all of our diverse forms of knowledge are made possible by this background of contextualized prejudgments, habits, and skills that inform our living in a communal world. The task of the shaping of rationality in theology and in the sciences requires our identifying the role that value judgments play in our decisions to commit ourselves—for what we see as the best possible reasons—to specific language games in specific forms of life.

Van Huyssteen's emphasis on value judgments in a post-foundationalist rationality leads him to insist that the human agent is taken to be basic. Rationality first of all characterizes an individual's decisions and beliefs, not propositions or communities. For post-foundationalist theology the recently much-neglected role of personal, responsible judgment in rational decision making must be retrieved as crucially important, but always within the larger context of the community. Van Huyssteen clearly moves beyond any narrow theoretical, cognitivist definition of rationality to include the evaluative and pragmatic dimensions of knowledge with the cognitive. Extremely significant for theology is the current recognition that epistemology must be creatively refigured. Our only cognitive access to reality is through interpreted experience. The question of objectivity (reference) should be approached pragmatically. It is a basic presupposition that we need for any performance of knowing. This pragmatic form of critical realism is a position we accept "not by the push of evidence, but by the pull of purpose."[10] Thus, "our commitment to a mind-independent reality arises not *from* experience but *for* experience."[11] While we are definitely shaped by our context, we are not totally determined by our context.

In this pragmatic or weak form of critical realism in theology we gain a quite limited but real conviction that what we are provisionally trying to conceptualize somehow really exists. We must attempt to find "a promising and suggestive hypothesis that can help us deal with some of the traditionally realist and meaning-giving assumptions of the Christian faith within a pluralist, postmodern context." This post-foundationalist option for a cognitive dimension in religious experience "opens up the possibility of interpreting religiously the ways we believe God comes to us in and through the manifold of our experiences of nature, persons, ideas, emotions, places, things, and events."[12] Our quest for ultimate meaning may find in these mediations an element of mystery, "which, when responded to, may be plausibly said to carry with it the potential for divine disclosure."[13] Van Huyssteen holds that this is the most crucial and telling difference between theology and the sciences: "This kind of mystery is unique to the experiential resources and epistemic focus of theology and very definitely sets it apart from the very focused empirical scope of the natural sciences."[14]

Postmodern Anthropology

While theology has returned to center stage for some postmodernists, the same cannot be said regarding anthropology. Common to all postmodern thinkers is a massive rejection of the modern "turn to the subject." We read of "the death of the self," "the death of the author," "the deconstruction of the self," "the end of the ego"—all summed up in Foucault's famous line "man is an invention of recent date" that will soon "be erased like a face drawn in the sand at the edge of the sea."[15] But just as theology cannot do without God, so theological anthropology cannot do without some version of the self. Responding to the anthropological challenge of postmodernism, theologians and philosophers with theological sensibilities have sought critically to retrieve a notion of the self beyond the monological cognitive subject of modernity. The self that emerges, ever so tentatively and modestly, is some version of the "decentered self," a self, however, with more theological potential than the autonomous self modern thought celebrated.[16] Indeed, the decentered self is the ideal of the Christian tradition whose paradigm is "the man for others." There are many ways of giving further precision to the decentered self, and one that seems nicely to fit the public theologian is the "rhetorical self." This is not the subject of "clear and distinct" ideas embraced by modern thought with its focus on epistemology. The rhetor today must be a decentered self.

The Rhetorical Self

The contemporary rehabilitation of rhetoric is a natural consequence of the "linguistic turn," a common feature of all postmodern thought. Perhaps the turn to language is the salient feature of postmodernity. While rhetoric is a pervasive feature of premodern thought, it was also central to early modern thought—if we accept Toulmin's portrayal of modernity in two distinct phases, the humanistic phase of the Renaissance preceding the rationalist phase, beginning with Descartes in the seventeenth century. Toulman describes the shift from modern humanism to modern rationalism as "four changes of mind— from oral to written, local to general, particular to universal, timely to timeless."[17] While these changes were distinct, if taken in their historical context, they had much in common. "All of them reflected an historical shift from *practical* philosophy . . . to a *theoretical* conception of philosophy: the effects of this shift were so deep and long-lasting that the revival of practical philosophy in our day has taken many people by surprise."[18] This shift began with Descartes, usually called the father of modern thought, who at the beginning of his influential *Discourse on Method* rejected rhetoric because "nothing solid could have been built on so insecure a foundation."[19] In this rationalist phase of modern thought which has recently come to its postmodern dead end, Lessing could sum up its cause in his famous "broad ugly ditch" between the accidental truths of history and the necessary truths of reason, the former being one damn thing after another while the latter enshrined rational truth. Now we know that "the 'ditch' simply does not exist: the truths of reason are never quite as necessary as those who formulate them may suppose, and historical contingency may bear the truth of God."[20]

No one can think of the rhetorical self in the context of Christian thought without remembering that self-confessed *venditor verborum*, Augustine of Hippo. In his *De doctrina christiana*, the converted Augustine converted pagan rhetoric for Christian purposes. The work was begun in 396, shortly after he became Bishop of Hippo, and completed in 427, twenty-four years later. While many contemporary rehabilitators of rhetoric look to Aristotle's *Rhetoric* as their ancient classic, the Western tradition of Christian rhetoric was shaped by the Roman treatises of Cicero and Quintilian.[21] Aristotle himself did not have a high regard for rhetoric; it was a way of persuading people who could not handle the rigors of rational discourse. Cicero, however, had an exalted view of the role of the rhetor. And Cicero was Augustine's teacher. Augustine's *Confessions* is a superb illustration of epideictic rhetoric, and the *De doctrina christiana* is the Christian classic on rhetorical hermeneutics. It is a rhetorical hermeneutics because it is a hermeneutics of praxis.[22] Its basic key for all biblical interpretation is the praxis of love of God and love of neighbor. According to David Tracy, this Augustinian *caritas* serves as a "foreknowing," that necessary pre-understanding of the subject matter in order to interpret the signs in texts correctly.[23] Like all hermeneuts, Augustine searched the scriptures for meaning, but as a "voluntarist" ("What are we but wills?"), he privileged the conative above the cognitive. Intellect serves will; knowing guides doing. And oftentimes the doing can do without the knowing!

> A person, supported by faith, hope, and charity, with an unshaken hold upon them, does not need the Scriptures except for the instruction of others. And many live by these three things in solitude without books.[24]

Maybe Augustine is responsible for the ignorance of the Bible among ordinary Christians (especially Catholics) so pervasive in the church until recently! For Augustine, instruction is the primary purpose of Christian rhetoric rather than the Ciceronian focus on plausibility. The truths of faith are not merely plausible—they are the ultimate truths about God, humanity, and the world. Their persuasive power comes from their content. Unlike Aristotle and Cicero, Augustine holds that the orator is not the creator of the message but only the vehicle for its transmission. The Christian preacher or teacher must interpret the message with as much clarity as possible.[25] The Christian audience wants to *know* the God they love.

Inspired by Augustine, Anselm delivered the classical definition of theology, "faith seeking understanding." For Augustine, again the "voluntarist," defined understanding as "that by which we understand while we are thinking: that is, when, after things that had been present to the memory but were not being thought about have been recovered, our thought is formed; and [it] further [includes] that will (*voluntas*) or love (*amor*) or desire (*dilectio*) which unites this offspring (knowledge) and parent (*ratio*) and is in a certain fashion common to both."[26]

David Tracy contends that some of Augustine's rhetorical principles are still alive today in new forms. Theological charity becomes Gadamerian prejudgment; spiritual obscurity becomes the priority of the symbolic and poetic; the divine surplus of meaning not determined by the author's meaning becomes the loss of the author in deconstruction; the demand for clarity in communication becomes arguments over the relation of a rhetoric of "invention" (*logos*) to a rhetoric of delight (*pathos*) and a rhetoric of *ethos* and all three to a fuller rhetoric of persuasion.[27] It seems that Augustine, "the first modern man," is thriving in postmodern places—as Derrida put it, "Augustine always haunts certain landscapes."[28] Indeed, he haunts even public theology! At the beginning of Book XIX of *The City of God* he makes his case for hope in

Michael J. Scanlon

God "not only by calling upon divine authority, but also, for the sake of unbelievers, by making as much use of reason as possible."[29]

With Augustine we can distinguish between finding the truth and communicating what we have found, but we cannot, again with Augustine, separate them. Calvin Schrag echoes Augustine when he claims that "the historico-communal situationality of reason disallows any separation of the act of knowledge and the achievement of truth from the context of community."[30] This Cartesian separation of knowing from communicating is the "most basic of all the presuppositions of modernity," the presupposition that led to the collapse of the modern epistemological paradigm.

> Communication is not an event ancillary to the conquest of knowledge and truth. Knowing and articulating, truth and communicability, are twin halves of an undivided occasioning. This intercalation of knowledge and truth with the articulatory and disclosive functions of rhetoric becomes evident when we understand, with Henry W. Johnstone, that "truth in philosophy is equivalent with the itinerary leading to it, and this itinerary is in principle an exercise in communication."[31]

Disdained by modern thought with the dismissive adverbs, "merely," "just," "only," rhetoric has returned to the center of attention in both philosophy and theology. Our consensus on the primacy of praxis and the postmodern focus on language meet in rhetoric which binds discourse with action. As persuasive discourse it is directed to and for the "other"—another major concern in postmodern thought.

But rhetoric, too, has its own postmodern challenges—especially in relation to postmodern thinkers who celebrate the incommensurability of our diverse discursive practices and who alert us to the effects of the intrusion of power into our uses of language—what Lyotard calls "rhetorical agonistics."

Responding to this postmodern challenge, Calvin Schrag locates rhetoric within the expansive terrain of communicative praxis—rhetoric is communicative rhetoric. Like Van Huyssteen, who refers to him often throughout his work, Schrag accepts and is stimulated by much of the current postmodern critique, but he rejects the inevitability of plurality sliding into the heterogeneity of self-contained language games as well as the identification of power with its negative expressions. Obviously, power can be destructive, but it can also be constructive in promoting social cohesion and solidarity. Schrag adopts the strategy of thinking *with* the postmoderns while thinking against their extreme positions—he wants to show how postmodern thought can be used against itself. He holds that "the occlusion of the ability to say 'we' may turn out to be the principal chink in the political armor of the new politics of postmodernism."[32] In response to this chink, Schrag urges us to remain in the situation of the "between," thinking with others, maintaining some kind of dialogue, keeping the conversation going. Then one is "between" affirmation and denial, acceptance and rejection, agreement and disagreement, consent and disavowal. Here we agree with and consent to the claims of postmodernity and in so doing reach a dialogic consensus—provisional to be sure, but not without some rather profound effects. The remarkable achievement in this is that we are able to say "we." And this "we" remains in effect whether one agrees or disagrees. "Even in the most adamant disagreeing and disputing I *address the other* as the one *with whom* I am in disagreement." What renders postmodern politics ineffective is this lack of acceptance of we-relationships and we-experiences without which there can be no I-experience, which requires some acknowledgment by an other in the context of we-relationships. For Schrag, our recovery of the space of communicative praxis "restores the dense network of we-relationships that supplies the binding topos of rhetoric."[33]

Schrag finds that critical reception of the postmodern challenge leads to very significant changes in the classical model of rhetoric, which recognized persuasive discourse as *to* and *for* the other, but which could not recognize the rhetorical situation as being *with* the other. The classical model envisioned the rhetor (with his *ethos* and his *logos*) as the agent, as the active articulator of his powerful message to a rather passive audience of recipients (*pathos*). Now the rhetor is decentered, and the situation is one of dialogical interaction and reciprocity of proposal and response. Communicative rhetoric replaces subject-centered rhetoric in an atmosphere of intersubjectivity. While ambiguity is never totally overcome, while the perfect rhetorical situation never exists, we can communicate as we do in everyday conversations with our commonsense rationality using the best reasons we can come up with here and now.

Conclusion

For philosopher Schrag and theologian Van Huyssteen, the postmodern challenge has clearly overcome many of the pretensions of modern epistemology with its monological thinking, its confidence in universal reason, its privileging of theory and its aversion to rhetoric, its domestication of the poetic, the symbolic, the metaphorical, and its privatizing of religion. Both of these thinkers are dedicated to the projects of interdisciplinarity and public theology. They affirm the human resources of rationality against the incommensurability of many isolated rationalities of some nonfoundationalists while they critically appropriate the positive contributions of postmodern thought. They constantly admit that human rationality is limited, fallible, and provisional. They resonate with the tone of philosopher Gianni Vattimo's *il pensiero debole*, "weak thought."[34]

Along the same lines are the reflections of philosopher Hans Blumenberg, who sees rhetoric as "a form of rationality itself—a rational way of coming to terms with the provisionality of reason."[35] With Blumenberg we learn that the *animal rationale* whose specific difference was celebrated by modernity is in fact a rather deficient creature who needs rhetoric precisely because of this deficiency: "The axiom of all rhetoric is the principle of insufficient reason (*principium rationis insufficientis*). It is a correlate of the anthropology of a creature who is deficient in essential respects."[36] If we could assign sufficient reasons for everything, there would be no need for rhetoric. On religious rhetoric, Blumenberg states that the "rhetoric that by its dissemination is the most important in our history, the rhetoric of prayer, always had to rely— contrary to the theological positions associated with rationalistic or voluntaristic concepts of God—on a God who allowed himself to be persuaded, and this problem recurs in the case of anthropology: the man [*sic*] whom it deals with is not characterized by the philosophical overcoming of 'opinion' by 'knowledge.' "[37]

In its deconstruction of the modern self, postmodernism returns us to the decentered self, deficient by modern standards but ripe for a rehabilitated rhetoric that can serve public discourse and, for our purposes, public theology. Fallible, feeble, finite, tentative, revisable as is our chastened rationality, effective in public theology, it may still be as God uses the weak to confound the strong.

NOTES

1. Paul Ricoeur, *Oneself as Another*, trans. Kathleen Blamey (Chicago: University of Chicago Press, 1992), 11.

2. See Paul Ricoeur, *Figuring the Sacred*, ed. Mark I. Wallace, trans. David Pellauer (Minneapolis: Fortress Press, 1995), 14.

3. Stephen Toulmin, *Cosmopolis: The Hidden Agenda of Modernity* (Chicago: University of Chicago Press, 1990), 11.

4. Ibid., 34.

5. Michael Himes and Kenneth Himes, *Fullness of Faith* (New York: Paulist Press, 1993), 4.

6. Paul Ricoeur, *Time and Narrative*, vol. 1 (Chicago: University of Chicago Press, 1984), 52.

7. Gary Comstock, "Two Types of Narrative Theology," *Journal of the American Academy of Religion* 55, no. 4 (1987): 687–717.

8. For a good defense of Wittgenstein against the charge of fideism, see Vincent Brümmer, "Wittgenstein and the Irrationality of Theology," in *The Christian Understanding of God Today*, ed. James Byrne (Dublin: Columba Press, 1983), 88–102.

9. (Grand Rapids: William B. Eerdmans Publishing Co., 1999).

10. Van Huyssteen, *The Shaping of Rationality* (Grand Rapids: William B. Eerdmans Publishing Company, 1999), 216.

11. Ibid.

12. Ibid., 220.

13. Ibid.

14. Ibid.

15. Michel Foucault, *The Order of Things: An Archaeology of the Human Sciences* (New York: Random House, 1970), 387.

16. For the notion of the decentered self, see Calvin Schrag, *The Resources of*

Rationality: A Response to the Postmodern Challenge (Bloomington: Indiana University Press, 1992) and *The Self after Postmodernity* (New Haven: Yale University Press, 1997).

17. Stephen Toulmin, *Cosmopolis: The Hidden Agenda of Modernity* (Chicago: University of Chicago Press, 1990), 34.

18. Ibid.

19. Quoted in Don H. Compier, *What Is Rhetorical Theology?* (Harrisburg, Pa.: Trinity Press International, 1999), 14.

20. Nicholas Lash, *The Beginning and the End of Religion* (Cambridge: Cambridge University Press, 1996), 18.

21. Compier, *What Is Rhetorical Theology?*, 2.

22. Werner Jeanrond, *Theological Hermeneutics: Development and Significance* (New York: Crossroad, 1991), 23.

23. David Tracy, "Charity, Obscurity, Clarity: Augustine's Search for Rhetoric and Hermeneutics," in *Rhetoric and Hermeneutics in Our Time: A Reader*, ed. Walter Jost and Michael Hyde (New Haven: Yale University Press, 1997), 264.

24. *St. Augustine on Christian Doctrine*, trans. D. W. Robertson, Jr. (Indianapolis: Bobbs-Merrill, 1958), 32. [*De doctrina christiana*, I, 39].

25. *De doctrina christiana*, 4, 10, 24.

26. Karl F. Morrison, *I Am You: The Hermeneutics of Empathy in Western Literature, Theology and Art* (Princeton: Princeton University Press, 1988), 179.

27. See Tracy, "Charity, Obscurity, Clarity," 272.

28. Jacques Derrida, *On the Name*, trans. David Wood, John Leavey, Jr., and Ian McLeod (Stanford: Stanford University Press, 1995), 40.

29. St. Augustine, *The City of God against the Pagans*, trans. R.W. Dyson (Cambridge: Cambridge University Press, 1998), 909.

30. Schrag, *The Resources of Rationality*, 136.

31. Ibid.

32. Ibid., 129–130.

33. Ibid., 130.

34. Gianni Vattimo, *The End of Modernity* (Baltimore: Johns Hopkins University Press, 1991), passim.

35. Hans Blumenberg, "An Anthropological Approach to Rhetoric," in *After Philosophy: End or Transformation?*, ed. K. Baynes, J. Bohman, and T. McCarthy (Cambridge: MIT Press, 1987), 452.

36. Ibid., 447.

37. Ibid.

Questioning God

Graham Ward

"Why then do you hide your face and regard me as your enemy?" Job asks, bowed beneath the devastation that has come upon him. "What then do I love when I love my God? Who is he who is higher than the highest element in my soul?" So Augustine voices two of the many thousands of questions which circulate throughout *Confessions*. "Is this place created by God? Is it part of the play? Or else is it God himself?" Thus Jacques Derrida inquires with respect to that which gives rise to the play of negative theology in *Sauf le nom*.

Three questionings of God, but what kind of questionings? The "of" slides between, schematically, Job's question posed *to* God for answering; Augustine's questioning installed *by* God; and Derrida's question *concerning* God. They are not then questions from the same vantage point, and we will have to come on to the nature of vantage points in a moment. Job speaks to God as with a powerful warrior Prince whom he has served as friend and obedient servant, and for whom the breaking of a covenant between Lord and servant would bring about the collapse of that servant's worldview. Job speaks from the fear of exclusion and the panic of possible alienation. He speaks to God from out of his distance. The speaking is attempting to close the space of distance not with just a communication but with the suggestion of an accusation: "Why do you do this?" It is a question demanding not only reparation but explanation, an explanation which is not simply the deliverance of knowledge as information. His is not an intellectual enquiry but a *cri de coeur*. What is required is an explanation which is at once an affirmation that the center still holds. It comes as the vantage point of someone who senses possible betrayal and has experienced an explicit confusion of expectations. It comes from a one-time intimate and familiar; an insider who is now wondering whether he is an outsider.

It is significant—and an enquiry into the kind of significance is highly relevant—that when God thunders back his reply in chapter 38, God answers Job with questions, turning the questioning about: "I shall put a question to you and you must answer." The doctrine of God as it emerges in the book of Job is a doctrine only possible in and through the process of mutual interrogation. The narrator stages this interrogation in which neither is answered and yet both are vindicated because both remain faithful. The answer Job receives is the reversal of his fortunes, not an explanation of why they had changed. He receives not the solution to a problem posed, but the resumption of a rhythm of relationship whereby his trust is strengthened.

Augustine's questioning opens a different reading of that same relation between questioning God and being questioned by Him. For he does not just *put* questions to God and never presumes (as Job can) to question the actions of this God, but Augustine questions what this might be who is called God and who calls him to call upon this God. There is no covenant of mutual obligations in the background here. The relationship is both more intimate—part of an amatory discourse intrinsic to the moral and epistemological architecture of his soul—and more distant (for more profoundly skeptical of what using these words might mean). The questions do not articulate the demands of "Why?," but the obfuscations of "Who?" and "what?"[1] The interrogative pronouns used dissolve the specificities of naming such as God and love so that the vantage point is more ambivalent, for the "I" has no standing outside and distinct from God (like Job's). The "I" is continually caught up in the circulations of love and the sublime verticalities of the superlatives: higher than the highest *in* my soul. Nevertheless, Job and Augustine share a similar economy of the question: In both cases the question is not answered. Job's discourse seems to suggest an answer is expected, whereas Augustine's does not. In both cases the question is not itself what is essential or what is most significant. The question is an occasion for something to occur—a theophany of a kind: the appearance of the divine not as the answerer but, nevertheless, the receiver of questions. What precedes, circumscribes, and follows the question is a relation; a relation liturgically formalized, for this interrogation constitutes prayer. The questioning keeps open the meaning and the nature of that relation such that prayer follows prayer. The question does not seek knowledge, as such, to assuage the pain of a privation (ignorance). It is a response internal to a

relationship already established, an economy of shared being already established. It is a response invoking meditation, the movement beyond things seen
into things mysterious, concealed, into *theoria*. Relation is the condition for
the question's possibility and that which follows the questioning. For the refusal to answer is not the refusal to speak (or act). The question, even Job's,
precipitates and perpetuates a process of yielding in hope, in the stillness
of affirmation. More explicitly for Augustine, the liturgy of this yielding—
confession—is an ecclesial sacrament benefiting not only himself but the
church. It is an exemplary and public act, an act to be imitated and repeated
(albeit differently), an act in imitation itself of all those others who have
yielded in such a manner, allowing themselves, through questioning, to be put
into question. Neither Job's nor Augustine's questioning is the questioning of
whether there is a God—the kind of questioning which begins to emerge in the
seventeenth and eighteenth centuries, when the presence or absence of God
has been liberalized, leading to wagers, on the one hand, and the fervent
assertions of various pietisms and evangelisms, on the other. This kind of
questioning led eventually to a new understanding of what it meant to be both
an atheist and a believer: the splits between those who claim he is dead and
those who set up TV networks and cyberspace stations to announce that he
lives. For Job will proclaim in his despair; "I know that my Redeemer lives,
And he shall stand at last on the earth." And Augustine opens his questioning
with a doxology: "You Lord are great, and highly to be praised."

Then what of Derrida's questioning with respect to Job's and Augustine's?
What kind of questioning is this? It is evidently not the questioning directed
to God. For in Job and Augustine the question presupposes, sets up, and
anticipates a relation between addressor and addressee. It places the addressee
under obligation to reply. Augustine is skeptical whether he has any substantial
knowledge of either himself or the one he names God. Nevertheless, the
question participates in the circulation of an economy of love and fealty. To
whom are Derrida's questions addressed? From whom is an answer being
elicited? Who can make the judgment that responds to his questions and make
a decision as to which of the three interpretations of the whence of negative
theology is correct? From whence can come the questions of the other? What
place does the other occupy? Is there another person (*autrui*) or just otherness
(*autre*), and can otherness (being an impersonal absence of the same) make a
response? We must observe here that, for Job and Augustine, the other is
neither just otherness nor, in being alterior, ever wholly other (*tout autre*). For
the relationship to be a relationship, a history of practiced believing is required, the memory (one's own and one's communities') of past engagement,
past epiphany, past revelations. The context of tradition and authoritative
narratives is implicit. Augustine may doubt his knowledge of what God is, and
Job may be confused by this activity as God's activity; nevertheless, the entrustment, hope, and assurance that makes their questioning possible is founded
upon this memory of past engagement in which *that* which they name God

has been demonstrated to be faithful. The *tout autre* as such puts an end to all revelation and inaugurates a discourse of the ineliminable yet impossible and undecidable trace. And, as Philippe Lacoue Labarthe observes about the representation which is necessary here: "The *logic* of the said representation . . . is, rigorously speaking, the interdiction of revelation."[2] To whom, then, are Derrida's questions addressed? Who receives them? The play in his book *The Post Card: From Socrates to Freud and Beyond* would suggest that these questions (both his and mine) are unanswerable.[3] But then what are the implications of unanswerability? It is not the questioning of one consciously committed to God. And I would greatly hesitate to suggest unconscious or anonymous commitment. For who can make such a suggestion, upon what grounds, from what elevated perspective, with what power?

I would suggest instead that a certain genealogy emerges here, but of what sort? What does the move from Job's kind of questioning to Augustine's to the interrogations of God in our present day depict? A genealogy of God? A genealogy of questioning? To be sure it must be both: For all our theological discourse is culturally embedded, and the kind of questions and the kind of questioning that discourse produces and promotes is determined by the cultural spaces that are available or can be opened for it.

What I wish to attempt today is twofold: a clarification of the kind of questioning of God, the kind of God-questions, that some forms of poststructuralism have articulated, and a configuration of an alternative spacing within which we might hear a different way of questioning God, a different approach to the question of God. Then, on the basis of this clarification and configuration, I am going to suggest that having, with Heidegger and Derrida, thought through the end of metaphysics, and the onto-theology of those metaphysics (having thought through the death of *that* God in the birth of a general aporetics, of the impossible and the undecidable), we are on the cusp of another thinking that is coming to be, another kind of questioning and, therefore, another kind of God.

I undertake this examination only with respect to Augustine, rather than with respect to Job, for several reasons: first, the time I have been given; second, Villanova's own commitments to research into Augustine; third, Augustine's Numidia is present-day Algeria and that makes Derrida, in ways he has pointed out in *Circumfession*, Augustine's *confrère*; fourth, and primarily, because it seems to me we stand, culturally, in a certain relation to Augustine's thinking. Poised as he was on the threshold between radical pluralism (which he called paganism) and the rise of Christendom, we stand on the other side of that history: at the end of Christendom and the re-emergence of radical (as distinct from liberal) pluralism.[4]

In the Tenth Book of his *Confessions*, Augustine informs us he has been told "that it is possible to ask three kinds of question—whether a thing is, what it is, and what sort it is [*an sit, quid sit, quale sit*]."[5] He is *put* into question—as placed into a space created by the interrogatives with which he begins and

which continue to punctuate his narrative. He thinks and writes interroga-
tively. The space of the question makes possible his communication—both as
an act of prayer (with respect to God) and as an act of pedagogy (with respect to
his readership). For the question, while not in itself dialogical, disturbs the
monologic of either autobiographical or exegetical discourse. It sets up a fold
in the discourse, a self-reflective divide. The *Confessions* is composed of auto-
biography and exegesis: the interpretation of one's life as a text written, in part,
from elsewhere and the interpretation of the Scriptures written, in part, from
elsewhere. Questioning as both rhetorical tool and theological method is foundational. Why?

Let us return to those three possible kinds of question and make explicit
the metaphysics that informs each kind, makes each of them possible *as* forms
of question, and relate this back to Augustine's own primary concerns: the
relationship between all that is created (most particularly human beings) and
the creator. Let me suggest that questioning God is all we can do, and that to
do so is most profoundly to participate in an economy of the fore-given: In the
beginning what is given is the reflection "Why?," and in the reflection invoked
by why is the reception of grace.[6]

But first, what makes a question a question? The paucity of inquiries into
the nature of the question among modern analytical philosophers of language
is somewhat surprising, given the attention to the semantics and logics of the
paradox, the optative, naming, the sentence, and predication which take up
pages in the work of Frege, Quine, Putnam, and Gareth Evans. What is the
logic of the question? What is its epistemic and ontic modality? Insofar as it is
dealt with, by Frege for example, the analysis proceeds as a subset of an inquiry
in the nature of assertions.[7] In Lewis the question is a subset of mands (a verbal
operation where the response is reinforced by a consequence—they include
commands, requests, and threats).[8] The assumption appears to be that questions are a mode of assertion or, at least, "similar to that of declarative sentences."[9] Some linguists place the question under the subheading "mood,"
describing its operation as a modification of the indicative—a modification
that can take the form of modified intonation, a different word order, an
interrogative particle, or pronouns. But is the question a mood, like the conditional or the passive? And is it the opposite of, but nevertheless sharing the
same epistemic and ontic logic of, assertion? Is all questioning the same kind
of operation?[10]

In Latin there are three forms of question, two rhetorical forms: One
implies either "Yes" or "No" and one implies the "open" form. It is with the
third form that we are concerned. For Augustine's three sets of questions are all
open questions. But what are they open to? What do they open? A question
does not necessarily imply an answer (as questions as a subset of assertions or
mands seems to assume). A question can be posed rather than asked. A question sets itself up in a wider conceptual field such that (a) a certain orientation
toward a set of related concepts is required and (b) in that orientation, relation-

ships between concepts are established such that the question initiates a procedure, a way of thinking through the relationships toward, if not an answer, then a better understanding of what the question involves. With the first of Augustine's kind of questions—"whether a thing is"—a conceptual orientation toward both "is" and "thing" is established. An orientation toward ontology—some model of the relationship between existence and existents, being and becoming—is necessary. The question also presupposes that an enquiry into the relationship is possible. The question demands that there is or can be an identification of "a thing," an understanding of thinghood. An enquiry into the nature of presence, the present and presentation, and the relationship between these concepts, is set up. A question about the nature of time begins to circulate. This is something of the conceptual field within which we make sense of the question and shape a method of enquiry. The field is more extensive still, in two significant ways. First, the subjunctive, "whether," introduces a set of conditionals such that if this thing is *not* then some understanding of non-existence, non-being, not-a-thing is necessary. Second, there is a set of presuppositions concerning the relationship between the discursive nature of questioning and what is being questioned: presuppositions about the nature of representation. What shape one's world is will determine how one makes sense of the question, the direction of the subsequent enquiry, and the possible answers that might emerge.

Each of Augustine's fundamental forms of question depends upon the field of concepts established by the previous question. There is, then, a movement in the forms of question. We cannot proceed in an enquiry into "what a thing is" without presupposing some conclusions to the question "whether a thing is," and we cannot proceed toward an enquiry about "what sort of thing it is" without presupposing some conclusions to the question of "what a thing is."

All this needs elucidating because the shape of the God-question as framed by, say, Heidegger's critique of onto-theology is not the same as the God-question as framed by Augustine's critique of materialism. Heidegger's (or Marion's) God beyond Being, God under erasure, is not Augustine's God as the source and sustainer of creaturely existence. Which is to say, questioning God at the end of Enlightenment's deisms and theisms is not the same as questioning God as a theological venture. That is not, let me hasten to add, because theology and philosophy are distinctive craft-bound discourses with their own intrinsic methods of enquiry. Such a view of the relationship between theology and philosophy is Averroist and is soundly condemned by Aquinas.[11] Augustine is as much philosophical as he is theological—as concerned as much with time, representation, Being, and Nothing as Heidegger. The philosophical and the theological are not distinctive domains, but, for Augustine, the trajectory of reasoning followed in the former is in accordance with a grammar of faith prescribed in the latter. So the God being questioned and putting Augustine into question is the triune God, the God who constitutes the fundamental community of love: the God who as Father is transcendent and as Son and Spirit is also immanent because implicated in the motions and energies of the creation, constituting within the world the structure of hope and the watermark of goodness, beauty, justice, and truth. And the world is not an emanation from the One, which would make it exist necessarily. The world is that which is born out of nothing as an act of grace, as gift issuing from the mutual givenness of the one for the other in the trinitarian sociality. The world exists in an order of the fore-givenness that eternally provides the structure for salvation: fore-givenness eternally offers forgiveness. Etymologically the "for" is a prefix indicating direction and that which goes on ahead. It is a world that does not possess its existence in its own right; its Being cannot *be* hypostasized. It exists in duration, in *distentio*, in time.

Its "thinghood" and the varieties of "thinghood" of which it is composed is never stable, never static. Its "thinghood" is in suspension, as the "what" is what it is in the fullness of its becoming, what Gregory of Nyssa calls its *skopus*—the trajectory of all its possibilities and transformations. The question then about what a thing is can only be ever answered provisionally. Similarly, whether a thing is can never be finally defined. That there *is* can be affirmed, but the nature of that *is* is not a thing that can be grasped or even experienced as an *is*, as presence, as that which can be isolated as present to itself. The now cannot be commodified, for it is not a discrete instant in a flow of such mind-independent instants—as Leibniz believed.[12] That which is can only be understood in the *distentio* of time as belonging to that which was and that which will be. Identity here is not indeterminate, is not endlessly undecidable, nor is the act of provisional identification arbitrary, one of any number of possible acts, the choosing of which forever makes one culpable of the sin of omission. All partial identifications participate in an ongoing pedagogy concerning the nature and truth of things. The lack of understanding, produced by the very excess of anything's meaning, fosters the questioning which participates in the unfolding of what things are. Things created "in the image of" or as the expression of, God's Word have only a symbolic presence. The thing's presence is not auto-referential, but is always pointing and existing beyond itself. The question installs a quest and suggests a wealth toward which one is being orientated. (In Latin *quaeso* is linked to *quaestio* and to *questus*.) Exposition is provoked. And in that exposition, the very demand for that exposition, God's active presence, is announced. What something is determines its identity as a thing performs what it is over time, gives an exposition and exegesis of itself. The present itself has no extension, Augustine tells us.[13]

The answer to the question "What sort of thing is it?" can only be given an answer if all things can be itemized, identified, frozen in their being fully present to themselves. Then a set of comparisons and contrasts can organize an identification of what sort of thing there is. It can be placed in a field of differentials and similitudes. But where *what is* can never be ascertained as such, only ascertained contingently, nor can *whether it is*, then any answers to the question of *what sort it is* also partake of the suspension of all things, their extension through time. Is this wine or the blood of Christ? Is this bread or the body of Christ or a Fish? (Augustine often uses the word Fish to speak of the Eucharist.) Am I the author of this text or am I authored from elsewhere? Where, as Augustine continually reminds us, "the manner of our existence shows that we have been made,"[14] and made "in the image of," then no thing can exist in and for itself. No entity can refer only to itself. A thing has not a reality adequate or equivalent to its appearance (the presupposition of empiricism) and nature, as it came to be constructed in the seventeenth century.[15] Nor is its reality given in some original manner (the presupposition of phenomenology). This is not the same as what Derrida felicitously calls "the disjunction of self-contemporaneity."[16] For nothing is present to itself; all is inherently mutable, for nothing and formlessness still haunt the perfection and salvation of all form. What an entity is has to be suspended, and hence all judgment about the *that*, the *what*, and the *sort of* is also suspended. All things are constituted in hope. Presence cannot be reified, made a literal thing itself; it is not a commodity and therefore does not issue as an event, an appropriating event such as Heidegger describes *Ereignis*.[17] Presence didn't become a commodity until the literalizing process began in the late Scholastic period, and it became central in the sixteenth century, when Protestant reformers disputed questions concerning *praesens* and *prasentia* with respect to the doctrine of transsubstantiation, and the Council of Trent framed its teaching on the Eucharist in terms of the real presence (*reali praesens*).[18] The thinghood of a thing is that which is most mysterious to it, that which is not closed but continually exposed. It exposes, gives an exposition of, itself as what it is, not in the present continuous (an endless succession of moments fully present to themselves) but in the duration, the *distentio*, of time past, present, and future.

If this is so of all *created* things, how much more so does this pertain to a creature's understanding of what God is in God's self? We are not depicting here a God beyond Being, for that would mean we grasp what "to be" is and what spatiality means with respect to a God who is distanced, who is beyond. Pace Karl Barth—who, to my mind, spent the latter part of his life supplementing the theology of wholly otherness through the quasi-transcendence of Christ—the God who is wholly other cannot be God at all. For there could be nothing at all that we could know about such a God, except by violent intervention and confrontation. It does not surprise me at all that such a doctrine of revelation—that for Barth, among others, forms the basis of his earlier dialectical theology—arose at the same time as speculation about aliens on other planets, or that science-fiction stories about alien invasion such as *The War of the Worlds* were circulating from the last years of the nineteenth century. The same kind of concept is involved—Christ as the man who fell to earth. Augustine's God is not some Darth Vader, nor is his Christ Luke Skywalker—who I notice now comes with a virgin mother. This interventionist model of revelation is the model implicit in recent post-structural critiques of the "historical revelation" at the origin of the Judaeo-Christian-Islamic religion group. I'm thinking here of Jacques Derrida's sidelining of an investigation into the rationality of faith practices by employing a Kantian distinction between dogmatic and moral religions and defining dogmatic as those religions founded upon historical revelation in *Faith and Knowledge* and of his identification of faith in this historical revelation with "the experience of non-relationship, or absolute interruption."[19] We will return to the structure of "absolute interruption" later. But such an account of revelation, as the punctuation of an arbitrary omnipotent will into the text of history, and the matrix of dualisms (faith/reason, name/object named, mind/world), which proceeded from this view of omnipotence, goes back to the philosophical precursors of modernity, the nominalists, most particularly William of Ockham.[20] For Augustine the revelation of God's love, which is ultimately what is revealed by God of God, has its origin (and he takes pains to demonstrate the complexity of words such as "origin" and "beginning") in creation itself. The opening line of Genesis, "In the beginning," he interprets as "in Christ."[21] So that in the historical incarnation, Augustine's Christ comes into his own: As Word, creation came to be through Him. That he was not recognized was only a fault of human memory; a fault produced through sin. If people, by a grace already given, could begin to understand what it was they truly desired, they would understand the God who had called them to be. An analogical relation maintains God's alterity and the integrity of creation's participation in the gift-exchange of trinitarian love. The language of quasi-transcendence may have application here: that is, no transcendent argument establishing that which makes possible all things—an argument only available through a univocity of being which Eric Alliez among others has shown to gain currency with Duns Scotus[22]—can be established. God cannot be made philosophically the first principle (actually, even Aristotle understood this, as anyone aware of the aporetics and rhetorics of Aristotle's *Metaphysics* will know).[23] Feuerbach was right: This is not God but a regulative ideal of human understanding. Nevertheless a quasi-transcendence might be said to operate (and I use the word advisedly)—in a way. For Augustine, the Spirit bears the gift of God's love to us, facilitating the participation of creation in the Godhead, yet nevertheless it is "borne above" the world, or bears the mutability of creation into the immutability of the divine.

God cannot then be a transcendental signifier. This does not name the one who comes to us continually, the creator-God, the triune by whom we are called to be and maintained in that being. This only names a conceptual idol, to employ Jean-Luc Marion's term.[24] Augustine's God cannot be a transcendental signifier. First, it is not logically possible, because although there remains a continual play between representation and significance (how something is perceived, understood, and the description of what that something *is*), God endlessly proceeds out of Godself such that meaning exceeds all interpretation or denotation. Hence the questioning of God (both subjective and objective genitive) never ends; it just plumbs deeper into the mystery of the Godhead as the Godhead unfolds its own infinite nature. Augustine is, then, quite prepared to admit that any passage of Scripture can be interpreted in an endless number of ways, that the death of the one who wrote it can be a further liberation of a writing's meaning which now has "more sublime authority."[25] All these ways, which may in fact contradict each other, may nevertheless deepen an understanding of some aspect of the Godhead. "What wonderful profundity there is in your utterances! The surface meaning lies open before us and charms beginners. Yet the depth is amazing, my God, the depth is amazing."[26] Hence judgment has to be suspended. God does not name the point of inertia that makes possible the *mathesis* of all motion. Such a God came to be with Newton, and it arose when a cultural concern with temporality and interrelatedness was eclipsed by a new concern to spatialize and itemize the material. This gave rise theologically to a line of questioning around the theme of "Where is God?"[27] God as transcendental signifier only gives *that* God a role to play in linguistics—rather, kinetics: the economies of both are very similar. The fundamental difference here is with the nature of knowledge: that there is some Archimedean point which makes possible and definitive all knowledge about all things *sub species aeternitatis*. But knowledge is not only partial and contingent; for Augustine, it is inseparable from pneumatology as the structure of eschatological hope: "The words 'it is not you that know' may rightly be said to those whose knowing is by the Spirit of God. . . . 'It is not you who see' is spoken to those who see it by the Spirit of God."[28]

This pneumatological element is the second reason why Augustine's God cannot be a transcendental signifier. The difference between the Spirit and the Father/Son relationship, the second or even third difference within the Godhead, entails that the meaning of the relationship, the meaning of the love that is continually given, received, and shared, is held open. It is held open before that which is not-God, that which is created rather than uncreated. Its significance is not endlessly deferred but endlessly deepened. The eternal significance of this God who from out of His *processio* extends a continual *missio* toward the world in which all things are called to be (and become what they are) cannot be hypostasized, given a spatialized point outside the system. It is no cultural coincidence that the absence of trinitarian theology coincides with the rise of Enlightenment deism, the God of the new sciences: mechanics, eventually linguistics. Pneumatology goes underground to thrive as Pietism and becomes one of the sources of Romanticism. Christology becomes caught up in the stage-effects of kenosis—those discourses on the messianic consciousness and the historicity of the Jesus-event.[29]

God cannot act as a transcendental signifier and therefore as the pure object of a transcendental questioning. God, in this mode of reasoning (a reasoning that cannot be divorced from the praxis upon which reasoning reflects), does not operate as a transcendental guarantor—of meaning, of trust, of testimony, of truth, of faithfulness, of the original "yes." God as guarantor is the God of capitalism: the God conceived in terms of commerce and the judiciary that regulates commercial transaction; *credo* as credit. This brings us back to a suggestion I made at the beginning of this chapter about the different modes of questioning, the genealogy of questioning with which we are involved here. There is a difference between what constitutes questioning (God) for Augustine and, say, those philosophers gathered in Capri on February 28, 1994—what constitutes questioning *as such*. I shall postpone examining that issue for the moment to clarify the distinction I am trying to make here between Augustine's God and the God of logocentrism. I wish to make two points here: one with respect to logocentrism and one with respect to Augustine's God. The concept of logocentrism is a magnification of modernity's obsession with the purity of the present, the isolation of the moment, the now, the instantaneous, the immediate. As such, the critique of logocentrism takes the form of attention to the mediated, the time lag of *re*presentation, that which is un*present*able. Logocentrism is implicated in a certain metaphysics, mathematics and technology of time. The God of logocentrism's questioning guarantees the possibility of living in, experiencing, being consumed by the eternal now, the daylight forever, what Certeau termed "the white ecstasy."[30] The univocity of being, which is the metaphysical condition for the possibility of onto-theology, proffers the purity of this present, eliding the difference between present and presence. As such, the God of logocentrism is a necessary part of creation: Creation is the necessary emanation of this God. The critique of logocentrism seeks that which is totally other, *tout autre*, that which cannot be reduced to the economy of the Same, variously labeled as the impossible, the unpresentable, and variously figured as the *khora* or death. The critique, then, of logocentrism and the questioning of logocentrism's God operates still within the metaphysics of modernity; it requires and maintains those metaphysics, locating aporia (but always and only aporia) within the certainties and certitudes of modernity's knowledge. Its questioning is *of* (both subjective and objective genitive) these certainties and certitudes. The critique is a further turn in Kantian thinking: where the denial of the univocity of being (which substantiates being as a predicate and makes possible, as Kant so clearly recognized, all three forms of the argument for the existence of God) makes the establishment of God as a necessary, but regulative, idea.

Augustine's God is not implicated in these metaphysics—nor are the dualisms installed by them (presence/absence, univocity/equivocity, immediacy/mediation, etc.). The present is not isolatable, for Augustine: It is part of a temporal distention. In fact, Augustine tells us in *The Confessions* that the present as such does not exist. The present is not identical to presence. God's presence in creation is governed by a fundamental *diastema* between the uncreated creator and creation: Presence as such is not part of the logic of univocity (or equivocity), and no necessity drives God to create. This presence establishes an analogical relation—which defies the categorical distinctions between *analogia attributionis* and *analogia proportionalis* developed by Cajetan in the sixteenth century in his *Commentary on St. Thomas Aquinas's Summa Theologiae* (1507–1522). It is a relation which exceeds our ability, as created, to comprehend. It is a relation which puts all things into question, which installs the desire to understand, to engage in a hermeneutical ontology. To reason is to question, to seek to understand this relation. To reason is to participate in the unfolding of this divine presence; to participate in the God who in being threefold is himself/herself/whatever in question, endlessly open to response, endlessly exceeding an answer.[31] To question is to pray, for Augustine; to question is to participate in God's own redemptive and creative activity. Only God as such is questionable, for God is both the subject and object of all questioning. To question is to be theological—it is Augustine's method, style, and content (as it later became Aquinas's, albeit in a different way).

The *questioning* of God in post-structural critical theory—those discussions on the island of Capri, for example, or Nancy's final chapters of *The Inoperative Community*,[32] or Baudrillard's extermination of the name of God in his *Symbolic Exchange and Death*,[33] or even Levinas's closing chapters of *Otherwise than Being*[34]—belong to a certain historical and cultural figuration of questioning itself. It belongs also to a certain historical and cultural figuration of God, the God who Hegel, Nietzsche, and Heidegger proclaimed dead, the God of *Kant's Religion within the Limits of Reason Alone*. It is a questioning of aporia; not a question-in-relation.

This is fundamental. Augustine and Derrida both argue for a necessary suspension of judgment in favor of an ungraspable excess and an openness to what has yet to come but is in the process of arriving. But Augustine's questions both structure the hope of final, eschatological judgment and participate, by that structuring, in the realization and arrival of that hope. The questioning is a movement in relation to the Good, the Just, the Beautiful and the True. Derrida's questioning is a "movement" in the continual expansion of aporia itself: promise, hope, the yes hover as never-to-be-realized, but nevertheless necessary, regulative ideals. The hope can never be enjoyed, as such, and the aporetic—with its tyrannous demand for infinite responsibility—can only be endured. Derrida's questioning seems locked, then, into the logic of Camus' Sisyphus[35]—which would therefore call into question whether, for all the use of the word economy, there is any movement at all; and, for all the employment of "responsibility," whether there is anything ethical about this position. The experience of infinite guilt as such is not in itself ethical.

For whom is this questioning undertaken; for what reason? It is not for a Wittgensteinian clarification, since aporia comes as that which is indefinable, unnameable, unpresentable. The aporetics installed by the questioning opens the aporia up not for inspection but for the generation of the undecidable. As such, God names Lacan's *objet petit a*,[36] that which keeps desire desiring: "'God' 'is' the name of this bottomless collapse, of this endless desertification of language," Derrida informs us.[37] God is a figure for what Hegel would call the bad infinite and the condition of infinite responsibility that did not participate in an economy of hope, the unhappy consciousness. For what is the aporia an index of? We return to Derrida's three questions concerning what gives rise or place to the playing of negative theology: "Is this place created by God? Is it part of the play? Or else is it God Himself?" They are reminiscent of Ricoeur's questions toward the end of *Oneself as Another*, when Ricoeur asks what aporetics is bearing witness to—God, the Unconscious, long-dead ancestors, the nihil, or what? Now to whom is this questioning addressed?[38] To what economy of exchange is it associated—if questioning *as such* is always open to exchange (rather than part of the logic of problem solving)? Does the structure of Derrida's questioning imitate and implement not the structure of exchange but onanism—"absolute interruption" as *coitus interruptus*: the dissemination of the philosopher's *logoi spermatikoi* on the sands of an infinite desertification? Is it the pleasure of the questioning, of the keeping in question, that really counts—the pleasure of not having what one desires: such as keeping the reader in suspense by endlessly deferring the denouement? Does questioning offer the pleasure of relief from the infinite guilt that threatens always to assail? Might we describe this as a hermeneutical meontology as distinct from Augustine's hermeneutical ontology? Compared to the ethics of entrustment that is performed and reaffirming in Job's and Augustine's questioning, what is the ethics of such an erotics and aesthetics of questioning? Is it a question of keeping modernity's philosophy of religion on a life-support machine? What is the ethics of such a questioning where there is no relation, no exchange, within which the interrogation functions? There is a yielding perhaps, a kenosis of discourse certainly, but not an entrustment or the deliverance of one's own judgment to the judgment of the Good, the Just, the Beautiful, and the True. Here there is only the starship *Enterprise* moving off into deeper space in search of further textual adventures. But then moving is always a pseudo-traveling: For what is discovered in this thinking through of aporia itself, since no one can take measurement in the infinite?

I draw to a close, but now wish to make a dramatic turn in my argument, to deepen and make it more complex. For I do not wish to suggest by my configuration of questioning God that we can naively return to Augustine or Job or put ourselves outside the questioning of God that has taken place prior to arriving at this point on the curve of the third millennium through thinkers such as Derrida. I have sketched both an archaeology and a genealogy of the questioning of God. We do not live in the cultural conditions that scarify Job's or Augustine's questioning. Our thinking is otherwise, for it is elsewhere. My configurations have constructed replicas, virtualities called "Augustine's questioning" or "Job's questioning." Coming after Gadamer, we cannot pretend to read them as they were; we read them in the ways they can be read today. I have come to a questioning of God brought to me by the philosophical and theological tradition I place myself within—by Hegel, Nietzsche, Heidegger, and Derrida. The questioning of Job and Augustine—and the God they question—is not available to me in the same way they understood the tasks they undertook. And Derrida is one of the people who taught me this through his construal of iteration. In *Identity and Difference*, Heidegger spoke of his thinking the thought of the metaphysics of the atomic age.[39] He spoke of the destiny of thinking as such. Have we thought through this thought such that today we are elsewhere and the questioning of God does not now involve the hypostasis of aporia? This is to say no more than Hegel understood (and Heidegger after him), that the matter or the task of thinking (or questioning) is in itself historical.

I suggest we are moving toward a new thinking of God-questioning, such that our questioning of God takes place in a space within which both questioning and God will be different because elsewhere. The clarification of that questioning now (Does it imitate the structural logic of onanism?) and the configuration of that questioning then (in an economy of the gift, the foregiven, an economy of hope) opens up differences and fosters a turning (a word I use after Heidegger) in thought itself—a turning out of the metaphysics of the death of God (which Heidegger and Derrida have thought through to their completion) into another place which is even now being determined, beyond deconstruction. Isn't that what Derrida's choice of topic for the discussion at the meeting in February 1994 on the island of Capri signals? To quote Vattimo, who also employs the language of Heidegger, "What we took to be the *Uberwindung* [of religion] is no more than a *Verwindung*."[40] Are we beginning to think and question God not now within the metaphysics of *techne* or the atomic bomb (where technological development was still seen in terms of furnishing bigger and better tools for human usage) but in the hyper-realities of cyberspace (where technology is creating not tools but an environment)? In the recent film by the Wachelski brothers, *The Matrix*, Neo lays aside Baudrillard's text *Simulacra and Simulation* to embark on a discovery of Zion within the matrix. Maybe we are turning out of the question of where is God toward the question of who or what is God, again.

NOTES

1. Every interrogative pronoun installs a different set of noetic relations and assumptions, different forms of knowledge and, therefore, what would constitute an answer in order to silence the interrogation. "Where," for example, establishes a question implicated in notions of space and objects with respect to that space; "when" is implicated in temporal concerns; "who" is implicated into construals of personhood and the constitution of identity; "what" and "which" are also concerned with identity, calling upon and triggering received ideas about "thinghood," "species," the "real."

2. *Typography: Mimesis, Philosophy, Politics* (Cambridge, Mass.: Harvard University Press, 1989), p. 118.

3. Trans. Alan Bass (Chicago: University of Chicago Press, 1987). Like the "postcards" addressed by Derrida to a number of real or imaginary correspondents in this book, the questions are open for all to read, answer, and endlessly disseminate without any sovereign source or destiny.

4. Bruno Latour, in his *We Have Never been Modern* (trans. Catherine Porter [London: Harvester Wheatsheaf, 1993]), and Homi Bhabha, in his *The Location of Culture* [London: Routledge, 1994]), both view this radical pluralism of contemporary culture in terms of hybrids and hybridity.

5. *Confessions,* trans. Henry Chadwick (Oxford: Oxford University Press, 1991), p. 217. The questions themselves are distinctly Aristotelian.

6. What I am suggesting here is that self-consciousness is constituted by the primacy of the question, that the question initiates reflexive thinking and such thinking participates in grace. I am aware that this brings Hegel much closer to Augustine and have discussed this possibility elsewhere. See *Cities of God* (London: Routledge, 2000).

7. For Frege's discussion of "sentential questions" and "auditional questions" see Michael Dummet, *Frege's Philosophy of Language* (London: Duckworth, 1973), pp. 306–308, 336–339.

8. D. Lewis, *Convention* (Cambridge, Mass: Harvard University Press, 1969), p. 156.

9. John Lyons *Semantic,* vol. 2 (Cambridge: Cambridge University Press, 1977), p. 754. See also Ruth M. Kempron, *Semantic Theory* (Cambridge: Cambridge University Press, 1977), pp. 61–63, on both interrogatives and imperatives as "non-declaratives."

10. Lyons himself recognizes an important distinction between asking and posing a question. In posing a question there is the expression or externalization of a doubt. To ask a "question of someone is both to pose the question and, in doing so, to give some indication to one's addressee that he is expected to respond by answering the question that is posed. But the indication that the addressee is expected to give an answer is not part of the question itself" (p. 755). Some questions oblige us; some are deliberative.

Posing questions is close to what Lyons called x-questions (p. 757) in which there is an unknown quantity requiring an interrogative pronoun. These kind of questions do not have a yes-or-no structure. Linguists have gone much farther than modern philosophy in discussing and analyzing the nature of questions and questioning. For an exploration of the presuppositions of different kinds of questions, see also A. N. Prior and M. Prior, "Erotetic Logic," *Philosophical Review* 64 (1955): 43–59; and Lennart Aqvist, *A New Approach to the Logic of Questions* (Philosophical Studies: University of Uppsala, 1965).

11. *Summa Theologiae,* Pt. I, Q.1.Art.1: "It was therefore necessary that, besides philosophical science built up by reason there should be a sacred science learned through revelation." Aquinas then would disagree with Heidegger's categorical distinction between theology, which is associated with onto-theology, and the discourse of faith.

12. "Time is an order of successions. . . . Instants apart from things are nothing, and they only consist in the successive order of things." *Leibniz: Philosophical Writings* (London: Dent, 1973), pp. 211–212.

13. *Confessions,* p. 232. See also Roland J. Teske, S.J., *The Paradoxes of Time in Saint Augustine* (Milwaukee: Marquette University Press, 1996).

14. *Confessions,* p. 224.

15. See Mary Poovey, *The History of the Modern Fact: Problems of Knowledge in the Sciences of Wealth and Society* (Chicago: University of Chicago Press, 1998); Jonathan Sawday, *The Body Emblazoned: Dissection and the Human Body in Renaissance Culture* (London: Routledge, 1995); Steven Shapin and Simon Schaffer, *Leviathan and the Air-Pump* (Princeton: Princeton University Press, 1985) and Stephen Shapin, *A Social History of Truth: Civility and Science in Seventeenth-Century England* (Chicago: University of Chicago Press, 1994).

16. Jacques Derrida, "Faith and Knowledge: The Two Sources of 'Religion' at the

Limits of Reason Alone," in *Religion*, ed. Jacques Derrida and Gianni Vattimo, trans. Samuel Weber (Cambridge: Polity, 1998), p. 15

17. See Martin Heidegger, *Time and Being*, trans. Joan Stambaugh (New York: Harper and Row, 1972).

18. See Chapter 6, "The Church as the Erotic Community," in my *Cities of God*.

19. Derrida, "Faith and Knowledge," p. 64.

20. For an account of Ockham's conception of the omnipotence of the divine will with respect to the world, see Etienne Gilson, *The Unity of Philosophical Experience* (New York: Charles Scribner's Sons, 1937), pp. 61–91; and Marilyn McCord Adams, *William Ockham*, 2 vols. (Notre Dame: University of Notre Dame Press, 1987), pp. 1233–1297. For Ockham's concern with the presence and the mind-independent present, see pp. 853–899.

21. *Confessions*, pp. 253–260.

22. See Eric Alliez, *Capital Times*, trans. Georges Van Den Abbeele (Minneapolis: University of Minnesota Press, 1996), pp. 196–238. The thesis reflects thinking among Catholic theologians in the twentieth century: Henri de Lubac, *Corpus Mysticum: L'Eucharistie et L'Eglise au Moyen-Age* (Paris: Aubier-Montaigne, 1949); Hans Urs von Balthasar, *The Glory of the Lord*, V: *The Realm of Metaphysics in the Modern Age*, trans. Oliver Davies et al. (Edinburgh: T. & T. Clark, 1991), pp. 16–29; Michel de Certeau, *The Mystic Fable*, trans. Michael B. Smith (Chicago: University of Chicago Press, 1992); and Catherine Pickstock, *After Writing: The Liturgical Consummation of Philosophy* (Oxford: Blackwell, 1997).

23. See my "Allegoria: Reading as a Spiritual Exercise," *Modern Theology* 15, no. 3 (July 1991): 271–295; and Edward Booth, *Aristotelian Aporetic Ontology in Islamic and Christian Thinkers* (Cambridge: Cambridge University Press, 1983).

24. Jean-Luc Marion, *God without Being*, trans. Thomas A. Carlson (Chicago: University of Chicago Press, 1991), pp. 16–17.

25. *Confessions*, p. 282.

26. *Confessions*, p. 254.

27. I am indebted here to Simon Oliver and the unpublished paper he gave comparing motion in Plato and Newton.

28. *Confessions*, p. 301.

29. See my essay "Kenosis: Death, Discourse and Resurrection," in *Balthasar at the End of Modernity*, ed. Lucy Gardner, David Moss, Ben Quash, and Graham Ward (Edinburgh: T. & T. Clark, 1999), pp. 15–68.

30. See "White Ecstasy," trans. Frederick Christian Bauerschmidt and Catriona Hanley in *The Postmodern God*, ed. Graham Ward (Oxford: Blackwell, 1997), pp. 155–158.

31. Again there are echoes here of Hegel, which I believe are entirely appropriate.

32. Jean-Luc Nancy, *The Inoperative Community*, trans. Peter Connor et al. (Minneapolis: University of Minnesota Press, 1991).

33. Jean Baudrillard, *Symbolic Exchange and Death*, trans. Iain Hamilton Grant (London: Sage, 1993).

34. *Otherwise than Being, or Beyond Essence*, trans. A. Lingis (The Hague: Martinus Nijhoff, 1981).

35. That is, Sisyphus as the absurd hero conscious of his own condition. "His scorn of the gods, his hatred of death, and his passion for life won him that unspeakable penalty in which the whole being is exerted towards accomplishing nothing." Albert

Camus, *The Myth of Sisyphus and Other Essays,* trans. Justin O'Brien (London: Hamish Hamilton, 1955), p. 97.

36. Slavoj Zizek observes "the futile movement of the *objet a,*" relating it, at one point (p. 5), to Sisyphus. He adds "The *objet a* is precisely that surplus, that elusive make-believe . . . it is nothing at all, just an empty surface" (p. 8). *Looking Awry: An Introduction to Jacques Lacan through Popular Culture* (Cambridge: Mass.: Harvard University Press, 1991).

37. Derrida, "Faith and Knowledge," pp. 55–56.

38. Paul Ricoeur, *Oneself as Another,* trans. Kathleen Blamey (Chicago: University of Chicago Press, 1992), p. 355.

39. Martin Heidegger, *Identity and Difference,* trans. Joan Stambaugh (New York: Harper Row, 1969).

40. Gianni Vattimo, "The Trace of the Trace" in *Religion,* p. 79.

twelve

What Do I Love When I Love My God? Deconstruction and Radical Orthodoxy

John D. Caputo

In "Circumfession," Derrida cites the Tenth Book of the *Confessions*, in which Augustine asks, "What do I love when I love my God (*quid ergo amo cum deum [meum] amo)*"? (X, 7), upon which Derrida comments "Can I do anything other than translate this sentence by SA [St. Augustine] into my language . . . the change of meaning, or rather reference, defining the only difference of the '*meum*.' "[1] Thus presented, and it is a surprising presentation, deconstruction is to be construed as a lifelong work of love, indeed, a love of God, where everything turns on the determination of this "love" and of the "my" and of the name of "God." The form this question takes is interesting because it seems to go without saying, for Derrida as for Augustine, that we love God. "It is with no doubtful knowledge, Lord, but with utter certainty that I love You," Augustine had just said (X, 6).[2] Who would be so hard of heart, or so timid, vacillating, and mediocre a fellow as not to love God? The name of God is the name of everything we love and desire, the name of our heart's desire. So the question for Augustine and Derrida is not *whether* we love God but *what* we love when we love our God. For there are many things that we might mean by God and many things that we might confuse with God—such as our own ego, our own will, our own pleasures, our own opinions, our own religion, our own nation—all of which are very good at masquerading under the name of God. So everything depends upon what we love when we love our God.

In "Circumfession," Derrida's work is cast in a very different light, one that, if pursued rightly, lays to rest the recurrent charges of nihilism by which deconstruction is so regularly visited, as if Derrida were someone who just tears things down, who celebrates the ruins of modernity, without the slightest affirmative intentions. But this more Augustinian approach to deconstruction, and the seriousness with which Derrida has embraced Augustine's question, are viewed with suspicion by Graham Ward. While Ward proved himself a perceptive and appreciative reader of Derrida in an earlier work, *Barth, Derrida and the Language of Theology*,[3] he has altered his tone in "Questioning God," his contribution to the present volume. Here he argues that Augustine's *Confessions* and Derrida's "Circumfession" are separated by an abyss: by the abyss that separates aesthetics from ethics, hopelessness from hope, paralysis from action, being lost and adrift from eschatology, and even, heaven save us, "onanism" or *coitus interruptus* from lovers with more serious intentions.[4] The result of Derrida's appropriation of the *Confessions* is what Ward calls an "aesthetics of questioning," where questioning is undertaken for the sheer masturbatory pleasure of questioning or seeking without the expectation or the desire of bringing this search to fruition, while Augustine's *Confessions* embody an "ethics of questioning," enclosed by trust and hope and weightiness of purpose. Derrida's is a hermeneutic me-ontology, interpretations that lead nowhere, as opposed to Augustine's hermeneutic ontology, seeking the living God. Derrida is giving himself pleasure, *jouissance*, while Augustine has an earnest ethical aim. Augustine's question arises within the framework of realizable eschatological hope, while Derrida's adaptation of it deals with unrealizable regulative ideals that leave us locked in aporias, unable to move, and subjugated to the tyrannous demand of infinite responsibility. Derrida's questioning is undertaken in order to expose the undecidability in things and to wallow in paralysis. For what is undecidability if not another name for what Hegel called a bad infinite, one that goes on and on without getting anywhere, resulting in hopeless desire and unhappy consciousness? Derrida's questioning is the onanism of an "absolute interruption,"[5] which disseminates its seeds on the desert sands of *khora*, even as it is sustained by the pleasure of not having what it desires. There is no

> entrustment or deliverance of one's own judgment to the judgment of the Good, the Just, the Beautiful, and the True. Here there is only the starship *Enterprise* moving off into deeper space in search of further textual adventures. But then moving is always a pseudo-traveling: For what is discovered in this thinking through of aporia itself, since no one can take measurement in the infinite?

Derrida's question does not "participate in the circulation of an economy of love and fealty," an economy of hope, prayer, and faith. Finally, the question that Augustine asks arises from a history and a tradition that bear continuous witness to its Addressee, while Derrida cannot tell us to whom he is speaking.

In sum, for Ward: (1) Derrida's "Circumfession" is devoid of faith, hope, and love in any seriously ethical or religious sense; (2) it is onanistic, deriving aesthetic pleasure from not having what it asks for; (3) it issues in the paralysis of undecidability and the bad infinite; (4) it does not know to whom it circumfesses.

Graham Ward is a lively, literate, and interesting writer who has engaging things to say about religion, literature, and the world of hyper-reality. His *Barth, Derrida and the Language of Theology* is a careful study that makes a number of astute comments about deconstruction and contributes significantly to our understanding of its relevance for theology. So it puzzles me to see him here embrace a reading of Derrida that adopts a stereotype of deconstruction—as a form of "aestheticism"—that he avoided and even warned us against in *BDLT*.[6] His present reading cuts short the chance of seeing what he had previously gone a long way to open up—"the theological significance of Derrida's work" (*BDLT*, 10), the possibility of a productive communication between deconstruction and "the language of theology." In what follows I will propose an explanation of how Graham Ward is led from the one view to the next—from seeing in Derrida what he calls a "theology" or "spirituality" of questioning (*BDLT*, 226) to what he now called an "aesthetics of questioning"—and then offer a rejoinder to his reading. Along the way I will venture some reflections on deconstruction and radical orthodoxy.

Derrida, Ward, and Theology

In *BDLT*, Ward starts out from the similarities between the projects of Barth and Levinas, each of whom is concerned with the problem of the "wholly other," with how to say and unsay the transcendence that stresses our language to the limits. Barth's theology of "the Word and words," of the Divine Word and human language, corresponds to Levinas's philosophy of *le dire* and *le dit*, each dealing with how a transcendent and infinite event both inspires and ruptures the immanence of finite human speech. Ward turns for help to Derrida's "negotiations" with Levinas, his critical reading and reinscription of Levinas within the terms of *différance*, in order to point out the difference between Barth and Levinas and the greater proximity, on this point at least, of Barth to Derrida. For Derrida's essays on Levinas demonstrate that a pure transcendence that would be *tout autre* pure and simple is impossible and even incoherent (the wholly other would always have to be wholly other "than" something, with which there would always be some analogy). The wholly other would necessarily implicate Levinas in some form of "analogical similarity" between the same and the other, and *différance* is the name of what imposes that necessity. Ward argues (1) that Derrida's recognition of the necessity of analogy and mediation permits at best a quasi-transcendence; (2) that Derrida's insistence on a certain structural betrayal of the wholly other by the very language that proclaims it, which is organized under the notion of the "economy of *différance*" ("betrayal" then became a central theme for Levinas in *Otherwise than Being*), supplies the "strategy" of Barth's dialectical theology, the deepest dialectical law of Barth's language, which is the *analogia fidei*. God's Word is mediated to us in human words, which are as necessary for this mediation as they are incapable of the mediation they are called upon to make. Seeing that the language of theology is both necessary and impossible, requiring the possibility of the impossible (*BDLT*, 155, 233, 256), Barth is in fact executing the very "rhetorical strategy" (*BDLT*, 247) that is being theorized by Derrida. God can only be understood in God's terms; we can only understand God in our terms. God is God, and humans are human (*BDLT*, 206). For Barth, the icon of the invisible God is the man who bore the proper name Jesus Christ, which is the point of mediation where the impossible becomes possible (*BDLT*, 233). Theological language thus does not crash against the rocks of "this incommensurable aporia" but, on the contrary, is set into motion by it (*BDLT*, 245). Just as Derrida would say that "we begin *by* the impossible," that we only get going when we see that it is impossible to move, Barth thinks that theology is set in motion by an undomesticatable alterity, by the dialectic without reconciliation of letting human words resonate with the Word even as we affirm their failure to do so. Both the Word and words, saying and the Said, God and man; it is not a question of choosing between them.

The identification of the structure of aporia constitutes a recognition on Derrida's part that "language is always and ineradicably theological" (*BDLT*, 9), that is, marked by an aporia that is the very life not only of language but of theology. But we must also remember that deconstruction is not theology, does not quite get as far as theology, but remains in suspense, at the threshold of the doors of faith and theology. If Barth's theology can be reframed in terms of *différance*, Derrida's philosophy can be reframed in terms of Barth's theology (*BDLT*, 175) and thereby led to transcendence. Each supplements the other. Throughout this analysis, Ward observes a fairly clear and even traditional distinction between philosophy and theology, where the former is marked by open-ended inquiry and the latter is marked by faith. If, for Ward, only faith can break this undecidability, end the endless deferral, and determine that there is something wholly other, for Derrida faith would always be a dogmatism (*BDLT*, 188–189). "Only dogmatic assertion can close the analysis" (*BDLT*, 211). In Derrida's democracy, all differences have equal rights (*BDLT*, 216). Philosophy keeps the question of the other of language alive, while faith determines that it is God, which is why Mark Taylor has precipitously determined deconstruction to be "a/theology" (*BDLT*, 225), a point that I too have complained about elsewhere.[7] If undecidability keeps Derrida always stuck

this side of faith, in Barth the anti-nomical clash of transcendence and immanence, of the Word and words, sets faith in motion.

In the final pages of his book, Ward notes a "change of tone" (*BDLT*, 221),
"a new note sounding" (*BDLT*, 229) in Derrida's more recent work, one more
congenial to and even reminiscent of theology than the earlier analyses of
différance, more "apocalyptic," and turned toward hope, the promise, the "yes,
yes," and the *viens*, a point upon which my own work on Derrida in *Prayers
and Tears* turns. This is the tone neither of "an atheist nor a nihilist," but of an
"agnosticism which must be open to the possibility of an impossible answer,"
marked by an "interminable openness" to an Other that we cannot determine
(*BDLT*, 220). By relentlessly pressing an open-ended question and desire—
"for the desire is the operation of this question"—Derrida "draws alongside"
the language of theology (*BDLT*, 225), constituting a certain "'theology' or
'spirituality' of questioning" (*BDLT*, 226). Ward points out that, like Heidegger
himself, questioning itself is put in question in virtue of a more primordial
"promise" lodged in the heart of language, a promise that precedes every
question, every assertion, to which every question is always already a response
(*BDLT*, 229–230).[8] Deconstruction is not paralysis (*BDLT*, 232) but a movement, a "healthy agnosticism" that draws alongside theology by situating us
between the promise of God's presence and its impossibility (*BDLT*, 232–233)
in a way that cries out for the supplement of faith. With "self-ironizing alertness" to the inadequacy of the language in which it is lodged, Christian faith
follows the traces of the promise—"I am with you always" (Matthew 28:20), the
promise of Emmanuel, God-with-us—recalling it and retracing it repeatedly,
"yes, yes," circulating between memory and the future (*BDLT*, 242–243).
Derrida has identified what he calls "the performative structure of the text in
general *as* promise," the "archi-promise" inscribed in all language, while theology carries out that performance in the name of Jesus Christ. That indeed is
why language itself has a theological character, is disturbed by a theological
restlessness. However, Derrida's "irreducible openness to the trace of a promise" is not to be confused with faith, which is a commitment over and beyond
recognizing the structure of textuality, a commitment to the Christian Word
proclaimed in the Church (*BDLT*, 251), from which Derrida will always
maintain his distance. Barth then would supplement deconstruction with the
movement of faith before which it hesitates, always trembling on the threshold, never crossing over.

Barth, Derrida and the Language of Theology is a perceptive study and
a significant addition to the literature of deconstruction and theology with
which I am in considerable agreement. Its central contribution for me is
the argument that by identifying the structure of language in terms of an
archi-promise, deconstruction has identified the fundamentally theological—I
would prefer to say religious—character of language itself. That goes to the
heart of what Derrida means by a "religion without religion." That also means

that the distinction between the sacred and the secular cannot be maintained in its purity (*BDLT*, 252), which is a point, perhaps the central point, on which both Derrida and radical orthodoxy agree (p. 67, this volume). Apart from the fact that the "secular" is already a religious category, framed from the standpoint of religion, the so-called secular world is always already inhabited by religious motifs such as the promise, an argument that is also at work in *Specters of Marx*, where Derrida claims that Marx has chased away one ghost too many.

The one point with which, for present purposes, I would take issue in *BDLT* is Ward's disjunction between faith and undecidability. Ward holds that Heidegger and Derrida have the same view of, and make the same distinction between, philosophy and faith. Just as Heidegger says the "thought of Being" would be closed down by faith, so also Derrida, on Ward's view, in virtue of the notion of "undecidability," advocates an endless questioning that would be arrested by faith (*BDLT*, 183, 226, 256). But in fact Derrida thinks that, precisely because of his notion of undecidability, everything begins and ends in faith while, on this point at least, by distinguishing faith and "thinking," Heidegger is being faithful to a rigorous Enlightenment distinction rejected by Derrida, who is being more "Jewgreek" on this point. "*Je ne sais pas. Il faut croire*" literally enframes *Memoirs of the Blind*, constituting both its opening and closing lines. Derrida does not oppose faith and reason, no more than he opposes the religious and secular, because he thinks that what we call reason turns on faith even as and precisely because he thinks that language is structured by the archi-promise. The operative distinction for Derrida is not between religious faith and philosophical reason but between a more deeply lodged structural faith, more indeterminate and determinable, and the determinate faiths of the concrete messianisms. Ward puts this very point well when he says at the end of his book, "His trace of a gift, a promise, a yes, a hope bears none of the *specifics* of Christian proclamation or Jewish eschatology" (*BDLT*, 256, my emphasis). Deconstruction is filled with faith and turns on the gift, the promise, the yes, the hope of something to come, but it always maintains a certain ironic distance from and alertness to the *specific* or determinate messianisms, be they Christian or Jewish, Heideggerian or Marxist. But that is *not* to say that deconstruction leaves us stuck in undecidability, on the threshold, unable to make a choice, questioning but never deciding, recognizing an archi-promise but unable to act on or respond to it, like a lover too timid to take the plunge. Rather, it means that we are always responding and at the same always asking what we are responding to, always choosing and at the same asking what we have chosen or has chosen us, what we are doing in the midst of the concrete decisions we always and invariably make. We are, just as he says in "Circumfession," always asking what do I love when I love my God? Deconstruction is not a philosophy of undecidability *tout court*, but of deciding-in-the-midst-of-undecidability, where for once I invoke these Heideggerian hyphens with utter seriousness. Barth does not differ from Derrida because

Barth decides and Derrida remains on the threshold, but rather because Barth casts his lot with a specific messianism, with the proper name and historical determinacy of Jesus Christ, while Derrida casts his lot with the love of a justice to come that *can always be determined otherwise,* of which Jesus Christ—or Judaism or Islam or the Buddhist great compassion—would also be a historically specific determination.

Undecidability is not indecision but the condition of possibility of a decision. The opposite of "undecidability" for Derrida is not "decision" but "decidability," which means programmability or formalizability. Derrida first came upon the term in connection with Gödel's theorem about the undecidability of formal systems, a theorem that Derrida says delimits "the ideal itself of decidability," that is, of "exhaustive deductivity."[9] If a decision is decidable in this sense, the decision can be made by formal rules that supply a decision procedure, by an algorithm, say, or by a mechanical process, and no human judgment or "decision" is needed; what we would then need is not good people but good software. The earliest antecedent of the idea is the undecidability that inhabits the ethical decision in Aristotle's *Ethics,* which differentiates ethical reasoning from mathematical reasoning, which is why I have elsewhere spoken of a certain form of "meta-*phronesis.*"[10] Without undecidability there is no decision or responsibility or faith. With faith, we do not cross over the "threshold" of undecidability and *leave it behind;* undecidability is not extinguished but persists as the medium in which faith, as the substance of things that are not seen, continually subsists. That is why Derrida says to Ward in the Roundtable:

> As to the aporia, on the one hand, I often say, perhaps not enough last night, that the aporia is not a paralyzing structure, something that simply blocks the way with a simple negative effect. The aporia is the experience of responsibility. It is only by going through a set of contradictory injunctions, impossible choices, that we make a choice. If I know what I have to do, if I know in advance what has to be done, then there is no responsibility. For the responsible decision to be envisaged or taken, we have to go through pain and aporia, a situation in which I do not know what to do. (p. 62)

This is not to say that a decision for Derrida is decisionistic or the work of some *übermenschlich* ego or phallic will, because a decision for Derrida is always the decision of the *other in me,* constituting a "passive decision," the decision of the other. "Of the absolute other in me, the other as the absolute that decides on me in me."[11] My decision is my response to a solicitation by the other in the singularity of the situation in which I find myself "before" the other, in Augustine's sense of *coram.*

In "Questioning God," Ward's contribution to the present volume, his view of faith and undecidability comes home to roost. Here Ward replays this same scenario, this time between Augustine and Derrida. Now Barth is characterized as a dualist who thinks of the Incarnation on the model of an alien invasion of earth, so that the affinity of Barth with Derrida, established earlier, now constitutes a criticism of both of them vis-à-vis the happy harmony of Augustine's analogy of being. This time the astute analyses of deconstruction are left at the door, undecidability is caricatured as onanism, and the judgment of Derrida is severe and uncompromising, indeed, I would say dogmatic. In my view, Ward has been misled by an untenable view of undecidability and consequently of the nature of faith and the promise in deconstruction. Thus, in what follows, I will go to go back to the structure of "promise" in deconstruction in order to make plain the place of faith, hope, and love—to adopt the categories of St. Paul—in Derrida's work and, in so doing, to counter Ward's current take on Derrida.

The questions Graham Ward raises are important and they are, in addition, in a manner characteristic of his work, clearly put. That is why I bother to contest them. It is also perfectly true that Derrida "quite rightly pass[es] for an atheist," as he says in "Circumfession."[12] So Graham Ward is right to say that we do not want to "theologize Derrida's work," to co-opt deconstruction for religion's purposes, and that, just as there are important differences between Barth and Derrida, so there are important differences between Augustine's question in the *Confessions* and Derrida's reinscription of that question in his "Circumfession." These differences require careful clarification and articulation, which is a task that I will take up in the final section of these remarks.

The Promise

Deconstruction, in a manner *not unlike* biblical religion itself, is called into being by a promise. Deconstruction arises, Derrida says, "from a certain experience of the promise."[13] Deconstruction is the affirmation of the promise. The promise is implicit in Derrida's presentation on forgiveness at the beginning of this volume: To speak is always also to ask forgiveness for our failure to deliver on the promise that language is. But who is promising what to whom? What are the "specifics" of this deconstructive "covenant"? The answer to that question is that deconstruction is or proceeds from a great, sweeping yes, a *oui, oui*, to the promise that "language" is, the promise that language makes, or that is made in language, that is embedded in the makeup of language. This is not a specific and determinate promise, like the promises that political candidates make during their campaigns, but the very structure of the promise itself, which precedes, accompanies, and follows upon all the specific promises that are made by individual conscious agents who make promises. This is the promise that is built right into language itself, if language has a self, and takes place as soon as we open our mouths—or turn on our word processors— in order to address the other. We must be careful here, of course, not to hypostasize language, as if "language" were "someone," and we must see exactly what Derrida is getting at. The promise is not made by some identifiable somebody about a specific ontical content but is embedded in the event of language, where language, which calls upon us, calls to us, and makes us promises, is taken to have a certain prophetic or messianic character. As Ward quite rightly pointed out earlier on, "language is always and ineradicably theological" (BDLT, 9).

In Being and Time, §44c, Heidegger said that the skeptic is "refuted," indeed, does not even need to be refuted, by the very existence of Dasein as being-in-the-world, because as soon as Dasein comes to be, and long before offering any "refutations of scepticism," long before any propositions or argument about truth and skepticism are formed, the event of truth as unconcealment happens and any possible skeptical denial of truth is undone. As soon as the skeptic comes to be, skepticism is undone. By a similar strategy, Derrida thinks that as soon as we open our mouth, we bear witness to the promise that language is. Inasmuch as this promise is not a determinate speech act, this promise is nothing egological. It is not so much something that I make as it is something that makes me, that is made to me, that opens my mouth, to which I am always already responding, constituting "a promise that has committed me even before I begin the briefest speech."[14] The "place" of deconstruction, the place in which it takes place, in which everything it asks and analyzes and agonizes over takes place, is the space or land of the promise. We might even say that deconstruction is sustained by its hope in the promised land.

So for Derrida, beyond, or rather before, the analysis or the enactment of any specific promise, deconstruction speaks *"from out of the experience"*—to borrow a Heideggerianism—of an "archi-promise":[15]

> I will thus not speak of this or that promise, but of that which, as necessary as it is impossible, inscribes us by its trace in language—before language. From the moment I open my mouth, I have already promised; or rather, and sooner, the promise has seized the *I* which promises to speak to the other, to say something. . . . The promise is older than I am. . . . It is older than I am or than we are. In fact, it renders possible every present discourse on presence.

As soon as I open my mouth, even if it is to denounce promising or even if it is to lie, I bear witness to the promise, to the structure of the promise. We who speak are the people of the promise, constituted by a certain analogate of the Shema, by an "archi-originary promise which establishes us *a priori* as people who are responsible for speech."[16] This is not a promise issuing from an intentional act and monitored for its fidelity by the conscious ego but the very promise that calls us, that calls our speaking, into being. Up to a point, as Ward shows in *BDLT*, this is one of Derrida's most Heideggerian moments, picking up on the saying of language,[17] what is being said in and by language rather than by a particular speaker. That is why Derrida can adapt Paul De Man's *die Sprache verspricht*, which is itself De Man's adaptation of Heidegger's *die Sprache spricht*. Not "language speaks" but "language promises," language is the promise.[18]

The promise of what? And specifically who—or what—is doing the promising? And why should we believe or trust him or her or it? Can there even be a promise if it is not made by someone in particular?

The promise is the promise of language itself, the promise issuing from language, which promises us the "other." Every discourse harbors within it the promise of the other, which is manifold: the other to which our language by its structure as language *refers*, the other one *whom* we address, the other one *by whom* we are addressed, and indeed the *other others* who witness our conversation, if only at times by being left out of it. To address the other is to promise to give the other the truth, to speak the truth, as a structural matter, for even if we are lying through our teeth, we depend upon the structure of *parrhesia*, of telling all, of hiding nothing, to get away our with our dissemblance. To speak or write is at least, as a structural matter, to purport to tell the truth, even if we are constantly perjuring ourselves. Likewise, to be addressed *by* the other is to be promised a new world, for the very idea of the other is that of the coming of someone from the other shore, from a place where I have never been, who can tell me of things I have not seen or heard, like a traveler from a distant land.[19] The very idea of the other is "magisterial," not maieutic, as Kierkegaard and Levinas have both argued, where the word coming from the other is a word of instruction and I am, as we say in English, "all ears."

But, as De Man also argues, *die Sprache verspricht* can also mean *verspricht*, mis-speaks. That means that language also fails to deliver the goods, not only when the other is lying to us or is in good faith but gets it wrong, but in the structural sense that language signs and traces things but is not to be confused with the things themselves. That is why Derrida can say that we are, as a structural matter, always asking for forgiveness. Language is the promise of things which also slip away from its grip, their absence being constitutive of a sign or a trace. Language is the memory and hope of things that are not now present. The very ideas of promise and of hoping in a promise is structured around deferral and absence, and they arise as ways of addressing this absence. A word is a like an arrow, not only Husserl's arrow of intentionality, but also an arrow of our longing, as Nietzsche might have said, pointing toward something that always slips away, delivering something to us that we do not quite have. The name of God is not God but the name of our desire for God, the name that points us to God. The other promised to us in and by language always remains out-standing, still to come, still promised, structurally, for as long as we are speaking, rather like a Messiah who does not show up.[20] To speak is to succumb to messianic longing, or rather to embrace and affirm it.

How does the promise issued in and by language arise? Who is making it? How is it authorized? What authority does it have? Why should we believe it?

"Our language" is not ours, not if that means our private possession or invention. If our language is ours, it is not because it belongs to us but because we belong to it. We are delivered over to our language and its mode of disclosing things. We grow up within it, inherit its presuppositions, sometimes curling up within its insights and intuitions and sometimes straining against its limits and feeling around within it for openings to allow the coming of something else. For language is the event of the coming of the other—that is the "calling" of language, its true vocation—rather than of more of the same. Very early on, in *Of Grammatology*, Derrida said, "We must begin *wherever we are*, and the thought of the trace, which cannot not take the scent into account, has already taught us that it was impossible to justify a point of departure absolutely. *Wherever we are*: in a text where we already believe ourselves to be."[21] Where else would we begin? How else could we begin? Like Kierkegaard's poor existing individual, we are utterly incapable of finding some absolute beginning, some absolutely originary point of departure, some completely presuppositionless starting point, some tabula rasa unmarked by the traces of anything that preceded us. We begin *with* the trace, *within* the trace, within a set of traces, in the text of a context which has us before we have it. As soon as I come to be I discover I am already there, as Heidegger says; answering a call I never heard, Levinas adds. We begin wherever we are—in the midst of a language, of a tradition, a heritage, of a complex and ultimately unfathomable web of intersecting, interweaving, and conflicting beliefs and practices, an inescapable cacophony of voices and counter-voices, a crazy quilt that we will never succeed in simply unstitching or simply bringing into harmony.

We begin in the promise, in whatever set of promises in which we find ourselves, in a set of conflicting promises. We are called upon and called into being by the cacophony of promises that have accumulated in our language, or languages, in our tradition, or traditions, in the irreducible multiplex that forms our world, that forms and informs us, that gives us things to hope for and things to fear, that encourages us and discourages us, in the gifts and poisons that our traditions harbor. "Language," then, is not "someone," not some hypostasis or super-person, but the multiple views of ourselves and our world embedded in the multiplicity of texts and contexts, histories and traditions, beliefs and practices, in which we "find ourselves" (*sich befinden*), which Jaspers and Heidegger called many years ago our "situation."

The radical orthodoxists mistakenly accuse deconstruction of a certain "indifferentism." Beginning with the idea that deconstruction is a philosophy of "differences," of differential spacing, which is true, they wrongly conclude that it is structurally incapable of differentiating among the play of differences and hence that it is deprived of the means to express a preference for one thing rather than another, which is not true.[22] This mistaken view seems to be based upon taking a short-sighted view of the famous 1967 essay "Différance," while neglecting the import of what came after that essay in the subsequent three decades since it was written, as also upon exaggerating the influence upon Derrida of Nietzsche, as opposed to Levinas. Derrida does not for a moment think that we simply splash about randomly and with abandon in this complex, multiplex sea of indifferent differences as if it were just a bad infinite. Graham Ward himself is aware of this in *BDLT* and cites a pertinent text in this regard.

In the "Afterword" to *Limited Inc.*, in a passage rejecting the charge of relativism, Derrida says:[23]

> To the extent to which it—by virtue of its discourse, its socio-institutional situation, its language, the historical inscription of its gestures, etc.—is itself rooted in a given context (but, as always, in one that is differentiated and mobile), it does not renounce (it neither can nor ought to do so) the "values" that are dominant in this context (for example, that of truth, etc.)

We associate ourselves with what is best in our tradition, or rather what we judge to be best, in our tradition, or rather in our *traditions*. For the idea of "the" tradition is a fiction, already a very violent and radical foreshortening and simplifying of what is handed down to us, of what we are handed over to. The whole idea of "*the one* history itself . . . *the one* tradition" needs to be "contested at its root," Derrida says.[24] To have a tradition is to have a responsibility to read and interpret and to know how to choose perspicaciously among its several strands:[25]

> An inheritance is never gathered together, it is never one with itself. Its presumed unity, if there is one, can consist only in the *injunction* to *reaffirm by choosing*. "One must" means *one must* filter, sift, criticize, one must sort several different possibles that inhabit the same injunction. . . . If the readability of a legacy were given, natural, transparent, univocal, if it did not call for and at the same time defy interpretation, we would never have anything to inherit from it.

That means that "conservatives" who want to cleave to what is "handed down" to us, let us say, to the best that has been said and written, have already made a "liberal" use of the tradition and have undertaken a series of risky choices. They may think, for example, that what is best is found among the "Fathers" of "the Church," a view that will not be shared by all. They have sorted through the multiplex of tradition and decided just what it is that the tradition is saying, just which of its many voices are the "best" and hence are worthy to be heeded and responded to. For *we* are responsible for the calls to which we say we are responding. The truth is that we associate ourselves, we try to associate ourselves, with what is best, with what we take to be the best, in our tradition, in our several and conflicting traditions, what we hope and pray is the best it has to offer. In that sense, Derrida too is a very conservative person.[26] For we love the good. Who would be so hard of heart as not to love the good? Even when what we love is as bad as bad can be, it is precisely insofar as we think, or make ourselves think, that it is good that we love it. That is why the question is never whether we love the good, or our God, but *what* we love (or *who*) when we love our God.

So even though we begin wherever we are, and where we "are" is wherever we "find ourselves," namely, tossed about in a sea of irreducible and conflicting differences, we do not begin with *just anything*, nor do we for a moment think that one thing is just as good as any another, which is one of the misconceptions that guides a good deal of the radical orthodoxist misinterpretation of deconstruction, which misconstrues the historical side of deconstruction as pure historicism. On the contrary, we are—this is where we are and where we begin—for the most part shielded from the full effect of the play of differences by the sheltering effects of family, community, and nation, by the highly defined choices that are always already built into the language that opens our mouth and into the books that are put into our hands, all of which collectively filters the flow of differences and selects among them for us and thereby gives our lives their initial form and shape and direction, of which any subsequent form will be a modification. Furthermore, insofar as we love the good, and we love our God, and we are on the look out for the good, the better, the best, we *gladly associate* ourselves with that with which we have been, willy-nilly, *always already associated.* We neither can nor ought to *not* associate ourselves with them. It belongs to our structure as historical beings to love and embrace that with which we are always and already associated, to prefer those who are closest to us. That is what it means to be a situated and historical being.

So now we get a better idea of who is promising what to whom. Our languages and traditions are built around the messianic structure of the promise and we are responding to their multiple promissory notes, which are not one. We have been promised fabulous things by them, things that dazzle us and compel our love—things such as "justice" and "democracy," "friendship" and "hospitality," the "gift" and "forgiveness," and "love"—let us not forget "love," which is one of our very best words, one of language's highest promises—and, let us also not forget, "God." The name of God is one that Derrida is intent on "saving," for we are always asking ourselves "What do I love when I love my God"? To open our mouth is to respond to the promises that our languages and traditions make to us, to be seduced by their charms, for our languages and traditions awaken our desire and hold out to us promises of things of which we can only dream.

I am thus proposing that we conceive of deconstruction, for the purposes of its present dispute with radical orthodoxy, as involving a twofold movement. The first moment I will call *historical association.* Deconstruction should be viewed, first, as a work of *associating* ourselves with, or of being already associated with, of being lodged and installed within, the powerful and compelling words that have been handed down to us, words that provoke us before we invoke them, that summon us, that summon up what is best in us, that call upon us for response. Why? And why do we settle on some words and not certain others? I do not believe there is a general formula with which to answer that question. It is answered in the singularity of each heart and in the singularity of the circumstance within which each of us finds ourselves. But insofar as such a question can be answered at all, the answer might be, without being impudent, because they are *there*. They are *given*, or, as Graham Ward would might say, they are *fore-given*, given in advance. We are formed and shaped by them.

We are, I would say, "made to love them," trading on the double sense that "made to" has in English. We are "made to" love them in the sense of "forced" by the force of circumstances, because the fore-given has the advantage of being there in advance, of being the first name on the ballot, like decisions that have been made for us in advance, before we arrived on the scene or had a chance to vote, without our ever having been consulted. But we are also "made to" love them in the sense that we have been "made *for*" love, brought into being by our love of the good, of God, which is the name of what we love. That is a phenomenological observation, a description of the structure of desire, of which the biblical idea that Augustine has so brilliantly worked out in the *Confessions*—that you have made us for yourself, O Lord, and our hearts will not rest until they rest in you (*Conf.* I, 1)—is a specific form. We are looking for love—that is the structure of our desire—and these are the first and most lovable things to present themselves to our love, and we fall head over heels in love with them. We are lovers, madly in love with the gift of what is given and fore-given.

We do not begin randomly, indifferently, because that would not be to begin at all; that would be a completely abstract, de-situated and historyless beginning that would not succeed in taking a single step forward, rather like a mime on a stage who makes a splendid show of moving while remaining all the while in place. We begin wherever we are, in a definite language and circumstance, shaped and formed by its determinate historical resources, moved by its motions, driven by the energy and dynamism of its loves. A tradition forms because we love something, and the love catches on, and we want to repeat what we love, to say yes to it, again and again. The *oui, oui* is the origin of tradition, and there are as many traditions or different strands in tradition as there are ways to say yes. Otherwise the tradition is sustained by violence, which it *also* is. That also happens, all the time, so that the bigger and the more prestigious the tradition, the harder it is to disentangle the violence and the love; it would be difficult, as an historical matter, to find one without the other.

That is why there is a second movement in deconstruction, one that arises precisely in order to remain faithful to the first movement, which means to remain faithful to the promise. For deconstructive thought and practice is *also* a work of dissociating itself from these names, in a movement that I will call *messianic dissociation,* which thus prevents these names from freezing over, from hardening and contracting themselves within their present limits, from becoming too prestigious and too containing. If the first moment, historical association, has to do with the *fore-given*, the second movement has to do with the *un-fore-seeable*, which is *never given*.

Let us illustrate this in terms of the issue of forgiveness, which is the theme of Derrida's address. In "To Forgive: The Unforgivable and the Imprescriptible," Derrida makes reference in a parenthetical remark to a situation in which he is "both in and *against* the concept of forgiveness, in and beyond, or against the idea of forgiveness that we inherit—and whose legacy we must question, perhaps contest the legacy while inheriting from it—and this is a reflection on inheritance that we are beginning here" (this volume, pp. 34–35). We begin with the inherited concept of forgiveness which we love and which we contest, both together. In the Roundtable, he says in answer to Kevin Hart, "I found the word and the concept, and a certain number of conflicts surrounding the concept in our tradition, in a number of traditions. This can be the object of knowledge, and from within this possible knowledge, I discover this extraordinary excess that I mentioned a moment ago" (this volume, p. 53). We begin in the tradition of "forgiveness" that we inherit, from the long and complex history of theological reflection on forgiveness in Judaism and Christianity and Islam, from the legal history of the king's or the state's right to grant clemency, and so forth. We love this concept of forgiveness, and then out of love we subject that tradition to a deconstructive analysis, by virtue of which we ask if there is not a *promise* within that tradition, an excess or messianic promise of a forgiveness to come that the tradition does not make good on, a "force that demands that forgiveness be granted just where the inherited and traditional concept argues that forgiveness may not or cannot be given," namely, in the case of the unforgivable. Still, this is not a demand that Derrida imposes on the traditional concept, but an aporetic or auto-deconstructibility that stirs within the classical concept. For even when we encounter something that is unforgivable in classical terms, still, Derrida says, "There is in forgiveness, in the very meaning of forgiveness, a force, a desire, an impetus, a movement, an appeal (call it what you will) that demands that forgiveness be granted" (this volume, p. 28), a force that he calls in this lecture "hyperbolic" and that I am calling here "messianic," an immanent force, internal to the dynamic of forgiveness that will not be contained by the classical conditions. Forgiveness thus is possible "only where it seems to be impossible, before the un-forgivable, and possible only when grappling with the im-possible" (this volume, p. 35). The very thing that the traditional concept takes to be impossible and the end of forgiveness is the condition of its possibility and its genuine beginning, whereas forgiving the venial and forgivable is hardly forgiving at all. We begin with the inherited concept and then by a deconstructive analysis we explore, unpack, release the messianic promise that the tradition contains but cannot contain, a promise that is astir in the auto-deconstructing tensions and aporias by which the classical concept is constituted.

That is why this messianic goes hand in hand with a sort of upbeat Babelianism and felicitous and very biblical or messianic "nominalism." The radical orthodoxists take to task William of Ockham,[27] who divides with Duns Scotus the dubious honor of assisting at the dawning of the doom of modernity, but in fact the view of divine omnipotence that they are complaining about goes back to the beginning of the high medieval ages, not the end, to Peter Damian's treatise *de divina omnipotentia*, where Damian defends the view that a world created by God cannot and does not offer any "ousiological resistance," as one might say, to the rule of God. That is something that is quite consistently testified to by the New Testament, in which the crippled are made straight, the lepers made whole, and the dead rise from their graves, not to mention the scandal of forgiveness, all of which seems to me have precious little to do with the Hellenistic essentialism defended by the radical orthodoxists. The biblical conception of the radical revisability of the things—the radical renewal of the earth and the transformation of the human heart—what I would call the "meta-noetic" structure of things in biblical religion, this felicitous and Babelian nominalism, is far bettered captured by the notion of "deconstructibility" or "auto-deconstructibility" than by the metaphysical essentialism defended by Ward.[28]

For "essences" are stills that have been cut from the flow of historical process, frozen moments of desire that want to contain or shut down the movement of hope, of hope against hope, of hope for something that eye hath not seen nor ear heard, closing off the dynamics of messianic desire itself. That is also why this "hyperbolic ethics," which turns on a hyperbolic love of things we love, with names such as "forgiveness" (or the "gift," "hospitality" or "friendship"), are not, as Graham Ward suggests, a matter of "regulative ideals." For a regulative ideal retains the mark of a fixed goal and determinate Idea, which is approached asymptotically over time, which puts a lid on our hope and contains it within the horizon of some historically limited ideal. Essences and regulative ideals are futile attempts to contain and stabilize the *becoming* of the *to come*, the hyperbolic force or impetus or desire, "call it what you will," which is so radical that when we speak of, say, the "democracy to come" the "to come" is more important than the "democracy." We cannot be sure at all that the democracy to come, the democracy we long for and desire, will in fact be or be called "democracy,"[29] or that we will not someday, in the name of forgiveness, have to dispense with the word "forgiveness." Or "deconstruction": just as, of course, as Ward contemplates with some satisfaction, it will be "beyond deconstruction" and *différance* (this volume, p. 286). But all this is so far removed from Ward's portrait of despair, hopelessness, onanism, and paralysis in "Questioning God" as to constitute its complete opposite.

That is also why the idea of radical orthodoxy is for me in the strictest and most rigorous terms incoherent, for the "radical" strains against and bursts the seams of the "orthodox." "Radical" is a word I love—I love radical hermeneutics so much that I want even more[30]—but the energy of something radical is contained and repressed by the "orthodox." The orthodox is the *given* and *foregiven*; the standard form; the straight rod of consensus; the ninety-nine that are found, not the one who is lost; the common teaching, not the coming of the other one, from the other shore, which eye has not seen nor ear heard, not yet. The very energy of the to come, which drives our love and drives the radical, shatters the limits of the orthodox, which seeks to contain the radical and make it safe. That is also why, I might add—since "violence" is a concern of radical orthodoxy—I do not see how any religious tradition or theological language can take shape *without* violence[31] (particularly one, God save us, bearing the name "radical orthodoxy"), whether institutionally or in the readings it makes of texts which differ from its point of view, unless it is through and through marked by thinking and acting in a deconstructive style.

In a deconstructive frame of mind, we are never satisfied that the promises lodged in our language and tradition have been kept. We are filled with a messianic discontent, with the impatience of the prophets who gave the Israelites hell over their infidelity to the promise that called them into being. We worry over what the filters of our languages and traditions have filtered out; over the voices tradition has drowned out or silenced; over the others whom it has excluded; the languages and traditions it has ignored, repressed, suppressed, or killed off; the *promises* which have been broken or have never been given a voice. We resist letting our horizons be saturated with the present, with what is presently available, presently thinkable and doable, presently possible, and we long for *the* impossible. We resist allowing the limits of the present horizon to restrict our view, to fill up the horizon of our hope. We can never be satisfied with what presently passes itself for "forgiveness." Or for "justice," for as long as the poor are with us, and Jesus tells us that they will *always* be, we will not have justice, not now, not yet. Rather, justice, which is something we dearly love and desire, is something to come, for which we work and pray. "Justice" is a promise which has not been kept, not yet, even as justice is urgent and needed now. We love the present laws that deliver justice now even as, restless lovers that we are, we are never satisfied that justice has been rendered, that what presently dares to call itself justice or democracy is democratic or just, that it has yet been loyal to itself. For whatever the blessings of living in the prosperous Western democracies, democracy is still to come so long as politicians are bought and sold by the highest campaign contributors and so long as political courage is displaced by polls that seek to find out in advance what the electorate wants to hear. Deconstruction is indeed driven and passionate, but this passion is not the "tyranny of infinite responsibility," as Ward says, but a messianic impatience, the impatience of love; it is the passion which can never do enough, which is never satisfied, which always puts itself in the wrong for the sake of the love and the beloved.

The same "logic"—or "prophetic"—of messianic dissociation applies likewise to the gift, or to friendship, or to any of these names that have been handed down to us and hold our love captive, including the name of God. Indeed, we are tempted to say that the name of God is not just another example in a list of names of things that we love, but that the name of God is paradigmatically the name of love. For "God is love, and those who abide in love abide in God and God abides in them" (I John 4:16). That is why Augustine's question "What do I love when I love my God?" is so perfect, so paradigmatic for deconstruction. Meister Eckhart said whatever you say God is, that is not true; but what you do not say of God, that is true. That was also why Meister Eckhart preached one day to what must have been a very astonished congregation, "I pray God to rid me of God."[32] Of course, the agents of the radical orthodoxy of the day, the Curia, made Eckhart pay for that and put him on trial for trying to let language be the event of the coming of the other. For God is always, structurally, greater than anything we have said or conceived God to be. The name of God is the name of that excess; that excess is what we mean by God, by love. And we can never rest until love is all in all.

It is in virtue of the complex interweaving of what I am calling here "historical association" and "messianic dissociation" that I described deconstruction in *The Prayers and Tears of Jacques Derrida* as itself *another* concrete Messianism.[33] That is, in spite of, or rather because of, the distinction Derrida draws between the concrete, historical messianisms and the absolute or pure messianic, deconstruction, too, must be viewed as one more messianism, as a style of thinking with a determinate historical identity and pedigree. Hence Ward is only partially right to say that the promise in deconstruction "bears *none* of the specifics" (*BDLT*, 256, my emphasis) of biblical religion. In fact, and short of its own intentions, by distinguishing the messianic from the messianisms, it is recognizably a reinscription of a biblical or messianic religion, of the religions of the Book (rather than of Buddhism or Zoroastrianism). Against its own purposes (and how could it be otherwise?) it does indeed bear specific traces of "Christian proclamation" and "Jewish eschatology" (*BDLT*, 256). Having begun where it is, deconstruction is identifiable and locatable within the political and biblical traditions of the west, within the Shema at the beginning and the call to "Come" at the end of the New Testament, as well as within the radical politics, the radical democratic utopianism and egalitarianism of the second half of the twentieth century. It is situated after the Holocaust and after Stalinism, to be sure (that is what thinkers of his generation meant by "totality"), but also after industrial capitalism, situated squarely in the high-tech, new world order of virtual reality and worldwide communication systems. It is a style of thinking marked by jet travel between continents, of speaking to, visiting with, and writing for an international audience that is increasingly conscious of having to speak Anglo-Christian English, in addition to the Christian Latin French that is Derrida's "native" language, if he has one. Derrida is a good Jewgreek and a good Greekjew and not a little Arab, American, and also something of a slightly atheistic Jewish Augustinian. He did not drop out of the sky one day in 1930 like a deconstructive avatar and just start talking funny. He has an historical pedigree that anyone who takes the time to carefully read a sometimes difficult text can discern, with all the inherited historical baggage of anybody else who pulls his or her pants on one leg at a time. He has situated himself within the play of the multiple and irreducible traditions and heritages, that is to say, within the play of the multiple and irreducible *promises* in which he finds himself, sorting and sifting among them with messianic longing and discontent, with the *cor inquietum* of a Jewish

Augustinian who asks himself night and day what he loves when he loves his God.

To describe such a position as "onanism" is, if not to indulge in a cynical joke, at the very least to misconstrue a complicated text.

Derrida versus Augustine

Still, Graham Ward is quite right to maintain that there is a world of difference between Derrida's question and St. Augustine's question, just as he was right to differentiate between Barth and Derrida. So let us return now to what are, in my view, the genuine differences that separate St. Augustine's *Confessions* from the "Circumfession" of Jacques Derrida. For if Ward mistreats deconstruction by marking the difference between these texts in terms of aestheticism, onanism, hopelessness, and paralysis, it would be foolish to try to assimilate Derrida to Augustine, as Derrida himself would be the first to insist.

Derrida says of himself that "I quite rightly pass for an atheist." When asked why he does not just say he *is* an atheist, Derrida replied that this is what others say of him and they are "right," but he is not saying so himself, because he does not know if he *is* one, that is, an atheist (as an American president said, it all depends upon what the meaning of "is" is.) Again, he does not know if he is *one*, that is, not two or more.[34] By the standards of the local pastor or rabbi, he is an atheist, but matters are not quite so simple and univocal in what Derrida calls a "religion without religion." One of the things I think those of us who have a religious tradition can learn from deconstruction is that we are, each of us, not "one." As he says in the Roundtable, there is someone inside him who is constantly approving of his actions and someone else who is very disapproving, even "merciless" with him, and the two are "constantly fighting." Just so, there is an atheist in the heart of every believer, who haunts and taunts the believer with disbelief, even as there is a believer in the heart of every atheist or agnostic, haunting and taunting them with God, and the two are always fighting. To "be" a believer or an atheist is to live with that dissension within ourselves. Derrida's formula is a good one, not only for himself, but for all of us, *mutatis mutandis*, for the faithful would do very well to say of themselves not that they "are" but that they "rightly pass for" Christians or Jews, Muslims or Hindus, not unlike the way that Johannes Climacus, given the "difficulty" of a being a Christian, preferred to speak of "becoming" Christian rather than of being one. We do not know who we are or what is to come, and we are more than one. To *be* a believer is to struggle with the disbeliever within us who will not give us peace, even as the disbeliever is always disturbed by the suspicion that he is just not listening closely enough to what is going on inside himself; we ought to suspect our disbelief as much as our belief. We are not who we are, and we are not necessarily who we say or think we are; we are not self-identical, not identical with ourselves, not if we are honest.

There is an interesting moment in the discussion following Kevin Hart's

John D. Caputo

chapter elsewhere in this volume, in which Derrida, taking up Hart's reference to the aporia as a gift, says to Hart:[35]

> If I am sure that aporia has been given to me by God, then that is the end; that is a reconciliation. To experience the aporia I will never know if it is being given to me as a gift or if it has been given to me as death or as a blow or as a punishment or torture. If you are sure that aporia was given as a gift, I envy you. (p. 202)

If I am sure that the paradoxes that surround the gift and forgiveness are given by God, then the paradoxes are not exactly paradoxes any longer but part of the ever-deepening mystery of God, and we can always trust God and his mysterious ways. The same thing might be said of an expression such as "the gift of faith": If we are sure that our faith in God has been given to us by God, then that makes things a lot easier, for the very thing in which we have faith is assured to us by the very fact of having faith, for God is where the faith has evidently originated. But that of course makes everything too easy and makes faith look like some sort of escape from the difficulty of life—the difficulty being that the very idea that faith is a gift *of* God depends upon having faith *in* God to begin with.

Now I think that something very much like that also applies to Ward's complaints that Augustine's *Confessions* are rooted in God, in the historical testimony of the God of Israel and the God whom Jesus dared call *abba*, while Derrida is whistling in the dark—or worse (giving himself *jouissance*). Augustine's faith in God is borne witness to by the history of Israel and Christianity just so long as Augustine reads that history to begin with in the light of his *faith that* God is at work in and testified to there. What Ward is in fact pointing to, in my view, is the phenomenon of what I called above the first movement of deconstruction, the movement of "historical association," of seizing upon the tradition and the heritage that we have been given. When Augustine heard the little child's voice say *"tolle, lege"* (VIII, 12), which constituted a kind of mystical decision procedure, the book he seized upon was the New Testament, and in Latin translation at that, not the Tanakh in Hebrew, not the Talmud, not the Koran, which had not been written yet, and not the words of ancient sages from the East whose languages he could not read and whose books were not handy. Augustine, like everyone else, begins wherever he is, in the midst of the complex, conflicting, and multiple play of voices in which he finds himself, with the materials at hand that are made available to him by what we call the "tradition," which he must sort through and appropriate. Had he been sitting in some other garden at some other time the results would have been different, because he would have picked up another book in another language in another tradition and been given other instructions. The *tolle, lege* experience is a function of the materials within arm's reach.

The difference between Augustine and Derrida, then, is *not* that Augustine is filled with faith and hope and love in the God before whom he confesses and whose actions are testified to in history while Derrida is playing with himself. The difference is *not* that Augustine has "entrusted" or "delivered" himself over to the Good while Derrida is just seeking new adventures on the starship *Enterprise*. That, I think, is a polemical reading that has abandoned the ground gained in *BDLT*, and it is, if I may say so, a dogmatic way to interpret the differences between them. The difference is that Augustine has seized and settled upon a determinate historical name for the object of his faith and hope and love, that he has "entrusted" or "delivered" himself over to the proper names that have been transmitted to him by his tradition, while for Derrida faith and hope and love make their way in the night as best they can. For night is their element, and the particular figures in which our faith and hope and love take shape can always be determined otherwise. The difference is that when Augustine asks "What do I love when I love my God?" his question is played out within the fixed and determinate limits of the historical tradition with which he associates himself, but Derrida asks this question with a certain detachment from the historical particularity of a determinate answer; he is really a little lost and leaves open other possible responses, something that Ward brought out in *BDLT* by underlining the open-endedness of Derrida's questioning as opposed to the particularism of Barth's commitment to Jesus Christ. Derrida is wrestling with his angel through the night and does not know if, when morning comes, he will find himself in the arms of an angel of the Lord, or the Lord himself, or what! None of this has anything to do with "onanism" or "aestheticism" but, on the contrary, with a radical affirmation of an unforeseeable ethical and political future and of the possibility of being otherwise. He has faith in faith, and hope in hope, but he has no guarantees. And he is in love with love, *not* in the sense that he is just playing with love, as the young Augustine accused himself (*Confessions* III, 1), which would have been a somewhat more polite and edifying way to frame Ward's charge of onanism, but in the sense that the determinate figures in which love takes shape—in the New Testament or the Tanakh or the Koran or in other great religious classics, or indeed in other forms that are not overtly "religious" at all—have an irreducible historical contingency. As beautiful and powerful and important as they are, and we can never finish reading them, or begin reading without them, it will always be true that a part of their beauty and power is to point to the possibility of what is to come, to serve as markers of a "perhaps" (*peut-être*), which is, perhaps, the best name of all for God.[36] As Richard Kearney argues in his contribution elsewhere in this volume, the best thing we can say of God is not that God is the act of all acts, but that God is the possibility of all possibilities, the possibility of the impossible, the highest possible "perhaps."[37] The name of God is one of our best names, and Derrida loves it very much and wants to save it. But however inescapable it is for us, here and now, it is not definitive or indispensable, and it may be that in time to come the name of God, and maybe even the name of love, will give way and that it will do so precisely in the name of what we now call love and now call God. Maybe. Perhaps. We do not know.

No more than does St. Augustine. For the *Confessions* confess Augustine's *faith*, what Augustine confesses, believes, and hopes for, the difference being that for Augustine the structure of faith and hope are lodged and fixed in the determinate historical figure of Jesus and the religion of Israel whose history he interprets as prefiguring the religion of Jesus (which not everyone agrees with, particularly the people of Israel, who could read the Hebrew). But for Derrida the determinate historical figure of Jesus, like the figures of Judaism or Islam, are so many *determinations* of a faith that remains *determinable* in *other* ways, that can take different forms in different times and different places, where these names are completely unknown, even as these figures harbor within themselves a future that eye hath not seen nor ear heard. So there would always be a certain movement of messianic dissociation, an awareness of the contingency of the proper names I have inherited, of the contingencies of my birth, the contingency, indeterminacy, and undecidability of what is foregiven, an inextinguishable restlessness in virtue of which this force, this desire, this impulse, "call it what you will" (p. 28) can assume other forms.

The difference between Augustine and Derrida is that while both decide-in-the-midst-of-undecidability, Derrida has made explicit the determinability and undecidability that inhabits the faith and hope and love that sustain him, whereas Augustine comes to rest in the historically determinate decision he has made in the midst of this undecidability. The difference is *not* that Augustine decides and Derrida does not, that Derrida lapses into undecidability but Augustine does not, that Augustine has faith and hope and love while Derrida does not, that Augustine has crossed the threshold of undecidability and left it behind while Derrida peers timidly before the doorway of decision unable to pass through. Augustine's faith and decision, no less than Derrida's, must be sustained across an abyss of undecidability that persists before, during, and after any determinate decision. I do believe, help thou my unbelief, which is co-constitutive of my belief. Derrida's love, no less than Augustine's, is a love of truth, of doing the truth, *facere veritatem.*

To decide-in-the-midst-of-undecidability is to decide in the midst of "mediations," a word that Ward and his movement much admire. But these are mediations that we cannot temporarily lay aside in order to look behind them for the Unmediated Truth that one of them contains in an absolute, definitive form, as if *one* of them were the one-holy-(Anglo)-catholic-and-apostolic "right" (*orthe*) one, the "orthodox" form, in which everyone else's mediations can only more or less "participate." Radical "mediation" means we are stuck *in medias res,* that we do not have "inside information" that hooks us up to the unmediated secret that is mediated by one of them, that God or Being or the Absolute prefers one of these mediations to the others, which thus represents the One and Only Mediator. That is to undo the idea of mediation which, radically conceived, means we are always already construing. Thus, if Augustine's is a hermeneutic ontology, Derrida's is a more radical hermeneutics,[38] not a hermeneutic me-ontology. Derrida once warned that when we are promised the "unmediated" and the *hors-texte* outside the mediations, the police cannot be far behind and we can expect to be soon subjected to the most dogmatic, "the most massively mediatizing machines."[39] In radical orthodoxy, we witness the opposite phenomenon: constant talk about mediation which seems always to have the Unmediated and Exclusive Mediator up its sleeve.

Because deciding-in-the-midst-of-undecidability is to continue to cope with an ineradicable undecidability, the *difference* between Augustine and Derrida should be seen to lie in the *relative determinacy* of the figures in which their faith, hope, and love are lodged. *Unless*, of course, one has dogmatically decided that Augustine's determinately *Christian* faith, hope, and love is the one definitive way of having faith, hope, and love and those who disagree with Augustinian Christianity are wrong, are indeed playing with themselves, are "aesthetes" who cannot be serious. Taking a course like that is a dogmatism that besets anything that calls itself "radical orthodoxy," which is of course an elliptical expression, a shorthand for "radical *Christian* orthodoxy," which should frighten Jews who have lived under centuries of Christian culture out of their wits, even as it besets its analogous forms: "radical *Jewish* orthodoxy," which should frighten Palestinians out of their wits, or "radical *Muslim* orthodoxy," which sent Salmon Rushdie heading for cover, and so on around the globe and over the ages. The list goes on. Fill in the blank: radical X orthodoxy, where X spells trouble: radical dogmatic and religious conflict. This movement thinks itself in tune with a Christian socialism and does not want to associate itself with the religious right, but I do not see how it can avoid "violence" *without* deconstruction. Expressions such as "radical orthodoxy" seem to me in fact to court violence. The best face I can put on this expression from which I would personally like to keep my distance is this: The "right teaching" will always be ineradicably *to come* and it is never one. The "more religious" (*religiosius*) thing to say, St. Augustine says, the more "radically" religious thing, is to love *all* of the right teachings, all of the ones to come, whose forms we cannot presently imagine, so long as all of them are true (*Conf.* XII, 31) and spring from love (*Conf.* XII, 18).

Thus, by saying that Derrida makes explicit the undecidability that inhabits faith, hope, and love I am not saying that he undermines faith, hope, and love and throws the three "theological" virtues to the four winds. On the contrary, he makes explicit the medium in which they subsist. Ward's take on undecidability, which I addressed at the beginning of these remarks, is, in my view, the one besetting, shall I say, the most radical confusion of the radical orthodoxists and the *radix* of a good deal of the *malum* that they mistakenly attribute to deconstruction—of the "paralysis," the "hopelessness," the "bad infinite," with which, as we have seen, Graham Ward confuses it, and of the nihilism that Milbank attributes to it. Undecidability does not undo faith, hope, and love but provides them with their condition of possibility, supplying their element, the night in which they are formed and performed. Faith is faith just when things are starting to look a little incredible and unlikely, even as faith vanishes entirely under the sun of knowledge. Faith is faith when it holds out against the voices of disbelief that grow stronger and stronger, voices from within and from without, when it holds on even as the evidence against it mounts up. You have believed because you saw, Thomas, but blessed are those who believe and have not seen (John 20:29). Hope is really hope just when things are starting to look hopeless, when the odds are mounting up against us, when reasonable people would cut their losses and head for cover. Hope is hope, as St. Paul said in a magnificent formulation, when it is hope against hope (Romans 4:18). And love is love when loving seems mad and impossible. It does not take much to love those who love us, but love is love, glows white-hot as love, just when we are asked to love what is unlovable, like loving those who do not love us, like loving our enemies (Matthew 5:43–48).

To this list drawn up by Paul we might add a virtue stressed by Jesus, which is also on Derrida's list: forgiveness, which gets to be itself the more impossible it gets. If your brother offends you seven times a day, you should forgive him. Even if he offends you seventy times seven, which is to say all the time. But is that not impossible?

Derrida describes the air that faith, hope, and love—and forgiveness—breathe, the ether in which they are sustained, even as he has adopted an Augustinian conception of truth as something to *do*, of *facere veritatem*, which has displaced truth in the sense of propositions, of the right propositions, the right *doxa*, the right doctrine, while having nothing whatever to do with aestheticism. Without undecidability, faith, hope, and love are a convenience, a source of dogmatic assurance, stoking the fires of triumphalism. Without undecidability, faith, hope, and love are melded into a straight rod (a "canon") with which to smite our enemies or those who differ with us.

What, then, do I love when I love my God? Can I do anything better than to translate that question into my own life, to ask myself that question night and day?

NOTES

1. Actually, Derrida's question is a collage of *Confessiones* X, 7: *quid ergo amo, cum deum amo* and X, 6, *quid autem amo, cum te amo . . . non haec amo, cum amo deum meum.* I am using the Latin text of *St. Augustine's Confessions*, trans. W. Watts, Loeb Classical Library (Cambridge: Harvard University Press, 1988). See Jacques Derrida, "Circumfession: Fifty-nine Periods and Periphrases," in Geoffrey Bennington and Jacques Derrida, *Jacques Derrida* (Chicago: University of Chicago Press, 1993), p. 122.

2. I prefer the English translation of the *Confessions* by F. J. Sheed (Indianapolis: Hackett, 1992).

3. In addition to *Barth, Derrida and the Language of Theology* (Cambridge: Cambridge University Press, 1995) (hereafter *BDLT*), see the "Introduction" to *The*

Postmodern God: A Theological Reader (Oxford: Blackwell, 1997). Ward is a much better reader of Derrida than the movement with which he has associated himself—a movement that wants to be known *as* a movement, that even has a "manifesto" of its own, and has baptized itself "radical orthodoxy" (which is a formidable name to give any child). See *Radical Orthodoxy*, ed. John Milbank, Catherine Pickstock, and Graham Ward (London: Routledge, 1999), especially the "Introduction," which sets out to save us all from the "nihilistic drift of postmodernism" (p. 1). See also page 3, which refers to the notion of "an illusion thrown up by the void," "a delusory and contradictory concealment of the void," a view that is attributed to "Derrida *et al.*"

4. I am summarizing the argument of Graham Ward, "Questioning God," elsewhere in this volume; see especially the concluding pages (pp. 285–287).

5. This phrase, which is the title of Kevin Hart's chapter elsewhere in this volume, where it is given a sensitive reading, is used by Derrida in "Faith and Knowledge: The Two Sources of 'Religion' at the Limits of Reason Alone," trans. Samuel Weber, in *Religion*, ed. Jacques Derrida and Gianni Vattimo (Cambridge: Polity Press, 1998), p. 64. Derrida is referring to the notion, whose "index" is Levinas and Blanchot, of the "distance" of the other. This distance gives the "community" the space to breathe, providing it with respiration by allowing for a certain separation, or non-relation, of the other and the same, which Derrida also describes as an "absolute interruption" of the same by the other. "Interruption" for Derrida is the condition of the possibility that something new can emerge in a relation, community, or tradition which must resist the ideal of "fusion." After saying that faith is a kind of "miracle," he says that it is the "ether" which sustains relation of the same to the "other," the shore that I never quite reach, whom I never know, but in whom I have faith. That Ward should appreciate this point is clear from his own exposition of the "rupture of revelation" in Barth and Levinas in *Barth, Derrida and the Language of Theology* (Cambridge: Cambridge University Press, 1995), p. 156. So to characterize what Derrida is talking about as a form of coitus interruptus or masturbation is surprising to me; it is long on polemics and short on conceptual content or textual basis.

6. I, for one, spelled out and responded to the charge of aestheticism, which was a commonplace of Derrida's critics twenty years ago, in "Beyond Aestheticism: Derrida's Responsible Anarchy," *Research in Phenomenology* 18 (1988): 59–73. The criticism persists, I think, because of an impression created in the first reception of Derrida by American literary critics and a failure to consider the more philosophical side of Derrida, which shows up especially in the writings of the last twenty years, writings that have taken on an ethical, political, and even messianic tone that Ward himself takes note of in *BDLT*, 221.

7. John D. Caputo, *The Prayers and Tears of Jacques Derrida: Religion without Religion* (Bloomington: Indiana University Press, 1997), p. 14; see my review of *Erring* in *Man and World* 21 (1988): 107–114.

8. Jacques Derrida, *Of Spirit: Heidegger and the Question*, trans. Geoffrey Bennington and Rachel Bowlby (Chicago: University of Chicago Press, 1989), p. 94.

9. Jacques Derrida, *Edmund Husserl's Origin of Geometry*, trans. John Leavey (Boulder: John Hays Co., 1978), pp. 53–56.

10. John D. Caputo, *Radical Hermeneutics: Repetition, Deconstruction and the Hermeneutic Project* (Bloomington: Indiana University Press, 1987), p. 262.

11. Jacques Derrida, *Politics of Friendship*, trans. George Collins (London & New York: Verso, 1997), p. 68.

12. Derrida, "Circumfession," p. 155.

13. Jacques Derrida, *Specters of Marx: The State of the Debt, the Work of Mourning, and the New International*, trans. Peggy Kamuf (New York: Routledge, 1994), p. 89.

14. Jacques Derrida, "How to Avoid Speaking: Denials," trans. Ken Friedan, in *Derrida and Negative Theology*, ed. Howard Coward and Toby Foshay (Albany: SUNY Press, 1992), p. 84. For Derrida, language is constituted by the promise; see pp. 82–85, 97–98.

15. Derrida, "How to Avoid Speaking," p. 84.

16. Ibid., pp. 86–87.

17. See Derrida's treatment of the promise in Heidegger's notion of language in *Of Spirit*, pp. 92–94, and Ward, *BDLT*, 229–230. Ward has also analyzed Heidegger's notion of language in Chapter 5 of *BDLT*.

18. Jacques Derrida, *Memoires: For Paul De Man*, trans. Cecile Lindsay, Jonathan Culler, and Eduardo Cadava (New York: Columbia University Press, 1986), pp. 94–98.

19. That would serve as a nice gloss on the expression "absolute interruption." See above, n. 6.

20. Jacques Derrida, *Politics of Friendship*, pp. 7, 46 n. 14, 173–174. This Coming One, this Messiah, is still to come, even in Christianity which, having been visited once by the Messiah, is opened up and constituted by the expectation of a coming *again*. Christianity opens its doors and is structured around the deferral of the Second Coming, and as such is made possible by *différance*, by an unforeseeable coming that comes like a thief in the night when we least expect it. The unforeseeability of the Messiah is built right into very structure of messianic expectation, which is built right into the idea of language and of history. History is over if the Messiah arrives once and for all.

21. Derrida, *Of Grammatology*, trans. Gayatri Spivak, New Corrected Edition (Baltimore: Johns Hopkins University Press, 1999), p. 162. See also Derrida, *Margins of Philosophy*, trans. Alan Bass (Chicago: University of Chicago Press, 1982), p. 6. See Ward, *BDLT*, p. 209 n. 1.

22. The charge of "indifferentism" underlies much of Milbank's "Ontological Violence or the Postmodern Problematic," in *Theology and Social Theory* (Cambridge: Cambridge University Press, 190, 1993), pp. 278–325. See pp. 302–305: As opposed to the analogy of being, which allows for hierarchical differentiations, Derrida and Deleuze follow the "univocal" scheme of Duns Scotus for whom "being" always means the same thing, while particular "beings" are each different, with the result that they are "absolutely indifferent to each particular difference." This issues in alleging either an "anything goes" licentiousness, which is why deconstruction is "nihilism," or an excessively "moralistic" form of moral rigorism. The latter can be found in John Milbank's question in the Roundtable, elsewhere in this volume (p. 65). Both objections proceed from a failure to grasp the fundamentally historically situated character of deconstructive thinking. That is why Derrida answers Milbank by saying that of course he experiences a greater obligation to those who are closest to him, but the point of a deconstructive analysis is to tug at the strains of that privilege and awaken us to the call of the other others. *Both* of these at once; it is not a matter of choosing between them. Ward intimates this criticism when he says that for Derrida, differences belong to a democracy where all differences are the same (*BDLT*, 216) but he also cites a text in which Derrida makes it clear that this is not a view he holds (*BDLT*, 216).

23. Derrida, *Limited Inc.* (Evanston: Northwestern University Press, 1988), p. 137.

24. Derrida, *On the Name*, ed. Thomas Dutoit (Stanford: Stanford University Press, 1995), p. 71.

25. *Specters of Marx*, p. 16. See also Derrida's response to Cleo Kearns at the Roundtable, pp. 58–59.

26. See *Deconstruction in a Nutshell: A Conversation with Jacques Derrida*, edited with a commentary by John D. Caputo (New York: Fordham University Press, 1997), pp. 8, 37.

27. See Ward, "Questioning God," p. 282 in this volume, and Laurence Hemming's treatment of Ockham in *Radical Orthodoxy*, pp. 93–4.

28. I have published a sketch of the argument to this effect in an anthology currently in preparation under the editorship of Graham Ward!

29. See "Politics and Friendship: An Interview with Jacques Derrida," trans. Robert Harvey, in *The Althusserian Legacy*, ed. E. Ann Kaplan and Michael Spinker (London: Verso Books, 1993), pp. 18–231; see pp. 197, 199, 213. Even *"différance"* must go one day; see *Margins*, p. 7.

30. See John D. Caputo, *Radical Hermeneutics* and *More Radical Hermeneutics: On Not Knowing Who We Are* (Bloomington: Indiana University Press, 2000).

31. For a reading of Derrida as a nihilist and author of a nihilistic and violent ontology, see John Milbank, "Ontological Violence, or the Postmodern Problematic," in *Theology and Social Theory: Beyond Secular Reason* (Oxford: Blackwell, 1990), pp. 278 ff. In radical orthodoxy, Derrida is portrayed as having a position like the young Nietzsche and Schopenhauer: Things in themselves are a violent and chaotic abyss (*Wille*) over which we have stretched a veil of fictions (*Vorstellung*). See also *Radical Orthodoxy*, p. 3. Unlike Graham Ward (*The Postmodern God*, p. xxx), I think the influence of Nietzsche upon Derrida *can* be overestimated.

32. I discuss these texts in reference to Derrida in the last chapter of *More Radical Hermeneutics*, pp. 249 ff.

33. John D. Caputo, *The Prayers and Tears of Jacques Derrida*, pp. 139–143.

34. Unpublished interview with Mark Dooley in Paris in Spring, 2000.

35. Derrida's response to Hart, pp. 201–202 in this volume.

36. See Jacques Derrida, *"Comme si c'était possible,* 'within such limits' . . . ,"* Revue internationale de Philosophie* 3 (1998): 497–529.

37. See also Richard Kearney, "The Possible God," in *Blackwell Readings in Continental Philosophy: The Religious*, ed. John D. Caputo (Oxford: Blackwell, 2001). Kearney makes an important use of Derrida's *"Comme si c'était possible"* (above).

38. That is the argument of *More Radical Hermeneutics*; see the "Introduction," pp. 1–13.

39. Jacques Derrida, *Truth in Painting*, trans. Geoff Bennington and Ian MacLeod (Chicago: University of Chicago Press, 1987), pp. 326–327.

The Scandals of the Sign

The Virgin Mary as Supplement in the Religions of the Book

Cleo McNelly Kearns

In Derrida's early critique of the metaphysics of presence, he notes that the persistent construct he there identifies as logocentrism is inextricably tied to the revealed monotheism of the three "religions of the book," Judaism, Christianity, and Islam. As a consequence, he implies that efforts simply to purge these monotheisms of their emphasis on the fully present, fully revealed Word guaranteed by patrilineal descent and offering title to a secure messianic possession of the land are bound, if pressed too hard, to miss the mark. At the same time, however, we may note that each of these monotheisms has generated a strong supplement to this logocentrism, a supplement which follows to the letter, as it were, Derrida's analysis of the ambiguous double function of supplementarity in Rousseau and others. Furthermore, in accordance with that supplementary function and from the perspective of its operations, the reified Word, the patriarchal line of descent, and what theologians would call the overly realized eschatology of the messianic promise may be seen as themselves supplements to other, perhaps less toxic, ways of meaning.[1]

One instance of this supplementarity—indeed, I would argue, one of the most paradigmatic—is to be found in the figure and cult of the Virgin Mary.

For Mary is both immaculate, untouched, and incorruptible, sealing the seed of God forever into a pure, eternal, logocentric meaning and at the same time the matrix of an extreme dissemination, vulnerability, and susceptibility to "corruption" that often goes well beyond the boundaries of cult, orthodoxy, and regulated tradition. Not only is she the mother of one who was disfigured and crucified and whose words, far from being maintained in purity, were not even preserved in their original spoken language, but she holds a singular generative position in a number of diverse and relatively incompatible religious discourses: in Islam, for instance, as the object of a widespread devotional cult (she is the only woman mentioned by name in the Qur'an) and in Haiti in tandem with Erzulie, the sponsor of eros and fertility, whose many children people the landscape of vodun devotion in what, from a monotheistic point of view, are highly unorthodox and uncanonical ways.[2]

Many of the dogmas and titles associated with Mary's name mark the various critical moments of this "double session" or crisscrossing of logocentrism and dissemination. She has been worshipped as, among many other things, the Theotokos, the Mother of God (as opposed to the mother of the merely human aspect of Jesus); as the typological fulfillment of a prophesy regarding Eve, whom Genesis describes as destined to crush the serpent under her foot; as the Immaculate Conception, herself conceived and born without sin; and as The Woman Clothed with the Sun, who appears in full-blown apocalyptic mode in Revelation as a figure of hope for the end time. At the same time and in the same breath, so to speak, Mary has insistently been defined—the point is most stressed by the most orthodox theologians—as an entirely human woman, not in herself a goddess. Indeed, a great part of her power stems from the fundamental assumption that she is not per se divine. In the extraordinary claims made for her, together with the denial or denegation of her divinity, lies a relationship to logocentrism that both uncovers its major aporia and disseminates its latent meanings in complex and surprising ways.

To show how such a figure can supplement a highly developed logo- and phallogocentric discourse like that of Christianity is a challenging task, and to do so without falling either into a repristination of dogma or a vacuous perennial philosophy is an almost impossible one. Even in broaching this topic, I am aware that I may be delaying or deferring from some of the more pressing questions of the hour: the demise of the secular hypothesis as a way of understanding history; the rise of "fundamentalism," whatever that may be; the increase in worldwide wars of religion in which monotheism often plays such a murderous role; the demands of women for a greater voice in public affairs; the expansion of Islam; and the hypertrophy of a technological and digital culture that both threatens religious discourse and ramifies it in ways that quickly move toward qualitative change. I hope to show, however, that the figure of the Virgin Mary bears more closely on these questions than might first appear and that in attending to the scriptures, sacraments, devotions, and theologies which seek to define her place and propagate her influence, we can trace something of the trajectories she makes and continues to make across these disparate fields.

To pick out only one strand of a complex pattern, the site Mary occupies is directly related to the fundamentalism of the word on the one hand and the fundamentalisms of a literal male priesthood, purity of culture, and possession of the land on the other. Not for nothing is there a web of metaphors and oppositions—pure/impure; immaculate/tainted; virgin/corrupt; seed/word; sterility/nourishment, to name only a few—which link the figure of Mary with the figure of the sacred text, the sacred ritual, and the sacred place. And not for nothing is there a deep connection between modes of gender and paternity, scriptural interpretation, sacramental decorum, and cultural identity, on all of which her figure has a direct bearing as well. Furthermore, in the quite un-precedented explosion of Marian apparitions from the mid-nineteenth to the late-twentieth century, an intimate connection may be traced with questions of scriptural authority, ecclesiastical control, political nationalism, messia-nism, and modes of dissemination in high and popular culture worldwide.[3] It may even be that by considering Mary as supplement we can shed some light on the question Derrida has posed most sharply in this context: the question as to whether the monotheisms are displaying a generic revealability, a *mes-sianicité*, of which they are merely examples, or whether they are themselves originary, incommensurate, and ineluctable; whether, that is to say, as in some sense creatures of a postmodern sensibility we are still in the familiar if dan-gerous Hebrew, Greek, and Latin desert of the *via negativa*, all of us, at least, headed in the same direction, or whether we are in a place even more dis-persed, even less mapped out, a *chora*—to use the deliberately ambiguous Platonic/Derridean term—lying beyond the purview of even the most radical "questioning of God."[4]

For the moment, however, I hope to adhere to a smaller, albeit equally daunting, agenda: first, to rehearse some of the reasons for the intimate im-brication of monotheism, logocentrism, and phallogocentrism; and second, to indicate some of the ways that the figure and cult of the Virgin Mary have supported, supplemented, and disseminated that formation. Before turning to this project, however, I must acknowledge some debts and enter some caveats. The usual conventions of the footnote are inadequate to express the impor-tance to religious studies of the thought of Jacques Derrida. Contrary to popu-lar opinion, Derrida offers insights into religious discourse informed both by consistent integrity of approach to the relevant texts and by a generous empa-thy with their horizons and aims. His work has supplied much of the theory and methodology for this project.[5] To Julia Kristeva's essay "Stabat Mater," more particularly, I owe an imaginative debt that far exceeds the limitations of her psychoanalytic framework; and to Marina Warner's *Alone of All Her Sex*, an awareness of the varieties of Marian experience that likewise exceeds the constraints of ideology in her work.

So much for debts; now for caveats. First, with respect to the use of the terms "supplement" and "dissemination," I have used them in a very particular sense, one that remains, I hope, faithful to the spirit and letter of Derrida's analysis. From the first, Derrida points out that while a "supplement" is by definition exterior, merely instrumental, making up the gap between ends and means, yet its very existence testifies to a lack in or absence of that to which it is supplementary and puts its supposed fullness in doubt. For instance, in opposing a "natural" but difficult and sometimes unobtainable intercourse of speech and sexuality to an "unnatural" but all-too-available supplementary secondary recourse of writing and self-stimulation, Rousseau puts himself in the impossible position of complete dependence on the very experiences he appears to disparage. By stressing what he sees as the fatal tendency of supplementary practices to lead desire "away from the good path," to make it "err far from natural ways" and guide it toward its "loss or fall," Rousseau passes a judgment that the logic of his argument cannot not sustain. Rousseau calls the move toward the supplement a sort of "lapse" or "scandal," one of the several allusions to that term which suggested the title for this essay. But this "scandal" is immensely productive, Derrida insists, for it not only carries forward, if only under erasure, the very values it seems to debase, it also adds new and divergent dimensions that are unforeseen. A further and even more provocative discussion of the function of supplementarity may be found in Derrida's essay on Mallarmé, where the supplement becomes not simply a scandal but the necessary condition of possibility of further signification and even more radically deconstructive of "natural" experiences and meanings.[6]

It is important to capture in summaries such as these a little of the scandal, the difficulty, the torque, as it were, that Derrida himself generates in his early work. He insists, for instance, that the supplement is, to use a term from *Of Grammatology*, "dangerous"; it often defaces what it pretends to cover up, and it can reveal fissures in a system of thought that generates quite incommensurable readings, readings which cannot either in theory or in practice be simply combined or treated within the same frame of reference. The supplement here is "always unfolding. . . .but it can never attain the status of a complement"; there can be no closure on the relationship between the added term and the primary one, not even the closure of assuming that the latter is always belated. Hence, as Derrida puts it, "the field is never saturated."[7]

Likewise with the related term dissemination, which indicates the process of dispersal of meaning across many readings and discourses. The disseminating activity is for Derrida not a matter of simple polysemy, for, as he says, "polysemy always puts out its multiplicities and variations within the horizon, at least of some integral reading, which contains no absolute rift, no senseless deviation—the horizon of the final parousia of a meaning at last deciphered, revealed, made present in the rich collection of its determinations" (*Dissemination*, 350). Dissemination, in contrast, operates only in and through rifts, undecipherable meanings, absences and erasures and, in a sense, through deviations. It cannot be confined within any hermeneutic procedure, even a dialectical one. Above all, it does not offer the spectacle of an array of complementary meanings whose relative degree of validity can be nicely adjudicated from some Archimedian point of view. As Edith Wyschogrod puts it, dissemination does not suppose a multiplicity of meanings, any or all of which might be in some sense true, but the "uncontrolled outflow of a textual stream whose interpretations cannot be brought to closure."[8] Dissemination is neither then a matter of pure replication of meanings nor of their total corruption; rather, it is an agonistic, destabilizing, and disconcerting process, as well as (or for that reason) a revelatory one. Parody and perversion, replication and kitsch, are, for instance, as Derrida has repeatedly argued, an inevitable aspect of signification, just as are reification and spiritualization, all entailing a perpetual and sometimes painful oscillation between debasement and elevation, fresh insight and crystallized dogma.

Dissemination and supplementation are not, then, terms we may employ simply to make peace among opposing understandings of a text or to recoup our losses by reducing the scandal of rebarbative ones to a matter of mere difference in interpretation. The temptation for the cultural critic is to seek to "save" the traditions by focusing exclusively on their more open-ended or least logocentric points and seeing them as in some way "already" deconstructed *avant la lettre*, as if all possible readings were anticipated, if only formally, in advance. This temptation is perhaps more pressing to those sympathetic to religious discourse than to their more skeptical or materialist colleagues, but it remains a danger to which several attempts to bring deconstruction into relationship with religion have fallen prey. As Barbara Johnson puts it in the prologue to her translation of *Dissemination*, Derrida coined this term not to abolish but to work a displacement of the "triangular"—dialectical, trinitarian, Oedipal—foundations of Western thought. True, he did not want to eradicate these foundations completely but rather to offer them a quasi-fourth dimension, a kind of wild card or new frame. That new frame, however, was meant to change the valences of that which it enfolded, so that the normalizing and domesticating tendencies of many neo-Hegelian, Christian-revisionist, and post-Freudian doctrines could no longer be sustained, even in their most apparently avant-garde moments. As Johnson admonishes, with particular relevance to the then fairly preliminary attempts at Christian appropriations of Derrida:

> This passage from three to four may perhaps be seen as a warning to those who, having understood the necessity for a deconstruction of metaphysical binarity, might be tempted to view the number "three" as a guarantee of liberation from the blindness of logocentrism. (*Dissemination*, xxxii)

This "passage from three to four" not only illuminates the transgressive and radical evolution of Marian piety and doctrine, which seeks both to exploit and to veil the scandalous dispersal of signs implied by Mary's willingness to bear the logos forth from her own body, but it helps to put even the more politically acute and engaged analyses of her role in a new light.[9] It allows for a critique not only of those who would vaporize her into a bloodless ideal of docile female piety but also of those who would rightly contest such a dubious spiritualization. It frees us to demur, for instance, from cultural critics such as Carroll, Kristeva, and Warner, who, though full of pregnant observations and responses, tend to see Mary as a construct of patriarchy, an ideal stick with which to beat real women; and even from liberation theologians such as Leonard Boff and Rosemary Reuther, who, though eloquent in her defense, wish to elevate her either to the position of a manifestation of Holy Spirit or that of the "feminine face of God."[10] Vis-à-vis the former, we might remark that not only do they offer a rather monological reading of a very complex figure disseminated across many religious and doctrinal formations, but in doing so also discountenance her extraordinary importance to the poor and marginalized, among whom she often finds her most spirited supporters. With respect to the latter, it can be said that seeing Mary as an alternative form of the Holy Spirit disallows, from a disseminative point of view, many of her most important and liberating functions, which require her human difference from divinity to proceed, while seeing her as the Great Mother restores her to a place in a highly mythologized and mystified masculine-feminine binary she seems better placed to deconstruct.[11]

Before wandering further into the wilds of this *marianicité*, however, I want to delineate more precisely the structure Mary both inhabits and uncenters by adumbrating some of the necessary connections between monotheism, logocentrism, and phallogocentrism on which her role is based. For Mary is first and foremost the handmaid of the Holy One of Israel and the singular, unique bride-to-be of the messianic promise. Her famous response at the Annunciation, *fiat mihi*, "be it done to me according to Thy word," recalls and re-enacts the great "yes, yes" or "here I am" of Father Abraham and the entire history of dogma associated with her may be read and read with reason as nothing more or less than the history of this obedience. We need to understand, then, something about that Holy One, not simply as a philosophical abstraction (though it is partly that, as many have argued, even in scripture) but also as a metaphorical trope and the center of a cult. Calling that center *logos, truth, monad, being,* or *essence* may help to provide a philosophical and a political location for discourse, but it must not obscure the semiotic as well as the symbolic resonance of the religious position it represents.

The presence of God as being, truth, logos and/or essence in the monotheisms is rooted, of course, in the great affirmation of Hebrew monotheism—"Hear, O Israel, the Lord your God is One God." The implications of this affirmation are wide, and so are those of its correlates, *credo in unum deum* from the Apostle's Creed and the Islamic Shahada, "there is no God but God." Suffice it to say that in these affirmations, all three monotheisms associate the linguistic sign very closely—so closely that only the thinnest fold of paper or the most fragile hymen might separate them—with the absolute priority of

God. Whether it be the God of the living Torah, of the incarnate Word, or of the Holy Qur'an, that God is in some way present, these credal assertions proclaim, perhaps even fully present, in the body of the text associated with His name. In making such an assertion, however, the monotheisms give rise as much to dismay as to comfort, for this postulate, taken as a religious rather than a purely metaphysical statement, subjects the logos or Word of God which we "hear" or "read" (or, as in Islam, "recite" or "write," an important distinction whose significance we cannot pursue here) to terrible potentials of sacrilege and contamination. If the linguistic sign—the very sign found on the lips and in the hand of mortals—is in some sense in direct contact with and perhaps even participatory in the divine essence on the one hand and the human being on the other, what then prevents it from profanation? What prevents it from sullying contact with physical decay, verbal negation, blasphemy, moral turpitude, and their issue in mortality, death, and corruption?[12]

Nor is this scandal accidental or extrinsic to the monotheistic systems. At the heart of revealed monotheism is the supposition that a unique, omnipotent, and absolutely originary deity is in some way *fully desiring of communication with human beings*, and this within the domain formed by human signifying practices, not simply in the context of a cult.[13] To use the old Sufi expression, God is a "hidden treasure" that "desires to be known." But this "desire to be known" troubles exactly the binary oppositions and distinctions most religious discourse is structured to establish and maintain. The multiple etymologies of the sacred, Derrida reminds us, draw what is holy toward the separate, pure, distinct, and self-contained, toward that which is indemnified from normal commerce among humans.[14] The desire to be known, on the other hand, draws the holy back from that indemnification toward the impure, the indistinct, the unconfined, the "corrupt," in the textual as well as material senses. It redefines the zone in which the quest for or question of God takes place, changing it into a force field, like that between unacknowledged lovers who seek each other but are also waiting to be found. We have here then a collision of maximum purity with maximum danger, to use the anthropologist Mary Douglas's terms, at once the possibility of divine contact and the potential of widespread contamination, as what is wholly other, wholly integral, enters fully, generatively and/or erotically into the realm of the contingent, the human, and the dispersed. From this point of view, the otherwise admirable Derridean slogan *tout autre est tout autre* begins to look less like a marker of a liberating philosophical distance than a talisman against disease.

The erotic desire of God to be known, known rather than merely propitiated, and known in the ordinary course of human signifying events and not simply in the context of a cult, is deeply constitutive of the religious formations of monotheism. Without a radical and disseminating desire manifesting in the fully present and highly charged sign in human history, there would be nothing at all remarkable in any of the religions of the book, and monotheism would be a either a nine-day wonder, a minor cult in Egypt, or a neutral and irenic point of view; one ethical, philosophical, or religious position among many, not a torment, a passion, and a form of possession, as it is throughout much of the world today. It is, furthermore, this generative and erotic desire of the Holy One for human communication that leads to the scandals of the sign to which the title of this essay, following a famous phrase of St. Paul's, alludes.

The whole *pharmakon* of the "religions of the book," their sometimes healing, sometimes toxic array of notoriously ramifying "logo-," "phallogo-," "carnephallogo-," and "latinocarnephallogocentric" formations may be seen from this point of view as strategies for mitigating these scandalous incursions. (These terms coined by Derrida are indeed baroque and in their own way deliberately comic, but he is more serious than meets the eye about the links between logocentrism, patriarchy, the sharing of meat, and the drawing of sharp boundaries between human and animal.) Among these strategies are the making of distinctions between insider and outsider, the evolution of a set of laws or norms to define order from disarray, the establishment of a scriptural hermeneutics which will make saving distinctions between cultic impurity conceived of as physical contamination and moral impurity conceived of as ethical transgression and, at some times and places, the institution of a sacrificial priesthood to maintain and defend these manifold differences. These ways of separating the God-bearing and God-consecrated sign from mundane signifying practices counterbalance the dangerous incursions of divine desire and inscribe that desire in an economy where its effects can be mitigated and managed—not to say manipulated—by human intent. And yet, however elaborate they are, the work of these religious discourses is ceaselessly undone, for, as modern linguistics has been so assiduous in telling us, no sign, even a divine one, can communicate without the contamination and dissemination which are its other face.

Among these strategies for handling the scandals of the sign, none is more striking and more problematic than the development, in the culture of the ancient Hebrews and in the Roman Catholic Church, among others, of a cult of sacrifice presided over by a male priesthood. We might even, with appropriate cautions and qualifications, call it a cult of "blood" sacrifice, or at least one in which blood is strongly emphasized.[15] The general function of such cults is, we are told by structural anthropologists, to mediate the binary oppositions of a culture, establish hierarchies within it and define its boundaries. This understanding is useful as far as it goes, but it requires a certain supplementation with respect to the monotheisms, especially, as recent work in anthropology has shown, when it comes to particulars of gender.

We may find one such supplement, I think, in the work of the late Nancy Jay, whose book on sacrifice, religion and paternity throws a sharp light on the *toledot*, or sacred genealogy of Israel, and its relationship to the temple cult and on the Roman Catholic *cultus*, with its extreme of phallogocentrism as well.[16] Jay sees one dimension of religious sacrifice in the need to establish a strong and enduring patriline over and against a latent quasi-natural matrilineal community. She argues that sacrifice, particularly expiatory as opposed to alimentary sacrifice, is one way in which religious discourse helps to establish a patriline vis-à-vis the "natural" community produced by the obvious and material connection between mother and child. The sheer facticity of this "natural" connection is counterbalanced by marking—usually in blood—a "cultural" connection with the father's line which is equally or more valid, equally or more binding. Jay argues that sacrifice, in a way, remedies the dreadful condition, the difference, of having been born of a woman, establishing bonds of intergenerational continuity between males that would otherwise not be easy to see, and helping the patriline transcend what seems its absolute dependence on childbearing.[17] Through religious sacrifice, then, father and son are bound together in a line of descent that will be clearly separated from others, clearly ordered in terms of hierarchy and securely extended through future generations. Participation in the sacrificial cult helps overcome the problem of being born of woman and subject to the decay and death which such a birth must entail.

Sacrificial priesthood then, according to Jay's analysis, reduces the multiplication of ties and endless disseminations of female procreativity to manageable dimensions. By constructing through culture a set of like and like-minded fathers and sons, sacrifice helps to assure—at least ideally—an enduring patriline and stamps an ineradicable seal on the dangerously undifferentiated stuff of material existence. As Jay states it, somewhat more precisely:

> It is by purification of the rule-governed (moral, not biological) relatedness of father and son in a ritually defined social order enduring continuously through time, that birth and death (continually changing the membership of the "eternal" lineage) . . . may be overcome.[18]

Such a structure tends, of course, toward replication and stasis and, taken too literally, can lead to something like an endless succession of homomorphic clones; at its best, however, it is one way, at least, of reproducing culture, making it cumulative and establishing both personal and collective identities in time. "Sacrifice," Jay says, "is childbirth done better." We might add that it creates all that is intended, both by definition and by implication, in the word *patrimony*.

Jay sees the workings of this reproductive function of sacrifice both in the genealogy of Israel and in the transmission of the Christian *cultus*. Israelite society, she reminds us, did not deny descent from women—nor could it, I would add by way of supplement to her argument, and still be a society structured around the universal and bilateral fatherhood of God.[19] This bilateral fatherhood, however, raises the issue of the role of the human father in procreation and perpetuation of the species in an especially acute way. So ancient Israel faced with special intensity the need to establish an enduring patriline through special emphasis on the male role. Religious sacrifices by males such as those entailed in circumcision and the temple cult, together with a certain hermeneutic agility in the interpretation of the signs of kinship, were effective ways of making that emphasis. Sarah, Rebecca, Rachel, and Ruth all represented a strong potential matriline which had to be incorporated and transumed into the eternal Israel by equally strong acts of sacrifice and prophetic reinterpretation of the "natural" ties of childbirth in order to restore the essentially patriarchal linear order. The strongest such act is, of course, Abraham's on Mt. Moriah, the *akedah*, or binding of Isaac, which deploys sacrifice at both literal and symbolical levels in the service of creating and guaranteeing the cultural patrimony of Israel.[20]

The Roman Catholic tradition faced the same problem of ensuring the patriline at perhaps an even greater level of risk. When Christian theory and practice chose to associate the link between the linguistic sign and divinity specifically with the person and body of Jesus Christ and with the material elements of bread and wine, the scandals of the sign entailed became potentially very intense. Again, it was St. Paul who said it most dramatically: The cross was a "scandal to the Greeks and a stumbling block to the Jews" (I Corinthians 23). For in Christian terms, during the crucifixion and its anamnesis in the Eucharist, the fully present divine Word is not only spoken and heard but seen, touched, and tasted and even violated as well. It is first born in blood, then broken on the cross, and then devoured in the actual mouths of physical creatures who copulate, bleed, excrete, and die. "In the juvescence of the year," intones Eliot's "Gerontion," "Came Christ the tiger / In depraved May . . . To be eaten, to be divided, to be drunk / Among whispers" by Hakagawa, by Madame de Tornquist, and the sinister and distressed Fraulein von Kulp. Here the potentially transgressive association between the body, divinity, and the linguistic sign reaches a level which threatens, from an anthropological point of view, the entire structure of linguistic, ethnic, and racial "purity" that religious discourse exists to erect and maintain.

To add insult to injury, Jesus's lineage comes, and comes famously, through the female line, and the Christian investment in maternal filiation and in spiritual as opposed to biological paternity creates serious problems of continuity for the tradition. Hence, when Catholicism emphasizes both the real presence of the divine in the elements of bread and wine and the literal truth of the Virgin Birth, it generates the need for correspondingly strong and emphasized prophylactics to contain the resulting anxieties of contamination, dispersal, and discontinuity. It is not surprising, then, to find the early church reinstating, after a time (though only in symbolic terms) a sacrificial cult long superseded in Judaism; one having scandalous aspects, from a modern point of view, that make it seem to come right out of the wilder pages of Sir James Frazer's *The Golden Bough*. This priesthood, however, performs several useful religious, psychological, and anthropological functions: It separates the elements of the cult, the bread and wine, the body and blood of Christ, from direct contact with the unclean, and it moderates the divine desire they convey by stepping it down, so to speak, until it is supportive of, rather than threatening to, the great binaries of human signifying practice. Above all, it protects the eucharistic elements from the extremities of uncleanness that are represented by the physical, material life of women and children: the blood of menstruation, of first intercourse or the breaking of the hymen, of childbirth, and of that "debt we owe to nature," death itself.

As Jay points out, the more the real presence of the divine is emphasized in the elements of the cult in Christian tradition, the more necessary such protections will appear to be, and the more gendered, masculine, celibate, and "pure" will be the priesthood entrusted with their mediation. Hence, in Protestantism, to the degree that the eucharistic elements are merely symbolic and the motif of sacrifice disappears in remembrance, priesthood can become ministry, at once more democratic, less hierarchical, and less gendered. In Catholicism, however, where the material elements of the sacrament themselves carry the burden of divine signifying presence, these controls cannot be so relaxed. When we add to this the intimate association of the anxieties of contamination with the anxieties of assuring the patriline, and both with the institution of writing (which is historically associated, Derrida reminds us, with genealogical concerns) we have a very strong imbrication of logocentrism with phallogo- and carnephallogo- and even latinocarnophallogocentrism. That is to say, we have a situation where the boundaries between male and female, insider and outsider, citizen and barbarian, man and animal may be established through language at one and the same stroke. In their own ways, both the *akedah* and the crucifixion function in just these terms—as sacrifices which might be specifically designed to ensure the patriline, defining the roles of male versus female in its construction, its species identity vis-à-vis the animal world, and its position in time and space. These sacrifices both threaten and restore the great binaries of human community, in the same stroke constructing the deep, the "real," the bloody connection of the son with the father and both with the natural world of the land, beyond even the bounds of death. We come here, I think, to something like the heart of the monotheistic faiths; perhaps, as Kierkegaard suggests, to the heart of religious observance itself.

And as is the case so often, Derrida has been here before us. There is a short excursus on the etymology of the word religion in *Religion* where, following Benveniste, Derrida ties this word by a somewhat obscure line of filiation to the Latin word *spondeo*, hope. The proof-text is an anecdote in Plautus in which a father receives news that a lost son lives and promises the bearer of that news that if it is true, he'll feed him all his days. "Is this a promise? *Sponden tu istud?*" the messenger asks. "*Spondeo* (I promise)," says the father. "All this goes on," Derrida says, in what we can "no longer isolate as simply a religious discourse" but must increasingly see as "at the heart of all human signification." It goes on, he continues, "in the experience of the promise or of the indemnificatory offering, of a word committing a future to the present but concerning an event that is past" (*Religion*, 31). Derrida even writes a little sketch or paraphrase of his own to dramatize this paradigmatic moment:

"I promise you that it happened." What happened? Who, to be precise? A son, yours. How beautiful to have an example. Religion, nothing less.[21]

Beautiful indeed, for it captures in a nutshell, as Caputo might say, all I am attempting to adumbrate about sacrifice, the patriline, violence, and messianic promise. And it takes us to exactly the place where the monotheistic covenants culminate: to the upper room, where the risen Christ reappeared to the disciples and Mary; and even before that, to the desert tent, where Sarah no doubt stood waiting when Abraham and Isaac came down from Mount Moriah. (Exalted? radiant? chastened? faintly sheepish? How is a mother to imagine that scene . . . ?) "If you tell me that my son lives, I will feed you all your days." "*Sponden tu istud?*" "*Spondeo*, I promise."

Without the divine desire of revealed monotheism, however, neither these great and touching promises nor their "guarantee" by willing sacrifice "to the very edge of doom," as Shakespeare put it, would exist in quite this way. If God were not in some sense, and even rather scandalously, the Father and, more transgressively, the Lover of humans, replicating the divine image promiscuously, as it were, in the line that passes from body to body and from mother to child in the natural world of death and decay, there would be no pressing need to reassert the construct of the human patriline as a counterbalance. Likewise, with the scandals of the linguistic sign, if the Word were not "of God" in some sense, it would not need to be marked off, contained, channeled, and protected by logocentrism, hermeneutics, and many a lesser ritual and observance surrounding the sacred text. Sacrificial priesthood and logocentric interpretation, whatever else they may be, are ways of performing the necessary mediations without which the monotheistic community would collapse into anarchy, entropy, and endless uncontrolled differance.[22] Either way, it's a bind. *Feu la cendre*, indeed.

It is over this structure of anxiety, sacrifice, and messianic promise that the Virgin Mary uniquely and pre-eminently presides. In Catholic churches all over the world her image gazes down from wall and window at these priestly sacrifices and the divine scandals of discontinuity, contamination, desire, and death that they mediate and attempt to contain. And Mary is present, too, in many more heterodox places, in households, on the windshields of cars, in museums and hospitals, in improvised shrines and backyard sanctuaries and cult and quasi-cult sites such as Guadelupe; Lourdes; Fatima; Knock; Medjugorie; Lubbock, Texas; and Bayside, New York. And as evidenced in a recent controversial exhibition in London and at the Brooklyn Museum, she is present in protest, parody, and perversion as well as in piety and obedience.[23] She is the protectress of women and the consolation of the poor, but she is also the conqueress of the indigenous, a talisman of anti-Communist and anti-Semitic piety, a pillar of nationalist ideologies, official patron of the Legion of Decency, and the perpetual dismay of many a libertarian.[24] So great are the recent proliferations of icons and cults of Mary, and so far have they moved from orthodoxy, that an attempt to contain or at least reassociate her with the eucharistic liturgy has had to be strongly reasserted in papal letters, orthodoxy being unerring in this way if no other, that it always puts its finger on a major contradiction.[25]

But what is she doing there in these churches, silent witness (for Mary, like Socrates, does not write) at the sacrificial death of her son and the beginning of its dissemination in the words of the apostles? What in the world can her "presence," so different from the presence of the Logos, possibly mean? It is hard to say, for Mary is herself at once ultimate scandal and ultimate containment of revealed monotheism, breaking the logo- and phallogo-centric model apart at its core, eluding its binaries and yet reinstating at another, sometimes toxic, but sometimes homeopathic level, the purity and order sought for by the system.[26] Representing pure exogamy by intercourse only with the *tout autre*, and then reinstating endogamy to the point of incest by asserting the identity of that *autre* with God the Father, Mary both constructs and deconstructs the kinship system of Israel. Matrix of the incarnate Word of God, the bearer of what Eliot called "the Word within a word, unable to speak a word," she both protects and disperses its multiple meanings. In the assertion of her simple humanity, and with that reticence or scruple which prevents her from either prophesying or "celebrating" the Eucharist, Mary not only accedes to logocentrism and phallogocentrism but demonstrates that she will not be contained within them. And in the oxymoronic virginal dissemination and fecundation she enables may be seen something like the two paths which, according to Derrida, lie before us with respect to religion today, 1) a turn to *messianicité* without messianism and 2) a move out into the zone indicated by the ambiguous term *chora*, which reorients, if that is the word, the monotheistic revelations toward that vast "desert within a desert" at their limits.

There are two particularly striking ways in which Mary acts as both support and supplement to the logos and as a prime point of dissemination into the *chora*, beyond the bounds of Christian and even monotheistic orthodoxy. The focal point for the first is her original, affirming yes at the Annunciation; and for the second her appearance as The Woman Clothed with the Sun, a title taken from the book of Revelation associated not only with a significant change in the cultural imaginary[27] but with a rising global tide of Marian apparitions, many of them widely disseminated through medals, holy pictures, television images, and photographs.[28] Her founding yes and her apocalyptic reappearance signal not only her significant role in the cultural imaginary of the monotheisms—a role sometimes quite divergent from orthodoxy—but her connection to the messianic promise and to her possible place in the great postmodern *chora*, in which even the name of God seems at times lost to view.

In the New Testament text of Luke 2, the story of the Annunciation, one of the most frequently read and frequently depicted texts in all of Western culture, the narrative begins with Mary as an espoused virgin. (The term "virgin" is a famous crux of textual criticism and exegetical debate.[29]) To that virgin or young woman comes an angel who announces that she shall bear a son and give him a name, Jesus. Unlike the case of the parallel birth story of John the Baptist, who is named by his father Zachariah, *she* will give him the name. Who else is there to do it? From one point of view, this is matriline pure and simple. When Mary immediately asks "How shall these things be, seeing that I know not a man?" the question is generic as well as practical. How can the human community go forward without fathers? Not to worry, says the angel. This line of filiation is a spiritual, not a biological, one; the Holy Ghost, as the old translation has it, will plant the seed, and that seed will "reign over the house of Jacob, and of His kingdom there shall be no end." The patriline is to be supported here by a new investment of seminal energy, and its duration through time is guaranteed. "Behold the handmaid of the Lord," says Mary in acquiescence: "be it done unto me according to Thy word." The logocentrism and phallogocentrism are clear here and so is their direct relationship to the messianic promise; but so also is another, a supplementary set of meanings to which we must in a moment turn.[30] In any case, it is to this whole structure that Mary says her founding "yes, yes," her *fiat mihi*, her "here am I."

Though Mary is most frequently paralleled here with Eve in Christian typology, her parallel with Abraham is, I think, though hitherto obscured by an excessive focus on gender, in many ways more revealing. For in undergoing the ritual purifications required by the cult, in presenting her child in the temple, taking him to Jerusalem for his ritual coming of age and arguably even in accompanying him to the cross, Mary is always, no more and no less, an Abrahamic figure, the faithful, prudent and circumspect daughter of the *akedah*, the binding of Isaac. Unlike Mary Magdalen, she is neither a fallen member of the old covenant nor an apostle of the new; and unlike her son, not one word is recorded of her in scripture that could not in theory be said by any faithful Jew, not even after the resurrection. She is exactly as one of her liturgical titles says, "The Chosen Daughter of Israel."[31]

But Mary's yes is Abrahamic not only in its obedience, but in the more extended, more ambivalent, more "deconstructed" sense given to it in a line of philosophical reflections stemming from Kierkegaard through Levinas to Derrida.[32] Indeed, we might apply to it one of Geoffrey Bennington's useful glosses on Derrida's understanding of this kind of discourse:

> To say "yes, yes" to the law . . . is in no way a passive obedience to a law whose justice is not even interrogated. To the contrary: it is only this preoriginary relation which makes possible the democratic discussion of the laws demanded in principle by the thought of the contact.[33]

For it may be noted that when she countersigns, Mary makes some terms. "Be it done to me," she says, but not "be it done to me in any old way": rather, "be it done to me according to Thy word." And what, after all, does Mary mean by "according to Thy word"? She means, among others things, according to the prior word of Hebrew scripture, the scripture on which she had been raised, that very "word" in which the story of the binding of Isaac, with its saving outcome, its undeconstructible justice, had repeatedly been told. By specifying her "be it done to me" in these terms, Mary indicates, of course, the sacrificial economy, but like the binding itself she also points to another symbolic order beyond that, to the possibility—the gift, if you like—of a line of descent without violation, one in which sex, childbirth, and kinship do not lead inevitably to closed systems and zero-sum games, and in which paternal and social identity, as well as maternal and ethnic difference, may be nonviolently sustained.

Sustained, but not reified. For this yes of Mary's at the Annunciation, seen as echo or countersignature to that of Father Abraham, deconstructs not only a number of metaphysical but a number of gender binaries as well. With Mary's Abrahamic consent, we are led to the "before" of binary oppositions in which the operative terms will certainly not be femininized but will no longer allow themselves simply to be marked for masculine gender without comment. Mary's yes, that is to say, throws into sharp relief the masculine attribute of God, which might otherwise have gone unremarked as a mere synonym for his mastery, propelling that masculinity (though not "all the way," as we say), toward the spousal, the hymen, the intermingled. What is feminine in this stance of Mary's is precisely to show how the opposition between masculine and feminine itself depends on its "lesser" term.[34] The overdetermined masculinity and mastery associated with God the Father is not contradicted but put *sous rature*, or framed by Mary's invagination of the divine, her consent to act as its matrix and, figuratively speaking (for gender is really a kind of figuration in this orbit of thought) as its spouse.

In framing the divine in this way, Mary gives birth to that decentered, deconstructive space in which, as Bennington puts it, "absolutely singular configurations have a chance to be events."[35] It is to this chance of the birth of a true singularity that Mary, in consenting to the Incarnation, says yes. In doing so, however, she activates the old paradox of exemplarity that so haunts deconstructive discourse, because so, of course, does every mother who says yes, who carries her child to term in that ultimate generic "throw of dice" which is the continuation through dissemination of the genetic code.[36] And it is only by means of this yes in both its particular and its generic forms, that is, as both incarnation and ordinary pregnancy, that we can achieve the "universalizable culture" of those singularities, as Derrida calls it, as opposed to the monological patriline of clones, toward which our political discourse and our struggle for justice would move.

The whole picture is, however, further complicated and even darkened when we turn to the extended implications of Mary's yes. For in the same chapter as the Annunciation in the gospel of Luke, we learn that her fiat is going to have to encompass not only the Incarnation, the birth, but also the cross, the death of her son, and its tragic aftermath for Judaism and in a way for the world as well. No deferring sacrificial ram is going to appear in *this* story. Not too long after the birth of the child, after the days set aside for her purification and after his circumcision—in their case technicalities because both are sinless, but ones that Mary pointedly observes—Luke's gospel tells us that Mary takes the baby to the temple, along with the requisite sacrificial turtledoves and pigeons. Accepting the offering, the priest Simeon says "Behold, this child is set for the fall and rising again of many in Israel: and for a sign which shall be spoken against. Yes, a sword shall pierce through Thy own soul also that the thoughts of many hearts may be revealed" (Luke 2:34ff.).

Tradition holds that sword to be the lance of the crucifixion, which Bernard of Clairvaux, the great Marian visionary, tells us pierced through the body of Jesus and into the heart of Mary at one and the same stroke.[37] Hence, as this prophecy of Simeon's implies, Mary's yes in the temple entails, shockingly enough, not only the sacrificial death of the innocent birds but the sacrificial death of her son as well. By extension of the trope, particularly in the gospel of John, that sword also entrains the violence that will in the future sever the children of the synagogue from the children of the church and split Mary's identity apart at the root. So Mary is here acceding not only to the precedent of the binding but to that precedent at its most extreme: the rift it opens between her own religious past and future, between the two covenants and between the life and death of her child.

We may note, however, that, structurally speaking, the extremity of that outcome matches the extremity of the problem it is designed to rectify. For given his ambiguous origins, Jesus is first and foremost the "natural" maternal child of a woman, who threatens as such to dissolve the particularity of Israel into a generic type, a self-evident, universally readable mother-and-son pair. Nothing to quarrel with, nothing unique to speak of there. To represent the one desiring God, he must also be reinserted into the patriline in the most conclusive way possible, and that patriline must assert a difference between particular Judaism and a universal *christianicité* in no uncertain terms. Indeed, Jesus is so paradigmatically a mother's son and universal innocent, and his crucifixion so paradigmatically rectifying of that unhappy condition, that the great New Testament letter to the Hebrews can say that here sacrifice has been performed "once and for all," ending the Judaic temple cult forever, even when it comes to substitute animals.[38]

Mary countersigns this sacrificial economy; she is obedient to it, scandalously obedient, we might even say, and her obedience is, scripture and tradition alike make clear, unalleviated by any direct foreknowledge of the resurrection or of the messianic promise of the harmony of the two covenants to come. Twice we are told that she "ponders" these things in her heart without apparent resolution, once at the Annunciation and the second time when Jesus, having been taken to Jerusalem, evades her to stay behind debating with the rabbis in the temple. Orthodox interpretation insists in both cases that Mary knows something is up, but she does not know what. For according to tradition, the Virgin is explicitly denied the kind of prophetic foreknowledge and/or consoling beatific vision associated with so many other saints.[39] She is the condition of the messianic sacrifice—she brings the child to biological birth and to the temple cult of the fathers—but she is neither its celebrant nor its apostle. She consents but she does not collude, nor could she, either from a psychological, an anthropological, or a theological point of view. If she were to become a celebrant or evangelist, not only would she make nonsense of her ethical position as mother while at the same time nullifying rather than fulfilling the temple cult by being a woman and impure, she would also disqualify herself from performing the witnessing function which stems from her place within the structure but by the same token allows her to stand outside of its restricted economy.

Mary's response to the call of the divine brings closure to the great "here I am" of Abraham, replacing or completing him typologically as founding father of Israel with herself as the founding mother of the Church. In doing so, this response offers to Judaism a dangerous supplement indeed. It also, however, moves Mary into a further position of supplementarity beyond even this deadly binary. For Mary's "according to Thy Word," it will be remembered, allows reference to a story in which not only are the lives of Isaac and his father at stake, but so are lives well outside that line of filiation, the lives in this case of Ishmael and Hagar, who were driven out into the wilderness but who survived and even flourished in that desert air. In the intertextual space between the scriptural word and Mary's yes are activated memories of both Isaac and Ishmael, because Mary is at once, like one and the other, the mother of an "illegitimate" child and of the heir to the house of David. Her countersigning word folds back here, then, not only to encompass the particularities of the cross and the *akedah* but the seed of Islam, and through Islam's generic insistence, all the children of Adam. Indeed, it is in part because of this fold that she can play the major role in the Qur'an that she does.

Further consideration of "how these things might be" and what resonance they might have for the relationships among the monotheisms must for moment be deferred. I would simply point out that we have here through Mary something like the classic fold or hymen of supplementation and dissemination indicated in the extravagant Derridean phrase "double chiasmic invagination of the edges," that is to say, a structure that most enfolds what it appears most to exclude. Judaism, Christianity and Islam are here braided into a complex knot which may be traced but never pulled apart, and they are interimbricated by an inviolate textuality, a never-broken hymen between logos and dissemination, in which no jot or tittle of the law is violated. For Mary is both within and outside their economies at one and the same time; indeed, she demonstrates the difference they can make to one another.

For this reason we may trace in Mary something of that stance toward the coming of the other that Derrida adumbrates in *Religion*: that is to say, *messianicité* without messianism, the opening to the future or to the coming of the other as the advent of justice but "without the horizon of expectation." Mary figures a kind of surprise at the advent of the other which fully admits that with it comes not only the possibility but the probability of death and radical evil; a suspicion that is confirmed by the words of Simeon and confirmed indeed in the event. Her founding and overturning yes takes place precisely in the Derridean quasi-messianic mode of "interrupting or tearing history itself apart, doing it by *deciding* [my emphasis] in a decision that can consist in letting the other come and that can take the apparently passive form of the other's decision."[40] That responsibility meets its acid test at the foot of the cross, where Mary loses her unique, her particular, son to gain the children of the world. "Mother," says Christ, pointing to the disciple John, "behold your son; son, behold your mother"—the proof-text, as it has always been taken, of Mary's founding of the Church, but also, as we have seen, of a generic motherhood that overflows its boundaries.[41]

This is not, however, Mary's last appearance, either in scripture or in history. Indeed, it may be said to be only the beginning of a proliferation of appearances in art, literature, and music and in the form of apparitions and visions which, far from abating, have grown in frequency, publicity, and intensity throughout the centuries, especially in recent times.[42] Marian apparitions are among the most striking phenomena of twentieth-century global religion, and they affect far more people than ever have or probably ever will identify themselves with the Catholic church or even with Christianity per se. What interests me here, however, is less the extent and distribution of these apparitions than their frequent iconographical and thematic association with the figure called The Woman Clothed with the Sun. This figure lies at the heart of the apocalyptic discourse of Chapter 12 of the book of Revelation:

> And there appeared a great wonder in heaven: a woman clothed with the sun, and the moon under her feet, and upon her head a crown of twelve stars. And she being with child cried travailing in birth, and pained to be delivered. . . . And the dragon stood before the woman which was ready to be delivered for to devour her child as soon as it was born. . . . And she brought forth a man child and the child was caught up unto God, and to his throne. And the woman fled into the wilderness where she hath a place prepared of God . . . where she is nourished for a time, and times, and half a time.

This wilderness is a remarkable, a significant, place. Among other things, it is truly terra incognita, a zone of indeterminacy which bears a close resemblance to the place, or no place, to which Derrida has assigned the Platonic term *chora*.[43] This place, Derrida says, is "radically heterogeneous to the safe and sound, to the holy and sacred," and it will never "admit of any indemnification." It is the habitat of infinite alterity, "before and after the logos which was in the beginning, before and after the Holy Sacrament, before and after the Holy Scriptures," a place as readily figured in terms of the monstrous dragon as of the divine child. Here, we might say, the Abrahamic religions find their own "outside;" the dangerous and war-torn place in which they must learn under pressure to submit to that which resists interrogation, that which "not allowing itself to be dominated by any theological, ontological or anthropological instance, without age, without history and more 'ancient' than all oppositions . . . does not even announce itself as 'beyond being.'" And the time of this *chora* is the time of ordeal, *l'épreuve de chora*, a secular time that seems twice as long as it is to some and yet not half long enough to others. "Now is the tryin' time" says the old spiritual, and the tryin' time, say the theologians who comment on Revelations 12, is the age, the wilderness, the crisis of lived experience today.[44]

It is into this wilderness that the "woman clothed with the Sun" is driven out, separated now alike from her child and from her proper name. And its monsters give her no quarter, just as Derrida warns; they offer, just as he says, "not the slightest generosity, whether divine nor human." "The dispersion of ashes is not even promised there nor death given"; it is a strange region, this "outside," or *chora*, one "founded," if that is the word, less on de-negation or absolute denial than on what Derrida calls "an always virgin impassability," a memory, a remote chance, a reservoir, a risk, a "chora of tomorrow in languages we no longer know or do not yet speak." In this indeterminacy, according to scripture, the woman is not only protected but nourished. In fact, she is safer than she would be inside some more particular, more precisely named, more officially sanctioned encampment. We are even given some notice that her son lives, though his name and messianic function are unspecified and we are told he is far away.[45]

Is this religion? "*Spondem tu istud? Spondeo*," Derrida might rejoin. "Religion, nothing less." Perhaps. But is it not from this place "before and after the logos that was in the beginning, before and after the Holy Sacrament, before and after the Holy Scriptures"—and before and after "religion," so-called—that Mary, and many like her, have uttered the words "yes, yes," "*viens*," "come O Lord," "here am I," "be it done to me according to Thy Word"?

NOTES

1. Derrida's analysis of logocentrism and of supplementarity may be found in *Of Grammatology*, trans. Gayatri Spivak (Baltimore: Johns Hopkins University Press, 1974), 14–64 and passim.

2. See also Terry Rey, *Our Lady of Class Struggle: The Cult of the Virgin Mary in Haiti* (Trenton, N.J.: Africa World Press, 1999), 99–237.

3. The association of Marian cults with national consciousness is well attested in almost every part of the globe, most notably perhaps in the cases of Poland and Cuba. For a close study of the latter, see Thomas Tweed, *Our Lady of the Exile: Diasporic Religion at a Cuban Catholic Shrine in Miami* (New York: Oxford University Press, 1997). For Mary and eschatology, see Sandra Zimdars-Swartz, *Encountering Mary: Visions of Mary from La Salette to Medjugorji* (New York: Avon Books, 1991) and "The

Marian Revival in American Catholicism: Focal Points and Features of the New Marian Enthusiasm," in *Being Right: Conservative Catholics in America,* ed. Mary Jo Weaver and R. Scott Appleby (Bloomington: Indiana University Press, 1995).

4. For the Derridean concept of the *chora,* see below, note 31. The phrase "questioning God" alludes to the title of October 1999 conference, "Religion and Postmodernism 2: Questioning God" at Villanova University, which occasioned this volume.

5. Among the few American scholars who have read Derrida well in this respect are John D. Caputo and Robert Magliola. Magliola is exact and exacting reader of Derrida with an extensive background in Christian theology and Buddhist philosophy as well as phenomenology. He is also, in fact, first in my knowledge to have advanced the notion of Mary as Derridean supplement, though in slightly different terms than mine and with a different point of departure. The aspect I am calling Mary's supplemental function Magliola calls Mary's "secondariness"; he goes on to show how that "secondariness" reverts to a form of priority at key points in the structure, especially in the Magnificat, Mary's song of triumph at the Annunciation. See *Shadow of Spirit* (London: Routledge, 1993), 211–226.

6. See also Jacques Derrida, *Dissemination,* trans. Barbara Johnson (Chicago: University of Chicago Press, 1981), 227–286

7. See also Jacques Derrida, "White Mythology: Metaphor in the Text of Philosophy," in *Margins of Philosophy,* trans. Alan Bass (Chicago: University of Chicago Press, 1982), 207–273.

8. Edith Wyschogrod, "Eating the Text, Defiling the Hands," in *God, the Gift, and Postmodernism,* ed. John D. Caputo and Michael J. Scanlon (Bloomington: Indiana University Press, 1999), 256.

9. Musings on threefold structures and their supplementation by some fourth term have a long history in theology and philosophy, drawing on roots deep in Christian and neo-Platonic thought, and this observation does not by any means exhaust their possibilities as resources for a critical theology. Derrida himself both indulges in and critiques such esoteric numerological meditations on threeness and fourness, most extensively in *Dissemination* and in *Truth in Painting.* For a discussion of trinitarian doctrine in the light of these musings and of the Buddhist logic of the third and fourth lemmas, see Robert Magliola, *Derrida on the Mend* (West Lafayette, Ind.: Purdue University Press, 1984).

10. See also Rosemary Radford Reuther, *Mary: The Feminine Face of the Church* (Philadelphia: Westminster Press, 1977), 43; and Leonard Boff, *The Maternal Face of God: The Feminine and Its Religious Expressions* (New York: Harper and Row, 1987), 189.

11. Warner is well aware of the pitfalls of the Jungian reading of Mary, but she does not thereby escape a certain kind of reduction. "The Virgin Mary," she writes "is not the innate archetype of female nature, the dream incarnate; she is the instrument of a dynamic argument from the Catholic Church about the structure of society, presented as a God-given code." *Alone of All Her Sex: The Myth and Cult of the Virgin Mary* (New York: Vintage Books, 1983), 338. Cited by Francoise Meltzer, "Re-embodying: Secularizing Virginity," in *God, the Gift, and Postmodernism,* 274.

12. This anxiety is intensified, in Israelite tradition, when the text comes in contact with sacred food. See Wyschogrod, "Eating the Text, Defiling the Hands," passim.

13. This point forms part of the argument of Richard Kearney's "Desire of God," in *God, the Gift, and Postmodernism,* 112–130.

14. Derrida affirms this classic definition in Derrida and Vattimo, *Religion* (Stanford, Calif.: Stanford University Press, 1996), 2.

15. See Stephen Geller's study of the Pentateuch, *Sacred Enigmas: Literary Religion in the Hebrew Bible* (London: Routledge, 1996), which points out the extreme emphasis on blood in the "P" tradition (62–87).

16. Nancy Jay, *Throughout Your Generations Forever: Sacrifice, Religion, and Paternity* (Chicago: University of Chicago Press, 1992).

17. Ibid., 147.

18. Ibid., 39.

19. Note that this is not to say that ancient Israel was a matrilineal society, a claim that Jay does not make; quite the contrary. On this point, see Shaye J. D. Cohen, *The Beginnings of Jewishness: Boundaries, Varieties, Uncertainties* (Berkeley: University of California Press, 1999), which argues that such matrilineal descent as Judaism shows is the creation of the second-century CE rabbinate.

20. For a different reading of the *akedah* and a critique of Jay see Carol Delaney, *Abraham on Trial: The Social Legacy of Biblical Myth* (Princeton: Princeton University Press, 1998). Delaney sees the *akedah* neither in terms of ritual in general nor of sacrifice in particular, but rather in terms of a discourse of paternity that regards the male as the transmitter of both biological and cultural identity, with the female acting only as a "vessel" of his seed. I think she is mistaken both in divorcing the *akedah* completely from a ritual context and in totalizing this assumption with respect to ancient Israel, where the child is first and foremost a child of God, rather than of man or woman. It is only by an act of cultural intervention—circumcision or legitimacy and/or marriage in the case of a female—that the child becomes a member of the house of Israel. See Shaye Cohen, "Why Aren't Jewish Women Circumcised?," *Gender and History* 9 (1997): 560–578.

21. Derrida and Vattimo, *Religion*, 31.

22. These needs could certainly be met, in theory at least, by "designating" a woman as occupying the masculine position for the purposes of the cult. But such a solution, if solution it be, would raise other problems without even fully addressing the feminist critique of patriarchal priesthood. In any case, the underlying structural and anthropological issues would have to be articulated, a task which conservative theology forecloses and liberal theology often fails to touch.

23. I refer to the painting *The Holy Virgin Mary* by Chris Ofili, in the controversial exhibit "Sensation," consisting of contemporary work by British artists, which opened in the United States on October 2, 1999, at the Brooklyn Museum. The painting shows the figure of the Virgin depicted as dark-skinned, spattered with elephant dung. At least a portion of the viewing public viewed this image as by intention a pious one, designed to make a statement about the fate of innocence in the world today.

24. See Michael Caroll, *Madonnas that Maim: Popular Catholicism in Italy since the Fifteenth Century* (Baltimore: Johns Hopkins University Press, 1992), an account of Marian cults in rural and southern Italy more nuanced than its title suggests; and William Christian, *Apparitions in Late Medieval and Renaissance Spain* (Princeton: Princeton University Press, 1989); and *Visionaries: The Spanish Republic and The Reign of Christ* (Princeton: Princeton University Press, 1996).

25. See the letters "*Marialis Cultus*: On Devotion to the Blessed Virgin Mary," Paul VI, 1974, and "*Redemptoris Mater*: On the Blessed Virgin Mary," John Paul II, 1987.

26. Her virginity is central to this problematic position. Some of the reasons that make it so are adumbrated in a different context by Meltzer, "Re-embodying: Secularizing Virginity," 260–282. Meltzer points out that according to traditional constructions of womanhood, a virgin is a subject only *in potentia*, a reservoir of fecundity awaiting an opening for release. As such, she is a kind of third term, in Edward Leach's sense, marking the place of danger and the sacred, if only under the rubric of monstrosity. When Meltzer comes to treat Mary directly, she follows Warner and Kristeva, finding Mary problematic as an exemplar of womanhood and hence "too confusing" to serve as a model for women. I am arguing that it is precisely this problematic and destabilizing position in the structure that allows her to function, for men and women, in both orthodox and unorthodox ways.

27. The iconography of the immaculate conception was developed by, among others, Titian, Tiepolo, Velasquez, Murillo, and Zurbaran. See also Edward Dennis O'Connor, *The Dogma of the Immaculate Conception: History and Significance* (Notre Dame, Ind.: University of Notre Dame Press, 1958), 124 ff.

28. For a suggestive discussion of some aspects of the association of Marian cults with dissemination through mass-produced replication, see Colleen McDannell, *Material Christianity: Religion and Popular Culture in America* (New Haven: Yale University Press, 1998); and for their illustration, Kay Turner's *Beautiful Necessity: The Art and Meaning of Women's Altars* (New York: Thames & Hudson, 1999). In the founding visions associated with the immaculate conception, Mary appears alone to the poor and humble, standing on the crescent moon or on a cloud of cherubs, often with an apocalyptic or eschatological message to share. Over time, these visions have acquired a standard iconography. Usually Mary appears without the child. In the case of the Lourdes grotto at Notre Dame University in Indiana, however, the child has been added to the image, standing before Mary with a flaming heart.

29. Christian exegesis relates Luke 1:32 to Isaiah 7:14, now most often translated as "and a young woman shall conceive, and bear a son." The Septuagint gives the term "young woman" the specific meaning virgin, *parthenos*, and the implication of that rabbinic decision is fully exploited in Roman Catholic theology of the Virgin Birth, though Protestants express a greater scruple with respect to the textual history and offer a more diverse, sometimes more naturalistic interpretation.

30. For an interesting revaluation both of generic virginity and of the Virgin Birth, see Luce Irigaray, *Entre Orient et Occident: De la singularité a la communaute* (Paris: Bernard Grasset, 1999), 72–72, 92–94.

31. See also Bertrand Buby, S.M., "The Jewishness of Mary," in *Mary of Galilee*, vol. II (New York: Alba House, 1995), 6–81.

32. The Abraham problem is canvassed and each of its turns of interpretation in modern and postmodern philosophy is well understood in Caputo's *Against Ethics: Contributions to a Poetics of Obligation with Constant Reference to Deconstruction* (Bloomington: Indiana University Press, 1993), 1–41 and passim.

33. Geoffrey Bennington and Jacques Derrida, *Jacques Derrida* (Chicago: University of Chicago Press, 1993), 254–255.

34. See also ibid., 215–216.

35. Ibid., 55.

36. Derrida, *Dissemination*, 122.

37. See also Donald Atwater, *A Dictonary of Mary* (New York: P. J. Kenedy and Sons, 1956), 282.

38. For a fuller discussion of the sacrifice of the son in Judaism and Christianity, see John Levenson, *The Death and Resurrection of the Beloved Son: The Transformation of Child Sacrifice in Judaism and Christianity* (New Haven: Yale University Press, 1993).

39. See Hans urs von Balthasar, *Mary for Today* (San Francisco: Ignatius Press, 1998), 36–37.

40. Derrida and Vattimo, *Religion*, 17.

41. Even in this, she is no more or less than a daughter of Israel. See Psalm 86:87: "Babylon and Egypt I will count / among those who know me /. . . . and Sion shall be called 'Mother' / for all shall be her children" (translation taken from *Daily Prayer from the Divine Office* [London: Collins, 1974]).

42. The escalation of these apparitions has, partly through the media, partly through their association with apocalyptic themes, by now become a worldwide and much-canvassed phenomenon. Not only do a million and half people a year visit the Rue du Bac, where Mary appeared to Catherine Laboure in 1830, but nearly two million a year visit Lourdes and twelve million a year the basilica of Our Lady of Guadelupe. When we add to these the many millions who have seen and still see material traces of her presence in such places as Medjugorie, Lubbock, and Bayside, New York, we have a phenomenon hard to understand, much less to control; one that is treated with marked caution by the Roman Catholic hierarchy.

43. The term arises from Derrida's close reading of Plato in *Khora* (Paris: Galilee, 1993); English translation by Ian McLeod in *On the Name*, ed. Thomas Dutoit (Stanford, Calif.: Stanford University Press, 1995). An illuminating discussion of Derrida's use of the term and his relationship to Plato may be found in J. D. Caputo's *Deconstruction in a Nutshell* (New York: Fordham University Press, 1997), 71–106.

44. Derrida and Vattimo, *Religion*, 21.

45. These and the following Derridean phrases are from Derrida and Vattimo, *Religion*, 20–22. This reading of Revelation 12 is based on the exegesis of von Balthasar's *Mary for Today*, 9–20. The text is often regarded as Balthasar's attack on the attempt of liberation theology to reappropriate Mary as a model of the active struggle for social justice rather than of passive obedience to the divine word. At one level this may be, but here, as elsewhere, conservative theology can offer important insights that liberal readings often overlook.

fourteen

Being, Subjectivity, Otherness

The Idols of God

Francis Schüssler Fiorenza

Theology should talk about God. Yet, whenever it does, it confesses the inadequacy of its very language about God. Theology lives off this tension between the need to speak of God and the inadequacy of its language about God. This tension is the motor driving theology to search for adequate language and at the same time to reflect critically on the inadequacy of its language about God. The categories of being, subjectivity, and otherness are common sites for talking about God. If, however, the adequacy of these sites is simply taken for granted, they can become not only inadequate categories but also substitutes for God. Taking the place of God, they become idols of God.

Hence, theology faces a dilemma. If theology stresses the inadequacy of its basic categories, it runs the risk of failing to say anything about God. At a time when the quest for meaning and the search for God is intensifying, the increased advocacy of a negative theology seems to imply that nothing can be said about God. If theology rejects the categories of being, subjectivity, and otherness, then it appears to be atheistic, denying being, subjectivity, and transcendence to God. If, however, theology uncritically accepts these categories, then it has locked God in an iron cage—a cage to keep "god," like an idol, safe and sound. Theology then talks about its safely secured idols rather than about a God that breaks out of the cages of the human imagination. In short, theology's dilemma is this: How can it talk about God except in such categories? How can it talk about God without such categories?

Today, many call our situation "postmodern,"[1] and many argue that it calls for a postmodern theology. The question then becomes: How does one talk about God in a postmodern situation? One solution offered is to reject the first two of the categories as idols of God but to exempt the third category from criticism.[2] Metaphysics, with its appeal to a universal rationality, and subjectivity, with its emphasis on autonomy, are often said to be specifically modern. Thus, the categories of being and subjectivity should be rejected. "Otherness," or "alterity," then becomes the only appropriate category for God in our postmodern age. I do not concur but shall argue that instead each one of these categories is problematic and ambiguous. Each category must be recast, and yet each category has significance as a site for language about God.

Some strains of *modern* theology oppose the God of Abraham with the God of Philosophy—and I emphasize the word "modern" because it is very modern to follow Pascal. Such a contrast departs from much of the theological tradition. Can one imagine Origen or Augustine, Anselm or Thomas Aquinas, Erasmus or Galileo, Cardinal Nicholas of Cusa or Cardinal Robert Bellarmine, not to mention Trent and Vatican I, making this contrast central to the theological task? The sectarian Montanist, Tertullian, but not the "Catholic," tradition can be adduced as a premodern foundation of such a sharp contrast. However, some even suggest the retrieval of a non-metaphysical Augustine, as if one could conceive of Augustine's theology without its intertwinement in Hellenistic metaphysics.[3] If such a sharp contrast is an event of *modern* theology in distinction to the long tradition of classical Christian theology, then one has to ask: What does a postmodern Christian theology mean? Does it mean that one follows the "modernist" post-Enlightenment dichotomy between the God of Abraham and the God of Philosophy? Or does it mean that one should go back to the "synthesis" created in classical Catholic Christian theology? Or, perhaps, as I shall suggest, does it mean that one should follow neither the sharp dichotomy nor the attuned synthesis, but, seeking to go beyond each, should develop a path between the contrast of otherness and sameness?

Emmanuel Levinas has written that "to ask oneself, as we are attempting to do here, whether God cannot be uttered in a reasonable discourse that would be neither ontology nor faith, is implicitly to doubt the formal opposition, established by Yehuda Halevy and taken up by Pascal, between the God of Abraham, Isaac, and Jacob, invoked without philosophy in faith, and on the other the god of philosophers. It is to doubt that this opposition constitutes an alternative."[4] As Levinas notes, this alternative is indeed a post-Enlightenment contrast: one he seeks to avoid. It is an alternative that should not be anachronistically projected back into the tradition. Moreover, the avoidance of such a sharp alternative has consequences not only for our language about God but also for our ethical language about love, justice, and forgiveness that flows from our belief and understanding of God. Therefore, in trying to avoid this contrast, I shall argue for the crisscrossing of these traditions and for a dialectical relationship between sameness and otherness in ways that Levinas's own understanding of otherness and his own conception of ethics may not allow. I proceed first by sketching the ambiguities and problems of the sites not only of being and subjectivity but also of otherness and alterity. Then a more constructive section seeks to take into account these ambiguities and recast these sites.

Being as the Site of God

The metaphysical site for language about God has come to be viewed recently as the dividing line between modernity and postmodernity. Such a dividing line might appear appropriate. After all, postmodernity is usually defined in terms of the radical contingency of reason. It is also viewed as the exodus from all essentialist and metaphysical thinking. Nevertheless, metaphysics in itself cannot be the dividing line between postmodernity and modernity. One of the hallmarks of modernity is the very critique of traditional ontology and metaphysics. When postmodern theologians accept the critique of metaphysics as integral to postmodernity, they need to examine the critique of metaphysics as it emerged within modernity and explore its import and consequences. In order to highlight the ambiguities of being as the site of language about God, I shall first examine the dilemmas in the metaphysical notion of God, the modern critique of metaphysics, and the theological reception of this critique.

The Dilemma of Otherness and Immanence in the Metaphysical Notion of God

Several basic tensions exist in traditional Christian conceptions of God. One such tension is the conflict between popular and metaphysical language about God. Popular religious language about God speaks of God in very anthropomorphic terms, whereas philosophical and metaphysical language about God is critical of such anthropomorphisms and seeks to avoid them.[5] However, philosophical and metaphysical understandings of God are themselves also not without tensions. On the one hand, they seek to conceive of God in categories that avoid reducing God to a being or an individual being. God is the "to be" of being or God is the "act of being." On the other hand, they refer to God as a perfect or supreme being, as if God were indeed a being but the most perfect and powerful one. The assertion that God is beyond being faces similar ambiguities. On the one hand, God is beyond being, even beyond the metaphysical category of "origin" (*arche*). On the other hand, God is the "cause" or "author" or maker (*poiein*) of being. Even though it is claimed that God is beyond being, categories are used that nevertheless integrate God into the chain of being, such as the metaphysical categories of cause and effect.[6]

This tension is also present in the contrast between transcendence and immanence within a metaphysical understanding of God. On the one side, God as infinite is contrasted with the world as finite. The infinite has its existence from itself, whereas the finite does not. The finite as finite is not only contingent but it is limited in space and time so that one cannot even think of a "created infinity." The contrast between eternity and time illustrates the difference between the infinite and finite. Eternity is not simply a time that goes on and on as if it were the path of time that simply continued onward. Such an understanding reduces eternity to a linear temporality. Instead, eternity contrasts with the very limitations and periodizations of time. Likewise, within the metaphysical notion of God, God is understood as the undifferentiated unity or as the first principle (beyond being) that is far removed from the multiplicity of the world. In such a conception, the distance or dissimilarity between God and the world is such that God is not to be conceived of as the most perfect form of what is creaturely. Instead, God is what cannot be comprehended within such worldly categories.

The other side of the metaphysical notion of God conceives of God as absolute and underscores the immanence of God to the world or, rather, the world to God. Such a conception of God considers God as "Being Itself" or the "To Be" of beings in contrast to finite individual beings. This approach to God does not employ metaphors that place God at a distance from the world. Instead, it conceives of God as the Creative Power, Principle of Creativity, Serendipitous Creativity, or Spirit that moves and waltzes through the world. This view interprets notions of creation as free and from nothing in ways that support rather than undercut the immanence of God. Creation as "self-communication" or as "donation" or "gift" of being underscores that God's own being becomes the principle of the being of creatures.

Thomas Aquinas's combination of the Aristotelian metaphysical categories of causality with the neo-Platonic categories of emanation and participation illustrates this tension. His commentary on Proclus's *Liber de Causis* (a neo-Platonic work mistakenly thought to be Aristotelian) combines two very different metaphysical categories. In addition to Aristotle's category of efficient causality, Thomas affirms that God contains all things (similar to Cusanus's *complicatio*).[7] This is not Aristotelian efficient causality, but Platonic form causality. The preservation of all things in God is explained with reference to neo-Platonic causality.[8] To the extent that being exists, it participates in the very being that is God.[9] This tension expresses the distinction between understanding the relationship between God and the world in terms of causal efficiency or in terms of participation in which the infinite is conceived of much more as the absolute ground of the world.

The metaphysical notion of God has two interlocking but distinct perspectives. Each challenges popular conceptions. If God is understood as the infinite in contrast to the finite, then metaphors of God as a person are inadequate if they depict God in ways that mirror the contingencies and limitations of individual persons or the relationality of personal subjectivity. Likewise, to understand God as the principle of being, even if one maintains that human subjectivity is closer to God's own being, is to describe God with a categorical framework that is other than the limitations of the categories of individual personhood.

The Theological Interpretation and Reception of the Critique of Metaphysics

Immanuel Kant's analysis of the aporia and antinomies of the rational metaphysics is a significant hallmark of modern philosophy. One can interpret Kant's critique as modern insofar as one views it as a much more radical development of the skeptical issues that David Hume had brought against metaphysics.[10] Nevertheless, both Kant's critique of rational theology and his criticisms of the proofs of God's existence provoked within modernity very diverse theological responses. One of these, the German Protestant Lutheran response, welcomed Kant's conclusion. Lutherans viewed Kant as furthering Luther's objections to natural theology. In setting out the limits of metaphysical reason, Kant liberated a space, a site, for faith. Hence, he was accorded the title "The Philosopher of Protestantism."[11] This view of Kant significantly influenced German Protestant liberal theology, from Albrecht Ritschl to Wilhelm Hermann and Adolf Harnack. It extended even to Karl Barth, a Reformed Calvinist theologian and a critic of Protestant liberal theology. These theologians sharply separated natural theology and Greek metaphysics from the Christian Gospel. They criticized metaphysics for the sake of what, in their eyes, was the purity of the Christian Gospel. In distinction to Roman Catholic theologians, they believed that Kant, like Luther, created a positive space for the distinctiveness of the Christian proclamation of God as a result of his critique of metaphysics.[12]

An analysis of Kant's critique shows that the import of his critique is not skepticism. It lies elsewhere. Kant's critique uncovers the dilemma of metaphysics, for his criticisms of rational theology underscore not only the antinomies of metaphysical reason but also reason's inability to specify the content and meaning of "absolute necessary being." It is indeed shortsighted to view Kant's critique primarily as limiting reason to make room for faith. Kant's critique presents a challenge that cannot easily be bypassed and points not just to the aporia of metaphysics but to our very ability to understand the meaning of absolute necessary being.

Inability of Defining Absolute Necessity: Transcendent or Immanent to the World?

Kant scholarship has demonstrated that Kant's critique of rational theology as well as his demolition of the proofs for God's existence has often been simplistically interpreted. Kant's critique has been falsely interpreted as directed mainly against the implication of the Cartesian proof that one can conclude from the concept of the infinite the necessary existence of the infinite. Likewise, Kant's argument has been characterized as entailing a subjectivization of the predicate of existence, as Hegel, for example, does in his caricature of Kant's argument about the difference between the idea and the existence of 100 talers. Dieter Henrich, however, has argued convincingly that "one misunderstands totally and fundamentally Kant's critique of onto-theology, if one attributes to Kant that he wanted to criticize generally and formally the transition from concept to existence."[13]

Kant's critique of the illusion of the transcendental ideal, which charges a confusion of concept and object, should be clearly distinguished from his critique of the cosmological and ontological proofs, which concerns the specification of the concept of necessary being. Concerning the latter, Kant writes: "Never can the cosmology decide if a necessary being exists in the world or outside of the world. Even less can it give an answer to the question [of] what an absolute necessary being means."[14] This statement points to an impossibility. As one interpreter of Kant explains: "In fact, the impossibility of specifying the notion of the absolute through the cosmological, especially the ontological deductions in the unambiguous sense of the moral concept of God of religion, is one of the essential points of Kant's critique of the proofs of God's existence."[15] Kant explicitly concludes his analysis by showing what cannot be demonstrated: "Now the pure cosmological proof can establish the existence of a necessary being in no other way than by leaving it unsettled whether this being is the world itself or a thing distinct from it."[16]

Kant's critique, therefore, raises both the problem of specifying the notion of absolute necessity and the problem of the indeterminability of whether this necessity is identical or separate from the world. Consequently, although Kant himself provided an avenue out of this dilemma through practical reason—an avenue often misunderstood[17]—his critique led also to the consequent development of a speculative metaphysics or to the advocacy of an empirical naturalism.

Speculative Idealist Metaphysics or Empirical Naturalism

The speculative idealist attempts at metaphysics immediately following Kant sought to conceptualize absolute necessity. Specifically, such speculative metaphysics sought to conceptualize the meaning of the totality and to grasp the ground of that meaning of the totality.[18] Hegel's philosophy sought to reconceptualize the metaphysical and ontological proofs of God's existence and to comprehend absolute necessity.[19] The work of Friedrich Schelling and Christian Hermann Weisse are other examples of such attempts to formulate modern idealist resolution in Germany.[20] Schelling sought to show that being is the ground of thought and freedom, the ground of necessity as a response to Kant's critique. Alfred North Whitehead's conception of God as the creative envisioning of relevant possibilities for processing occasions[21]and Charles Hartshorne's criticism of classical metaphysics represent, along with successive generations of North American process thinkers, from John Cobb to Robert Neville, attempts to produce a modernist synthesis of science and metaphysics.[22] They exemplify modern concerns with reconciliation of scientific thinking and philosophical thought and are thereby thoroughly modernists.[23]

From traditional to modern theology one talks of God in terms of creativity and being. God is the creator of all being; God is the cause of being. Even when God is conceived of as independent of being, God is understood as the cause of being. Even when contemporary theologians such as Gordon Kaufman talk about God in terms of serendipitous creativity, the same issue arises, because creativity, no matter how it is conceived, is the basis of what is and of what has become.[24] Both good and evil have to be viewed as the effects of creativity; to look at evil simply as the privation of goodness (as in classic metaphysics) or as Nothingness (as Karl Barth does) overlooks its creative power. The creativity that takes place in the growth of empires—for example, the emergence of National Socialism out of the economic ruins of the World War I—exemplifies the intertwinement of creativity, power, and evil. The identification of God with the creative principle of being that runs the risk of identifying God and being or the creativity of being needs to reflect on creativity manifesting itself as creative evil force.

Speculative idealism represents one reaction to Kant's critique. It attempts to specify the idea of an absolutely necessary being and to understand it in a way that integrates the necessary ground of being with freedom. Another and quite different reaction is that of empirical naturalism. In contrast to an idealist metaphysics, this naturalism understands totality in terms of a material and physical explanation of life.[25] Much of contemporary analytical philosophy offers a completely materialistic and physical explanation of life and consciousness as an adequate explanation of the nature of humans within the cosmos. The naturalist view realistically acknowledges that human life is a passing phenomenon within the material world. The proper consciousness of humans should be one of resignation; they should resign themselves before the insignificance of human life within the cosmos.[26] Many versions of naturalism (metaphysical as well as ethical) exist within contemporary philosophy.[27] A weak version of naturalism proposes that an adequate scientific account of human life should not conflict with the understanding of humans as material objects and as products of an evolutionary natural selection. A strong version of naturalism (for example, Quine) maintains that the philosophical quest for the meaning of human knowledge and rationality is met adequately by empirical and a posteriori scientific research. In the advocacy of naturalism, the question of meaning, let alone that of God, becomes lost, "for naturalism begins with the assumption that communicative activities—indeed, all of those which involve the 'understanding' of 'meanings' can ultimately be viewed as a series of functions in the cerebral cortex."[28]

Francis Schüssler Fiorenza

In short, the philosophical responses to Kant's critique took two directions. One direction, especially present in German Idealism, interpreted the creative principle in relationship to the totality of being. A transcending creativity, which is immanent within the totality of being, is not only a creativity of good but also of evil. The response of radical naturalism reduces conceptions of meaning and linguistic exchange to natural processes. In the face of these two directions, the simple appeal to a skepticism that makes room for faith overlooks the depth of the consequences of Kant's critique as well as Kant's own appeal to practical philosophy as a solution.

Subjectivity as the Site of God

Many twentieth-century theologians, influenced by Protestant neo-orthodoxy, take issue with subjectivity as the site of God. They view the site of subjectivity as constituting the "modern" approach to God that carries with it the following flaws: the Renaissance's glorification of human nature, the Cartesian search for certitude, the a priori nature of Kant's transcendentalism, and an emphasis on human autonomy. For them, modern theology as anthropocentric or centered on the human subject is in reality a thinly veiled cover for Feuerbach's atheistic humanism.[29]

These charges against the site of subjectivity are not without their historical and systematic problems. Subjectivity as a site for the knowledge of the divine is not simply modern. Indeed, it has its roots in classical antiquity, not only in neo-Platonic worldviews, but also in the Christian reception, modification, and reinterpretation of those worldviews. This is not to deny that the modern understanding of subjectivity as the site of God differs significantly from the antique view of the relationship between subjectivity and God. In antiquity, the spiritual nature of the soul placed it within an ontological hierarchy, where it was closer to the spiritual God. In modernity, the infinite horizon of the human consciousness becomes the avenue of infinity and access to knowledge of God. The spiritual interiority of antiquity becomes in modernity an interiority of subjective certainty. Consequently, a certain foundationalism, either Cartesian or empirical, often underlies modern appeals to subjectivity.[30] Hence, modern appeals to religious experience sometimes exhibit the Cartesian concern with immediacy and certainty as the foundation of knowledge. Or they exhibit the empirical concern with the evidentiary immediacy of religious experience, as if religious experience were analogous to sense perception and could ground religious knowledge in the same manner that sense perception grounds empirical knowledge.[31]

Subjectivity as Site of the Infinite and of the Divine

The connection between human subjectivity and interiority has its roots in classical metaphysical presuppositions. Interpretations of the modern theological appeal to subjectivity as a site of the divine should take into account the degree to which modern theologians are indeed indebted to traditional and classical theology in their appeals to subjectivity. An example is Karl Rahner's transcendental existential approach. Although Rahner is readily criticized for his modernist anthropocentricism by Hans Urs von Balthasar, he is indebted to antiquity as well as to modernity—to Augustine as well as to Descartes (via Maréchal).[32]

Augustine asks How do we know how to search for God unless we already know what we are searching for?[33] To search presupposes a knowledge of that for which one is searching. The discovery of God is the discovery of a truth that is in some way already present in the searching person.[34] Augustine's theory of knowledge and his manner of questioning correlate with his emphasis on interiority and ascent and with his fusion of the two.[35] Augustine finds in the soul the image of God, not as Plotinus did in the acquired personal moral perfection, but rather in the cognitive and volitional ability in which the mind reflects upon its memory, understanding, and will. By examining one's intellectual powers, one discovers the unchangeable powers that provide traces of the unchangeable truth. This Augustinian tradition continues in the Middle Ages. Christian mystics, who view the human soul as the locus of the divinity, often use language that borders upon an identification of the soul and the divine (e.g., Eckhart).[36]

Karl Rahner re-interprets this Augustinian tradition with insights borrowed from diverse sources: a specific reading of Thomas (in a way that assimilates Thomas and Dionysius), a reception of the Cartesian-Maréchalian emphasis on the infinity of subjectivity, an adaptation of Martin Heidegger's existential categories, and a Christian interpretation of human nature in relationship to Christology.[37] The Dionysian reading of Thomas equates the hierarchy of being and spiritual forms and the perfection of being with the intellectual return to the self. This reinterpretation combines Heidegger's notion of pre-understanding with Maréchal's dynamism of the intellect. Rahner relates the infinity of consciousness, the unlimited dynamism to know and to choose, and especially the freedom of responsibility, with the pre-apprehension that makes language about God intelligible and meaningful. Rahner's interpretation of human personhood as constituted by transcendence in freedom and responsibility models that transcendence of freedom exhibited in Jesus's death with the help of Ignatian categories. Consequently, his interpretation of human finitude and subjectivity alters Heidegger's understanding of *Entschlossenheit* (resoluteness) and opens subjectivity to the givenness and mystery of God's transcendence.

The Ambiguities of Subjectivity

Nevertheless, the site of subjectivity has its own ambiguities, among which are its foundationalism, its conception of the self, its anthropocentrism, and its elitism. Although the self exists within a biological, evolutionary, and historical cultural matrix, it can mistakenly assume the translucence of consciousness so that the appeals to the self betray what has been labeled a Cartesian foundationalism. Appeals to the creativity and autonomy of the self as a model of divine creativity and responsibility can overlook both the subjection of the self as well as the abyss of evil within the self. In addition, the interpretation of the self as a site of the divine has to face up to the ambiguity of subjectivity that underlies the neo-orthodox charge of anthropocentrism. It rightly warns that making subjectivity a site of connection (*Anknüpfüngspunkt*) between the human and the divine can too easily make human subjectivity the standard of the divine.

The critique of onto-theology points to more than the inadequacy of metaphysical conceptions of God as a being. As it relates to subjectivity as the site of the divine, it also raises the question whether God is conceived of in the light of the ontological qualities of the human person. Why does the human intellect and will (knowing and loving) become the locus of language about God? Is this the residue of a neo-Platonic theory of participation in which the intellect and will participate much more in the divine and, consequently, mirror the divine much more than materiality does? Hence, the intellect and will are seen as sites of the divine by virtue of an ontological proximity. When the spontaneity and creativity of the modern subject are taken as sources for understanding God, then are not God's act and creativity understood in categories of human subjectivity? The critique of subjectivity as a site of the divine raises the central question: How can one articulate one's belief in God without reducing God to a being and without reducing God to the norms of human experience or to the finite qualities of human personhood?

Otherness as the Site of God

The third category is alterity, or otherness, as the site of God. In his book on Jacques Derrida, John Caputo's first subtitle "God Is Not Differánce" clearly rejects identifying the category of "difference" with God.[38] Derrida's early criticism of Levinas in "Violence and Metaphysics" and his later essay on negation clearly show the inadequacy of some appeals to "otherness" or "alterity" or the "negative" of "negative theology."[39] Some contemporary theologians appeal to the otherness of God or the transcendence of God simply to criticize natural theology, metaphysics, and transcendental or experiential approaches to God. They often claim that only revelation, faith, and theology overcome the evil and even violence of metaphysical and anthropological approaches to God.

Otherness as Otherness to both Metaphysical and Transcendental Theology

Twentieth-century Protestant neo-orthodoxy appealed to the transcendent otherness of God in a critique of both natural theology and the anthropocentrism of modern theology.[40] The critique of natural theology was directed not only against Roman Catholic neo-Scholastic theology but also against the secular naturalism of National Socialism. The critique of experience was directed not only against Schleiermacher but also against various forms of pietism. The goal of this critique is clear; its de facto execution is less clear.

Critique of Natural Theology: The neo-orthodox critique of the anthropocentrism of modern theology does not escape its own critique. It criticized the freedom and autonomy of the human subject. Within postmodern theology, this critique is accepted, and human subjectivity is interpreted with the categories of subjection, vulnerability, and hostage. Yet neo-orthodoxy criticized the anthropocentrism of modern theology in order to preserve the absolute freedom and sovereignty of God.[41] It emphasized the actuality of revelation over against the essentialism of natural theology with language that resonates in today's critique of the violence of metaphysics. Nevertheless, its characterization of God in terms of freedom and sovereignty in some way mirrors in some of these theologians not only the freedom and sovereignty of the modern absolute monarchy but also the freedom of the possessive bourgeois.

Some have criticized metaphysical natural theology for reducing God to an object within the cosmos and to a being within the chain of being and thereby overlooking the ontological difference between being and beings. Others have criticized the transcendental subject as a site of God for making human subjectivity the standard and measure of God. The question is whether those who criticize metaphysics and transcendental subjectivity adequately deal with metaphysics or subjectivity so that their appeal to otherness as the site of God does not surreptitiously and unreflectively introduce ontic models of freedom and otherness in such a way that their understanding of God does not represent genuine transcendence.

Otherness as an Alternate Symbolic and Linguistic System: When the Christian tradition is viewed as an alternative symbolic system, the otherness of God is often formulated in terms of a sharp contrast between Judaism and Christianity or, more often, between Hellenism and Christianity. One sees such a contrast among many biblical, historical, comparative, and systematic theologians, such as, for example, Theorleif Boman, Oscar Cullmann, and Jürgen Moltmann.[42] Here, biblical categories are contrasted with Greek categories. Biblical categories understand the world as history, have space for God's act, and maintain an openness to the future. In contrast, Greek categories are said to be static, without genuine history, without space for God's historical acts, and closed to the future, viewing the cosmos as cyclic. Moltmann distinguishes the two in the following way: "If the mythical and magic cults of the epiphany religions have the purpose of annihilating the terrors of history by anchoring life in the original sacred event, and if in tendency they are 'anti-historical' (M. Eliade), then the God who gives his promises . . . makes possible for the very first time the feeling for history in the category of the future, and consequently has a 'historicizing' effect.' "[43] For Moltmann, these epiphany religions form "the presupposition and abiding foundation of the natural theology of Greek philosophy of religion, and of oriental philosophies of religion.[44]

Kevin Hart has recently argued that the strictures against metaphysics do not apply to theology, that a theology based on revelation can escape the chains in which metaphysics is caught.[45] John Milbank has argued that the conventional, social, constructed character of language allows one to contrast linguistic systems. To the extent that theology acknowledges this conventional character of language, it acknowledges that it creates a meaningful linguistic system that is distinct. Therefore, he makes the claim that only theology can overcome metaphysics.[46] Metaphysics is overcome here to the extent that a more general ontology or metaphysics has been replaced with a specifically Christian theological conceptuality. This conceptuality, which should be specifically and uniquely Christian, is often expressed in neo-Platonic categories despite its goal to free itself from the constraints of metaphysical discourse.

Other as Other to the Very Ontological Difference: Third, one can "attempt" to conceive this otherness of God as so radically other that there is an absolute asymmetry between God and Being, as Jean-Luc Marion has done.[47] God is so other that God is beyond being and beyond the ontological difference. To the extent that God is beyond being, the relationship between God and the world is not a difference which takes place within being. Just as Aristotle affirmed that difference takes place within the same genus, this position consistently argues that God is beyond difference since God and being are not within the same genus, as if being were perhaps univocally understood. God is free from the "tyranny" of being when being is understood as that which links our knowledge of being to God.[48]

To affirm or to know that God is other from the world and is radically other presupposes that one knows what the world is and what God is. Likewise, it requires that one specify the meaning of that otherness. Marion makes God beyond being in order that being not diminish God's freedom. God is sovereignly free, even to the extent that he is free from being.[49] When God is beyond being, the defining characteristic of God becomes the freedom of the event of giving. Does Marion, by releasing liberation and freedom from the constraints of being, make as a key characteristic of God the defining characteristic of the modern subject with its liberation and freedom?[50] The emphasis on love, grace, and donation is an answer to that objection. Nevertheless, Marion's distinction between freedom and being enables him to mirror Heidegger's distinction and enables *nolens volens* his parallel distinction that one finds in the heritage of both liberal Protestantism and Protestant neo-orthodoxy.

A theology that makes the fear of idols central may be a theology that ends up having room for neither icons of the divine nor the divine. Such a position may be ultimately much more neo-Platonic than it acknowledges if it underscores the gift and the donation yet undercuts the value of the gift and the being of the donation.[51] It tends to overemphasize the sublime in contrast to the beautiful, in the way it stresses the invisibility of otherness and criticizes visibility as idolatry. Consequently, it diminishes the place for the sacramentality of the visible within being. Does this position leave room for the sacramental within the ontic manifestations of being?[52]

Moreover, one has to ask about the ethical consequences of this position. Is the being of the world relegated to a sphere of boredom and indifference?[53] Does the critique of the metaphysical lead to a theological indifference toward human experiences of the world? One has to ask whether this position has adequately reflected on the ethical consequences of its emphasis on indifference. Within modern theology, the "death of God" theology emerged in the 1950s against a similar background. Because neo-orthodoxy emphasized so strongly the otherness of God, it diminished the sacramental presence of God within the natural world. Could not the same be argued against this position?

Critical Reflections

Some might object that I have brought together three very different theological positions under the category of otherness. Yet they share some common threads: their criticism of both classical and modern natural theology, their rejection of the traditional analogy of being, and their objection to a transcendental starting point of theology. They base the analogy of faith upon a conception of the divine in which the divine is viewed in terms of sovereign freedom and autarchy. Consequently, the attributes of the modern human subject and even the attributes of the modern royal national state have been applied to God. Thus, although these theological positions have attempted to avoid either contamination of the metaphysical being or the pitfalls of modern subjectivity, their conception of God draws on characteristics that are central to the modern conception of the self.

This criticism has been most often brought against Karl Barth's emphasis on the sovereign freedom of God. Trutz Rendtorff and his students have consistently argued that Karl Barth's conception of God mirrors the attributes of the modern subject, namely, autonomy, autocracy, and freedom.[54] Consequently, although he is most critical of the anthropocentricism of modern theology, he has transferred the qualities of modern subjectivity to God, thus crafting God in the image of the modern subject—the product of the Renaissance and the Enlightenment. A similar result is in seen in those theologians that emphasize God's acts in history in contrast to the metaphysical view of God as the ground of being. The result is that God's acts are described on the analogy of the human person, hidden except in their free acts that reveal personality and personhood. God's acts are then like those of an acting person, conceived of in the dimensions of time and place and in terms of choices among alternatives.

The emphasis upon theology's overcoming of metaphysics often appeals to Hans Urs Balthasar's elaboration of the drama and logic of God. His theology moves from aesthetics to action and logic in order to profile a specifically Christian vision of the historical drama of salvation. Yet these appeals to von Balthasar overlook the nuance and philosophical presuppositions of his argument. Von Balthasar emerged on the theological scene with his critical sketch of modern Promethean man.[55] But in his sympathetic dialogue with Karl Barth, he argued that the analogy of faith cannot be understood independently of the analogy of being. It is not my intention here to defend von Balthasar's adoption and defense of Erich Przywara's conception of analogy over against Barth's analogy of faith.[56] I merely want to suggest for consideration that the assertion of an analogy of faith as independent from our logical and metaphysical categories easily remains just an assertion. Von Balthasar argues that "every real 'contra' presupposes a constantly to be understood relationship and thus at least a minimal community in order to be really a 'contra' and not a totally unrelated 'other.' "[57]

To the extent that revelation and faith uses language, they cannot simply escape the meaning of this language. Concepts such as freedom, agency, and donation presuppose a specific understanding of reality. The use of language, even if one defines language as a conventional rather than natural set of arbitrary signs, does not escape the problem of the meaning of such terms as freedom, existence, and reason. The same could be said of intratextuality, with its solipsist and claustrophobic character of formalist criticism that isolates the texts from their social, political, and anthropological contexts. In the face of the isolationist and solipsist character of such formalist criticism, Paul De Man recalls the image of the grandmother in Proust's novel, for she constantly seeks to push the young Marcel out into the garden away from the "unhealthy inwardness of his closeted reading."[58]

Beyond Metaphysical Naturalism to Fragile Interpretive Experiences

The previous argument has been that the ambiguities of being and of subjectivity are not avoided by an appeal to otherness or alterity. Not only does this appeal itself have its own ambiguities, but one must also explicitly confront (and not bypass) the challenges of a naturalistic interpretation of being and a transcendental interpretation of subjectivity. Taking up each of the three sites in the same order, I shall suggest the following: *first*, one should go beyond a naturalistic metaphysics by appealing to fragile interpretive experiences; *second*, one can elucidate these experiences not in terms of transcendental subjectivity but in relationship to an ethical and religious intersubjectivity; *finally*, one should provide a thicker description of metaphysical language and the relationship between sameness and otherness and show the ethical consequences of this thicker description.

Fragile Interpretations of Transcending Meaning

Some search for an incomprehensible meaning of life. Some interpret the events of life and the encounter with others in terms of a meaning that points to what is unconditional and absolute in the midst of a life that appears to be contingent and a world in which contingency is celebrated. It is possible to interpret these experiences in purely naturalistic terms. In *Philosophy and the Mirror of Nature*, Richard Rorty seeks not only to demolish metaphysics but also to defend naturalism.[59] He describes a planet on the other side of the galaxy inhabited by featherless bipeds like ourselves. They treat members of their own species with mutual respect even though they do not have metaphysical concepts, such as personhood. Moreover, they have developed the disciplines of neurology and biochemistry before other disciplines, thus their conversations concern their nerves. They refer to touching hot stoves as "stimulating C fibers," or to looking at surprising art as "causing g-14s to quiver," or to solitude as "placing oneself in S-296." They list the fibers for love, kindness, and generosity. When a young couple meet, each can say to the other: "When I meet you, neurological fiber 114 quivers. Therefore, we should arrange a permanent social tie. It will stimulate our neurological fibers and our biological organisms will continue our species."

Such language cannot simply be substituted for our language as if it said the very same thing. We do not interpret our encounters with others simply in terms of neurological fibers and the continuation of the human species. Instead, we interpret and experience our encounters with categories such as "love" and "unconditional commitment." This interpretation of our experience as an unconditional commitment is in some ways a counterfactual experience. It cannot be justified exclusively on the basis of empirical evidence, yet it provides a meaning of this experience.

Conscience is likewise such an experience. Conscience can be explained away in many ways as just freedom and responsibility. Conscience can be explained as a Freudian taboo or a Nietszchean will to power. However, when conscience is understood in neither of these naturalistic ways, then it expresses the responsibility and accountability of freedom. What takes place through the experience of conscience, interpreted as conscience, is the acknowledgement of freedom and responsibility that transcends natural, psychological, and social causes. To call these experiences "fragile interpretive experiences" is to affirm that they are not experiences prior to interpretation. Instead, the self-interpretation of the experience constitutes the experience itself. The interpretations are fragile in the sense that they are counter-factual or counter-natural and can be explained by means of a completely naturalistic interpretation. However, insofar as one does not give a naturalistic interpretation, one experiences what transcends, and what is other than, a contingent naturalistic interpretation. One's experience is constituted through an interpretation pointing to the transcendence of the experience.

The reference to these experiences does not constitute a claim that transcendence exists, as the traditional demonstration claimed to prove that "God exists." Such interpretative experiences are indeed fragile because an alternative interpretation is always possible. Such an alternative interpretation may appeal to a scientific methodology that considers explanation to be the reduction of an event to the lowest common denominator. Nevertheless, fragile experiences of meaning are such that they constitute our very experience because it is their meaning that constitutes and gives our experiences their significance. Moreover, it is this "fragility of the transcending meaning of our experience" that constitutes us as human persons.

It is this transcending meaning that gives meaning to our existence and according to which we often act and understand ourselves. Interpretation is what gives meaning to the experience. This transcending meaning has been interpreted in categories of ultimacy or as the "whence" or "whither" of human existence. I would rather avoid such spatial images. The examples of "fragile interpretive experiences" were selected in order to avoid any type of language that objectifies transcendence. Despite all criticisms of anthropomorphic images and of reducing God to a finite object like other objects, too often the treatment of God overlooks the problem of the ontological difference. Too often it reduces the meaning of transcendence to a claim about an object, such as whether a certain moon exists around Jupiter. The interpretation of life in relationship to transcendence presupposes that another interpretation remains possible: Language about conscience can be explained as social taboo; language about responsibility for the other as an altruistic social gene; and language about God as love as an objectification of the most admired attributes of the human species to that which is other than the human species.

Nevertheless, the possibility of denial is at the same time the possibility of denial of what constitutes the depth of meaning of human existence. The question becomes: Does interpreting conscience as conscience, responsibility as responsibility, or God as ultimacy alienate human existence or not? The answer depends on how conscience, responsibility, and God are interpreted. What is experienced in terms of its counter-factual transcendence gives meaning to the extent that the rejection of that transcendence eliminates the very meaning of the experience. This meaning relates to the human subject with regard to the constitution of the self and its responsibility to society and history.

Beyond Subjectivity to an Ethical Intersubjectivity

Subjectivity as the site of knowledge of God deals with the ambiguities of human subjectivity. These ambiguities challenge the classic ontological prioritizing of subjectivity as well as the hubris of modern transcendental subjectivity, which sets itself up as the norm of knowledge and action. Levinas advances elements of subjection, receptivity, and responsibility to counter the centrality given to autonomy and freedom in the modern conception of the self. His phenomenological description, however, needs to be complemented by George Herbert Mead's elaboration of the social nature of the self and its ethical implications. Both provide an understanding of subjectivity as an ethical intersubjectivity. From the perspective of this ethical intersubjectivity, the meaning of religious transcendence needs to be elaborated.

Subjectivity as Ethical Intersubjectivity

George Herbert Mead underscores the social structure of the human self. In distinction to the transcendental and idealist approaches to the self, he does not begin with self-reflection as the immediate and original given of experience. Instead, he seeks to understand the self within social interaction with others. The self involves a becoming that emerges in social experience.[60] Mead writes: "The individual experiences himself as such, not directly, but only indirectly, from the particular standpoints of other individual members of the same social group, or from the generalized standpoint of the social group as a whole to which he belongs."[61] What is important about Mead's insight is not simply the distinction between the ego and self (derived from William James).[62] In Mead's view, the self understands its identity and continuity in the context of a social identity from which it understands itself, such as a social group, or, in the most generalized sense, from the human race.[63] Transcendental philosophy has an a priori conception of the self that assumes that this self as consciousness is the condition of the unity of experience and precedes all experience. In contrast, Mead's position understands that the genesis of the self takes place within the interaction of experience itself. Such a perspective questions the adequacy of the individualism of the a priori transcendental interpretation of the idea of God from either the unlimited openness of individual subjectivity or from the idea of infinity within individual consciousness. One should explore how what "transcends" emerges within the interaction of experience. It is within intersubjectivity and community.

Mead explicated the ethical consequences of his interactive understanding of the self in terms of such concepts as the "generalized other." Whereas Mead interrelates the social constitution of the self and ethics, he does not deal with the relationship of the self and religious transcendence. On this point Levinas's critique of Heidegger's analysis of Dasein advances the argument. He goes beyond the critique of the transcendental self entailed in Heidegger's analysis of the historicity, facticity, and thrownness of Dasein insofar as he defines conscience beyond the courage to be and beyond the *conatus essendi*. Through becoming hostage for the other in responsibility for the other, one goes beyond one's own *conatus essendi* and testifies to transcendence.

Moreover, Levinas argues that Heidegger ends up "affirming a tradition in which the same dominates the other, in which freedom, even the freedom that is identical with reason, precedes justice. Does not justice consist in putting the obligation with regard to the other before obligations to oneself, in putting the other before the same?"[64] By emphasizing the letting-be (*Gelassenheit*) of humans and their potentiality for being, Heidegger prioritizes possibility and potentiality. He gives priority to the a-ethical modality of existence and sets freedom over responsibility and being over ethics.

Intersubjectivity and Ethical Religious Responsibility

Mead's social constitution of the self and ethics and Levinas's setting of ethics and responsibility over ontology provide the basis for a social and religious interpretation of responsibility and transcendence. The responsible self within a responsible community is a site of transcendence. This transcendence of the self takes place in a broader realm than the contexts of fragile interpretations of meaning and commitments to others. The parable in Matthew 25 has significance for how we understand the self as well as the site of transcendence. In short, the self constituted by intersubjectivity becomes a self within a community and by means of its acts of transcending commitments. It is an intersubjective member of a community and at the same time a site of the presence of the divine. But a self conceived of in such terms is not the transcendental self of modern philosophy that is autonomously self-legislative. This view of the self does not arise as an alternative to a purely naturalistic interpretation through reflection upon itself as a transcendental self, but rather through reflection upon transcending intersubjective commitments. In other words, instead of being, subjectivity, and otherness as sites for language about God, the responsible community becomes the site of transcendence and the site of the transcendence of the self in responsibility.

Fragile interpretive experiences of transcendence are not meanings derived simply from the intentionality of individuals. Instead, these meanings are shared intersubjectively. They constitute a meaning that is shared pragmatically and ethically. In other words, persons not only understand the transcendence of the meaning but they relate toward one another and to others in terms of this meaning. The pragmatic and ethical constitution of community both constitutes and expresses the interpretive experiences of transcendence, just as ethical and pragmatic behavior gives testimony to transcendence. It does not suffice simply to develop ethics as first philosophy, as Levinas does,[65] or to criticize the naturalistic fallacy, as Anglo-Saxon analytical philosophy does, in dealing with the complex relationship between the "is" and the "ought."[66] Instead, my introduction of Mead's notion of the intersubjective constitution of the self suggests that fragile interpretive experiences of transcendence are meanings that are not only intersubjectively constituted but are also constitutive of how we relate to one another.

Intersubjectivity as Religious: A Community of Prayer

This notion of intersubjectivity impacts our understanding of the relationship of praxis and transcendence. In theology, Johann Baptist Metz and Helmut Peukert have argued for the primacy of practical reason as a basis of fundamental theology.[67] Whereas Karl Barth has argued for the priority of dogmatics to ethics and Wolfhart Pannenberg has argued that the ethical pre-supposes a vision of the totality, Gerhard Ebeling argues for the primacy of the ethical and the primacy of prayer as sites and criteria for the knowledge of God.[68] What are the consequences of giving primacy to a practical reason that takes into account the critique of the priority of ontology and the naturalistic fallacy for the knowledge of God? In his emphasis on ethics over ontology, Levinas writes that "one seeks to think God in this way without recourse to ontology, that is to say that one seeks a thought that breaks with the philosophical tradition, where God is understood as being par excellence, as being supremely being, and where the idea of God has its philosophical signification in conformity with the rational rules of knowledge."[69] Goodness conceived of as excellence within the hierarchy of being and measured by such distinctions as spirit over matter or intellect over flesh often mirrors societal distinctions between the contemplative life of the elite intellectual class and the active life of the working class.[70] Instead of positing the relation to transcendence in a way that mirrors ontological qualities, one has to understand transcendence in relation to actions of responsibility and actions of ethical transcendence whereby we transcend the *conatus essendi*. My critique of a naturalistic metaphysics seeks to affirm a meaning that transcends the empirical, just as my emphasis on ethical responsibility emphasizes that responsibility gives testimony to a transcending of what is. The ethical does not mirror reality understood naturalistically but acts in a transcending manner and understands the human community in relation to transcendence, as in the belief in humans as icons of God.

The interrelating of ethical intersubjectivity and communal responsibility with transcendence raises the issue of the relationship between prayer and ethics. Prayer and ethics are often distinguished within an individualistic conception of prayer, for such an individualistic conception divides them. Prayer expresses one's relationship with God, whereas ethics expresses an individual's relationship to other individuals or a person's relationship to a particular community or to a social group. Instead, if we stand in relation to God in and through a community, we are created by God not as individuals but as part of the earth, its plants and animals, and its people, and we relate to God in and through God's creation: the earth and all its living creatures.

The communal aspect of prayer is brought out by the prophetic critique of prayer. This critique is not so much a critique of prayer as an understanding of the communal nature of our relationship to God. We relate to God in and through our relationships to one another and our community's relationship to other communities. This dual relation is expressed in the Christian liturgical practice of the Eucharist, where thanksgiving, remembrance, offering, and gifts for the poor are interrelated. The religious act of thanksgiving and giving offerings was linked in Christian tradition with the ethical concern for the poor rather than with the ontological issue of the value or hierarchy of being.

Beyond Otherness: To the Dialectics of Otherness and Sameness

Contemporary philosophical and theological efforts to use otherness as a site of language about God are fruitful when they do not simply appeal to otherness as if it were a deus ex machina solution to philosophical, linguistic, social, and ethical issues of language about God. Denys Turner's perceptive remark sets the challenge before us when he writes: "Therefore, the only way in which we can attest to the absolute transcendence of God is by transcending the language of similarity and difference itself."[71] Such a challenge suggests that we first give a thicker description of the metaphysical than is sometimes done. Such a thicker description can then be applied to the categories of sameness and otherness, viewing them as not simply contrasts but as interrelated. Such a description should likewise show the interrelation and criss-crossing between language about transcendence and language about ethics in which the categories of sameness and otherness are dialectically interrelated.

Thicker Description of the Metaphysical Language about Sameness and Otherness

A "thicker description" of language about sameness and otherness must deal with the charge that metaphysical language overlooks otherness and reduces everything to the tyranny of sameness. This criticism, of course, has various roots in our century, notably in Martin Heidegger's critique of onto-theology and Ernst Bloch's critique of Greek reduction of knowledge to knowledge of the same.[72] However, these roots extend to the very first criticisms of Enlightenment rationality. Herder had already associated the rationality of the Enlightenment with the evils of colonialism. His critique of the Enlightenment contended that the bonds of natural reason can be oppressive. This takes place when the cultures of minorities are eliminated for the sake of the allegedly superior Eurocentric colonial culture. Herder writes: "The universal dress of philosophy and philanthropy can conceal repression, violations of the true personal, human, local, civil, and national freedom, much as Cesare Borgia would have liked it."[73]

Similar criticisms abound in regard to language about rights as expressions of an allegedly universal European rationality. For example, George Lindbeck argues: "As current East Asian challenges to the discourse of international human rights illustrate, the universal languages (or 'Esperantos' as some have called them) in which Enlightenment modernity seeks to deal with the common problems of the global village are not likely long to survive the Western cultural hegemony under which they developed."[74] Likewise, Richard Rorty argues how much of the appeal to human rights is based upon an essentialism and foundationalism.[75] This metaphysical view of human rights represents a quasi-Platonic worldview that is simply an "outmoded attempt."[76] Instead he advocates the sentimentality of feeling, a feeling more comprehensive.

In historical cases, such as the treatment of the Mexicans, the emancipation of African Americans in the United States, and suffrage for women, the question is What role was played by the appeal to a greater sentimentality or to a common humanity? In the case of the treatment of Mexicans, Barthleme le Casus argued that basic human sameness versus ontic difference—they were fellow humans—required the critique of the unjust treatment of the Mexicans.[77] While the feelings aroused by *Uncle Tom's Cabin* did indeed do much, were those feelings also not based upon an empathic identification with African Americans as fellow humans? The women's rights movement argued a political understanding of women as equals over against conceptions of women as different and therefore incapable of participating in the electoral process.

A thicker description of modern rights languages should include first the historical roots of rights language within our religious heritage and the historical defense of minority religious groups. It should also consider Levinas's argument that rights have meaning when they refer to the rights of the other and when their interpretation is such that they entail a respect for the other rather than merely one's own right or an abstract resolution.[78] This suggests that one can argue on the basis of practical reason against not only the sharp contrast between modern rationality as secular and Christian faith as religious, but also against the sharp post-Enlightenment contrast between the God of the Philosophers and the God of Abraham; one can also argue against the distinction between Greek metaphysical thought and Hebrew thought—an inadequate comparison that contrasts the Athenian period as the measure of Greek thought (to the neglect of the Homeric period and Stoic thought, Hebrew thought, and biblical thought) to the neglect of wisdom literature and the Hellenistic New Testament or Christian Scriptures. The overlapping and crisscrossing between the dignity accorded to the human community in Christian interpretation and the dignity of all humans shows a convergence rather than a contrast between Christian and modern conceptions of human dignity.

In short, a thicker historical description is possible not only historically but also systematically. A thick systematic description has to point to a crisscrossing and an overlapping rather than a specific difference between Christian, metaphysical, and modern conceptions of human dignity. This crisscrossing requires that with regard to the ethical and political consequences of our beliefs, one thinks dialectically about difference and sameness. It moves beyond the language of the transcendence of others to a language in which similarity and difference overlap and crisscross.

Justice and the Ethical and Social Character of Language about God

In his commentary on Genesis, John Calvin explains that because humans are created in the image of God, an injury against anyone is an injury against God.[79] In this belief system, every human person is an image of God, and the unity of God's creation of all humans as brothers and sisters points to an understanding of how human persons, despite all differences among themselves, have a unique dignity because they are images of God and therefore to injure them is to injure God. One can point to the Stoic notions of equality, the humanism of the Renaissance, and the Enlightenment's understanding of freedom and autonomy in the development of rights language. However, the conception of human dignity and equality that language about rights seeks to express owes its origin not simply to an Enlightenment universal rationality but also has its roots in the diverse traditions of the West, including the Judaic and Christian traditions. Historians have shown that the Western understanding of rights is in no small degree due to the struggles of religious minorities over against a majority.[80]

It is because of this overlapping between the Christian belief in God and the dignity of all human beings that sameness and otherness needs to be interrelated. The belief in the transcendence of God has functioned to view all races and nations in relation to God and to view them as a unity and as images of the reality of transcendence. In Jewish and Christian traditions the concern with the stranger, the widow, the orphan, and the poor flows out of the belief that our concern and responsibility for these groups is a site that testifies to God's presence.[81] In reflecting on responsibility as a site for the divine, one does not bypass religious and ethical intersubjectivity, nor does one bypass the question of one's understanding of others as images and icons of God. Instead, one links one's understanding of one's self and one's community in relation to the self and community of others.

Conclusion

In summary, being, subjectivity, and otherness are contested sites for talking about God. Language about God from the site of being can reduce God to an object among other objects or to the totality of being itself. Language about God from the site of subjectivity can see God as the mirror of our anthropocentric images and desires. Language about God from the site of alterity, insofar as it employs language, often uses anthropomorphic categories. It is important to underscore the ambiguities of all three sites, even the site of alterity. In his *Dialectics of the Enlightenment*, Max Horkheimer expressed the hope of the possibility of a non-instrumental rationality. Such a rationality would have its roots in the religious-metaphysical heritage of the West.[82] Horkheimer did not simply seek the "wholly other in negative theology"; he also saw that solidarity as a "universal compassion among all suffering creatures" was connected with "the longing, that the reality of the world in all its horror is not ultimate or final," and that this longing "unites and binds all human beings who cannot come to terms with the injustice of this world."[83]

This longing leads me to point to fragile interpreted experiences of transcending as fragments of meaning that contrast with a naturalist metaphysics. Such experiences of meaning involve formulations that do not reduce God to an object among objects. Second, the constitution of subjectivity through intersubjectivity rather than through transcendental consciousness makes room for the ethical dimension of intersubjectivity and for transcendence through responsibility. Third, I have suggested that a thicker description of metaphysical language about sameness and otherness points much more to a dialectical relationship rather than to a dichotomous relation. This dialectical relationship also expresses the relationship between Christianity and modernity. In this Christian view, language about God in and through a responsible community, with its liturgical practice and concern for justice and for others, is not supplementary but constitutive of knowledge and language about God. My arguing for fragile interpretations of transcendence against a naturalistic understanding of reality, for the responsible community as a site of transcendence, and for the necessity for a thicker description of the relation between sameness and otherness seeks to overcome the ambiguities of each site and yet still finds resources in them, as is the tradition within Roman Catholic theology.

NOTES

1. For surveys of the term "postmodern" see David Lyon, *Postmodernity* (Minneapolis: University of Minnesota Press, 1994); Charles Jenck, *The Post-modern Reader* (New York: St. Martin's Press, 1992); and Paul Lakeland, *Postmodernity: Christian Identity in a Fragmented Age* (Minneapolis: Fortress, 1997).

2. See Graham Ward, *The Postmodern God: A Theological Reader* (Malden, Mass.: Blackwell Publishers, 1997); and Phillip Blond, ed., *Postsecular Philosophy: Between Philosophy and Theology* (New York: Routledge, 1998).

3. See Wayne John Hankey, "Re-Christianizing Augustine Postmodern Style," *Animus* 2 (1977).

4. Emmanuel Levinas, *Of God Who Comes to Mind*, trans. Bettina Bergo (Stanford, Calif.: Stanford University Press, 1998), 57.

5. See Francis Schüssler Fiorenza and Gordon Kaufman, "God," in *Critical Terms for Religious Studies*, ed. Mark C. Taylor (Chicago: University of Chicago Press, 1998), pp. 136–159.

6. Maximos the Confessor, "Two Hundred Texts on Theology and the Incarnate Dispensation of the Son of God, Written for Th, 1,4," in *The Philokalia*, vol 2., trans. and ed. G. E. Palmer et al. (Boston: Faber and Faber 1986), pp. 114–117. "God is not a being either in the general or in any specific sense of the word and so He cannot be an origin. . . . On the contrary, He is the author of being and simultaneously an entity transcending being. . . . In short, He is the author of all being, potentiality and actualization, and of every origin, intermediary state and consummation."

7. Thomas Aquinas, *Commentary on the Book of Causes* (Washington, D.C.: Catholic University of America Press, 1996). See the exposition by Klaus Kremer, "Die Creatio nach Thomas von Aquinas," in *Ekklesia* (Trier: Paulinus, 1962), pp. 321–344.

8. See Klaus Kremer, *Die Neuplatonische Seinsphilosophie und Ihre Wirkung auf Thomas von Aquin* (Leiden: Brill, 1966). See also Wayne J. Hankey, "Theology as System and as Science: Proclus and Thomas Aquinas," *Dionysius* 6 (1982): 83–93.

9. Thomas's understanding of the proofs for God's existence is based not so much

on the notion of contingency as on participation; see Norbert Hinske, "Teilhabe und Distanz als Grundvoraussetzung der Gottesbeweise des Thomas Aquin," *Philosophisches Jahrbuch* 75 (1968): 279–293.

10. David Hume, *Enquiry concerning the Human Understanding*, ed. L. A. Selby-Bigge, rev. Peter Nidditch (1748; rep. Oxford: Oxford University Press, 1975).

11. Friedrich Paulsen, *Kant der Philosoph des Protestantismus* (Berlin: Reuther & Reichard, 1899); Ernst Katzer, *Luther und Kant: Ein Beitrag zur innern Entwicklungsgeschichte des deutschen Protestantismus* (Giessen: A. Topelmann, 1910); and Werner Schultz, *Kant als Philosoph des Protestantismus* (Hamburg: H. Reich, 1960).

12. In general, Roman Catholic theologians sought to refute Kant's critique as an aberration. They argued for an intellectual metaphysical intuition and for the return to the metaphysics of Thomas Aquinas. The transcendental Thomism, exemplified by Karl Rahner and Bernard Lonergan, sought to respond through a transcendental philosophy and without an appeal to intuition. See Francis Schüssler Fiorenza, "Transcendental Thomism," in *Modern Christian Thought*, vol. 2: *The Twentieth Century*, by James Livingston and Francis Schüssler Fiorenza (Upper Saddle River, N.J.: Prentice Hall, 2000), pp. 197–232; and Francis Schüssler Fiorenza, "Introduction: Karl Rahner and the Kantian Problematic," in Karl Rahner, *Spirit in the World*, trans. William J. Dych (New York: Herder and Herder, 1968), pp. xiv–xlv.

13. Dieter Henrich, *Der ontologische Gottesbeweis* (Tübingen: Mohr, 1960), p. 176 (my own translation). See also Josef Schmucker, *Die Primären Quellen des Gottesglaubens* (Freiburg: Herder, 1967).

14. Henrich, *Der Ontologische Gottesbeweis*, p. 154.

15. Schmucker, *Die Primären Quellen des Gottesglaubens*, p. 53. See his own constructive approach in Josef Schmucker, *Das Problem der Kontingenz der Welt: Versuch einer positiven Aufarbeitung der Kritik Kants am kosmologischen Argument* (Freiburg: Herder, 1969).

16. Kant, *Critique of Pure Reason* A/456B484 (New York: Cambridge University Press, 1997), p. 492.

17. Alois Winter, "Der Gotteserweis aus praktischer Vernunft. Das Argument Kants und seine Tragfähigkeit vor dem Hintergrund der Vernunftkritik," in *Um Möglichkeit oder Unmöglichkeit natürlicher Gotteserkenntnis Heute*, ed. Klaus Kremer (Leiden: E. J. Brill, 1985), pp. 109–178.

18. For the difference between the notion of totality and transcendent ground, see Friedrich Schleiermacher, *Dialektik* (Darmstadt: Wissenschaftliche Buchgesellschaft, 1976), pp. 297–314. See also Wolfhart Pannenberg, *Metaphysics and the Idea of God* (Grand Rapids, Mich.: William B. Eerdmans, 1990).

19. For the treatment of Hegel, Weisse, and Schelling, see Dieter Henrich, *Ontologische Gottesbeweise*, pp. 189–262.

20. Walter Kasper, *The God of Jesus Christ* (New York: Crossroads, 1984).

21. Alfred North Whitehead, *Process and Reality*, corrected edition by David Ray Grinn and Donald W. Sherburne, eds. (New York: Free Press, 1978).

22. Charles Hartshorne, *The Logic of Perfection and Other Essays in Neoclassical Metaphysics* (LaSalle, Ill.: Open Court, 1962). On the differences between Whitehead and Hartshorne, see David Ray Griffin, "Hartshorne's Differences from Whitehead," in *Two Process Philosophers: Hartshorne's Encounter with Whitehead*, ed. Lewis S. Ford (Tallahassee, Fla.: American Academy of Religion, 1973). Note the shift from the first generation, where one criticizes classical metaphysics in order to put in its place an

alternate metaphysics, to more recent, but very different, advocates of process thought; for example, John Cobb, A *Christian Natural Theology* (Philadelphia: Westminster Press, 1965); and Robert Neville, *God the Creator: On the Transcendence and Presence of God* (Chicago: University of Chicago Press, 1968).

23. For a contrary view, David Ray Griffin seeks to locate process thinking within postmodernism. See David Ray Griffin, ed., *God and Religion in the Postmodern World: Essays in Postmodern Theology* (Albany: SUNY Press, 1989).

24. Gordon Kaufman, *In Face of Mystery: A Constructive Theology* (Cambridge, Mass.: Harvard University Press, 1993).

25. See Levinas's treatment of naturalism in Emmanuel Levinas, *The Theory of Intuition in Husserl's Phenomenology*, 2nd ed. (Evanston: Northwestern University Press, 1995), pp. 3–16.

26. On the two types of ethical naturalism, see John McDowell, "Two Sorts of Naturalism," in John McDowell, *Mind, Value, and Reality* (Cambridge, Mass.: Harvard University Press, 1998), pp. 167–197.

27. See Chrisopher Hookway, "Naturalism and Normativity: Some Issues concerning Naturalised Epistemology," unpublished paper. See also Christopher Hookway, *Scepticism* (New York: Routledge, 1996).

28. Dieter Henrich, "What Is Metaphysics—What Is Modernity? Twelve Theses against Jürgen Habermas," in *Habermas: A Critical Reader*, ed. Peter Dews (Malden, Mass.: Blackwell, 1999), pp. 291–319. For the original German and other related essays, see Dieter Henrich, *Konzept* (Frankfurt: Suhrkamp, 1987), pp. 11–43.

29. Francis Schüssler Fiorenza, "The Response of Barth and Ritschl to Feuerbach," *Sciences religieuses/Studies in Religion* 7 (1978): 149–166. See also Fiorenza, "Feuerbach's Interpretation of Religion and Christianity," *The Philosophical Forum* 11 (Winter 1979/1980): 161–181

30. See Jean-Luc Marion, *On Descartes' Metaphysical Prism: The Constitution and the Limits of Onto-theo-logy in Cartesian Thought* (Chicago: University of Chicago Press, 1999); and Richard J. Bernstein, *Beyond Objectivism and Relativism: Science, Hermeneutics and Praxis* (Philadelphia: University of Pennsylvania Press, 1983).

31. For example, William P. Alston's critique of the classic position of Thomas because it seems to exclude this perceptive knowledge of knowledge in his *Perceiving God: The Epistemology of Religious Experience* (Ithaca: Cornell University Press, 1991).

32. Hans Urs von Balthasar, *Love Alone: The Way of Revelation* (London, 1968). See also Eamonn Conway, *The Anonymous Christian: A Relativised Christianity?—An Evaluation of Hans Urs von Balthasar's Criticisms of Karl Rahner's Theory of the Anonymous Christian* (New York: P. Lang, 1993). Rahner's approach to God has been likened, for example, by Joseph Cardinal Ratzinger to Bonaventure's *Itinerarium* ("The Path of the Soul's Journey to God"), see his "Vom Vertsehen des Glaubens: Anmerkungen Zu Rahners Grundkurs des Glaubens," *Theologische Revue* (1978): 177–186. Of course, Augustine is the ultimate, and perhaps more appropriate, point of comparison.

33. Though Augustine rejected the argument that learning is a form of memory. This statement coincides with the centrality of memory for Augustine, for whom knowledge is a form of recognition.

34. Even though Augustine had rejected Plato's argument in Phaedo that learning was an anamnesis (a remembering of what we knew before birth), he nevertheless held on to the view of knowledge as a recognition (recognition of eternal truths).

35. See Augustine, *Confessions* (New York: Modern Library, 1999), 10, 6 (also

earlier 7, 17 and 9, 10); see John M. Rist, *Augustine: Ancient Thought Baptized* (New York: Cambridge University Press, 1994), pp. 67–91.

36. See Denys Turner, *The Darkness of God: Negativity in Christian Mysticism* (New York: Cambridge University Press, 1995).

37. Rudolf Bultmann has already noted the link between the Augustinian search and Heidegger's pre-understanding, see his "The Problem of Pre-understanding," For Heidegger's early writings on Augustine, see Theodore Kisiel, *The Genesis of Heidegger's Being & Time* (Berkeley: University of California Press, 1993), pp. 192–217.

38. John D. Caputo, *The Prayers and Tears of Jacques Derrida: Religion without Religion* (Bloomington: Indiana University Press, 1997), p. 1.

39. Jacques Derrida, "Violence and Metaphysics," in Derrida, *Writing and Difference* (Chicago: University of Chicago Press, 1967), 79–153; and "How to Avoid Speaking: Denials," in *Derrida and Negative Theology*, ed. Harold Coward and Toby Foshay (Albany: SUNY Press, 1992), 73–142.

40. There are similar criticisms today that are formulated in terms of the failure to acknowledge the particularity of Christian revelation and linguistic categories and the attempt to think of God beyond the confines of metaphysics.

41. Karl Barth, *Church Dogmatics*, II, 1 (Edinburgh, T & T Clark, 1957), pp. 257–321. For an interpretation of divine power, see Sheila Greeve Davaney, *Divine Power* (Philadelphia: Fortress, 1986), pp. 21–61.

42. Anders Nygren, *Agape and Eros* (Philadelphia: Westminster Press, 1953); Thorleif Boman, *Hebrew Thought Compared with Greek* (Philadelphia: Westminster Press, 1960); Oscar Cullmann, *Salvation in History* (London: S.C.M. Press, 1967); Jürgen Moltmann, *Theology of Hope: On the Ground and the Implications of a Christian Eschatology* (New York: Harper & Row, 1967). For a criticism of this distinction, see Catherine Osborne, *Eros Unveiled: Plato and the God of Love* (Oxford: Clarendon, 1994)

43. Moltman, *Theology*, p. 100.

44. Ibid., p. 101.

45. Kevin Hart, *The Trespass of the Sign* (New York: Cambridge University Press, 1989).

46. John Milbank's "Only Theology Overcomes Metaphysics," in Milbank, *The Word Made Strange: Theology, Language, and Culture* (Cambridge: Blackwells, 1997).

47. In his development of his conception of God beyond, Jean-Luc Marion recurred to neo-Platonic authors in contrast to Thomas Aquinas; see Jean-Luc Marion, *L'Idole et la distance* (Paris: Grasset, 1977). Because he has become more aware of the neo-Platonic character of Aquinas's theology, he has retracted his earlier critique of Aquinas. See for example, Jean-Luc Marion, "Saint Thomas d' Aquin et l'onto-théologie," *Revue Thomiste* 95 (1995): 31–66.

48. See Jean-Luc Marion, *God without Being* (Chicago: University of Chicago Press, 1991), p. 105. See also his *On Descartes' Metaphysical Prism: The Constitution and the Limits of Onto-theology in Cartesian Thought* (Chicago: University of Chicago Press, 1999).

49. Jean-Luc Marion, *God without Being: Hors-Texte—Religion and Postmodernism* (Chicago: University of Chicago Press, 1991).

50. Jean-Luc Marion, *L'Idole et la Distance* (Paris: Grasset, 1977), pp. 247–309.

51. See the discussion between Jacques Derrida and Jean-Luc Marion on the gift

in John D. Caputo and Michael J. Scanlon, eds., *God, the Gift, and Postmodernism* (Bloomington: Indiana University Press, 1999). See also Merold Westphal, ed., *Postmodern Philosophy and Christian Thought* (Bloomington: Indiana University Press, 1999); and Hent de Vries, *Philosophy and the Turn to Religion* (Baltimore: John Hopkins University Press, 1999).

52. John Milbank has criticized Marion for not going far enough, for not recognizing the neo-Platonic character of donation, and for overemphasis of the sublime in contrast to the beautiful and thereby not seeing the visible in the invisible; see his "Only Theology Overcomes Metaphysics," in *The Word Made Strange*. See also Anthony Godzieba, "Ontotheology to Excess: Imaging God without Being," *Theological Studies* (1995): 1–20. See also Rudolf Gasche, *Inventions of Difference: On Jacques Derrida* (Cambridge, Mass.: Harvard University, 1984), pp. 82–106.

53. Compare Marion's emphasis on and interpretation of boredom with Martin Heidegger's three forms of boredom. See Jean-Luc Marion, *Reduction and Givenness: Investigations of Husserl, Heidegger, and Phenomenology* (Evanston, Ill.: Northwestern University Press, 1998), pp. 167–202; and Martin Heidegger, *The Fundamental Concepts of Metaphysics: World, Finitude, Solitude* (Bloomington: Indiana University Press, 1995), pp. 78–184.

54. Trutz Rendtorff, ed., *Die Realisierung der Freiheit* (Güterslohr: Gerd Mohn, 1975).

55. Hans Urs von Balthasar, *Apokalypse der deutschen Seele*, 3 vols. (Salzburg: Anton Pustet, 1937–1939).

56. See the third volume of Erich Przywara, *Analogia Entis*, Schriften, vol. 3 (Einsiedlen: Johannes Verlag, 1962). See Bernhard Gertz, *Glaubenswelte also Analogie. Die theologische Analogielehre Erich Przywaras und Ihr Ort in der Auseinandersetzung um die Analogie fides* (Düsseldorf: Patmos Verlag, 1969); and Hans Urs von Balthasar, *The Theology of Karl Barth* (Garden City: Doubleday, 1972). For an analysis of Balthasar's own constructive interpretation of the analogy of charity, see Manfred Lochbrunner, *Analogie Caritatis: Darstellung und Deutung der Theologie Hans Urs von Balthasars* (Freiburg: Herder, 1981). (For the importance of Maximus the Confessor, see Hans Ottmar Meuffels, *Einbergund des Mensch in das Mysterium der dreieinigen Liebe. Eine trinitarische Anthropologie nach Hans Urs von Balthasar* [Würzburg: Echter Verlag, 1991].)

57. Hans Urs von Balthasar, "Analogie und Dialektik," *Divus Thomas* 22 (1944): 196.

58. Paul De Man, *Allegories of Reading: Figural Language in Rousseau, Nietzsche, Rilke, and Proust* (New Haven: Yale University Press, 1979), p. 4.

59. See Richard Rorty, *Philosophy and the Mirror of Nature* (Princeton: Princeton University Press, 1979),

60. George Herbert Mead, *Mind, Self and Society* (Chicago: University of Chicago Press, 1934). This volume, published posthumously from student notes, lacks the usual precision of his essays.

61. Mead, *Mind*, p. 138.

62. Pannenberg argues that the unity of the ego and self cannot be understood except in such interaction. Wolfhart Pannenberg, *Anthropology in Theological Perspective* (Philadelphia: Westminster Press, 1985).

63. Pannenberg suggests that "the abiding merit of Mead is that he went beyond

the broad personalist thesis that the ego is constituted by its relation to the Thou and understood a concrete and nuanced description of this dependence." *Anthropology*, pp. 189–190.

64. Emmanuel Levinas, *Collected Philosophical Papers*, Phaenomenologica 100 (Boston: Nijhoff, 1987), 53.

65. Emmanuel Levinas, "Ethics as First Philosophy," in *The Levinas Reader*, ed. Seán Hand (New York: B. Blackwell, 1989),

66. See William D. Hudson, ed., *The Is-Ought Question: A Collection of Papers on the Central Problems in Moral Philosophy* (London: Macmillan, 1969). See also John L. Mackie, *Ethics: Inventing Right and Wrong* (Harmondsworth: Penguin, 1977); and Christine Korsgaard, *The Sources of Normativity* (Cambridge: Cambridge University Press, 1996).

67. Johann Baptist Metz, *Faith in History and Society: Toward a Practical Fundamental Theology* (New York: Seabury, 1980); and Helmut Peukert, *Science, Action, and Fundamental Theology: Toward a Theology of Communicative Action* (Cambridge, Mass.: MIT, 1994).

68. See the debate between Ebeling and Pannenberg in Wolfhart Pannenberg, "Die Krise des Ethischen und die Theologie," *Theologische Literaturzeitung* (1962): 7ff.; and Wolfhart Pannenberg and Gerhard Ebeling, "Briefwechsel," *Zeitschrift für Theologie und Kirche* 70 (1973): 448–473.

69. Emmanuel Levinas, *Dieu, la mort et le temps* (Paris: Editions Grasset et Fasquelle, 1993), p. 177 (my own translation).

70. An order of contemplative systems between two classes—those who were contemplative and wore one habit, and those who did the labor and wore another. The former spent more hours in the chapel than the latter, who worked. Applicants were often divided in terms of social class.

71. Denys Turner, *The Darkness of God: Negativity in Christian Mysticism* (New York: Cambridge University Press, 1995), p. 45.

72. Martin Heidegger, *Identity and Difference* (New York: Harper & Row, 1969); and Ernst Bloch, *The Principle of Hope* (Cambridge, Mass.: MIT Press, 1986).

73. Johann Gottfried Herder, *Herders Werke*, ed. Theodor Matthias (Leipzig: Bibliographisches Institut, 1903), 5: 578. Quoted translation from Allen W. Wood, *Kant's Ethical Thought* (New York: Cambridge University Press, 1999), p. 233.

74. George Lindbeck, "The Gospel's Uniqueness: Election and Untranslatability," *Modern Theology* 134 (1997): 423–450, quote from p. 427. For a contrasting viewpoint to Lindbeck, see Joseph Ratzinger's defense of human rights as a basis for democracy and pluralism in Joseph Ratzinger, *Wahrheit, Werte, Macht. Prufsteine der pluralistischen Gesellschaft* (Freiburg: Herder, 1993); on the relation between religious belief and rights, see Michael Perry, *The Idea of Human Rights: Four Inquiries* (Oxford: Oxford University Press, 1988).

75. Richard Rorty writes:

> The moral to be drawn . . . is that Serbian murderers and rapists do not think of themselves as violating human rights. For they are not doing these things to fellow human beings but to *Muslims*. They are not being human, but rather are discriminating between true humans and pseudo-humans. They are making the same sort of distinctions the Crusaders made between humans and infidel dogs, and Black Muslims make between humans and blue-eyed devils. The founder of my univer-

sity was able both to own slaves and to think it self-evident that all men were endowed by their creator with certain inalienable rights.

"Human Rights, Rationality, and Sentimentality," in Rorty, *Truth and Progress* (New York: Cambridge University Press, 1998), pp. 167–185. Quotation from p. 167.

76. Ibid., p. 170. See also his *Philosophy and Social Hope* (New York: Penguin, 1999).

77. See Bartolome de Las Casas (1474–1566) in *In Defense of the Indians: The Defense of the Most Reverend Lord, Don Fray Bartolomé de las Casas, of the Order of Preachers, Late Bishop of Chiapa, Against the Persecutors and Slanderers of the Peoples of the New World Discovered Across the Seas*, ed. Stafford Poole (DeKalb: Northern Illinois University Press, 1974); de Las Casas, *Brevisima relacion de la destruccion de las Indias* (Barcelona: Fontamara, 1974); Fernando Mires, *En nombre de la cruz. Discusiones teológicas y políticas frente al holcausto de los indios, período de conquista* (San José: Departmento Ecumenico de Investigaciones, 1986). Lewis Hanke, *All Mankind Is One: A Study of the Disputation Between Bartolome de Las Casas and Juan Gines de Sepulveda in 1550 on the Intellectual and Religious Capacity of the American Indians* (DeKalb: Northern Illinois University Press, 1974).

78. Emmanuel Levinas, "The Rights of Man and Good Will," in Levinas, *Entre Nous: Thinking-of-the Other* (New York: Columbia University Press, 1998), pp. 155–158.

79. "This doctrine, however is to be carefully observed that no one can be injurious to his brother without wounding God himself." John Calvin, *Commentary on Genesis* (Grand Rapids, Mich.: Baker Book House, 1981), Chapter 12 n. 7.

80. Arthur J. Dyck, *Rethinking Rights and Responsibilities* (Cleveland: Pilgrim, 1994); J. B. Schneewind, *The Invention of Autonomy* (New York: Cambridge University Press, 1998); R. Tuck, *Natural Rights Theories: Their Origins and Development* (New York: Cambridge University Press, 1979); Brian Tierney, *Religion, Law, and the Growth of Constitutional Growth* (New York: Cambridge University Press, 1982); and James A. Brundage, *Medieval Canon Law: The Medieval World* (London and New York: Longman, 1995).

81. See Francis Schüssler Fiorenza, "The Works of Mercy: Theological Perspective," in *The Works of Mercy*, ed. Francis Eigo (Villanova: Villanova University Press, 1991).

82. For an analysis of Horkheimer's understanding of religious meaning, see James Bohman, "Entwertende und bewahrende Kritik: Wahrheit und Religion in Spatphilosophie Horkheimers," in *Kritische Theorie und Metaphysik*, ed. M. Lutz-Bachmann (Wurzburg: Echter Verlag, 1996), pp. 164.

83. Max Horkheimer, "Bermerkungen zur Liberalisierung der Religion," *Sozialphilosophische Studien* (Frankfurt: Fisher Verlag, 1972), pp. 135–136.

CONTRIBUTORS

JOHN D. CAPUTO holds the David R. Cook Chair of Philosophy at Villanova University. His most recent publications include *More Radical Hermeneutics: On Not Knowing Who We Are* (2000), *On Religion* (2001), *The Prayers and Tears of Jacques Derrida: Religion without Religion* (1997), *Deconstruction in a Nutshell: A Conversation with Jacques Derrida* (1997), *Against Ethics* (1993), and *Demythologizing Heidegger* (1993). He is editor of *Blackwell Readings in Continental Philosophy: The Religious* (2001) and *God, the Gift, and Postmodernism* (1999). He also serves as editor of the Fordham University Press book series "Perspectives in Continental Philosophy."

JACQUES DERRIDA, Ecole des Hautes Etudes en Sciences Sociales (Paris) and the University of California, Irvine, is one of the most important philosophers of our time. Among his more recent works are *Etats d'âme de la psychanalyse: Adresse aux Etats Généraux de la Psychanalyse* (2000), *Voyager avec Jacques Derrida: La Contre-Allée* (with Catherine Malabou, 1999) and *Le Toucher, Jean-Luc Nancy* (2000). His most recent work to be translated into English is *Adieu: To Emmanuel Levinas* (1999); *Demeure: Fiction and Testimony* (2000), *Of Hospitality* (with Anne Dufourmantelle, 2000), and *On Cosmopolitanism and Pardon* (2001). He has recently been lecturing on forgiveness, perjury, and capital punishment.

MARK DOOLEY is John Henry Newman Scholar in Theology at University College Dublin, Ireland, where he has taught philosophy and theology since 1993. He co-edited, with Richard Kearney, *Questioning Ethics* (1999), and his forthcoming book with Fordham University Press, *The Politics of Exodus* (2001), is an exploration of the way in which the work of Kierkegaard and Derrida can act as a basis for a postmodern politics. Dooley has just completed editing a volume dedicated to the work of John D. Caputo entitled *From Aquinas to Derrida*.

FRANCIS SCHÜSSLER FIORENZA, the Stilman Professor of Catholic Theology at the Harvard Divinity School, is the author of *Foundational Theology: Jesus and the Church* (1984) and *Beyond Hermeneutics: Theology as Discourse*. He has also co-edited *Systematic Theology: Roman Catholic Per-*

spectives (with John P. Galvin, 1991), *Handbook of Catholic Theology* (with Wolfgang Beinert, 1995), *Modern Christian Thought*, Vol. II: *The Twentieth Century* (with James C. Livingston), and *Habermas, Modernity, and Public Theology* (with Don S. Browning, 1992).

ROBERT GIBBS, Professor of Philosophy at the University of Toronto, teaches Continental Philosophy and Jewish Thought. His writings include *Correlations in Rosenzweig and Levinas* (1992) and *Why Ethics: Signs of Responsibilities* (2000). He is also co-author with Peter Ochs and Steven Kepnes of *Reasoning after Revelation: Dialogues in Postmodern Jewish Philosophy* (1998). Current research includes a larger project on Law and Ethics, and a current book entitled *Messianic Epistemology.*

JEAN GREISCH is Director of the doctoral program in philosophy at the Institut Catholique de Paris. A native of Luxembourg, he has published *Herméneutique et Grammatologie* (1977), *L'âge herméneutique de la Raison* (1985), *La Parole Heureuse. Martin Heidegger entre les choses et les mots* (1986), *Hermeneutik und Metaphysik. Eine Problemgeschichte* (1993), *Ontologie et Temporalité. Esquisse d'une interprétation intégrale de Sein und Zeit* (1994), *L'arbre de vie et l'arbre du savoir. Les racines phénoménologiques de l'herméneutique heideggérienne* (2000), *Le Cogito herméneutique. L'herméneutique philosophique et l'héritage cartésien* (2000). He is currently preparing a book under the title *De l'homme faillible à l'homme capable. La phénoménologie herméneutique de Paul Ricoeur* and a book on the philosophy of religion.

KEVIN HART is Professor of English and Comparative Literature at Monash University in Melbourne, Australia. His most recent book is entitled *The Dark Gaze: Maurice Blanchot and Friends.* He is the author of *The Trespass of the Sign* (expanded edition, 2000), *A. D. Hope* (1992), and *Samuel Johnson and the Culture of Property* (1999) and is the editor of *The Oxford Book of Australian Religious Verse.* He is currently at work on another book entitled *The Experience of God.* He has also published several award winning books of poetry and serves as the Director for the Center of Religion and Theology at Monash.

RICHARD KEARNEY is Professor of Philosophy at University College Dublin and Boston College. In addition to his well-known *The Wake of Imagination* (1988), his most recent books include *Poetics of Imagining* (1998), *Postnationalist Ireland* (1997), and *Poetics of Modernity* (1995). He is editor of *Continental Philosophy in the Twentieth Century* and co-editor of *Questioning Ethics: Contemporary Debates in Philosophy* and *The Continental Philosophy Reader.* Richard Kearney is also a novelist (*Sam's Fall,* 1994 and *Walking at Sea Level,* 1997), a poet (*Angel of Patrick's Hill,* 1991), and a cultural critic. His book on God will appear soon from Indiana University Press.

CLEO MCNELLY KEARNS writes on theology, literature, and literary theory. She is the author of *T. S. Eliot and Indic Traditions: A Study in Poetry and Belief* (1987) and has contributed essays on the theological implications of postmodern critical theory to many periodicals and anthologies, including, most recently, "Jacques Lacan: an Introduction" in *The Postmodern God*, edited by Graham Ward (1997). She is working on a book on the figure of the Virgin Mary in Judaism, Christianity, and Islam.

JOHN MILBANK is Frances Myers Ball Professor of Philosophical Theology at the University of Virginia. Previously he was Reader in Philosophical Theology at the University of Cambridge and a Fellow of Peterhouse. He is the author of *Theology and Social Theory: Beyond Secular Reason* (1990), *The Word Made Strange: Theology, Language and Culture* (1997), and *Truth in Aquinas* (with Catherine Pickstock). He is a co-editor (with Graham Ward and Catherine Pickstock) of *Radical Orthodoxy*.

MICHAEL J. SCANLON, O.S.A. has held the Josephine C. Connelly Chair in Christian Theology at Villanova University since 1992. He is a Past President of the Catholic Theological Society of America (1988). Michael Scanlon, who was one of the founders of the Washington Theological Union, a graduate school of theology, has published numerous studies in such journals as *The Thomist, Theological Studies, Augustinian Studies*, the *Proceedings of the CTSA*, the *American Ecclesiastical Review, Proceedings of the Theology Institute*, and several chapters in various collections and encyclopedia.

REGINA M. SCHWARTZ is Professor of English and Religious Studies at Northwestern University and director of the Institute of Religion, Ethics, and Violence. She works at the intersections of philosophy, theology, and literature. She is the author of *The Curse of Cain: The Violent Legacy of Monotheism* (1997), *Remembering and Repeating: On Milton's Theology* (1988), editor of *The Book and the Text: The Bible and Literary Theory* (1990), and co-editor of *The Postmodern Bible* (1995) and *Desire in the Renaissance: Literature and Psychoanalysis* (1994). Her contribution to *Questioning God* is part of her forthcoming book on the Eucharist.

GRAHAM WARD is Professor of Contextual Theology and Ethics at the University of Manchester. His books include *Barth, Derrida and the Theology of Language* (1995), *Theology and Contemporary Critical Theory* (1999) and, most recently, *Cities of God* (2000). Among the several books he has edited are *The Postmodern God* (1998), *The Certeau Reader* (1999) and (with John Milbank and Catherine Pickstock) *Radical Othodoxy*. For the last five years he has been executive editor of the Oxford University Press journal *Literature and Theology*.

INDEX

Index

Index